Internet Multimedia Search and Mining

Editors

Xian-Sheng Hua
Microsoft Research, USA

Marcel Worring
University of Amsterdam, The Netherlands

Tat-Seng Chua
National University of Singapore, Singapore

CONTENTS

contd.....

FOREWORD

Multimedia information started receiving serious attention only about 20 years ago. It was that time that researchers started exploring how to deal with increasing volumes of multimedia document. The rise of search and mining of multimedia information grew in parallel to text search, but was slower in the early stages. In the last decade, it has accelerated to the stage where much of the new information being created is multimedia. Research in search and mining of multimedia contents has been intensifying over the last few years. The need for this technology has become essential, rather than just desirable, due to the volumes and diversity of information being created. Several factors have contributed to this surge in the volume of information and hence urgent need for research in multimedia search and mining. The first factor is the low-cost and widespread use of Internet and intelligent mobile devices. This allows most urban users to access, search and share media contents conveniently at any time and from any location. This gives rise to the second factor which is the popularity of media sharing services and mobile media apps. People are now sharing a huge amount of multimedia contents on the social network sites, though primarily on their personal activities, but increasingly include social events, social commentaries, and informational contents such as the "howto" videos. This offers a huge repository of multimedia and social contents that permits a wide variety of knowledge to be extracted to facilitate better media search, recommendation and social analysis applications. The third factor for the surge in media research is due to the maturity and success of some media technologies for internet applications. This includes media indexing, search, duplicate detection and recommendation techniques, which are adopted in many large-scale public search engines, media social sharing sites and online shopping sites. These partial successes motivated further research in internet media applications.

As a result of the above three factors, active research has gone beyond the traditional areas of media content analysis and search, to the new topics motivated by the emergence of social media and mobile devices. These include research on social media analysis and mining, techniques for Web-scale media indexing and sharing, personalization and recommendations, as well as new user interface and interaction techniques to meet the need of social mobile media applications. These works are currently reported in diverse forums, such as the latest conference proceedings and journals, and are not easily accessible and comprehensible to most people. There was an urgent need to bring together this variety of research into a single complied volume.

This is therefore a long awaited eBook that addresses a comprehensive range of modern topics in search and mining of multimedia contents over the internet. It organizes both the traditional as well as social media research topics into a structure suitable for both researchers and practitioners in the field. It will be of great benefits to the community as a useful guide for latest research and practices in this exciting emerging field. To make it useful and authoritative, this collection is edited by three very active researchers in the field who are expert in different aspects of multimedia search and mining. I believe that this eBook will be very useful to researchers in the field to find all relevant information at one place and thus be a strong reference source.

Ramesh Jain
University of California
Irvine
USA

PREFACE

With the explosion of video and image data available on the Internet, desktops, and mobile devices, multimedia search is becoming more and more important. Mining semantics and other useful information from large-scale multimedia data to facilitate online and local multimedia content analysis, search, and related applications is gaining attention from both academia and industry.

On the one hand, the rapid growth of multimedia data brings new challenges to multimedia content analysis and retrieval, especially in terms of scalability. Both computational costs and accuracy are still far from satisfactory. On the other hand, large-scale multimedia data provides new ways to meet these challenges and solve conventional problems in media analysis and computer vision. That is, the massive associated metadata, context, and social information available on the Internet, desktops, and mobile devices, as well as the massive number of grassroots users, are valuable resources that can be leveraged to address the aforementioned difficulties.

Today, researchers are realizing that both the challenges and the opportunities presented by the rapid growth of multimedia content, users, metadata, context, and social information. This eBook brings together high-quality research and recent insights into multimedia search and mining. It focuses on online and social multimedia techniques, systems, and applications in order to advance research and development in this promising area. The eBook is organized into five sections with a total of seventeen chapters.

Section I introduces recent research on content-based image and video indexing, and consists of three chapters. In the first chapter, Zhang *et al.* present an efficient visual indexing technique for large-scale image search, the basic idea of which is to decompose a document-like representation of an image into two components, one for dimension reduction and the other for residual information preservation. In the second, Wu *et al.* review various approaches to near-duplicate web video detection, including combining global features and local features, integrating content and contextual information, and visual-word based scalable retrieval. Finally, Zhang *et al.* present recent advancements in web scale video retrieval and discuss two methods for efficient visual representation and efficient visual indexing of web videos.

Section II has four chapters addressing concept and tag based multimedia indexing. The first chapter, by Qi *et al.* introduces large-scale online active annotation for

Internet multimedia using the two basic techniques - active learning and online computing, and proposes to combine these two techniques in a unified framework, where scalable multimedia annotation can be achieved in an online manner so that both annotation accuracy and efficiency are able to be significantly improved. Li *et al.* in the second chapter, tackle two issues in social image indexing, that is, the subjectiveness and the incompleteness of the social tags. The third chapter, authored by Borth *et al.* introduces visual learning of automatic concept detectors from web video as available from services like YouTube, where domain change problem is addressed and a novel approach, which performs a highly efficient online adaptation on the target domain after an initial training on web content. In the last chapter of this section, Liu *et al.* present techniques to improve the quality of social tags on social media websites, including filtering, refinement and ranking.

Section III, containing four chapters, discusses data mining from Internet multimedia content. Negoescu *et al.* present a review of current work that leverages on large online social networks' meta-information, in particular Flickr Groups, in the first chapter. The second chapter, by Li *et al.* explores how to leverage the web image collection and knowledge databases to convert a textual word into its visual counterpart with sets of high quality, precise, diverse and representative images. In the third chapter, Wu *et al.* estimate semantic distance of two textual terms through mining visual content from the Internet, where semantic concepts are modeled based on visual language models. And last, Ahlers *et al.* introduce techniques for mining location of a web image and mining images of a location.

Section IV mainly addresses search and recommendation problems for Internet multimedia with four chapters. Wilkins *et al.* present an overview of data fusion and how it can be applied to the internet multimedia search, specifically content-based multimedia search. Efrat *et al.* introduce cross-modality indexing, browsing and search of distance learning media on the Web. Lu and Li present a music indexing scheme by exploiting and utilizing two data sources: surrounding text of the music on web pages and mete-data describing music attributes. Mei and Aizawa introduce the basic techniques for general recommender systems and specific research for video recommendation.

The last section introduces two novel search interfaces for Internet media. The first chapter, authored by Zha *et al.* proposes a new query suggestion scheme named visual query suggestion to help users precisely express their search intents by joint text and image suggestions. In the second chapter, Wang *et al.* present an interactive image search interface, color sketch, which enables users to interactively indicate the search intention, in particular, how the colors are spatially distributed in desired images, by scribbling a few color strokes or dragging an image and highlighting a few regions of interest in an intuitive way.

This eBook is well suited for graduate students and senior researchers working in the field of multimedia search and mining, as well as practitioners, including search engine developers, and multimedia content providers. We hope readers find that this eBook enhances their study of and work in internet multimedia search and mining.

Many exceptional colleagues made a significant impact on the development of this eBook. First of all, we would like to thank all the authors for their irreplaceable contributions to the eBook and their patience for the long process of editing this eBook. We would also like to acknowledge our reviewers for their insightful and valuable comments that improved the quality and readability of the eBook: Kiyoharu Aizawa, Susanne Boll, Daniel Gatica-Perez, Winston Hsu, Gang Hua, Xirong Li, Zhu Li, Wei Liu, Yan Lu, Jiebo Luo, Tao Mei, Chong-Wah Ngo, Shin'ichi Satoh, Nicu Sebe, Jialie Shen, Alan Smeaton, Cees Snoek, Dacheng Tao, Meng Wang, Lei Wu, Xing Xie, Changsheng Xu, Rong Yan, and Lei Zhang. Special thanks to Dr. Kuiyuan Yang, who helped us check and correct all the format issues and integrated all the chapters into the final version.

Finally, we are deeply indebted to each of our family members for their patience and understanding as we were creating this eBook.

Xian-Sheng Hua
Microsoft Research
USA

Marcel Worring
University of Amsterdam
The Netherlands

Tat-Seng Chua
National University of Singapore
Singapore

LIST OF CONTRIBUTORS

Alexander G. Hauptmann
Carnegie Mellon University, 5000 Forbes Avenue, Pittsburgh, PA 15213, USA

Adrian Ulges
German Research Center for Artificial Intelligence, Gemany

Alan F. Smeaton
Centre for Sensor Web Technologies, Dublin City University, Ireland

Alon Efrat
The University of Arizona, Tucson, AZ 85721, USA

Arnon Amir
IBM Almaden Research Center, San Jose, CA 95120, USA

Chong-Wah Ngo
City University of Hong Kong, Hong Kong

Cees G.M. Snoek
University of Amsterdam, The Netherlands

Damian Borth
University of Kaiserslautern & German Research Center for Artificial Intelligence, Germany

Dong Liu
Department of Electrical Engineering, Columbia University, New York, NY 10027, USA

Daniel Gatica-Perez
Idiap Research Institute and Ecole Polytechnique Fédérale de Lausanne, Switzerland

Dirk Ahlers
NTNU - Norwegian University of Science and Technology, Trondheim, Norway

Gang Hua
Stevens Institute of Technology, Hoboken, NJ 07030-5991, USA

Guo-Jun Qi
Beckman Institute, University of Illinois at Urbana-Champaign, Urbana, IL 61801, USA

Guangda Li
School of Computing, National University of Singapore, Singapore

Heung-Yeung Shum
Microsoft Research Asia, Beijing, China

Hong-Jiang Zhang
Microsoft Advanced Technology Center, Beijing, China

Haojie Li
School of Software, Dalian University of Technology, Liaoning, China

Jinhui Tang
School of Computer Science, Nanjing University of Science and Technology, Nanjing, China

Jingdong Wang
Microsoft Research Asia, Beijing, China

Kobus Barnard
The University of Arizona, Tucson, AZ 85721, USA

Kiyoharu Aizawa
University of Tokyo, Tokyo, Japan

Lei Zhang
Microsoft Research Asia, Beijing, China

Lei Wu
University of Pittsbugh, PA 15213, USA

Lie Lu
Dolby Laboratories, Beijing, China

Linjun Yang
Microsoft Research Asia, Beijing, China

Marcel Worring
University of Amsterdam, The Netherlands

Meng Wang
Hefei University of Technology, Anhui, China

Philipp Sandhaus
CEWE Color AG & Co. OHG, Oldenburg, Germany

Peter Wilkins
Centre for Sensor Web Technologies, Dublin City University, Ireland

Quanfu Fan
Exploratory Computer Vision Group, Thomas J. Watson Research Center, Hawthorne, NY 10532, USA

Radu-Andrei Negoescu
Idiap Research Institute and Ecole Polytechnique Fédérale de Lausanne, Swizerland

Susanne Boll
University of Oldenburg, Oldenberg, Germany

Tat-Seng Chua
National University of Singapore, Singapore

Thomas M. Breuel
University of Kaiserslautern, Germany

Tao Mei
Microsoft Research Asia, Beijing, China

Wei-Ying Ma
Microsoft Research Asia, Beijing, China

Wan-Lei Zhao
City University of Hong Kong, Hong Kong

Xian-Sheng Hua
Microsoft Research Redmond, WA 98052, USA

Xiao Wu
Southwest Jiaotong University, Chengdu, Sichuan, China

Xiao Zhang
Institute for Advanced Study, Tsinghua University, Beijing, China

Xirong Li
Renmin University of China, Beijing, China

Yinghai Zhao
University of Science and Technology of China, Hefei, China

Zhiwei Li
Microsoft Research Asia, Beijing, China

Zheng-Jun Zha
Institute of Intelligent Machines, Chinese Academy of Science, Hefei, China

Internet Multimedia Search and Mining, 2013, 3-25

CHAPTER 1

An Image Decomposition Approach to Large-scale Image Retrieval

Xiao Zhang

Institute for Advanced Study, Tsinghua University, Tel: +86-13146526618, Email: andypassion@gmail.com

Zhiwei Li

Microsoft Research Asia, Tel: +86-10-59173195, Email: zli@microsoft.com

Lei Zhang*

Microsoft Research Asia, Tel: +86-10-59173197, Email: leizhang@microsoft.com

Wei-Ying Ma

Microsoft Research Asia, Tel: +86-10-59173197, Email: wyma@microsoft.com

Heung-Yeung Shum

Microsoft Corporation, Tel: +1-425-703-8165, Email: hshum@microsoft.com

Abstract:

Thanks to the fast development of Internet and image capturing devices, the available images online have gone through an exponential growth. Efficient indexing and retrieval methods are crucial in order to leverage the web image dataset. This has important impact to a number of research areas such as image recognition, image retrieval and computer graphics. In this chapter, we review the current popular image representation and corresponding large-scale index technologies. For global representation, we review tree and hash based index structures. For local features, which recently receive lots of attention for their invariance properties to lighting,

***Correspondence Author:** Lei Zhang, Microsoft Research Asia, Email: leizhang@microsoft.com.

Xian-Sheng Hua, Marcel Worring & Tat-Seng Chua (Eds.)

scale and rotation, we review inverted list indexing and the related "long query problem". Then we introduce an image decomposition approach to convert the local feature representation from high dimensional sparse feature vectors to (relatively) low dimensional dense feature vectors with residual information. We also discuss a specially designed index structure to facilitate efficient storage and retrieval for this image representation. At the end of the chapter, we present extensive experiment results on a 2.3 million image database to demonstrate the efficacy of the image decomposition approach.

Keywords

Image retrieval, image indexing, data driven image understanding, inverted list, long query, search engine, image search, visual search, bag of words, dimension reduction, latent dirichlet allocation.

1 Introduction

With the explosive growth of the available image data, a large amount of research efforts has been dedicated to large-scale image retrieval [1, 20, 30] and data driven image understanding [4, 29]. The research efforts have led to advancements in both academic research[29] and industrial application, e.g. Google Goggles and Bing Image Search.

In this chapter, we introduce the technical advancement on an image decomposition based approach for large scale image retrieval. This approach improves local feature based bag-of-words model by applying dimension reduction and a specially designed index structure. We start our discussion from a brief review of previous large-scale image retrieval methods.

Existing image retrieval methods

Currently, two categories of approaches are popular for large-scale image retrieval. One is global descriptors based approaches, and another is based on a "bag of visual terms" (BOV). Next we briefly review these two approaches and discuss their advantages and drawbacks.

Image retrieval by global features

The early research on content based image retrieval represents images by global descriptors. A group of descriptors that are particularly popular are color based descriptors such as color histogram and correlogram[3]. Although these descriptors are not sensitive to the pose changes of the objects in the images, they become unreliable when the lighting condition changes. Recent development in the vision community has led to descriptors that are more robust to lighting changes. One that receives increasingly more attention is GIST[7]. GIST is a low dimensional representation of the scene, comprised of a set of perceptual dimensions including naturalness, openness, roughness, expansion, etc.. These dimensions are designed to represent the dominant spatial structure of a scene. It was shown that these dimensions may be reliably estimated using spectral and coarsely localized information. An evaluation of GIST based image retrieval methods can be found in [8].

To index the large amount of feature vectors for efficient retrieval, various methods have been proposed, among which two types of methods are particularly popular. The first type corresponds to tree-based approaches. For example, k-d tree has been used to index large number of SIFT descriptors [30]. A k-d tree (short for k-dimensional tree) is a space-partitioning data structure for organizing points in a k-dimensional space. Every node in a k-d tree partitions the data along one dimension with a certain threshold. There are various methods for choosing the dimension and threshold for each node. One common approach is to pick the dimension with the highest variance as the dimension for partition and use the median value as the threshold to balance the tree. To mitigate the quantization error of the spatial partition tree, a randomized version of the k-d tree can be constructed by choosing the splitting dimension at random from among a set of the dimensions with highest variance and the splitting threshold using a randomly selected point close to the median. An ensemble of the randomized k-d trees creates an overlapping partition of the feature space and helps to mitigate quantization effects. This robustness is especially important in high-dimensions, where due to the "curse of dimensionality", points will be more likely to lie close to a boundary.

Another type of methods for indexing high dimensional feature vectors are hash-based solutions. One of the most famous methods of this kind is locality sensitive hashing (LSH)[16]. The foundation of this algorithm is LSH functions. An LSH function h is called (R, cR, P_1, P_2)-sensitive if $\forall \mathbf{x}, \mathbf{y} \in \mathcal{R}^d$, we have:

- if $||\mathbf{x} - \mathbf{y}|| \leq R$ then $P[h(\mathbf{x}) = h(\mathbf{y})] \geq P_1$
- if $||\mathbf{x} - \mathbf{y}|| \geq cR$ then $P[h(\mathbf{x}) = h(\mathbf{y})] \leq P_2$

To make h useful, it must satisfy that $P_1 > P_2$. In real systems, h is used in the following way. First the "gap" between P_1 and P_2 is amplified by concatenating K LSH functions into K dimensional signatures. In this way, the precision of the retrieval is improved but since $P_1^k < P_1$ the recall is sacrificed. To improve recall, L hash tables are constructed, each of which use a different set of K LSH functions. Given a query, a union of the items found in each hash tables is returned. In this chapter, we use LSH to index large-scale image dataset and adjust K and L to achieve a good balance between precision and recall. However, it is worth noting that a potential disadvantage of LSH is that it needs to store multiple hash-table in the memory to achieve efficient retrieval, so the memory cost is possibly high, especially for a large L. Recently, researchers have proposed a single hash-table based LSH technologies[5] which retrieves not only the data points in the hash bucket that query maps to, but also the data in the adjacent hash buckets.

LSH is a randomized version of hash algorithms that map visually close images to the same hash-table entry with high probability. Recent studies of the hash algorithms try to learn the hash functions based on given similarity metrics. Torralba *et al.* introduced two methods that convert Gist descriptor [7] to a compact binary code with a few hundred bits per image[4]. The goal is to retrieve millions of images using one single PC. The first method is based on GentleBoost. The input labels indicate the neighborhood relationship between pairs of data points. The learned weak classifiers are decision stumps, each of which uses one dimension of input feature vectors to generate binary values. The binary code of an image is a concatenation of such binary values of the weak classifiers. The second method is based on the dimensionality reduction framework of restricted Boltzmann machines (RBMs). Another representative approach of this kind is Spectral Hashing [36], which learns the hash projection from the affinity matrix of the training data. The authors introduced a spectral method whose solutions were simply a subset of thresholded eigenvectors of the graph Laplacian. By utilizing recent results on convergence of graph Laplacian eigenvectors to the Laplace-Beltrami eigenfunctions of manifolds, the authors showed how to efficiently calculate the binary code of a novel data point. Recently, Gong *et al.* [6] proposed a simple method that minimized the quantization loss by a alternating optimization scheme. It was shown that the resulted binary code outperformed state-of-the-art methods.

Image retrieval by local features

Due to good invariant properties to lighting conditions, scale and rotation changes, local features (e.g. SIFT[18]) receives lots of attention recently [30]. However, by local features, an image is represented by a set of features, where the number of features is changeable and thus difficult to use. Thus, in state-of-the-art local feature-based image retrieval systems, "bag of visual terms" (BOV) model is widely adopted to convert local features of an image to a fixed-length histogram [20].

A typical local feature-based large-scale image retrieval system could be divided into three parts: feature extraction, feature quantization and indexing.

Feature extraction and quantization is to convert an image into BOV representation. An image is usually represented by 500-5000 local descriptors. *k-means* clustering is the most popular approach to get BOV representations. [22] and [22] demonstrated the accuracy of retrieval increases with the increasing of the number of clusters (i.e. vocabulary size). However, the time to train a vocabulary with 1 million words by *k-means* is extremely long. [22] proposed to train the lexicon by a top-down hierarchical clustering manner. [22] proposed to index local descriptors by *KD*-tree and use an approximate *k-means* to achieve this goal. Their following works used soft assignment[25] and hamming embedding[32] to alleviate information loss suffered by hard quantization.

To speed up the process of finding relevant images for a query image, indexing techniques are necessarily adopted to organize images. In state-of-the-art systems, a popular indexing technique is the so called *inverted lists* structure [20, 22, 25, 30], which has an entry for each visual term followed by a list of all the images in which the visual term occurs. Based on an index structure, we expect the relevance scores can be efficiently computed for images in the database and a small number of candidate images can be proposed. As in this step we need to find relevant images from a database with millions of images, the indexing design is very critical for a large-scale system.

A fundamental difference between an image query and a text query is that an image query usually contains much more information than a text query (e.g. 1,000 visual words v.s. 3 text terms). This is called the **Long Query Problem** in the search engine literature and is largely ignored in the existing index design for content-based image retrieval. This difference makes the inverted list inappropriate to index images. For example, given a query with three terms, all images containing them can be obtained by intersecting three rows in the inverted list. However, given a real image query which consists of 1000 visual terms, we have to intersect 1000 rows in the list. Thus, when inverted list is applied to index images, both its storage cost and time complexity to respond a query are unacceptably high. In this case, the performance of inverted list may be even worse than linear scan (say, without index). In a well known image retrieval system which index about 1 million images [22, 30], the memory cost to host its index is 4.3GB which exceeds the maximum physical memory of a 32-bit machine. Thus, the average time to answer a query is 15-35 seconds. In contrast, it was reported that a commercial web search engine can index more than 5 million web pages by a 32-bit machine with the same data structure, and answer a query in a few milliseconds [34]. This creates a strong need to an efficient index structure specifically designed for visual search.

Despite of the heavy investigation of the feature extraction and quantization components, efficient indexing design has been given less attention since its first introduction in [20]. In the rest of the chapter, we'll discuss an efficient index structure to solve the long query problem based on image decomposition

Solving the long-query problem by dimension reduction

The BOV model represents each image with a fixed-length high-dimensional feature vector, which may contain more than 1 million components [22]. Although the dimensionality of the new image representation is very high, most of its components are zero. That is, the image feature is extremely high-dimensional and sparse. These characteristics bring difficulties to existing high-dimensional indexing techniques, e.g. Locality Sensitive Hashing (LSH) [14], Spectral Hashing [36], and *KD*-tree[26]. Although known as effective techniques to index dense features, LSH and Spectral Hashing are not good solutions to index sparse features because the L2 distance of sparse features is not as reliable as that of dense features [16]. Similarly, *KD*-tree, , can only be applied when the dimensionality of the feature space is about a dozen [26], otherwise its performance may be even worse than linear scan.

It is worth noting that dimension reduction algorithms could be a solution to address this problem because they are capable of finding compact and dense representations of images in a low-dimensional space. Two kinds of dimension reduction approaches could be adopted for large scale visual search. One is matrix factorization approaches(e.g. PCA, NMF [35]), the other is probabilistic topic models. The former algorithm is easy to implement while the latter is more interpretable. Moreover, both of them could be easily paralleled. In[33], Latent Dirichlet Allocation is used to model higher level semantics and represent images for large scale image retrieval, and superior evaluation results are obtained on a large scale image dataset.

Dimension reduction algorithms have two major merits. First, by capturing high level semantics, the projected low dimensional space could facilitate information retrieval. Second, high-dimensional indexing technique such as *KD*-tree or LSH performs better in the projected space, because image feature vectors in this space are compact and dense. However, retrieving images in a low dimensional space has a critical drawback because dimension reduction will inevitably result in the loss of some important information. That is, some image specific information (say, residual) which cannot be effectively represented in the low-dimensional space. For example, when a user inputs a query image which contains a building facade, the projected low dimensional space may capture the general aspects of this image such as windows, pillars, roofs, etc. but may lose some specific information about this image like company logo or some special artifacts. However, from a user's perspective, this kind of specific information is important. This problem will further affect the performance when the type of information contained in the query image is not contained in the training corpus used for dimension reduction algorithms. That is, the query image could not be well represented in the low dimensional space and the information loss is large.

Overview of our approach

The image decomposition approach was originally proposed in [1]. More discussions about related work, the proposed algorithm, and additional experiment results are provided here. The proposed solution consists of a feature decomposition model and a specifically designed indexing scheme.

1. We compute a compound representation for each image by a feature decomposition model. Both general and special aspects of an image can be extracted by

the model. Beyond traditional dimension reduction algorithms, this model enables us to take the residual information into account. In the model, we explicitly know which visual terms in an image cause most of the re-construction error. That is, we can identify and preserve the most special/important local features for an image. Thus, an image is represented by a low-dimensional vector and a few important key terms.

2. We design an appropriate indexing scheme by fully considering the physical meanings and storage characteristics of the two components of the compound representations. The low-dimensional representations of images can be efficiently indexed by LSH [14]. By indexing only those most important visual terms (say, 30 terms in our experiments), which cause the most of the reconstruction error, and taking them into account in the ranking algorithm, we achieve significant performance improvement.

We evaluate the proposed solution on some benchmark datasets as well as a dataset with 2.3 million images. With a postprocessing technique (RANSAC based image matching [22]), we achieve comparable performance with state-of-the-art approaches [22], but both the time to answer a query and memory cost to host index are significantly reduced.

2 Image Decomposition

Basic idea

Our image decomposition idea is motivated from dimension reduction approaches because once we obtain low-dimensional and dense representations of images, many existing indexing techniques can be used to index images, e.g. LSH [14, 16]. A common objective function for dimension reduction algorithm is

$$min \sum_{i=1}^{N} \|p_i - V \times h_i\|$$

where p_i is the high-dimensional histogram representation of an image [20, 22] (We assume that the means of feature vectors are removed), V is a matrix whose column vectors span a low-dimensional space, and h_i is the coefficients to reconstruct the image by column vectors of V. h_i is the compact representation of the original histogram feature p_i in the low-dimensional subspace V.

However, as we have discussed in Section 1.2, h_i does not contain complete semantics of an image. The lost semantics of an image in the dimension reduction process is likely to be very discriminative. Therefore, we propose a compound image representation which consists of a low-dimensional vector h_i and some important residual information lost in dimension reduction. Actually, an image p_i can be

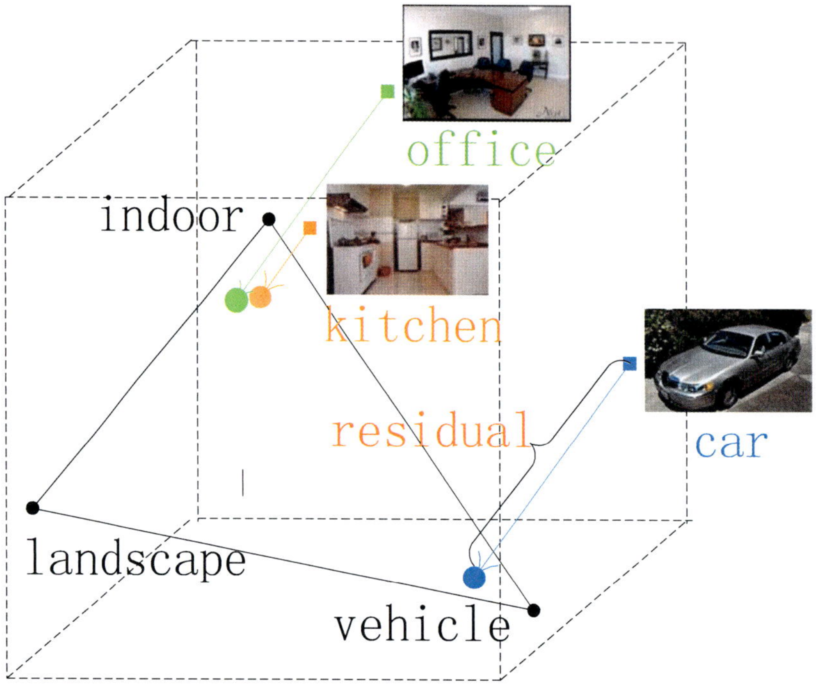

Fig. (1): Illustration of the image decomposition idea. The cube denotes a vector space of images represented by bag of words, the triangle denotes a simplex spanned by three bases, a rectangle point denotes an image, a circle point denotes an embedding of an image in the subspace, and the distance of an image to the subspace is its residual.

mathematically represented as follows

$$p_i = V \times h_i + \epsilon_i \qquad (1)$$

where ϵ_i is residual of the reconstruction. ϵ_i has the same dimensionality as p_i. However, only components with the largest absolute values in ϵ_i, which are more important than other components in terms of reconstructing the image, need to be preserved. We will show in Section 4 that this compound representation has a very natural indexing scheme.

We further illustrate in Fig. (1) the key observation motivating the image decomposition idea. The two images about kitchen and office are projected to almost the same position(indoor) in the subspace, while the image about car is projected to a position(vehicle) far from them. Thus, it's easy for us to distinguish kitchen and car or office and car in the low dimensional subspace. However, only from their coefficients in the subspace, we may not be able to distinguish the two indoor im-

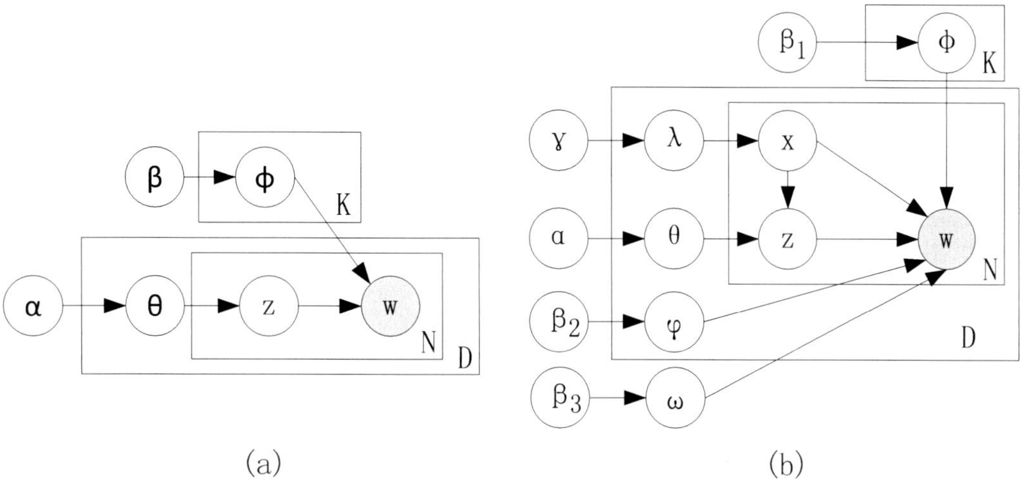

Fig. (2): Probabilistic topic models. (a) latent Dirichelt allocation(LDA), (b) Image decomposition model (IDM).

ages(kitchen and office). Fortunately, the two images can be distinguished by their distances to the subspace, i.e. their residual (ϵ_i).

Two kinds of approaches could be considered for implementing the proposed idea. One is matrix factorization approaches, the other is probabilistic topic models. Most of matrix factorization approaches, e.g. PCA and non-negative matrix factorization (NMF) [35] could be adopted for this purpose. Although the computations of topic models are more complex than matrix factorization approaches, they offer better ways to understand problems and easy to be generalized to unseen data. Therefore, in this paper, we will mainly implement the image decomposition idea in a topic model way.

A probabilistic decomposition model

Represented by a BOV model, an image can be deemed as a document. A way to implement the proposed decomposition idea is to use an Image Decomposition Model(IDM), which is an extension of the popular LDA model [13], which was first proposed to model documents, as shown in Fig. **(2)**(b). IDM was first proposed in [23] to detect important words of a document. To generate a visual word, a random variable x is first drawn from $Multinomial(\lambda)$, then

- if $x = 1$, draw $z \sim Multinomial(\theta)$, and then draw a visual word $w \sim Multinomial(\phi_z)$
- if $x = 2$, draw a visual word $w \sim Multinomial(\psi)$
- if $x = 3$, draw a visual word $w \sim Multinomial(\omega)$

The conditional probability of a visual word w given an image d in IDM could be written as

$$p(w|d) = \sum_z p(w|z)p(z|x=1,d)p(x=1|d)$$
$$+p(w|x=2,d)p(x=2|d) + p(w|x=3,d)p(x=3|d)$$

The key idea of IDM is to use a switch variable x to control the generation of visual words. x can take value in 1, 2, 3, which controls that a visual word is generated from either a topic distribution (ϕ_z), an image-specific distribution (ψ_d), or a corpus background distribution (ω). It provides a natural way to partition an image into three types of visual words. Intuitively, a visual word which appears in almost all images is likely to be a background/stop word; a visual word which only appears in a few images but seldom appears in other images is likely to be an image-specific word; a visual word which widely appears in images with a common semantic but seldom appears in other images is likely to be a topic related word.

Mapping to the matrix factorization formulation, the work of IDM can be understood as simultaneously finding a group of basis vectors (ϕ_z, a set of distributions over vocabulary), coefficients (θ_d, topic mixture proportion), and residual (ψ_d, an image-specific distribution), which correspond to V, h_i and ϵ_i in Eq.(1), respectively. The visual terms generated from the background distribution correspond to the mean of image histograms. The compound representation of an image obtained by IDM is a pair $< \theta_d, \psi_{large} >$, where ψ_{large} means part of ψ components which have the largest values.

Parameter estimation

Because the maximum likelihood estimation of IDM is intractable [13, 23], we adopt the Monte Carlo EM algorithm to estimate parameters [15]. MCEM consists of two steps. In E-step, instead of computing the posterior of latent variables, we draw samples from it. Gibbs sampling is a popular method to sample complex posterior [12]. We adopt the collapsed Gibbs sampling algorithm proposed in [23], in which x and z are jointly sampled while other hidden variables are integrated out. The Gibbs sampling equations are listed as follows

$$p(x_i = 1, z_i = k|x_{-i}, z_{-i}, w, \alpha, \gamma, \beta_1, \beta_2, \beta_3)$$
$$= \frac{\gamma_1 + n^1_{d,-i}}{\sum_{j=1}^3 \gamma_j + n^{\cdot}_{d,-i}} \times \frac{\alpha_1 + n^{1,k}_{d,-i}}{\sum_{j=1}^K \gamma_j + n^{1,(.)}_{d,-i}} \times \frac{\beta_1 + n^{1,k,w_i}_{.,-i}}{\sum_{j=1}^W \beta_j + n^{1,k,w_j}_{.,-i}}$$
$$p(x_i = 2|x_{-i}, z_{-i}, w, \alpha, \gamma, \beta_1, \beta_2, \beta_3)$$
$$= \frac{\gamma_2 + n^2_{d,-i}}{\sum_{j=1}^3 \gamma_j + n^{\cdot}_{d,-i}} \times \frac{\beta_{2,w_i} + n^{2,w_i}_{d,-i}}{\sum_{j=1}^W \beta_{2,j} + n^{2,w_j}_{d,-i}}$$
$$p(x_i = 3|x_{-i}, z_{-i}, w, \alpha, \gamma, \beta_1, \beta_2, \beta_3)$$
$$= \frac{\gamma_3 + n^3_{d,-i}}{\sum_{j=1}^3 \gamma_j + n^{\cdot}_{d,-i}} \times \frac{\beta_{3,w_i} + n^{3,w_i}_{.,-i}}{\sum_{j=1}^W \beta_{3,j} + n^{3,w_j}_{.,-i}}$$

where K is the number of topics, W is the size of visual vocabulary, $-i$ in subscript means whole variables excluding the i-th variable; $n^1_{d,-i}$, $n^2_{d,-i}$ and $n^3_{d,-i}$ mean the numbers of words generated from topics, image-specific distribution and background distribution in image d; $n^{1,k}_{d,-i}$ means the number of words assigned to topic k in image d; $n^{1,k,w_i}_{\cdot,-i}$ means the number of times of word w_i assigned to topic k in the whole corpus; $n^{2,w_i}_{d,-i}$ means the number of times of word w_i assigned to image-specific distribution in image d; and $n^{3,w_i}_{\cdot,-i}$ means the number of times of word w_i assigned to background distribution in the whole corpus.

In M-step, we maximize the expectation with respect to model parameters. The expectation can be approximated by

$$\arg\max_{\alpha,\gamma,\beta_{1,2,3}} \frac{1}{M} \sum\nolimits_{j=1}^{M} \log(p(w, x_j, z_j|\alpha, \gamma, \beta_{1,2,3}))$$

where M is the number of samples drawn in E-step. Because all hidden variables are observed, the joint probability can be decomposed to a product of some simple probabilities, which can be estimated separately. We take the Newton-Raphson algorithm to estimate Dirichlet hyper-parameters [13].

Inference of unseen images

After we estimate a model from training images, we need to infer latent variables for images to be indexed in the database as well as query images. For IDM, the inference algorithm is the same as the estimation. However, part of model parameters will be fixed to be those obtained in the estimation step. The two terms $\frac{\beta_1+n^{1,k,w_i}_{\cdot,-i}}{\sum_{j=1}^{W}\beta_j+n^{1,k,w_j}_{\cdot,-i}}$ and $\frac{\beta_{3,w_i}+n^{3,w_i}_{\cdot,-i}}{\sum_{j=1}^{W}\beta_{3,j}+n^{3,w_j}_{\cdot,-i}}$ are replaced by ϕ_{k,w_i} and ω_{w_i}.

It is remarkable that the inference of different images are independent to each other. This fact can be easily verified by checking the Gibbs sampling equations for inference: the factors in these equations only depend on variables related to one image. That is, we can distribute images to different processors/machines and decompose them in a parallel way. Thus, the scalability of IDM algorithm is not a problem.

Similarity measure

Given a query image, we use a heuristic method to compute its similarity to each image in the database. The similarity function is a linear combination of two evidences

$$sim(d, q) = \gamma_{d1}\gamma_{q1}sim(\theta_d, \theta_q) + \gamma_{d2}\gamma_{q2}sim(\psi_d, \psi_q) \tag{2}$$

where θ_d, θ_q stand for the topic mixture proportion of the two images, ψ_d, ψ_q stand for image-specific distributions ($p(w|x = 2, d)$), and $\gamma_{\cdot 1}$ and $\gamma_{\cdot 2}$ stands for

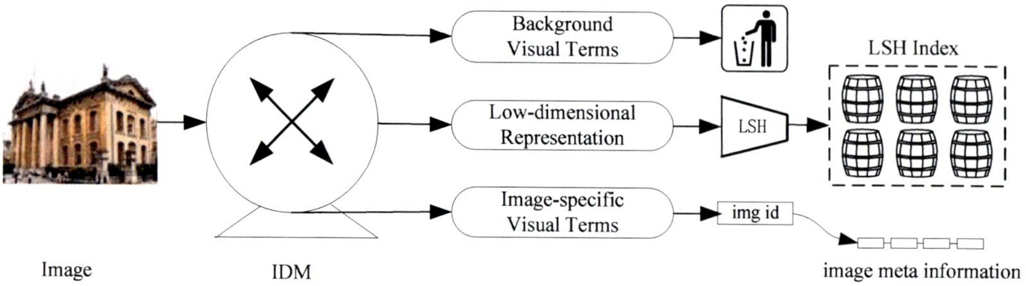

Fig. (3): Work flow of our indexing framework. IDM is a centrifugal machine which decomposes an image to three components which are indexed in appropriate ways.

the word ratios of topic related terms and image-specific terms. These variables can be obtained by the inference algorithm. An advantage of this simple ranking function is that it does not introduce additional parameters. Actually, we can use any similarity function to compute $sim(\theta_d, \theta_q)$ and $sim(\psi_d, \psi_q)$. In our experiments, we adopted *cosine* similarity to compute them.

Here, two observations of Eq.(2) should be highlighted. First, Eq.(2) provides an alternative way to compute cosine similarity. If the low dimensional distribution θ and image specific distribution ψ are orthogonal(e.g. if they are obtained by PCA), Eq.(2) will be exactly equivalent to the cosine similarity between a query image and an image in the database. Otherwise, it could be considered as a close approximation to the cosine similarity. Second, θ and ψ are separately computed, so they could be organized by different data structures in the index to optimize the retrieval performance.

3 Indexing and Ranking

If we rank images according to Eq.(2), we have to linearly scan all images in the database. In case the database is huge, the time complexity is unacceptable. To speed up the ranking process, we need a specifically designed indexing and fast ranking solution. The overall work flow of the proposed indexing solution is shown in Fig. **(3)**.

Indexing scheme

As we have illustrated in Fig.(**1**), different kinds of image representations have different functionalities and storage characteristics. Thus, we choose different approaches to index them. It is worth noting that background visual terms are common for all images in a database, that is, they cannot discriminate images with different semantics. Thus, they are discarded from index.

Indexing Low-dimensional Representations. We choose Locality Sensitive Hashing (LSH) [14] to index the low-dimensional representations of images (i.e. θ). Previous research [16] and our experiments demonstrated that the LSH is an effective approach to indexing compact and dense feature vectors. LSH will assign a group of hash values to an image. These hash values can be deemed as a new discrete representation of this image. Therefore, the memory requirement of LSH index is only $O(L * D)$, where L (e.g. 60 in our experiments) is the number of hash functions of LSH and D is the number of images.

Indexing Image-Specific Words. As we have mentioned, we can preserve only a small amount of visual words of an image as its image-specific words. These words can be selected according to the image-specific distribution ψ. In our experiments, we demonstrated the number of image-specific visual words could be very small. In our experiments, we obtained satisfied retrieval accuracies with only 30 image-specific words. We organize the image-specific words of an image as a fixed-length array, in which each component is a $< wordid, weight >$ pair. This array is termed as image meta information. The most notable advantage of the fixed-length array is that we can randomly access meta information of any image efficiently. The memory cost of this index in our implementation is only $O(30 * D)$.

Ranking scheme

Considering the functionalities (in terms of representing semantics of an image) of the two components of the compound representation of an image, we develop an efficient ranking scheme. The similarity $sim(\theta_d, \theta_q)$ in Eq.(2) can distinguish images belonging to different visual categories, while $sim(\psi_d, \psi_q)$ is a complement to the first similarity and it can further distinguish images belonging to different sub visual categories. This observation motivates a two-step re-ranking approach for querying an image. A query image q is processed as follows

- Extract θ_q (topic mixture proportion) and ψ_q (an image-specific word distribution) from the query image.
- Generate an initial candidate set of relevant images (e.g. 200 images in our experiments) by approximately computing $cosine(\theta_d, \theta_q)$ using LSH.
- Assign final scores to images in the candidate set by using Eq.(2).
- Rank all candidate images according to the final scores and return the most relevant images to the user.

As shown above, in the first step, we use $sim(\theta_d, \theta_q)$ to select top k images as a candidate set. In our implementation, θ_d is indexed by LSH. Thus, we can get an approximately accurate set efficiently. In the second step, we combine information from topic related words and image-specific words to re-rank images in this set. Our experimental results show that this approach is capable of obtaining almost the same results as the "accurate algorithm" (i.e. Eq.(2)).

It is worth noting that, using the ranking algorithms based on the proposed index scheme, we cannot get the same results as the accurate algorithm(Eq.(2)) because: 1) LSH is an approximate nearest-neighbor algorithm; 2) only a few most salient image-specific visual terms are kept in index. Although this ranking scheme is only an approximation, its retrieval results are almost as good as the accurate algorithm in our experiments. The little sacrifice of accuracy significantly reduce the response time to queries and save memory cost. The two ranking approaches are termed as "*accurate*" and "*index*" in our experiments.

4 Experiments

In this section, we report the performance comparison of the proposed solution with serveral state-of-the-art approaches over a 2.3 million image database. To the best of our knowledge, this database is the largest one in this research direction.

Datasets

Four datasets (including two benchmark databases) were used in our experiments.

Oxford5K (*5062 images, 18M descriptors, 55 queries*) This dataset consists of 5062 images with extensively associated groundtruth for 55 queries: 5 queries for each of 11 Oxford landmarks [22]. This dataset served as the groundtruth in all experiments.

Paris (*6300 images, 19M descriptors*) This dataset consists of 6300 images obtained from Flickr [25]. Similar as the *Oxford5K* dataset, most of images in this dataset are buildings.

PhotoForum2M (*2.3M images, 4165M descriptors*). We collected these images from some professional photo forums, which cover various topics such as people, buildings and natural scenes. Some sample images of the two datasets are shown in Fig. (**4**). To test the impact of vocabularies constructed on different types of images, we construct a subset of *PhotoForum2M*, **PhotoForum7K** (*7769 images, 22M descriptors*).

Implementation

SIFT features were chosen as local features to represent images. We used the binary code shared by David Lowe to detect salient points and generate descriptors

Fig. (4): Sample images from PhotoForum2M.

[18]. In feature extraction, we used default parameters of the tool. Visual vocabulary was generated by *k-means*, which was accelerated by the *KD*-forest algorithm proposed in [22]. In all probabilistic model-based approaches, we constructed vocabularies with 50k words, while in other approaches, we constructed vocabularies with 1 million words. For the proposed image decomposition model(IDM), the dimensionality of low dimensional subspace is set to be 250(excluding Sec. 4), and only 30 visual words(i.e. image specific words) are preserved in the index.

Experiment design

All experiments were carried out over a dataset constructed by mixing images from *Oxford5K* and *PhotoForum2M*. Images in *PhotoForum2M* served as distractors. The combined dataset contains 2, 277, 584 images. As we have summarized in Section 1.1, a typical image retrieval system consists of three major components: feature extraction and quantization, indexing, and postprocessing. To evaluate the performance of the proposed indexing solution, we varied settings of each component. These variations include:

- Construct visual vocabularies based on different types of images, i.e. *Oxford5K* and *PhotoForum7K*.
- Train IDM on both groundtruth dataset, i.e. *Oxford5K*, and a similar dataset, i.e. *Paris*.

Tab. (1): Performance comparison for some variations of the proposed algorithm, LDA-based approach and TF-IDF approach. The vocabulary was constructed over *PhotoForum7k*.

Approaches	**Training data for IDM**	
	Oxford5K	**Paris**
Accurate	0.4227	0.3542
Low-dim Only	0.3632	0.2315
Index	0.3901	0.3387
Index with reranking	0.6304	0.5571
LDA[33]	0.3927	0.2405
TFIDF[22]	0.4116	
TFIDF with reranking[22]	0.6047	

- Change the number of image-specific words in index.
- Perform postprocessing or not.

We implemented two baseline approaches. The first one is the approach proposed in [22], in which images are represented by BOV models, weighted by TF-IDF scheme, and indexed by inverted list. It has the state-of-the-art performance of large-scale visual search. The second one is the approach proposed in [33], in which images are projected to a latent space obtained by training a latent Dirichlet allocation (LDA) model, and image similarities are measured in the latent space.

In retrieval applications, a popular and simple accuracy measure is the precision of top search results. In all experiments, we use the precision of top 10 search results (P@10), to measure the performances of all approaches.

Accuracy comparison

Results of all approaches on two vocabularies are summarized in Tab. **(1)** and Tab. **(2)**. In the tables, "Accurate" corresponds to use Eq.(2) as similarity measure and perform a linear scan over the entire database, "Index" corresponds to use Eq.(2) on the proposed indexing structure and ranking scheme introduced in Sec. 3, "Low-dim Only" corresponds to use only the image representation projected in the low dimensional subspace learned via the training data, "LDA" and "TFIDF" are the baseline approaches we compare with, and "Index with reranking" and "TFIDF with reranking" corresponds to use spatial verification for reranking.

Overall, the proposed approach "Accurate" achieved even better accuracies than state-of-the-art approaches. Moreover, the accuracy of "Index" is quite close to state-of-the-art approaches, with significantly faster retrieval speed and lower memory consumption. Next, we provide more detailed analysis of the experiment results.

Tab. (2): Performance comparison for some variations of the proposed algorithm, LDA-based approach and TF-IDF approach. The vocabulary was constructed over *Oxford5K*.

Approaches	Training data for IDM	
	Oxford5K	**Paris**
Accurate	0.6371	0.5774
Low-dim Only	0.5713	0.4105
Index	0.6207	0.5654
Index with reranking	0.8727	0.7803
LDA	0.6091	0.4674
TFIDF	0.6274	
TFIDF with reranking	0.8451	

Impact of vocabulary and models

The two vocabularies were constructed over *PhotoForum7K* and *Oxford5K*. And two IDM models are trained on *Paris* and *Oxford5K*. From these tables, we can see: 1) The proposed approach "Accurate" performs better than state of the art approaches when vocabularies are trained either on *PhotoForum7K* or *Oxford5K*. 2) The model trained on *Oxford5K* achieved slightly better performance than the model trained on *Paris*. In contrast, the performances of LDA-based approach[33] dropped dramatically. When we decompose some kind of images, e.g. *Oxford5K*, using model trained on a different dataset, e.g. *PhotoForum7K*/*Paris*, more information will be preserved in the residual (image-specific words) instead of the low dimensional representation. This is the reason why the proposed index method, which combines information from both image-specific words and the low-dimensional representations obtained by dimension reduction, has better generalization ability. This is very important for real word applications.

To further verify this explanation, we reported the performance of a ranking approach which only depends on low-dimensional representations obtained by IDM, which is termed as "*Low-dim only*" in these tables. We found its performance is almost the same as the LDA based approach. However, compared "Low-dim only" with "Accurate", we could see that once taking the image-specific words into account, the accuracy was significantly improved. This demonstrates that especially when the model or vocabulary cannot well explain images to be indexed, image-specific words must be included in index.

Impact of subspace dimensionality

A common obstacle of applying dimension reduction algorithm to real world problems is to determine the dimensionality of the projected subspace. Therefore we compare the parameter sensitivity of proposed algorithm("Accurate") with LDA [33] regarding the dimensionality of the low dimensional subspace. In this ex-

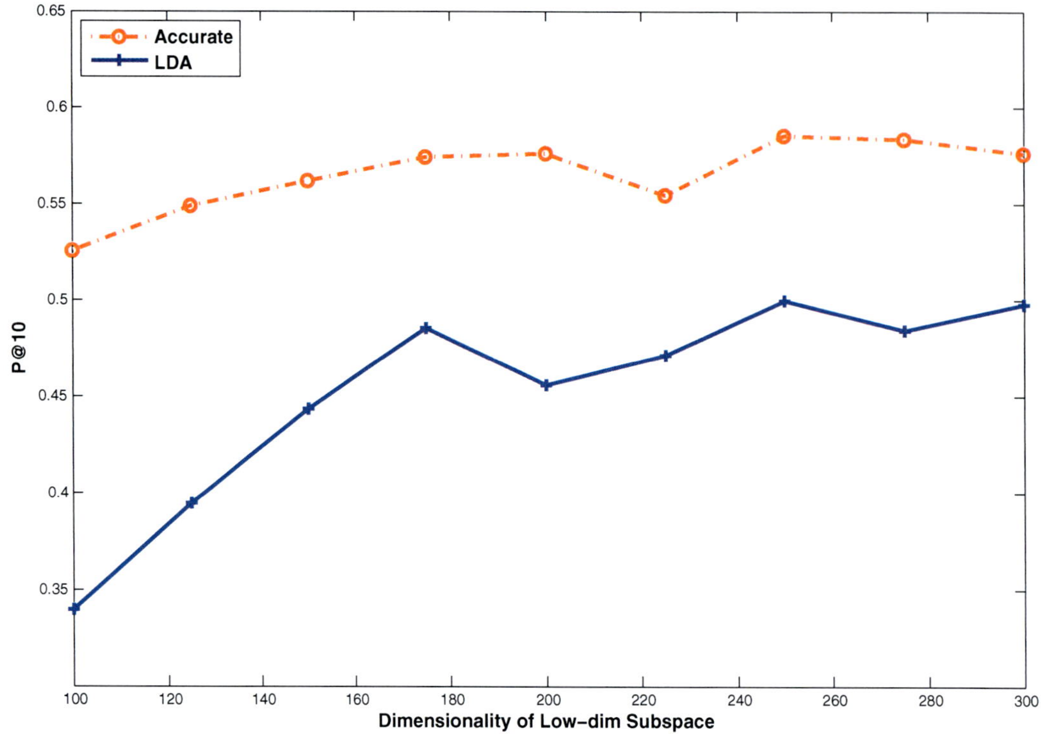

Fig. (5): Accuracy comparison between proposed algorithm and LDA with change in the dimensionality of learned subspace.

periment, the training data includes all images from *Oxford5K*. For each algorithm to be compared, we vary its subspace dimensionality and evaluate its precision of top 10 results using the 55 queries provided in *Oxford5K*. The result is shown in Fig. (**5**). From the figure, we could see that the accuracy of LDA drops apparently when the dimensionality is reduced because of the increasing information loss. However, the curve of the proposed algorithm("Accurate") is much more flat, thanks to the information preserving capability of image specific words.

The implication of this experiment result is two fold. First, the proposed algorithm is less sensitive to the subspace dimensionality thus less parameter tuning needs to be performed. Second, when the dimensionality of low-dimensional space is very small and information loss is large, the proposed algorithm achieves significantly better performance than LDA[33], thanks to the explicit representation of residual error(i.e. image specific distribution) in the proposed image decomposition model. This observation is aligned with the previous experiment results in which the proposed algorithm achieve superior performance than LDA when the training data(Paris) is different from testing data(Oxford5K) and the information loss of dimension reduction is large.

Tab. (3): Performances of the proposed approaches under different numbers of image-specific words in index with visual vocabulary trained on *PhotoForum7K*.

Approaches	The number of image specific words				
	30	**60**	**90**	**120**	**150**
Accurate	0.4227	0.4306	0.4369	0.4428	0.4475
Index	0.3901	0.3957	0.3996	0.4013	0.4072

Improvement with postprocessing

We rerank a short list of images obtained by our indexing scheme based on the estimation of an affine transformation with an implementation of [22]. Tab. **(1)** and Tab. **(2)** also shows that the results obtained by reranking a short list of 100 images, which is termed as "index with reranking" in these tables. We observed further performance improvement. The performance gain of our approach is larger than the TF-IDF based approach. This results indicates that the proposed indexing and ranking scheme has better recall rate than the TF-IDF based approach.

The number of image-specific words

Tab. **(3)** shows the performances of the proposed approach under different numbers of image-specific words kept in the indexing structure, with vocabulary trained on *PhotoForum7K* and IDM trained on *Oxford5K*. No obvious improvement could be observed after the number of image-specific words kept in the indexing structure is more than 30 in the index scheme. This result demonstrates that a small number of image-specific words is enough for the proposed indexing scheme.

Cost comparison

We compared the memory cost and time cost of the proposed approach with the inverted list based approach [22]. The results (Memory cost for 10 million images is estimated without real implementation.) are summarized in Tab. **(4)**.

Memory Cost: In a real system, index should be able to be loaded in memory to enable fast search. For the proposed indexing algorithm, the memory cost consists of two parts, i.e. memory cost of indexing low-dimensional representations and indexing image-specific words. Therefore, memory consumption of proposed algorithm is determined by LSH parameters L(set to 60) (In our implementation, LSH is implemented by inverted index. Thus L integers are used to represent low dimensional distribution for each image.) and the number of image-specific words(set to 30). In total, the memory cost of indexing 2.3 million images is 1.1GB. Thus, all index data can be loaded in memory. In contrast, assuming each image contains 1000 visual words, then the index made by inverted list for 2.3 million images costs 18 GB (In our implementation, each visual word is represented by a <word id,

Tab. (4): Cost comparison between the proposed Image Decomposition Model and inverted index.

Database	Cost	Image decomposition model	Inverted index
2.3M Images	Time Cost(s)	**0.04**	25
	Memory Cost(GB)	**1.1**	18
10M Images	Memory Cost(GB)	**4.8**	78.3

weight>pair.) and could not be loaded into memory for a typical workstation with 8GB memory. In theory, a common back-end server with 8GB memory is capable of indexing 10 Million images using the proposed indexing scheme.

Time Cost: The time cost of proposed indexing algorithm consists of two parts, time to decompose an query image to get its topic distribution (θ) and image-specific words, and time to query the database. As we use LSH to index the topic related word, querying image database is very fast. The average time to inferring an image is about 4.2 milliseconds. The average time for querying an image on the 2.3 Million database costs about 0.04 seconds (not including the RANSAC based spatial re-ranking step [22]).

5 Conclusion

In this paper, we have presented a novel indexing solution for local feature-based large-scale image retrieval systems. The solution consists of two key components: an image decomposition model, and an indexing and ranking scheme. The major contributions can be highlighted as follows. Based on the image decomposition model, the representation of an image can be decomposed to a compact vector as well as a few key visual terms. Retrieval accuracy based on the new representations is comparable to or even better than existing approaches in our experiments. Moreover, the proposed indexing and ranking scheme, which fully considers the characteristics of the new representations of images, is effective and efficient. With this scheme, both the computational and memory cost of online search service are significantly reduced, while the search results are almost as good as the accurate algorithm.

Both theoretic cost analysis and experiments over a 2.3 million image database demonstrate that this solution can be scaled up to index large-scale image databases for fast and accurate visual search.

6 References

[1] Xiao Zhang, Zhiwei Li, Lei Zhang, Wei-Ying Ma and Heung-Yeung Shum Efficient Indexing for Large Scale Visual Search. In *ICCV*, 2009.

[2] Fei-Fei Li and Pietro Perona. A Bayesian Hierarchical Model for Learning Natural Scene Categories. In *CVPR*, 2005.

[3] Jing Huang, Ravi Kumar, Mandar Mitra, Wei-Jing Zhu and Ramin Zabih Image Indexing Using Color Correlograms. In *CVPR*, 1997.

[4] A. Torralba, R. Fergus and Y. Weiss Small codes and large image databases for recognition. In *CVPR*, 2008.

[5] Q. Lv, W. Josephson, Z. Wang, M. Charikar,and K. Li Multi-probe LSH: efficient indexing for high-dimensional similarity search In *VLDB*, 2007

[6] Yunchao Gong and Svetlana Lazebnik. Iterative quantization: A procrustean approach to learning binary codes In *CVPR*, 2011

[7] A. Oliva and A. Torralba Modeling the shape of the scene: a holistic representation of the spatial envelope. In *IJCV*, 2001.

[8] Matthijs Douze, Herve Jegou, Harsimrat Sandhawalia, Laurent Amsaleg and Cordelia Schmidt Evaluation of GIST descriptors for web-scale image search. In *International Conference on Image and Video Retrieval*, 2009.

[9] Navneet Dalal and Bill Triggs Histograms of Oriented Gradients for Human Detection. In *CVPR*, 2005.

[10] J. Philbin, O. Chum, M. Isard, J. Sivic and A. Zisserman Object retrieval with large vocabularies and fast spatial matching. In *CVPR*, 2007.

[11] Y. Amit and D. Geman. Shape quantization and recognition with randomized trees. In *Neural Computing*, 1997.

[12] Thomas L. Griffiths, Mark Steyvers, David M. Blei and Joshua B. Tenenbaum. Integrating Topics and Syntax In *NIPS*, 2004.

[13] David M. Blei, Andrew Y. Ng and Michael I. Jordan. Latent Dirichlet Allocation. In *Journal of Machine Learning Research*, 2003.

[14] Alexandr Andoni and Piotr Indyk. Near-optimal hashing algorithms for approximate nearest neighbor in high dimensions. In *Commun. ACM.*, 2008.

[15] Wei Gang and Martin Tanner. A Monte Carlo implementation of the EM algorithm and the poor man's data augmentation algorithms In *Journal of American Statistics Association*, 1990.

[16] Piotr Indyk and Nitin Thaper. Fast Image Retrieval via Embeddings. In *3rd International Workshop on Statistical and Computational Theories of Vision*, 2003.

[17] I. T. Jolliffe. Principal Component Analysis. In *Springer Series in Statistics*, 2002.

[18] M. Belkin and P. Niyogi. Laplacian Eigenmaps for Dimensionality Reduction and Data Representation. In *Neural Computation*, 2003.

[19] A. Bosch, A. Zisserman and X. Munoz Scene Classification via pLSA. In *ECCV*, 2006.

[20] Josef Sivic and Andrew Zisserman. Video Google: A Text Retrieval Approach to Object Matching in Videos. In *ICCV*, 2003.

[21] David Lowe. Distinctive image features from scale-invariant keypoints. In *IJCV*, 2004.

[22] David Nister and H. Stewenius. Scalable Recognition with a Vocabulary Tree. In *CVPR*, 2006.

[23] C. Chemudugunta, P. Smyth and M. Steyvers. Modeling general and specific aspects of documents with a probabilistic topic model. In *NIPS*, 2006.

[24] Thomas Hofmann. Probabilistic latent semantic indexing. In *SIGIR*, 1999.

[25] Serge Brin and Larry Page. The Anatomy of a Large-Scale Hypertextual Web Search Engine. In *WWW*, 1998.

[26] Ting Liu, Andrew W. Moore, A. Gray and Ke Yang. An Investigation of Practical Approximate Nearest Neighbor Algorithms. In *NIPS*, 2004

[27] Chris Ding, Tao Li and Wei Peng. On the Equivalence Between Nonnegative Matrix Factorization and Probabilistic Latent Semantic Indexing. In *Computational Statistics and Data Analysis*, 2008

[28] L. A. Barroso, J. Dean, and U. Holzle. Web Search for a Planet: The Google Cluster Architecture. In *Proc. of Micro*, 2003

[29] A. Torralba, R. Fergus and W. T. Freeman. 80 million tiny images: a large dataset for non-parametric object and scene recognition. In *MIT-CSAIL-TR-2007-024*, 2007

[30] O. Chum, J. Philbin, J. Sivic, M. Isard and A. Zisserman Total Recall: Automatic Query Expansion with a Generative Feature Model for Object Retrieval. In *ICCV*, 2007

[31] J. Philbin, O. Chum, M. Isard, J. Sivic and A. Zisserman Lost in Quantization: Improving Particular Object Retrieval in Large Scale Image Databases. In *CVPR*, 2008.

[32] Herve Jegou, Matthijs Douze and Cordelia Schmid. Hamming Embedding and Weak Geometric Consistency for Large Scale Image Search. In *ECCV*, 2008.

[33] Eva Hörster, Rainer Lienhart and Malcolm Slaney. Image retrieval on large-scale image databases. In *CIVR*, 2007.

[34] Luiz André Barroso, Jeffrey Dean and Urs Hölzle. Web Search for a Planet: The Google Cluster Architecture. In *IEEE Micro.*, 2003.

[35] Daniel D. Lee and H. Sebastian Seung. Algorithms for Non-negative Matrix Factorization. In *NIPS*, 2000.

[36] Y. Weiss, A. Torralba and R. Fergus. Spectral Hashing In *NIPS*, 2009.

[37] Zhong Wu, Qifa Ke, Michael Isard, and Jian Sun. Bundling Features for Large Scale Partial-Duplicate Web Image Search. In *CVPR*, 2009

Internet Multimedia Search and Mining, **2013, 26-57**

CHAPTER 2

Near-Duplicate Web Video Detection

Xiao Wu*
Southwest Jiaotong University, Tel: +86-28-87600744,
Email: wuxiaohk@home.swjtu.edu.cn
Wan-Lei Zhao
City University of Hong Kong, Email: wzhao2@cs.cityu.edu.hk
Chong-Wah Ngo
City University of Hong Kong, Tel: +852-3442-4390, Email: cwngo@cs.cityu.edu.hk
Alexander G. Hauptmann
Carnegie Mellon University, Tel: +1-412-268-1448, Email: alex@cs.cmu.edu

Abstract: The explosive expansion of the social web makes overwhelming amounts of web videos available, among which there are a large number of near-duplicate videos. Current web video search results rely exclusively on text keywords or user-supplied tags. A search on the keywords of a typical popular video often returns many duplicate and near-duplicate videos in the top results. Efficient near-duplicate web video detection is essential for effective search, retrieval, browsing and annotation. Due to the large variety of near-duplicate web video types ranging from simple formatting to complex editing, accurate detection generally comes at the cost of time complexity, particularly for web scale video applications. On the other hand, timely response to user queries is one important factor that fuels the popularity of the social web. This chapter will review approaches for near-duplicate web video detection from different technical viewpoints: combining global features and local features, integrating content and contextual information, and visual-word

***Correspondence Author:** Xiao Wu, Southwest Jiaotong University and City University of Hong Kong; Email: wuxiao@cs.cityu.edu.hk.

Xian-Sheng Hua, Marcel Worring & Tat-Seng Chua (Eds.)

based scalable retrieval.

Keywords

Near-Duplicates, Video Copy Detection, Web Video, Content, Context, Local Points, Novelty and Redundancy Detection, Similarity Measure, Data-driven, Video Retreival, Social Web, Bag of Word

1 Introduction

With the exponential growth of social media in Web 2.0, the huge volume of videos being transmitted and searched on the Internet has increased tremendously. Users can obtain web videos easily, and distribute them again with some modifications. For example, in July 2006 users uploaded 65,000 new videos each day on the video sharing website YouTube and the daily video views were over 100 million. And it is estimated that 24 hours of new videos are uploaded to the site every minute in March 2010 [28]. Among these huge volumes of videos, there exist large numbers of duplicate and near-duplicate videos.

Near-duplicate web videos are identical or approximately identical videos close to an exact duplicate of each other, which have similar time duration/length, but may be different in file formats, encoding parameters, photometric variations (color, lighting changes), editing operations (caption, logo and border insertion), and certain modifications (frames added/removed) [29]. Fig. (1) shows a set of examples of near-duplicate web videos. A video is a duplicate of another, if it looks the same, corresponds to approximately the same scene, and does not contain new and important information. For videos having remarkably different time durations, e.g. full version and short version, by definition, will not be regarded as near-duplicates. A user would clearly identify the videos as "essentially the same." A user searching for entertaining video content on the web, might not care about individual frames, but the overall content and subjective impression when filtering near-duplicate videos. Exact duplicate videos are a special case of near-duplicate videos, which are frequently returned by video search services. Recently, the semantic aspect is also considered when defining near-duplicate web videos in [2]. In this chapter, near-duplicate web videos do not take into account the semantic component. *Video copies* refer to videos derived from the same source but re-produced under different editing. The editing effects could range from simple insertion of patterns and re-encoding to dramatic decreasing in video quality. As a result, the purpose of video copy detection is to trace different copies of the same video content. Generally speaking, content-based video copy detection (VCD) can be viewed as a sub-issue of near-duplicate detection.

Based on a sample of 24 popular queries from YouTube, Google Video and Yahoo! Video, on average there are 27% redundant videos that are duplicate or

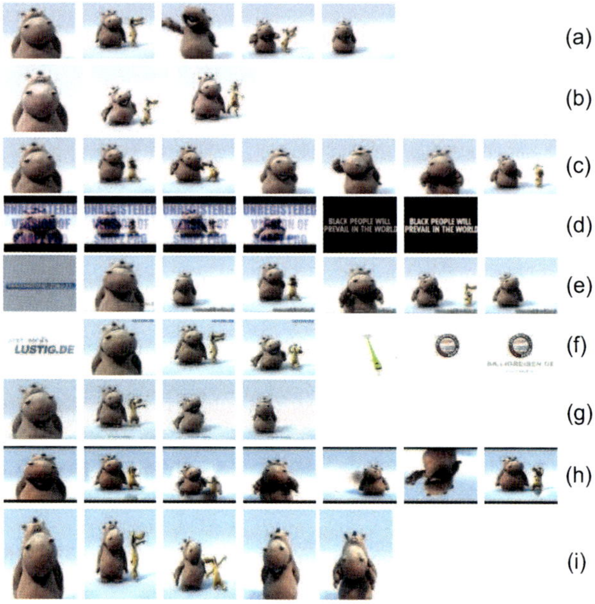

Fig. (1): A set of near-duplicate web videos (each row corresponds to one video). (a) is the standard version (b) brightness and resolution change (c) frame rate change (d) adding overlay text, borders and content modification at the end (e, f) content modification at beginning and end (g) longer version with borders (h) resolution differences.

nearly duplicate to the most popular version of a video in the search results [29]. For certain queries, the redundancy can be as high as 93%. As a consequence, users are often frustrated when they need to spend significant amount of time to find the videos of interest, having to go through different versions of duplicate or near-duplicate videos streamed over the Internet before arriving at new, interesting video. An ideal solution would be to return a list which not only maximizes precision with respect to the query, but also novelty (or diversity) of the query topic. To avoid getting swamped by almost identical copies of the same video in any search, near-duplicate web videos should be detected and eliminated. From new perspectives, the visual redundancy can act as a useful feature, which can be exploited to find new videos of user interest, identify the dominant video version, and annotate incoming videos [26]. It becomes important to manage these videos in an automatic and efficient way. Efficient near-duplicate video detection plays critical role in effective search, retrieval, browsing and annotation.

Due to the large variety of near-duplicate web videos ranging from simple formatting to complex editing, near-duplicate detection remains a challenging problem. Among existing content based approaches, many focus on the rapid identification of duplicate videos with global signatures, which are able to handle almost identical videos. However, duplicates with changes in color, lighting and editing artifacts can only be reliably detected through the use of more reliable local features. Local point based methods have demonstrated impressive performance in a wide range of vision-related tasks, and are particularly suitable for detecting near-duplicate web videos having complex variations. Unfortunately, their potential is undermined by matching and scalability issues. The local point based method remains expensive considering the prohibitively large number of keyframe pairs within two videos and local points within even a single keyframe. Accurate detection generally comes at the cost of time complexity particularly in a large scale web video corpus. Timely response to user queries is one important factor that fuels the popularity of Web 2.0. Therefore, computation becomes the bottleneck for large-scale near-duplicate web video detection.

In this book chapter, we explore two applications based on near-duplicate web video detection: *"Unsupervised" near-duplicate detection* and *near-duplicate video retrieval through query*. "Unsupervised" near-duplicate detection refers to near-duplicate detection without the need of inputting query video, while near-duplicate video retrieval through query means the traditional near-duplicate retrieval by a given query video, that is, query by video example. For "unsupervised" near-duplicate detection, we discuss the novelty re-ranking. Given a list of videos ranking according to text relevance, novelty re-ranking aims to provide novel videos by eliminating all near-duplicate videos. While near-duplicate web video retrieval through query seeks to find all videos that are near-duplicates to a query video. We will review approaches for near-duplicate web video detection from different technical viewpoints. Novelty re-ranking is achieved through a hierarchical approach combining global features and local features, and then a novel solution integrating content and contextual information is proposed to further improve the efficiency. An efficient near-duplicate retrieval based on visual words is proposed, which integrates a couple of techniques, including visual word indexing, keyframe-level pruning, and video-level localization. The rest of this chapter is organized as follows. Section II gives a brief overview of related work. Section III introduces the hierarchical approach combining global signature based on color histograms and local feature based pair-wise keyframe comparison. Section IV presents the method integrating content and context. Section V outlines the efficient algorithm based on visual words for near-duplicate search. Section VI describes our experimental setup, and section VII details the performance evaluation. Finally, section VIII concludes this chapter.

2 Related Works

Video copy and similarity detection has been actively studied for its potential in search [3], topic tracking [31] and copyright protection [17]. Video copy detection has been extensively studied partly due to the initiative contests on content based video copy detection (VCD) in CIVR [18] and TRECVID [19]. Various approaches using different features and matching algorithms have been proposed, which can be applied to near-duplicate video detection. Existing works can be broadly grouped into two categories. One category demands speedy response while the other emphasizes detection effectiveness.

The first category aims for rapid identification of duplicate videos with compact and reliable global features. These features are generally referred to as signatures or fingerprints which summarize the global statistic of low-level features. Typical features include color, motion and ordinal signature [8, 21, 32] and prototype-based signature [3, 4]. One successful example is the retrieval of commercial clips in large database with high speed [16]. It is based on the accumulation of frame signatures. These global feature based approaches are suitable for identifying almost identical videos, and can detect minor editing in the spatial and temporal domain [3, 4, 8, 9, 32]. However, for videos with partial duplicate, either spatially or temporally, global features are known to be less reliable.

The second category addresses the robustness issue by mainly employing local point features [22]. Local points (keypoints) are salient local patches detected over different scales, which are tolerant to geometric and photometric variations. Salient regions in each keyframe can be extracted with local point detectors (e.g. DOG [22], Hessian-Affine [24]) and their descriptors (e.g., SIFT [23]) are mostly invariant to local transformations. Keypoint based local feature detection approaches (e.g. OOS [25]) avoid the shortcomings of global and segment-level features, and give an accurate measurement even for images that have undergone drastic transformations. Their effectiveness has been demonstrated by various works (e.g., [13, 17, 20, 33, 34]), where near-duplicates with considerable variations in background, color and lighting can be successfully identified.

Although local points have been largely acknowledged as reliable and robust features, efficiently matching a large amount of local points remains a difficult problem. To tackle this problem, different approaches have been proposed. Locality sensitive hashing (LSH) is adopted in [17], while a distortion-based probability similar search algorithm based on LSH is proposed for fast duplicate search in [14]. Another popularly adopted technique is retrieval by visual keywords (VK) [27], also known as bag-of-words. Under this technique, keypoints are quantized into groups (forming a dictionary) and each group (an entry in the dictionary) is viewed as a word. As a result, instead of representing video content with hundreds to thousands of keypoint features in high dimensions (e.g., 128 dimensions for the SIFT descriptor [22]), VK characterizes video content as a histogram of words which facilitates fast matching. A VK histogram is often a sparse feature vector in high dimensional space (e.g., 10,000 words). Thus, an inverted file index can be employed for fast matching of visual words [27]. A major weakness of VK is the visual ambiguity caused by keypoint quantization. Specifically, a large (small) dictionary leads to miss (false) matching. Several approaches have been proposed to address this problem, for instance, Hamming embedding (HE) [10], soft-weighting (SW) [12] and weak geometric consistency (WGC) [10]. HE keeps a bit-pattern signature for each visual word for pruning false positives due to histogram matching, while SW assigns multiple words to keypoints to resolve visual ambiguity. WGC is a weighting scheme which re-ranks the quality of histogram matches by checking their geometry consistency. VK normally operates on keyframe-level. Specifically one keyframe is represented by a histogram. To match two videos, the Hough Transform (HT) [7] is another technique often employed to measure the degree of match between videos. HT considers time lags between the matched keyframes from two videos. The time lags are utilized as the cue to measure video similarity.

3 A Hierarchical Approach for Novelty Re-Ranking

To guarantee effective near-duplicate detection while meeting the speed requirements for large-scale video collections, a hierarchical method is proposed for novelty re-ranking in [29], which utilizes both global signatures and local keypoints for detecting near-duplicate web videos. A global signature from color histograms is first used to detect the near-duplicate videos with high confidence and filter out very dissimilar videos. For videos that cannot be clearly classified as novel or near-duplicate using global signatures, a local feature based near-duplicate detection is adopted, which provides very accurate duplicate analysis through more costly computation.

It is common for web users to upload exact duplicate videos with minimal change. This demands an approach for fast detection of duplicate videos. A global signature from color histograms is just this kind of fast measures suitable for matching videos with identical and almost identical content with only minor changes. The global signatures are basically the global statistics or summaries of low-level color features in videos. A video signature (VS) is defined as an m-dimensional vector of a normalized color histogram over all keyframes in the video. $VS = (s_1, s_2, \cdots, s_m)$, where $s_j = \frac{1}{n}\sum_{j=1}^{n} h_{ij}$, n is the number of keyframes in the video, and h_{ij} is the ith bin of the color histogram at keyframe j. We compute the distance of two signatures VS_i and VS_j based on the Euclidean distance:

$$R(V_i|V_j) = d(VS_i, VS_j) = \sqrt{\sum_{k=1}^{m} (x_k - y_k)^2} \quad (1)$$

where $VS_i = (x_1, \cdots, x_m)$, and $VS_j = (y_1, \cdots, y_m)$. Two videos are regarded as near-duplicate if their distance is considered close. Certain videos with small distance can be directly identified as near-duplicate videos, while other videos with large distance can safely be labeled as novel ones. With this filtering, a large portion of videos can be successfully identified, which reduces the computation for more expensive pairwise comparison.

However, for videos with major editing, content modification, dramatic photometric and geometric transformations, global signatures tend to be inadequate. Especially, when multiple variations are mixed together, the near-duplicate detection becomes even harder. Furthermore, due to different frame rates, and content modifications such as the insertion of commercials or title frames at the beginning and credits at the end, the extracted keyframe sequence could be different. And even non-duplicate videos could have similar color distribution as duplicate videos, which will be falsely detected as similar videos.

For web videos that cannot be determined to be novel or near-duplicate using global signature, local feature based near-duplicate detection is adopted to provide very accurate duplicate analysis, at higher cost. A local feature based method is used to measure the similarity of keyframes by pairwise comparison of keyframes from two videos. Pairwise keyframe comparison treats each keyframe as an independent node and two videos are compared by measuring the pairwise similarity among these nodes. To find all near-duplicate/similar keyframes in two videos, the traditional method is to exhaustively compare each keyframe pair. The time complexity is the product of the number of keyframes in the two videos. When the videos consist of a large number of keyframes, it is expensive and not feasible for large scale web video collections. Based on the observation that the corresponding keyframes of near-duplicate web videos have consistent mapping, a *sliding window scheme* is applied to reduce the computation. Each keyframe is only compared to the corresponding keyframes in another video within a certain sliding window. Although the sliding window scheme might miss part of near-duplicate keyframes for a single keyframe in videos of simple scenes, these missed near-duplicate keyframes will be eventually included by transitive closure considering the fact that keyframes for simple scene videos are usually very similar. Once the similar keyframes have been identified, a normalized set difference is used as the metric to evaluate the similarity between two videos. The redundancy of two videos can be determined by comparing the ratio of the number of similar keyframes.

The hierarchical approach combing the global signature and pairwise comparison is a reasonable solution to provide effective and efficient near-duplicate web video detection. Coupled with the use of a sliding window scheme, considerable savings have been made to relieve the computational burden. The combination of global feature and local feature can balance performance and cost.

4 Novelty Re-Ranking with Content and Context

Good performance has been achieved with the hierarchical approach. Unfortunately, the local point based method remains expensive considering the prohibitively large number of keyframe pairs within two videos and local points within a single keyframe. The number of keyframes could exceed one hundred for a four minute

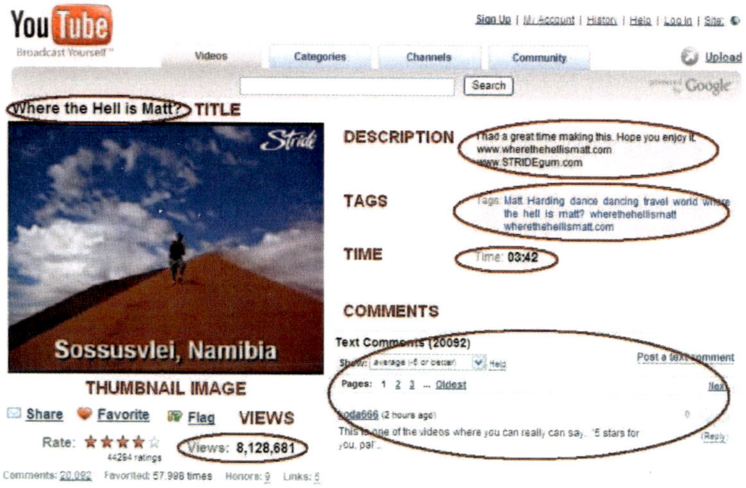

Fig. (2): Rich context information is associated with web videos, e.g., title, tags, thumbnail image, time, views, etc.

music video with fast changing scenes, while the number of local points could reach hundreds to thousands per keyframe. Efficiency is an important factor for web applications. Therefore, computation becomes the bottleneck for efficient near-duplicate elimination. Fortunately, the social web provides much more than a platform for users to interact and exchange information. This has resulted in the rich sets of context information associated with web videos. Careful coupling of context and content is a promising way to hit a balance between speed and accuracy for practical elimination of near-duplicate web videos. In this section, we novelly exploit contextual cues, integrated with content information, for the fast filtering of near-duplicate web videos. The contextual information is first introduced, followed by the approach combining context and content.

Contextual information

One attractive aspect of social media is the abundant amount of context metadata associated with videos as shown in Fig. (2). The metadata includes different aspects of information such as tags, time durations, titles, thumbnail images, number of views, comments, usernames, and so on.

Different from still images and text documents, video describes scenes through displaying a sequence of consecutive frames. An interesting observation is that near-duplicate web videos more or less have similar time duration, with a difference of only a few seconds. As such, *time duration* becomes a critical feature for efficient filtering of dissimilar videos.

A *Thumbnail image* is another critical context metadata associated with videos.

In social media, thumbnail images are usually extracted from the middle of videos. These images give users a basic impression of the video content. In most cases, it is sufficient to categorize two videos as near-duplicates if (a) their thumbnail images are near-duplicate and (b) their time durations are close to each other. This dramatically reduces computation time compared to conventional content-based approaches, which involve all pairwise permutations of keyframes/shots. However, near-duplicate videos with complex variations might sample different thumbnail images due to different video length, particularly when frame insertions or deletions corrupt the time-line of the original video clips. An example illustrating the problem is shown in Fig. (3)(b). This might lead to inadequate near-duplicate detections.

View count is an important indication of the popularity of videos. The larger number of views indicates that it is either a relatively important video or an original video. The popularity count of a video carries implicit information about the intention and interest of the users. Therefore, when presented with a group of potentially near-duplicate videos, view count provides clues to identify the original video sources from which other near-duplicate videos are transformed.

In addition to time duration, thumbnail image and view count, other frequently employed context features include title, tags, description, and so on. These features, while known to be useful for video retrieval, are not particularly helpful for near-duplicate detection. So they will not be discussed in this work.

Context information can accelerate the detection of near duplicates in two manners. First, context can be used jointly with content as a basis to perform near-duplicate decision. Second, context information can be used to uncover the set of dominant near-duplicate groups. These contextual cues can be exploited in a complementary way. Time duration provides a useful hint for rapid identification of dissimilar (novel) videos. On the other hand, thumbnail images reveal the near-duplicate identity of web videos. View count indicates the popularity of a web video and provides cue for the selection of source videos which being popularly modified into different versions of near-duplicate videos.

Novelty re-ranking with content and context

With the fact that a contextual cue is cheaper to acquire from social media while content is expensive to process, a framework exploiting both cues is illustrated in Fig. (4). As a preprocessing step, time duration is used to rapidly but coarsely identify the preliminary groups of near-duplicate videos, where we term each group as a *dominant version*. For each dominant version, a *seed video*, which potentially is the original source from which other videos are derived, is selected. To be efficient, the selection is based on the color histograms of thumbnail images and their view counts. Since seed videos are potential sources, the final step of near-duplicate detection is reduced to compare thumbnail images of candidate videos to the selected seed videos. To ensure accurate detection, this step is performed by matching local

Fig. (3): Near-duplicate web videos can be identified by checking their time duration and thumbnails. They usually have similar time duration, and thumbnail images are commonly matched to the middle part of the dominant video.

points. In brief, the framework integrates context and content information, seeking a balance between real-time processing and detection accuracy. The three main processes (*dominant version identification*, *seed video selection*, *near-duplicate video elimination*) are briefly described as below.

Dominant version identification. In an entertainment web video search, there usually exist a couple of dominant videos. Other videos in the search result are usually derived from them. For example, there are a short version and a full version in the query "The lion sleeps tonight." For each query, dominant version identification is performed by analyzing the distribution of time duration. For each query, the time duration of all videos in this query is first collected, from which we can have a basic understanding of the time distribution and potential peaks. To increase robustness towards editing effects and quantization errors, in addition to the frequency of a single bin, neighboring bins could also be taken into account when computing the significance of a time duration. A simple strategy to consider the neighboring bins is:

$$T = \begin{cases} t_i|(\sum_{j=i-d}^{j=i+d}|t_j|) > \theta \\ t^*|\forall t_i : |t_i| \leq |t^*| & otherwise \end{cases} \tag{2}$$

where $|t_j|$ is the cardinality of the time duration bin t_j, d is the length of neighborhood window, and θ is a threshold. The peaks satisfying the above conditions will be treated as the dominant versions.

Seed video selection. Seed video selection is performed to pick one seed video for each dominant time. Seed video is defined as a potential source from which most near-duplicate videos derived. Videos falling within a specified time range are then filtered by matching the thumbnail images. Color histogram (CH) is extracted for every thumbnail image. Without delving into the content detail inside the videos, the color histogram of thumbnail images and the number of views are combined to select the seed videos. A relative distance distribution is first built where an arbitrarily selected video is used as reference video. The distances between the thumbnail image of the reference video and all other videos in the set are computed, and the relative distance distribution in the form of a histogram is constructed. The set of videos that fall into the largest distance bin thus forms the dominant near-duplicate group for the corresponding dominant time duration. To pick the seed video, another context feature, view count, is employed. A higher number of clicks (views) indicates that a particular video is potentially the original version or it is more popular. The video with the biggest number of views will be picked as the seed video. For each seed video, the representative keyframes are extracted from the middle part of this video. We call these representative keyframes as *prototype keyframes* since they are the potential "prototypes" from which other near-duplicates are transformed, either directly or indirectly. While each video is represented by one thumbnail image, the seed video has multiple prototype keyframes extracted from the middle part. Therefore, the matching of videos is implemented as the comparison of thumbnail images and prototype keyframes, which significantly reduces computational time.

Near-duplicate video elimination. According to the original ranking from the search engine, each video is compared with the seed videos and every novel video to see whether they are duplicates. The comparison is carried out in two ways, by using context and content information respectively. First, time duration information is treated as a filter to avoid the comparison between videos with considerably different length. If the difference of time durations is large enough, the two videos will not be compared and they will be directly regarded as dissimilar. Otherwise, the thumbnail image of the video will be compared with the thumbnail images of previously novel videos and the prototype keyframes of the seed videos to evaluate the degree of redundancy. Second, content features based on local points extracted from the thumbnail images and prototype keyframes are matched using [35]. To

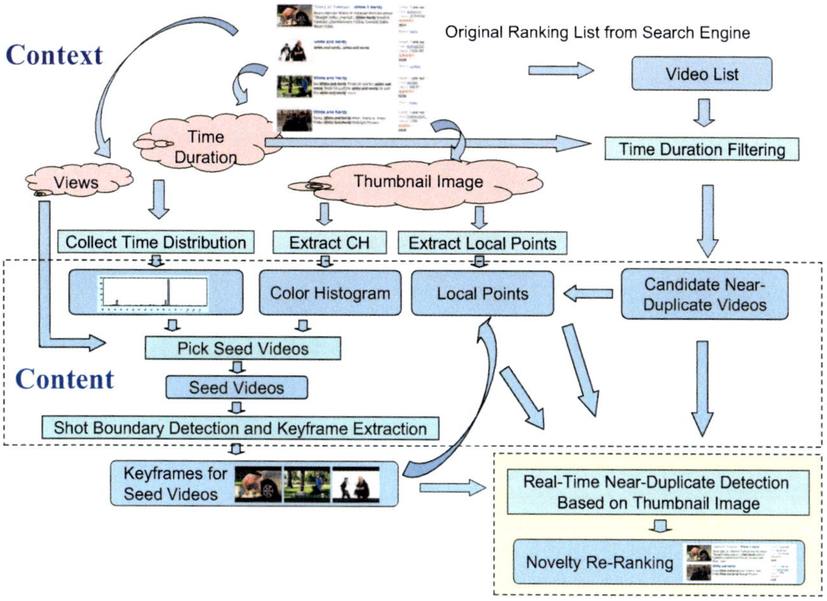

Fig. (4): Framework for novelty re-ranking with content and context.

increase efficiency, comparison is performed only on thumbnail images, instead of exhaustively between all keyframe pairs of two videos. Similar to [29], we treat two images as near-duplicate if they have enough number of local point matching pairs. The first step speeds up detection by avoiding unnecessary comparison, while the second step keeps the expensive content processing as low as possible. After that, if the thumbnail image of a video is found to be a duplicate of the seed video or some previous novel videos, it will be labeled as a near-duplicate video and filtered out. Otherwise, the video is considered novel and will be returned to the users.

5 Efficient Near-duplicate Video Retrieval

In this section, we discuss efficient near-duplicate video retrieval for a given query. Recently, analogous to text information retrieval, visual vocabulary has been proposed by quantizing points into visual words, and inverted file index is employed for fast matching of visual words. However, a major weakness of visual words is visual ambiguity caused by keypoint quantization. To make the near-duplicate detection applicable to web scale video corpus, we propose an efficient and effective near-duplicate video retrieval approach by considering three aspects: indexing of local visual features, fast pruning of false matches at frame-level, and localization of near-duplicate segments at video-level. This approach integrates enhanced weak geometric constraint (E-WGC), Hough Transform (HT), and reverse entropy (RE).

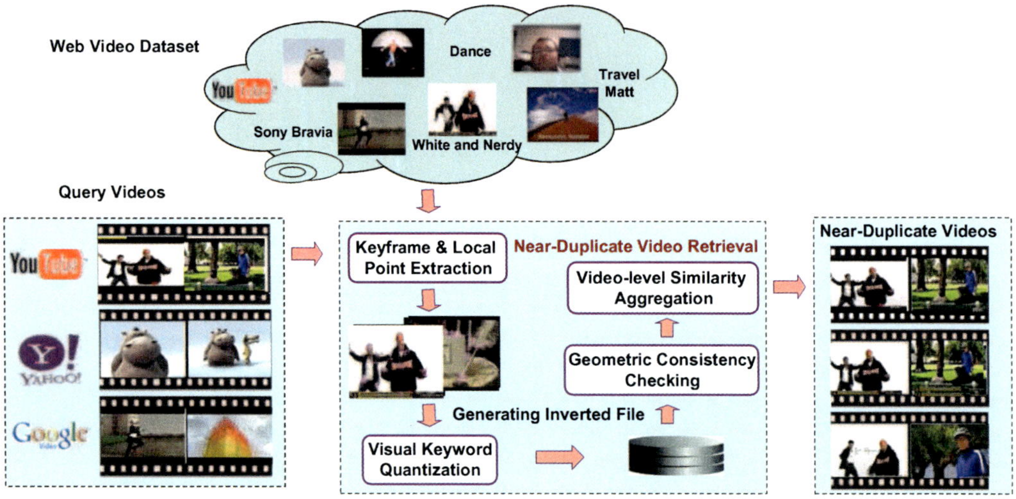

Fig. (5): Framework for efficient near-duplicate retrieval based on visual keywords.

It has shown its efficiency, effectiveness and superior capability in pruning out false alarms compared to the-state-of-art techniques.

Framework

Fig.(5) illustrates the proposed framework for efficient near-duplicate web video retrieval. For offline indexing, web videos are pre-processed by performing shot boundary detection and then keyframe selection. Local keypoints are extracted from the keyframes and clustering is carried out to quantize the keypoints into a visual dictionary. Each keypoint in the keyframes is then encoded with a visual word in the dictionary, and this forms a bag of words for each keyframe. Inverted file indexing is employed for supporting scalable keyframe retrieval with fast similarity evaluation. Similar procedure is applied to the given queries for generating a bag of words to describe video content.

In near-duplicate search, the keyframes which are similar to query keyframes are retrieved from video corpus via visual keywords and inverted file (Section V-B). The retrieved keyframes are further re-ranked according to their geometric consistency with the query. An efficient evaluation based on weak geometric consistency checking is proposed (Section V-C). Finally, the similarity of a video is determined by aggregating the scores of keyframes in the video while weakly considering their temporal consistency with the query. The video-level similarity aggregation is based on 2D Hough Transform together with a proposed reverse-entropy measure (Section V-D).

Visual Keywords (VK) and Inverted File indexing

For reliable retrieval, we adopt local keypoint descriptors as the features for near-duplicate retrieval. Nonetheless, the number of keypoints in a keyframe can range from hundreds to thousands, while the dimension of descriptor is typically high. Matching keypoints between two keyframes becomes extremely slow. Thus, we employ clustering approach by first quantizing keypoints into a visual dictionary (codebook). Each entry in the dictionary (or centroid of a cluster) corresponds to a word. By mapping each keypoint in a frame to the nearest word, this forms a bag-of-words, which is represented in the form of histogram, describing the visual content of the keyframe. Each bin in the histogram accumulates the number of words found in the keyframe. Measuring the similarity between two keyframes is then performed by bin-to-bin matching of their histograms. We use cosine distance to measure the closeness between keyframes.

To ensure the coverage of dictionary, the number of words is usually large (e.g., $\geq$ 10,000). Direct matching two histograms will not be extremely fast in this case. Nevertheless, since the histogram is normally very sparse, the matching can be efficiently conducted by exploiting structure such as inverted file index [27] which is popularly used in text information retrieval. The index stores the keyword-image relationship, in which each entry (or row) corresponds to a keyword and links to the list of keyframes which contain the word. As a consequence, given a keyframe, the words are hashed into the index and the matched keyframes are retrieved. Cosine similarity is thus only evaluated for a subset of keyframes in the dataset and for those no-zero entries in the histograms only.

We adopt 2-level vector quantization (VQ) to further speed up the online retrieval time. Multiple-level VQ allows efficient encoding of keypoints to keywords without exhaustive search of the nearest words. In our experiment, querying a keyframe against a dataset of 632,498 keyframes only requires 0.08 seconds to complete.

Keyframe-level geometric consistency checking

The keypoint quantization introduces ambiguity in visual matching. For example, words from the same bin are always matched regardless of their actual distance measured by keypoint descriptors. For words from large clusters, this could cause excessive number of false matches. Thus geometric consistency checking is a post-processing step aiming to examine the coherency of matches between two sets of visual words. Fig.(6) and (7) show examples that two pairs of keyframes have similar matching scores as computed by cosine distance. However, visually the keyframes in Fig.(7) are very different. Ideally, by recovering their underlying geometric transformation from the word matches as shown in Fig.(6), the dissimilar keyframes can be pruned.

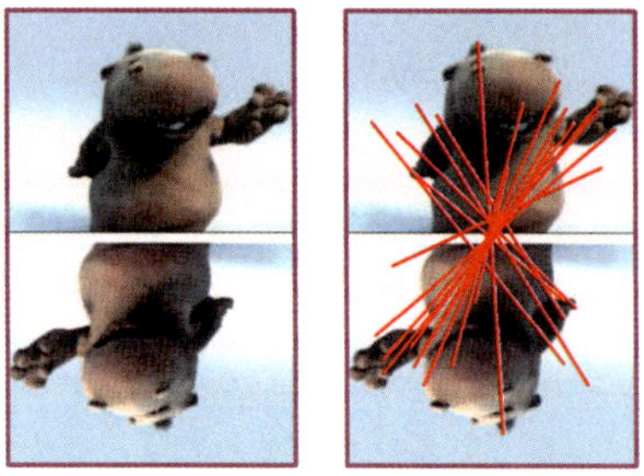

Fig. (6): Near-duplicate keyframes (left) with similar matching scores based on cosine distance. Portion of the matched visual words are highlighted (right).

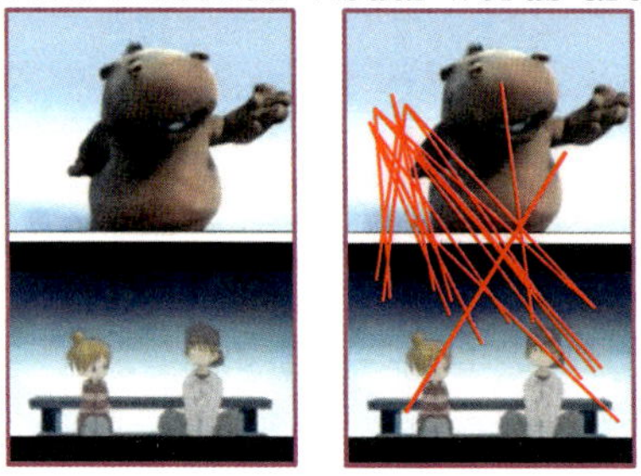

Fig. (7): Dissimilar keyframes (left) with similar matching scores based on cosine distance. Portion of the matched visual words are highlighted (right).

Weak geometry consistency (WGC)

Recovery of transformation is often done by RANSAC [24]. However, such estimation is always costly and not appropriate when large number of keyframes are required to be investigated. WGC [10] is a recently proposed technique which exploits the weak or partial geometric consistency without explicitly estimating the transformation by checking the matches from one keyframe to another. Given two matched visual words $p(x_p, y_p)$ and $q(x_q, y_q)$ from two keyframes respectively, WGC estimates the transformation from p to q as:

$$\begin{bmatrix} x_q \\ y_q \end{bmatrix} = s \times \begin{bmatrix} \cos\theta & -\sin\theta \\ \sin\theta & \cos\theta \end{bmatrix} \times \begin{bmatrix} x_p \\ y_p \end{bmatrix} + \begin{bmatrix} T_x \\ T_y \end{bmatrix}, \quad (3)$$

where (x_p, y_p) and (x_q, y_q) are the 2D spatial positions of p and q in x-y coordinate. In Eq.(3), there are three parameters to be estimated: the scaling factor s, the rotation parameter θ and the translation $[T_x, T_y]^t$. In WGC, only the parameters s and θ are estimated. For efficiency, the scale and rotation can be derived directly from the local patches of p and q without explicit estimation of Eq.(3). The scale s is approximated as:

$$\widetilde{s} = 2^{(s_q - s_p)}, \quad (4)$$

where s_p, s_q are the characteristic scales of words p and q respectively. The scale values of words are known by the time when their corresponding keypoints (or local patches) are detected. For instance, the value s_p indicates the scale level which p resides in the Laplacian of Gaussian (or Difference of Gaussian) pyramid [22, 24]. Similarly, the orientation θ is approximated as:

$$\widetilde{\theta} = \theta_q - \theta_p, \tag{5}$$

where θ_p and θ_q are the dominant orientations of visual words p and q estimated during keypoint detection [22]. WGC computes $log(\widetilde{s})$ and $\widetilde{\theta}$ for each matched visual word between two keyframes. By treating scale and rotation parameters independently, two histograms h^s and h^θ, referring to the scale and orientation consistency respectively, are produced. Fig.(8) and (9) show the scale and rotation histograms according to the matches of words in Fig. (6) and (7) respectively. Each peak in a histogram means one kind of transformations being performed by a group of words. Ideally, a histogram with one or few peaks hints the consistency of geometry transformation for most visual words in the keyframes. WGC utilizes the consistency clue to adjust the similarity of keyframes by:

$$sim_{wgc}(i, j) = min(max(h^s), max(h^\theta)) \times sim_{ij}. \tag{6}$$

The similarity is boosted, by a factor corresponding to the peak value in scale or orientation histogram, for keyframe pairs which show consistency in geometry transformation.

Enhanced weak geometry consistency (E-WGC)

The merit of WGC lies in its simplicity and thus efficiency in transformation estimation. Nevertheless, such estimation is not always reliable. For example, despite that the keyframes in Fig. (6) are rotated version of one another, there are two peaks found in the difference of $\widetilde{\theta}$ histogram of (8). Similarly, by observing the histograms in Fig. (9) computed from the keyframes in Fig. (7), there are apparent peaks in both histograms, though the keyframes are dissimilar. The re-ranking scheme in Eq.(6) may incorrectly boost their similarity in this case. The main reason for such unreliable estimation is due to the fact that the characteristic scale and dominant orientation estimated from keypoint detection are not always discriminative enough. For example, although DoG (Difference of Gaussian) detector adopts 5 levels of Gaussian pyramid for keypoint localization, most points are detected at level 1. As a consequence, the scale histogram always has a peak corresponding to level 1.

We propose the enhancement of WGC by also including translation information. Combining equations 3, 4 and 5, we have the WGC estimation as:

$$\begin{bmatrix} \widetilde{x_q} \\ \widetilde{y_q} \end{bmatrix} = \widetilde{s} \times \begin{bmatrix} \cos\widetilde{\theta} & -\sin\widetilde{\theta} \\ \sin\widetilde{\theta} & \cos\widetilde{\theta} \end{bmatrix} \times \begin{bmatrix} x_p \\ y_p \end{bmatrix}. \tag{7}$$

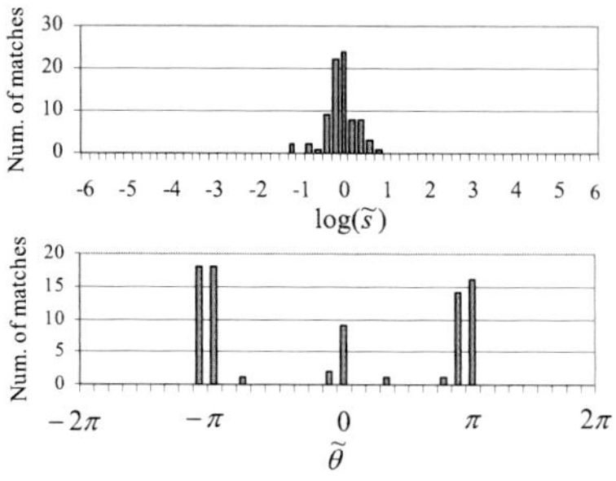

Fig. (8): Scale and rotation histograms of WGC for Fig.(6).

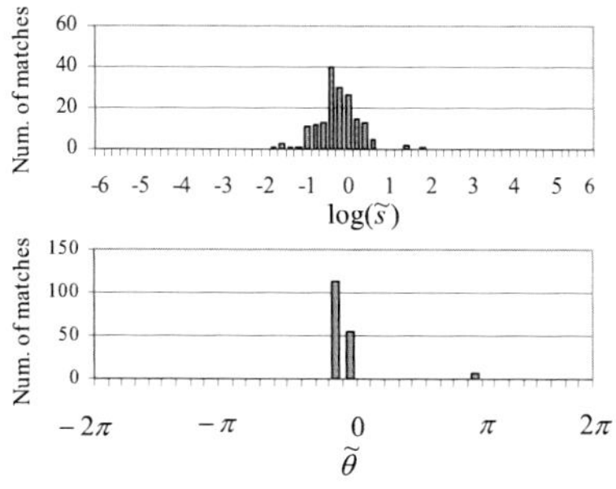

Fig. (9): Scale and rotation histograms of WGC for Fig.(7)

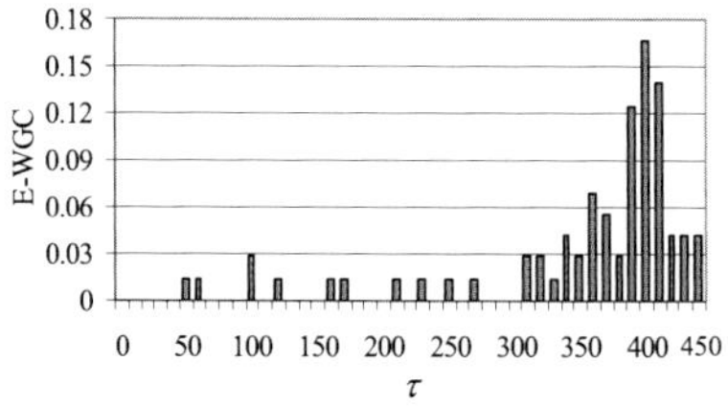

Fig. (10): Translation histograms of E-WGC for Fig.(6).

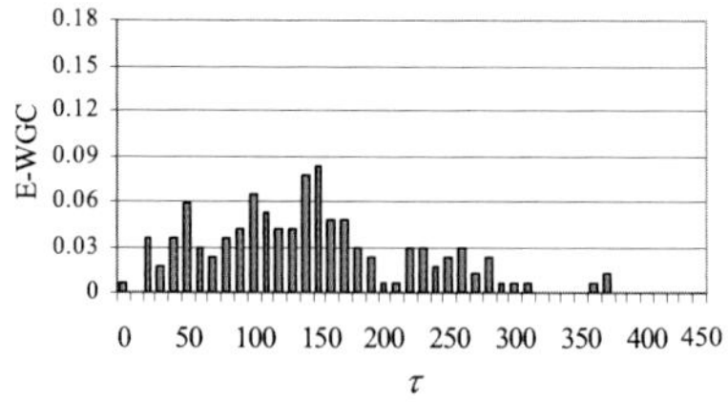

Fig. (11): Translation histograms of E-WGC for Fig.(7).

Deriving from equations 3 and 7, the translation τ of the visual word q can be efficiently estimated by

$$\tau = \sqrt{(\widetilde{x_q} - x_q)^2 + (\widetilde{y_q} - y_q)^2}. \tag{8}$$

Ideally, the matched visual words which follow consistent transformation should have similar values of τ, and thus τ can be used to directly adjust the keyframe similarity as in Eq.(6). There are two advantages with this simple scheme. First, the inclusion of translation information provides another geometric clue in addition to scale and rotation. Second, Eq.(8) has jointly integrated the clues from scale, rotation and translation, thus generating one histogram of τ is enough for similarity re-ranking. In addition, Eq.(8) can be trivially computed without incurring additional computational cost. Since Eq.(8) is an enhanced version of equations 4 and 5, we name our approach *enhanced* WGC, or E-WGC in short.

In E-WGC, only one histogram is generated based on the values of translation τ. Similar to WGC, histogram peak is located to re-rank the keyframe similarity. For robustness, the peak is smoothed by considering the moving average of two neighboring bins. As a result, the value of peak is computed as:

$$\tau_{peak} = |h_i| + |h_{i-1}| + |h_{i+1}| - 2 \times \frac{\sum_{j=1}^{m} |h_j|}{m}, \tag{9}$$

where h_i is the bin with peak value, and m is the number of histogram bins. Ultimately, the keyframe is re-ranked as:

$$sim_{ewgc}(i,j) = (\frac{\tau_{peak}}{M_{vk}})^{\gamma} \times sim_{ij}, \tag{10}$$

where τ_{peak} is normalized by M_{vk} which denotes the number of matched visual words in two keyframes. We amplify the ratio of τ_{peak} to M_{vk} by a factor of γ so as to increase the gap between similar and dissimilar keyframes. The factor γ is a parameter empirically set equal to 3, which will not affect the re-ranking result.

Fig.(10) and (11) show the translation histograms generated by E-WGC for keyframe pairs in Fig.(6) and (7). Note that the histograms are normalized by M_{vk}. The histogram shows an apparent peak for the near-duplicate pair in Fig.(6), while there is no peak with high score for the dissimilar keyframes in Fig.(7). The re-ranking formula in Eq.(10) therefore boosts the similarity of Fig.(6) but not Fig.(7). This is in contrast to the histograms generated by WGC as shown in Fig.(8) and (9). In these figures, peaks are observed in both scale and orientation histograms regardless of whether the videos are similar. As a result, the similarities are incorrectly ranked by Eq.(6). Compared to WGC, E-WGC can more effectively distinguish near-duplicates from dissimilar keyframes.

Video-Level similarity aggregation

Similarity aggregation involves the measure of sequence similarity for videos where their keyframes are fully or partially matched to the keyframes of a query video. Given a set of keyframe pairs from a video V_k and a query Q, the similarity between V_k and Q can be simply counted by aggregating the number of keyframe matches. Such measure, nevertheless, does not consider temporal consistency and the noisy matches can be easily included in similarity counting. Hough Transform (HT) is a technique aiming to aggregate the keyframe matches by weakly considering their temporal consistency [7]. HT is basically a voting scheme which accumulates scores from matches with similar time lags. Given a keyframe pair I_i and I_j with similarity score $sim_{ewgc}(i,j)$ as computed in Eq.(10) and temporally located at time t_1 and t_2 of videos V_k and Q respectively, the time lag is computed as:

$$\delta_{i,j} = t_1 - t_2. \tag{11}$$

HT aggregates the similarity score as a result of one keyframe match into a 2-dimensional histogram, with one dimension as the video ID and the other dimension as the time lag. In this histogram, video ID is a unique integer assigned to a video, and the range of time lag is quantized into bins by a bandwidth of δ_0. Each keyframe matching pair I_i and I_j contributes a score of $sim_{ewgc}(i,j)$ to the bin $[k,b]$, where k is the video ID of V_k and $b = \lfloor \frac{\delta_{i,j}}{\delta_0} \rfloor$. Consequently, a peak in the histogram, in the form of a triple $[k, b, score_{kb}]$, corresponds to an accumulated score $score_{kb} = \sum_{i,j} sim_{ewgc}(i,j)$ of keyframes in V_k which are temporally aligned with the query video Q (i.e., $b = \lfloor \frac{\delta_{i,j}}{\delta_0} \rfloor$). In other words, peaks in the histogram hint the video segments which are similar to Q. Detecting the peaks is basically equivalent to finding the partial near-duplicates of Q.

Let $\mathcal{H}[k,b]$ be the 2D Hough histogram, where $1 \le k \le n$, and n is the number of videos having the matched keyframes with query Q. HT measures the similarity of video V_k to Q by

$$\mathcal{S}im_{ht}(V_k, Q) = max_b(\mathcal{H}[k,b]), \tag{12}$$

In other words, the similarity of two videos is determined by the maximum aggregated similarity score of keyframes from both videos which are consistently matched along the temporal dimension.

Reverse-Entropy ranking

While Hough Transform is efficient to implement, it has the deficiency that the influence of noisy matches is not carefully tackled. As indicated in [7], the similarity aggregation is often mixed with considerable portion of false positive matches. The reasons are mainly due to two practical concerns. First, shot boundary detection is not always perfect. False detection can cause excessive number of shots (and keyframes) which are similar to each other within a video. As a consequence, this often results in one keyframe from a video being matched to several keyframes in another video or vice versa. Second, the imprecise matching of visual words due to quantization error, as well as E-WGC which only weakly considers the geometric transformation, also introduces random false matches. These practical concerns jointly make the similarity aggregation in HT lack robustness.

To solve this problem, we revise Eq.(12) by taking into account the granularity of matching. The intuitive idea is that a keyframe which matches to multiple keyframes in another video is given less priority when determining the video similarity. Thus, the aim is to lower the scores of video segments which include excessive matching. Let the 2D Hough bin $[k, b]$ as the peak which gives rise to the similarity between videos V_k and Q as in Eq.(12), and assume that the bin corresponds to a segment S_v from V_k and another segment S_q from Q. Let N_q be the number of keyframes in S_q, and η_l be the number of keyframes from S_v with matches to the lth keyframe of S_q. We employ entropy to measure the associative mapping from S_q to S_v as

$$RE(S_q \to S_v) = \frac{-1}{\log Z}(\sum_{l=1}^{N_q} \frac{\eta_l}{Z} \times log\frac{\eta_l}{Z}), \tag{13}$$

where $Z = \sum_{l=1}^{N_q} \eta_l$ is the total number of keyframe matches between videos V_k and Q. The value of entropy ranges within $[0, 1]$. The measure of entropy depends upon the granularity of matches from one video to another. Matching which exhibits one-to-one correspondence will receive the highest entropy value of 1. In contrast, for the cases of one-to-many or many-to-one matching, the entropy value will be low. A special case happens when only one keyframe in S_q has matches, and the keyframe matches to all the keyframes in S_v. In this case, the value of entropy will be 0. Since the definition of entropy here is different from convention where a value of 1 indicates uncertainty while a value of 0 indicates confident match, we name the entropy measure in Eq.(13) as *Reverse-Entropy (RE)* measure.

The measure of RE is not symmetric, meaning that the matches for $S_q \to S_v$ will have different RE value from that of $S_v \to S_q$. Thus the final value of RE is defined as:

$$RE(V_k, Q) = min(RE(S_q \to S_v), RE(S_v \to S_q)). \tag{14}$$

We use the RE measure in Eq.(14) to estimate the similarity between videos V_k and Q as following:

$$\mathcal{S}im_{re}(V_k, Q) = \begin{cases} Sim_{ht}(V_k, Q) \times RE(V_k, Q)^2 & \text{if } RE(V_k, Q) \neq 0 \\ Sim_{ht}(V_k, Q) \times \frac{1}{\sqrt{Z}} & \text{Otherwise} \end{cases} \tag{15}$$

The original similarity is devalued by the square of RE so as to penalize more on video segments having noisy matches. Notice that when RE equals to 0, it indicates that only one keyframe of a video (either Q or V_k) is matched to keyframes of another video. In this case, the similarity is weighted by $\frac{1}{\sqrt{Z}}$ so as to avoid the similarity score abruptly dropping to zero.

Time and space complexity

While the framework involves a variety of components, the retrieval speed is highly efficient mainly due to the use of inverted file which is essentially a hashing technique. There are several factors which govern the time complexity of retrieval. These include the size of visual words (w), number of keyframes (m) per query, and number of keypoints (p) per keyframe.

Mapping a keypoint to a word and eventually retrieving the list of keyframes containing the word takes $O(w)$ time. The speed can be improved to $O(log(w))$ with the use of multi-layer vector quantization. Thus mapping an entire query video to visual words for retrieval costs $O(mplog(w))$. The size of candidate videos retained for E-WGC and HT is query dependent. Assuming that there are n keyframes being retrieved and each keyframe contains q keypoints, in worst case E-WGC will take $O(mnpq)$ to verify every matching point, and HT will take $O(mn)$ to check temporal alignment. Summing up all the components, the complexity is $O(mplog(w))+O(mnpq)+O(mn)$. Let K as the total number of keyframes indexed in dataset. In practice, $m, n << K$, and the average number of keypoints (p and q) is typically about 260. Due to the use of HE, the number of keypoints to be verified by E-WGC can be reduced by another 70-85%. In brief, the time complexity is sub-linear to the number of keyframes and keypoints of a dataset, and in practice, the retrieval speed can be very efficient.

In terms of space complexity, each visual word in the inverted file stores the keyframe ID (4 bytes), spatial location of keypoint (4 bytes), scale (2 bytes), dominant orientation (2 bytes), and Hamming signature (4 bytes). Thus, the space is linear to the number of keypoints to be indexed. For our dataset of 144G bytes and 1,040 hours of videos, the size of inverted file is 2.45G.

6 Experiment Setup

Datasets

To verify the robustness, effectiveness and efficiency of the approaches for near-duplicate web video detection, two web video datasets (DS_SOURCE and DS_TIME) are collected to evaluate the performance. Dataset DS_SOURCE is the same dataset used in [29, 30] and was publicly released recently, which is also called CC_WEB_VIDEO [1]. The dataset was collected in November, 2006. Our aim is to re-rank videos according to novelty, and to retrieve Google and Yahoo! videos using YouTube resources. We select 24 queries designed to retrieve the most viewed and top favorite videos from YouTube. Each text query is issued to YouTube, Google video, and Yahoo! video respectively and we collect all retrieved videos as our dataset. This collection consists of 12,790 videos. The query information and the number of near-duplicates in DS_SOURCE are listed in Tab.(1). The 3rd column shows the number of videos from YouTube, while the number of web videos from Google and Yahoo! is listed in the 4th column. The 5th and 6th columns list the amount and percentage of near-duplicates among which videos from Google and Yahoo! can find the corresponding near-duplicates in the YouTube. For example, 85 out of 93 videos from Google and Yahoo! in Query 19 ("Sony Bravia") have corresponding near-duplicate videos in YouTube. On average, there are 38.6% videos from Google and Yahoo! having counterparts in YouTube.

Since the distribution of video data evolves as the time goes by, it is expected that the uploaded videos might deviate from the original ones, and the number of near-duplicate videos should diminish. To verify the robustness of proposed method, dataset DS_TIME was collected in December 2008, using the same queries as in DS_SOURCE but crawled at different time. The objective is to retrieve the newly added videos using previous data. Tab.(2) shows the details. For each topic, we retrieve top 500 videos returned by YouTube search engine. Among these videos, the ones having time overlapping with videos in the first dataset DS_SOURCE are removed. In Tab. (2), the third column lists the number of videos in the DS_SOURCE dataset, while the fourth shows the number of web videos newly collected. The 5th and 6th columns demonstrate the amount and percentage of newly crawled videos that can find the near-duplicate in the DS_SOURCE dataset. Query "I will survive Jesus" still has high percentage of near-duplicates (73.3%) for videos uploaded during December 2006 to December 2008. Based on our statistics, the average percentage of near-duplicate videos is 13.5%, which is smaller than the percentage in DS_SOURCE. Currently a portion of fully duplicate videos has been removed by YouTube, and there is a two year interval between these dataset collections. The topics may become unpopular and the contents can deviate from the original ones. These reasons cause the relatively low percentage of near-duplicates if compared to DS_SOURCE.

Pre-Processing

Shot boundaries are detected and each shot is represented by a keyframe. Totally, there are 398,009 keyframes in CC_WEB_VIDEO. To compare the performance, we extract the global features (color moment and color histograms) and local keypoint features. Each keyframe is depicted with the first three color moments (i.e., mean, standard deviation, and skewness) extracted in Lab color space over 5×5 grid partitions, which results in a 225 dimensional feature vector. Color histogram is based on the HSV color space, which is the same as [29, 31]. A color histogram is concatenated with 18 bins for Hue, 3 bins for Saturation, and 3 bins

Tab. (1): The information of dataset DS_SOURCE. Annotating videos of Google and Yahoo!(G+Y) by using YouTube (YT).

ID	Topic	YT	G+Y	ND	%
1	The lion sleep tonight	664	128	61	47.7
2	Evolution of dance	354	129	29	22.5
3	Fold shirt	337	99	61	61.6
4	Cat massage	293	51	22	43.1
5	Ok go here it goes again	263	133	17	12.8
6	Urban ninja	682	89	40	44.9
7	Real life Simpsons	249	116	40	34.5
8	Free hugs	489	50	32	64
9	Where the hell is Matt	196	39	9	23.1
10	U2 and green day	277	39	8	40.0
11	Little superstar	229	148	18	12.2
12	Napoleon dynamite	769	112	33	29.5
13	I will survive Jesus	376	40	30	75.0
14	Ronaldinho ping pong	79	28	11	39.3
15	White and Nerdy	1495	276	70	25.4
16	Korean karaoke	180	25	16	64.0
17	Panic at the disco I write sins not tragedies	609	38	9	23.7
18	Bus uncle	453	35	23	65.7
19	Sony Bravia	473	93	85	91.4
20	Changes Tupac	178	16	9	56.3
21	Afternoon delight	412	37	10	0.27
22	Numa Gary	360	62	34	54.8
23	Shakira hips don't lie	1146	176	42	23.9
24	India driving	220	67	13	19.4
	Total	12790	1870	722	38.6%

for Value. The local points of images are located by Hessian-Affine detector [24]. The local points are then described by PCA-SIFT [17], which is a 36 dimensional vector for each local point. With a fast indexing structure LIP-IS [25], local points are matched based on a point-to-point symmetric matching scheme [25]. For visual keywords based approaches, local keypoints are detected by Harris-Laplace and described by SIFT [22]. For learning visual dictionary, we collect 742,139 local features from 2,000 keyframes which are randomly selected from the DS_SOURCE dataset. The publicly available toolkit CLUTO [15] is employed to cluster local points into 20,000 clusters.

Performance metrics

To generate the ground-truth, two assessors are asked to watch videos one query at a time. The videos are ordered according to the sequence returned by the video search engines. The assessors are requested to label the videos with a judgment

Tab. (2): The information of dataset DS_TIME. Annotating newly crawled dataset DS_TIME (NEW) by previously crawled DS_SOURCE (OLD).

ID	Topic	OLD	NEW	ND	%
1	The lion sleep tonight	792	395	82	20.8
2	Evolution of dance	483	414	9	2.2
3	Fold shirt	436	355	35	9.9
4	Cat massage	344	433	10	2.3
5	Ok go here it goes again	396	255	13	5.1
6	Urban ninja	771	337	53	15.7
7	Real life Simpsons	365	304	20	6.6
8	Free hugs	539	324	0	0.0
9	Where the hell is Matt	235	437	7	1.6
10	U2 and green day	297	328	54	16.5
11	Little superstar	377	397	0	0.0
12	Napoleon dynamite	881	326	47	14.4
13	I will survive Jesus	416	326	240	73.6
14	Ronaldinho ping pong	107	160	61	38.1
15	White and Nerdy	1771	334	76	22.8
16	Korean karaoke	205	350	11	3.1
17	Panic at the disco I write sins not tragedies	647	375	48	12.8
18	Bus uncle	488	250	0	0.0
19	Sony Bravia	566	392	65	16.6
20	Changes Tupac	194	446	75	16.8
21	Afternoon delight	449	426	37	8.7
22	Numa Gary	422	375	89	23.7
23	Shakira hips don't lie	1322	342	92	26.9
24	India driving	287	378	8	2.1
	Total	12790	8459	1141	13.5%

(redundant or novel) and to form the ground truth. To evaluate the re-ranking results, the assessors are requested to identify the near-duplicate clusters in an incremental way and the final ranking list is formed based on the original relevance ranking after removing near-duplicate videos. For near-duplicate video retrieval, assessors are asked to watch the query and then browse through the videos in datasets to manually find the corresponding near-duplicate videos. Partial near-duplicate videos, with at least one shot being near-duplicate, are also included as the ground-truth.

In order to evaluate the performance of novelty re-ranking, we use the *novelty mean average precision* (NMAP) to measure the ability to re-rank relevant web videos according to their novelty. The NMAP measures the mean average precision of all tested queries, considering only novel and relevant videos as the ground truth set. In other words, if two videos are relevant to a query but near-duplicate to each other, only the first video is considered as a correct match. For a given query, there are total of N videos in the collection that are relevant to the query. Assume that the system only retrieves the top k candidate novel videos where r_i is the number of novel videos seen so far from rank 1 to i. The NMAP is computed as:

$$NMAP = \frac{(\sum_{i=1}^{k} r_i/i)}{N} \tag{16}$$

The value of NMAP is in the range of 0 to 1. A value of 0 means all videos in the top-k list are near-duplicate of each other. In contrary, a value of 1 indicates that all top-k ranked videos are novel.

For near-duplicate video retrieval, we measure the *average precision* (AP) of each query topic. AP is a measure indicating the area under a precision-recall curve.

7 Evaluation

Performance of novelty Re-Ranking

The objective of search results novelty re-ranking is to list all the novel videos while maintaining the relevance order. To evaluate the performance of novelty re-ranking, we compare the re-ranking results based on (a) context information only, where the time duration (*Duration*), title (*Title*) and tag (*Tags*) context are evaluated separately; (b) content information only, i.e., the hierarchical method (*HIRACH*) proposed in [29] and global signatures (*Signature*) using color histogram; and (c) the approach (*CONT+CONX*) that integrates the content and context information [30]. The original ranking (*Original*) from the search engine serves as the baseline, while HIRACH serves as the upper limit performance. For the time duration context, if the time difference between two videos is within an interval (e.g. 3 seconds), they will be treated as redundant. Similarly, for the global signature, two videos were regarded as duplicate when their signature difference is close enough (e.g. less than 0.15). The titles and tags are compared using set difference measurement. If the titles or tags are same for two videos, they will be treated as duplicate.

The performance comparison up to top 30 search results is illustrated in Fig. (12). It is obvious that the performance for original search results is not good because duplicate videos often dominate the top list. In general, content-based methods, i.e. HIRACH and global signature, are able to consistently improve upon the baseline performance over all top k novel topics. As expected, HIRACH achieves the best performance. Although the global signature method can identify duplicate videos to some extent, its capability to discover more difficult duplicate videos is limited. A lot of near-duplicate videos cannot be correctly detected. Therefore the re-ranking list still consists of some duplicate videos and many novel videos are falsely removed.

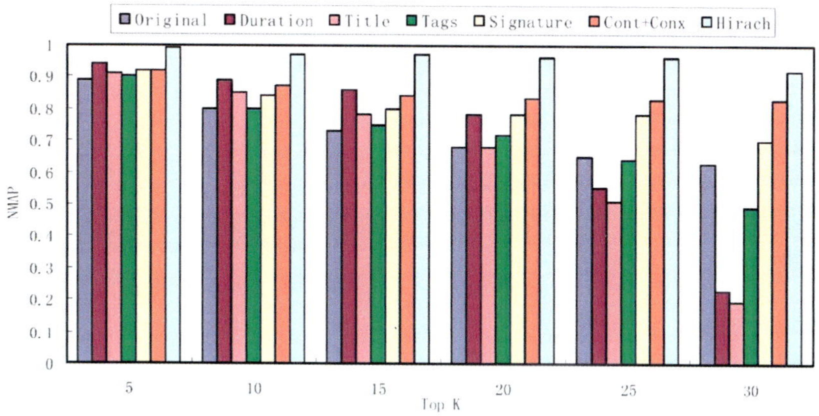

Fig. (12): Performance comparison for web video novelty re-ranking.

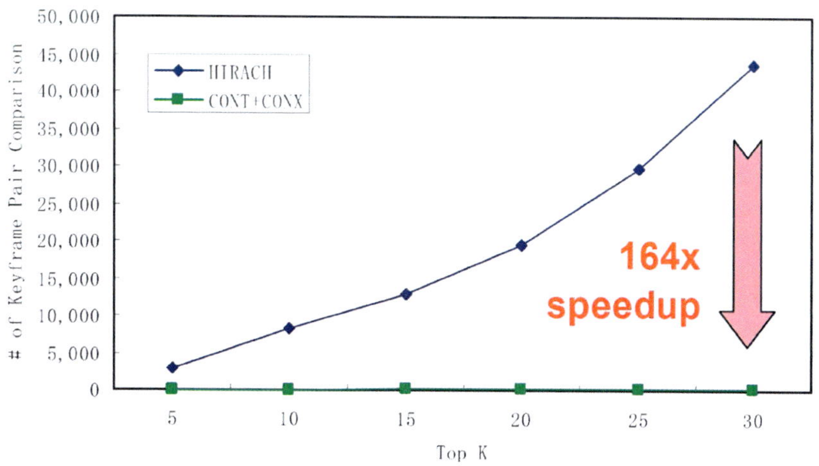

Fig. (13): Computation comparison for novelty re-ranking.

The approach integrating content and context information (CONT+CONX) achieves stable performance across all top k levels. The compensation from content and context makes this approach reliable. Certain videos can be filtered out simply based on time duration information. The local point based detection on thumbnail images guarantees the performance. Although the performance is slightly worse than the hierarchical method, the integration of content and context is able to compensate and overcome the limitations faced by each context as a separate entity.

As search engines demands for quick response, the computation time is an important factor for consideration. The average number of keyframe pair comparison for top k re-ranking over 24 queries is showed in Fig. (13). Although HIRACH has been able to reduce the computation through the use of global signature filtering and the sliding window scheme, it is still infeasible for large scale duplicate elimination. The situation becomes worse as k becomes larger since it still requires a large number of comparisons among keyframes. In contrast, CONT+CONX is extremely efficient, achieving real-time elimination. A huge number of comparisons are filtered out with the time duration information. Furthermore, CONT+CONX only compares the thumbnail images or the prototype keyframes of seed videos, thus avoiding comprehensive keyframe pair comparisons. The speedup is especially evident for videos with fast changing scenes. By using a small number of prototype keyframes for the seed videos and the thumbnail for the unprocessed video, the number of comparisons required by CONT+CONX to match two videos has a constant time complexity. From Fig. (13), we can see that the average number of keyframe pair comparison grows almost exponentially using HIRACH. On the other hand, CONT+CONX only has a linear increase. The speedup of CONT+CONX is around 164 times faster than the hierarchical method when re-ranking the top 30 novel videos. The acceleration will be more conspicuous as k becomes larger.

Performance of Near-duplicate video retrieval

We compare the performance of efficient near-duplicate retrieval for following approaches: 1) LSH-E: locality sensitive hashing embedding on color moment, 2) VK: visual keyword search together with inverted file index and 2D HT for video similarity measure, 3) VK+ [10]: visual keyword search with WGC checking and 2D HT, 4) VK++: visual keyword search plus E-WGC checking and 2D HT, and 5) VK#: VK++ with RE ranking. LSH-E is a recently proposed technique in [6] for scalable video search. Using LSH, the technique embeds color moment into a long and sparse feature vector. Inverted file is then applied to support the fast retrieval of long vectors. We use the same implementation provided by [6]. Cosine distance measure is used for forming the embedded space. We use the best possible setting of bin width equal to 200 for all approaches. To confirm the retrieval performance of five approaches, we measure AP of up to top-500 retrieved items. The mean AP (MAP) of the five approaches in DS_SOURCE and DS_TIME datasets is listed in Tab. (3). The experiments are conducted for queries with near-duplicates. Therefore, 722 and 1,141 queries are tested for DS_SOURCE and DS_TIME, respectively. Overall, VK based approaches show significantly better performance than LSH-E. LSH-E is based on color feature, which lacks discriminative power as the dataset becomes larger. Local feature is a more favorable choice than global features. Visual keyword based search generally returns a high recall of near-duplicate keyframes but mixed with a large portion of false matches. Although geometric consistency constraint WGC is employed by VK+, there is no obvious improvement over VK. On the contrary, E-WGC significantly enhances the performance of VK++ and VK#. Compared to VK+, the improvement of VK++ is significant. In addition to scale and rotation transforms, E-WGC also integrates the translation transform,

Tab. (3): Performance Comparison of Near-duplicate Video Retrieval on DS_SOURCE and DS_TIME.

Metrics	Dataset	LSH-E	VK	VK+	VK++	VK#
MAP	Cross Source	0.514	0.690	0.684	0.849	**0.869**
MAP	Cross Time	0.290	0.463	0.519	0.721	**0.762**

Tab. (4): Time cost comparison.

Method	KF Extr.	Feat. Extr.	VK Quant.	Online Retr.
LSH-E	1.0 s	0.4 s	-	0.016 s
VK	1.0 s	1.1×53 s	0.41×53 s	0.082×53 s
VK+	1.0 s	1.1×53 s	0.41×53 s	0.35×53 s
VK++	1.0 s	1.1×53 s	0.41×53 s	0.35×53 s
VK#	1.0 s	1.1×53 s	0.41×53 s	0.35×53 s

The average number of keyframes in one query video is 53.

which is a more discriminative measure. Only matches following the same linear transformation will be kept, which filters out large amount of false-positives while maintaining a high recall. Hough Transform (HT) weakly considers the temporal consistency. Unfortunately, its effectiveness can be affected by noisy matches. With the assistance of reverse entropy (RE), the performance is further boosted. VK# achieves the best performance. Noisy keyframe matches are effectively pruned out.

The efficiency is a critical factor for web scale applications. Mainly the following factors affect the computation cost: keyframe extraction, local point feature extraction, visual keyword quantization, and near-duplicate video retrieval on inverted file. The time cost of these four factors is listed in Tab.(4). According to our experiment, time cost for HT, RE and tag recommendation is negligible. Our programs are implemented with C++, and performed on a PC with Intel Duo Core 3.2GHz CPU and 3G memory. Among all approaches, LSH-E is the fastest. For one query video, it takes less than 1.5s to fulfill the retrieval. Time costs for VK based approaches are much higher because they are operated at the keyframe level and using local features. In our dataset, the average length of a query is approximately 3 minutes with about 53 keyframes, and 260 keypoints per keyframe. To process a query of average length, as shown in Tab. (4), in total it takes 84 seconds for VK, and 98.6 seconds for VK+, VK++ and VK#. Without geometric consistency checking, VK is about 0.15 times faster. From our observation, the use of HE indeed helps prune significant amount of potential matches to be checked by WGC and E-WGC. Compared to more costly but widely used geometric checking such as RANSAC, WGC and E-WGC are approximately 40 times faster in our experiments.

8 Conclusions

With the rival growth of social media, abundant video resources are freely available online. Among them, there exists a huge number of near-duplicate videos returned from current video search engines. Near-duplicate web video detection is a critical task for web video search, retrieval, annotation and mining. However, the diversity of near-duplicate videos ranges from simple formatting to complex mixture of different editing effects, which causes the near-duplicate video detection a challenging task. In this book chapter, we review various strategies for effective and efficient near-duplicate web video detection, including a hierarchical approach combining global signature based on color histograms and local point based pairwise comparison, a novel solution integrating context filtering and content analysis, and an efficient retrieval method based on visual words applicable for large scale web videos. Experiments demonstrate that the approach combining content and context is a proper way for "unsupervised" near-duplicate detection, and the near-duplicate video retrieval based on visual words achieves efficient and effective performance.

The scalability is a critical factor for large scale web video applications. In order to improve the efficiency of near-duplicate video detection, two feasible techniques can be explored: feature compression and distributed computing. One is to compress the keypoint representation for images/videos. Possible directions are to aggregate keypoint features or extract stable and representative keypoints from images and video sequences. Meaningful attempts have been made in this direction (e.g., [11]). As indicated in [11], the memory consumption and computing cost can be decreased by at least one magnitude while maintaining satisfactory performance. The other promising direction for scalability is to adopt distributed computing or cloud computing. The indexing structure employed in this work can be implemented in a distributed manner. Our algorithms are easily adapted to parallel computing model, such as Mapreduce [5]. They can be decomposed into several pieces so that each component can be carried out in parallel. As a consequence, near-duplicate web video detection is able to work in real-time model.

The next chapter will present another two techniques towards efficient web scale near-duplicate video retrieval from the viewpoint of efficient visual representation and indexing. A more discriminative video representation named interest seam image is first presented. It generates a compact synopsis of a video shot and keeps important spatio-temporal information in a computationally efficient manner. A retrieval system combining local and global features is then introduced.

Acknowledgement

The work described in this book chapter was supported by the Fundamental Research Funds for the Central Universities (Project No. SWJTU09CX032 and

SWJTU09ZT14) and a grant from City University of Hong Kong (Project No. 7002438).

9 References

[1] Xiao Wu, Chong-Wah Ngo, and Alexander G. Hauptmann. CC_WEB_VIDEO. http://vireo.cs.cityu.edu.hk/webvideo/.

[2] M. Cherubini, R. de Oliveira, and N. Oliver. Understanding Near-Duplicate Videos: A User-Centric Approach. In *ACM Multimedia*, 2009.

[3] S. C. Cheung and A. Zakhor. Efficient Video Similarity Measurement with Video Signature. In *IEEE Transactions on Circuits and Systems for Video Technology*, 2003.

[4] S. C. Cheung and A. Zakhor. Fast Similarity Search and Clustering of Video Sequences on the World-Wide-Web. In *IEEE Transactions on Circuits and Systems for Video Technology*, 2005.

[5] J. Dean and S. Ghemawat. Mapreduce: Simplified Data Processing on Large Clusters. In *Communications of the ACM*, 2008.

[6] W. Dong, Z. Wang, M. Charikar and K. Li. Efficiently Matching Sets of Features with Random Histograms. In *ACM Multimedia*, 2008.

[7] M. Douze, A. Gaidon, H. Jegou, M. Marszatke and C. Schmid. INRIA-LEAR's Video Copy Detection System. In *TREVCID*, 2008.

[8] A. Hampapur and R. Bolle. Comparison of Sequence Matching Techniques for Video Copy Detection. In *Conf. on Storage and Retrieval for Media Databases*, 2002.

[9] T. C. Hoad and J. Zobel. Fast Video Matching With Signature Alignment. In *MIR*, 2003.

[10] H. Jégou, M. Douze and C. Schmid. Hamming embedding and weak geometric consistency for large scale image search. In *ECCV*, 2008.

[11] H. Jégou, M. Douze, C. Schmid, and P. Pérez. Aggregating Local Descriptors into Compact Image Representation. In *CVPR*, 2010.

[12] Y.-G. Jiang and C.-W. Ngo. Visual Word Proximity and Linguistics for Semantic Video Indexing and Near-Duplicate Retrieval. In *Computer Vision and Image Understanding*, 2009.

[13] A. Joly and O. Buisson. A Posteriori Multi-Probe Locality Sensitive Hashing. In *ACM Multimedia*, 2008.

[14] A. Joly, O. Buisson and C. Frelicot. Content-Based Copy Detection using Distortion-Based Probabilistic Similarity Search. In *IEEE Transactions on Multimedia*, 2007.

[15] G. Karypis http://glaros.dtc.umn.edu/gkhome/views/cluto/.

[16] K. Kashino and T. Kurozumi and H. Murase. A Quick Search Method for Audio and Video Signals based on Histogram Pruning. In *IEEE Transactions on Multimedia*, 2003.

[17] Y. Ke, R. Suthankar and L. Huston. Efficient Near-Duplicate Detection and Sub-image Retrieval. In *ACM Multimedia*, 2004.

[18] J. Law-To and A. Joly and N. Boujemaa. Muscle-VCD-2007: A Live Benchmark for Video Copy Detection. Available at: http://www-rocq.inria.fr/imedia/civr-bench/.

[19] J. Law-To and A. Joly and N. Boujemaa. TREC Video Retrieval Evaluation (TRECVID). Available at: http://www-nlpir.nist.gov/projects/trecvid/.

[20] J. Law-To, B. Olivier, V. Gouet-Brunet and B. Nozha. Robust Voting Algorithm Based on Labels of Behavior for Video Copy Detection. In *ACM Multimedia*, 2006.

[21] L. Liu, W. Lai, X.-S. Hua and S.-Q. Yang. Video Histogram: A Novel Video Signature for Efficient Web Video Duplicate Detection. In *Multimedia Modeling*, 2007.

[22] D. Lowe. Distinctive Image Features from Scale-Invariant Keypoints. In *International Journal of Computer Vision*, 2004.

[23] K. Mikolajczyk and C. Schmid. A Performance Evaluation of Local Descritors. In *IEEE Transactions on Pattern Analysis and Machine Intelligence*, 2005.

[24] K. Mikoljczyk and Schmid, C. Scale and Affine Invariant Interest Point Detectors. In *International Journal of Computer Vision*, 2004.

[25] C.-W. Ngo, W.-L. Zhao and Y.-G. Jiang. Fast Tracking of Near-Duplicate Keyframes in Broadcast Domain with Transitivity Propagation. In *ACM Multimedia*, 2006.

[26] S. Siersdorfer, J. S. Pedro and M. Sanderson. Automatic Video Tagging using Content Redundancy. In *ACM SIGIR*, 2009.

[27] J. Sivic and A. Zisserman. Video Google: A Text Retrieval Approach to Object Matching in Videos. In *ICCV*, 2003.

[28] Wikipedia. In *http://en.wikipedia.org/wiki/YouTube*

[29] X. Wu, A. G. Hauptmann and C.-W. Ngo. Practical Elimination of Near-Duplicates from Web Video Search. In *ACM Multimedia*, 2007.

[30] X. Wu, C.-W. Ngo, A. G. Hauptmann, and H.-K. Tan. Real-Time Near-Duplicate Elimination for Web Video Search with Content and Context. In *IEEE Transactions on Multimedia*, 2009.

[31] X. Wu, C.-W. Ngo and Q. Li. Threading and Autodocumenting News Videos. In *Signal Processing Magazine*, 2006.

[32] J. Yuan, L.-Y. Duan, Q. Tian, S. Ranganath and C. Xu. Fast and Robust Short Video Clip Search for Copy Detection. In *Pacific Rim Conf. on Multimedia*, 2004.

[33] D.-Q. Zhang and S.-F. Chang. Detecting Image Near-Duplicate by Stochastic Attributed Relational Graph Matching with Learning. In *ACM Multimedia*, 2004.

[34] W.-L. Zhao and C.-W. Ngo. Scale-Rotation Invariant Pattern Entropy for Keypoint-based Near-Duplicate Detection. In *IEEE Transactions on Image Processing*, 2009.

[35] W.-L. Zhao, C.-W. Ngo, H.-K. Tan and X. Wu. Near-Duplicate Keyframe Identification with Interest Point Matching and Pattern Learning. In *IEEE Transactions on Multimedia*, 2007.

Internet Multimedia Search and Mining, 2013, 58-79

CHAPTER 3

An Efficient Visual Representation and Indexing Scheme for Large Scale Video Retrieval

Xiao Zhang

Institute for Advanced Study, Tsinghua University, Tel: +86-13146526618, Email: andypassion@gmail.com

Gang Hua*

Stevens Institute of Technology, Tel: +1-2012168073, Email: ghua@stevens.edu

Lei Zhang

Microsoft Research Asia, Tel: +86-10-59173197, Email: leizhang@microsoft.com

Abstract: This chapter presents technical advancements toward web scale video retrieval. Two methods for efficient visual representation and efficient visual indexing of web videos are discussed. First, a video representation named interest seam image is presented, which considers both spatial and temporal information contained in a video. Therefore it is more discriminative than previous video representations (such as those based on key-frames). Second, an indexing system is presented, which is capable of dealing with web-scale data. The system combines both local and global descriptors, and embeds geometric configuration information of interest points into the index to simultaneously improves retrieval accuracy, speed and memory footprint. The efficacy and efficiency of the proposed methods are demonstrated in large scale experiments on real web-videos.

***Correspondence Author:** Gang Hua, Stevens Institute of Technology; Email: ghua@stevens.edu.

Xian-Sheng Hua, Marcel Worring & Tat-Seng Chua (Eds.)

Keywords

Video Representation, Efficient Indexing, Video Retrieval, Seam, MinHash, Temporal, Keyframe, global descriptor, GIST, geometric information

1 Introduction

The far reach of the internet has created gigantic amount of online videos. This is largely due to the ever more popular social video sharing activities supported by online social media web-sites, such as YouTube. To address the growing demand for users to search, share and manage this increasingly larger online video repository, tremendous effort has been made on Internet video search and mining, which can be roughly categorized into two types: the first category of research tries to search/cluster videos by content similarity (i.e. query-by-example). For example, Peng *et al.* [1] leveraged bipartite graph matching algorithms to compute video clip similarity and applied in a large scale video clip retrieval scenario. Another group of efforts aim to automatically generate textual description for online videos (i.e. concept-detection), so that users could search videos using natural language queries. For an instance, a scalable multi-label video annotation system is developed in [2] to facilitate large scale content-based video search. Multi-modal information is fused in [3] to form "audio-visual atom" for generic video concept classification.

Although plenty of work has been done in the literature of content-based video retrieval, the magnitude of Internet videos induces severe scalability challenges for state-of-the-art algorithms, both in terms of computational cost and memory usage. A content-based video retrieval system is often composed of two components. In the first component, a visual representation algorithm shall convert a video into a numerical vector representation. Then in the second component, these vectors are organized in an index structure for efficient access and ranking. To meet the demand of web scale multimedia search and mining, the visual representation must be not only informative to discriminate various types of video content, but also computationally *super efficient*. Moreover, the visual representation should be compact to keep memory cost in an affordable manner. Regarding indexing and ranking, they should maintain high level of accuracy while being memory efficient, and should also have sub-linear retrieval complexity w.r.t. the number of videos.

To mitigate the scalability challenges, we propose a novel video synopsis scheme, namely *interest seam image* [4]. The interest seam image generates a compact synopsis of a video shot and keeps important spatiotemporal information in a computationally efficient manner. Based on a spatiotemporal energy map extracted from a video, an optimal vertical seam which encompasses the highest energy is identified and used to extract a seam of pixels from each video frame. These seams of pixels are placed column by column to compose the interest seam image. To cope with the visual variations among near duplicate videos, local invariant features are extracted from each interest seam image and a MinHash scheme [5] is further leveraged to convert an interest seam image to a numerical vector.

We also present a novel indexing algorithm to build an inverted file structure for the video database, which improves traditional inverted lists indexing [22, 27]. We incorporate geometric information of the local features detected from the video synopsis into the index, and hence achieve more efficient and accurate retrieval performance. We further present a new post verification scheme, namely scene verification. Scene verification is performed in a holistic appearance level by leveraging global descriptors such as GIST [21, 29], and is found to simultaneously improve retrieval accuracy, speed and memory efficiency.

The proposed algorithms are evaluated on large scale near duplicate video retrieval problem. Near duplicate videos refer to different videos generated from the same video source, but have undergone different visual editings, such as re-compression, gamma correction, resizing, aspect ratio changes, contrast stretch, and cutting, etc.. With the proliferation of online videos, such as the massive number of videos uploaded daily to YouTube, efficient near duplicate video retrieval becomes an emerging need. It may greatly facilitate users to obtain videos according to their needs, advertisers to monitor the online distribution of their advertisement, and content owners to detect infringement to their copy-rights, etc.. The evaluation results demonstrate the superiority of the proposed methods compared with state-of-the-art.

2 Related Work

Previous work related to this chapter can be put into two categories: visual representations for videos, and large scale video indexing and retrieval schemes. In this section, we discuss some of the most relevant ones and clarify how the proposed algorithms differ from them.

Visual representations

The visual representations could be classified into three categories. The first category [7, 8] extracts spatiotemporal local invariant features from the raw video, from which a visual representation, e.g., a *bag-of-word* or a more complicated statistical model, is induced. Although the feature extraction may be sped up by using certain computational paradigms such as integral videos [11], still they are not efficient enough to handle billions of videos.

Some other approaches convert video content into fingerprints for fast processing. Most of them, such as the color signature and the video histogram [20], are based on global histogram of visual features. They usually do not consider the rich temporal context in a video sequence, neither are they robust to visual transformations such as lighting enhancement, contrast sharpening, and gamma rectification, etc..

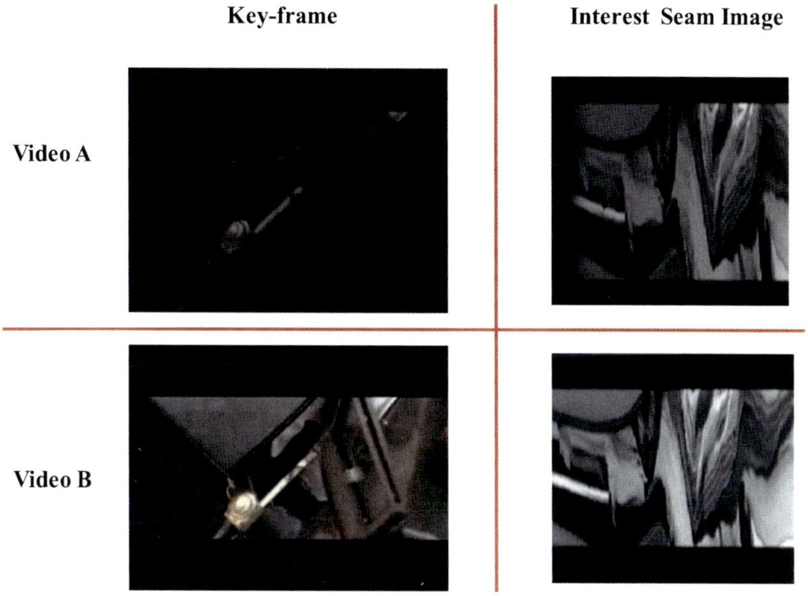

Fig. (1): Key-frames and interest seam images from a pair of near duplicate videos. The key-frames contain the same object with different poses which are difficult to match. In contrast, interest seam images are near duplicates which could be matched easily.

The third category of approaches is most relevant to this chapter. Firstly a condensed synopsis of the video is generated, from which low level features are extracted to build the final visual representation for the video. The video synopsis could be generated, for example, from key-frames of a video shot [10], or from temporal slice [9], which is a set of two dimensional images extracted along the time dimension of a video sequence. Since low-level features are only extracted from the synopsis of the video [5, 18, 19], approaches in the third category have great potential to be both computationally and memory efficient, and therefore to be scalable to web-scale data.

However, there are serious defects for both key-frame and temporal slice image based approaches. For key-frame based approach, how to ensure the stability and repeatability of key-frame detection is an open problem. This is exemplified in the first column of Fig. (1), where two key frames extracted from two near duplicate videos are actually quite different. Besides, key-frame based synopsis neglects temporal information, which is obviously very valuable for video content analysis. On the other hand, temporal slice based method may discard valuable spatiotemporal visual information since no visual saliency information is accounted for.

In contrast, the proposed interest seam images are more repeatable for near duplicate videos because they aggregate information from all frames. For example, in the second column of Fig. **(1)**, we present the two interest seam images extracted from the two videos. It is shown that the two interest seam images are visually very similar to each other, which is in contrast to the two key frames extracted. Compared with temporal slice images, interest seam images contain more valuable information about the original video because the generation of interest seam image is guided by gradient and motion information. A comparison is shown in Fig. **(2)(b)** and Fig. **(2)(c)**.

Large scale video indexing and reranking

We proceed to discuss large scale indexing and ranking algorithms for the video synopsis based visual representations. The state-of-the-art indexing approach is to first quantize local features extracted from the video synopsis to a visual word ID, and then index them by inverted lists. Each list corresponds to a visual word, and the entries in the list correspond to the IDs of the videos, whose synopsis contain the visual word. Although inverted list index enjoys great success for text search, it may not be directly suitable for image/video search, as discussed by [26]. Inverted list index is suitable for text search because a text query usually contains only a few words so a intersection of the inverted lists corresponding to the query words is able to return relevant documents. However, images and videos often contain thousands of visual words thus a intersection of corresponding inverted lists is highly probable to return an empty set. This is why the current state-of-the-art needs to perform a union of the inverted lists instead of an intersection. Since a union operation need to access every entry in the corresponding inverted lists, it is much slower than intersection and can not power efficient large scale visual search.

A number of efforts have been made to solve this problem. Zhang *et al.*[26] uses topic model to convert the bag-of-words representation to a low dimensional vector and residual error, and then invent an indexing structure to combine the two parts in an efficient manner. However, as this method needs to collect training data to model the topic space, it might fail when the distribution of the testing data is unknown. Another work that tries to overcome the limitation of the inverted index is the work of Wu *et al.*[17], in which a color histogram based feature is used to filter out a large portion of the database videos and then use bag-of-words model to rerank the rest videos. Although the algorithm is scalable, it fails to tackle the color change in the near duplicate videos, which is common on the web.

In the proposed indexing structure, geometric configuration of local features are leveraged to arrange the entries of the inverted lists so visual search based on the proposed index only access a small subset of the corresponding inverted lists. In this way, not only the retrieval speed is significantly improved, but also the retrieval accuracy is improved because geometric information is used to perform binary search to match visual words to enhance the bag-of-word model based matching.

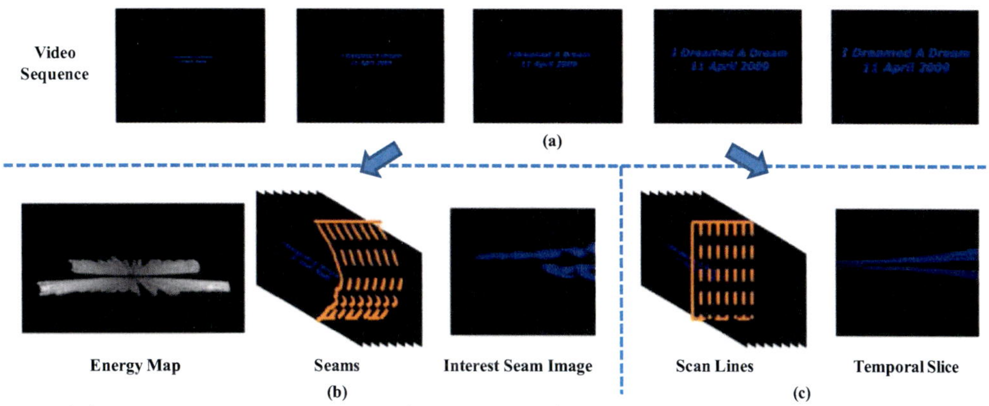

Fig. (2): Interest seam image (bottom left) v.s. temporal slice(bottom right): interest seam image incorporates more information about the original video than temporal slice(best viewing in color format). Here the energy map visualizes E_{ST} in Eq.(3).

Post verification is also a critical component for the retrieval system. Previous works mostly use spatial configuration of local features for post verification[22, 25]. However, this kind of approaches assume a rigid transformation between images and require heavy computation. Moreover, it is almost impossible to store spatial positions of all local features in a video synopsis in the memory, meaning that the spatial verification step needs disk access, which prevents spatial verification to be scalable.

The proposed verification algorithm uses scene descriptor(GIST) to rerank the videos on a holistic level, which is fast to compute and compact enough to be stored in the memory (in our implementation, we quantize each dimension of GIST to 3 bits). The resulted post verification algorithm is much more efficient than spatial verification and significantly improves retrieval accuracy, for both key-frame and interest seam image based video synopsis.

3 Interest Seam Image

A video clip could be considered as a 3 dimensional spatiotemporal cube. Interest seam image is a synopsis of the clip which represents the most informative 2 dimensional curvature manifold in this cube. A naive method, namely temporal slice [9], obtains a slice by getting one column per frame and concatenate them together as an image. But slice images obtained this way might be very uninformative and can not represent the video content very well, as shown in the bottom right of Fig. **(2)**. The reason resides in the fact that the spatiotemporal informativeness of the pixels are not taken into consideration. To improve this naive method, we need to define an energy function in the image plane to measure the spatiotemporal saliency of each pixel, and then pick a group of pixels with the highest energy. Since our goal is to identify an efficient and compact visual synopsis of the video content, we propose to define the group of pixels to be vertical seams on consecutive frames which encompasses the highest energy. This leads to the proposed *interest seam image*, which provides a flexible and rich representation, and is yet efficient to compute.

Seam based video synopsis

To obtain an interest seam image, for each frame I, we extract a "seam" **s** and concatenate seams of pixels from all frames column by column to form the interest seam image. Formally, let the resolution of an input video be $m \times n$, where m is the width and n is the height of I, following the definition of [14], a vertical *seam* is defined as

$$\begin{aligned} \mathrm{s} &= \{s_i\}_{i=1}^{n} = (x(i), i)_{i=1}^{n} \\ s.t.\ & \forall i,\ \ |x(i) - x(i-1)| \leq 1 \end{aligned} \qquad (1)$$

where x is a mapping $x : [1, ..., n] \rightarrow [1, ..., m]$. That is, a vertical seam **s** is an 8-connected path of pixels in the image from top to bottom, containing only one pixel in each row of frame I. The pixels on the path of the seam $\{s_i\}_{i=1}^{n}$ will therefore be $\mathbf{I_s} = \{\mathbf{I}(s_i)\}_{i=1}^{n} = \{\mathbf{I}(x(i), i)\}_{i=1}^{n}$

With this definition, we proceed to extract interest seam image from a sequence of video frames. Simply obtaining a seam with the highest energy from each frame separately will introduce serious discontinuity into the resulted interest seam image, which may render it very difficult to extract meaningful low level features. Therefore, we choose to extract a seam in the image plane that are of the highest energy on an aggregated spatiotemporal energy map. That is, the configuration of the seams in different video frames are the same. We proceed to introduce the spatiotemporal energy function we adopt.

Spatiotemporal energy map

The visual saliency energy function we adopt is

$$E(i,j) = E_{ST}(i,j) + \beta E_{prior}(i,j), \qquad (2)$$

where $i \in [1, n]$, and $j \in [1, m]$. Recall from the previous section, m and n are defined as the width and height of the video frames. The first component of the energy function, E_{ST}, takes both spatial and temporal saliency information into consideration. This is done by computing the gradient and motion information in each frame independently and then use an operator f (e.g. average, max, median, etc.) to aggregate energy value at each pixel location from different frames, which is a generalization of the formulation of [6]. Specifically, given a video sequence $\{I_t\}_{t=1}^T$, its spatiotemporal energy function E_{ST} is defined as follows

$$E_{ST}(i,j) = (1-\alpha)E_S(i,j) + \alpha E_T(i,j) \tag{3}$$

$$E_S(i,j) = f(\{|\frac{\partial}{\partial x}I_t(i,j)| + |\frac{\partial}{\partial y}I_t(i,j)|\}_{t=1}^T) \tag{4}$$

$$E_T(i,j) = f(\{|\frac{\partial}{\partial t}I_t(i,j)|\}_{t=1}^T) \tag{5}$$

where $\alpha \in [0,1]$ balances the spatial and temporal energies.

Since we prefer seams with high energy, solely relying on E_{ST} may be prone to noises. Therefore, we introduce E_{prior}, a spatially central Gaussian prior, to the energy function in Eq.(2). It is defined as

$$E_{prior}(i,j) = exp(-(\frac{i-\frac{m}{2}}{\sigma m})^2) \tag{6}$$

The introduction of this prior is based on our observation that most web videos will place the most important and interesting content in the central part of the video frames. Indeed, this is probably true for almost any video framing.

Therefore it is reasonable for the seam to be biased toward the central part of the video frame, which in general enhance the repeatability of the seam, as demonstrated in our experiments. The strength of the Gaussian central prior is adjusted by $\beta \geq 0$ in Eq.(2). The effectiveness of Gaussian prior and the sensitivity of the interest seam image against β is tested in the experiment section.

Interest seam image identification

Given E, the energy that a seam contains is

$$E(\mathbf{s}) = \sum_{i=1}^{n} E(s_i) = \sum_{i=1}^{n} E(x(i), i). \tag{7}$$

We look for an optimal seam with highest energy, i.e.,

$$\mathbf{s}^\star = \max_{\mathbf{s}}(E(\mathbf{s})) \tag{8}$$

Let $\mathbf{s}_k = \{s_i\}_{i=1}^k$ be a sub-seam of $\mathbf{s}$, we denote

$$E_m(p,k) = \max_{\mathbf{s}_k : x(k)=p} \sum_{i=1}^{k} E(x(i), i). \tag{9}$$

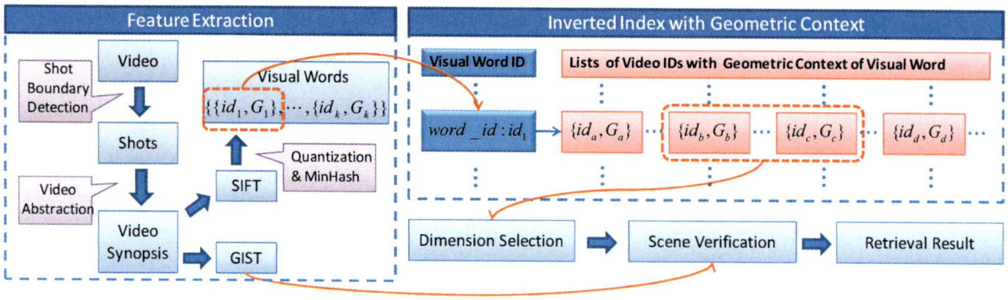

Fig. (3): The retrieval system pipeline: as each inverted list is sorted by the geometric context of the visual words(i.e. $G_a < G_b < G_c < G_d$), only a small subset(i.e. the middle part) of the list needs to be visited, because $G_a < G_1 - c < G_b < G_c < G_1 + c < G_d$.

as the maximum energy up to seam position (p, k) in $\mathbf{s}_k$, it is easy to figure out that

$$\begin{aligned} E_m(p, k+1) &= E(p, k+1) \\ &+ \max_{\Delta \in \{-1,0,1\}} \{E_m(p+\Delta, k)\} \end{aligned} \tag{10}$$

From Eq.(10), the optimal seam $s^\star$ can be obtained efficiently using dynamic programming.

With the optimal seam $\mathbf{s}^\star$, the interest seam image is obtained by placing seams of pixels from consecutive frames column by column. Examples of energy map, seam and interest seam image are shown in Fig. **(2)**. From this figure, we could see that the interest seam image contains more information about the original video, e.g. the letters, while temporal slice only contains blue strips.

4 Efficient Video Indexing and Reranking

Our video retrieval pipeline is shown in Fig. **(3)**. In offline stage, the system automatically segments the database videos into shots [30]. Next, a video synopsis(e.g. key-frame or interest seam image) is computed for each shot, from which both local feature(MSER [17]) and global feature(GIST [29]) are extracted. SIFT [16] is used to describe the gradient information in the neighborhood of the local features. To make the representation to be more compact, we quantize SIFT descriptors using vector quantization [22] to convert a video synopsis to a *bag-of-word* representation, i.e.,

$$V = \{P_i^V\}_{i=1}^N, P_i^V \in \{id_i^V\}, \tag{11}$$

where each local feature P_i^V is represented by a visual word ID (i.e. id_i^V) obtained during the quantization process. The problem of this representation is that N is

Tab. (1): Images I_1 and I_2 represented in visual codebook space.

	A	B	C	D
I_1	1	1	1	0
I_2	0	1	1	1

often very large and varies for different videos. Therefore, we use MinHash to reduce the memory cost and convert the interest seam image to a fixed length feature vector. We briefly review the technique of MinHash in the following subsection. More details could be found in [5].

MinHash review

With k hash functions $\{H_j\}_{j=1}^{k}$, we convert an interest seam image into a k dimensional *MinHash signature*

$$H(V) = \{P_{m_j}^V\}_{j=1}^k, P_{m_j}^V = H_j(\{P_i^V\}_{i=1}^N), m_j \in \{1, ..., N\} \tag{12}$$

where the jth dimension is a selected visual word obtained by applying the jth hash function on the entire bag of visual words. Here,

$$H_j(\{P_i^V\}_{i=1}^N) = \arg\min_{P_i^V}\{\pi_j(P_i^V)_{i=1}^N\}, \tag{13}$$

where π_j is a random permutation of visual codebook, i.e. a mapping from original visual word id to new visual word id. For example, suppose there are four visual words in the visual codebook, {A, B, C, D}. And two images I_1 and I_2 contain visual words {A, B, C} and {B, C, D} respectively, as shown in Tab. (1). Two random permutations are applied on the visual codebook, and the visual words with lowest permuted visual word id are selected as MinHash signature, as shown in Tab. (2). From the table, we can see that with the two random permutations, the MinHash signatures of I_1 and I_2 are $\mathbf{H}(I_1) = (B, C)$ and $\mathbf{H}(I_2) = (B, D)$, respectively. This indicates that

$$P(H(I_1) = H(I_2)) = \frac{I_1 \cap I_2}{I_1 \cup I_2} \tag{14}$$

Actually, the above property can be proved mathematically. Since the probability of the matching of MinHash signatures equals the jaccard distance between two visual word sets, MinHash is a good approximation of the bag-of-words representation.

Note that the dimensionality of MinHash signature, i.e. k in Eq.(12), determines the memory cost of indexing. Therefore, k is usually set to be much smaller than N in Eq.(11) to reduce memory cost. After the MinHash algorithm is applied, an indexing structure is built to quickly return a small candidate set of relevant videos for any specific query. Each inverted list is sorted based on the geometric context of the video synopsis for efficient access. Finally, a scene verification component using

Tab. (2): Examples of random permutations π and resulted MinHash signatures.

Random Permutations				MinHash Signatures	
A	**B**	**C**	**D**	I_1	I_2
2	1	3	4	B	B
4	3	2	1	C	D

GIST features extracted from the video synopsis is used to re-rank this candidate set and improve retrieval accuracy. In the next two subsections, we will introduce the video indexing structure and the scene verification algorithm in detail.

Inverted index with geometric context

In this section, we introduce the technical detail of the efficient inverted file indexing scheme with geometric context, which effectively improves retrieval accuracy and speed by leveraging the geometric information contained in the local features detected from the video synopsis.

Denote geometric context of a local feature as G, its mathematical definition is

$$G = \{X, Y, S, \theta\}, \tag{15}$$

where X and Y are the spatial positions of local feature and S and θ are its scale and angle. With geometric context, the MinHash signature for video synopsis in Eq.(12) is expanded as

$$V = \{\{id^V_{m_j}, G^V_{m_j}\}\}^k_{j=1}. \tag{16}$$

To reduce the storage cost, entropy is computed to select the most informative dimension to represent G, which transforms G from a vector to a scalar. The most informative dimension may differ based on the training dataset. In our experiments, we found the spatial position Y has the highest entropy. Therefore Y is used to represent G in subsequent experiments of this chapter.

Then the similarity between the query video and a database video is measured as

$$Sim(Q, V) = \sum_{j=1}^{k} I(id^Q_{m_j} = id^V_{m_j}, |G^Q_{m_j} - G^V_{m_j}| < c), \tag{17}$$

where $I(\cdot)$ equals 1 if all conditions in the parenthesis holds and 0 otherwise, and the parameter c introduces flexibility to this similarity measure to a certain degree. It confines that only local features with similar geometric context could be matched in our system.

The geometric constrained similarity in Eq.(17) shares similar idea with spatial verification for large scale image search [22, 25]. Both methods utilize spatial configuration of the local features to improve the discriminality of image representation. The difference is, the proposed algorithm embeds the geometric information in the visual index and thus could be computed quickly for every video in the database, while the spatial verification in [22, 25] only works for a small subset of images because of the heavy computational and the IO burden.

Besides the increase of accuracy, the efficiency of the video indexing structure is also improved. In the proposed indexing structure, the MinHash signatures of the database videos are organized by inverted lists, as shown in the middle of Fig. (**3**). Inverted list index has an entry for each visual word in the database followed by a list of all the videos (and the geometric context in the video synopsis of each video) in which the visual word occurs. The advantage of the inverted lists is that a linear scan for the entire database is avoided, i.e. only lists corresponding to the visual words of the query need to be scanned. However, for a large scale database, the lists themselves are very long and a linear scan over the entire list will reduce the retrieval speed.

In the proposed video indexing algorithm, geometric context is leveraged to sort the entries in each list thus by binary search we can efficiently identify a small subset of the list, in which the geometric configuration of the visual words are similar to that of the query video. For example, in Fig. (**3**), as the first dimension of the MinHash signature of query video has value $\{id_1, G_1\}$, thus the list corresponding to visual word id_1 is looked up. According to Eq.(17), we only want to return videos containing visual word id_1 with geometric context G subject to $(G_1 - c) < G < (G_1 + c)$. Therefore instead of enumerating all the entries in the list, only the middle part of that list need to be scanned, because $G_a < (G_1 - c) < G_b < G_c < (G_1 + c) < G_d$. In the experiments, the retrieval speed of this indexing structure is orders of magnitude faster than the state-of-the-art methods.

Dimension selection for MinHash signature

Although geometric context can significantly improve the retrieval efficiency in most cases, the retrieval speed may still be harmed when query video contains visual words of high *document frequency* (DF), because in this case the geometric constrained subset of the corresponding inverted list would comprise a large number of entries. Besides, visual words of high DF hurt the accuracy because they are not discriminative. Therefore, for an input query video, dimensions corresponding to visual words of DF higher than a threshold will be ignored to improve efficiency and accuracy. Despite its simplicity, this method is found to be effective in our large scale experiments.

Scene verification

After a small candidate set of videos is generated by local feature based index, a re-ranking mechanism using scene descriptor is added to further improve the precision of top search results. This is achieved by extracting GIST descriptors G

from interest seam images [21, 29]. Then we compute the Cosine similarity of the scene descriptors between the query video and each video in the candidate set, i.e.,

$$Sim_{Gist}(Q, V) = \frac{G_Q \cdot G_V}{\|G_Q\|\|G_V\|}. \tag{18}$$

We then use a linear combination of the two similarities defined in Eq.(18) and Eq.(17) as the final ranking score to rerank the videos in the candidate set, i.e.

$$R(V) = \gamma Sim_{Gist}(Q, V) + (1 - \gamma) Sim(Q, V) \tag{19}$$

The higher $R(V)$ is, the more relevant V is to Q. This design is based on our observation that the visual scenes of the interest seam images extracted from near duplicate videos are usually very similar, although there may be subtle local differences. Therefore, performing scene verification can improve the search accuracy.

A nice property of this approach is that, with the help of the scene verification, empirically we find that not only the retrieval accuracy is improved, but the dimensionality of MinHash signature (i.e. k in Eq.(12) can be greatly reduced as well, which implies that much less information nodes need to be stored and visited in the inverted lists. Therefore, the memory efficiency, retrieval speed and accuracy are improved simultaneously.

5 Dataset and evaluation criterion

To conduct large scale video retrieval experiments, 10382 videos, which covers a variety of genres including TV shows, dramas, movie trailers and MTVs etc., are crawled from Internet and automatically segmented [30]. Among them, two labeled dataset **Qr** and **Qt** are used as queries, with 400 video shots and 1500 video shots respectively, and a dataset **D** with 246551 video shots are used as distracters to further test the scalability of our algorithm. Each shot in our collection ranges from 2 to 10 seconds.

Qr: The near duplicate videos in this dataset are videos that contain the same content but have undergone a combination of transformations such as scaling, compression, color change, caption overlay, and logo insertion, etc., as shown in Fig. (**4**). We manually label the near duplicate relationships and use these ground-truth label to compare the performance of our system with state-of-the-art systems in real world settings.

Qt: A group of 150 video shots is randomly selected from the crawled videos. Each of them undergoes several artificial transformations including scale change, horizontal mirror, blur, contrast stretch, and gama correction, which results in 9 transformed versions of each original video. Therefore, the dataset contains

Fig. (4): Examples of the near duplicate videos in **Qr**.

1500 videos in total. In our experiments, the original 150 video shots are used as queries to test whether the transformed ones can be successfully retrieved. This dataset is used to compare the interest seam image synopsis with key-frame based methods.

With these query datasets, two groups of experiments are conducted, in which the evaluation strategy is similar to the leave-one-out strategy commonly used in object recognition. For the first group, each video shot from **Qr** is used in turn to query the database which combines **D** and **Qr** with the query video excluded. The other group of experiments is conducted similarly but **Qr** is replaced by **Qt**. We compute Average Precision by averaging precision over all recall levels for each query. Then we get the mean value of average precisions for all queries, namely Mean Average Precision (**mAP**), to serve as the main performance evaluation criterion, which is also widely adopted for multimedia retrieval evaluation [17, 22, 25].

6 Experiments

In this section, we present a variety of experiments conducted to demonstrate the effectiveness and efficiency of the proposed video retrieval algorithms. First, the performance of the proposed video synopsis and retrieval system is compared with several state-of-the-art methods. Then, the parameter sensitivity of the proposed retrieval algorithm is tested. After that, the impact of dimension selection for MinHash signature is presented. Finally, the strength of scene verification and inverted index with temporal context are investigated.

Tab. (3): Average video processing and retrieval time of the proposed algorithms.

Feature extraction		Retrieval
Interest seam image Identification	**MinHash signature Generation**	
0.6424s	0.2186s	0.24s

Tab. (4): Performance comparison between interest seam image and key-frame on local feature(MSER) and global feature(GIST). The evaluation is carried on **Qt**.

	mAP	
Video representation	**MSER**	**GIST**
Interest Seam Image	**0.9699**	**0.9766**
Keyframe	0.894	0.9062

Before introducing the experimental results, we briefly discuss the implementation details of the proposed algorithms. All experiments are carried out on a 2.33GHZ PC. The β, α, σ, c, γ, in Eq.(2), Eq.(3), Eq.(6), Eq.(16), Eq.(19), are set to be 40, 0.7, $\frac{\sqrt{2}}{7}$, 30, 0.7, respectively. If not specifically stated, the dimensionality of MinHash signatures is 60. Besides, in all experiments, *max* is used to implement operator f in Eq.(4) and Eq.(5).

Processing speed

In this section, we present the speed of interest seam image extraction and its application to near duplicate video retrieval, as shown in Tab. (3). From the table, we could see that the speed of interest seam image identification, MinHash indexing and video retrieval are very fast and thus can handle web scale video dataset.

Retrieval accuracy

To demonstrate the superiority of interest seam image over key-frame, we compare them with different low level features, using **Qt** as testing data. The result is shown in Tab. **(4)**. It is clear that no matter we use MSER [17] or GIST [29], the accuracy of interest seam image based method is much higher than the key-frame based approaches.

We also compare the proposed video retrieval systems with several recent methods [5, 9, 17, 21] on **Qr**. In [5], interest points were extracted from key-frames and indexed by Min-Hash. In [17] local and global features extracted from key-frames were combined in a hierachical framework to improve efficiency and preserve accuracy. GIST was used in [21] as global feature to index web images and good result is achieved. Therefore, we also use key-frame combined with GIST as a baseline in the experiment. Finally, we compare interest seam image with [9] which used temporal slice. The comparison results are summarized in Tab. **(5)**.

Tab. (5): Performance comparison between proposed algorithms and state-of-the-art methods on **Qr**. The last two columns indicate whether each method uses global/local feature.

Approaches	**mAP**	**Global**	**Local**
Interest Seam Image + Geometric Context + Scene Verification	**0.9401**	Y	Y
Interest Seam Image + Geometric Context	**0.896**	N	Y
Keyframe + Geometric Context + Scene Verification	**0.889**	Y	Y
Keyframe + Geometric Context	**0.866**	N	Y
Keyframe + MinHash [5]	0.8179	N	Y
Keyframe + GIST [21]	0.8472	Y	N
Temporal Slice [9]	0.8388	Y	N
Hierachical Framework [17]	0.8828	Y	Y

From the evaluation result, it can be seen that only with local feature, interest seam image already achieve 0.896 retrieval accuracy, which is better than all competing methods, including [17] which utilizes both global feature and local feature. After the scene verification based reranking step is added, the accuracy of the proposed video retrieval system is further improved to reach 0.94.

Also, we can see that for both interest seam image and key-frame based retrieval systems, the performance is improved when geometric context is considered in the index and scene verification is added, demonstrating the effectiveness of the proposed indexing and reranking algorithms.

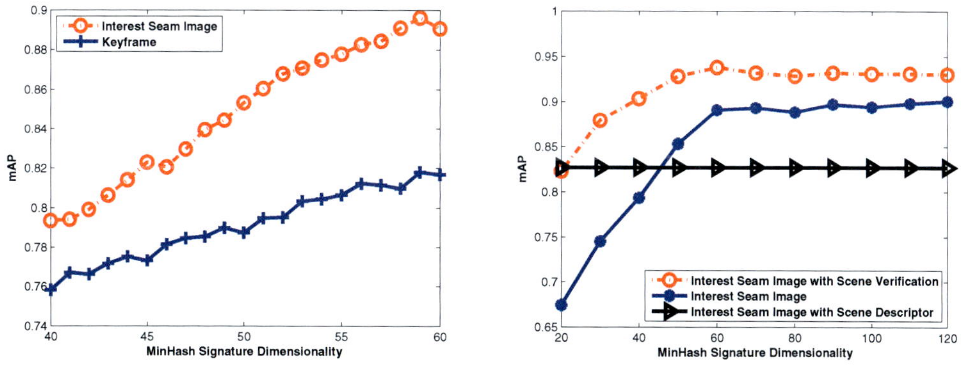

(a) (b)

Fig. (5): (a). Performance comparison between interest seam image and key-frame with changes in the MinHash signature dimensionality; (b). performance comparison among interest seam image, interest seam image with scene descriptor, and interest seam image with scene verification.

Tab. (6): Performances with and without dimension selection for MinHash signature, using different video representations, without scene verification. The evaluation is carried on **Qr**.

Video representation	mAP	Speed	Dimension selection for MinHash signature
Interest Seam Image	**0.9165**	**0.47**	Y
	0.9076	1.2	N
Key-frame	**0.8656**	**0.73**	Y
	0.8534	1.3	N

Impact of dimensionality of MinHash signature

Recall from Sec. 4 that the signature dimensionality k in Eq.(12) determines both the representation capacity of the signature and the memory cost of the retrieval system. Therefore we vary k, and compare the accuracy of the proposed retrieval system with key-frame combined with MinHash [5] on **Qr**. The result is shown in Fig. **(5)(a)**. This figure shows that interest seam image based indexing performs better than key-frame on all levels of k. Besides, it also shows that even with a small dimensionality (e.g. 60), our retrieval system could achieve good retrieval result, i.e. 0.896 in terms of mAP. This indicates that our video retrieval system can be scaled to web video dataset.

Impact of dimension selection for MinHash signature

In this experiment, the efficacy of DF based dimension selection algorithm is demonstrated by comparing the performance of proposed retrieval systems with and without dimension selection, using both interest seam image (The dimension of MinHash signature for interest seam image is set to be 180 in this experiment.) and keyframe as video representation. The result is summarized in Tab. **(6)**. From the result, we can see that with the help of dimension selection, both accuracy and speed of the retrieval system improve consistently, no matter what video representation is used. This is because dimension selection not only removes noisy dimensions from MinHash signature but also reduces the computational burden for the retrieval system.

Impact of scene verification

To fully justify the benefit of scene verification, we compare the proposed retrieval system with two of its variants: interest seam image without scene verification(the curve for "Interest Seam Image" in Fig. **(5)(b)** and interest seam image with only scene descriptor. The first variant only uses local feature, the second variant only uses scene descriptor, while the proposed retrieval system combines both features. The comparison result is shown in Fig. **(5)(b)**. We could see that the scene verification approach performs much better than using either kind of feature individually. Also, it can be seen that with the help of scene verification, the accuracy of the proposed retrieval system is improved even with much less dimensions of MinHash signature, which implies that both accuracy and memory efficiency of the retrieval system are improved.

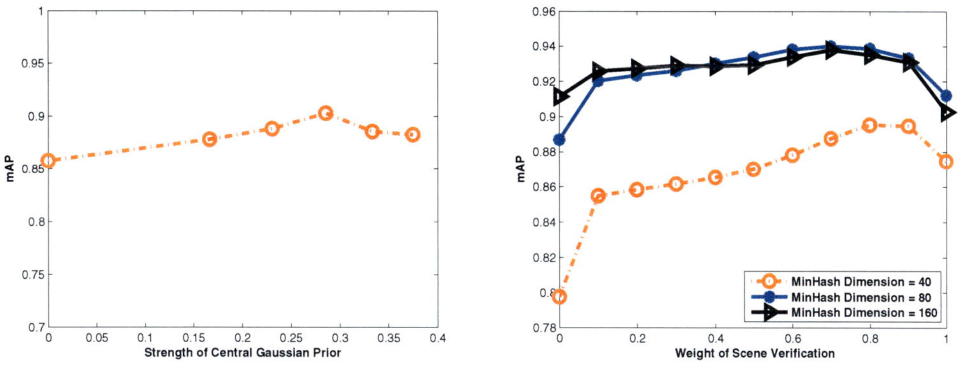

(a) (b)

Fig. (6): (a). Retrieval accuracy influenced by gaussian prior strength; (b). Retrieval accuracy influenced by scene verification strength.

Impact of gaussian prior weight and scene verification weight

In this section, we study the influence of gaussian prior weight and scene verification weight, i.e. parameters in Eq.(2) and Eq.(19). The results are shown in Fig. (6).

From Fig. (6)(a), we can see that if no Gaussian prior is enforced on the generation of seam, the seam will become less repeatable and lead to performance degradation. Increasing the strength of Gaussian prior will make an remarkable improvement on the retrieval accuracy(mAP improved from 0.8577 to 0.9029) but if the Gaussian prior is too strict, the seam will be less flexible and hurt the retrieval results.

From Fig. (6)(b), we can see that when the dimension of MinHash signature is fixed, the performance of the retrieval system is stable across a wide range(from 0.1 to 0.9) of γ in Eq.(19). That is, the video retrieval system is not sensitive to the change of this parameter.

Tab. (7): The mAP and cost comparison of MinHash, MinHash with geometric context, MinHash with geometric context and scene verification.

Approaches	mAP	Memory	Speed
MinHash	0.8886	720 Bytes	4.09s
MinHash + Geometric Context	0.9165	1080 Bytes	0.47s
MinHash + Geometric Context +Scene Verification	**0.9401**	**480 Bytes**	**0.24s**

Efficiency comparison

In this section, we compare the efficiency of the proposed retrieval algorithm with [5], one of the most efficient multimedia retrieval algorithms. Here, the MinHash signature dimensionality is an important parameter which trades off efficiency and accuracy. In this experiment, we adjust this parameter to ensure each retrieval algorithm achieves the best mAP. Then we compare their mAP, memory cost per video shot, and retrieval speed per query. The result is summarized in Tab. (**7**). From the table, we can see that by incorporating geometric information into the inverted index, our retrieval algorithm achieves better accuracy and 9 times speedup but sacrifices memory efficiency. However, after combining scene descriptor with local feature, not only the retrieval accuracy is improved from 0.8886 to 0.9401, but also the memory cost is reduced from 720 bytes to 480 bytes and retrieval speed is 17 times faster. This is because performing scene verification enables us to use MinHash signature of smaller dimensionality to represent each video.

7 Limitations

From our experiments, generally interest seam image based approach outperforms their key-frame based correspondences. However, there is also a limitation of interest seam image. It can not model video shots with little motion very well, e.g., a TV scene comprising a static background and an actor standing still and talking. For this kind of video shots, the interest seam image is mainly composed of colored bars, from which it is difficult to extract discriminative features. Therefore, for this kind of video shots, one may want to use key-frame as video synopsis, instead of interest seam image. Overall, an algorithm combining the power of the interest seam image and key-frame might further improve the performance of retrieval system. We leave that for future investigation.

8 Conclusion and future work

This chapter has presented interest seam image, a novel approach to generating discriminant and efficient video synopsis for web-scale near duplicate video retrieval.

A spatiotemporal energy map is defined to guide the extraction of prominent seams in the video, from which interest seam image is composited. Therefore, interest seam image preserves both spatially and temporally salient visual information in the videos.

Two novel video retrieval algorithms have been developed. The first one is an efficient inverted indexing scheme that takes advantages of the geometric context in the video synopsis, and a general post verification method, namely scene verification, which is manifested to be able to boost both retrieval accuracy and efficiency. Comparisons with state of the art near duplicate video retrieval systems on a large scale web video database demonstrate that the proposed approaches simultaneously improve retrieval accuracy, retrieval speed, and memory efficiency.

Future works include further exploration of invariant visual representations for videos which are robust to more types of video editings, methods to combine interest seam image and key-frame in a unified framework, and extensive tests using different types of query videos.

9 References

[1] Yuxin Peng and Chong-Wah Ngo. Clip-Based Similarity Measure for Query-Dependent Clip Retrieval and Video Summarization. In *IEEE Transactions on Circuits and Systems for Video Technology*, 2006.

[2] Xian-Sheng Hua and Guo-Jun Qi. Online multi-label active annotation: towards large-scale content-based video search. In *ACM Multimedia*, 2008.

[3] Wei Jiang, Courtenay V. Cotton, Shih-Fu Chang, Dan Ellis and Alexander C. Loui Short-term audio-visual atoms for generic video concept classification. In *ACM Multimedia*, 2009.

[4] Xiao Zhang, Gang Hua, Lei Zhang and Heung-Yeung Shum. Interest Seam Image. In *CVPR*, 2010.

[5] Ondrej Chum, James Philbin, Michael Isard and Andrew Zisserman. Scalable near identical image and shot detection. In *CIVR*, 2007.

[6] Michael Rubinstein, Ariel Shamir and Shai Avidan. Improved Seam Carving for Video Retargeting. In *ACM TOG (SIGGRAPH)*, 2008.

[7] Ivan Laptev. On Space-Time Interest Points. In *IJCV*, 2005.

[8] Krystian Mikolajczyk, Tinne Tuytelaars, Cordelia Schmid, Andrew Zisserman, Jiri Matas, Frederik Schaffalitzky, Timor Kadir and Luc J. Van Gool. A Comparison of Affine Region Detectors. In *IJCV*, 2005

[9] Chong-Wah Nog, Ting-Chuen Pong, Hong-Jiang Zhang. On Clustering and Retrieval of Video Shots Through Temporal Slices Analysis. In *IEEE Transactions on multimedia*, 2002

[10] Changick Kim and Jenq-Neng Hwang. Object-based video abstraction for video surveillance systems. In *IEEE Trans. Circuits Syst. Video Techn.*, 2002.

[11] Yan Ke, Rahul Sukthankar and Martial Hebert. Efficient Visual Event Detection Using Volumetric Features. In *ICCV*, 2005

[12] Robert C. Bolles, H. Harlyn Baker and David H. Marimont. Epipolar-plane image analysis: An approach to determining structure from motion. In *IJCV*, 1987

[13] Fang Liu and Rosalind W. Picard Finding Periodicity in Space and Time. In *ICCV*, 1998

[14] Shai Avidan and Ariel Shamir. Seam Carving for Content-Aware Image Resizing. In *ACM Transactions on Graphics(SIGGRAPH)*, 2007

[15] K. Mikolajczyk and C. Schmid. Scale and affine invariant interest point detectors In *IJCV*, 2004.

[16] D. Lowe Distinctive image features from scale-invariant keypoints In *IJCV*, 2004

[17] Xiao Wu, Alexander G. Hauptmann and Chong-Wah Ngo. Practical elimination of near-duplicates from web video search In *ACM Multimedia*, 2007

[18] Hung-Khoon Tan, Xiao Wu, Chong-Wah Ngo, Wanlei Zhao. Accelerating near-duplicate video matching by combining visual similarity and alignment distortion. In*ACM Multimedia*, 2008

[19] Hung-Khoon Tan, Chong-Wah Ngo, Richang Hong and Tat-Seng Chua Scalable Detection of Partial Near-Duplicate Videos by Visual-Temporal Consistency. In *ACM Multimedia*, 2009

[20] Lu Liu, Wei Lai, Xian-Sheng Hua and Shi-Qiang Yang. Video Histogram: A Novel Video Signature for Efficient Web Video Duplicate Detection. In *MMM*, 2007

[21] Matthijs Douze, Hervé Jégou, Harsimrat Singh, Laurent Amsaleg and Cordelia Schmid. Evaluation of GIST descriptors for web-scale image search. In *CIVR*, 2009.

[22] Philbin, J., Chum, O., Isard, M., Sivic, J. and Zisserman, A. Object retrieval with large vocabularies and fast spatial matching. In *CVPR*, 2007.

[23] Chum, O., Philbin, J., Sivic, J., Isard, M. and Zisserman, A. Total Recall: Automatic Query Expansion with a Generative Feature Model for Object Retrieval. In *ICCV*, 2007.

[24] Alexandr Andoni, Piotr Indyk. Near-Optimal Hashing Algorithms for Near Neighbor Problem in High Dimensions. In *Proceedings of the Symposium on Foundations of Computer Science*, 2006.

[25] Philbin, J., Chum, O., Isard, M., Sivic, J. and Zisserman, A. Lost in Quantization: Improving Particular Object Retrieval in Large Scale Image Databases. In *CVPR*, 2008.

[26] Xiao Zhang, Zhiwei Li, Lei Zhang, Wei-Ying Ma and Heung-Yeung Shum. Efficient Indexing for Large Scale Visual Search. In *ICCV*, 2009

[27] Sivic, J. and Zisserman, A. Video Google: A Text Retrieval Approach to Object Matching in Videos. In *ICCV*, 2003.

[28] J.Matas, O. Chum, M. Urban and T. Pajdla. Robust wide baseline stereo from maximally stable extremal regions. In *BMVC*, 2002.

[29] Aude Oliva and Antonio B. Torralba. Modeling the Shape of the Scene: A Holistic Representation of the Spatial Envelope. In *IJCV*, 2001.

[30] H.J. Zhang, Atreyi Kankanhalli and Stephen W. Smoliar. Automatic partitioning of full-motion video. In *Multimedia Systems*, 1993.

Internet Multimedia Search and Mining, 2013, 80-110

CHAPTER 4

Large-Scale Online Multi-Labeled Annotation for Multimedia Search and Mining

Guo-Jun Qi*
Beckman Institute, University of Illinois at Urbana-Champaign, Email: qi4@illinois.edu
Hong-Jiang Zhang
Microsoft Advanced Technology Center, Email: hjzhang@microsoft.com

Abstract: In this chapter, we briefly review the online learning algorithms applied to enable content-based multimedia annotation, which is scalable to handle large-scale multimedia data as well as the associated semantic concepts. Multimedia search uses annotated semantic concepts to approach efficient content-based indexing. This is a promising direction to enable real content-based multimedia search. However, due to large amounts of multimedia samples and semantic concepts, existing techniques for automatic multimedia annotation are not able to handle large-scale multimedia corpus and concept set, in terms of both annotation accuracy and computation cost. To enable large-scale semantic concept annotation, a practical multimedia annotation method ought to be scalable on both multimedia sample dimension and concept label dimension. In real-world cases, large-scale unlabeled multimedia samples arrive consecutively in batches with an initial prelabeled training set, based on which a preliminary multi-label classifier is built. For each arrived batch, a multi-label active learning engine is applied, which selects a set of unlabeled samples with selected set of labels to get label confirmation from

***Correspondence Author:** Guo-Jun Qi, Beckman Institute, University of Illinois at Urbana-Champaign; Email: qi4@illinois.edu.

data labelers. And then an online learner updates the original classifier by taking the newly labeled sample-label pairs into consideration. This process repeats until all data are arrived. During the process, new labels, even without any pre-labeled training samples, can be incorporated into the process anytime. In this chapter, we review the large-scale online active annotation for Internet multimedia in the above two basic techniques - active learning and online computing. By combining these two techniques in a unified framework, scalable multimedia annotation can be achieved in an online manner so that both annotation accuracy and efficiency are able to be significantly improved.

Keywords

large-scale multimedia search and mining, online learning, multi-label annotation, multimedia sample dimension, concept label dimension, sample-label pair, multi-label active learning, large-scale online active annotation, Correlative Multi-Label, 2D Active Learning

1 Introduction

Existing Multimedia search engines are all based on indexing "text metadata" with few support from multimedia content analysis and understanding. That is, surrounding text (the text in a web page that may be related to the video), multimedia descriptions (the textual description of the target multimedia, including title, author, content description, tags, comments, etc.), recognized speech, and multimedia metadata (such as format, bitrates, frame size, etc) are used to index multimedia documents. The advantage of this design is that, we can directly use text-based indexing and ranking technologies to do multimedia search. The disadvantage is that this "direct text" frequently is far from the real content of the multimedia.

Multimedia search moves one-step ahead, which takes advantages of content analysis, especially semantic concept annotation. Machine learning techniques are applied to convert visual information into textual description to realize content-based video search. We argue this is a promising direction to enable real content-based multimedia search. However, due to the complexity of both multimedia data and semantic concepts, existing techniques on automatic multimedia annotation are suffering the difficulties in scaling them up to handle large-scale multimedia documents and concept set, in terms of both annotation accuracy and computation cost. Generally, to overcome these difficulties, huge training datasets and high computation powers are required, but they are difficult, if not impossible, to be obtained in many real-world large-scale problems.

To address this difficulty, a scalable framework is proposed for annotation-based multimedia search. This online multi-label active learning approach enables large-scale semantic concept annotation in terms of both multimedia samples and concept labels. In this framework, large-scale unlabeled multimedia samples are assumed to arrive consecutively in batches with an initial pre-labeled training set for the first batch, based on which an initial multi-label classifier is built. For each arrived batch, an online multi-label active learning engine is applied to efficiently update the classifier which maximizes its performance on all current-available data. This process repeats until all data are arrived and resumes when a new data batch is available, during which new concept labels are allowed to be introduced into the online multi-label active learning framework at any batch, even though these labels have no any pre-labeled training samples. The core approach, online multi-label active learning, has three major modules, multi-label active learning, online multi-label learning and new label learning from zero-knowledge.

Active learning is well-known for its efficiency in saving labeling cost by exploiting the redundancy in samples. The multi-label active learning strategy in this chapter exploits the redundancy in both samples and semantic labels to further reduce the labor cost of labeling. The primary difference between multi-label active learning and typical active learning is that, we will iteratively ask people to confirm the labels of selected set of sample-label pairs instead of samples (with all labels by default) to minimize an estimated classification error.

Online learning is designed to reduce the computation cost in multi-label active learning. Generally, retraining is required when new sample-label pairs are obtained, which is computation-intensive. The computation cost increases remarkably with the increase of labeled sample-label pairs. On the contrary, online multi-label learning is able to incrementally update the multi-label classifier by adapting the original classifier to the newly labeled data, which significantly saves computation cost. Different from existing online learning approaches, the one proposed in this paper exploits the correlations among multiple labels to improve the performance of the classifier. New label learning is to make the proposed framework scalable to new semantic labels. Existing semantic annotation schemes are only applicable for a closed concept set, which is not practical for real world video search engines. The aforementioned online learner can be naturally extended to handling new labels, even though these new labels have no any pre-labeled training data. The annotation performance of the new labels will be gradually improved through the iterative active learning process.

The remaining of this chapter is organized as follows. First in Section 2 we briefly introduce the multi-label multimedia annotation problem and show why it is important for real-world annotation. Then we briefly review active learning in Section 3 and extend it to multi-label case, which makes the multimedia annotation scalable on the dimension of concept labels. On the other hand, online algorithm is proposed in Section 4, which makes annotation scalable on the dimension of multimedia samples.

2 Multi-label Multimedia Annotation

Before we state the online algorithm for large-scale multimedia search and mining, we briefly introduce the multi-labeled multimedia annotation which scales the multimedia database along the label dimension. The goal of multimedia annotation is to assign a set of labels to multimedia documents based on their semantic content. In most existing approaches, multimedia annotation has been formulated as either multi-class or multi-label problem. As multi-class problem, each multimedia document, such as an image and video, can be labeled by one and only one class. An example under such an annotation problem is the Caltech 101 [13] annotation, in which each image in this data set is classified as only one object category. However in most real-world problems, multiple labels can be assigned to a multimedia document. For example, in many online video/image sharing websites (e.g., Flickr, Picasa, and Youtube), most of the multimedia documents have more than one tags manually labeled by users. These real cases result in a multi-label multimedia annotation problem which is more complex and challenging compared to multi-class annotation problem. In this chapter, we will focus on multimedia annotation under the multi-label cases.

Research on multi-label multimedia annotation evolved through three paradigms: individual concept detection and annotation, *Context Based Conceptual Fusion* (CBCF) [16] annotation, and the third paradigm: *integrated multi-label annotation*. We next review these three paradigms.

First paradigm: Individual Concept Annotation

In this paradigm, multiple multimedia concepts are detected *individually* and *independently* without considering correlations between them. That is, the multi-label multimedia annotation is translated into a set of binary detectors with presence/absence of the label for each concept. A typical approach is to independently train a concept model using *Support Vector Machine*(SVM) [8] or *Maximum Entropy Model* (MEM) [26] etc. The leftmost flowchart of Fig.(1) illustrates the first paradigm – a set of individual SVMs for multimedia concept detection and annotations. A mathematical alternative is to stack this set of detectors into a single discriminative classifier [35]. However, both the individual detectors and the stacked classifier at their core are independent binary classification formulations.

The first-paradigm approaches only achieved limited success. In real world, multimedia concepts do not exist in isolation. Instead, they appear correlatively and naturally interact with each other at the semantic level. For example, the presence of "crowd" often occurs together with the presence of "people" while "boat ship" and "truck" commonly do not co-occur. Furthermore, while simple concepts can be modeled directly from low level features, it is quite difficult to individually learn the models of complex concepts, e.g., "people marching", from the low-level features.

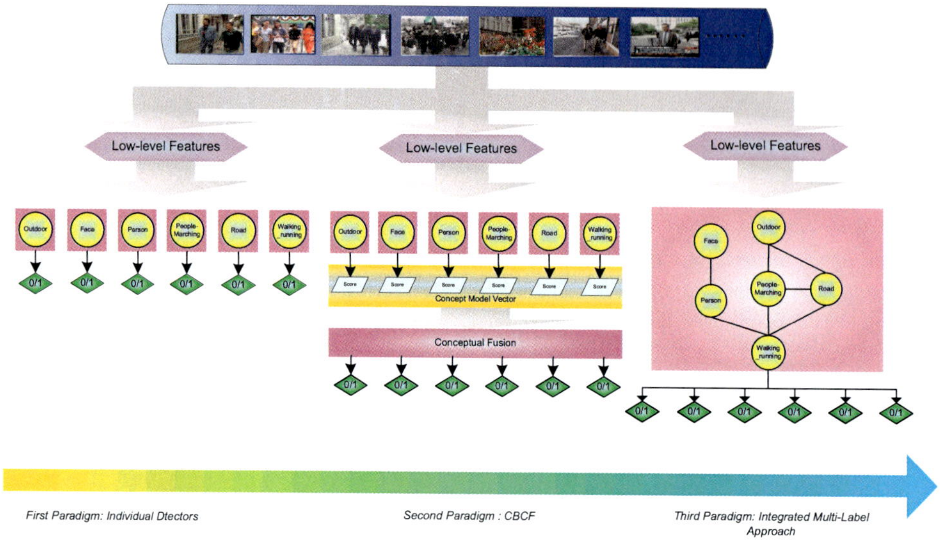

Fig. (1): The multi-label multimedia annotation methods in three paradigms. From leftmost to the rightmost, they are the individual SVM, CBCF and our proposed CML.

Instead, the complex concepts can be better inferred based on the correlations with the other concepts. For instance, the presence of "people marching" can be boosted if both "crowd" and "walking running" occurs in a video clip.

Second paradigm: Context Based Conceptual Fusion Annotation

One of the most well-known approaches in this paradigm is to refine the detection results of the individual detectors with a *Context Based Concept Fusion* (CBCF) strategy. For instance, Naphade *et al.* [25] proposed a probabilistic Bayesian Multinet approach to explicitly model the relationship between the multiple concepts through a factor graph which is built upon the underlying multimedia ontology semantics. Wu *et al.* [41] used an ontology-based multi-classification learning for multimedia concept detection. Each concept is first independently modeled by a classifier, and then a predefined ontology hierarchy is investigated to improve the detection accuracy of the individual classifiers. Smith *et al.* [36] presented a two-step Discriminative Model Fusion (DMF) approach to mine the unknown or indirect relationship to specific concepts by constructing model vectors based on detection scores of individual classifiers. A SVM is then trained to refine the detection results of the individual classifiers. The center flowchart of Fig.(1) shows such a second-paradigm approach. Alternative fusion strategy can also be used, e.g. Hauptmann *et al.* [14] proposed to use Logistic Regression (LR) to fuse the individual detections. Jiang *et al.* [16] used a CBCF-based active learning method. Users were involved in their approach to annotate a few concepts for extra video clips, and these manual annotations were then utilized to help infer and improve detections of other concepts.

Although it is intuitively correct that contextual relationship can help improve detection accuracy of individual detectors, experiments of the above CBCF approaches have shown that such improvement is not always stable, and the overall performance can even be worse than individual detectors alone. For example, in [14] at least 3 out of 8 concepts do not gain better performance by using the conceptual fusion with a LR classifier atop the uni-concept detectors. The unstable performance gain is due to the following reasons:

1. CBCF methods are built on top of the independent binary detectors with a second step to fuse them. However, the output of the individual independent detectors can be unreliable and therefore their detection errors can propagate to the second fusion step. As a result, the final annotations can be corrupted by these incorrect predictions. From a philosophical point of view, the CBCF approaches do not follow the *principle of Least-Commitment* espoused by D. Marr [24], because they are prematurely committed to irreversible individual predictions in the first step which can or cannot be corrected in the second fusion step.

2. A secondary reason comes from the insufficient data for the conceptual fusion. In CBCF methods, the samples needs to be split into two parts for each step and the samples for the conceptual fusion step is usually insufficient compared to the samples used in the first training step. Unfortunately, the correlations between the concepts are usually complex, and insufficient data can lead to "over fitting" in the fusion step, thus the obtained prediction lacks the generalization ability.

Third paradigm: Integrated Multi-label Annotation

To address the difficulties faced in the first and second paradigms, the third paradigm of an integrated multi-label annotation is proposed. The key of this paradigm is to simultaneously model both the individual concepts and their interactions in a single formulation. The rightmost flowchart of Fig.(1) illustrates such an algorithm - *Correlative Multi-Label* (CML) method [27]. This approach has the following advantages compared with the second paradigm, e.g., CBCF methods:

1. The approach follows the *Principle of Least-Commitment* [24]. Because the learning and optimization is done in a single step for all the concepts simultaneously, it does not have the error propagation problem as in CBCF.

2. The entire samples are efficiently used simultaneously in modeling the individual concepts as well as their correlations. The risk of overfitting due to the insufficient samples used for modeling the conceptual correlations is therefore significantly reduced.

To summarize, the first paradigm does not address concept correlation. The second paradigm attempts to address it by introducing a separate second correlation step. The third paradigm, on the other hand, addresses the correlation issue at the root in a single step.

3 Multi-Label Active Learning

Active learning is one of the most widely-used approaches in image classification, as it can significantly reduce the effort in labeling training samples [11, 15, 30, 42]. Specifically, active learning approaches iteratively annotate a set of elaborately selected samples so that the expected classification error is minimized in each iteration. As a result, the total number of training samples that need to be labeled is smaller than non active learning approaches. The core of any active learning approach is the sample selection strategy. In the past decade, a number of active learning approaches were developed using different sample selection strategies [5, 15, 37]. For example, [17, 20] have explored reduction in uncertainty as the sample selection criterion and competitive performances have been achieved. Most of these approaches focus on the binary classification. However, in many real-world applications [3, 21, 27], a sample is usually associated with multiple labels rather than a single one. Under such a multi-label setting, each sample will be annotated as either "positive" or "negative" for each and every label. As a result, active learning with multi-label samples is much more challenging than that with binary-label ones, especially when the number of labels is large.

A direct way to tackle active learning under multi-label setting is to translate it into a set of binary problems, i.e., each category/label is independently handled by a binary active learning algorithm. For example, in [4, 21] two research groups have proposed such a binary-based active learning algorithm for multi-label classification problem, respectively. However, these approaches do not take into account the inherent relationship among multiple labels. To incorporate the inherent label correlations, an active learning strategy is proposed, which iteratively selects sample-label pairs to minimize the expected classification error. Specifically, in each iteration, human annotators are only required to annotate/confirm a selected part of labels of selected samples while the remaining unlabeled part can be inferred according to the label correlations. We call this strategy 2 Dimensional Active Learning (2DAL) [29] because it considers not only the samples to be labeled along the sample dimension but also the labels associated with these samples along the label dimension. An intuitive explanation of this strategy is that there exist both

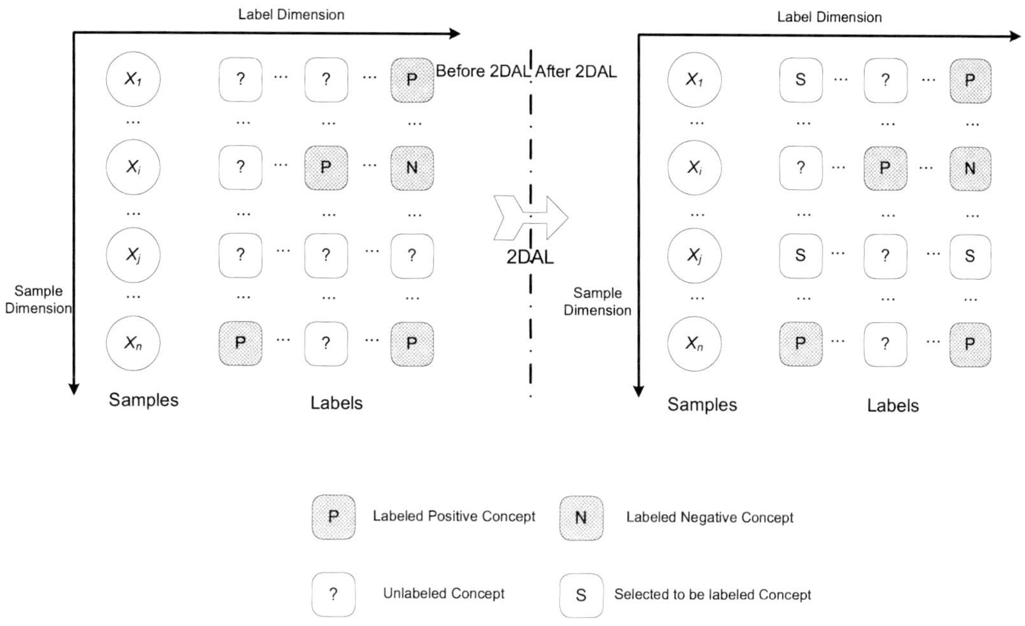

Fig. (2): Two-dimension active learning (2DAL) strategy.

sample and label redundancies for multi-label samples. Therefore, annotating a set of selected sample-label pairs provides enough information for training the classifiers since the information in these pairs can be propagated to the rest along both the sample "dimension" and the label "dimension". Such a strategy significantly can reduce the required human labor. For example, "field" and "mountain" tend to occur simultaneously in an image. Therefore, it is reasonable to select only one label (e.g., "mountain") for annotation since the uncertainty of the other label can be remarkably decreased after annotating this one. Another example is "mountain" and "urban". In contrast to "field" and "mountain", these two labels often do not occur simultaneously. Thus, annotating one of them will probably eliminate the existence of the other one.

Two dimensional Multi-Label active learning

The research work on multi-label active learning is proposed in [29]. Different from the typical binary active learning formulation that selects the most "informative" samples for manual labeling, we jointly select both the samples and labels simultaneously. The underlying assumption is that different labels of a certain sample have different contributions to minimizing the expected classification error of the to-be-trained classifier. And annotating a portion of well selected labels may provide sufficient information for learning the classifier.

In essence, the multi-label classifiers do have uncertainty along different labels as well as different samples. Traditional active learning algorithms can be seen as a one-dimension active selection approach, which only reduces the sample uncertainty. In contrast, multi-label active learning is a two-dimensional active learning strategy, which selects the most "informative" sample-label pairs to reduce the uncertainty along the dimensionalities of both sample and label. More specifically, along label dimension all of the labels correlatively interact. Therefore, once partial labels are annotated, the left unlabeled concepts can then be inferred based on label correlations.

In detail, Fig.(2) illustrates the Two-Dimensional Active Learning (2DAL) strategy. Different from the typical binary active learning formulation that selects the most informative samples for annotation, we jointly select both the samples and labels simultaneously. The underlying assumption is annotating a portion of well-selected labels provides sufficient information for learning the classifier. As shown in Fig.(2), this strategy trades off between the annotation labor and the learning performance along two dimensions, i.e., the sample and label dimensions. In contrast, traditional active learning algorithms can be seen as a one-dimension active selection approach along only sample dimension. More specifically, along label dimension all of the labels correlatively interact. Therefore, once labels are partially annotated, the remaining unlabeled concepts can be inferred based on label correlations. Theoretically, the label correlations have a connection with the expected Bayesian Error Bound, and thus these label correlations can help to reduce the prediction errors in the testing set during the active learning procedure. This approach saves much labor compared to fully annotating multiple labels especially when the number of labels is huge.

This approach significantly saves the labor cost for data labeling compared with fully annotating all labels. Thus, it is far more efficient when the number of labels is huge. For instance, an image may be associated with thousands and hundreds of concepts. That means a full annotation strategy will pay large labor costs for only one image. On the contrary, multi-label active learning only manually annotates the most informative labels. It is worth noting that during multi-label active learning process, some samples may be lack of some labels since only a partial of labels are annotated. This is different from traditional active learning algorithm. The missing labels for a certain sample can be seen as hidden variables and the corresponding classifier with such incomplete labeling can be trained by the standard Expectation-Maximum (EM) [10] algorithm accordingly.

To explain the multi-label active learning algorithm, we begin by defining some notations. For each sample $\boldsymbol{x}$, it has m labels $y_i (1 \leq i \leq m)$ each of which indicates whether its corresponding concept occurs. As stated before, in each 2DAL iteration, some of these labels have already been annotated while others not. Let $U(\boldsymbol{x}) \triangleq \{i|(\boldsymbol{x}, y_i) \text{ is unlabeled sample-label pair.}\}$ denote the set of indices of unlabeled part and $L(\boldsymbol{x}) \triangleq \{i|(\boldsymbol{x}, y_i) \text{ is labeled sample-label pair.}\}$ denote the labeled part for $\boldsymbol{x}$.

Note that $L(\boldsymbol{x})$ can be an empty set $\varnothing$, which indicates that no label has been annotated for $\boldsymbol{x}$. Let $P(\boldsymbol{y}|\boldsymbol{x})$ be the conditional distribution over samples, where $\boldsymbol{y} = \{0,1\}^m$ is the complete label vector and $P(\boldsymbol{x})$ be the sample distribution.

We are concerned with *pool-based active learning*, i.e., a large pool $\mathcal{P}$ is available to the learner sampled from $P(\boldsymbol{x})$ and then the proposed 2DAL elaborately selects the sample-label pairs from this pool to reduce the *sampled* expected classification error. We first write the expected Bayesian classification error over all samples in $\mathcal{P}$ before selecting a sample-label pair $(\boldsymbol{x}_s, y_s)$

$$\mathcal{E}^b(\mathcal{P}) = \frac{1}{|\mathcal{P}|}\sum\nolimits_{\boldsymbol{x}\in\mathcal{P}} \mathcal{E}\left(\boldsymbol{y}|y_{L(\boldsymbol{x})}, \boldsymbol{x}\right) \tag{1}$$

where $\mathcal{E}\left(\boldsymbol{y}|y_{L(\boldsymbol{x})}, \boldsymbol{x}\right)$ denotes the classification error of labeling $\boldsymbol{y}$ given the annotated $y_{L(\boldsymbol{x})}$ for the sample $\boldsymbol{x}$. We can use the above classification error on the pool to estimate the expected error over the full distribution $P(\boldsymbol{x})$, i.e., $E_{P(\boldsymbol{x})}\mathcal{E}\left(\boldsymbol{y}|y_{L(\boldsymbol{x})}, \boldsymbol{x}\right) = \int P(\boldsymbol{x})\mathcal{E}\left(\boldsymbol{y}|y_{L(\boldsymbol{x})}, \boldsymbol{x}\right)d\boldsymbol{x}$, because the pool not only provides a finite set of samples but also an estimation of $P(\boldsymbol{x})$. After selecting the pair $(\boldsymbol{x}_s, y_s)$, the expected Bayesian classification error over the pool $\mathcal{P}$ is

$$\begin{aligned}&\mathcal{E}^a(\mathcal{P})\\ &= \tfrac{1}{|\mathcal{P}|}\left\{\mathcal{E}\left(\boldsymbol{y}|y_s; y_{L(\boldsymbol{x}_s)}, \boldsymbol{x}_s\right) + \sum\nolimits_{\boldsymbol{x}\in\mathcal{P}\setminus\boldsymbol{x}_s} \mathcal{E}\left(\boldsymbol{y}|y_{L(\boldsymbol{x})}, \boldsymbol{x}\right)\right\}\\ &= \tfrac{1}{|\mathcal{P}|}\{\mathcal{E}\left(\boldsymbol{y}|y_s; y_{L(\boldsymbol{x}_s)}, \boldsymbol{x}_s\right) - \mathcal{E}\left(\boldsymbol{y}|y_{L(\boldsymbol{x}_s)}, \boldsymbol{x}_s\right)\\ &+ \sum\nolimits_{\boldsymbol{x}\in\mathcal{P}} \mathcal{E}\left(\boldsymbol{y}|y_{L(\boldsymbol{x})}, \boldsymbol{x}\right)\}\end{aligned} \tag{2}$$

Therefore, the reduction of the expected Bayesian classification after selecting $(\boldsymbol{x}_s, y_s)$ over the whole pool $\mathcal{P}$ is

$$\Delta\mathcal{E}(\mathcal{P}) = \mathcal{E}^b(\mathcal{P}) - \mathcal{E}^a(\mathcal{P}) \tag{3}$$

The goal is to select $(\boldsymbol{x}_s^\star, y_s^\star)$ to maximize the above expected error reduction. That is,

$$\begin{aligned}&(\boldsymbol{x}_s^\star, y_s^\star) = \arg\max\nolimits_{\boldsymbol{x}_s\in\mathcal{P}, y_s\in U(\boldsymbol{x}_s)} \Delta\mathcal{E}(\mathcal{P})\\ &= \arg\min\nolimits_{\boldsymbol{x}_s\in\mathcal{P}, y_s\in U(\boldsymbol{x}_s)} -\Delta\mathcal{E}(\mathcal{P})\end{aligned} \tag{4}$$

Applying Lemma 1 and Theorem 1 in [29], we can select the sample-label pair for annotation as

$$\begin{aligned}&(\boldsymbol{x}_s^\star, y_s^\star)\\ &= \mathop{\arg\min}_{\boldsymbol{x}_s\in\mathcal{P}, y_s\in U(\boldsymbol{x}_s)} \tfrac{1}{|\mathcal{P}|}\left\{\epsilon - \tfrac{1}{2m}\sum_{i=1}^{m} MI\left(y_i; y_s|y_{L(\boldsymbol{x}_s)}, \boldsymbol{x}_s\right)\right\}\\ &= \mathop{\arg\max}_{\boldsymbol{x}_s\in\mathcal{P}, y_s\in U(\boldsymbol{x}_s)} \sum\nolimits_{i=1}^{m} MI\left(y_i; y_s|y_{L(\boldsymbol{x}_s)}, \boldsymbol{x}_s\right)\end{aligned} \tag{5}$$

4 Multi-Label Online Computing

Online learning has a long history which can be traced bake to F. Rosenblatt's work on perceptron algorithm for linear discriminant functions [31]. Since then, many striking results have been obtained which solve various online learning problems, from Winnow family of algorithms [22] to the milestone Back Propagation (BP) [32] learning method on Artificial Neural Networks. In this chapter, we give a brief review about some new progresses in online learning algorithm from both practical and theoretical perspectives. A general online learning framework is introduced which can be applied into many different scenarios from binary classification, multi-label classifier, and conditional random field to metric learning and PCA (principal component analysis). In this framework, a regret bound can be deduced which bounds the total loss between online learners and the best offline solution.

A General Framework for Online Learning

Given a sequence of trials $\mathcal{S} = \{(x_i, y_i)|i = 1, \cdots, \ell\}$, online learning algorithm dynamically maintains a sequence of parameters $\{\theta_t\}$ over a hypothesis space $\mathcal{H}$ for $t = 1, \cdots, \ell$. Before trial t, the model with parameter θ_t is learned from the information in the past trials $\{(x_i, y_i)|i = 1, \cdots, t-1\}$. After the tth trial (x_t, y_t) comes, the parameter θ_t is updated according to some rule which results in a new model in $\mathcal{H}$. In general, the model observes a new instance x_t and makes a prediction $\hat{y}(x_t, \theta_t)$ on it. Then the new parameter θ_{t+1} is obtained which depends on the true outcome y_t, the prediction $\hat{y}(x_t, \theta_t)$ and the learning rate η.

To design a proper updating rule, two criteria should be obeyed [19, 29].

- Conservativeness. It ought to preserve the old knowledge that has already existed in the current model, because this knowledge stores the rich historical information about the previous trials;
- Correctiveness. Its performance should be improved on the new trial.

Following this idea, the new model parameter θ_{t+1} is updated by minimizing an objective function

$$F(\theta_{t+1}) = d(\theta_{t+1}, \theta_t) + \eta_t L(y_t, \hat{y}_t(x_t, \theta_{t+1})) \tag{6}$$

where d is a distance measure between two parameterized models with θ_{t+1} and θ_t. L is a loss function between the true outcome y_t and the prediction $\hat{y}_t$, and η_t is the learning rate.

There are many options for the distance measure d, however, it is not necessary that it must be a metric which must satisfy the triangle inequality. For example, when $\mathcal{H}$ is a hypothesis space consisting of linear predictors, θ_t is a weighting vector. Then d can be a squared Euclidean distance or the relative entropy if θ_t is probability vector (i.e., each entry of θ_t is nonnegative and the sum of all entries is equal to 1). On the other hand, the loss function L also has many various forms which depend on the specific problems for studying. Take the example of linear predictors above, L can be the squared loss between y_t and $\hat{y}_t$ for regression problem, or the 0/1 loss for the classification problem. By choosing different d and L, different online learners can be defined. In the following, we give some examples which have already been proposed in the literature.

Some examples of online learners

In [19], some simple examples of online learners have been defined by following (6). These examples include GD (Gradient Descent) with d as the squared Euclidean distance and L as the squared loss, EG (Exponentiated Gradient) with d as unnormalized relative entropy, AEG (Approximated Exponentiated Gradient) with d as χ^2 distance.

Besides these relatively simple examples, there are many other which have been applied into real problems in practice. In this chapter, we enumerate some examples as follows.

Neural Network [1] studied how to learn a family of exponential distributions, including Boltzmann machine, multi-layer perceptron and mixtures of expert neural nets, from an information geometry point of view. In this work, kullback-leibler divergence between the model submanifold $\mathcal{M}$ and observed data submanifold $\mathcal{D}$ is defined as the measure distance d. In general, their online learning algorithm contains two steps optimizations.

- Guess the unobserved variables in neural network (e.g., the hidden variables in the middle layer) based on the observed variable at trial t. This is done by calculating e-projection from the current model in $\mathcal{M}$ into the conditional expectation of the unobserved variables. About e-projection, please refer to the introduction into information geometry. Then the observed point at t is modified to a new observed point based on the new guess of the unobserved variables.

- Calculate the new m.l.e. (maximum likelihood estimation) model in $\mathcal{M}$.

The method given in [1] investigates the learning procedure by jointly e-projection and m-projection between $\mathcal{M}$ and $\mathcal{D}$, which leads to a powerful analysis tool for the family of exponential distributions. Next, we review another online algorithm for multi-label classifier which also employs kullback-divergence as distance measure, but instead it directly optimize the distance in a single distribution space rather than using e-projection and m-projection to iteratively project from one space to another.

Support Vector Machine Another example of online learner for binary classification problem was given in [43]. In this work, the squared Euclidean distance between the parameters of two successive linear models w_{t+1} and w_t was used as d and the hinge loss on the new trial (x_t, y_t) served as L in (6). Hence the new parameter w_{t+1} was solved by minimizing

$$||w_{t+1} - w_t||_2^2 + \eta_t(1 - y_t w_{t+1} \cdot x_t)_+ \tag{7}$$

where $(a)_+ = \max(0, a)$ and $|| \cdot ||_2$ is the norm 2 for a vector.

Metric Learning Besides the online learner which involves a sequence of single training examples like (x_t, y_t), [9] proposed another form of online learner which updated a metric model with a pair of examples $(x_t^{(1)}, x_t^{(2)}, d_t)$, where d_t is the target distance metric for learning at trial t. In their method, the Bregman divergence over the positive definite convex cone is used to measure the progress between two successive metric models parameterized by Mahalonobis matrix M_{t+1} and M_t. Meanwhile, the squared loss between the prediction $\hat{d}_t = (x_t^{(1)} - x_t^{(2)})^T M_{t+1}(x_t^{(1)} - x_t^{(2)})$ and the target d_t was used to measure the correctiveness of new model on trial t. Formally, M_{t+1} was computed by minimizing

$$D_{ld}(M_{t+1}, M_t) + \eta_t(\hat{d}_t - d_t)^2 \tag{8}$$

where D_{ld} is the Bregman distance between two positive definite matrices.

Besides the above concrete examples, there are still many other online learner recently proposed. See more materials about online PCA algorithm in [39], a new stochastic gradient method for SVM [34] and CRF (conditional random field) [33]. These online learners follow the main idea in (6) but may use some approximations to update the model instead of exactly minimizing it.

Multi-Label online learner

This multi-label classifier was proposed in [29]. In this work, kullback-leibler divergence was used exactly as d in (6), and a submanifold $\mathcal{H}$ satisfying multi-label constraints set by the current trial t is formed which acts as the loss function in (6).

To explain the multi-label online learner in detail, we begin our discussion with the definition of some notations. Under the online setting, we are given an existing old multi-label model $P^{\tau}(\boldsymbol{y}|\boldsymbol{x})$, which is trained from the historically-acquired images. Then a set of new images and their corresponding labels $\{\boldsymbol{x}_i, \boldsymbol{y}_i\}_{i=1}^n$ is obtained in each 2DAL iteration. Each $\boldsymbol{x}_i \in \mathbb{R}^d$ is the feature vector and $\boldsymbol{y}_i \in \{0, 1\}^m$ is a m-dimensional label vector, in which m is the number of image labels and each element in $\boldsymbol{y}_i$ indicates the membership for the corresponding label. Our goal is to learn a new model $P^{\tau+1}(\boldsymbol{y}|\boldsymbol{x})$ based on the existing model $P^{\tau}(\boldsymbol{y}|\boldsymbol{x})$ and $\{\boldsymbol{x}_i, \boldsymbol{y}_i\}_{i=1}^n$. In contrast to the retraining-based learning algorithm, the online learner does not utilize the historical training set but only the current new coming samples. It assumes

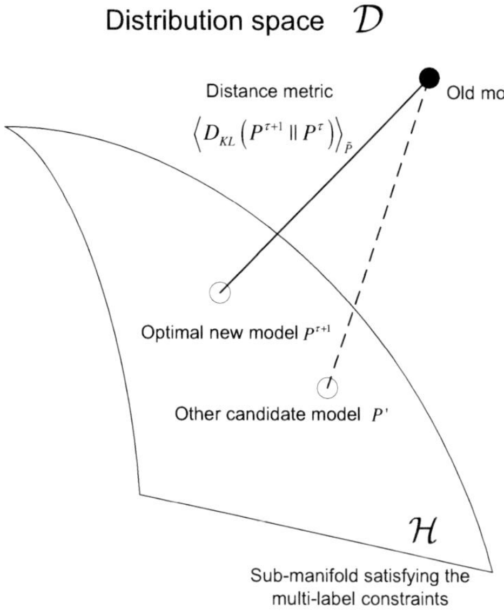

Fig. (3): A Geometry explanation of the proposed online learner. $\mathcal{D}$ is a space of all potential distributions for the new model. It is equipped with KLD as its distance measure. All the distributions satisfying the multi-label constraints constitute a sub-manifold $\mathcal{H}$. The optimal new model $P^{t+1}(\boldsymbol{y}|\boldsymbol{x})$ at trial t can be seen as the projection of the old model $P^{t}(\boldsymbol{y}|\boldsymbol{x})$ to the sub-manifold $\mathcal{H}$. In this figure, P^{t+1} is the optimal new model and we can see its distance to the old model is less than that of any other candidate models P' in the sub-manifold $\mathcal{H}$. The figure originally appears in [29].

the information about the historical training samples has been preserved in the old model $P^{\tau}(\boldsymbol{y}|\boldsymbol{x})$, which is learned from these old samples. Thus with much fewer of only new coming samples, the online learner can train a new model efficiently.

As aforementioned, this new model $P^{\tau+1}(\boldsymbol{y}|\boldsymbol{x})$ ought to satisfy the two requirements: preserving the existing knowledge in $P^{\tau}(\boldsymbol{y}|\boldsymbol{x})$ while revealing the information in new samples $\{\boldsymbol{x}_i, \boldsymbol{y}_i\}_{i=1}^{n}$. These two requirements can be satisfied by formulating the following probabilistic variational problem. In this paper, we use the Kullback-Leibler Divergence (KLD)[7] to measure the degree of the new model preserving the existing knowledge contained in the old one, under a set of multi-label constraints revealing the information contained in the new samples:

$$l\widehat{P}^{\tau+1}(\boldsymbol{y}|\boldsymbol{x}) = \arg\min_{P^{\tau+1}} \left\langle D_{KL}\left(P^{\tau+1}(\boldsymbol{y}|\boldsymbol{x})||P^{\tau}(\boldsymbol{y}|\boldsymbol{x})\right)\right\rangle_{\widetilde{P}(\boldsymbol{x})} \tag{9}$$

$$s.t. \langle y_i\rangle_{P^{\tau+1}(\boldsymbol{x},\boldsymbol{y})} = \langle y_i\rangle_{\widetilde{P}(\boldsymbol{x},\boldsymbol{y})} + \eta_i, 1 \le i \le m \tag{10}$$

$$\langle y_i y_j\rangle_{P^{\tau+1}(\boldsymbol{x},\boldsymbol{y})} = \langle y_i y_j\rangle_{\widetilde{P}(\boldsymbol{x},\boldsymbol{y})} + \theta_{ij}, 1 \le i < j \le m \tag{11}$$

$$\langle y_i x_l\rangle_{P^{\tau+1}(\boldsymbol{x},\boldsymbol{y})} = \langle y_i x_l\rangle_{\widetilde{P}(\boldsymbol{x},\boldsymbol{y})} + \phi_{il}, 1 \le i \le m, 1 \le l \le d \tag{12}$$

$$\sum_{\boldsymbol{y}} P^{\tau+1}(\boldsymbol{y}|\boldsymbol{x}) = 1 \tag{13}$$

where $\left\langle D_{KL}\left(P^{\tau+1}(\boldsymbol{y}|\boldsymbol{x})||P^{\tau}(\boldsymbol{y}|\boldsymbol{x})\right)\right\rangle_{\widetilde{P}(\boldsymbol{x})}$ is the KLD between the new model $P^{\tau+1}(\boldsymbol{y}|\boldsymbol{x})$ and the old one $P^{\tau}(\boldsymbol{y}|\boldsymbol{x})$ over the sample frequency $\widetilde{P}(\boldsymbol{x}) = \frac{1}{m}\sum_{i=1}^{m}\delta(\boldsymbol{x}-\boldsymbol{x}_i)$ taken from $\{\boldsymbol{x}_i\}_{i=1}^{n}$ where $\delta(\cdot)$ is the indicator function. Thus we have

$$\begin{aligned}&\left\langle D_{KL}\left(P^{\tau+1}(\boldsymbol{y}|\boldsymbol{x})||P^{\tau}(\boldsymbol{y}|\boldsymbol{x})\right)\right\rangle_{\widetilde{P}(\boldsymbol{x})}\\ &= \sum_{\boldsymbol{x}} \widetilde{P}(\boldsymbol{x}) D_{KL}\left(P^{\tau+1}(\boldsymbol{y}|\boldsymbol{x})||P^{\tau}(\boldsymbol{y}|\boldsymbol{x})\right)\\ &= \sum_{i=1}^{n} D_{KL}\left(P^{\tau+1}(\boldsymbol{y}|\boldsymbol{x}_i)||P^{\tau}(\boldsymbol{y}|\boldsymbol{x}_i)\right)\end{aligned}$$

$\langle\cdot\rangle_{P^{\tau+1}(\boldsymbol{x},\boldsymbol{y})}$ and $\langle\cdot\rangle_{\widetilde{P}(\boldsymbol{x},\boldsymbol{y})}$ in Eq.(10) $\sim$ (12) denote the expectation w.r.t. model distribution $P^{\tau+1}(\boldsymbol{x},\boldsymbol{y})$ and empirical distribution $\widetilde{P}(\boldsymbol{x},\boldsymbol{y}) = \frac{1}{m}\sum_{i=1}^{m}\delta(\boldsymbol{x}-\boldsymbol{x}_i)\cdot\delta(\boldsymbol{y}-\boldsymbol{y}_i)$ on the training samples $\{\boldsymbol{x}_i,\boldsymbol{y}_i\}_{i=1}^{n}$, respectively. y_i, y_j and x_l in these $\langle\cdot\rangle$ represent the ith and jth elements in label vectors $\boldsymbol{y}$ and lth element in feature vectors $\boldsymbol{x}$, respectively. It is worth noting that the joint model distribution $P^{\tau+1}(\boldsymbol{x},\boldsymbol{y}) = P^{\tau+1}(\boldsymbol{y}|\boldsymbol{x})\widetilde{P}(\boldsymbol{x})$, i.e., we only care about the conditional distribution $P^{\tau+1}(\boldsymbol{y}|\boldsymbol{x})$ and thus use the sample frequency $\widetilde{P}(\boldsymbol{x})$ on the training samples to approximate the true sample distribution $P^{\tau+1}(\boldsymbol{x})$. Constraints (10) $\sim$ (12) restrict the new model to comply with the statistics on the new samples. It is similar to the conventional offline model used in the previous work [28, 44]. $\eta_i \sim N(0,\sigma_\eta^2)$, $\theta_{ij} \sim N(0,\sigma_\theta^2)$ and $\phi_{il} \sim N(0,\sigma_\phi^2)$ are the estimation errors following the Gaussian distribution which serve to smooth $P^{\tau+1}(\boldsymbol{y}|\boldsymbol{x})$ to improve the model's generalization ability. These estimation error distributions can be due to the noise in the training samples. Note that we do not assume any specific probabilistic form of $P^{\tau+1}(\boldsymbol{y}|\boldsymbol{x})$ and $P^{\tau}(\boldsymbol{y}|\boldsymbol{x})$. Therefore, the objective function is minimized by exploring all possible input functions instead of some parameterized functions like in the conventional optimization problem. This type of optimization objective is called variational optimization (see more detail about variational optimization in [2]). With no assumption of any specific probabilistic form, the variational optimization problem can search in a much larger functional space to find a more optimal one.

The above objective function (14) has a rather intuitive explanation. From the perspective of the information theory [7], the KLD measures the distance between two different distributions. Thus by minimizing the KLD between $P^{\tau+1}(\boldsymbol{y}|\boldsymbol{x})$ and

$P^{\tau}(\boldsymbol{y}|\boldsymbol{x})$, the new model $P^{\tau+1}(\boldsymbol{y}|\boldsymbol{x})$ can preserve the old knowledge in the existing model $P^{\tau}(\boldsymbol{y}|\boldsymbol{x})$ as much as possible. This is consistent with the first requirement above. On the other hand, in the multi-label constraints (10) (11) (12), we force the new model $P^{\tau+1}(\boldsymbol{y}|\boldsymbol{x})$ to comply with three statistics on the new samples $\{\boldsymbol{x}_i, \boldsymbol{y}_i\}_{i=1}^{n}$. It satisfies the second requirement that the new model must comply with the information contained in the new samples. It is worth noting that by modeling the label correlations in Eq.(11), the obtained model reveals the underlying correlations between different labels. Finally, the constraint (13) just serves to normalize $P^{\tau+1}(\boldsymbol{y}|\boldsymbol{x})$. Fig.?? illustrates the geometry explanation of this online learner. Here $\mathcal{D}$ denotes a space in which each point is a potential conditional distributions $P(\boldsymbol{y}|\boldsymbol{x})$ for the new model. This space is equipped with KLD as its distance metric. All the distributions satisfying the multi-label constraints constitute a sub-manifold $\mathcal{H}$ embedded in $\mathcal{D}$. Therefore, the above optimization problem equals to find an optimal new model $P^{\tau+1}(\boldsymbol{y}|\boldsymbol{x})$ in $\mathcal{H}$ with the minimum distance from the old model $P^{\tau}(\boldsymbol{y}|\boldsymbol{x})$. Equivalently, from the Geometrical prospective, the optimal solution $P^{\tau+1}(\boldsymbol{y}|\boldsymbol{x})$ to this problem is a projection of the old model $P^{\tau}(\boldsymbol{y}|\boldsymbol{x})$ to the sub-manifold $\mathcal{H}$.

Actually, when learning the new model we should balance between the existing knowledge and the new information. The Gaussian error estimations in (10) (11) (12) serve to provide such a trading-off scheme. When the variances of Gaussian errors η_i, θ_{ij} and ϕ_{il} are larger, the new model $P^{\tau+1}(\boldsymbol{y}|\boldsymbol{x})$ will be biased to be the existing model $P^{\tau}(\boldsymbol{y}|\boldsymbol{x})$ since the multi-label constraints become more relaxed with relatively large noises η_i, θ_{ij} and ϕ_{il} in the current training set. In contrast, the small variances will make $P^{\tau+1}(\boldsymbol{y}|\boldsymbol{x})$ bias on the new information in $\{\boldsymbol{x}_i, \boldsymbol{y}_i\}_{i=1}^{n}$. Extremely, the removal of these error estimations will lead to a new model that completely comply with the new information. Furthermore, as to been derived later, these Gaussian errors will introduce a regularizer term in the dual form of this formulation. As suggested in [6, 44], they assume the joint probability of estimation errors should be reasonably large, e.g., $P(\eta_i, \theta_{ij}, \phi_{il}|1 \leq i < j \leq m, 1 \leq l \leq d) \geq \varepsilon$. Substitute $\eta_i \sim N(0, \sigma_\eta^2) = \frac{1}{\sqrt{2\pi}\sigma_\eta}\exp\{-\frac{\eta_i^2}{2\sigma_\eta^2}\}$, $\theta_{ij} \sim N(0, \sigma_\theta^2) = \frac{1}{\sqrt{2\pi}\sigma_\theta}\exp\{-\frac{\theta_{ij}^2}{2\sigma_\theta^2}\}$ and $\phi_{il} \sim N(0, \sigma_\phi^2) = \frac{1}{\sqrt{2\pi}\sigma_\phi}\exp\{-\frac{\phi_{il}^2}{2\sigma_\phi^2}\}$ into this inequality and assume these estimate errors are independent to each other, we have

$$\sum_i \frac{\eta_i^2}{2\sigma_\eta^2/n} + \sum_{i<j} \frac{\theta_{ij}^2}{2\sigma_\theta^2/n} + \sum_{i,l} \frac{\phi_{il}^2}{2\sigma_\phi^2\Big/n} \leq C \tag{14}$$

Before moving further, we briefly discuss how the above online formulation tackles "concept drift" over time. There already exist literatures working on this "concept drift" problem [18, 40]. From statistical perspective, "concept drift" can be modeled as the change of empirical distribution of the samples and the labels (i.e., the joint distribution of the samples and the labels) over time [18]. As indicated by Eq.(10) $\sim$ (12), the proposed online model adapts to the new empirical distribution

$\widetilde{P}(\boldsymbol{x}, \boldsymbol{y})$ by complying with the first and second order statistics of $\widetilde{P}(\boldsymbol{x}, \boldsymbol{y})$. Through such a model adaptation, "concept drift" can be automatically captured by this online adaptation model.

Combining the formulations (14) $\sim$ (13) and (14), according to Karush-Kuhn-Tucker (KKT) conditions $P^{\tau+1}(\boldsymbol{y}|\boldsymbol{x})$ can be solved by maximizing the dual Lagrange function

$$\begin{aligned}
&\mathcal{L}\left(P^{\tau+1}(\boldsymbol{y}|\boldsymbol{x}), \eta, \theta, \phi, \boldsymbol{b}, \boldsymbol{R}, \boldsymbol{W}, \gamma, \varsigma\right) \\
&= \left\langle D_{KL}\left(P^{\tau+1}(\boldsymbol{y}|\boldsymbol{x}) || P^{\tau}(\boldsymbol{y}|\boldsymbol{x})\right)\right\rangle_{\widetilde{P}(\boldsymbol{x})} \\
&+ \sum_i b_i \left(\langle y_i\rangle_{\widetilde{P}(\boldsymbol{x},\boldsymbol{y})} + \eta_i - \langle y_i\rangle_{P^{\tau+1}(\boldsymbol{x},\boldsymbol{y})}\right) \\
&+ \sum_{i<j} R_{ij}\left(\langle y_i y_j\rangle_{\widetilde{P}(\boldsymbol{x},\boldsymbol{y})} + \theta_{ij} - \langle y_i y_j\rangle_{P^{\tau+1}(\boldsymbol{x},\boldsymbol{y})}\right) \\
&+ \sum_{i,l} W_{il}\left(\langle y_i x_l\rangle_{\widetilde{P}(\boldsymbol{x},\boldsymbol{y})} + \phi_{il} - \langle y_i x_l\rangle_{P^{\tau+1}(\boldsymbol{x},\boldsymbol{y})}\right) \\
&+ \gamma\left(\sum_i \frac{\eta_i^2}{2\sigma_\eta^2/n} + \sum_{i<j}\frac{\theta_{ij}^2}{2\sigma_\theta^2/n} + \sum_{i,l}\frac{\phi_{ij}^2}{2\sigma_\phi^2/n} - C\right) \\
&+ \sum_x \varsigma(x)\left(1 - \sum_y P^{\tau+1}(\boldsymbol{y}|\boldsymbol{x})\right)
\end{aligned} \tag{15}$$

where $\boldsymbol{b}, \boldsymbol{R}, \boldsymbol{W}, \gamma, \varsigma$ are Lagrangian multipliers, in which $\boldsymbol{b} = [b_1, b_2, \cdots, b_m]^T$ is a $m \times 1$ column vector, $\boldsymbol{R} = [R_{ij}]_{m\times m}$ is a strict upper matrix with $R_{ij} = 0$ for $i \geq j$, and $\boldsymbol{W} = [W_{ij}]_{m\times d}$ is a $m \times d$ matrix. Then following the standard KKT techniques, we obtain

$$P^{\tau+1}(\boldsymbol{y}|\boldsymbol{x}) \propto P^{\tau}(\boldsymbol{y}|\boldsymbol{x}) \exp\left\{\boldsymbol{y}^T(\boldsymbol{b} + \boldsymbol{R}\boldsymbol{y} + \boldsymbol{W}\boldsymbol{x})\right\} \tag{16}$$

Considering the normalization condition (13), we can get

$$P^{\tau+1}(\boldsymbol{y}|\boldsymbol{x}) = \frac{1}{Z^{\tau+1}(\boldsymbol{x})} P^{\tau}(\boldsymbol{y}|\boldsymbol{x}) \exp\left\{\boldsymbol{y}^T(\boldsymbol{b} + \boldsymbol{R}\boldsymbol{y} + \boldsymbol{W}\boldsymbol{x})\right\} \tag{17}$$

$$\eta_i = -\frac{\sigma_\eta^2}{n\gamma} b_i, \theta_{ij} = -\frac{\sigma_\theta^2}{n\gamma} R_{ij}, \phi_{il} = -\frac{\sigma_\phi^2}{n\gamma} W_{il} \tag{18}$$

where

$$Z^{\tau+1}(\boldsymbol{x}) = \sum_{\boldsymbol{y}} P^{\tau}(\boldsymbol{y}|\boldsymbol{x}) \exp\left\{\boldsymbol{y}^T(\boldsymbol{b} + \boldsymbol{R}\boldsymbol{y} + \boldsymbol{W}\boldsymbol{x})\right\} \tag{19}$$

is the partition function.

The Lagrangian Function and the corresponding dual optimization problem can be obtained to solve the parameters $\boldsymbol{b}, \boldsymbol{R}, \boldsymbol{W}$

$$\begin{aligned}
&\boldsymbol{b}^\star, \boldsymbol{R}^\star, \boldsymbol{W}^\star = \arg\max_{\boldsymbol{b},\boldsymbol{R},\boldsymbol{W}} \mathcal{L}(\boldsymbol{b}, \boldsymbol{R}, \boldsymbol{W}) \\
&\arg\max_{\boldsymbol{b},\boldsymbol{R},\boldsymbol{W}} \left\langle \boldsymbol{y}^T(\boldsymbol{b} + \boldsymbol{R}\boldsymbol{y} + \boldsymbol{W}\boldsymbol{x}) - \log Z^{\tau+1}(\boldsymbol{x})\right\rangle_{\widetilde{P}(\boldsymbol{x},\boldsymbol{y})} \\
&-\tfrac{\alpha_b}{2n}||\boldsymbol{b}||_2^2 - \tfrac{\alpha_R}{2n}||\boldsymbol{R}||_F^2 - \tfrac{\alpha_W}{2n}||\boldsymbol{W}||_F^2 \\
&= \arg\max_{\boldsymbol{b},\boldsymbol{R},\boldsymbol{W}} \sum_{i=1}^{n}\left\{\boldsymbol{y}_i^T(\boldsymbol{b} + \boldsymbol{R}\boldsymbol{y}_i + \boldsymbol{W}\boldsymbol{x}_i) - \log Z^{\tau+1}(\boldsymbol{x}_i)\right\} \\
&-\tfrac{\alpha_b}{2n}||\boldsymbol{b}||_2^2 - \tfrac{\alpha_R}{2n}||\boldsymbol{R}||_F^2 - \tfrac{\alpha_W}{2n}||\boldsymbol{W}||_F^2
\end{aligned} \tag{20}$$

with

$$\alpha_{\boldsymbol{b}} = \sigma_\eta^2/\gamma, \alpha_{\boldsymbol{R}} = \sigma_\theta^2/\gamma, \alpha_{\boldsymbol{W}} = \sigma_\phi^2/\gamma. \tag{21}$$

where $||\cdot||_2$ and $||\cdot||_F$ are norm-2 and Frobenius norm respectively. Here, $-\frac{\alpha_{\boldsymbol{b}}}{2n}||\boldsymbol{b}||_2^2 - \frac{\alpha_{\boldsymbol{R}}}{2n}||\boldsymbol{R}||_F^2 - \frac{\alpha_{\boldsymbol{W}}}{2n}||\boldsymbol{W}||_F^2$ serves as regularization term. Note that in this dual optimization problem, the old model $P^\tau(\boldsymbol{y}|\boldsymbol{x})$ affects the objective function through the partition function $Z^{\tau+1}(\boldsymbol{x})$ of Eq.(19). Moreover, according to the last equality in Eq.(20) the summation is only taken over the newly-acquired samples, instead of all the historically-accumulated training set like the offline learner. Thus with a rather smaller number of new samples, the above optimization problem can be solved much more efficiently for the proposed online learner.

Take the derivatives of $\mathcal{L}(\boldsymbol{b}, \boldsymbol{R}, \boldsymbol{W})$ w.r.t. $\boldsymbol{b}, \boldsymbol{R}, \boldsymbol{W}$

$$\begin{aligned} \frac{\partial \mathcal{L}}{\partial b_i} &= \langle y_i \rangle_{\widetilde{P}(\boldsymbol{x},\boldsymbol{y})} - \langle y_i \rangle_{P^{\tau+1}(\boldsymbol{x},\boldsymbol{y})} - \frac{\alpha_{\boldsymbol{b}}}{n} b_i \\ \frac{\partial \mathcal{L}}{\partial R_{ij}} &= \langle y_i y_j \rangle_{\widetilde{P}(\boldsymbol{x},\boldsymbol{y})} - \langle y_i y \rangle_{P^{\tau+1}(\boldsymbol{x},\boldsymbol{y})} - \frac{\alpha_{\boldsymbol{R}}}{n} R_{ij} \\ \frac{\partial \mathcal{L}}{\partial W_{il}} &= \langle y_i x_l \rangle_{\widetilde{P}(\boldsymbol{x},\boldsymbol{y})} - \langle y_i x_l \rangle_{P^{\tau+1}(\boldsymbol{x},\boldsymbol{y})} - \frac{\alpha_{\boldsymbol{W}}}{n} W_{il} \end{aligned} \tag{22}$$

Given the above derivatives, we can use the efficient gradient descent methods (such as L-BFGS [23]) to maximize (20).

Here we would like to have a brief discussion about the optimization problem (20). By setting the larger variances $\sigma_\eta^2, \sigma_\eta^2, \sigma_\phi^2$, it says there exists considerable noise in the new samples $\{\boldsymbol{x}_i, \boldsymbol{y}_i\}_{i=1}^n$ (see Eq.(10), (11), (12)). At this time, according to the regularization term in (20), the smaller parameters $\boldsymbol{b}, \boldsymbol{R}, \boldsymbol{W}$ are preferred. Thus, the new model $P^{\tau+1}(\boldsymbol{y}|\boldsymbol{x})$ will approach to the old one. Conversely, $P^{\tau+1}(\boldsymbol{y}|\boldsymbol{x})$ will more consider the new samples. So by setting different $\sigma_\eta^2, \sigma_\eta^2, \sigma_\phi^2$, we can make balance between old knowledge in $P^{\tau+1}(\boldsymbol{y}|\boldsymbol{x})$ and new information in $\{\boldsymbol{x}_i, \boldsymbol{y}_i\}_{i=1}^n$. Such a balance is useful when the semantic meaning of image concept is changing over time, as well as the number of the new training samples is rather smaller than that of historical training samples.

Note that when deriving $P^{\tau+1}(\boldsymbol{y}|\boldsymbol{x})$ in Eq.(17), we do not assume any specific probabilistic form of the old model $P^\tau(\boldsymbol{y}|\boldsymbol{x})$. Thus any statistical model can be used as $P^\tau(\boldsymbol{y}|\boldsymbol{x})$, such as logistic regression model and Gaussian process model. However without loss of generality, we can assume $P^\tau(\boldsymbol{y}|\boldsymbol{x})$ has the following form

$$P^\tau(\boldsymbol{y}|\boldsymbol{x}) = \frac{1}{Z^\tau(\boldsymbol{x})} \exp\left\{\boldsymbol{y}^T(\boldsymbol{b}^\tau + \boldsymbol{R}^\tau \boldsymbol{y} + \boldsymbol{W}^\tau \boldsymbol{x})\right\} \tag{23}$$

where $Z^\tau(\boldsymbol{x}) = \sum_{\boldsymbol{y}} \exp\left\{\boldsymbol{y}^T(\boldsymbol{b}^\tau + \boldsymbol{R}^\tau \boldsymbol{y} + \boldsymbol{W}^\tau \boldsymbol{x})\right\}$ is the partition function. Thus, according to Eq.(17), the new model $P^{\tau+1}(\boldsymbol{y}|\boldsymbol{x})$ is

$$\begin{aligned} &P^{\tau+1}(\boldsymbol{y}|\boldsymbol{x}) \\ &= \tfrac{1}{Z^{\tau+1}(\boldsymbol{x})} \exp\left\{\boldsymbol{y}^T\left((\boldsymbol{b}^\tau + \boldsymbol{b}^\star) + (\boldsymbol{R}^\tau + \boldsymbol{R}^\star)\boldsymbol{y} + (\boldsymbol{W}^\tau + \boldsymbol{W}^\star)\boldsymbol{x}\right)\right\} \end{aligned} \tag{24}$$

Note that when the number of labels become large, the computation of partition function Z^{τ} can be intractable. In this case, efficient algorithms, such as Loopy Belief Propagation and Expectation Propagation, can be applied to compute the partition function. Interested readers could refer to [29] for more implementation details. We can find $P^{\tau+1}(\boldsymbol{y}|\boldsymbol{x})$ has the same probabilistic form like $P^{\tau}(\boldsymbol{y}|\boldsymbol{x})$ except their parameters have been adapted as

$$\boldsymbol{b}^{\tau+1} \leftarrow \boldsymbol{b}^{\tau} + \boldsymbol{b}^{\star} \quad (25)$$

$$\boldsymbol{R}^{\tau+1} \leftarrow \boldsymbol{R}^{\tau} + \boldsymbol{R}^{\star} \quad (26)$$

$$\boldsymbol{W}^{\tau+1} \leftarrow \boldsymbol{W}^{\tau} + \boldsymbol{W}^{\star}$$

Therefore, such an online adaptation can then be iterated in the same manner in each iteration. Here, the initial model P^0 can be started with the parameters $\boldsymbol{b}^0 = 0$, $\boldsymbol{R}^0 = 0$, $\boldsymbol{W}^0 = 0$.

5 Human Computer Interface for Multi-label Online Annotation System

An effective User Interface (UI) is a critical factor to improve the interaction efficiency between human beings and computers when annotating images. Traditionally, the image annotation interface is designed to annotate all the concepts simultaneously for each image before proceeding to the next one (see Fig.(4) for an example of this interface). However we argue such an interface is not the most suitable choice to annotate images with multiple labels, because the annotators must switch their minds between different concepts to annotate these images and it can exhaust annotators' energy more quickly. An alternative choice is to annotate all the images exhaustively with a concept before proceeding to the next one. In this interface, annotators can focus on only one concept at one time so that they can quickly browse a group of images to judge if the concept exists in these images. That is because the vision system of human beings can rapidly respond to visual information of multiple images in a very short time. For example, given the images in an annotation interface illustrated in Fig.(5), annotators can find which images contain the concept "airplane" in a rather short time, instead of having to judge these images one by one. In contrast, in the traditional annotation interface of Fig.(4), annotators cannot focus on one concept to annotate all the images before proceeding to the next concept, and it reduces the annotators' efficiency. Therefore, we organize the image annotation by concept as illustrated in Fig.(5) rather than by image as in Fig.(4). In addition to the consideration of annotation efficiency, organizing annotation by concept can also lead to more accurate and complete annotation than annotating all concepts for each image simultaneously. Past experience has shown that the latter can cause many concepts to be missed (i.e., causing false negative labeling) [38].

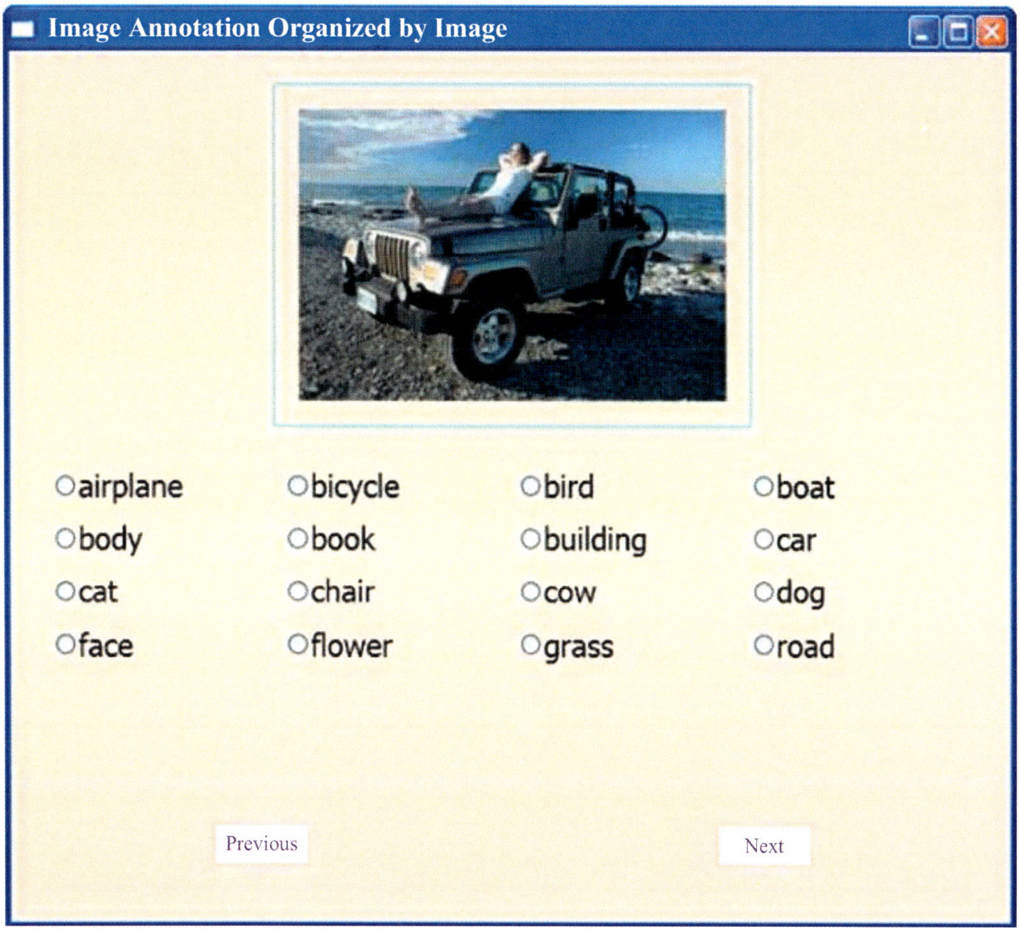

Fig. (4): The user interface that organizes image annotation by image. Users annotate all the concepts simultaneously for each image before proceeding to the next one.

In the user interface that organizes image annotation by concept as Fig.(5), the annotation workload is proportional to the number of sample-label pairs rather than the number of distinct images associated with these pairs, because the time used to annotate a certain concept for an image (i.e., a sample-label pair) can be assumed to be a constant on average. Therefore in this interface, it is reasonable to compare the performances of 2DAL against the other active learning approaches under the same number of selected sample-label pairs as the basic unit to measure the annotation costs.

To verify the assumption that image annotation workload is proportional to the number of label-sample pairs rather than the number of distant images in the annotation interface organized by concept, we conduct a user study on this interface.

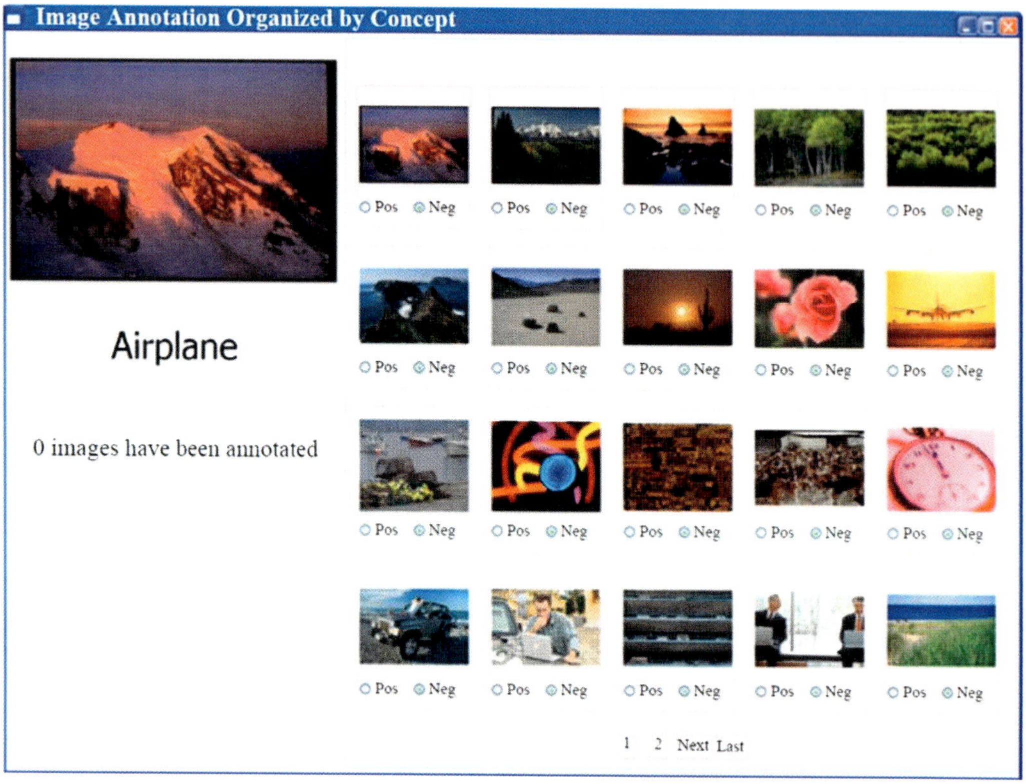

Fig. (5): The user interface that organizes image annotation by concept. Users annotate all the images exhaustively with a concept before proceeding to the next one.

Each of three users annotated 200 sample-label pairs that are associated with *varying* number of images in each step. This step was repeated ten times, yielding 2,000 sample-label pairs per user. First, we compare the annotation efficiency on the interface organizing annotation by image as Fig.(4) and that by concept as Fig.(5). In Tab.(1), we report the time used on these two interfaces by these three users. Obviously organizing annotation by concept is much more efficient than that by image especially considering the annotation is usually very sparse for images, and thus we will adopt the former one to annotate images. Second we verify the image annotation workload is related to the number of label-sample pairs on the interface as Fig.(5). Fig.(6) shows the linear relationship between annotation time and the number of annotated sample-label pairs. We can find the annotation time is proportional to the number of annotated sample-label pairs. It verifies the annotation workload can be measured by the number of sample-label pairs.

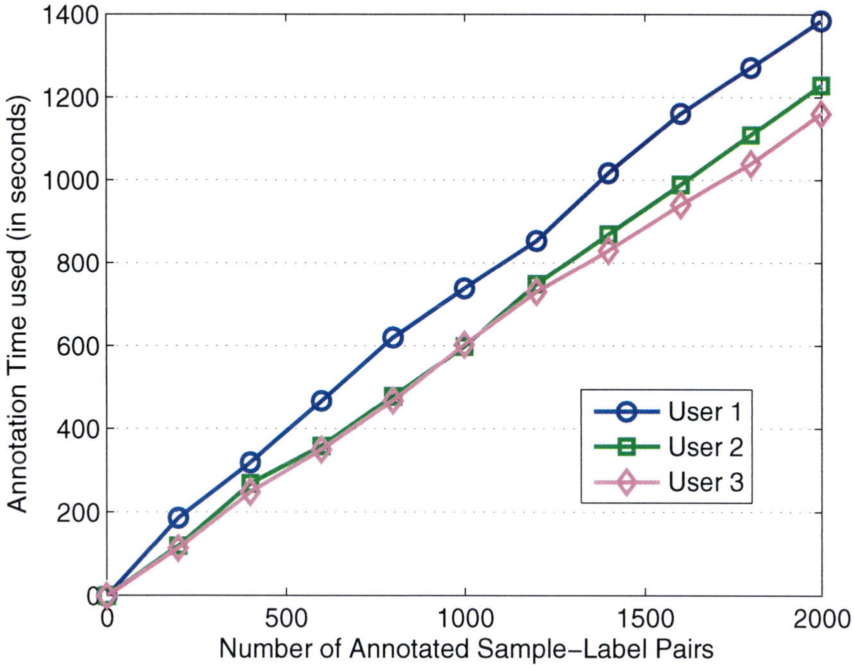

Fig. (6): User study for the user interface for image annotation organized by concept.

Tab. (1): Comparison between the interface organizing annotation by image and that by concept.

User ID	Organizing annotation by image	Organizing annotation by concept
1	3660	1386
2	3138	1230
3	3138	1162

6 Empirical Evaluation

In this section, we compare the different algorithms on two publicly available datasets.

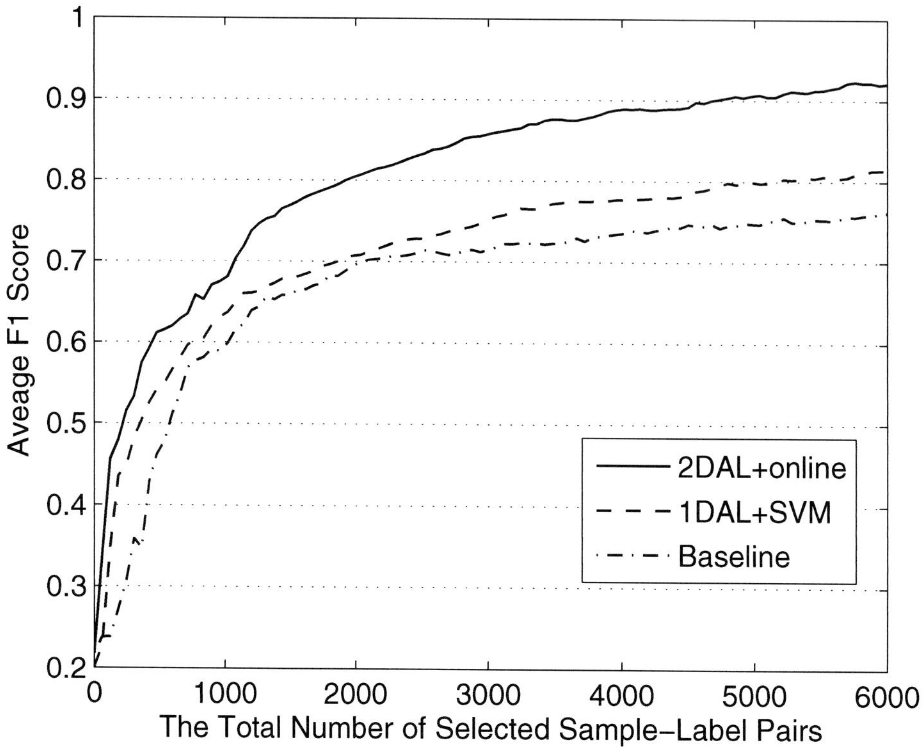

Fig. (7): Performance of three active learning strategies over the *Scene* data set.

Natural scene classification

This natural scene data set is first used in a previous research on the multi-label image scene classification problem [3] (This data set is publicly available at http://www.csie.ntu.edu.tw/~cjlin/libsvmtools/datasets/multilabel .html#scene-classification.). It contains 2,407 natural images belonging to one or more of six natural scene categories including beach, sunset, fall foliage, field, mountain, and urban. Since the data sets are multi-labeled, there are 14,442 sample-label pairs in this set.

An image is first converted into CIE Luv color space and then the first and second color moments (mean and variance) are extracted over a 7×7 grid on the image. The end result is a $49 \times 2 \times 3 = 294$ dimension feature vector [3].

In this experiment, the following three active learning strategies are compared

1 2DAL strategy (2DAL+online): using the proposed sample-label pair selection criterion, associated with the online adaptation statistical model (17) as

Tab. (2): *Scene* data set

Class	Total	Class	Total
Beach	369	Beach+Mountain	38
Sunset	364	Foliage+Mountain	13
Foliage	360	Field+Mountain	75
Field	327	Field+Foliage+Mountain	1
Beach+Field	1	Urban	405
Foliage+Field	23	Beach+Urban	19
Mountain	405		

the underlying classifier.

2 1D active learning strategy (1DAL+SVM): using the mean-max loss active learning strategy that has been proposed in [21] on multi-label active learning. This strategy selects only along the sample dimension. It does not take advantage of the label correlations to reduce human labeling cost. To the best of our knowledge, there exist very limited literatures on the multi-label active learning [4, 21] and 1DAL here is among these methods. All these existing methods are 1D-style active learning which only selects samples rather than sample-label pairs. Thus we compare with the existing 1DAL method to verify the effectiveness of the proposed 2DAL.

3 Baseline: the random strategy - selecting the sample-label pairs at random. For the sake of fair comparison with the proposed 2DAL, we also use the online adaptation learner (17) as the classifier.

We use the average $F1$ score over all different labels for performance evaluation, i.e., $F1 = \frac{2rp}{r+p}$ where p and r are precision and recall respectively. It is the harmonic mean of precision and recall. In statistics, the $F1$ score measures a test's accuracy and has been widely used in information retrieval. For this Scene data set, we use 241 (10%) images as the initial training set. In each iteration, 60 sample-label pairs are selected by the 2DAL. Note that, for 1DAL, it requests annotation on the basis of samples rather than sample-label pairs, so in each iteration, it selects 10 images for annotating all the six labels or equivalently 60 image-label pairs. The average $F1$ score is then computed over all the remaining unlabeled data. In Fig.(7), we show the performance of these three strategies versus the number of the

Tab. (3): $F1$ scores after 100 iterations on six scene categories.

Class	2DAL+online	1DAL+SVM	Baseline
Beach	0.9523	0.8652	0.6744
Sunset	0.9916	0.9421	0.9002
Fall Foliage	0.9887	0.9338	0.8927
Field	0.9588	0.8813	0.8071
Mountain	0.7806	0.6457	0.6122
Urban	0.8534	0.6162	0.6856

selected sample-label pairs. The proposed 2DAL has the best performance in all the iterations. With the number of selected pairs increasing, the improvement becomes more and more significant. Tab.?? compares the $F1$ scores after 100 iterations over all the six scene categories, which illustrates 2DAL outperforms the other strategies on all the labels. In particular, the improvement is obvious on "Urban". Such an improvement is obtained by considering its significant correlations with other labels, such as "Mountain" and "Fall foliage". It confirms 2DAL can obviously improve the classification performance.

Note that in the above comparison, the performances of different active learning approaches are compared under the same number of sample-label pairs. As indicated in the last section, the labor cost for image annotation is linear to the number of sample-label pairs in the user interface. Therefore it is reasonable to prove the superiority of an active learning algorithm if it can improve the classification accuracy with the same number of selected sample-label pairs.

Gene classification

The second benchmark data set is the Yeast data set which consists of micro-array expression data and phylogenetic profiles with 2,417 genes. Each gene in the set belongs to one or more of 14 different functional classes (This data set is publicly available at http://www.csie.ntu.edu.tw/~cjlin/libsvmtools/datasets/multilabel .html#yeast), yielding 33,838 sample-label pairs. Fig.(9) illustrates the distribution of the label numbers for the gene samples on this Yeast data set. The detailed description about this biological data set can be found in [12].

In the experiment, 242 (10%) genes with their labels are used as the initial training set. In each iteration, 140 sample-label pairs are selected. Similar to the above subsection, 1DAL selects 10 samples for annotating all their labels, which is 140 sample-label pairs. Fig.(8) compares the performance of the three strategies.

From the above two experiments, we have observed:

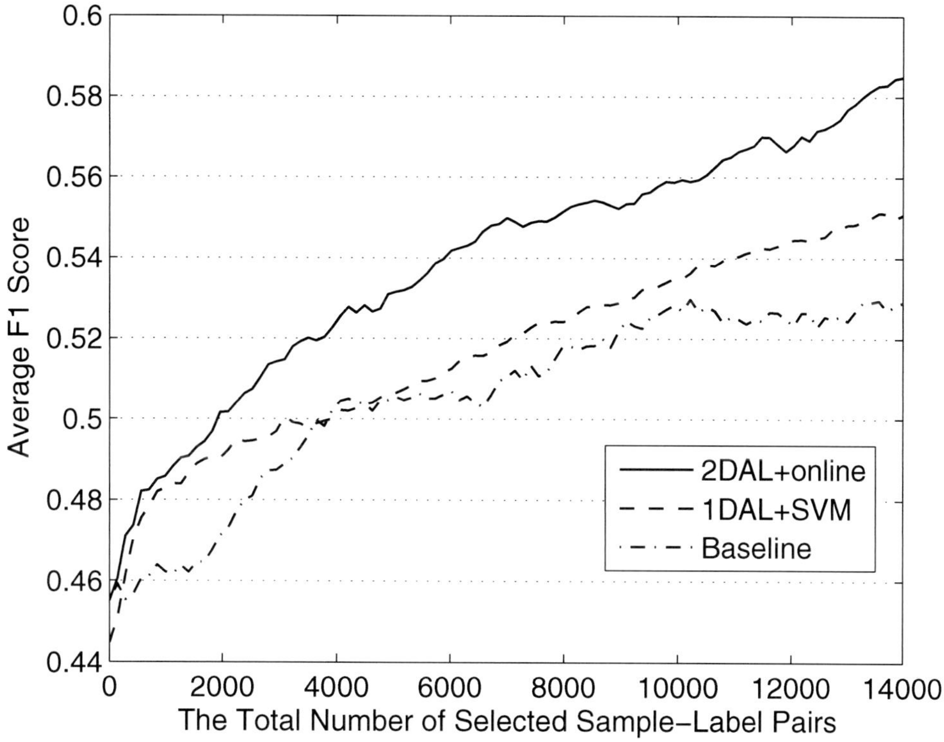

Fig. (8): The performance of three active learning strategies over the *Yeast* data set.

1 Given a fixed number of annotations, 2DAL outperforms 1DAL over all the active learning iterations. This is because the former considers both sample and label uncertainty for selecting sample-label pair, while 1DAL only considers the sample uncertainty. Therefore, the informative label correlations associated with each sample can help to reduce the expensive human labor needed to construct the labeled pool.

2 2DAL gives good performance on diverse data sets, ranging from natural scenes to gene images. This is an important character of a good algorithm to be used in real-world applications.

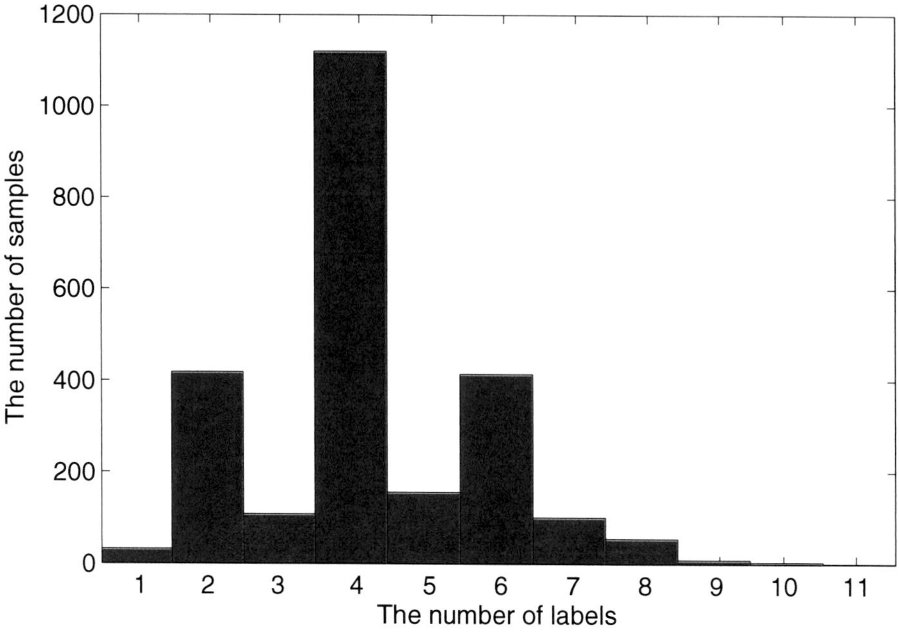

Fig. (9): The distribution of the label numbers for the gene samples on the *Yeast* data set.

7 Conclusion

In this chapter, We review the large-scale online active annotation for Internet multimedia in the two basic techniques - active learning and online computing. By combining these two techniques in a unified framework, scalable multimedia annotation can be achieved in an online manner so that both annotation accuracy and efficiency are able to be significantly improved.

In detail, to enable large-scale semantic concept annotation, a practical multimedia annotation method ought to be scalable on both multimedia sample dimension and concept label dimension, a two-dimensional multi-label active learning algorithm asks for human annotation along both sample and label dimensions. In contrast to the typical one-dimensional active learning algorithm that asks to annotate all the labels of the selected image samples, this 2DAL strategy only requires to annotate a part of label set given the selected samples and the remaining part can be inferred according to the learned label correlations. This strategy can effectively reduce the unnecessary annotation labor to construct the training set for a classifier. Specifically, a multi-label Bayesian error bound is derived and the new sample-label pairs are selected to minimize it.

Furthermore, to make the learning process more efficient, an online adaptation model is proposed which update the existing model with only the newly-acquired samples. Most of the existing learning algorithm has to be retrained with all historically-acquired training samples. This learning scheme becomes impractical when more and more training samples are accumulated into the training set over time during the active learning iterations. Instead, the online learner can efficiently update the existing model without retraining it. In detail, the new model is obtained by minimizing its Kullback-Leibler distance from the existing one under a set of multi-label constraints.

8 References

[1] S. Amari. Information geometry of the em and em algorithms for neural network. Technical Report METR 94-4, University of Tokyo, 1994.

[2] C.M. Bishop. *Pattern recognition and machine learning*, chapter Approximate Inference, pages 461–473. Springer, 2006.

[3] M. R. Boutell, J. Luo, X. Shen, and C. M. Brown. Learning multi-label scene classification. *Pattern Recognition*, 2004.

[4] K. Brinker. On active learning in multi-label classification. *"From Data and Information Analysis to Knowledge Engineering" of Book Series "Studies in Classification, Data Analysis, and Knowledge Organization"*. Springer, 2006.

[5] E. Y. Chang, S. Tong, K. Goh, and C. Chang. Support vector machine concept-dependent active learning for image retrieval. *IEEE Transactions on Multimedia*, 2005.

[6] S. F. Chen and R. Rosenfeld. A gaussian prior for smooting maximum entropy models. Technical Report CMU-CS-99-108, School of Computer Science, Carnegie Mellon University, 1999.

[7] T. Cover and J. Thomas. *Elements of information theory, second edition.* Wiley Series in Telecommunications, John Wiley and Sons, New York, 2006.

[8] N. Cristianini and J. Shawe-Taylor. *An introduction to support vector machines and other kernel-based learning methods.* Cambridge University, 2000.

[9] J. V. Davis, B. Kulis, P. Jain, S. Sra, and I. S. Dhillon. Information-theoretic metric learning. In *ICML*, 2007.

[10] A. P. Dempster, N. M. Laird, and D. B. Rubin. Maximum-likelihood from incomplete data via em algorithm. *Journal of the Royal Statistical Society (Series B)*, 1977.

[11] A. Dong and B. Bhanu. Active concept learning for image retrieval in dynamic databases. In *ICCV*, 2003.

[12] A. Elisseeff and J. Weston. A kernel method for multi-labelled classification. In *NIPS*, 2002.

[13] L. Fei-Fei, R. Fergus, and P. Perona. One-shot learning of object categories. *IEEE Transactions on Pattern Analysis and Machine Intelligence*, 2006.

[14] A. Hauptmann, M.-Y. Chen, and M. Christel. Confounded expectations: Informedia at TRECVID 2004. In *TREC Video Retrieval Evaluation Online Proceedings*, 2004.

[15] S. C. H. Hoi and M. R. Lyu. A semi-supervised active learning framework for image retrieval. In *CVPR*, 2005.

[16] W. Jiang, S.-F. Chang, and A.C. Loui. Active concept-based concept fusion with partial user labels. In *ICIP*, 2006.

[17] A. Kapoor, K. Grauman, R. Urtasun, and T. Darrel. Active learning with gaussian processes for object categorization. In *ICCV*, 2007.

[18] A. Kapoor and E. Horvitz. On discarding, caching, and recalling samples in active learning. In *UAI*, 2007.

[19] J. Kivinen and M. K. Warmuth. Exponentiated gradient versus gradient descent for linear predictors. Technical Report UCSC-CRL-94-16, Baskin Center for Computer Engineering and Information Sciences, University of California, Santa Cruz, 1994.

[20] A. Krause, A. Singh, and C. Guestrin. Near-optimal sensor placements in gaussian processes: Theory, efficient algorithms and empirical studies. *Journal of Machine Learning Research*, 2008.

[21] X. Li, L. Wang, and E. Sung. Multi-label svm active learning for image classification. In *ICIP*, 2004.

[22] N. Littlestone. *Mistake Bounds and Logarithmic Linear-threshold Learning Algorithms*. Phd thesis, University of California Santa Cruz, 1989.

[23] D. C. Liu and J. Nocedal. On the limited memory BFGS method for large scale optimization. *Mathematical Programming B*, 1989.

[24] D. Marr. *Vision*. W. H. Freeman and Company, 1982.

[25] M. Naphade, I. Kozintsev, and T. Huang. Factor graph framework for semantic video indexing. *IEEE Transactions on Circuits and Systems for Video Technology*, 2002.

[26] K. Nigam, J. Lafferty, and A. McCallum. Using maximum entropy for text classification. In *IJCAI-99 Workshop on Machine Learning for Information Filtering*, 1999.

[27] G.-J. Qi, X.-S. Hua, Y. Rui, J. Tang, T. Mei, and H.-J. Zhang. Correlative multi-label video annotation. In *ACM Multimedia*, 2007.

[28] G.-J. Qi, X.-S. Hua, Y. Rui, J. Tang, and H.-J. Zhang. Two dimensional active learning for image classification. In *CVPR*, 2008.

[29] G.-J. Qi, X.-S. Hua, Y. Rui, J. Tang, and H.-J. Zhang. Two-dimensional multi-label active learning with an efficient online adaptation model for image classification. *IEEE Transactions on Pattern Analysis and Machine Intelligence*, 2009.

[30] G.-J. Qi, Y. Song, X.-S. Hua, L.-R. Dai, and H.-J. Zhang. Video annotation by active learning and cluster tuning. In *International Workshop on Semantic Learning Applications in Multimedia, in association with CVPR*, 2006.

[31] F. Rosenblatt. *Principles of Neurodynamics: Perceptrons and the Theory of Brain Mechanisms.* Spartan Books, 1962.

[32] D.E. Rumelhart, G.E. Hinton, and R.J. Williams. *Parallel Data Processing*, 1986.

[33] Mark Schmidt S. V. N. Vishwanathan, Nicol N. Schraudolph and Kevin Murphy. Accelerated training conditional random fields with stochastic gradient methods. In *ICML*, 2006.

[34] S. Shalev-Shwartz, Y. Singer, and N. Srebro. Pegasos: Primal estimated subgradient solver for svm. In *ICML*, 2007.

[35] X. Shen, M. Boutell, J. Luo, and C. Brown. Multi-label machine learning and its application to semantic scene classification. In *International Symposium on Electronic Imaging*, 2004.

[36] J. R. Smith and M. Naphade. Multimedia semantic indexing using model vectors. In *Proceeding of IEEE International Conferences on Multimedia and Expo*, 2003.

[37] S. Tong and E. Y. Chang. Support vector machine active learning for image retrieval. In *ACM Multimedia*, 2001.

[38] T. Volkmer, J. R. Smith, and A. Natsev. A web-based system for collaborative annotation of large image and video collections. In *ACM Multimedia*, 2005.

[39] M. K. Warmuth and D. Kuzmin. Randomized online pca algorithms with regret bounds that are logarithmic in the dimension. *Journal of Machine Learnign Research*, 2008.

[40] J. Wu, X.-S. Hua, and B. Zhang. Tracking concept drifting with gaussian mixture model. In *International Conference on Visual Communications and Image Processing*, 2005.

[41] Y. Wu, B. L. Tseng, and J. R. Smith. Ontology-based multi-classification learning for video concept detection. In *ICME*, 2004.

[42] R. Yan, J. Yang, and A. Hauptmann. Automatically labeling data using multi-class active learning. In *ICCV*, 2003.

[43] J. Yang, R. Yan, and A. Hauptmann. Cross-domain video concept detection using adaptive svms. In *ACM Multimedia*, 2007.

[44] S. Zhu, X. Ji, W. Xu, and Y. Gong. Multi-labelled classification using maximum entropy method. In *ACM SIGIR*, 2005.

CHAPTER 5

(Un)Tagged Social Image Retrieval

Xirong Li*
Renmin University of China, Tel: +86-(0)10-62514526, Fax: +86-(0)10-62515228, Email: xirong.li@gmail.com

Cees G.M. Snoek
University of Amsterdam, Tel: +31-(0)20-525-7528, Fax: +31-(0)20-525-7490, Email: cgmsnoek@uva.nl

Marcel Worring
University of Amsterdam, Tel: +31-(0)20-525-7521, Fax: +31-(0)20-525-7490, Email: m.worring@uva.nl

Abstract: Social image retrieval is increasingly important for managing and accessing the rapidly growing social-tagged images. In this chapter, we address social image retrieval from two directions which tackle the subjectiveness and the incompleteness of social tagging, respectively. To make subjective social tagging objective, we introduce a simple and effective neighbor voting algorithm to estimate the relevance of a tag with respect to the visual content it is describing. To build a concept index for untagged or incompletely tagged images, we study a new learning scenario where concept detectors are trained with negative examples created by social tagging, rather than by traditional expert labeling. Empirical studies on realistic subsets of Flickr data demonstrate the potential of the proposed algorithms for searching (un)tagged social images.

***Correspondence Author:** Xirong Li, Renmin University of China (work performed while the author was at University of Amsterdam); Email: xirong.li@gmail.com.

Xian-Sheng Hua, Marcel Worring & Tat-Seng Chua (Eds.)

Keywords

Image retrieval, social tagging, machine tagging, tag relevance learning, concept detection, negative examples, neighbor voting, concept index, expert labeling, untagged

1 Introduction

Social images tagging, assigning tags or keywords to images by common users, is creating massive amounts of tagged visual data. Photo sharing websites such as Flickr (`http://www.flickr.com`) and Facebook (`http://www.facebook.com`) host billions of user-generated images, many of which are labeled with tags. Apart from their usage for general purpose search, the increasing amounts of social-tagged images are triggering many innovative research topics as diverse as landmark detection [7, 19], concept similarity measurement [43], tag suggestion [31, 38], and automated image tagging [9, 25, 40]. For all these applications, tag-based image retrieval is a starting point.

Despite the success of social tagging, however, tags contributed by common users are known to be subjective and inaccurate. This is not surprising because of the uncontrolled nature of social tagging and the diversity of knowledge and cultural background of its users. Although the relevance of a tag with respect to an image can be subjective for a specific user, an objective criterion is desirable for general-purpose search and visual content understanding. We consider a tag objective and relevant with respect to an image if the tag accurately describes objective aspects of the visual content. In other words, users with common knowledge relate the tag to the visual content easily and consistently. Objective tags reflect visual concepts such as objects, scenes, and events. In contrast to free text descriptions wherein tag relevance might be reflected by their statistics, individual tags are mostly used once per image in the social tagging paradigm. Tag frequency is thus not a good measure of tag relevance [24], as opposed to the practice in text retrieval [1]. Hence, a fundamental problem in social image retrieval is how to accurately and efficiently learn the relevance of a tag with respect to the visual content the tag is describing.

Besides its subjective nature, social tagging is also incomplete. Namely, only part of the visual content is described by user-contributed tags. To search unlabeled or incompletely labeled images, machine tagging is an important prerequisite. To that end, visual concept detectors which estimate the relevance of concepts or tags with respect to unlabeled visual content are demanded. To train a visual classifier for a given concept, the status quo requires three elements: 1) a set of well-labeled examples, to be specific, positive examples with the concept visible and negative examples with the concept invisible, 2) low-level features such as color and texture to represent the visual content, 3) supervised machine learning techniques mapping visual features to semantic concepts using the labeled examples. Though the

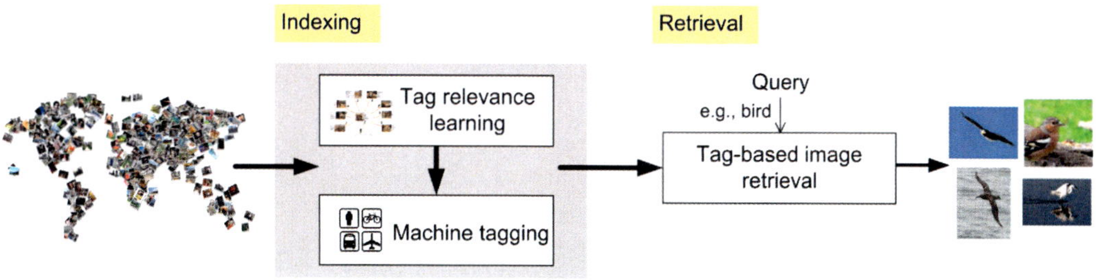

Fig. (1): (Un)Tagged social image retrieval. To search labeled images, we introduce the idea of tag relevance learning to attack the problem of subjective social tagging. To build concept detectors for searching untagged or incompletely tagged images, we present a new learning scenario wherein negative training examples of machine tagging are harvested from social-tagged images.

continuous progress in feature extraction [2, 48], and statistical machine learning [20, 33], keeps improving the accuracy of visual categorization, a large set of diverse examples are required to model the significant intra-concept variance and inter-concept ambiguity in visual appearance. However, the number of training examples is often limited due to the expense of skilled manual labeling conducted by experts. The lack of training examples often results into unreliable classifiers [45]. Given social-tagged images widely accessible for free, an important question in searching untagged social image is whether social tagging can substitute expert labeling for learning visual classifiers.

We show in this chapter how the above two problems of social tagging, namely subjectiveness and incompleteness, can be partially solved by leveraging a large amounts of social-tagged images. First, to address the problem of subjective social tagging, we propose a neighbor voting algorithm which accurately and efficiently learns tag relevance by accumulating votes from visual neighbors. Second, to tackle the problem of incomplete social tagging, we propose to harvest *negative* training examples for social tagging, based on the simple yet important fact that negative examples are the majority for most concepts. In this new learning scenario, since only positive training examples require manual verification, expert annotation is reduced.

This chapter is based on our previous work, mainly [26] for tagged social image retrieval and [23] for untagged social image retrieval. In this chapter, we present a conceptual framework, as illustrated in Fig.(1), in which the previously developed approached are integrated and applied to attack the social image retrieval problem.

2 Literature Review

We structure our literature review in terms of whether the focus is on searching tagged images or searching untagged images.

Searching tagged images

Many methods have appeared in literature to improve tag-based image search, either by re-ranking search results in terms of their visual consistency [13, 16] or by query expansion [6, 27, 47].

Re-ranking methods assume the majority of search results are relevant with respect to the query and relevant examples tend to have similar visual patterns such as color, texture, and shape. To find the dominant visual patterns, density estimation is often used, typically in the form of clustering [13] or a random walk on a graph wherein each node is a result image and each edge is weighted by pairwise visual (dis)similarity [16]. It is known that density estimation is inaccurate when feature dimensionality is high and samples are insufficient for computing the density [36]. Besides, density estimation is computationally expensive. Though caching pre-computed search results is possible for some common queries, it is challenging to cover diverse user queries in general. Query expansion methods augment the original query by automatically adding extra terms [6, 27]. In [6], for instance, the authors use synonyms from a dictionary, whereas in [27] and [47], statistically correlated tags are selected from text snippets returned by web search engines. Adding more query terms may retrieve more relevant results, how to choose appropriate expansion terms requires further research [3]. Notice that the fundamental problem of subjective social tagging is unaddressed in the above methods.

As the first attempt to social tag relevance learning, we proposed a neighbor voting algorithm which infers the relevance of a tag with respect to an image from the image's visual neighbors [24, 26]. In this chapter, we will show how image search accuracy is improved after tag relevance learning. Besides, our tag relevance learning results can be used as a better input for tag processing such as refinement and ranking discussed in Chapter 7 of this book [29].

Searching untagged images

To search untagged images at the semantic level, automatic visual categorization is a base component [8, 12]. It is worth pointing out that an alternative solution to search unlabeled images is content-based image retrieval [39], which aims to find images which are visually, and hopefully semantically, similar to a query image. Since we focus on tag-based image retrieval which copes more easily with semantic queries, we do not discuss the content-based solution. Since expert labeling is labor-intensive and time-consuming, however, only a limited number of visual classifiers can be effectively modeled at present. In a strike towards replacing expert labeling with social tagging, most existing methods [21, 35, 44] focus on automated approaches to collecting positive examples for a given concept. A common strategy among these approaches is to take tag-based image search results as a starting point and refine the results by online learning afterwards. As aforementioned, since social tagging is known to be subjective and inaccurate, the search results might be unsatisfactory. Empirical evidence from earlier studies [4, 18, 37] and Chapter 6 of this book [5] has demonstrated that classifiers directly trained on social-tagged examples are inferior to classifiers trained on well-labeled instances. As an alternative, some try to encourage web users to label examples as volunteers [34, 42]. Still, automatically obtaining positive examples with a sufficient accuracy for learning classifiers is an open research problem.

In contrast to the intensive effort devoted to the positive examples, the importance of negative examples for visual categorization is overlooked. Since negative examples of a concept belong to many other concepts, they often demand more manual labeling. In video retrieval, the authors in [32] create pseudo negative examples by random sampling. Their results suggest that adding the pseudo negatives obtains a better retrieval results versus solely using query images. Similar ideas have been studied for document classification [11, 28], where negative examples are automatically selected by weak classifiers trained on expert-labeled positive examples and unlabeled examples. To the best of our knowledge, however, the problem of leveraging negative examples from social tagging for visual categorization remains largely unexplored and its importance underestimated.

3 Tagged Social Image Retrieval

Intuitively, if different persons label visually similar images using the same tags, these tags are likely to reflect objective aspects of the visual content. This intuition suggests that the relevance of a tag given an image might be inferred from how visual neighbors of that image are tagged: the more frequent the tag occurs in the neighbor set, the more relevant it might be, as illustrated in Fig.(2). However, some frequently occurring tags, such as '2007' and '2008', are unlikely to be relevant to the majority of images. Hence, a good tag relevance measurement should take into account the distribution of a tag in the neighbor set and in the entire collection, simultaneously.

Motivated by the informal analysis above, we propose a neighbor voting algorithm for learning tag relevance, as depicted in Fig.(2). Concretely, given an image labeled with tag w, let the image represented by a specific visual feature $\mathbf{x}$. Given a large collection of N social-tagged images, let N_w be the number of images labeled with w and k_w the number of images labeled with w in x's k-nearest neighbors

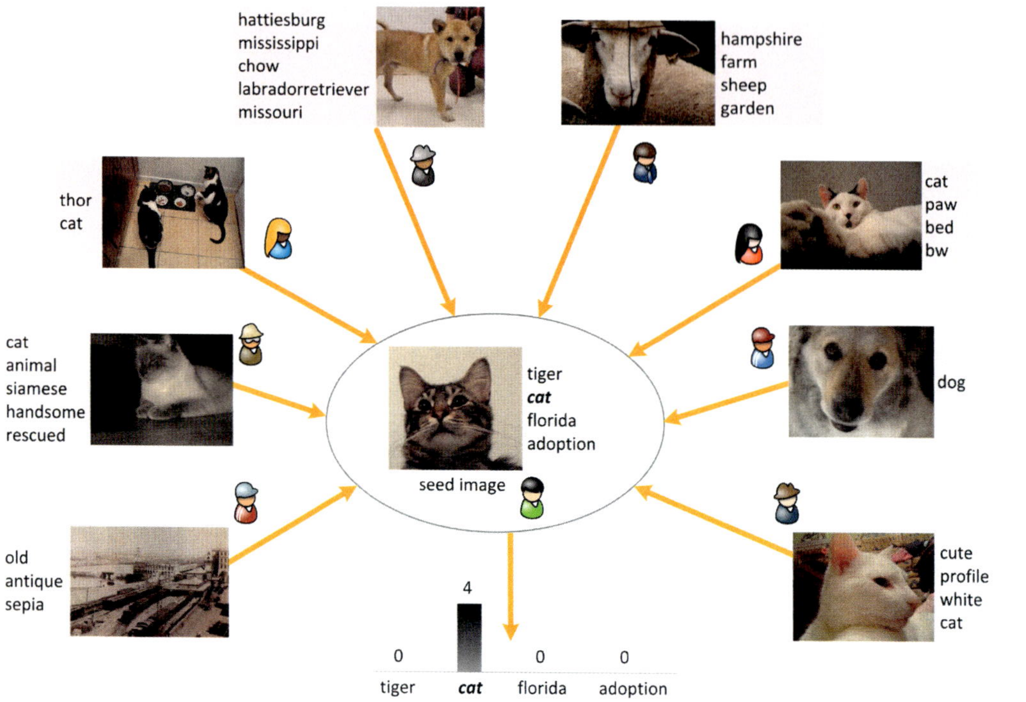

Fig. (2): Learning tag relevance by neighbor voting for searching tagged images. The tag relevance value of each tag is estimated by accumulating the neighbor votes it receives from visually similar images of the seed image. In this example, since four neighbor images are labeled with *cat*, the tag relevance value of *cat* with respect to the seed image is 4. Hence, we update the tag frequency of *cat* from 1 to 4.

computed using the visual feature. The tag relevance is computed as

$$tagRelevance(x, w) = max(k_w(x) - Prior(k, w), 1), \tag{1}$$

where $Prior(k, w) = k \cdot \frac{N_w}{N}$.

The tag relevance function in Eq.(1) consists of two components which representing the distribution of the tag in the local neighborhood and in the entire collection. If the learned tag relevance value is less than 1, the max function is applied to reject the learning result. We show that when 1) the probability of correct user tagging is larger than the probability of incorrect user tagging and 2) content-based visual search is better than random sampling, our algorithm produces a good tag relevance measurement for image ranking. A detailed proof can be found in [26]. The advantages of the proposed algorithm are as follows. First, by updating original tag frequency with the learned tag relevance value, we seamlessly embed visual information into the standard tag-based retrieval paradigm which is known to be scalable. Second, in contrast to previous image ranking approaches which are

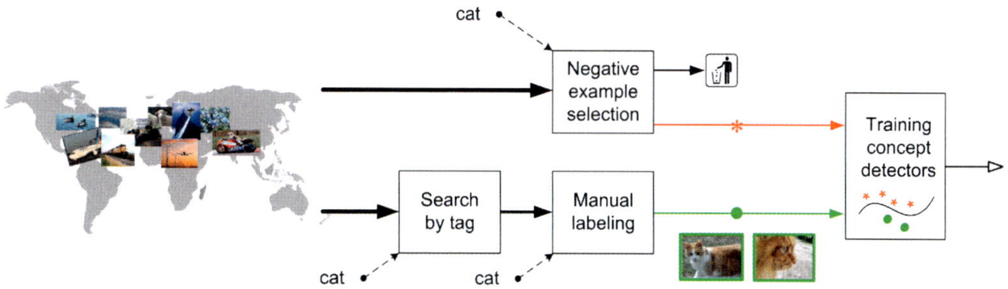

Fig. (3): Learning visual concept detectors using social-tagged negative examples for searching untagged images. Given a set of expert-labeled positive examples, we harvest negative examples from a large amount of social-tagged images. Since only positive examples require manual verification, expert annotation is reduced.

query-dependent, our algorithm is query-independent. This property allows us to run the algorithm offline without imposing extra waiting time on users. Moreover, since the algorithm does not require any model training for any visual concept, it is efficient in handling large-scale image data sets. Finally, the algorithm is easy to implement.

4 Untagged Social Image Retrieval

Visual concept detectors are base components for users to search unlabeled image collections by semantic concept. In this section, we describe an approach to learning visual concept detectors where negative examples are automatically obtained by social tagging without manual verification [23].

As illustrated in Fig.(3), we harvest negative examples from numerous social-tagged images. Since only positive examples require manual verification, expert annotation is thus significantly reduced. We term this new learning scenario as *visual categorization with negative examples for free*, or negative-for-free. A natural question is how to obtain accurate negative examples. For unlabeled data, the problem is difficult to solve. Notice however that social-tagged images are associated with several user-uploaded tags. Though the tags tend to be subjective and inaccurate, they might be important clues to indicate the presence of a concept in the visual content. We introduce a simple anti-tag filtering strategy to address the problem. Given a concept, say aeroplane, multiple words may refer to the same concept, e.g., plane and airplane for aeroplane. For example, we observe that the two tags, boeing and airbus, are likely to indicate images of an aeroplane also. Bearing these in mind, we introduce a selection strategy called random sampling after anti-tag filtering. That is, we first identify a set of possible synonyms of the concept by computing tag co-occurrence within a large social-tagged image collec-

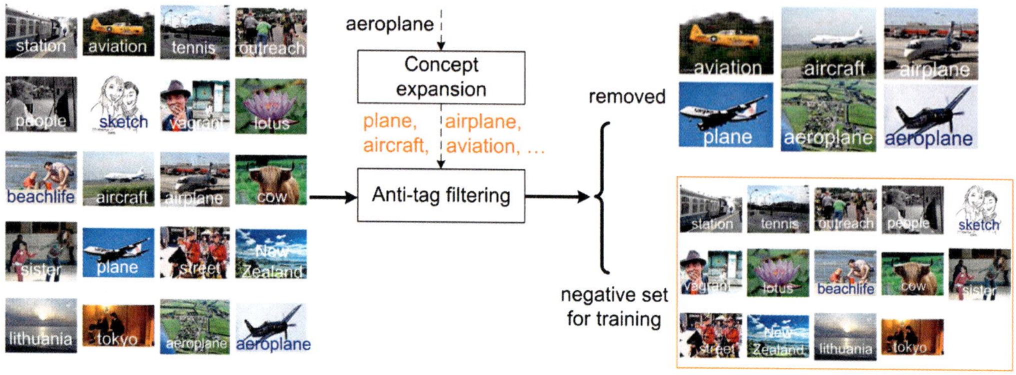

Fig. (4): Selecting negative examples by anti-tag filtering. Given a concept, e.g., aeroplane in this figure, we find a set of tags semantically and visually related to the concept, say by computing tag co-occurrence. After removing images labeled with these tags, we obtain negative examples which are more accurate than examples randomly sampled from the social-tagged image collection.

tion. By removing images labeled with the concept and its most correlated tags, we obtain negative examples which are more accurate than examples created by random sampling. The anti-tag filtering idea is illustrated in Fig.(4).

It is worth pointing out that, although getting positive examples in an automated manner is still challenging, candidate images obtained by the query-by-tag paradigm already provides a better starting point than using an unlabeled collection for labeling positive training examples. One main, perhaps obvious, reason is that the chance of finding positive examples in images tagged with the concept is much larger than in an unlabeled collection. Hence, combining the proposed negative-for-free scenario and positive labeling enhanced by query-by-tag, as shown in Fig.(3), might be a promising solution for scalable concept detection.

5 Experimental Setup

Experiments

Experiment 1. Searching tagged images

We have proposed a neighbor voting algorithm to learn tag relevance. To study whether tag relevance learning improves image retrieval, we design tag-based image retrieval experiments as follows. We adopt Okapi BM25 [17], a well founded ranking function in text retrieval, to compute the relevance score of an image with respect to a text query. We take image ranking using original tags as a baseline. For each image, we perform the neighbor voting algorithm. Then, for each tag of the image, we update its tag frequency using the learned tag relevance value.

Experiment 2. Searching untagged images

We build visual concept detectors to search unlabeled images. For visual concept detection with negative examples for free, there are two research questions to answer. Namely, 1) is the anti-tag filtering better than random sampling for creating negative examples, and 2) is the negative-for-free scenario competitive with the classical scenario wherein both positive and negative examples are manually labeled? To answer the two questions, we design the following two experiments.

Experiment 2.1: Anti-tag filtering versus random sampling. We compare two strategies for negative example selection. One is the proposed anti-tag filtering. The other is fully random sampling. In anti-tag filtering, for each concept we filter out images labeled with the concept and top 50 tags with the highest co-occurrence with the concept. Since the candidate set is still very large, we further perform down sampling to make the classifier learning feasible. For both strategies, we choose 1000 and 5000 negative examples for training, respectively.

Experiment 2.2: Social-tagged negative examples versus expert-labeled negative examples. Given a set of expert-labeled positive examples available, we compare concept detectors trained using social-tagged negative examples and those trained using expert-labeled negative examples. We follow the same procedure as in Experiment 1 for negative example selection and use 5000 negative examples for the negative-for-free scenario.

Datasets

Experiment 1. Searching tagged images

To create a large set of neighbor voting, we randomly downloaded 3.5 million labeled images from the Flickr webiste using its public API. We use a ground truth dataset from [26] (The groundtruth set and the 3.5 million image set are available at `http://staff.science.uva.nl/~xirong/tagrel/`). The dataset has 20 queries covering diverse visual concepts such as bridge, classroom, kitchen, and street. Each concept has 1000 Flickr images labeled with the concept by common users. For the baseline system and the new system using tag relevance value as tag frequency, we use leave-one-out strategy on the 20 queries to optimize the OKAPI-BM25 parameters.

Experiment 2. Searching untagged images

We adopt the PASCAL VOC 2008 development set as our benchmark data, which is collected from Flickr with expert verification [10]. The set consists of two predefined subsets, one for training and the other for validation with 2111 and 2221 images, respectively. To resemble the VOC set, we collected 6.5 million Flickr images using the 20 VOC concepts as queries. We refer to [23] for the data statistics.

Implementation

Experiment 1. Searching tagged images

To implement the neighbor voting algorithm, we need to define visual similarity between images and then search visual neighbors in our 3.5 million Flickr photo database. Visual similarity between two images is measured using corresponding visual features. We adopt a 64-dimensional global feature, as a tradeoff between effectiveness and efficiency, combing the 44-d color correlogram [14], the 14-d texture moments [46], and the 6-d RGB color moments.

To search millions of images by content, efficient indexing methods are imperative for speed. We adopt a K-means clustering based method for its empirical success in large-scale content-based image retrieval, e.g., [15, 22]. First for indexing, we divide the whole dataset into smaller subsets by the K-means clustering. Each subset is indexed by a cluster center. Then for a query image, we find neighbors within those subsets whose centers are closest to the query. The search space is thus reduced. Since the search operation in individual subsets can be executed in parallel, we execute neighbor search on a distributed super computer.

Experiment 2. Searching untagged images

Since representing images by bag-of-words is well recognized as the state-of-the-art feature for visual categorization [10], we follow this convention. In particular, we adopt dense sampling for point detection and SIFT [18] for point description, using a recently developed fast implementation of the dense-SIFT [41]. We create a codebook of 4000 bins by running K-means clustering on the VOC dataset. By mapping the SIFT features to the bins, each image is represented by a 4000-d bag-of-words feature.

We follow the definition of the VOC categorization task. For each concept we predict the presence of that concept in a test image with a real-valued confidence. All test images are then ranked according to their confidences in descending order. Here we choose the Support Vector Machine (SVM) as a supervised learner with the χ^2 kernel, which has proven to be a solid choice. For both experiments, we train SVM models by three-fold cross validation.

Evaluation criteria

For all experiments, we use average precision (AP) as our evaluation criterion. Given a ranked list of l test instances, AP is defined as $(1/R)\sum_i^l (R_i/i)\delta_i$, where R

is the number of positive examples in the list, R_i the number of positive instances in the top i ranked instances, and indicator function $\delta_i = 1$ if the i-th instance is positive and 0 otherwise.

Random guess baseline. Since frequent concepts tend to have higher average precision scores than rare concepts like cow, we also report a random baseline for the ease of analysis, which is calculated as follows. For each concept, we randomly rank the validation set and calculate average precision. We run the process 100 times and take as the random baseline an averaged score over the 100 runs.

6 Results

Experiment 1. Searching tagged images

As shown in Fig.(5), for all queries, we improve upon the baseline method by using learned tag relevance value as updated tag frequency. On average, we obtain a relative improvement of 24.3% in terms of average precision. Due to the social tagging paradigm, directly using original tags for retrieval does not yield good results. For some concepts such as horse and street, the baseline method is even worse than random guess. In contrast, relevant tags are identified and reinformed after tag relevance learning, resulting a significant improvement in the retrieval performance. The results clearly show the effectiveness of the proposed neighbor voting algorithm for tag relevance learning for social image retrieval.

The proposed algorithm is also robust to changes in the number of neighbors used for voting. To show this property, we first run leave-one-out cross validation on the 20 queries to determine the optimized OKAPI-BM25 parameter b for *tag baseline* and our method, which is 0.8 and 0.3, respectively. As shown in Fig.(6), *tagRelevance* consistently outperforms *tag baseline*. More precisely, we reach at least 20% relative improvement in terms of MAP when the number of neighbors is between 200 and 20,000.

Experiment 2. Searching untagged images

Experiment 2.1: Anti-tag filtering versus random sampling for negative example selection. As shown in Fig. (7), with anti-tag filtering, we achieve better categorization performance. We observe that as more negative examples are selected, from 1000 to 5000, the performance of the random sampling result degenerates from 0.296 to 0.270 in terms of MAP. By contrast, the performance of random sampling after anti-tag filtering improves by 4.5%, from 0.308 to 0.322 in terms of MAP. This result demonstrates that with the anti-tag filtering algorithm, we create a better candidate set for negative example selection.

Experiment 2.2: Social-tagged negatives versus Expert-labeled negatives. As shown in Fig. (8), social tagging fully substitutes expert labeling for

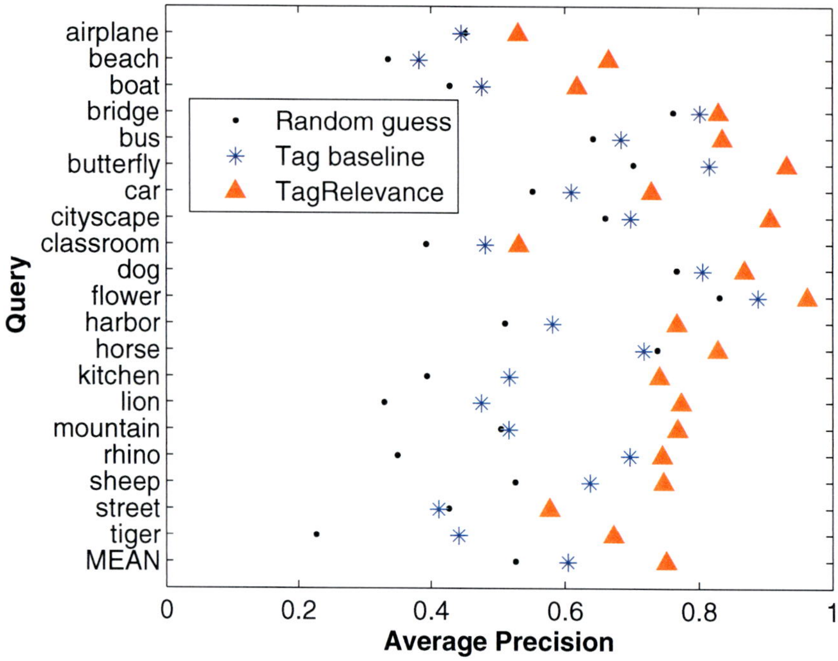

Fig. (5): Experiment 1. Searching tagged images. Per-query comparison between image retrieval with and without tag relevance learning. We apply tag relevance learning for tag-based image retrieval by updating the original tag frequency with the learned tag relevance values. For all queries, TagRelevance outperforms the tag baseline, with a relative improvement of 24.3% in terms of mean average precision.

creating negative examples, with a relative loss of only 4.3% in terms of MAP. Recalling that over 90% of the VOC 2008 expert labeling effort is spent on negative examples, we believe the small loss in the classification accuracy is worth the immense annotation effort saved. Note that the expert-labeled negative set is closed in the sense that the number of visual classes is fixed. In contrast, our social-tagged negative set is more diverse as we sample from an open collection. Therefore, on one hand, the performance of social negatives on the closed validation set degrades to some extent for 14 concepts. On the other hand, we expect classifiers trained on a more diverse set to have a better generalization ability. Due to the limit of the validation set, however, this advantage is not obvious in the current experiments. As a future work, it would be interesting to reveal the generalization issue, say by diversifying the validation set.

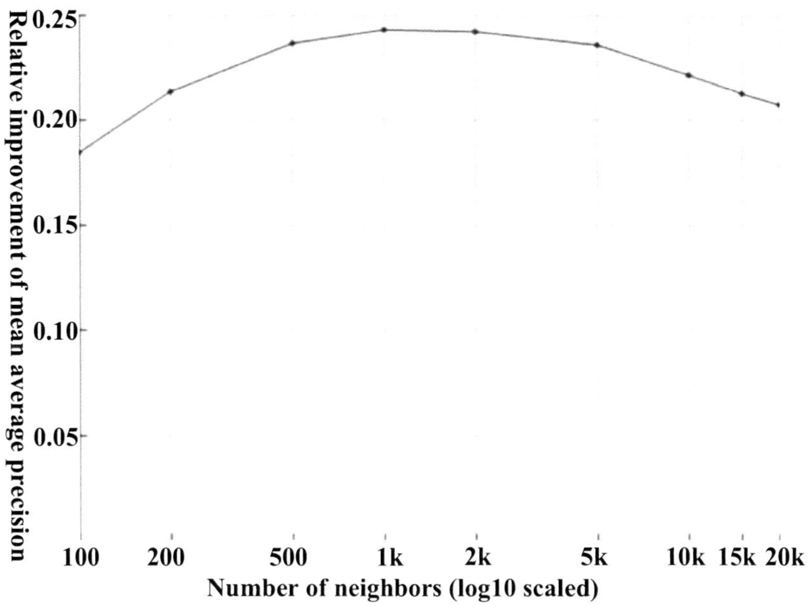

Fig. (6): The impact of the number of the neighbors on image retrieval performance. This figure shows the relative improvement in terms of mean average precision (MAP) over the best *tag baseline* with respect to changes in the number of neighbors for learning tag relevance. We obtain at least 20% relative improvement in terms of MAP when the number of neighbors is between 200 and 20,000. The result shows the robustness of the proposed tag relevance learning algorithm.

7 Conclusions

In this chapter, we approach social image retrieval from two directions which target at the subjectiveness and the incompleteness of social image tagging.

To make subjective social tagging objective, we propose a neighbor voting algorithm. The key idea is to infer the relevance of a tag with respect to an image from tagging behaviors of visual neighbors of that image. The proposed algorithm produces a good tag relevance measure for image retrieval. Moreover, since the algorithm does not any model training for any visual concept, it is efficient in handling large-scale image data. Learning tag relevance from 3.5 million Flickr photos, tag-based image retrieval experiments show that retrieval with tag relevance learning outperforms retrieval without tag relevance learning, with a 24.3% improvement in terms of mean average precision.

To search untagged or incompletely tagged images, building a semantic index by concept detection is a promising direction. We discuss a new scenario to learn visual concept detectors where negative training examples are automatically collected from tremendous social-tagged images. We present an empirical study using 6.5 million

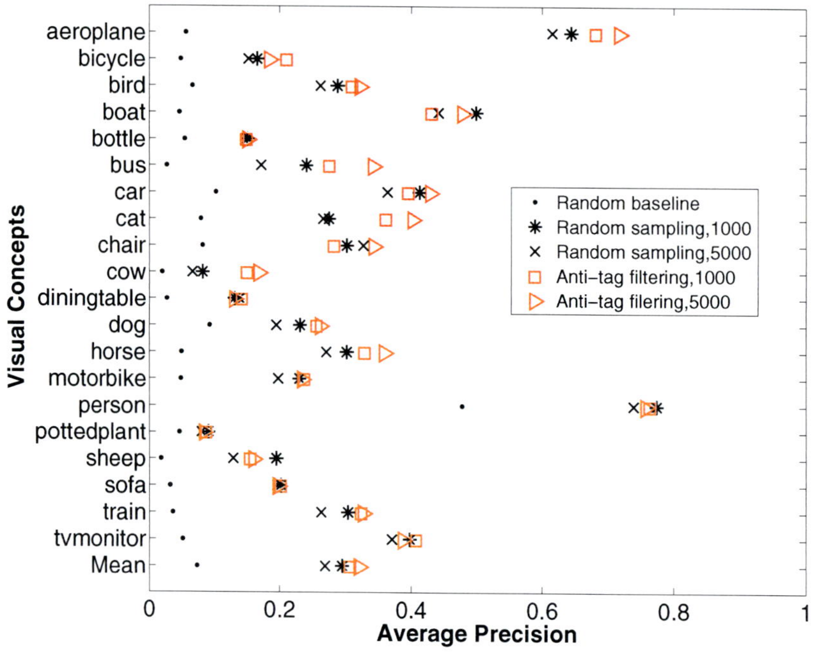

Fig. (7): Experiment 2.1: Comparing the two strategies for negative example selection. For both random sampling and random sampling after anti-tag filtering, we choose 1000 and 5000 negative examples for training, denoted as "Random sampling,1000", "Random sampling,5000", "Anti-tag filtering,1000", and "Anti-tag filtering,5000". With anti-tag filtering, we create a better candidate set for negative example selection.

Flickr photos as a source of social-tagged negative examples. Our experiments on the PASCAL VOC challenge 2008 show that with a relative loss of 4.3% in terms of mean average precision, expert-labeled negative examples can be replaced by social-tagged negative examples for building concept detectors to search untagged images.

For their simplicity and effectiveness, we consider the proposed approaches promising for making massive amounts of user-generated visual data more accessible.

Acknowledgements

This work was supported by the EC-FP6 VIDI-Video project and the STW SEARCHER project. The authors thank Dr. Mark Everingham for providing VOC08 statistics for untagged social image retrieval.

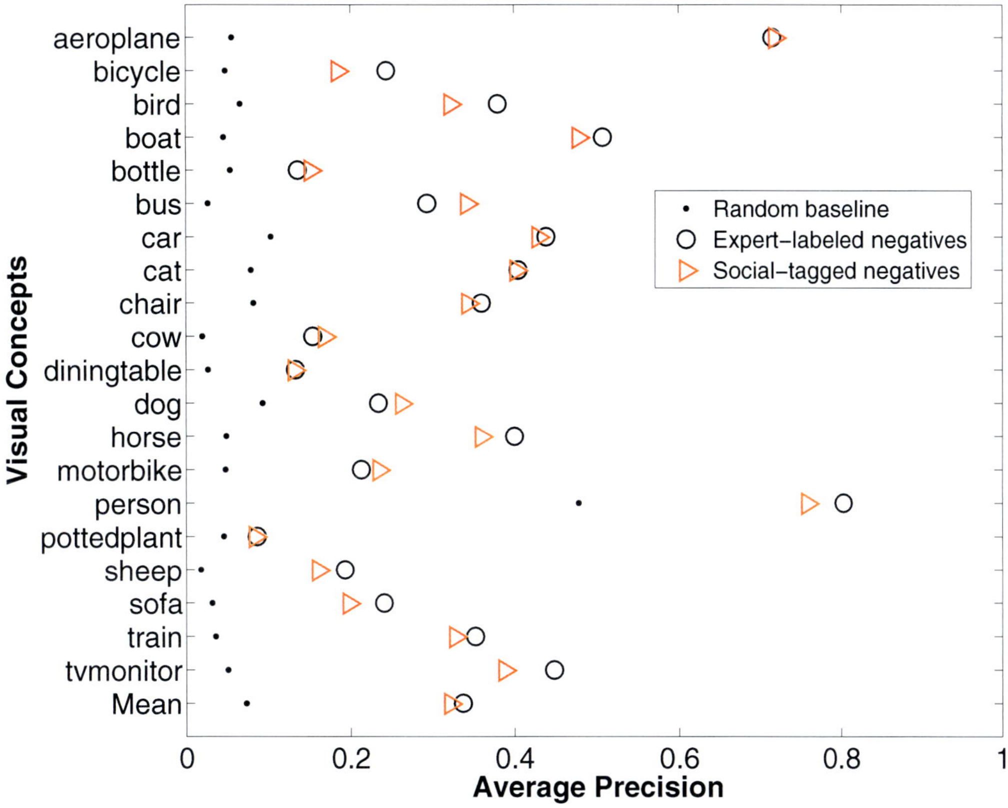

Fig. (8): Experiment 2.2: Social-tagged negatives versus expert-labeled negatives. By fixing the positive examples, we compare two-class learning with expert-labeled negative examples (denoted as "Expert-labeled negatives") and learning with 5000 social-tagged negative examples (denoted as "Social-tagged negatives"). With a relative loss of only 4.3% in terms of mean average precision, social tagging fully substitutes expert labeling for creating negative examples.

8 References

[1] R. Baeza-Yates and B. Ribeiro-Neto. *Modern Information Retrieval*. Addison Wesley, 1999.

[2] H. Bay, A. Ess, T. Tuytelaars, and L. van Gool. Speeded-up robust features (SURF). *CVIU*, 2008.

[3] B. Billerbeck and J. Zobel. Questioning query expansion: an examination of behaviour and parameters. In *Australasian database conference*, 2004.

[4] A. Ulges, C. Schulze, M. Koch, and T. Breuel. Learning automatic concept detectors from online video. *CVIU*, 2010.

[5] D. Borth, A. Ulges, and T. Breuel. *Internet Multimedia Search and Mining*, chapter Adapting Web-based Video Concept Detectors for Different Target Domains. Bentham, 2010.

[6] T.-S. Chua, S.-Y. Neo, K.-Y. Li, G. Wang, R. Shi, M. Zhao, and H. Xu. TRECVID 2004 search and feature extraction task by NUS PRIS. In *Proc. TRECVID Workshop*, 2004.

[7] D. Crandall, L. Backstrom, D. Huttenlocher, and J. Kleinberg. Mapping the world's photos. In *ACM WWW*, 2009.

[8] R. Datta, W. Ge, J. Li, and J. Wang. Toward bridging the annotation-retrieval gap in image search by a generative modeling approach. In *ACM Multimedia*, 2006.

[9] R. Datta, D. Joshi, J. Li, and J. Wang. Tagging over time: real-world image annotation by lightweight meta-learning. In *ACM Mutlimedia*, 2007.

[10] M. Everingham, L. van Gool, C. Williams, J. Winn, and A. Zisserman. The PASCAL Visual Object Classes Challenge 2008 Results. http://www.pascal-network.org/challenges/VOC/voc2008/workshop/index.html.

[11] G. Fung, J. Yu, H. Lu, and P. Yu. Text classification without negative examples revisit. *IEEE Transactions on Knowledge and Data Engineering*, 2006.

[12] A. Hauptmann, R. Yan, W.-H. Lin, M. Christel, and H. Wactlar. Can high-level concepts fill the semantic gap in video retrieval? *IEEE Transactions on Multimedia*, 2007.

[13] W. Hsu, L. Kennedy, and S.-F. Chang. Reranking methods for visual search. *IEEE Multimedia*, 2007.

[14] J. Huang, S. Kumar, M. Mitra, W. Zhu, and R. Zabih. Image indexing using color correlograms. In *CVPR*, 1997.

[15] H. Jégou, M. Douze, and C. Schmid. Hamming embedding and weak geometric consistency for large scale image search. In *ECCV*, 2008.

[16] Y. Jing and S. Baluja. VisualRank: Applying pagerank to large-scale image search. *IEEE Transactions on Pattern Analysis and Machine Intelligence*, 2008.

[17] K. Jones, S. Walker, and S. Robertson. A probabilistic model of information retrieval: development and comparative experiments. *Inf. Process. Manage.*, 2000.

[18] L. Kennedy, S.-F. Chang, and I. Kozintsev. To search or to label?: predicting the performance of search-based automatic image classifiers. In *ACM MIR*, 2006.

[19] L. Kennedy, M. Naaman, S. Ahern, R. Nair, and T. Rattenbury. How flickr helps us make sense of the world: context and content in community-contributed media collections. In *ACM Multimedia*, 2007.

[20] J. Li and J. Wang. Real-time computerized annotation of pictures. *IEEE Transactions on Pattern Analysis and Machine Intelligence*, 2008.

[21] L.-J. Li and L. Fei-Fei. OPTIMOL: Automatic online picture collection via incremental model learning. *International Journal of Computer Vision*, 2010.

[22] X. Li, L. Chen, L. Zhang, F. Lin, and W.-Y. Ma. Image annotation by large-scale content-based image retrieval. In *ACM Multimedia*, 2006.

[23] X. Li and C. Snoek. Visual categorization with negative examples for free. In *ACM Multimedia*, 2009.

[24] X. Li, C. Snoek, and M. Worring. Learning tag relevance by neighbor voting for social image retrieval. In *ACM MIR*, 2008.

[25] X. Li, C. Snoek, and M. Worring. Annotating images by harnessing worldwide user-tagged photos. In *ICASSP*, 2009.

[26] X. Li, C. Snoek, and M. Worring. Learning social tag relevance by neighbor voting. *IEEE Transactions on Multimedia*, 2009.

[27] W.-H. Lin and A. Hauptmann. Web image retrieval re-ranking with relevance model. In *WIC*, 2003.

[28] B. Liu, W. S. Lee, P. S. Yu, and X. Li. Partially supervised classification of text documents. In *ICML*, 2002.

[29] D. Liu, X.-S. Hua, and H.-J. Zhang. *Internet Multimedia Search and Mining*, chapter Tag Processing for Internet Social Images. Bentham, 2010.

[30] D. Lowe. Distinctive image features from scale-invariant keypoints. *International Journal of Computer Vision*, 2004.

[31] E. Moxley, J. Kleban, and B. Manjunath. Spirittagger: a geo-aware tag suggestion tool mined from flickr. In *ACM MIR*, 2008.

[32] A. Natsev, A. Haubold, J. Tešić, L. Xie, and R. Yan. Semantic concept-based query expansion and re-ranking for multimedia retrieval. In *ACM Multimedia*, 2007.

[33] A. Quattoni, M. Collins, and T. Darrell. Transfer learning for image classification with sparse prototype representations. In *CVPR*, 2008.

[34] B. Russell, A. Torralba, K. Murphy, and W. Freeman. Labelme: A database and web-based tool for image annotation. *International Journal of Computer Vision*, 2008.

[35] F. Schroff, A. Criminisi, and A. Zisserman. Harvesting image databases from the web. In *ICCV*, 2007.

[36] D. Scott. *Multivariate Density Estimation: Theory, Practice, and Visualization*. Wiley, 1992.

[37] A. Setz and C. Snoek. Can social tagged images aid concept-based video search? In *ICME*, 2009.

[38] B. Sigurbjörnsson and R. van Zwol. Flickr tag recommendation based on collective knowledge. In *ACM WWW*, 2008.

[39] A. Smeulders, M. Worring, S. Santini, A. Gupta, and R. Jain. Content-based image retrieval at the end of the early years. *IEEE Transactions on Pattern Analysis and Machine Intelligence*, 2000.

[40] J. Tang, S. Yan, R. Hong, G.-J. Qi, and T.-S. Chua. Inferring semantic concepts from community-contributed images and noisy tags. In *ACM Multimedia*, 2009.

[41] J. Uijlings, A. Smeulders, and R. Scha. Real-time bag-of-words, approximately. In *CIVR*, 2009.

[42] L. von Ahn and L. Dabbish. Labeling images with a computer game. In *SIGCHI*, 2004.

[43] L. Wu, X.-S. Hua, N. Yu, W.-Y. Ma, and S. Li. Flickr distance. In *ACM Multimedia*, 2008.

[44] K. Yanai and K. Barnard. Probabilistic web image gathering. In *ACM MIR*, 2005.

[45] J. Yang and A. Hauptmann. (Un)Reliability of video concept detection. In *CIVR*, 2008.

[46] H. Yu, M. Li, H.-J. Zhang, and J. Feng. Color texture moment for content-based image retrieval. In *ICIP*, 2002.

[47] Z.-J. Zha, L. Yang, T. Mei, M. Wang, and Z. Wang. Visual query suggestion. In *ACM Multimedia*, 2009.

[48] J. Zhang, M. Marszalek, S. Lazebnik, and C. Schmid. Local features and kernels for classification of texture and object categories: A comprehensive study. *International Journal of Computer Vision*, 2007.

 Internet Multimedia Search and Mining, 2013, 130-167

CHAPTER 6

Adapting Web-based Video Concept Detectors for Different Target Domains

Damian Borth*
University of Kaiserslautern & German Research Center for Artificial Intelligence (DFKI), Tel: +49 (631) 20575-4184, Email: d_borth@cs.uni-kl.de
Adrian Ulges
German Research Center for Artificial Intelligence, Tel: +49 (631) 20575-4190, Email: adrian.ulges@dfki.de
Thomas M. Breuel
University of Kaiserslautern, Tel: +49 (631) 205-3456, Email: tmb@cs.uni-kl.de

Abstract: In this chapter, we address the visual learning of automatic concept detectors from web video as available from services like YouTube. While allowing a much more efficient, flexible, and scalable concept learning compared to expert labels, web-based detectors perform poorly when applied to different domains (such as specific TV channels). We address this *domain change problem* using a novel approach, which – after an initial training on web content – performs a highly efficient online adaptation on the target domain.

In quantitative experiments on data from YouTube and from the TRECVID campaign, we first validate that domain change appears to be the key problem for web-based concept learning, with a much more significant impact than other phenomena like label noise. Second, the proposed adaptation approach is shown to improve the accuracy of web-based detectors significantly, even over SVMs trained

***Correspondence Author:** Damian Borth, University of Kaiserslautern, Germany; Email: d_borth@cs.uni-kl.de.

Xian-Sheng Hua, Marcel Worring & Tat-Seng Chua (Eds.)

on the target domain. Finally, we extend our approach with active learning such that adaptation can be interleaved with manual annotation for an efficient exploration of novel domains.

Keywords

content-based video retrieval, concept detection, visual learning, web video, domain change, cross-domain, online learning, classifier adaptation, TRECVID, YouTube

1 Introduction

Currently, the media landscape experiences a major shift towards more distributed structures called *social media* or *citizen journalism* as illustrated by the Hudson River airplane crash or the public protest in Iran after the presidential election in 2009. One key element of this is the upload and distribution of images and videos over the Internet minutes after such incidents happened.

Focusing on video, this trend is only one example of the increasing presence of digital video in our everyday's life. Nowadays, we are used to generate large amounts of video material and to publish it online via video portals like "YouTube", "Vimeo" or "Blinkx" (www.youtube.com, www.vimeo.com, www.blinkx.com). For example, YouTube, as the market leader, is storing about 24 hours of new video content per minute in its database [9]. Additionally to online video portals, live-streaming services like "Ustream", "Justin.tv" and "Livestram" (www.ustream.com, www.justin.tv, www.livestream.com) create another quickly growing area for digital video. Such companies offer video live streams which combined with social networks lead to a new form of interactive TV experience as being already streamed in massive amounts over the web [43]. Putting it together, there is not only an immense amount of digital video already stored but also a rapidly growing trend to make even larger quantities of video content available online. This is particularly reflected in a recent report by CISCO [28], where digital video is estimated to occupy around 91% of all Internet traffic by 2013.

However, making video content available online does not imply to make it searchable to the end user. While community efforts like collaborative tagging (also called *folksonomy*) are aiming to provide searchable annotations (or tags) [23], they are prone to spam [36], include misspellings, numbers [15] or are subjective or incomplete [38, 71]. Therefore, the lack of accurate and detailed metadata is still a major problem in video search, making it a cumbersome and frustrating task for end users.

Concept-based video retrieval

In the literature two groups of access mechanisms to video databases can be found: "query-by-example" [2, 7, 17] where an image is given as an example and similar images are retrieved from the database, and "textual-search", where the user types in a textual query and the retrieval system connects the given keywords with videos stored in the database. While the first query approach might favor a browsing alike exploration of the database, the later one is considered to be a more natural querying mechanism by the end user and therefore is used more in the context of folksonomy driven environments as well as regular search engines.

One way to build a textual index might be to let experts label the database manually according to well defined semantic concepts describing objects ("airplane flying"), scene type ("cityscape") and activities ("person playing soccer") appearing in the videos. This, however, is infeasible due to the huge size of current video databases. Concluding, the question is if this can be done automatically i.e. can a machine build such an index? This challenging task is referred to as *concept detection* [65] and is subject of intensive research by a large research community [45].

Following, concept detection systems aim to infer the probability for predefined target concepts to appear in a given video clip. This is accomplished by treating concept presence as a binary classification problem under the usage of extracted low-level features like color, texture or motion from the video stream and statistical learning methods. The difficulty behind this can be summarized by the semantic gap [63], the mismatch between low-level features of a video stream on the one side and a user's high-level interpretation of the video on the other. Although the performance of state-of-the-art concept detection systems [64, 82] is yet not as good as manual annotation [61], the idea of automatically mining large video databases for semantic concepts is considered to be a key building block of video search prototypes [1, 62, 65].

Visual learning from web video

One particular problem of concept detection is its demand for labeled training sets, which serve as a foundation for supervised machine learning as being the underlying technology of current concept detection systems. So far, the required training samples have been acquired manually i.e. a human operator labels videos or video shots with respect to concept presence. Thereby, concepts are well defined according to a concept vocabulary [40]. This time-consuming and cost-intensive effort [4, 66] indeed leads to high quality training material, but, however, suffers from a scalability problem which raises the question if alternative sources for concept detector training exist.

Recently, the usage of socially tagged web images & video as alternative training source for semantic concept detection has become more prominent [38, 57, 72, 74].

Utilizing such data offers the following advantages over a training from a small set of expert labels: first, it allows to learn large concept vocabularies which is required to cover users' information need [25]. Second, it enables concept detection systems to be more flexible in learning new emerging concepts like "Michael Jackson", "Inauguration Day" or "iPod" (top ranked searches 2009 by "Google Insights for Search" for web search, news search and product search respectively - as retrieved Nov. 2009). Third, it prevents overfitting as learning from only a small set of sample videos tends to deliver overfitted detectors which generalize poorly [83].

Web video in particular is publicly available at large scale from online portals like YouTube, Vimeo or Blinkx and is associated with a noisy but rich corpus of tags, comments and ratings that are provided by large communities. Utilizing this information might replace expert labeled datasets in automatically harvesting training material from the web. For example, to learn a concept like "person playing soccer" a search query has to be formulated and sent to one of the previously mentioned web video portals. The resulting list of relevant videos can now be downloaded and used as training material. For this purpose tags are used as positive labels for concept learning. Web video has already been proven to train more general detectors performing better on unseen datasets as compared to detectors trained on specific expert labeled data [74] and demonstrated its potential as a comprehensive training source for visual concept learning [72].

However, the usage of web videos as training material for concept detection systems faces two challenges: first, web video is *weakly labeled* i.e. its annotations are often noisy, subjective, unreliable and coarse containing a great amount of non-relevant content. For example, at YouTube where tags can only be given at video level the fractions of non-relevant content lies between $50-80\%$ leading to a performance loss of web-based concept detectors when compared to ones trained on labels given by experts [71]. To deal with this *label noise problem*, several approaches have been proposed, either filtering non-relevant material [8, 73, 78] or focusing on tag coarseness [22]. Second, when concept detectors are trained on web video and afterwards applied to a different source of video data (or *domain*) we face the so-called *domain change problem*: a significant discrepancy of the visual appearance between given domains. This challenge is the focus of this chapter and will be described in the next section in more detail.

The domain change problem

One key problem with concept detectors is that they work well on the data they are trained on but generalize poorly to other data sources (or *domains*) [83]. In this context, the definition of a domain is the following [85]:

> ***Domain:*** A domain refers to data of a certain type, from a certain source, or generated in a certain period in time.

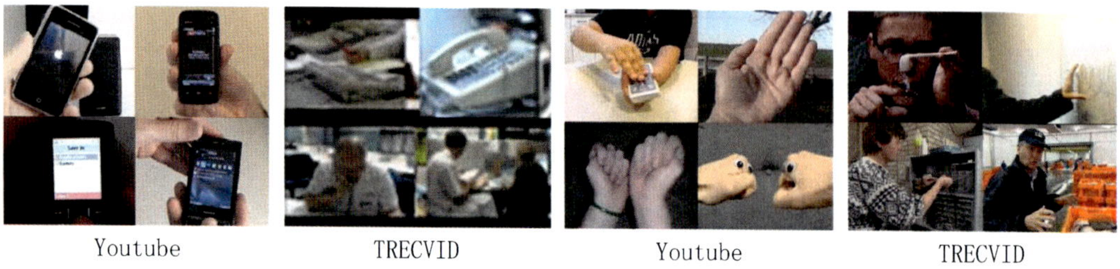

Fig. (1): Frames from YouTube and TRECVID videos tagged with "Telephone" (left) and "Hand" (right). The domain change leads to a different visual appearance of both concepts.

Following, a domain can be a particular TV channel, a content provider, or a video genre like documentary content. Particularly, web video also defines its own domain considering the definition above. In practice, concept detectors are often trained on one domain and applied to another one. This has been reported to degrade detector performance [74, 84], a phenomenon that is commonly referred to as *domain change problem* and is illustrated in Fig. **(1)**: imagine training a detector for the concepts "Telephone" or "Hand" on web video (here, YouTube data), which shows mostly close-ups, and applying it on TV broadcast data (here, the TRECVID dataset [45]), which shows mostly office telephones or hands in interview scenes. Obviously, the web-based detectors will perform poorly on this particular dataset.

This raises the question whether detectors trained on one domain (the "source domain") can be *adapted* to another one (the "target domain"). So far, this challenge has been addressed using techniques like *cross-domain learning* or *domain adaptation* in the context of switching between different TV domains [20, 30, 84, 85].

Outline

This chapter addresses the training of concept detectors on web video and their application to different domain of video data. Particularly, the associated challenges resulting from the domain change problem are addressed. The goal of this work is to analyze the impact of the domain change between web video and specific target domains and to adapt web-based detectors by a novel domain adaptation technique as illustrated in Fig. **(2)**: a first training on large-scale web material leads to an initial detector, which is then used as a starting point for a few cycles of adaptation utilizing labels from the target domain. In the context of web-based learning, where we want to learn *many* concepts from *large-scale* training data, several new questions need to be answered:

1. Can social-tagged web video improve detectors compared to training only on domain-specific data?

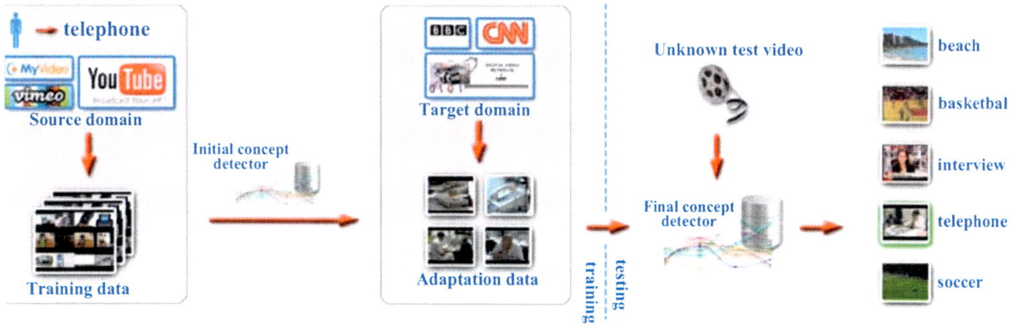

Fig. (2): To learn a concept, the proposed system downloads videos from web video portals and trains an initial detector. This detector is adapted efficiently using few labeled samples from the target domain, obtaining a final domain-specific detector.

2. How much does the associated label noise of web video affect domain adaptation?

3. Can we do an efficient, light-weight adaptation of web-based detectors to other domains (enabling adaptation in an "interactive search" fashion [57])?

4. How many samples from the target domain are needed for a successful adaptation?

In details, the contribution of this chapter are the following:

- **domain change impact**: first, the impact of domain changes on concept detectors is analyzed. This includes different supervised learning methods and combinations of training data. It will be demonstrated that domain changes degrade concept detection performance significantly.

- **adaptation**: a novel and efficient adaptation approach is proposed and demonstrated to lead to significant improvements – adapted detectors can outperform purely web-based ones and also one trained on the target domain.

- **adaptation with few samples**: as the acquisition of training samples is cost-intensive, a minimal amount of target domain samples should be required for adaption. For this purpose, active learning methods [4] are evaluated. These offer the advantage that user feedback can be incorporated into the domain adaptation framework.

The remaining chapter is organized as follows: the second section covers recent work related to concept detection, domain adaptation and active learning. Section 3 outlines the proposed approach of an online learning domain adaptation technique whereas Section 4 presents experimental results on newscast from the TRECVID benchmark and web video data. Finally, Section 5 provides a conclusion and an appendix summarizes the used YouTube query formulations.

2 Related Work

In this section, we will introduce supervised concept detection, then we will continue with general domain adaptation techniques where classifier are trained on particular source domains and are applied to different target domains. Finally, an overview of active learning will be given and how it helps to label unknown datasets.

Concept detection

Concept detection is the task of inferring semantic concepts in video streams. This is achieved by computing posterior probabilities which indicates the likelihood of presence of concepts from a vocabulary. A comprehensive overview of the field can be found in [65].

A major research effort in the context of concept detection is the TRECVID [60] benchmark, which addresses concept detection in its High-Level Feature Extraction task [61]. This benchmark aims to evaluate the performance of different concept detection systems on a common, standardized dataset and allows the community to exchange experience and drive this area of research forward. The architecture of most concept detection systems as benchmarked at TRECVID can be described by five major blocks:

1. **Pre-processing** A video consists of a sequence of shots being separated by cuts or gradual transitions. Since the basic unit of information in concept detection is a shot, the first step is to temporarily segment a video into its shots. From this keyframes can be extracted, which serve as input for visual concept learning in the next processing steps.

2. **Feature Extraction** The purpose of feature extraction is to transform keyframes into n dimensional feature vectors $x \in \mathbb{R}^n$ which can be used during the subsequent classification step. Many different descriptors have been proposed, ranging from global color, texture and motion descriptors to patch-based ones. For details please refer to evaluations in [19, 76].

3. **Statistical Classification** Given feature vectors $x \in \mathbb{R}^n$ the next processing step is the inference of concepts using statistical classification. A popular choice to achieve this are Support Vector Machines (SVMs) [55], which are used in most systems nowadays [65]. SVMs, configured as binary classifiers,

deliver scores which transformed into posterior probabilities $P(t)$ indicate the absence or presence of a concept t. Such supervised machine learning requires a labeled training set prior to classification. This training data can be acquired by an expert [4] or by alternative sources like web video [57, 72]

4. **Fusion** Many systems utilize multiple types of features and supervised learners. A fusion or combination of such components can be performed on two different levels: features fusion i.e. the concatenation of features vectors previous to detector learning or classifier fusion where detector results are put together after classification. An overview of different fusion approaches can be found in [79].

5. **Concept Relation Modeling** One additional step, is semantic relation modeling between concepts [41, 50, 64]. Here, the presence of a concept serves as an additional indicator for a related concept e.g the presence of a "sky" indicates an increased probability of an "airplane" being present. Such co-occurrences or correlation between concepts can be modeled with different approaches. For a more details please refer to [65].

Domain adaptation

This section discusses domain adaptation from different points of view. A common setup is defined as follows: a supervised learner is trained initially on labeled samples $x_1, \ldots, x_n \wedge y_1, \ldots, y_n \in \{+1, -1\}$ from a source domain $\mathcal{D}^s$ and is employed on a specific target domain $\mathcal{D}^t$. In such a setup it is likely that the data distribution of the source and target domain are different and therefore the performance of the supervised learner will not be optimal. To reduce the effect of such a domain change, different techniques have been proposed (for a detailed survey refer to [29, 86]):

Domain Adaptation Approaches A first approach towards domain adaptation is **Sample Bias Correction** or **Covariance Shift**, where the focus lies on dealing with different distributions of training and test data. Here, the basic assumption is that the expected loss on the test distribution equals a weighted expected loss on the training distribution. Transferring this idea to domain adaptation, Blitzer proposed an approach [6], where pivot features that appear frequently in both domains are selected by heuristic methods and reweighed appropriately. A more theoretical investigation of this method can be found in [5]. Related approaches which additionally utilize the structure of unlabeled samples are proposed as covariate shift [68] or sample selection bias [27]. Another data manipulation technique is **Feature Replication** [16], where features are augmented for kernel function construction. The idea of feature replication is to combine source and target domain datasets to find common feature characteristics so that the source domain can provide missing data for the target domain. A disadvantage of this method is the increased dimensionality of the feature vector and the resulting increase of model complexity.

Another area in machine learning similar to the domain adaptation setup is **Transfer Learning**. In transfer learning, knowledge from one related task (in case of multiple related tasks it is called **Multi-Task Learning**) is used to improve performance of a target task. One group of such methods uses weighted auxiliary or prior data in combination with SVMs [80, 81], whereas another group of methods focus on unsupervised transfer learning [46, 51].

An alternative to this is **Incremental Learning** or **Online Learning**. Here, classifiers are successively updated according to a continuous sample input and therefore can adapt naturally to a new model given a sufficient number of samples from the target domain. Our approach in this chapter can be seen as an example of online learning adaptation. Other examples of SVM-based online learning can be found in [10, 33].

Another field close to domain adaptation is **Drifting Concept Detection** known from the data mining community. A drifting concept is a statistical property of a predicted target variable which changes over time due to the change of an incoming data stream. Here, two major approaches exist: first, the reweighing of training samples depending on a fixed or adaptive window moving over the stream [18, 34]. Second, fusion of weighted ensemble classifier from different parts of the data stream [35, 77].

Domain Adaptation for Concept Detection Finally, we consider domain adaptation in concept detection, where it is commonly referred to as **Cross-domain Learning**. One of the first studies in this area was motivated by a dataset change of the TRECVID campaign. The dataset changed from the previously used *news video* (2005 + 2006) to the newly introduced *documentary video* (2007), which was leading to the situation where robust detectors for the news domain were available but could not be used naively on the new documentary domain. On the other side, the initially small amount of positive samples on the documentary dataset might not have been sufficient for new domain specific detector training.

A first straightforward approach to domain adaptation is **Data Aggregation**, where labeled samples from both domains are put together for classifier training $\mathcal{D}_l = \mathcal{D}_l^s \cup \mathcal{D}_l^t$. Data aggregation – often used as a baseline [30, 85] is usually biased towards larger dataset. However, this method proved to be helpful during a cold start (or kickstart), where a source domain dataset is successively enriched by labeled target domain samples [57].

A first domain adaptation approach, where an existing classifier is reused is **Adaptive-SVM** (A-SVM) [85]. An A-SVM learns a specific *delta function* to compensate the domain change. In particular, the adapted classifier $f^a(x)$ is a combination of the source classifier $f^s(x)$ and the delta function $\Delta f(x) = \mathbf{w}^T \phi(x)$ leading to $f^a(x) = f^s(x) + \Delta f(x) = f^s(x) + \mathbf{w}^T \phi(x)$ where $\mathbf{w}$ is the parameter to be derived from the labeled target domain samples $\mathcal{D}_l^t$. The goal of an A-SVM is to learn a new decision boundary which is close to the original decision boundary but also separates well labeled target samples.

Another SVM-based approach has been introduced in [30]. Here, a **Cross-Domain SVM** (CDSVM) aims not to learn a delta function but to directly utilize the knowledge about the source domain compressed in the support vectors $\mathcal{V}^s = \{(\mathbf{v}_1^s, y_1^s), \ldots, (\mathbf{v}_M^s, y_M^s)\}$ representing the source classifier $f^s(x)$. The underlying idea is that if a support vector $\mathbf{v}_i^s$ falls into the neighborhood of a target data sample it tent to be drawn from a distribution similar to $\mathcal{D}^t$ and therefore help to classify $\mathcal{D}^t$.

An additional approach applied in the context of concept detection are **Transductive SVMs** (TSVM) [30, 84], a semi-supervised learning method. Since a large dataset on the target domain is available but only few samples are labeled it seems reasonable to employ semi-supervised learning. Note, however, that one key assumption – namely that the underlying data distribution of both domains is similar – can not be expected to hold in concept detection. Other drawbacks are computational cost and non-convex optimization.

The same idea of utilizing unlabeled target domain samples inspired **Domain Transfer SVM** (DTSVM) [21]. This approach is based on simultaneously learning a kernel function and minimizing the mismatch of data distributions of source and target domain by employing the structure of the unlabeled target data.

A similar approach from the same authors are **Domain Adaptation Machines** (DAMs) [20]. DAMs are multiple source learners based on Least-Squares SVM and enhanced by a data-dependent smoothness regularizer leading to an adapted classifier. An advantage of DAMs are their sparse characteristic and the resulting computational efficiency. Additionally, DAMs do not depend on the assumption that source and target domain samples come from the same data distribution.

A different direction of domain adaptation in concept detection is the utilization of relations between concepts (or correlated concepts). The idea of adapting *contextual models* based on source classifier was practically used in [41], where a graph based approach called **Domain Adaptive Semantic Diffusion** (DASD) [32] was used in combination with an ontology based word similarity named *Flickr Context Similarity* (FCS) [31]. However, the aforementioned methods are particularly used for semantic context adaptation targeting the domain-shift-of-context problem [41] and not for direct classifier adaptation as in case of the SVM based approaches previously described. In our case, we particularly aim to perform domain adaptation in terms of data distribution shifts and the resulting different visual appearance of semantic concepts as illustrated in Fig. (**1**).

So fare, the proposed domain adaptation techniques were based on SVMs and compared either domain change influences between news channels or between news vs. documentation material. In our study, we investigate the impact of web video as alternative source for concept detector training, a more challenging task due to its intrinsic label noise and subjectivity. Furthermore, a key benefit of the proposed adaptation approach is its ability to incorporated user feedback where techniques like active learning might help to further reduce the need for target domain samples.

Active learning

In supervised learning, classifier training is performed on a labeled dataset. Prior to training such a labeled dataset must be manually acquired by annotating unlabeled samples. This is an expensive and cost-intensive effort. The main goal of active learning is to select only the "most informative" samples for manual annotation and therefore to minimize the effort of labeling new datasets [56]. In particular, active learning works in iterative cycles, where each cycle consist of the following steps: first, a model training. Second, a "query sample" selection based on this model, and third, the manual annotation of the selected sample. This user feedback is then included in the next cycle of active learning leading to a successively improved classifier.

Pool-based Methods The first appearance of active learning alike algorithms can be tracked back to the *Query-by-Committee* (QBC) algorithm [58], where the query sample is selected according to the principle of maximal disagreement among different learners. One particular family of active learning algorithms which is specifically suitable for retrieval is pool-based active learning. In pool-based active learning the learner has access to a pool of unlabeled data and can request the user to label a certain amount of instances in the pool to improve retrieval results. A straightforward method of selecting samples is *most relevant sampling* [53] as it is originated by the idea of relevance feedback. In the context of text retrieval, Lewis and Gale [37] introduced *uncertainty sampling*, which is also known as the close-to-boundary criterion [54, 70].

Applications in Image & Video Retrieval In the context of image retrieval, Tong and Chang [12, 69] proposed a version space reduction approach for sample selection. Clustering-based approaches were presented in [42, 48], where the structure of the underlying data distribution is utilized. This provides good means for the cold start of active learning and improves performance by not labeling redundant samples belonging to the same cluster. Considering the annotation of image databases, a combination of online learning with active learning have been proposed in [49]. Such an approach is able to efficiently update existing models every time a new batch of labeled samples is available.

Active learning also finds application in video retrieval [67]. A large-scale evaluation of standard active learning sample selection methods can be found in [3], where close to ground truth detector performance could be achieved by labeling only 15% of the original TRECVID 2006 dataset. Particularly interesting is the performance improvement when taking temporal information into account for sample selection, i.e actively selecting neighborhood shots of already positive annotated shots. Ayache and Quenot also embedded active learning methods within the TRECVID collaborative annotation effort [4]. A more general view of active learning for multimedia can be found in [14, 26], where active learning is the method behind the feedback mechanism of the proposed retrieval system. Another scenario where active learning proofed to be helpful is relevance filtering of noisy web video material [8]. Here, the combination of automatic filtering techniques with successively refined labels by active learning improved concept detector performance up to expert level by refining only 25% of the positive labeled samples.

Summarizing, active learning can be employed in three practical video retrieval situations. First, in situations where only few annotations are given, active learning can help to efficiently identify and annotate the most "informative samples" to increase training data size. Second, in relevance filtering setups, where a labeled but noisy dataset is available but must be refined, and third, in using a robust classifier trained on a particular source domain to acquire training samples from a specific target domain.

3 Approach

In this section, a novel domain adaptation approach for concept detection will be outlined. This approach is based on previous work on passive aggressive online learning [24, 47], where a similar method was introduced as a fast and accurate alternative to SVMs for concept learning. The extension of those methods to domain adaptation as proposed in this chapter is particularly designed to be highly efficient in terms of computational cost. This allows to process large amount of web video data and to incorporate domain adaptation as a part of an interactive relevance feedback loop. Such feedback on the target domain can be seen as a strong requirement in a real world domain adaptation scenario.

First, we will introduce some basic notation, followed by an overview of the proposed domain adaptation framework. After this, the underlying statistical learning procedure will be outlined and a novel adaptation method will be introduced: it will be shown how this method can be used in batch processing mode where a set of labeled target domain samples is available and how adaptation can be performed simultaneously with sample acquisition using active learning.

Problem overview

For the sake of simplicity the methods throughout this chapter will be discuss in terms of a single concept. Video content is represented as a set of keyframes $x \in X$, associated with feature vectors $\mathbf{x} \in \mathbb{R}^d$. Additionally, let $(\mathbf{x}_i, y_i)$ be a sample consisting of a feature vector and a binary class label $y_i \in \{+1, -1\}$ indicating the presence of a concept. Let $\mathcal{D}^s$ denote the dataset acquired from the source domain. In our case this dataset is fully labeled i.e. $\mathcal{D}^s = \mathcal{D}^s_l$. Note that web video is defined as source domain, which is *weakly* labeled i.e. labels are only weak indicators of concept presence because of their noise and subjectivity [71]. Further, $\mathcal{D}^t$ is denoted as the target domain dataset consisting of two subsets: a labeled dataset $\mathcal{D}^t_l$ and an unlabeled one $\mathcal{D}^t_u$. Here we assume that $|\mathcal{D}^s_l| \gg |\mathcal{D}^t_l|$, the amount of labeled source domain samples is much higher than the amount of target domain samples. This corresponds to the practical situation, as web video is available at large scale through online portals like YouTube.

In a domain adaptation scenario, distributions of $\mathcal{D}^s$ and $\mathcal{D}^t$ are assumed to be different and therefore the classifier $f^s(\mathbf{x})$ trained from the source domain will not perform well classifying $\mathcal{D}^t_u$. However, to learn a new classifier $f^t(\mathbf{x})$ alone from the labeled samples of the target domain may not give robust performance due to the small amount of training samples. Concluding, the core question of domain adaptation is how to utilize the knowledge given by the source domain (compressed in $f^s(\mathbf{x})$) in combination with target domain $\mathcal{D}^t_l$ to improve classification of $\mathcal{D}^t_u$.

Proposed framework

The core interest of this work is to adapt web trained classifiers to specific target domains other than web video. To achieve this, we propose the following framework, which consists of a training, adaptation and testing phase as illustrated in Fig. (**3**). To learn a particular concept like "telephone", training material is downloaded from an online video platform (i.e. the source domain $\mathcal{D}^s$). This material is used for initial concept detector training resulting in a source classifier $f^s(\mathbf{x})$. The source classifier $f^s(x)$ is then adapted efficiently in an online fashion to a classifier $f^a(\mathbf{x})$ in utilizing a few samples from the target domain $\mathcal{D}^t$. This can be performed in two different modes:

1. *batch adaptation*, where adaptation is done on a set of a priori available labeled samples from the target domain

2. *active adaptation*, where adaptation is alternated with sample acquisition by active learning. Such an alternated user feedback is only possible if the underlying domain adaptation approach is highly efficient. This mode aims at practical scenarios where no target domain labels are available a priori.

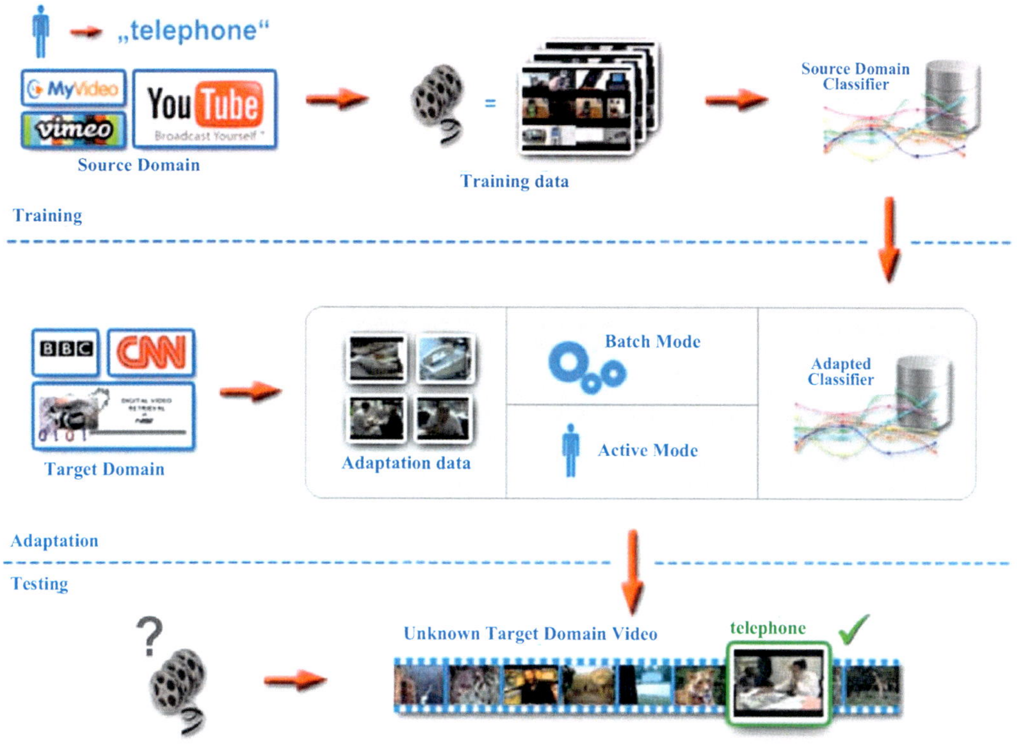

Fig. (3): To learn a concept, the proposed system downloads videos from web video portals and trains an initial source domain classifier. This classifier is adapted efficiently either in a *batch adaptation* mode or an *active adaptation* mode obtaining a final domain-specific detector.

Passive aggressive online learning

Because one core requirement for the illustrated domain adaptation framework is efficiency in terms of learning and classification, the passive aggressive online learning approach (PAMIR) of Grangier [24] is adapted as its underlying statistical learning method. Additionally, its online learning nature makes its particularly applicable for domain adaptation. PAMIR has also been demonstrated to serve as a competitive alternative to SVMs in concept detection [47].

The goal of PAMIR is to find a linear projection from the feature space to a concept score. Such a projection is represented by a *weight vector* $\mathbf{w}$. Given an unlabeled sample $\mathbf{x}_i$, classification scores for a concept are calculated by a dot product:

$$f(\mathbf{x}_i) = <\mathbf{w}, \mathbf{x}_i> \tag{1}$$

Concept learning means here to find a suitable weight vector $\mathbf{w}$ for a concept. This is accomplished by minimizing the following optimization problem:

$$\arg\min_{\mathbf{w}} \; || \mathbf{w} ||^2 \quad + \mathcal{C} \sum_{\forall(\mathbf{x}_p,\mathbf{x}_n)\in\mathcal{D}} l(\mathbf{w};\mathbf{x}_p,\mathbf{x}_n) \tag{2}$$

where $\mathbf{x}_p \in \mathcal{D}$ is a positive sample ($y_p = +1$) drawn from the training data $\mathcal{D}$ and $\mathbf{x}_n \in \mathcal{D}$ is a negative sample ($y_n = -1$), $\mathcal{C}$ being a cost parameter, and $l(\cdot)$ being the hinge loss function:

$$l(\mathbf{w};\mathbf{x}_p,\mathbf{x}_n) = \begin{cases} 0 & \mathbf{w}(\mathbf{x}_p - \mathbf{x}_n) > 1 \\ 1 - \mathbf{w}(\mathbf{x}_p - \mathbf{x}_n) & otherwise \end{cases} \tag{3}$$

Intuitively, optimization of Eq. (**2**) results in high classification scores of videos where learned concept appears and low classification scores for videos where the concept is not present. Following, the minimization criterion directly optimizes *Average Precision* (AvgP), a standard performance metric in video concept detection. The optimization problem of finding a suitable weight vector $\mathbf{w}$ can now be solved with the help of an iterative procedure [47]:

$$\mathbf{w}^i = \arg\min_{\mathbf{w}} \frac{1}{2} \, || \mathbf{w} - \mathbf{w}^{i-1} ||^2 \; + \; c \, l(\mathbf{w};\mathbf{x}_p,\mathbf{x}_n) \tag{4}$$

where i is the number of optimization steps, c is the hyper-parameter of the system controlling the *aggressiveness* of optimization, $\mathbf{x}_p$,$\mathbf{x}_n$ a positive and negative labeled random pair of samples and $l(\cdot)$ being the previously introduced loss function (Eq. **3**). In particular, Eq. (**4**) consist of two terms: the first term $\frac{1}{2} \, || \mathbf{w} - \mathbf{w}^{i-1} ||^2$ forces the new weight vector to be nearby to the previous one. It can be understood as a regularizer performing a smoothing between successive optimization steps. Whereas the second term $c \, l(w, (\mathbf{x}_p; \mathbf{x}_n))$ represents the ability to discriminate correctly between positive and negative samples.

The optimization algorithm starts with iteration $i = 0$ and a weight vector initialization of $\mathbf{w}^{i=0} = 0$. At each iteration a random pair of samples $(\mathbf{x}_p, \mathbf{x}_n)$ is drawn from $\mathcal{D}$ and evaluated. For this pair the new weight vector $\mathbf{w}^i$ is obtained by solving Eq. (**4**). According to [24] the solution to this equation is:

$$\mathbf{w}^i = \mathbf{w}^{i-1} + \Gamma^i(\mathbf{x}_p - \mathbf{x}_n) \tag{5}$$

where the Lagrange multiplier Γ^i is:

$$\Gamma^i = \min\left\{\mathcal{C}, \frac{l(\mathbf{w};\mathbf{x}_p,\mathbf{x}_n)}{|| \mathbf{x}_p - \mathbf{x}_n ||^2}\right\} \tag{6}$$

After a appropriate number of iterations $i = n$ the procedure is stopped and model training is finished.

Domain adaptation

The previously introduced algorithm is an online learning method. Online learning methods build a model by processing a sequence of labeled samples, where each single sample is viewed as one instance at a time by the learner during training and therefore contributes only gradually to the learned model. This is also true for the iterative optimization of Eq. (**4**), where each pair of samples represents one step of optimization. This characteristic fits smoothly into the domain adaptation framework. The idea is to first, train a source classifier by iteratively picking samples from $\mathcal{D}^s$ and then to adapt this classifier by picking samples explicitly from the target domain $\mathcal{D}^t$.

Batch Adaptation In batch adaptation mode a new weight vector is learned from the target dataset $\mathcal{D}_l^t$ with the support of $\mathcal{D}^s$. A detailed description of the adaptation procedure can be found in Tab. (**1**): Let f^s be the classifier trained on the source domain $\mathcal{D}^s$ by optimizing Eq. (**2**) and substituting $\mathcal{D} = \mathcal{D}^s$. Then, adaptation of f^s is performed as a second optimization of Eq. (**2**), but here with $\mathcal{D} = \mathcal{D}_l^t$ and more importantly instead of initializing the weight vector with $\mathbf{w}^{s^{i=0}} = 0$, the second optimization starts with the previously learned model from the source domain: $\mathbf{w}^{a^{j=0}} = \mathbf{w}^s$. This provides a reasonable foundation for adaptation in providing knowledge from the source domain. Now, every optimization step j of Eq. (**4**) aims to find a weight vector $\mathbf{w}^{a^j}$ which is close to the source domain model and can separate sample pairs drawn explicitly from the target domain $\mathcal{D}_l^t$.

Note that this approach is not simply a data aggregation approach, where source domain data and target domain data are put together leading to one optimization procedure with $\mathcal{D} = \mathcal{D}^s \cup \mathcal{D}_l^t$. Instead, the proposed adaptation can be seen as belonging to the "function level classifier adaptation" schema proposed by Yang [84] as it seeks to learn a decision boundary close to the source domain decision boundary and tries to separate the labeled target domain samples. However, here, the computation of the new model is different due to the underlying online learning optimization so that the regularization condition of finding a "close" boundary is only valid in the scope of one single optimization iteration. Controlling the number of iterations allows the model to gradually change over time and therefore adapt to target domains which are not "close" to the source domain.

Adaptation Stopping Criterion One remaining question is: how much adaptation is enough i.e. how many iterations of optimization steps should be performed? While it can be expected that adaptation improves concept detector performance in general, it may have negative impact on some concepts where the source domain may already provide comprehensive training material resulting in a robust source classifier. In such cases an adaptation could harm the final classification performance, an effect which is known as "negative transfer" [52] in transfer learning.

Tab. (1): After a first model training on the source domain (step 1. and 2.) a second optimization cycle (step 3. and 4.) performs adaptation on the target domain.

1. initialize **source classifier training** with weight vector $\mathbf{w}^{s^{i=0}} = 0$
2. for $i = 1, \ldots, n$ do:
   - select randomly $(\mathbf{x}_p, \mathbf{x}_n) \in \mathcal{D}^s$
   - obtain new weight vector $\mathbf{w}^{s^i}$ by Eq. (**4**):
     - perform update according to Eq. (**5**) and Eq. (**6**)

   Once the first optimization cycle is finished the source domain classifier $f^s(\mathbf{x})$ is represented by the weight vector $\mathbf{w}^s$.
3. initialize **target domain adaptation** with weight vector $\mathbf{w}^{a^{j=0}} = \mathbf{w}^s$
4. for $j = 1, \ldots, m$ do:
   - select randomly $(\mathbf{x}_p, \mathbf{x}_n) \in \mathcal{D}^t_l$
   - obtain new weight vector $\mathbf{w}^{a^j}$ by Eq. (**4**):
     - perform update according to Eq. (**5**) and Eq. (**6**)

   Once the second optimization cycle is finished the adapted classifier $f^a(\mathbf{x})$ is represented by the weight vector $\mathbf{w}^a$.

Domain adaptation according to the proposed method consists of two major optimization cycles, namely training on the source domain and adaptation to the target domain. For source domain training, the number of iterations is fixed. For adaptation, however, the question of when to stop is tackled by testing the following rules:

1. **oracle**, where adapted classifier $f^a(\mathbf{x})$ performance is evaluated on the target domain $\mathcal{D}^t_u$. Adaptation is stopped in the very moment when performance on the target domain is best. While this is not feasible in reality it provides an upper bound for adaptation performance.
2. **sample**, where a small set of additional labels from the target domain data $\mathcal{D}^t_u$ is made available for adaptation evaluation. This criterion is similar to oracle but uses a much smaller fraction of $\mathcal{D}^t_u$ ($\approx 5\%$), making it feasible in a real application scenario.

3. **predict**, where a validation set from $\mathcal{D}_l^t$ is defined on which adaptation performance can be evaluated and accordingly stopped if degradation is observable.

4. **fix**, where a fixed number of iterations is set. This straightforward setup always assumes that domain adaptation on the target domain is necessary and that this should be performed with a fixed number of iterations. A good value was empirically evaluated in [47] showing a stable behavior of the online learning optimization. Therefore, the number of iterations is set s to the same value, namely $i = 10^6$ for both source domain training and target domain adaptation.

Domain adaptation extended by active learning

While so far labeled samples from the target domain $\mathcal{D}_l^t$ are assumed to be available, in a real world application this may not be the case. In such a situation, label acquisition from the target domain $\mathcal{D}^t$ is necessary but should be kept to a minimum. Taking also into account that not all samples from the target domain are equally informative, an efficient sample selection is preferable. For this purpose active learning is particularly suitable, where samples are selected according to different heuristics.

Relevance Feedback as a Wrapper In the following setup, a manual labeling of selected samples from $\mathcal{D}_u^t$ is placed as a wrapper around the proposed domain adaptation procedure. Note that initially $\mathcal{D}_l^t = \emptyset$ i.e. we do not have any labeled samples from the target domain.

The procedure is illustrated in detail in Tab. (**2**): initially a source classifier $f^s(\mathbf{x})$ is trained on the source domain $\mathcal{D}^s$. This classifier provides an initial set of classifications scores $p_i^{j=1}$ on the target domain $\mathcal{D}_u^t$. For each iteration j of adaptation a sample from $\mathcal{D}_u^t$ is selected according to an active learning criterion based on the previous scores p_i^j. This sample is manually labeled and belongs now to $\mathcal{D}_l^t$ being available for the next batch of domain adaptation resulting in an adapted classifier $f^{a^j}(\mathbf{x})$. This new classifier will provide new scores p_i^{j+1} for the next iteration of active learning sample selection. Continuing further, this procedure increases the amount of labeled samples from the target domain successively, providing an improved basis for adaptation.

Sample Selection Methods In the literature, different active learning strategies for sample selection exist. Here, we compare the ones that proofed to be successful in previous concept detection experiments [3]:

1. **random sampling**: samples are selected randomly.

Tab. (2): Active learning wrapped around domain adaptation selects informative samples from the target domain for manual annotation. Once the sample is labeled, the system takes this newly acquired knowledge into account for the next iteration of adaptation.

1. train source classifier $f^s(\mathbf{x})$ on source domain $\mathcal{D}^s$
2. $\forall \mathbf{x}_i \in \mathcal{D}_u^t$ obtain classification scores $p_i^{j=1}$ using $f^s(\mathbf{x}_i)$
3. for $j = 1, \ldots, m$ do:
   - select sample s^* according to an *active learning* criterion Q:

     $$s^* := \arg\max_i \; Q(p_i^j)$$

   - get label y_{s^*}
   - add sample $s^* = (\mathbf{x}_{s^*}, y_{s^*})$ to $\mathcal{D}_l^t$
   - perform domain adaptation on $\mathcal{D}_l^t$ obtaining an adapted classifier $f^{a^j}(\mathbf{x})$
   - $\forall \mathbf{x}_i \in \mathcal{D}_u^t$ obtain classification scores p_i^{j+1} using $f^{a^j}(\mathbf{x}_i)$

2. **most relevant**: samples are selected which are most likely to be relevant and are therefore associated with the highest posterior [53]:

$$Q_{REL}(p_i^j) := p_i^j$$

3. **uncertainty**: samples are selected for which the relevance filtering method is least confident, i.e. $p_i^j \approx 0.5$ [37]:

$$Q_{UNC}(p_i^j) := 1 - |p_i^j - 0.5|$$

Note that the proposed active learning approach does not incorporate shot neighborhood information into the sample selection mechanism as in [3].

4 Experimental Results

In the previous section, a domain adaptation framework for concept detection has been proposed to tackle the domain change problem. We study this approach in the following experiments, whereas the focus is on web video downloaded from

YouTube as a source domain and television content from the TRECVID campaign [44] being the target domains. In particular, this raises three key questions: first, how strong is the impact of the domain change in terms of performance degradation, second, how successful is domain adaptation in terms of detector performance and efficiency and third, how much can active learning help when adaptation data must be acquired manually.

Datasets

Several datasets are used to benchmark domain adaptation for concept detection (an overview is given in Tab. (**3**). Two datasets belong to the source domain: *Web Video*, and two datasets to the target domain: the TRECVID 2007 *Sound & Vision (S&V)* data. These datasets are additionally denoted as "training data", where the source classifier is trained on, "adaptation data", where labeled samples from the target domain are given or "test data" serving for performance evaluation. As a concept vocabulary, we use the 20 test concepts from the TRECVID 2009 High-Level Feature Extraction task (http://www-nlpir.nist.gov/projects/tv2009/tv9.hlf.for.eval.txt). In the following the datasets are described in more detail.

Web Video Web video material was retrieved from YouTube through the provided API (http://code.google.com/apis/youtube/overview.html). For each concept, representative keywords and YouTube categories were chosen manually and used for searching videos at YouTube (for a detailed overview, please refer to the App. (**5**). For each concept, 150 video clips were downloaded, obtaining the dataset `yt-direct` with 120 hours total length and 2500 videos (for some concepts not all requested 150 videos could be downloaded from YouTube). A simple change detection approach for keyframe extraction was leading to roughly 50,000 keyframes.

As our focus is on web video, domain change is also studied in combination with *label noise*, given the fact that web-based training sets contain significant amounts of non-relevant material which is another challenge for web-based concept detection. To evaluate if domain change or label noise has a stronger impact on system performance, we acquired a second manually refined dataset for the following 12 concepts: "airplane flying","boat ship", "bus", "cityscape", "classroom", "demonstration", "doorway", "female human face closeup", "people dancing", "person eating", "person playing soccer", "traffic intersection". For these concepts, only keyframes were kept that were manually validated to show the concept as defined by TRECVID. The resulting dataset of about 29,000 keyframes (`yt-refined`) allows us to study concept detection with domain change but free of label noise.

TRECVID Sound & Vision (S&V) As a first target domain dataset the TRECVID S&V dataset (`tv7`) is used. This dataset consists of documentary video and was initially used in the TRECVID 2007 evaluation. It contains 50 hours of

Tab. (3): Overview of datasets used in the experiments.

	Source domain: raw	refined	**Target domain:** S&V
training data ($\mathcal{D}^s$)	`yt-direct`	`yt-refined`	
adapt. data ($\mathcal{D}^t_l$)			`tv7-devel`
test data ($\mathcal{D}^t_u$)			`tv7-test`

training data (`tv7-devel`) and 50 hours of test data (`tv7-test`). As in TRECVID the basic unit of evaluation is a shot, the dataset was segmented into the provided ground truth shot sequences and multiple keyframe per shots were extracted, leading to about $68,000$ keyframes. Further, the publicly available annotation set from the TRECVID collaborative effort [4] was used as label information. Comparing this expert labeled dataset to `yt-direct`, annotation quality is much higher than for raw web video, but many concepts are very rare i.e. there are ten time more negative samples than positive ones [13]. Correspondingly, the majority of the keyframes does not show any target concept. This renders domain adaptation challenging, considering positive labels as the core information from the target domain.

In all experiments we employ the well-known bag-of-visual-words approach for feature extraction [59, 75]: for each keyframe a regular patch sampling was performed at several scales, describing each patch by SIFT [39]. Patches were matched against a 2000-dimensional visual word codebook – build by K-Means – forming a feature histogram representing the keyframe. Further, as all classification is based on keyframes but performance evaluation is done on shot level, an averaging of keyframe scores to video shot scores was performed.

Domain change impact

In a first experiment we quantify the impact of domain changes by comparing classification performance of systems beings trained on the source domain vs. systems being trained on the target domain.

Setup Two runs are performed: (1) a classifier trained on `yt-direct` and (2) a classifier trained on `tv7-devel`. Both classifiers are tested against `tv7-test`. For each setup, two statistical models are evaluated: the PAMIR method as introduced before with $i = 10^6$ as the fixed number of optimization steps and $\mathcal{C} = 0.001$, and SVMs [55] (which constitute the state-of-the-art in video concept detection), with a χ^2 kernel ($\mathcal{C}$ and γ are evaluated in a grid-search cross validation). SVM scores were mapped to class posterior estimates using LIBSVM [11].

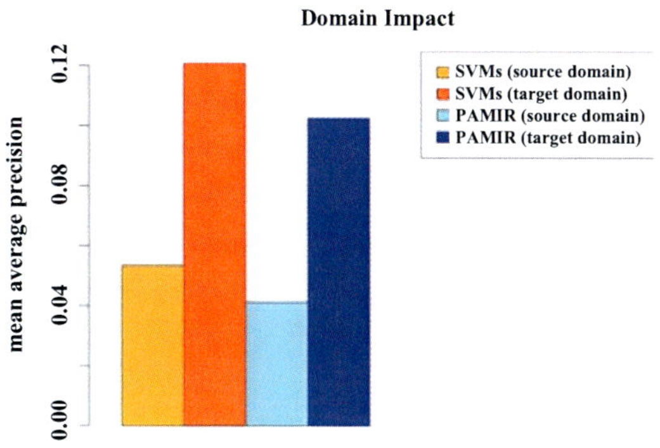

Fig. (4): Results illustrating the domain change impact for SVMs and PAMIR based concept detectors. A significant performance drop can be observed when training is performed on the source domain instead of the target domain.

Results As a performance measure, average precision is used, i.e. the area under the recall-precision curve over the ranked list of test videos. By averaging over all 20 concepts, the mean average precision (MAP) is obtained, a standard evaluation metric for video concept detectors [45]. Quantitative results for the `tv7` dataset are given in Fig. **(4)**, as averaged over 5 repeated runs. It can be seen that the domain change leads to a significant performance drop in MAP by up to 6.1% for PAMIR (which corresponds to a relative loss of 60%) and up to 6.75% for SVMs (relative loss 55%) when training and test data are not from the same domain. This performance drop can be explained by the different visual appearance of the same semantic concept e.g. in `yt-direct` training samples of the concept "airplane flying" show mostly civil planes whereas in `tv7-devel` the concept is represented by historical aircrafts in black and white documentary material. Considering each single concept (Tab. **(5)**), similar performance degradations can be observed. However, four exceptions have to be pointed out when performing adaptation to the `tv7` target domain: "demonstration or protest", "female human face closeup", "person playing a musical instrument" and "person playing soccer". For these concepts the training on `yt-direct` leads to a more robust classifier than training on `tv7-devel`.

Domain adaptation

As shown in the previous experiments, performance of web-based concept detectors degrades significantly when they are applied to target domains different than web video. The purpose of this experiment is to study domain adaptation in a controlled setting where the size $\alpha \in \{0.0, \ldots, 1.0\}$ of adaptation data ($\mathcal{D}_l^t$) is predefined with respect to the number of positive samples per concept. Here, $\alpha = 0.0$ corresponds to applying the source domain classifier $f^s(\mathbf{x})$ with no adaptation and

$\alpha = 1.0$ to perform domain adaptation on the entire adaptation data $\mathcal{D}_l^t$. For any number in between, the total amount of both positive and negative adaptation samples is reduced to a fraction of α. In particular, small fractions of α are interesting for adaptation because such a situation reflects real application scenarios where only few samples from the target domain are available and adaptation of robust source classifier is highly desired. Similar to the previous experiments, 5 runs are executed for each of the methods described below:

- **Target-SVM**: the control run setup from the fist experiment, performed on different α values. For this control run, $\alpha = 1.0$ is equivalent to target domain classifier training, whereas $\alpha = 0.0$ is equivalent to random guessing.
- **Target-PAMIR**: same as **Target-SVM** but for the PAMIR model.
- **Aggregation-SVM**: a simple data aggregation i.e. training a classifier on both the source domain and the target domain (i.e., $\mathcal{D}^s \cup \mathcal{D}_l^t$).
- **Aggregation-PAMIR**: same as **Aggregation-SVM** but for the PAMIR model.
- **Adapt-SVM**: an SVM based domain adaptation approach by Yang [85]. An RBF kernel was used and an optimal C was evaluated using cross validation (The author would like to thank Jun Yang for his help and tips regarding Adaptive-SVMs).
- **Adapt-PAMIR**: the domain adaptation extension based on PAMIR with $c = 0.001$ and $i = 10^6$ iterations for source classifier training, whereas the number of iterations for adaptation was determined by the proposed stopping rule.

Results Results are given in Fig. (**5**) and Tab. (**4**) for `tv7`, where concept detection accuracy on the target domain $\mathcal{D}_u^t$ is plotted against α. For *Adapt-PAMIR*, two stopping rules are tested, namely the *oracle* runs and the *fix* runs as defined in the previous section. As adaptation performance depends on the adapted concept, detailed results on concept level are also given for a full adaptation ($\alpha = 1.0$) in Tab. (**5**).

A first observation for `tv7` is that the SVM classifier (*Target-SVM* run) performs uniformly better when trained on the target domain than the linear but more efficient PAMIR classifier (*Target-PAMIR*). This already has been observed in [47]. The next observation is that data aggregation (*Aggregation-SVM* and *Aggregation-PAMIR* runs) does not truly overcome the domain change problem. Finally, when considering domain adaptation, the *Adapt-PAMIR* run outperforms the *Target-PAMIR* run, where a stable performance increase of 2.8% (a relative gain of 20%)

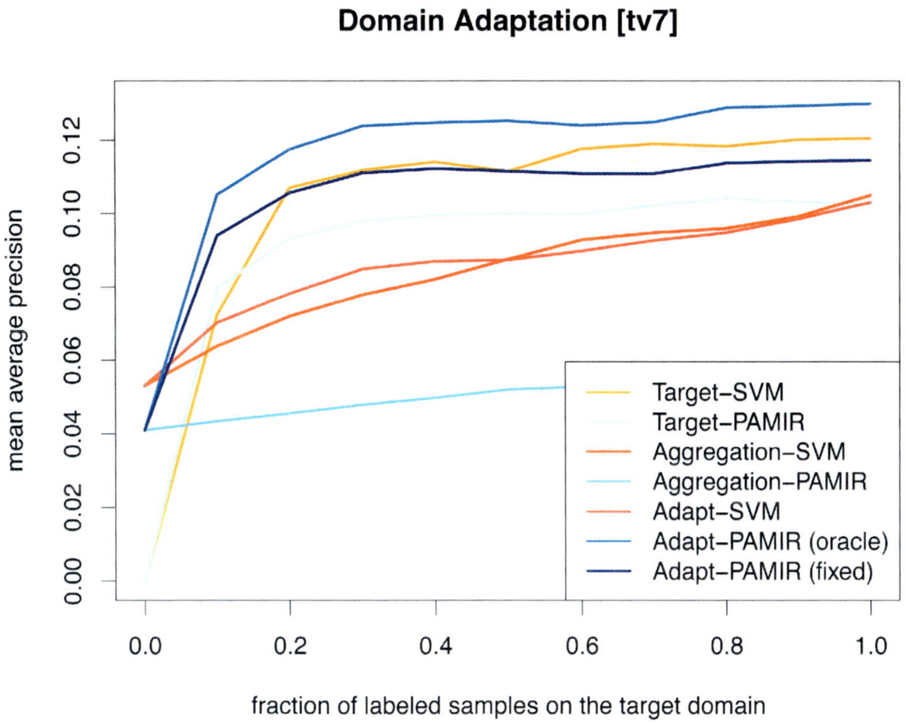

Fig. (5): Results of domain adaptation. Performance is plotted against the size α of the adaptation dataset, where *Adapt-PAMIR* (oracle) outperforms all other methods.

Tab. (4): Results in MAP of domain adaptation runs ($n = 34,000$) on `tv7` averaged over all concepts for all values of α.

Fraction α	**0.0**	**0.1**	**0.2**	**0.3**	**0.4**	**0.5**	**0.6**	**0.7**	**0.8**	**0.9**	**1.0**
Target-SVM	0.005	0.072	0.107	0.112	0.114	0.112	0.118	0.119	0.119	0.120	0.121
Target-PAMIR	0.005	0.080	0.093	0.098	0.099	0.100	0.100	0.102	0.104	0.103	0.102
Aggr-SVM	**0.053**	0.064	0.072	0.078	0.082	0.088	0.093	0.095	0.096	0.099	0.105
Aggr-PAMIR	0.041	0.044	0.046	0.048	0.050	0.052	0.053	0.054	0.056	0.057	0.056
Adapt-SVM	**0.053**	0.070	0.078	0.085	0.087	0.087	0.090	0.093	0.095	0.099	0.103
Adapt-PAMIR**	0.041	**0.105**	**0.118**	**0.124**	**0.125**	**0.125**	**0.124**	**0.125**	**0.129**	**0.129**	**0.130**
Adapt-PAMIR$^+$	0.041	0.094	0.106	0.111	0.112	0.112	0.111	0.111	0.114	0.114	0.115

**oracle*, $^+$*fixed*

Tab. (5): Results (AvgP) of domain adaptation runs per concept for $\alpha = 1.0$. Note, *Source-SVM* and *Source-PAMIR* are placeholders for pure source domain runs i.e. Target-SVM and Target-PAMIR with $\alpha = 0.0$

Concept	**Source-SVM**	**Source-PAMIR**	**Target-SVM**	**Target-PAMIR**	**Adapt-SVM**	**Adapt-PAMIR-fix**	**Adapt-PAMIR-oracle**
classroom	0.005	0.007	0.016	0.013	0.013	0.018	**0.026**
chair	0.008	0.007	0.010	0.011	0.008	0.012	**0.012**
infant	0.031	0.037	0.053	0.009	0.023	0.046	**0.102**
traffic intersection	0.021	0.014	**0.447**	0.327	0.348	0.372	0.372
doorway	0.003	0.004	**0.030**	0.016	0.010	0.018	0.025
airplane flying	0.05	0.035	0.042	0.113	0.093	0.175	**0.176**
person playing a musical instrument	**0.052**	0.032	0.022	0.037	0.036	0.031	0.041
bus	0.028	0.012	**0.036**	0.014	0.008	0.021	0.030
person playing soccer	**0.387**	0.261	0.211	0.071	0.341	0.114	0.272
cityscape	0.089	0.079	**0.237**	0.212	0.187	0.213	0.213
person riding a bicycle	0.009	0.014	0.253	**0.313**	0.128	0.297	0.297
telephone	0.002	0.002	0.016	**0.018**	0.005	0.011	0.011
person eating	0.004	0.004	**0.445**	0.425	0.377	0.415	0.415
demo. or protest	**0.110**	0.083	0.053	0.012	0.109	0.060	0.089
hand	0.063	0.047	0.144	**0.146**	0.085	0.143	0.144
people dancing	0.006	0.006	0.008	0.007	0.011	0.008	**0.014**
nighttime	0.077	0.089	0.145	0.140	0.097	**0.149**	**0.149**
boat ship	0.061	0.048	**0.188**	0.127	0.086	0.125	0.126
female human face closeup	0.041	0.023	0.029	0.016	**0.055**	0.039	0.042
singing	0.017	0.019	0.029	0.024	0.031	0.028	**0.047**
MAP	0.053	0.041	0.121	0.103	0.103	0.115	**0.130**

could be measured for all values of α. Comparing no adaptation and full adaptation, the *Adapt-PAMIR* run shows an improvement from 4.1% to 13.0% (oracle run), which corresponds to a relative gain of 225%. The more surprising result is, however, that the *Adapt-PAMIR* run outperforms the *Target-SVM* run by 3.2% when starting adaptation ($\alpha = 0.1$) and by 1.0% when finishing adaptation. Concluding, the kickstart setup where a web-based classifier is used for adaptation is demonstrated to perform better than training only on the target domain, even if

Fig. (6): Top ranked frames of source domain classifier (top) vs. adapted classifier (bottom). For some concepts the visual appearance changes successfully during adaptation. For other concepts, the classifier adapts to redundant material in the dataset (person eating).

using a stronger classifier e.g. an SVM.

A visualization of the adaptation performance by *Adapt-PAMIR* for $\alpha = 1.0$ can be seen in Fig. **(6)**. The image mosaics illustrate top ranked keyframes provided by the source classifier (top row) and top ranked keyframes provided by the adapted classifier (bottom row). As seen, domain adaptation leads to an improved classifier for the concepts "cityscape", "airplane flying" whereas for the concept "person eating" domain adaptation results in an adaptation to the redundant material in the dataset which is not desired but indeed provides better classification performance.

Evaluating the proposed early stopping rules for domain adaptation (*Adapt-PAMIR*), the following results were obtained. In general, a successful early stopping is important because it prevents negative transfer as observed in the domain impact experiment for the concepts "demonstration or protest", "female human face closeup", "person playing a musical instrument" and "person playing soccer". In Fig. **(7)** a visualization of MAP development over all target concepts is plotted against the number of iterations i. Here, the first $i = 10^6$ iterations train the source classifier and the next $i = 10^6$ iterations are dedicated to domain adaptation on the full adaptation data ($\alpha = 1.0$). Particularly, right after beginning adaptation a strong improvement can be observed for several concepts, whereas for some concepts adaptation leads to the known performance loss. A good stopping rule should identify such negative transfer and stop adaptation for such concepts. Results of the proposed stopping rules can be seen in the table of Fig. **(7)**.

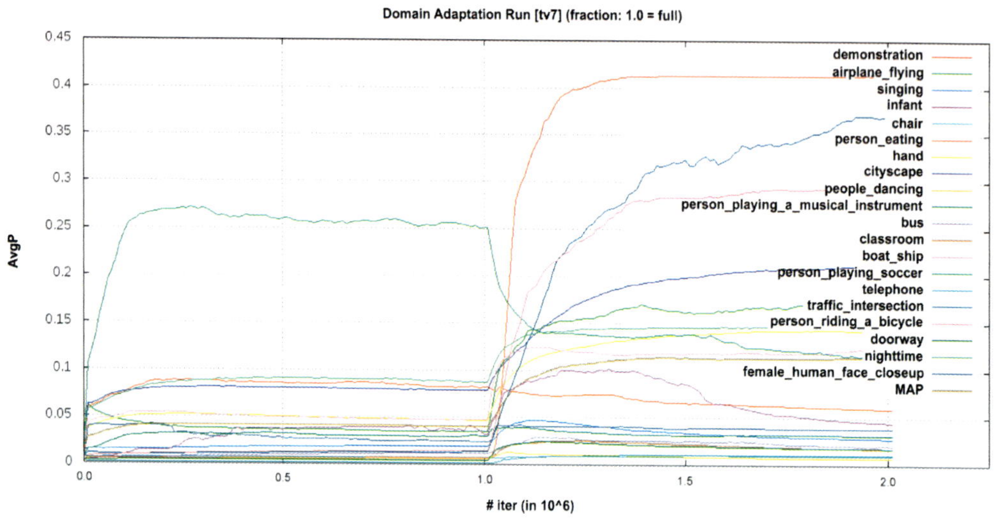

Performance (MAP)							
oracle	13.01	*sample*	12.45	*predict*	11.33	*fixed*	11.47

Fig. (7): Results of domain adaptation as performed by *Adapt-PAMIR* for a $\alpha = 1.0$. AvgP is plotted against the number of iterations. While for a majority of concepts performance increases during adaptation, for some a performance loss can be observed. To prevent this, different early stopping rules have been proposed leading to the MAP values illustrated in the table below.

Label noise problem vs. domain change problem

In the previous experiments, classifier trained on web video as source domain were adapted to a specific target domain. In the next experiment, the effect of label noise present in web video datasets is investigated. The question to be answered is if label noise has a stronger influence on system performance than domain change.

Setup The experiments were performed with systems comparable to the *Adapt-PAMIR* run i.e. the same setup and adaptation fractions α were used. But now source classifier are trained separately on two different training datasets: `yt-direct`, a noisy web video dataset, and `yt-refined`, a manually refined dataset. Both source domain classifiers are now adapted to the target domain with appropriate sizes of α and detector performance is measured. This experiments is evaluated on the subset of 12 concept from the `yt-refined` dataset.

Results Results are illustrated in Fig. (8). It can be observed that the source classifier trained on `yt-refined` starts with an 1.7% higher MAP as compared to the

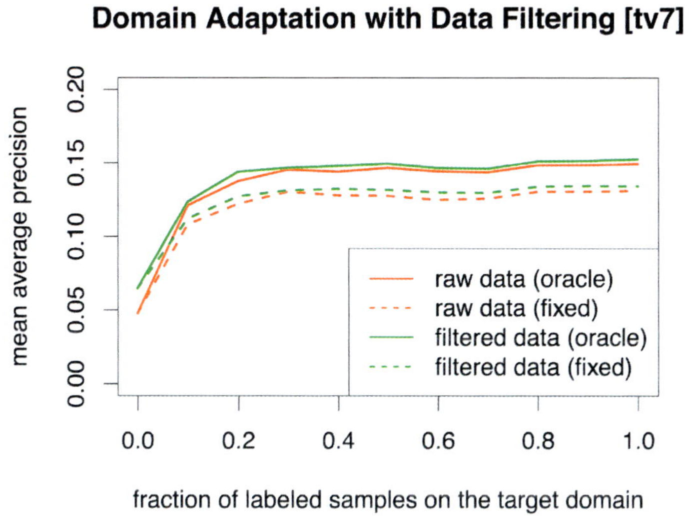

Fig. (8): Comparing domain adaptation performance of systems initially trained on noisy web video (red) and on refined web video (green). Noisy training material has initially a negative influence on system performance, which, however, is negligible after domain adaptation.

`yt-direct` trained source classifier (a relative loss of 30%) showing that label noise is a significant problem for web-based concept detectors. However, when performing adaptation the advantage of having *clean* source domain data is neglectable leading to the conclusion that label noise becomes irrelevant when performing adaptation.

Domain adaptation extended by active learning

Finally, the extension of domain adaptation with active learning is evaluated. One major benefit of the proposed domain adaptation method is its efficiency. For one concept, adaptation (about 50,000 samples from `yt-direct` and about 34,000 samples from `tv7.devel`) with the method takes on average 76 sec. for training and 64 sec. for adaptation (SVM: 16540 sec. for training on `tv7.devel`) whereas testing (about 34,000 samples from `tv7.test`) takes on average less than 1 sec. (SVM: 3509 sec.). Being able to retrain classifiers this efficient allows to incorporate user feedback within the adaptation process as proposed in the previous section.

Setup A source classifier is trained on `yt-direct` and adapted by simultaneously acquiring labels from the target domain `tv7-devel`. Due to efficiency, 1,000 samples out of the available 34,000 from the target domain are annotated. For each active learning cycle 20 samples are selected for human annotation. The hyper-parameter

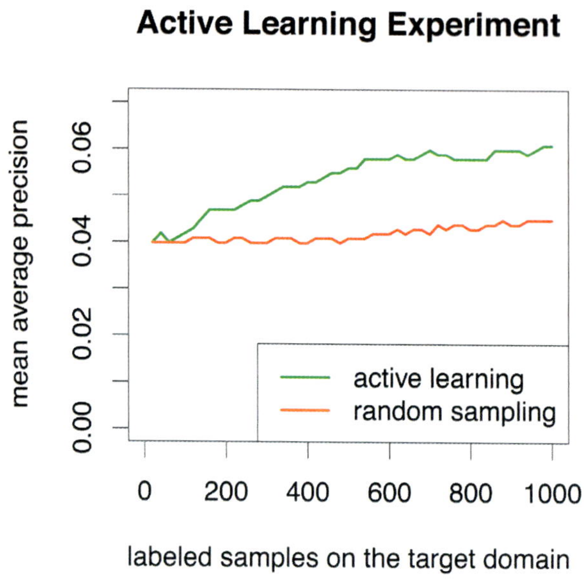

Fig. (9): Results on the active learning extension to domain adaptation. As illustrated, active learning with most relevant sampling outperforms random sampling as a baseline, demonstrating its potential for domain adaptation when only very few samples are available from the target domain.

of *Adapt-PAMIR* is set to the same value $c = 0.001$ as before and the source classifier was trained as previously with $i = 10^6$ iterations. Note that annotating only $1,000$ samples is both realistic and very challenging as the number of positive samples in the given target domains is very sparse.

Results Results of the active learning vs. random sampling are illustrated in Fig. (**9**). Performance is plotted against the number of annotated samples. When starting adaptation the performance is equal to the source domain classifier trained on `yt-direct`. With increasing amounts of samples being annotated, domain adaptation improves system performance. Thereby active learning outperforms a random selection of manually annotated samples, which can be explained by the fact that this approach better finds positive labels for a concept to be learned.

In such a situation, a robust source domain classifier provides valuable samples for domain adaptation leading to significant improvements of the detector. For example, with only $1,000$ samples and *most relevant* sampling an MAP of 6.1% can be reached compared to initial source classifier performance of 4.1%. When considering per concept results we can see that classification improvements are very concept dependent e.g. for "airplane flying" a similar MAP is reached by only labeling 1,000 *most relevant* selected samples instead of 12,000 *randomly selected* samples. However, concepts with a high redundancy (e.g. "person eating") gain more from a source classifier independent selection (*random sampling*) than from active learning (*most relevant selection*).

5 Conclusions

In this chapter the domain change problem was addressed in the context of using web video as source domain for visual concept detector training. Classifiers, trained on web video as an alternative, freely available source for concept learning experience a significant performance degradation when being applied on specific target domains. This impact can cause a loss by up to 60% showing that the domain change problem influences detection accuracy more than label noise.

To overcome this problem, an efficient framework for domain adaptation was proposed. In contrast of the previous work on cross-domain learning, adaptation is conducted in an online learning fashion. The framework trains source classifiers based on web video and adapts them to defined target domain in utilizing a small fraction of labeled data from the target domain. In quantitative experiments, it was demonstrated that domain adaptation can be performed successfully and improves system performance from 4.1% to 13.0% (a gain of 225%) being also able to outperform SVMs trained on the target domain. Facing the situation where no adaptation dataset is available, an extension of the proposed method was introduced, which employs active learning strategies to support domain adaptation in providing target domain samples. This way, with the help of a proper sample selection method, domain adaptation can also be performed on very few samples from the target domain.

As shown in the experiments, domain adaptation depends strongly on robust source classifier which is related to the acquisition of qualitative training material from the source domain. In the context of web video, future work might focus on retrieving video material from online video portals which is visually similar to the target domain to further improve domain adaptation.

Acknowledgments This work was supported by the German Research Foundation (DFG), project MOONVID (BR 2517/1-1).

Appendix: YouTube Query Definition

This section provides query information used to retrieve training videos from YouTube (http://code.google.com/apis/youtube/). Query formulations as well as the additional category identifier are listed for every concept in Tab. (**6**).

Tab. (6): Query definitions for YouTube video downloads regarding the 20 concepts used in the experiments.

TRECVID number	**Concept name**	**YouTube query***	**YouTube category***
001	classroom	classroom school -secret	-
002	chair	office chair -wheel -trailer, bürostuhl	howto&style
003	infant	infant baby, kleine babys	people&blog
004	traffic intersection	traffic intersection, strassen kreuzung	autos&vehicles
005	doorway	doorway doors and gates, türen öffnen	entertainment
006	airplane flying	airplane flying -jefferson -indoor -school -kids	autos&vehicles
007	person playing a musical instrument	playing instrument, learn to play instrument	music
008	bus	bus -van -suv -vw -ride	autos&vehicles
009	person playing soccer	people playing soccer, fussball spielen	sports
010	cityscape	cityscape -slideshow -emakina	travel&places
011	person riding a bicycle	riding bicycle, fahrrad fahren	sports
012	telephone	phone device	-
013	person eating	food eating contest, essen und kochen	entertainment
014	demo. or protest	protesting	-
015	hand	hand draft	-
016	people dancing	people dancing, learn to dance	people&blogs, sports
017	nighttime	by night	travel&places
018	boat ship	ship queen, ship freedom, ship royal	autos&vehicles
019	female human face closeup	female videoblog girl makeup	people&blog howto&style
020	singing	singing gospel, singing choir	-

* *Values used for YouTube API calls*

6 References

[1] R. Aly and D. Hiemstra. Concept Detectors: How good is good enough? In *ACM Multimedia*, 2009.

[2] J. Ashley, M. Flickner, J. Hafner, D. Lee, W. Niblack, and D. Petkovic. The

Query by Image Content (QBIC) System. *SIGMOD Rec.*, 1995.

[3] S. Ayache and G. Quenot. Evaluation of active learning strategies for video indexing. *Signal Processing: Image Communication*, 2007.

[4] S. Ayache and G. Quenot. Video Corpus Annotation using Active Learning. In *ECIR*, 2008.

[5] S. Ben-David, J. Blitzer, K. Crammer, and F. Pereira. Analysis of Representations for Domain Adaptation. *NIPS*, 2007.

[6] J. Blitzer, R. McDonald, and F. Pereira. Domain Adaptation with Structural Correspondence Learning. In *EMNLP*, 2006.

[7] D. Borth, C. Schulze, A. Ulges, and T. Breuel. Navidgator - Similarity Based Browsing for Image & Video Databases. In *Proc. KI*, 2008.

[8] D. Borth, A. Ulges, and T. Breuel. Relevance Filtering meets Active Learning: Improving Web-based Concept Detectors. In *ACM MIR*, 2010.

[9] BroadCasting Ourselves - The Official YouTube Blog. Oops Pow Surprise... 24 Hours of Video all up in Your Eyes! available from `http://youtube-global.blogspot.com/2010/03/oops-pow-surprise24-hours-of-video-all.html` (retrieved: March 2010), 2010.

[10] G. Cauwenberghs and T. Poggio. Incremental and Decremental Support Vector Machine Learning. In *NIPS*, 2001.

[11] C.-C. Chang and C.-J. Lin. *LIBSVM: A Library for Support Vector Machines*, 2001. Software available at `http://www.csie.ntu.edu.tw/~cjlin/libsvm`.

[12] E.Y. Chang, S. Tong, KS Goh, and C.W. Chang. Support Vector Machine Concept-Dependent Active Learning for Image Retrieval. *IEEE Transactions on Multimedia*, 2005.

[13] S.-F. Chang, J. He, Y.-G. Jiang, E. El Khoury, C.-W. Ngo, A. Yanagawa, and E. Zavesky. Columbia University/Video-CityU/IRIT TRECVID2008 High-Level Feature Extraction and Interactive Video Search. In *Proc. TRECVID Workshop (unreviewed workshop paper)*, 2008.

[14] M. Chen, M. Christel, A. Hauptmann, and H. Wactlar. Putting Active Learning into Multimedia Applications: Dynamic Definition and Refinement of Concept Classifiers. In *ACM Multimedia*, 2005.

[15] S. Choudhury, J. G. Breslin, and A. Passant. Enrichment and Ranking of the YouTube Tag Space and Integration with the Linked Data Cloud. In *Int. Semantic Web Conference*, 2009.

[16] H. Daumé. Frustratingly Easy Domain Adaptation. In *Annual Meeting: Association for Computational Linguistics*, 2007.

[17] O. de Rooij, C.G.M. Snoek, and M. Worring. MediaMill: Fast and Effective Video Search using the Forkbrowser. In *CIVR*, 2008.

[18] S.J. Delany, P. Cunningham, A. Tsymbal, and L. Coyle. A Case-based Technique for Tracking Concept Drift in Spam Filtering. *Knowledge-Based Systems*, 2005.

[19] T. Deselaers, D. Keysers, and H. Ney. Features for Image Retrieval: An Experimental Comparison. *Information Retrieval*, 2008.

[20] L. Duan, I.W. Tsang, D. Xu, and T.S. Chua. Domain Adaptation from Multiple Sources via Auxiliary Classifiers. In *ICML*, 2009.

[21] L. Duan, I.W. Tsang, D. Xu, and S.J. Maybank. Domain Transfer SVM for Video Concept Detection. In *ICPR*, 2009.

[22] U. Gargi and J. Yagnik. Solving the Label Resolution Problem in Supervised Video Content Classification. In *Proc. Int. Conf. on Multimedia Retrieval*, 2008.

[23] S.A. Golder and B.A. Huberman. Usage Patterns of Collaborative Tagging Systems. *Journal of Information Science*, 2006.

[24] D. Grangier and S. Bengio. A Discriminative Kernel-based Model to Rank Images from Text Queries. *IEEE Transactions on Pattern Analysis and Machine Intelligence*, 2008.

[25] A. Hauptmann, R. Yan, and W. Lin. How many High-Level Concepts will Fill the Semantic Gap in News Video Retrieval? In *Proc. Int. Conf. Image and Video Retrieval*, 2007.

[26] A.G. Hauptmann, W.H. Lin, R. Yan, J. Yang, and M.Y. Chen. Extreme Video Retrieval: Joint Maximization of Human and Computer Performance. In *ACM Multimedia*, 2006.

[27] J. Huang, A.J. Smola, A. Gretton, K.M. Borgwardt, and B. Scholkopf. Correcting Sample Selection Bias by Unlabeled Data. In *NIPS*, 2007.

[28] Cisco Systems Inc. Cisco Visual Networking Index: Forecast and Methodology, 2008-2013. available from `http://www.cisco.com` (retrieved: June'09), 2009.

[29] J. Jiang. A Literature Survey on Domain Adaptation of Statistical Classifiers. 2007.

[30] W. Jiang, E. Zavesky, S.-F. Chang, and A. Loui. Cross-domain Learning Methods for High-level Visual Concept Classification. In *ICIP*, 2008.

[31] Y.G. Jiang, C.W. Ngo, and S.F. Chang. Semantic Context Transfer across Heterogeneous Sources for Domain Adaptive Video Search. In *ACM Multimedia*, 2009.

[32] Y.G. Jiang, J. Wang, S.F. Chang, and C.W. Ngo. Domain Adaptive Semantic Diffusion for Large Scale Context-based Video Annotation. In *ICCV*, 2009.

[33] J. Kivinen, A.J. Smola, and R.C. Williamson. Online Learning with Kernels. *IEEE Transactions on Signal Processing*, 2004.

[34] R. Klinkenberg and T. Joachims. Detecting Concept Drift with Support Vector Machines. In *ICML*, 2000.

[35] J.Z. Kolter and M.A. Maloof. Dynamic Weighted Majority: An Ensemble Method for Drifting Concepts. *The Journal of Machine Learning Research*, 2007.

[36] Georgia Koutrika, Frans Adjie Effendi, Zolt´n Gyöngyi, Paul Heymann, and Hector Garcia-Molina. Combating spam in tagging systems: An evaluation. *ACM Transactions on Web*, 2008.

[37] D. Lewis and W. Gale. A Sequential Algorithm for Training Text Classifiers. In *Proc. Int. Conf. Research and Development in Information Retrieval*, 1994.

[38] X. Li, C. Snoek, and M. Worring. (Un)Tagged Social Image Retrieval. In *Internet Multimedia Search and Mining*. Bentham Science Publishers, 2010.

[39] D. Lowe. Distinctive Image Features from Scale-Invariant Keypoints. *International Journal of Computer Vision*, 2004.

[40] M. Naphade, J. Smith, J. Tesic, S. Chang, W. Hsu, L. Kennedy, A. Hauptmann, and J. Curtis. Large-Scale Concept Ontology for Multimedia. *IEEE MultiMedia*, 2006.

[41] C.-W. Ngo, Y.-G. Jiang, X.-Y. Wei, W. Liu, S. Zhu, and S.-F. Chang. VIREO/DVMM at TRECVID 2009: High-Level Feature Extraction, Automatic Video Search, and Conctent-based Copy Detection. In *Proc. TRECVID Workshop*, 2009.

[42] H.T. Nguyen and A. Smeulders. Active learning using Pre-Clustering. In *ICML*, 2004.

[43] Online Inauguration Videos set Records. available from `http://edition.cnn.com/2009/TECH/01/21/inauguration.online.video/` (retrieved: Jan'10), 2009.

[44] P. Over, G. Awad, W. Kraaij, and A. Smeaton. TRECVID 2007 - An Overview. In *Proc. TRECVID Workshop (unreviewed workshop paper)*, 2007.

[45] P. Over, G. Awad, T. Rose, J. Fiscus, W. Kraaij, and A. Smeaton. TRECVID 2009–Goals, Tasks, Data, Evaluation Mechanisms and Metrics. In *Proc. TRECVID Workshop*, 2009.

[46] S.J. Pan, J.T. Kwok, and Q. Yang. Transfer Learning via Dimensionality Reduction. In *Proceedings of the AAAI Conf. on Artificial Intelligence*, 2008.

[47] R. Paredes, A. Ulges, and T. Breuel. Fast Discriminative Linear Models for Scalable Video Tagging. In *Proc. Int. Conf. on Machine Learning and Applications*, 2009.

[48] G. Qi, Y. Song, X.S. Hua, H.J. Zhang, and L.R. Dai. Video Annotation by Active Learning and Cluster Tuning. In *Computer Vision and Pattern Recognition Workshop*, 2006.

[49] G. Qi and H. Zhang. Large-Scale Online Multimedia Annotation. In *Internet Multimedia Search and Mining*. Bentham Science Publishers, 2010.

[50] G.J. Qi, X.S. Hua, Y. Rui, J. Tang, T. Mei, and H.J. Zhang. Correlative Multi-Label Video Annotation. In *ACM Multimedia*, 2007.

[51] R. Raina, A. Battle, H. Lee, B. Packer, and A.Y. Ng. Self-taught Learning: Transfer Learning from Unlabeled Data. In *ICML*, 2007.

[52] M.T. Rosenstein, Z. Marx, L.P. Kaelbling, and T.G. Dietterich. To Transfer or not to Transfer. In *Proceedings of NIPS 2005 Workshop on Inductive Transfer: 10 Years Later*, 2005.

[53] G. Salton and C. Buckley. Improving Retrieval Performance by Relevance Feedback. *Journal of the American Society for Information Science*, 1990.

[54] G. Schohn and D. Cohn. Less is More: Active Learning with Support Vector Machines. In *ICML*, 2000.

[55] B. Schölkopf and A. Smola. *Learning with Kernels: Support Vector Machines, Regularization, Optimization, and Beyond.* MIT Press, Cambridge, MA, USA, 2001.

[56] B. Settles. Active Learning Literature Survey. Computer Sciences Technical Report 1648, University of Wisconsin–Madison, 2009.

[57] A. Setz and C. Snoek. Can Social Tagged Images Aid Concept-Based Video Search? In *ICME*, 2009.

[58] HS Seung, M. Opper, and H. Sompolinsky. Query by committee. In *Proc. of the fifth annual workshop on Computational learning theory*, 1992.

[59] J. Sivic and A. Zisserman. Video Google: A Text Retrieval Approach to Object Matching in Videos. In *ICCV*, 2003.

[60] A. Smeaton. Large Scale Evaluations of Multimedia Information Retrieval: The TRECVid Experience. In *CIVR*, 2005.

[61] A. Smeaton, P. Over, and W. Kraaij. High-Level Feature Detection from Video in TRECVid: a 5-Year Retrospective of Achievements. In *Multimedia Content Analysis, Theory and Applications*, 2009.

[62] A. Smeaton, P. Wilkins, M. Worring, and O. de Rooij. Content-Based Video Retrieval: Three Example Systems from TRECVid. *International Journal of Imaging Science and Technology*, 2008.

[63] A. Smeulders, M. Worring, S. Santini, and A. Gupta R. Jain. Content-Based Image Retrieval at the End of the Early Years. *IEEE Transactions on Pattern Analysis and Machine Intelligence*, 2000.

[64] C. Snoek and et al. The MediaMill TRECVID 2009 Semantic Video Search Engine. In *Proc. TRECVID Workshop (unreviewed workshop paper)*, 2009.

[65] C. Snoek and M. Worring. Concept-based Video Retrieval. *Foundations and Trends in Information Retrieval*, 2009.

[66] C. Snoek, M. Worring, J. van Gemert, J. Geusebroek, and A. Smeulders. The Challenge Problem for Automated Detection of 101 Semantic Concepts in Multimedia. In *ACM Multimedia*, 2006.

[67] Y. Song, X.S. Hua, L.R. Dai, and M. Wang. Semi-automatic Video Annotation based on Active Learning with Multiple Complementary Predictors. In *Proceedings of the Int. Workshop on Multimedia Information Retrieval*, 2005.

[68] M. Sugiyama, M. Krauledat, and K.R. Muller. Covariate Shift Adaptation by Importance Weighted Cross Validation. *The Journal of Machine Learning Research*, 2007.

[69] S. Tong and E. Chang. Support Vector Machine Active Learning for Image Retrieval. In *ACM Multimedia*, 2001.

[70] S. Tong and D. Koller. Support Vector Machine Active Learning with Applications to Text Classification. *The Journal of Machine Learning Research*, 2002.

[71] A. Ulges, D. Borth, and T. Breuel. Visual Concept Learning from Weakly Labeled Web Videos. In *Video Search and Mining*. Springer-Verlag, 2010.

[72] A. Ulges, M. Koch, D. Borth, and T. Breuel. Tubetagger - youtube-based concept detection. In *Proc. Int. Workshop on Internet Multimedia Mining*, 2009.

[73] A. Ulges, C. Schulze, D. Keysers, and T. Breuel. Identifying Relevant Frames in Weakly Labeled Videos for Training Concept Detectors. In *CIVR*, 2008.

[74] A. Ulges, C. Schulze, M. Koch, and T. Breuel. The Challenge of Tagging Online Video. *Compuper Vision and Image Understanding*, 2009.

[75] K. van de Sande, T. Gevers, and C. Snoek. A Comparison of Color Features for Visual Concept Classification. In *CIVR*, 2008.

[76] K.E.A. Van De Sande, T. Gevers, and C.G.M. Snoek. Evaluation of Color Descriptors for Object and Scene Recognition. In *CVPR*, 2008.

[77] H. Wang, W. Fan, P.S. Yu, and J. Han. Mining Concept-Drifting Data Streams using Ensemble Classifiers. In *Proceedings of Int. Conf. on Knowledge Discovery and Data Mining*, 2003.

[78] M. Wang, X.-S. Hua, Y. Song, X. Yuan, S. Li, and H.-J. Zhang. Automatic Video Annotation by Semi-supervised Learning with Kernel Density Estimation. In *ACM Multimedia*, 2006.

[79] P. Wilkins and A. Smeaton. Weighted Data Fusion for Content-Based Multimedia Information Retrieval. In *Internet Multimedia Search and Mining*. Bentham Science Publishers, 2010.

[80] P. Wu and T.G. Dietterich. Improving SVM Accuracy by Training on Auxiliary Data Sources. In *ICML*, 2004.

[81] X. Wu and R. Srihari. Incorporating Prior Knowledge with Weighted Margin Support Vector Machines. In *Proceedings of Int. Conf. on Knowledge Discovery and Data Mining*, 2004.

[82] A. Yanagawa, S.-F. Chang, L. Kennedy, and W. Hsu. Columbia University's Baseline Detectors for 374 LSCOM Semantic Visual Concepts. Technical report, Columbia University, 2007.

[83] J. Yang and A. Hauptmann. (Un)Reliability of Video Concept Detection. In *Proc. Int. Conf. Image and Video Retrieval*, 2008.

[84] J. Yang and A.G. Hauptmann. A Framework for Classifier Adaptation and its Applications in Concept Detection. In *ACM MIR*, 2008.

[85] J. Yang, R. Yan, and A. Hauptmann. Cross-Domain Video Concept Detection using Adaptive SVMs. In *ACM Multimedia*, 2007.

[86] J. Yang, R. Yan, and A. Hauptmann. Learning to Adapt Across Multimedia Domains. In *ACM Multimedia*, 2007.

Internet Multimedia Search and Mining, **2013, 168-203**

CHAPTER 7

Social Tag Processing for Internet Images

Dong Liu*
Department of Electrical Engineering, Columbia University, Tel: 1-917-566-3084, Fax: 212-854-3105, Email: dongliu@ee.columbia.edu
Xian-Sheng Hua
Microsoft Research, Email: xshua@microsoft.com
Hong-Jiang Zhang
Microsoft Advanced Technology Center, Email: hjzhang@microsoft.com

Abstract: Online social image websites such as Flickr and Zooomr allow users to manually annotate their uploaded images with freely-chosen tags, which are then used as indexing keywords to facilitate image search and other applications. However, although the tags are provided by the users, they are generally imprecise and incomplete, and many of them are intrinsically unrelated to the visual content. Besides, the tags associated with social images are generally uniform without any importance or relevance information with respect to the content. The imprecise, incomplete and uniform characteristics of the tags have significantly limited tag-based applications, such as social image search and browsing. In this chapter, we discuss the tag processing techniques for improving the quality of the manually input tags for the social images on the Internet, which includes tag filtering, completing and ranking. We will also show various applications benefiting from the processed tags.

Keywords

social images, tag filtering, tag ranking, tag refinement, tag completion, tag enrichment, visual similarity, semantic similarity, ontology, graph, optimization

Xian-Sheng Hua, Marcel Worring & Tat-Seng Chua (Eds.)

1 Introduction

The prevalence of digital cameras and the growing practice of photo sharing in community-contributed image websites like Flickr [6] and Zooomr [2] have led to a flourish of social images on the Web. Besides plain visual information, such large-scale images are augmented with user-provided tags, which greatly benefit a wide variety of applications such as image search, organization and management.

Despite the high popularity of manually tagging social images, the quality of the tags associated with images is still far from satisfactory. Currently, the image tagging on the image sharing websites solely relies on the manual inputs, which is an extra burden for grassroots Internet users and often prohibits accurate and comprehensive textual descriptions of the visual content. A recent study reported in [5, 13] reveals that the user-provided tags are rather imprecise, with only about 50% precision rate. On the other hand, the average number of tags for each social image is relatively small [3], which is far from the number that can fully describe the content of an image. Finally, as investigated in [17], the relevance levels of the tags associate with a social image cannot be distinguished from the current tag list, where the rank order of each tag is just based on the manual input and thus carries little information about the importance or relevance information, which further limits the effectiveness of tags in search and other applications.

Fig. (1): An example image from Flickr and its associated tags. The tags marked in red color truly describe the content of the image and the other tags are content-unrelated or irrelevant. On the other hand, the most relevant tag "kitty" does not locate at the top position in the tag list.

As an example, Fig. **(2)** illustrates an image from Flickr and its associated tags. From the figure we can observe that only "kitty" and "animal" truly describe the visual content of the image, and the other tags are imprecise or subjective. Meanwhile, some other tags that should be used to describe the visual content are missed, such as "grass" and "flower". Moreover, if we further consider the lexical variation and the hierarchy of semantic concepts, the tags such as "kitten", "pussy" and "feline" also need to be included. Finally, we can also observe that "kitty" is the most relevant tag with respect to the image, but this cannot be discovered from the tag list directly.

Without reliable tags, social images on the Web cannot be well indexed by the search engine, and consequently cannot be well accessed by the users. Therefore, effective methods to process these unreliable tags have become emerging needs. In this chapter, we will discuss some research advances along this direction and present effective solutions on the following three issues.

1. Tag Filtering. Many tags provided by users are intrinsically unrelated to the visual content of the images and are almost only meaningful for the image owners(such as the name of a dog). Involving such tags in the content-based tag processing procedure will bring significant noises to algorithms. Therefore, we need to filter out these content unrelated tags to ensure that the content-related tags can be significantly enhanced and the detailed process will be discussed in section 2.

2. Tag Completion. We will introduce a solution to refine the tags so that they can better describe the visual content of social images. It is based on the consistency of visual and semantic similarities between images as well as the prior preference to the original tags provided by users. To further improve the coverage of the tags, a knowledge based method is also developed to enrich the tags with appropriate synonyms and hypernyms. We will introduce the tag completion scheme in section 3.

3. Tag Ranking. A ranking scheme that aims to differentiate the tags with various degrees of relevance levels will be introduced. The ranked tags will benefit visual search performance and in turn improve the relevance in the social media applications. Section 4 describes the tag ranking scheme.

2 Related Works

Ames *et al.* [3] explored the motivation of manual tagging on the Flickr website and claimed that most users tag images to make them better accessible to the general public. Yan *et al.* [28] proposed a model that can predict the time cost of manual image tagging. Sigurbjörnsson *et al.* [23] provided the insights on how users tag their photos and what type of tags they are providing. Kennedy *et al.* [13] evaluated the performance of the classifiers trained with Flickr images and their associated tags, and demonstrated that tags provided by Flickr users contain many noises. Weinberger proposed a method to analyze the ambiguity of tags [27]. Although these works have shown encouraging results, they focus on directly utilizing the tags as a knowledge source or simply analyzing the relation between images and their associated tags, whereas there is still a lack regarding improving the quality of tags.

The previous research on improving unreliable descriptive keywords of images has focused on annotation refinement, i.e., identifying and eliminating the imprecise annotation keywords produced by the automatic image annotation algorithms. As a pioneering work, Jin *et al.* [11] used WordNet [7] to estimate the semantic correlation among the annotated keywords and then those weakly-correlated ones are removed. However, this method can only achieve limited success since it totally ignores the visual content of the images. To address this problem, Wang *et al.* [26] proposed a content-based approach to re-rank the automatically annotated keywords of an image and only reserve the top ones as the refined results. Despite these efforts, existing methods typically focus on selecting a coherent subset of keywords from the automatically annotated keywords. This is reasonable since the underlying assumption for annotation refinement is that the generative likelihoods between visual content and annotation keywords have been maximized by the automatic annotation algorithms. On the other hand, the tags associated with social images are often imprecise and incomplete, and thus their descriptive capability to the visual content cannot be guaranteed. Therefore, the reranking-and-removing strategy in annotation refinement methods is not applicable in our scenario and we need to design new methods to accomplish the task.

3 Tag Filtering

The aim of tag processing is to improve the quality of the tags based on content analysis techniques. However, this is mainly applicable for "content related" tags (In this work, we regard whether or not a tag is content-related as its **intrinsic** property. For example, the tag "cool" in Fig. **(2)** is content-unrelated. In contrary, we call a tag irrelevant with respect to an image if it does not describe the image's visual content, such as the "dog" and "boy" in Fig. **(2)**. Thus, content-related tags can also be irrelevant.). That is, those tags that have high correspondence with the visual content. If we introduce "content unrelated" tags into the above optimization framework, we may even degrade the performance of the tag processing procedure. This is actually also one of the main difficulties in all automatic learning based image annotation approaches [9, 14], as well as one of the main reasons causing "semantic gaps" except for representative features and learning models. Accordingly, we propose a method to filter out those content unrelated tags to ensure that the quality of content related tags can be significantly improved.

To differentiate content-related tags from content-unrelated ones in a large tag set is not a trivial task. The most straightforward way is to check each word in an authoritative dictionary (such as Merriam-Webster dictionary) and ask humans

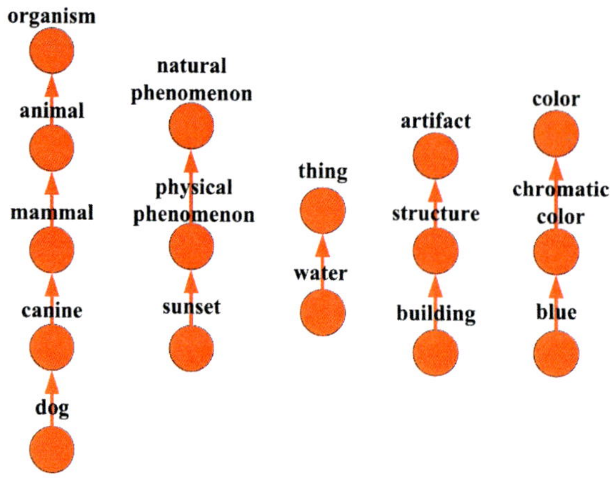

Fig. (2): The decision process of some exemplary tags. Each tag successfully matches one of our pre-defined visual categories and thus is decided as content-related.

to decide whether it is content-related or not based on their knowledge and understanding. However, it needs intensive labor costs. Another possible approach is to mine the relationship between tags and the content of images from large-scale data, such as the works in [19, 29]. However, a limitation of this approach is that it needs to be accomplished based on a set of low-level features. There is always a gap between these features and the actual image content. For example, the tags "red" and "green" are of course content-related, but these approaches may decide them as content-unrelated if SIFT feature is applied. In our work, we solve this difficulty by taking advantage of lexical and domain knowledge, which is analogous to the approach in [20].

First, from the part-of-speech of words, we only consider nouns. For example, many photos on Flickr are tagged with verb "delete", adjective "beautiful", adverb "heavily" or numerals such as "2", "131", and "1001". Actually it is hard to say the non-noun words are definitely not related to image content, since there also may be several visual patterns for these words. For example, "beautiful" may relate to flower, scene or woman with high probability. But these non-noun words are difficult to be analyzed or learned. Thus we restrict ourselves in the noun set of WordNet lexicon [7], which contains 114, 648 noun entries and the tags that are out of this set will be out of the scope of this work.

Then we further observed that noun tags are not always content-related. Some abstract nouns such as "science", "lifetime" and "distance", have weak connection with image content and thus also need to be filtered out. To this end, we adopt an automatic process to detect the visual property of the tags as follows.

1. We first empirically select a set of high level categories as a taxonomy of our domain knowledge in vision field. In this work, we choose "organism", "artifact", "thing", "color" and "natural phenomenon", since they cover most of the frequently used concepts in computer vision and multimedia domains.

2. For each entry in WordNet, there are one or more senses (a sense can be viewed as a meaning or explanation of the entry), in which WordNet provides a set of synonyms and hypernyms [25]. For each noun entry in WordNet lexicon, we traverse along the path that is composed of hypernyms of the given word until one of the pre-defined visual categories is matched. If the match succeeds, the word is decided as content-related, and otherwise it is decided as content-unrelated.

Fig. **(2)** illustrates the decision process of several exemplary tags. In this way, we obtain a content-related vocabulary that contains 57,623 noun entries. Tab. **(1)** illustrates the number of entries for each category.

Tab. (1): Number of entries for each visual category in our content-related vocabulary.

Visual Category	Number of entries	Percentage
Color	423	0.73%
Thing	4,484	7.78%
Artifact	14,087	24.45%
Organism	37,672	65.38%
Natural phenomenon	957	1.66%

It is worth noting that although our approach involves several heuristics, it can achieve fairly consistent results with humans (the detailed results will be demonstrated in Section 6). Our method is also with high flexibility. For example, the Wordnet lexical knowledge base can be easily replaced with other lexical base such as Wikipedia. Besides, we can easily further add categories to cover more entries. The vocabulary can also be manually refined by adding or removing entries. In addition, the number of content-related tags is still very large (57,623 entries) and we believe the description capability of this tag set is still high enough to describe most of the entities in general images.

Now we conduct a simple testing to evaluate the above tag filtering strategy. We randomly select 500 tags from the 11,861 noun tags and then ask human assessors to label each tag as "content-related" or "content-unrelated". We invite five researchers in multimedia research community to perform the labeling task based on their knowledge. The voting results are considered as the ground truths of these tags. We regard our method as a binary classification process, and employ accuracy measurement as evaluation metric. Tab. **(2)** illustrates the results, from which we can see that the accuracy measurement is as high as 0.83. Considering the simplicity and the computational efficiency of our method, the result is satisfactory (Recently Overell *et al.* [20] have conducted a study on classifying tags into 25 semantic categories. They have leveraged the knowledge sources of both Wikipedia and WordNet and used a SVM classifier. The study demonstrates that this approach significantly outperforms other methods, but the classification error rate is still as high as 0.38. This result indicates that tag classification is actually a challenging task.).

Tab. (2): Confusion matrix obtained by our content-related tag detection method. The evaluation is carried out on 500 tags randomly selected from our social image collection.

	Related	**Unrelated**
Related	132	58
Unrelated	27	283
Accuracy	0.83	

4 Tag Refinement

In this section, we introduce the tag refinement scheme that aims at improving the tag quality. The most straightforward approach to address this task is to ask humans to check the tags associated with each image, but obviously this way is infeasible considering the large number of images and tags. Therefore, an automatic method based on the available information, such as the content of images and their existing tags, is desired. The refining process, including denoising and enriching, is formulated as an optimization framework based on the following two observations in real-world social images. First, consistency between visual similarity and semantic similarity, that is, similar images often reflect similar semantic theme, and thus are annotated with similar tags. Second, user-provided tags, despite imperfect, still reveal the primary semantic theme of the image content. In our approach, the improved tag assignments are automatically learned by maximizing the consistency between visual similarity and semantic similarity while minimizing the deviation from initially user-provided tags. This is actually using information from different channels to complement each other in a collective way.

Though the above tag refinement approach is able to add some new tags to an image (for example, a tag of an image may be transferred into a similar image originally without this tag), it is not able to "invent" new tags for a particular image if the tags are not assigned to its similar images. Therefore, as a post-processing step, we propose to use an external knowledge base to further enrich the tags to a certain extend, that is, adding synonyms and hypernyms (In search, this issue can also be solved by "query expansion", that is, expanding query term with its synonyms and hyponyms. But enriching image tags will be useful for other tag-based applications as well, such as image organizing and automatic annotating untagged images.).

Tag refinement framework

Denote by $\mathcal{D} = \{x_1, x_2, \ldots, x_n\}$ a social image collection, where n is the size of the image set. All unique tags appearing in this collection are gathered in a set $\mathcal{T} = \{t_1, t_2, \ldots, t_m\}$, where m denotes the total number of unique tags. The initial tag membership for the whole image collection can be presented in a binary matrix $\widehat{\mathbf{Y}} \in \{0, 1\}^{n \times m}$ whose element $\widehat{Y}_{ij}$ indicates the membership of tag t_j with respect to image x_i (i.e., if t_j is associated with image x_i, then $\widehat{Y}_{ij} = 1$, and otherwise $\widehat{Y}_{ij} = 0$). To represent the refinement results, we define another matrix $\mathbf{Y}$ whose element $Y_{ij} \geq 0$ denotes the confidence score of assigning tag t_j to image x_i. Denote by $\mathbf{y}_i = (y_{i1}, y_{i2}, \cdots, y_{im})^\top$ the confidence score vector of assigning the tags to the i-th image.

The tag refinement is accomplished based on two assumptions. The first is the consistency between visual similarity and semantic similarity in social images, i.e., the tags of two visually close images are expected to be similar. The second is that the user-provided tags are relevant to the semantic theme of the image with high probability. We then introduce a regularization framework which contains two terms that indicate these two assumptions. Note that these assumptions may not hold for all images, but they are reasonable in most cases and the regularization scheme is able to automatically deal with several outliers.

We first compute the visual similarity between images. Let $\mathbf{W}$ denote a similarity matrix whose element W_{ij} indicates the visual similarity between images x_i and x_j, which can be directly computed based on a Gaussian function with a radius parameter σ, i.e.,

$$W_{ij} = exp(-\frac{\| x_i - x_j \|^2}{\sigma^2}). \tag{1}$$

The semantic similarity of two images is defined based on their tag sets. The most simple approach is to define it as the overlap between the two tag sets, i.e., $\mathbf{y}_i^\top \mathbf{y}_j$. However, this approach actually treats all tags independently without considering their correlation. For example, it will give zero similarity for two images that do not share any common tag, but the images can still be very semantically similar if their tags are strongly correlated. To leverage the correlation of tags, we introduce the tag similarity matrix $\mathbf{S}$, in which the element $S_{ij} \geq 0$ indicates the tag similarity between tags t_i and t_j. In this work, we adopt Lin's similarity measure [15], a knowledge-based similarity metric which utilizes WordNet as knowledge base. It estimates the semantic similarity between t_i and t_j as

$$S_{ij} = \frac{2 * IC(lcs(t_i, t_j))}{IC(t_i) + IC(t_j)}, \tag{2}$$

where $IC(t_i)$ and $IC(t_j)$ are the information content of t_i and t_j respectively, and $lcs(t_i, t_j)$ is their least common subsumer(LCS) in the WordNet taxonomy which represents the common ancestor of these two entries that has the maximum information content. But it is worth noting that our method is flexible, and the semantic similarities can be computed through other approaches as well, such as using Google distance [6].

Then we define the semantic similarity of images by a weighted dot product, i.e., $\mathbf{y}_i^\top \mathbf{S}\mathbf{y}_j = \sum_{k,l=1}^{m} Y_{ik}S_{kl}Y_{jl}$.

According to our consistency assumption, the visual similarity is expected to be close to semantic similarity, i.e., $W_{ij} \approx \mathbf{y}_i^\top \mathbf{S}\mathbf{y}_j$. This leads to the following formulation:

$$\begin{aligned} \min_{\mathbf{Y}} \quad & \sum_{i,j=1}^{n} (W_{ij} - \sum_{k,l=1}^{m} Y_{ik}S_{kl}Y_{jl})^2 \\ s.t. \quad & Y_{jl} \geq 0, \;\; i,j = 1,2,\ldots,n, \; k,l = 1,2,\ldots,m. \end{aligned} \tag{3}$$

We then consider the assumption that user-provided tags are relevant with high probability. Here we introduce the minimization of $\sum_{j=1}^{n}\sum_{l=1}^{m}(Y_{jl} - \widehat{Y}_{jl})^2 exp(\widehat{Y}_{jl})$. A problem with the above formula is that Y_{ij} and $\widehat{Y}_{ij}$ may lie at different scales(from Eq. (3) we can see that Y_{ij} may be much smaller than 1, whereas the value of the initial tag membership $\widehat{Y}_{ij}$ is restricted to 0 or 1). To deal with this problem, we introduce a scaling factor α_j for each image and thus the optimization term turns to

$$\sum_{j=1}^{n}\sum_{l=1}^{m}(Y_{jl} - \alpha_j\widehat{Y}_{jl})^2 exp(\widehat{Y}_{jl}). \tag{4}$$

Formally, we can summarize the above two assumptions into the following optimization problem:

$$\begin{aligned} \min_{\mathbf{Y},\boldsymbol{\alpha}} \; \mathcal{L} = & \sum_{i,j=1}^{n} (W_{ij} - \sum_{k,l=1}^{m} Y_{ik}S_{kl}Y_{jl})^2 \\ & + C\sum_{j=1}^{n}\sum_{l=1}^{m}(Y_{jl} - \alpha_j\widehat{Y}_{jl})^2 exp(\widehat{Y}_{jl}) \\ & s.t. \; Y_{jl}, \alpha_j \geq 0, \; i,j = 1,2,\ldots,n, \; k,l = 1,2,\ldots,m, \end{aligned} \tag{5}$$

where C is a weighting factor to modulate the two terms.

The above equation can be written in matrix form as

$$\begin{aligned} \min_{\mathbf{Y},\mathbf{D}} \quad & \mathcal{L} = \| \mathbf{W} - \mathbf{YSY}^\top \|_F^2 + C\|(\mathbf{Y} - \mathbf{D}\hat{\mathbf{Y}})\circ\mathbf{E}\|_F^2 \\ s.t. \quad & Y_{jl}, D_{jj} \geq 0, \end{aligned} \tag{6}$$

where $\circ$ indicates the pointwise product of matrices, the element E_{ij} of matrix $\mathbf{E}$ represents the weighting factor $exp(\widehat{Y}_{jl})$ in Eq. (4), and $\mathbf{D}$ is a $n \times n$ diagonal matrix whose element $D_{jj} = \alpha_j$.

Solution of the optimization problem

The coupling of $\mathbf{Y}$ and $\boldsymbol{\alpha}$ and the positive constraints of Y_{jl} and α_j make the above optimization framework difficult to solve. In this work, we propose an efficient iterative bound optimization method to obtain its solution, which is analogous to [18]. The basic idea is to first bound the objective function with a computationally feasible function, and then implement an iterative algorithm to obtain its optimal solution. The following two theorems provide the upper bound of $\mathcal{L}$ and its solution.

Theorem 1 *The objective function $\mathcal{L}$ in Eq. (5) has an upper bound $\mathcal{L}'$ as follows.*

$$\begin{aligned} \mathcal{L} \leq \mathcal{L}' = \sum_{i,j=1}^{n} \Big(& W_{ij}^2 + \sum_{l=1}^{m} [\widetilde{\boldsymbol{Y}}\boldsymbol{S}\widetilde{\boldsymbol{Y}}^\top]_{ij} [\widetilde{\boldsymbol{Y}}\boldsymbol{S}]_{il} \frac{Y_{jl}^4}{\widetilde{Y}_{jl}^3} \\ & - 4\sum_{l=1}^{m} W_{ij} [\widetilde{\boldsymbol{Y}}\boldsymbol{S}]_{il} \widetilde{Y}_{jl} log Y_{jl} - 2W_{ij}[\widetilde{\boldsymbol{Y}}\boldsymbol{S}\widetilde{\boldsymbol{Y}}^\top]_{ij} \\ & + 4\sum_{k=1}^{m} W_{ij} [\boldsymbol{S}\widetilde{\boldsymbol{Y}}^\top]_{kj} log \widetilde{Y}_{ik} \Big) \\ & + C\sum_{j=1}^{n}\sum_{l=1}^{m} \Big(Y_{jl}^2 - 2\alpha_j \widehat{Y}_{jl}\widetilde{Y}_{jl}(log\frac{Y_{jl}}{\widetilde{Y}_{jl}} + 1) \\ & + \alpha_j^2 \widehat{Y}_{jl}^2 \Big) exp(\widehat{Y}_{jl}), \end{aligned} \tag{7}$$

where $\tilde{\boldsymbol{Y}}$ can be any $n \times m$ matrix.

Theorem 2 *The optimal solution of the upper bound $\mathcal{L}'$ is given by*

$$\begin{cases} Y_{jl} = \left[\frac{-Cexp(\hat{Y}_{jl})\tilde{Y}_{jl}^3 + \sqrt{M}}{4[\tilde{\boldsymbol{Y}}\boldsymbol{S}\tilde{\boldsymbol{Y}}^\top\tilde{\boldsymbol{Y}}\boldsymbol{S}]_{jl}} \right]^{\frac{1}{2}}, \\ \alpha_j = \frac{\sum_{l=1}^{m} \tilde{Y}_{jl}(log Y_{jl} - log\tilde{Y}_{jl} + 1)}{\sum_{l=1}^{m} \hat{Y}_{jl}}. \end{cases} \tag{8}$$

where $M = (C\exp(\hat{Y}_{jl}))^2 + 8U_{jl}\tilde{Y}_{jl}^4(2[\boldsymbol{W}\tilde{\boldsymbol{Y}}\boldsymbol{S}]_{jl} + C\alpha_j\hat{Y}_{jl}\exp(\hat{Y}_{jl}))$ with $U_{jl} = [\tilde{\boldsymbol{Y}}\boldsymbol{S}\tilde{\boldsymbol{Y}}^\top\tilde{\boldsymbol{Y}}\boldsymbol{S}]_{jl}$.

Both of the two theorems can be verified with algebraic manipulations, and their proofs can be found in our recent work [16].

With the obtained solution in Eq. (8), we present an iterative algorithm to approximate the optimal solution of the upper bound function $\mathcal{L}'$, as shown in Algorithm 1.

Algorithm 1 Iterative Optimization Algorithm

Input: Visual similarity matrix $\mathbf{W}$, Semantic similarity matrix $\mathbf{S}$, Weighting parameter C.
Output: $\mathbf{Y}$,$\boldsymbol{\alpha}$.

1. Randomly initialize $\mathbf{Y}$ and $\boldsymbol{\alpha}$ that satisfy the constraints in Eq. (5). Their initial values will not influence the final results.
2. Repeat the following steps until convergence:
   - Fix $\boldsymbol{\alpha}$, update $\mathbf{Y}$ using the upper equation in Eq. (8).
   - Fix $\mathbf{Y}$, update $\boldsymbol{\alpha}$ using the lower equation in Eq. (8).

In fact the procedure above not only minimizes the upper bound function $\mathcal{L}'$ but also obtains the optimal solution of the objective function $\mathcal{L}$, i.e., we have the following theorem:

Theorem 3 *The process in Algorithm 1 will converge and leads to the minimum of the objective function $\mathcal{L}$.*

The proof of this theorem can be found in [16]. With the computed confidence score matrix $\mathbf{Y}$, we can easily generate the refined tags of an image x_i by setting a threshold for the confidence scores Y_{ij}.

Further enrichment

Although the tag refinement approach can effectively improve the quality of tags, it is still unable to introduce new tags for an image if these tags do not exist in the original image collection. However, this difficulty can be alleviated in certain extend through adding synonyms and hypernyms. Actually, the synonym and hypernym are both valuable indexing keywords that can be utilized to describe the visual content. As an example, Fig. **(3)** illustrates an image annotated with the tag "kitty" from Flickr. We can see that the synonyms and hypernyms of "kitty", such as "kitten", "pussy", "feline" and "animal" are also precise textual descriptors to the image content. However, most users will not spend time to enter these tags. Here is a simple empirical validation. We randomly select 1,000 images that are tagged with "kitty" on Flickr and then check the synonyms and hypernyms. Tab. **(3)** illustrates several statistical results, including the percentages of images that are also tagged with its synonyms ("kitten" or "pussy") or hypernyms ("feline"

Fig. (3): An example image on Flickr and its associated tags. The synonyms and hypernyms are not simultaneously provided by the user.

Tab. (3): Percentage of images that are simultaneously tagged with "kitty" and its synonyms ("kitten", "pussy") as well as hypernyms("feline", "animal").

Relation with "kitty"	Exists with "kitty" together	Percentage of images
Synonym	*kitten*	30.6%
	pussy	2.3%
Hypernym	*animal*	24.8%
	feline	28.0%

or "animal"). As can be seen, only a small percentage of images are simultaneously tagged with "kitty" and its synonyms or hypernyms.

The missing of such tags will degrade the performance of tag-based applications. For example, when users perform search with query "kitten" or "animal", the photo in Fig. **(3)** will not be returned. To address this issue, we adopt a tag enrichment step based on lexical knowledge to expand the synonyms and hypernyms of the refined tags, and this will be an effective strategy to improve the coverage of the tags.

We take advantage of the WordNet lexicon again. As discussed previously, the tags after filtering and refinement are all content-related nouns, and each of them has a coordinate in WordNet. Hence, we apply the lemma entries in WordNet lexicon as the potential enrichment candidate words. Take tag "kitty" for example, it matches the visual category "organism" in its 4-th sense, and thus we collect all the synonyms and hypernyms in this sense, as illustrated in Fig. **(4)**.

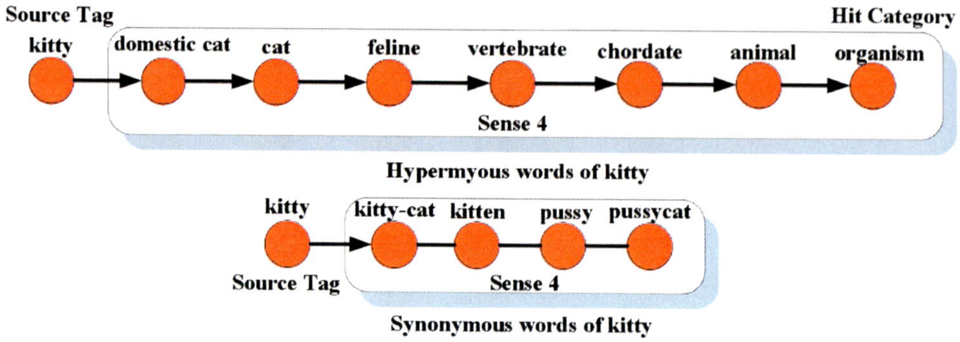

Fig. (4): The hypernyms and synonyms of tag "kitty" can be collected based on the WordNet lexicon.

Experiment result

Data set

We evaluate our tag refinement approach on social images that are collected from Flickr. We select ten most popular queries, including *cat*, *automobile*, *mountain*, *water*, *sea*, *bird*, *tree*, *sunset*, *flower* and *sky*, and then perform tag-based image search with "ranking by interestingness" option. The top 5,000 returned images for each query are collected together with their associated information, including tags, uploading time, user identifier, etc. In this way, we obtain a social image collection consisting of 50,000 images and 106,565 unique tags.

For each image, we extract 428-dimensional features, including 225-dimensional block-wise color moment features generated from 5-by-5 fixed partition of the image, 128-dimensional wavelet texture features, and 75-dimensional edge distribution histogram features.

As aforementioned, we have constructed a content-related vocabulary which is a subset of the WordNet lexicon. We first match each of the 106,565 tags in our social image collection with the noun entries in WordNet. In this way, 11,861 noun tags are obtained, occupying only 11% of all tags in our collection. We then further match these tags with the entries in the content-related vocabulary that includes 5 high level categories, and thus obtain 4,556 tags. Tab. (4) illustrates the detailed results.

Experimental result

The proposed tag refinement method is evaluated on the Flickr dataset. To reduce computational cost, we first perform the K-means clustering algorithm to divide the 50,000 images into 20 groups. Then the tag refinement algorithm is

Tab. (4): Statistics of our tag detection results. There are 4,556 content-related tags in all in our social image collection.

Categories		Tag number	Percentage
Content-Unrelated		7,305	61.6%
Content-Related	*Color*	83	0.70%
	Thing	483	4.07%
	Artifact	2,511	21.2%
	Organism	1,259	10.6%
	Natural Phenomenon	220	1.85%

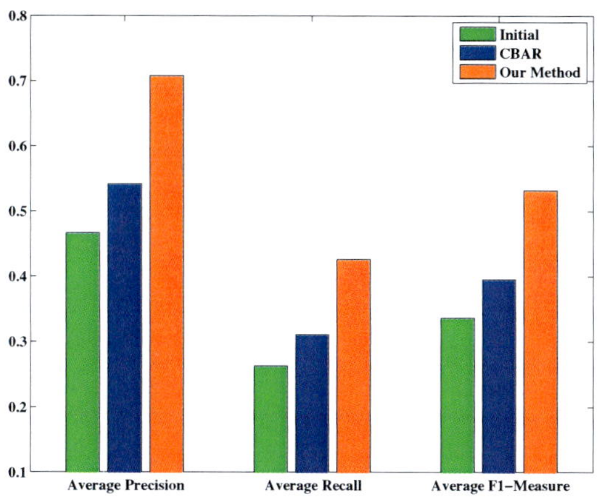

Fig. (5): Performance comparison of the baseline and the two tag refinement methods.

implemented for each group separately. As introduced in Section 4, our tag refinement algorithm is developed mainly based on the similarities of images. Since most similar images will be clustered into the same groups, the clustering strategy will not degrade the performance of refinement while being able to significantly reduce computational costs. The radius parameter σ in Eq. (1) is set to the median value of all the pair-wise Euclidean distances between images in the same cluster, and the parameter C in Eq. (5) is empirically set to 10. We compare the following three methods:

- Baseline, i.e., keeping the original tags.
- Content Based Annotation Refinement (CBAR). We adopt the method proposed in [26].
- Our tag refinement method.

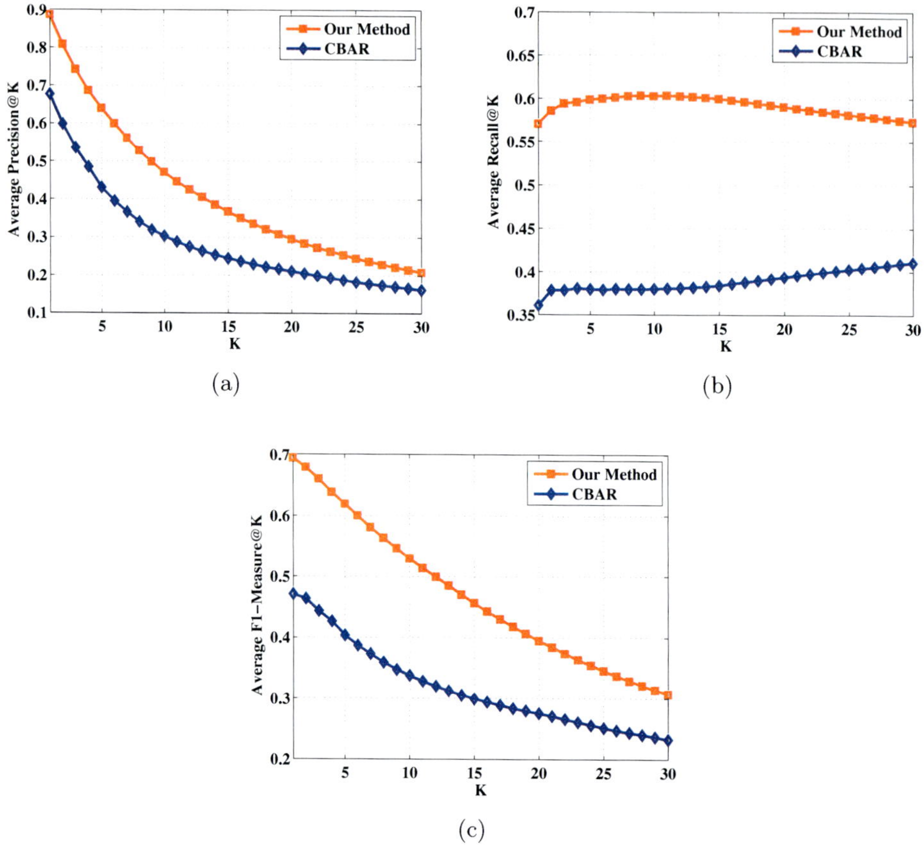

Fig. (6): Performance comparison of the CBAR and our methods when keeping different number of tags.

Note that actually CBAR and our tag refinement method both produce confidence scores for tags. Therefore, for these two methods we rank the tags of each image based on their confidence scores and then keep the top m tags where m is the number of the original tags. The ground truths of the tags are voted by three volunteers. If a tag is relevant to the image, it is labeled as positive, and otherwise it is negative. However, manually labeling all the image-tag pairs will be labor-intensive, and thus here we randomly select 2,500 images as the evaluation set. We adopt precision/recall/F1-measure as performance measurements. But a problem is that the estimation of recall measurement needs to know the full set of relevant tags for each image, while in our case it is unknown. So here we adopt an alternative strategy. We gather the tags obtained by CBAR and our method as well as the original tags for each image, and then the positive tags among them are regarded as the full relevant tag set.

Fig. **(5)** shows the precision, recall and F1-measure measurements obtained by the three methods, averaged over all evaluation images. We can see that CBAR and our method both outperform the baseline method, but the improvement of CBAR is limited. As analyzed in Section 2, this is due to the fact that visual information has not been sufficiently explored in CBAR. Our tag refinement method performs much better than the baseline and the CBAR methods.

We also study the performance of keeping varied number of tags. Here we only compare CBAR and our tag refinement method, since there is no ranking in the original tags. The results are illustrated in Fig. **(6)**. From the figure we can clearly see that our method consistently outperforms the CBAR method.

Furthermore, as introduced previously, we obtain the synonyms and hypernyms of each tag based on the WordNet lexicon, and then a tag-based search is performed on Flickr website to obtain their usage frequencies to decide whether to enrich them. We empirically set the threshold to $10,000$ in this work, i.e., the tags with usage frequencies under $10,000$ will not be enriched.

We still utilize the $2,500$ evaluation images to validate performance of tag enrichment. The ground truths of the enriched tags are also decided by the three labelers. The performance measurements before and after enrichment are illustrated in Tab. **(5)**(the recall measurement is computed in the same way as in the last section, i.e., collect all the relevant tags obtained by different methods and regard them as the full set). From the table we can see that all performance evaluation measurements are improved after enrichment. We can see that the recall measurement is improved from 0.34 to 0.66, and this indicates the coverage of the tags is significantly improved. Actually our experimental results show that the average number of relevant tags for an image is improved from 3.09 to 9.34 after enrichment.

Tab. (5): Quality comparison of the tags before and after enrichment. Each measurement has been averaged over all evaluation images.

Method	Precision	Recall	F1-Measure	Relevant tag number
Before Enrichment	0.71	0.34	0.46	3.09 (4.80 in all)
After Enrichment	0.90	0.66	0.76	9.34 (10.38 in all)

Applications

It is widely acknowledged that user-generated tags are valuable metadata and can be used in many applications. In this section, we will evaluate the effectiveness of image retagging on two applications.

- Tag-based image search. The images that contain the query tag are returned in descending order in terms of their confidence scores.

- Tag-based automatic annotation. For a given image, we provide the tags of its visual neighbors as the potential labels of the image.

Tag-Based image search

Since the retagging scheme improves the quality of tags, tag-based image search can be naturally improved. In addition, our retagging scheme also brings a ranking scheme for tag-based image search since it not only adds and removes tags but also assigns them confidence scores. Current online image-sharing websites support different ways to facilitate tag-based image search and browsing. Take Flickr for example, it provides two options to rank tag-based image search results. One is "most recent", which ranks the most recently uploaded images on top, and the other is "most interesting" which ranks images by "interestingness", a measure that takes clickthrough, comments and so on into consideration. As introduced in Section 4, our retagging scheme can obtain the confidence scores of tags with respect to their associated images, and we can regard them as an indication of relevance levels and provide a new ranking method.

To demonstrate the effectiveness of this approach, we conduct experiment on the 50,000 Flickr images and perform tag-based image search with ten tags, i.e., *cat, automobile, flower, sea, bird, sunset, mountain, water, sky* and *tree.* For each ranking list, the images are decided as "relevant" or "irrelevant" with respect to the query tag by human labelers, and we employ Average Precision (AP) as our evaluation metric. Give a ranked list L with length n, AP is defined as

$$AP = \frac{1}{R}\sum_{j=1}^{n} \frac{R_j}{j} I_j \tag{9}$$

where R is the number of relevant instances in L, R_j the number of relevant instances among the top j instances, $I_j = 1$ if the j-th instance is relevant and 0 otherwise. To evaluate the overall performance, we use Mean AP, the mean value of AP scores over all queries.

We compare our approach with the two schemes provided by Flickr: (1) interestingness-based ranking; and (2) uploading time-based ranking. Fig. (**7**) illustrates the mean AP measurement at different return depths and we can see that our approach consistently outperforms the other two ranking methods. This demonstrates our approach can remarkably improve the performance of tag-based image search.

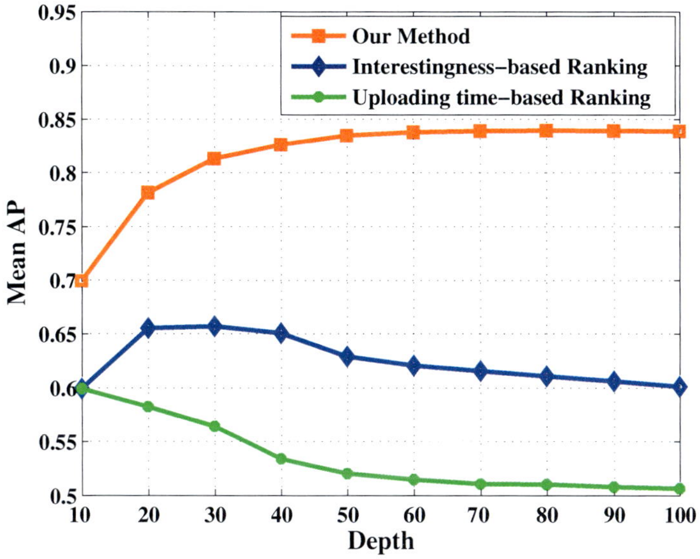

Fig. (7): The performance comparison of different ranking methods for tag-based image search.

Tab. (6): Performance comparison of annotation before and after performing retagging.

Methods	Using images with original tags	Using retagged images
Precision in average	0.221	0.340

Tag-Based automatic annotation

Automatic image annotation algorithms [9, 24] frequently suffer from the insufficiency of training data. Fortunately, nowadays we can easily collect enormous tagged images (such as from Flickr), and these images can be used as labeled data to help annotation, such as the work in [4]. However, the low quality of these tags limits the performance of the automatic annotation approaches. Here we will show that it can obviously benefit from our retagging scheme, since the tag quality has been significantly improved.

The experimental setting is as follows. We randomly select 500 images from a personal photo album as a testing set. Then for each testing image, we perform the k-NN method to decide its labels. More specifically, we find its k-nearest neighbors in our tagged Flickr data $(50,000$ in all) and then collect their tags. The confidence

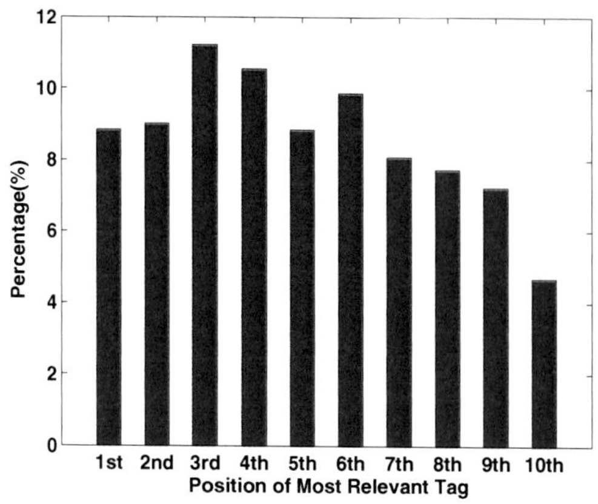

Fig. (8): Percentage of images that have their most relevant tag at the n-th position in the associated tag list, where $n = 1, 2, 3 \ldots, 10$.

of each tag is estimated as its appearing frequency in the neighborhood. We then regard the T most confident tags as the labels of the image. In our experiments, the parameters K and T are both empirically set to 10.

The experimental results are illustrated in Tab. **(6)**. We can see that performing retagging on the training data can help improve the precision measurement from 0.221 to 0.340, i.e., there are 2.2 true labels for a testing image in average if we use the original tags, and there will be 3.4 true labels if we perform retagging. The relative improvement is 53.8%. Therefore, our retagging method can help obtain more accurate tag-based annotation results.

5 Tag Ranking

As discussed in section 1, the tags associated with social images are generally in a random order without any relevance information. To justify this claim, we randomly select 1,200 Flickr images with at least 10 tags. For each image, its most relevant tag from the list is labeled based on the majority voting of five volunteers. Fig. **(7)** shows the position (in terms of the tag list) distribution of the most important tags. As can be seen, only less than 10% of the images have their most relevant tag at the top position in their attached tag list. This illustrates that the tags are almost in a random order in terms of relevance to the associated image.

Tag relevance ranking

In this section, we will introduce our tag ranking method. We firstly give an overview of our tag ranking approach, and then introduce the probabilistic relevance score estimation and random walk-based refinement in detail.

Overview

The tag ranking scheme mainly consists of two steps: initial probabilistic tag relevance estimation and random walk refinement. Given an image and its associated tags, we first estimate the relevance score of each tag individually through a probabilistic approach. We will simultaneously consider the probability of the tag given the image and the descriptive ability of the tag in the relevance score estimation, and we show that it can be accomplished by using the Kernel Density Estimation (KDE) [22]. Although the scores obtained in this way reflect the tag relevance, the relationships among tags have not been taken into account. Thus we further perform a random walk-based refinement to boost tag ranking performance by exploring the relationship of tags. Finally, the tags of the image can be ranked according to their refined relevance scores. In the next two sub-sections, we will detail the probabilistic relevance score estimation method and the random walk-based refinement process, respectively.

Probabilistic tag relevance estimation

First, we estimate the relevance scores of the tags from the probabilistic point of view. Given a tag t, its relevance score to an image x is defined as

$$s(t, x) = p(t|x)/p(t). \tag{10}$$

Now we will explain the rationality of Eq. (10). In fact, the most straightforward way is to directly regard $p(t|x)$ as the relevance score, since it indicates the probability of tag t given image x. However, the tag may not be so descriptive when it appears too frequently in the dataset. For example, for the tag "image", the probability $p(t|x)$ will be always 1, but obviously this tag is non-informative. Therefore, we normalize $p(t|x)$ by $p(t)$, i.e., the prior probability of the tag, to penalize frequently-appearing tags. This principle has actually been widely investigated in information retrieval, e.g., in the design of tf-idf features.

Based on Bayes' rule, we can easily derive that

$$s(t, x) = \frac{p(x|t)p(t)}{p(x)p(t)} = \frac{p(x|t)}{p(x)}, \tag{11}$$

where $p(x)$ and $p(x|t)$ are the prior probability density function and the probability density function of images conditioned on the tag t, respectively. Since the target is to rank the tags for the individual image and $p(x)$ is identical for these tags, we can simply redefine Eq. (11) as

$$s(t, x) \doteq p(x|t). \tag{12}$$

We adopt the classical Kernel Density Estimation (KDE) method to estimate the probability density function $p(x|t)$. Denote by X_i the set of images that contain tag t_i, the KDE approach measures $p(x|t_i)$ as

$$s(t_i, x) = p(x|t_i) = \frac{1}{|X_i|} \sum_{x_k \in X_i} K_\sigma(x - x_k), \tag{13}$$

where $|X_i|$ is the cardinality of X_i and K_σ is the Gaussian kernel function with the radius parameter σ, i.e.,

$$K_\sigma(x - x_k) = exp(-\frac{||x - x_k||^2}{\sigma^2}). \tag{14}$$

The relevance score computed in Eq. (13) actually has a very intuitive explanation. For each image x, the neighbors X_i can be regarded as its friends. The sum of the similarities estimated based on Gaussian kernel function can be regarded as the soft voting from the friends. Therefore, such relevance is actually estimated based on "collective intelligence" from friend images.

Random Walk-based refinement

The probabilistic tag relevance estimation, which takes the image "friends" into consideration, has not taken into account the relationship among tags which will be helpful. For example, consider the image which has a lot of closely related tags, such as "cat", "animal" and "kitten", and an isolated tag such as "Nikon". In this case, intuitively we can infer that the isolated tag "Nikon" is less descriptive than the others.

To investigate the relationship between tags, we perform random walk over the tag graph for each image to propagate the relevance scores among tags. The nodes of the graph are the tags of the image and the edges are weighted with pairwise tag similarity. Here we propose two tag similarity measurements, i.e., exemplar similarity and concurrence similarity, and combine them in the tag graph construction.

Tag graph construction. We estimate the tag exemplar similarity and concurrence similarity and then combine them to form the weights of tag graph edges.

We first estimate tag exemplar similarity from visual clue. For a tag t associated with an image x, we collect the N nearest neighbors from the images containing tag t, and these images are regarded as the exemplars of the tag t with respect to

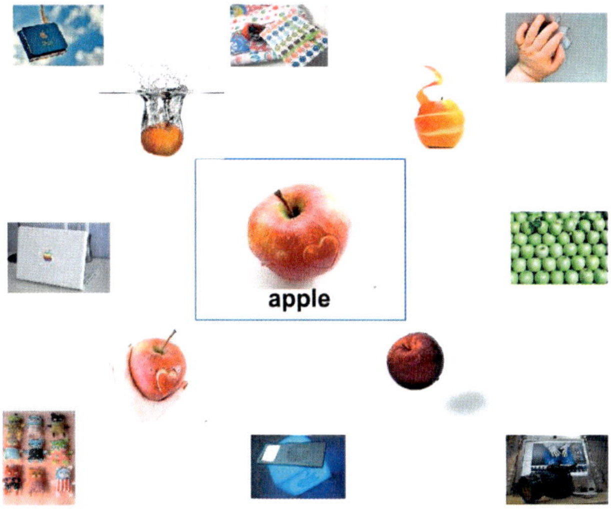

Fig. (9): The images containing tag "apple" are diversified and only using nearest neighbors of the central image will help produce better representative exemplars.

x (more exactly, the images are the local exemplars of the tag since we have only used the neighbors of image x). The purpose of adopting nearest neighbor strategy here is to avoid noise introduced by polysemy. Take the central image in Fig. **(4)** as an example. The images in Fig. **(4)** are all with tag "apple" and we can see that they are highly diversified. But actually the tag "apple" of the central image only indicates a fruit. So, only using the neighbors of this central image will reduce noise and lead to better tag representative collection.

Denote by Γ_t the representative image collection of tag t. Then the exemplar similarity between tags t_i and t_j is defined as follows

$$\varphi_e(t_i, t_j) = exp(-\frac{1}{N * N}\Sigma_{x\in\Gamma_{t_i}, y\in\Gamma_{t_j}}\frac{||x-y||^2}{\sigma^2}) \tag{15}$$

Note that here we have used the same radius parameter σ as in Eq. (3).

We then define the concurrence similarity between tags based on their co-occurrence. Analogous to the principle of Google distance [6], we first estimate the distance between two tags t_i and t_j as follows.

$$d(t_i, t_j) = \frac{max(logf(t_i), logf(t_j)) - logf(t_i, t_j)}{logG - min(logf(t_i), logf(t_j)))} \tag{16}$$

where $f(t_i)$ and $f(t_j)$ are the numbers of images containing tag t_i and tag t_j respectively and $f(t_i, t_j)$ is the number of images containing both t_i and t_j. These numbers can be obtained by performing search by tag on Flickr website using the tags as keywords. Moreover, G is the total number of images in Flickr. The concurrence similarity between tag t_i and tag t_j is then defined as

$$\varphi_c(t_i, t_j) = exp(-d(t_i, t_j)) \tag{17}$$

To explore the complementary nature of exemplar similarity and concurrence similarity, we combine them as

$$s_{ij} = s(t_i, t_j) = \lambda \cdot \varphi_e(t_i, t_j) + (1 - \lambda) \cdot \varphi_c(t_i, t_j) \tag{18}$$

where λ belongs to $[0, 1]$. In Section 3 we will demonstrate that their combination is better than using each one individually. The combined similarity is used as the weight of the edge between t_i and t_j in the tag graph.

Random walk over tag graph. Random walk methods have been widely applied in machine learning and information retrieval fields [8, 12, 21]. Here we perform random walk process over the tag graph in order to boost the performance of tag ranking by using the relationship among tags. Given a tag graph with n nodes, we use $r_k(i)$ to denote the relevance score of node i at iteration k. Thus, the relevance scores of all the nodes in the graph at iteration k form a column vector $\mathbf{r}_k \equiv [r_k(i)]_{n\times1}$. Denote by $\mathbf{P}$ an n-by-n transition matrix. Its element p_{ij} indicates the probability of the transition from node i to node j and it is computed as

$$p_{ij} = \frac{s_{ij}}{\sum_k s_{ik}} \tag{19}$$

where s_{ij} denotes the pairwise tag similarity(see Eq. (18) between node i and j.

The random walk process is thus formulated as

$$r_k(j) = \alpha \sum_i r_{k-1}(i) p_{ij} + (1 - \alpha) v_j \tag{20}$$

where v_j is the initial probabilistic relevance score of tag t_j, and α is a weight parameter that belongs to $(0, 1)$. The above process will promote the tags that have many close neighbors and weaken isolated tags.

Performance evaluation

Experimental settings

All the experiments in this work are conducted on a dataset comprising $50,000$ images collected from Flickr. We select ten most popular tags, including *cat, automobile, mountain, water, sea, bird, tree, sunset, flower* and *sky*, and use them as query keywords to perform tag-based search with ranking by interestingness option. Then the top $5,000$ images are collected together with their associated information, including tags, uploading time, etc. for each query. We notice that the collected tags (more than $100,000$ unique tags) in this way are rather noisy and many of them are misspelling or meaningless words. Hence, a pre-filtering process is performed for these tags. We match each tag with the entries in a Wikipedia thesaurus, and only the tags that have a coordinate in Wikipedia are kept. In this way, $13,330$ unique tags in total are obtained. For each image, we extract 353-dimensional features, including 225-dimenaional block-wise color moment features generated from 5-by-5 partition of the image and a 128-dimensional wavelet texture features.

We use $NDCG$ [10] as the performance evaluation measure. $10,000$ images are randomly selected from our Flickr set for labeling by five persons. For each image, each of its tags is labeled as one of the five levels: Most Relevant (score 5), Relevant (score 4), Partially Relevant (score 3), Weakly Relevant (score 2), and Irrelevant (score 1). Given an image with ranked tag list $t_1, t_2, \ldots, t_n$, the $NDCG$ is computed as

$$N_n = Z_n \sum_{i=1}^{n} (2^{r(i)} - 1)/log(1 + i) \tag{21}$$

where $r(i)$ is the relevance level of the ith tag and Z_n is a normalization constant that is chosen so that the optimal ranking's $NDCG$ score is 1. After computing the $NDCG$ measures of each image's tag list, we can average them to obtain an overall performance evaluation of the tag ranking method. The radius parameter σ in Eq. (3) and Eq. (15) is set to the median value of all pair-wise Euclidean distances between images, and the parameter N in exemplar similarity computation in Eq. (15) is empirically set to 50. The parameters λ and α in Eq. (18) and Eq. (20) are set to 0.8 and 0.5 respectively and their sensitivities will be analyzed in detail in section 3.2.

Experimental results

We compare our proposed tag ranking strategy with the following two methods in terms of average $NDCG$.

1. Probabilistic Tag Ranking (PTR). In this method, we use the relevance score obtained in Eq. (13) without implementing random walk among tags;

2. Random Walk-based Tag Ranking (RWTR). We conduct random walk along the tag correlation graph with $v_i = 1/n$, i.e., do not utilize probabilistic relevance estimations.

Our proposed approach can be viewed as a combination of the above two methods. The experimental results are shown in Fig. (**10**). We have also computed the $NDCG$ of the original tag lists as baseline. From the results we can see that all the three methods can bring better order to the tags, and the combination method outperforms PTR and RWTR. Fig. (**11**) illustrates several exemplary results, from

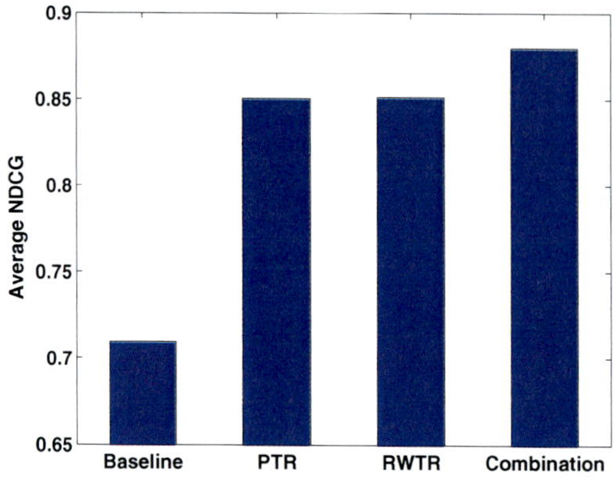

Fig. (10): Performance of different tag ranking strategies. Baseline is the average $NDCG$ of the original tag lists and the others are average $NDCG$ values after performing tag ranking with different methods, where PTR is Probabilistic Tag Ranking, PWTR is Random Walk-based Tag Ranking, and the last one is their combination.

which we can clearly see the tag ranking lists are better than the original ones in terms of relevance ordering.

As shown in Fig. **(7)**, only less than 10% of the images have their most relevant tag at the top position in their attached tag list. We also illustrate the same histogram for the ranked tag list, as shown in Fig. **(8)**. We can clearly see that our tag ranking approach has successfully promoted the most relevant tags. Nearly 40% images have their most relevant tags ranked at top.

We then further conduct experiments to analyze the sensitivity of our tag ranking scheme with respect to the two parameters λ (see Eq. (18)) and α (see Eq. (18)). The parameter λ is a trade-off to balance the contributions of concurrence-based similarity and exemplar-based similarity in tag graph, and the parameter α controls the impact of probabilistic relevance scores in the random walk process.

First we simply set α to 0.5 and range λ from 0 to 1.0. Fig. **(9)**(a) illustrates the results. From the results we can see that basically setting λ in $(0, 1)$ is better than setting λ to 0 or 1 individually. This demonstrates the complementary nature of the concurrence similarity and exemplar similarity. Interestingly, we find that the optimal performance is achieved when the weighting parameter λ for exemplar similarity is set to 0.8, which confirms the significance of visual modality for our tag ranking. We then set λ to 0.8 and range α from 0 to 1. As can be observed in Fig. **(9)**(b), the performance curve is smooth when α varies in a wide range $[0.3, 0.8]$. We can also see that the result is always better than PTR and RWTR

Fig. (11): Several exemplary tag ranking results.

when α ranges from 0.1 to 0.9. This indicates the robustness of our approach. According to the results, the optimal values of λ and α are around 0.8 and 0.5 respectively, and thus in the tag ranking-based applications introduced in the next section we will empirically adopt these settings to generate tag ranking results.

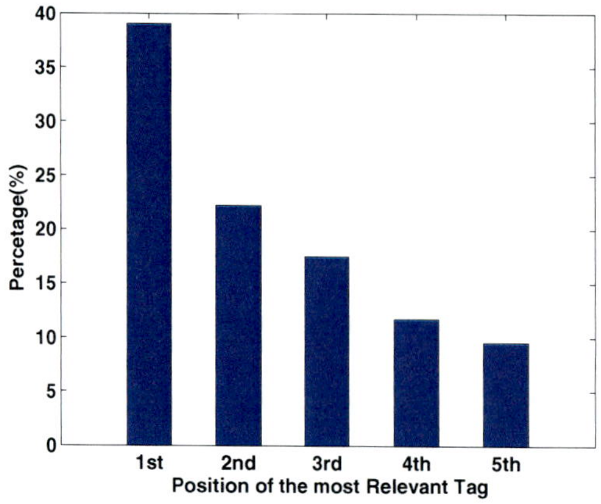

Fig. (12): The percentage of images that have their most relevant tag appear at n-th position in the associated tag list after performing tag ranking, where $n = 1, 2, ..., 5$.

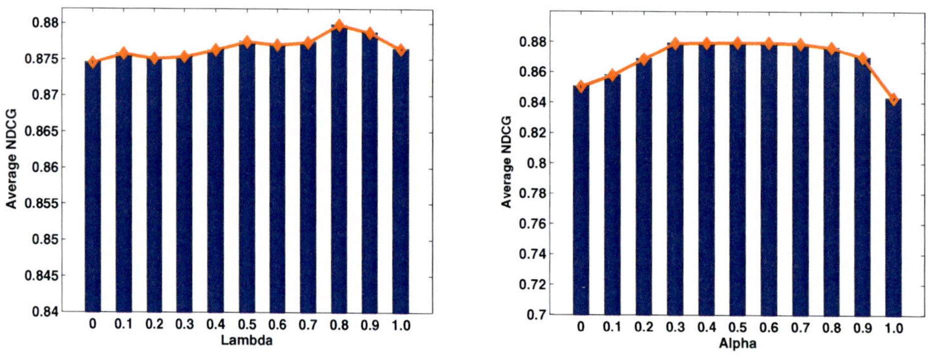

(a) (b)

Fig. (13): The performance curves of our tag ranking method with respect to the parameters λ and α.

Applications

In this section, we introduce three potential application scenarios of tag ranking:

1. Tag-based image search, in which the image ranking list is generated based on the given tag's position in these images' ranked tag lists.

2. Tag recommendation. For a given image, we provide the most relevant tags

of its neighbors as recommendation.

3. Image group recommendation. Given an image, we use the top tags in the ranked tag list to search for possible groups for sharing purpose.

Tag-Based image search

As introduced in Section 1, currently Flickr provides two tag-based image search services that rank images based on interestingness and uploaded time, respectively. Based on the tag ranking results, we develop a method to rank search results based on their relevance, which will be useful in most of the situations when users want to search for information about a topic.

Given the query tag, we estimate the relevance levels of images based on the position of the query tag in each image's tag ranking list. Generally, the more advanced position the query tag is located in an image's tag ranking list, the more relevant the image will be with the query. Fig. **(14)** illustrates an example. The query tag "dog" lies at the first and second positions in the tag lists of (a) and (b) respectively, and we can see that obviously (a) is more relevant to the query than (b).

(a) dog tree

(b) tree dog

Fig. (14): The tag positions can be used to identify the relevance of images with respect to the query. The query "dog" locates at first and second position in (a) and (b) respectively and we can clearly see that (a) is more relevant than (b) for query "dog".

Our image ranking method is designed as follows. Given a query tag q, denote by τ_i the rank position of q in the ranked tag list of image x_i. Since we only consider the images that contain tag q, we have $\tau_i > 0$. Let n_i denote the number of tags of image x_i, we then estimate relevance score for image x_i as

$$r(x_i) = -\tau_i + 1/n_i \tag{22}$$

The rationality of Eq. (22) lies on the following two facts:

1. If $\tau_i < \tau_j$, we will always have $r(x_i) > r(x_j)$. This indicates that we assign higher relevance score to the image that contains the query tag at more advanced positions in its ranked tag list.

2. If $\tau_i = \tau_j$, the relationship is decided by n_i and n_j. If $n_i < n_j$, we have $r(x_i) > r(x_j)$. It implies that, if the positions of the query tag are the same for two images, then we will prefer to the image that has fewer tags. This is intuitive since fewer tags indicate the image is more simple and it is thus with higher probability to be relevant with the given query tag.

With the ranking scores obtained in Eq. (22), we rank image search results with the scores in descending order.

Fig. (15): The top results of query "bird" and "car" using our image ranking strategy.

To evaluate the proposed tag-based search strategy, we conduct experiment on the 50,000 Flickr image collection described in section 3.1 and use the 10 tags, i.e., *cat, automobile, mountain, water, sea, bird, tree, sunset, flower* and *sky*, as query keywords. We use $NDCG$ as the performance evaluation measure. Each image is labeled as one of four levels: Most Relevant (score 4), Relevant (score 3), Weakly Relevant (score 2) and Irrelevant (score 1). We compare our method with

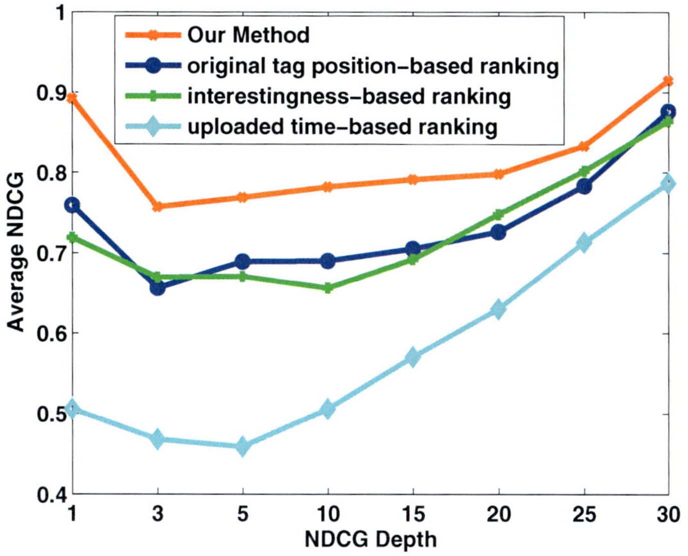

Fig. (16): NDCG comparison with varied depths using different ranking methods for tag-based image search.

the following three methods: (1) interestingness-based ranking; (2) uploading time-based ranking; and (3) original tag position-based ranking. The first two methods are both the services provided by Flickr website, which generate image ranking lists based on their interestingness and uploading time records, respectively. In the third method, we use Eq. (22) to generate ranking score with the original tag lists, i.e., do not perform tag ranking. Fig. **(15)** illustrates the first 12 results of query "bird" and "car" using our method. We can clearly see that our top results are more relevant. The average $NDCG$ results with different depths are illustrated in Fig. **(16)**, and the results demonstrate that our method can achieve better search performance, in terms of relevance ranking with respect to the query tag.

Tag recommendation

Based on the tag ranking results, we propose a content-based tag recommendation method. As stated in section 5, current tag recommendation approaches can be categorized into automatic and semi-automatic approaches. Our method is one of the automatic approaches and the recommendation process does not require users to provide initial tags. The proposed method is as follows. Given an image, we first find its K nearest neighbors from the image dataset. Then we collect the top m tags of each neighboring image according to its tag ranking list. As a result, $m \times K$

Tab. (7): Performance of tag recommendation.

	Prec@1	Prec@5	Prec@all
Original(Baseline)	0.5858	0.4980	0.4980
Recommendation	0.7255	0.5799	0.5772
Improvement(%)	23.9	16.5	15.9

Fig. (17): Tag recommendation example.

tags are collected in total. The unique tags in the collection are then recommended to the users, sorted according to the occurrence frequency in the collection.

To demonstrate the effectiveness of the tag recommendation method, we randomly select 500 images from Flickr collection to perform tag recommendation. We set $m = 2$ and $K = 10$ empirically. We also invite people to label the recommended tags as "relevant" or "irrelevant". We use precision as the performance evaluation measure. The average precisions with different depths are illustrated in Tab. **(7)**. From the table we can see that our tag recommendation results are surprisingly good. The precision is even higher than that of the tags provided by Flickr user (the precisions of the original tags and recommended tags are 0.4980 and 0.5772, respectively). Fig. **(17)** illustrates some sample images and their recommended tags.

Fig. (18): An example for group recommendation. Based on the tag ranking results, we use the first three tags of the given image, i.e., *bird*, *nature* and *wildlife* to search for suitable groups, and we can find a series of possible groups.

Group recommendation

Groups in Flickr are self-organized communities with common interests. Users can add their images to suitable groups such that they can be more easily accessed. The group information is thus useful for users to share and browse images. However, nowadays there are a large number of groups in Flickr and it is not easy for general users to find a suitable group for his photos. Therefore, a group recommendation service is highly desired.

We propose a group recommendation approach based on the tag ranking. Since groups are usually titled and described with words corresponding to the image content in its image pool, we can use the top tags of an image as query keywords to search for its potentially suitable groups. Since the top tags in the ranked tag list are the keywords that can best describe the visual content of the query image, the group will be found with high probability. Fig. **(18)** shows a typical image and its group recommendation results. The top three tags in the ranked tag list are used as keywords to find the groups which contain these tags. After recommending the potential groups, users can select the preferred groups from the recommended ones.

To objectively evaluate the performance of group recommendation, we randomly select 50 images from our Flickr collection. For each image, we use the top n tags in the tag ranking list to search for groups. The top three groups in each search result are collected (Currently Flickr supports four text-based group search strategies, including "ordering by most relevant", "ordering by most recent activity", "ordering by group size" and "ordering by date created". We adopted the first strategy.) and thus we obtain $3n$ recommended groups in total. The recommended groups

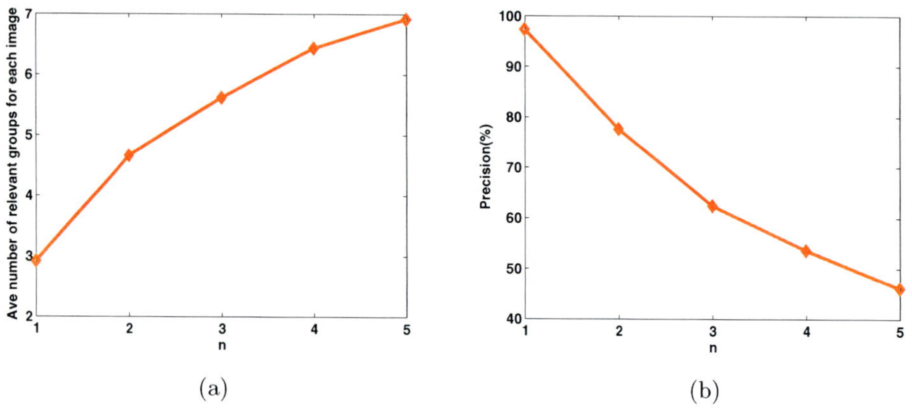

Fig. (19): Performance of group recommendation with different n. (a) illustrates the average numbers of relevant recommended groups and (b) illustrates the recommendation precisions.

for each image are then manually labeled as "relevant" or "irrelevant" according to whether the image can be categorized into the groups for evaluation purpose. We calculate group recommendation precision for each image and average them as final evaluation measure. n varies from 1 to 5, and Fig. **(19)** illustrates the average results. Fig. **(19)**(a)shows the average number of relevant groups for an image and Fig. **(19)**(b) illustrates the recommendation precision, i.e., the percentage of relevant ones in the recommended groups. From the figure we can see that the number of relevant groups keeps increasing when n increases, but the recommendation precision actually decreases. This can be easily understood, since using more tags can always find more groups and there will be more relevant ones, but the group recommendation precision will be worse than only using one or two most relevant tags. If we only use the top tag for search, we can see that the recommended groups will nearly be all relevant, and this demonstrates the effectiveness of our approach. In practical application, we can establish n by compromising the number of recommended groups and the recommendation precision or providing several options for user customization.

6 Conclusions

In this chapter, we have introduced the tag processing techniques that aims at improving the quality of the tags associated with social images. A series of tag processing issues including tag filtering, tag refinement and tag ranking have been addressed. Experiments on real-word social image dataset have demonstrated their effectiveness in improving the quality of the tags. Although we mainly focus on Flickr in this chapter, the tag processing techniques are flexible and can be easily extended to deal with a variety of online media repositories, such as Zooomr as well as any other image databases with noisy and incomplete tags. We will also investigate the tag processing techniques for social video website such as Youtube in the future.

7 References

[1] http://www.flickr.com.

[2] http://www.zooomr.com.

[3] Morgan Ames and Mor Naaman. Why we tag: motivations for annotation in mobile and online media. In *SIGCHI*, 2007.

[4] Shih-Fu Chang, Junfeng He, Yu-Gang Jiang, Akira Yanagawa, Eric Zavesky, Elie Khoury, and Chong-Wah Ngo. Columbia university/vireo-cityu/irit trecvid2008 high-level feature extraction and interactive video search. In *TRECVID*, 2008.

[5] Tat-Seng Chua, Jinhui Tang, Richang Hong, Haojie Li, Zhiping Luo, and Yantao Zheng. Nus-wide: a real-world web image database from national university of singapore. In *CIVR*, 2009.

[6] Rudi Cilibrasi and Paul M. B. Vitányi. The google similarity distance. *IEEE Transactions on Knowledge and Data Engineering*, 2007.

[7] Christiane Fellbaum, editor. *WordNet: an electronic lexical database.* MIT Press, 1998.

[8] Winston H. Hsu, Lyndon S. Kennedy, and Shih-Fu Chang. Video search reranking through random walk over document-level context graph. In *ACM Multimedia*, 2007.

[9] Xian-Sheng Hua and Guo-Jun Qi. Online multi-label active annotation: towards large-scale content-based video search. In *ACM Multimedia*, 2008.

[10] Kalervo Järvelin and Jaana Kekäläinen. Cumulated gain-based evaluation of ir techniques. *ACM Trans. Inf. Syst.*, 2002.

[11] Yohan Jin, Latifur Khan, Lei Wang, and Mamoun Awad. Image annotations by combining multiple evidence & wordnet. In *ACM Multimedia*, 2005.

[12] Yushi Jing and Shumeet Baluja. Pagerank for product image search. In *ACM WWW*, 2008.

[13] Lyndon S. Kennedy, Shih-Fu Chang, and Igor Kozintsev. To search or to label?: predicting the performance of search-based automatic image classifiers. In *ACM MIR*, 2006.

[14] Jia Li and James Ze Wang. Real-time computerized annotation of pictures. *IEEE Transactions on Pattern Analysis and Machine Intelligence*, 2008.

[15] Dekang Lin. Using syntactic dependency as local context to resolve word sense ambiguity. In *ACL*, 1997.

[16] Dong Liu, Xian-Sheng Hua, Meng Wang, and Hong-Jiang Zhang. Image retagging. In *ACM Multimedia*, 2010.

[17] Dong Liu, Xian-Sheng Hua, Linjun Yang, Meng Wang, and Hong-Jiang Zhang. Tag ranking. In *ACM WWW*, 2009.

[18] Yi Liu, Rong Jin, and Liu Yang. Semi-supervised multi-label learning by constrained non-negative matrix factorization. In *AAAI*, 2006.

[19] Yijuan Lu, Lei Zhang, Qi Tian, and Wei-Ying Ma. What are the high-level concepts with small semantic gaps? In *CVPR*, 2008.

[20] Simon E. Overell, Börkur Sigurbjörnsson, and Roelof van Zwol. Classifying tags using open content resources. In *WSDM*, 2009.

[21] Jia-Yu Pan, Hyung-Jeong Yang, Christos Faloutsos, and Pinar Duygulu. Gcap: Graph-based automatic image captioning. In *MDDE*, 2004.

[22] Emanuel Parzen. On estimation of a probability density function and mode. *The Annals of Mathematical Statistics*, 1962.

[23] Börkur Sigurbjörnsson and Roelof van Zwol. Flickr tag recommendation based on collective knowledge. In *ACM WWW*, 2008.

[24] Simon Tong and Edward Y. Chang. Support vector machine active learning for image retrieval. In *ACM Multimedia*, 2001.

[25] Antonio B. Torralba, Robert Fergus, and William T. Freeman. 80 million tiny images: A large data set for nonparametric object and scene recognition. *IEEE Transactions on Pattern Analysis and Machine Intelligence*, 2008.

[26] Changhu Wang, Feng Jing, Lei Zhang, and Hong-Jiang Zhang. Content-based image annotation refinement. In *CVPR*, 2007.

[27] Kilian Q. Weinberger, Malcolm Slaney, and Roelof van Zwol. Resolving tag ambiguity. In *ACM Multimedia*, 2008.

[28] Rong Yan, Apostol Natsev, and Murray Campbell. A learning-based hybrid tagging and browsing approach for efficient manual image annotation. In *CVPR*, 2008.

[29] Keiji Yanai and Kobus Barnard. Image region entropy: a measure of "visualness" of web images associated with one concept. In *ACM Multimedia*, 2005.

Internet Multimedia Search and Mining, 2013, 204-222

CHAPTER 8

Flickr Groups: Multimedia Communities for Multimedia Analysis

Radu-Andrei Negoescu*
Idiap Research Institute and Ecole Polytechnique Fédérale de Lausanne, Tel: +41 27 721 77 11 / 12, Email: phd@radunegoescu.ch
Daniel Gatica-Perez
Idiap Research Institute and Ecole Polytechnique Fédérale de Lausanne, Tel: +41 27 721 77 11 / 12, Email: gatica@idiap.ch

Abstract: We present in this chapter a review of current work that leverages on large online social networks' meta-information, in particular Flickr Groups. We briefly present this hugely successful feature in Flickr and discuss the various ways in which metadata stemming from users' interactions with and within groups has been exploited by researchers to improve on state-of-the-art search and browsing algorithms. We then review recent works that have already made use of Flickr Groups, either as a data source, as a way of filtering content, or as a way to reach users for automatic analysis or user studies, and conclude by pointing out to potential directions of future research.

Keywords

virtual communities, automatic analysis, Flickr Groups, content funnelling, social metadata, large-scale data sources, survey, social network, metadata stemming,

***Correspondence Author:** Radu-Andrei Negoescu, Idiap Research Institute and Ecole Polytechnique Fédérale de Lausanne; Email: radu.negoescu@idiap.ch.

Xian-Sheng Hua, Marcel Worring & Tat-Seng Chua (Eds.)

users' interaction

1 Introduction

It is common nowadays to hear people talking about how "on the internet you can find anything". While this may not hold true for really anything, the amount of information available electronically is staggering. As electronic devices become more ubiquitous, from mobile phones to internet-enabled refrigerators, more and more consumers become producers of content. As of the writing of this piece, YouTube, arguably the world's most popular video sharing website, was boasting 20 hours worth of video uploads each minute [22]. Flickr on the other hand, one of the most popular photo sharing websites, showed an average of 2000 photos uploaded per minute. This average was computed by counting the time it took to upload 1 billion photos starting from the 3rd billionth one in November 2008: less than a year.

One of the more interesting aspects of social media today, apart from the sheer amount of data available to the research community, is the even richer metadata. People create, upload, and then annotate content, be it through tags, regions of interest, or comments. Annotation is just one of the explicit ways through which metadata is created - and the most visible, but many other actions also lead to the generation of metadata, such as rating, adding photos or videos to favorite lists, organizing content in sets or collections, and even simply viewing content. This type of implicit metadata is also useful for the understanding of the dynamics of social media. Another way in which social media collections can be enriched is through the social sphere itself, like user-to-user relationships, or online communities, such as Flickr Groups. These groups are user-managed communities that form around a specific interest, such as a photographic technique, geographical location, event, or simply as a result of a desire for social interaction. There is a great number of groups on Flickr, currently in the range of 300,000. By nature, Flickr Groups become content filtering mechanisms, and this has great potential for multimedia mining.

In this book, the reader has already seen Flickr being used as a data source in Chapters 5 and 7, and some of the following chapters will present further research based on Flickr data. In this chapter we take a comprehensive look at Flickr Groups as one of the most importantn instances of social media communities. While other online photo sharing communities also exist (PicasaWeb, Photobucket, Zooomr), none is as popular as Flickr and indeed none of them offers the same ease of access to their data as Flickr does, through its API. This is the main reason why a lot of multimedia mining research uses Flickr as a data source in the first place.

After briefly describing Flickr Groups, we first analyze how users make use of groups, and then review how the research community has recently begun to take advantage of them in order to address fundamental multimedia problems like image retrieval or search results ranking and re-ranking. We also discuss ways in which the research community, by combining visual content, textual descriptions, and social data, are making progress towards providing users with better content and entity discovery options or personalized content filtering options. The main advantage of metadata over visual content is, still, the computational cost and relatively lower complexity, and this explains why it has been so far the most common source of data for analysis. On the other hand, one of the drawbacks is the relatively higher noise of such metadata, like poor or incomplete annotations. Fortunately, by taking advantage of the massive amount of data available, noise can be somewhat reduced through aggregation techniques. All of these issues are discussed in this chapter. To our knowledge, this represents the first review of the use of Flickr Groups for multimedia analysis.

This chapter is structured as follows: first we present Flickr Groups, from both a functional and a data source perspective. We then review research that has taken advantage of Flickr Groups so far. We end this hapter with a brief discussion in the last section about future directions.

2 What are Flickr Groups?

Flickr was founded in 2004 and in the following five years became one of the major players in the online photo management market. Part of its success seems to be related to the way photos are central to the website experience: rather than becoming an online photo album storage site like other existing systems, Flickr from the very beginning encouraged users to share their photos with the rest of the world. Why exactly users share photos online is a question that received tentative answers in several recent studies like those of Van House [19] and Ames and Naaman [1]. Apart from simply needing a place to store their photos online, most users seem driven by social motives like self-expression and self-promotion, and social interaction is indeed one of the key aspects of the Flickr experience. Users can explore random photos automatically ranked by "interestingness", leave comments, add tags, mark-up regions within a photo with notes, list a specific photo as a favorite, or add other users as contacts. All these public displays of interaction have a strong impact on community building.

In Flickr, apart from the previously described interaction mechanisms, users can organize themselves in self-managed communities, called Flickr Groups. As the name suggests, Flickr Groups are sets of users who are brought together by a common feature, and who share photos in the so called *group pool*. There is quite a wide range of interests that bring people together. As a few examples, it may be an interest in a specific kind of photographic technique, leading to groups like *Black and White*, *Closer and Closer Macro Photography*, or *Digital Infrared*. It can also be an interest in a specific geographical location, with groups like *New York City*, *Paris*, or even smaller geographic communities, like the *2010 Olympic Athletes' Village*.Yet again, it may be an interest in promoting one's images, which leads to groups like *Views 7-25* or *Views 1250-1500*, groups in which people share their photos that have reached the respective number of views on Flickr. Within the same category there are groups like *Nature's Finest (Invited Images Only)*, or *Your Best Shot 2009*.These are communities of sometimes tens of thousands of people, whose common goal is the gathering and exposure of high quality photography. The list of interests that brings people together in groups does not end here: there are the charity oriented groups, the photojournalism ones, the groups for political activism, and even the groups for corporate marketing.

In previous research on a Flickr dataset[12], we analyzed the way users of Flickr use the system, and its groups. First, there are two types of users, ones who have free accounts, and ones who pay in order to have unlimited access to the site's features. The two types of users (paying and non-paying) were almost equally represented (51.4% and 48.6% respectively) in our data set. We show in Fig. (1) the relation between the size of the users' photo collections (in number of photos) and the fraction of photos shared in groups. As a first observation, the sizes of the photo collections for users who shared no photos at all were evenly spread over the entire range of sizes (the thick line overlapping the x axis). Furthermore, the sharing fractions for the users who had the maximum number of photos allowed in our dataset (we collected at most 500 photos per user), were also evenly spread over the entire interval $[0, 1]$ (the thick line at $x = 500$). The correlation coefficient between the two measures was 0.1417, indicating a weak correlation. While the restrictions on free accounts do seem to influence the number of photos users had in their accounts (with an average of around 220 photos for non-paying members as opposed to 450 for paying members) and also the number of groups they shared photos with (on average 60 for paying members, with a median of 23 and an average of 24.7 with a median of 7 for non-paying members), we found that the ratio of photos shared in groups was similar for both categories of users: paying members in our data shared on average 29.4% of their photos (median 17.2%) and non-paying members shared on average 30% (median 17.1%). Our results on the same data showed that, on average, a user shared a small number of photos with each group (mean 9.6, median 5.1) and shared the same photo in multiple groups in even smaller numbers (mean 3.1, median 1.5), with small differences between paying and non-paying members, despite the large differences in the average number of groups noted above. This was an interesting result, showing that users' group-sharing behavior was not influenced by their paying or non-paying status, or by the amount of photos they uploaded. Overall, the analysis showed that through relatively modest photo repurposing, small but persistent group loyalty and active participation in groups, Flickr users contribute a significant proportion of their content to communities, which emerge as rich Flickr entities through the aggregation of their members'

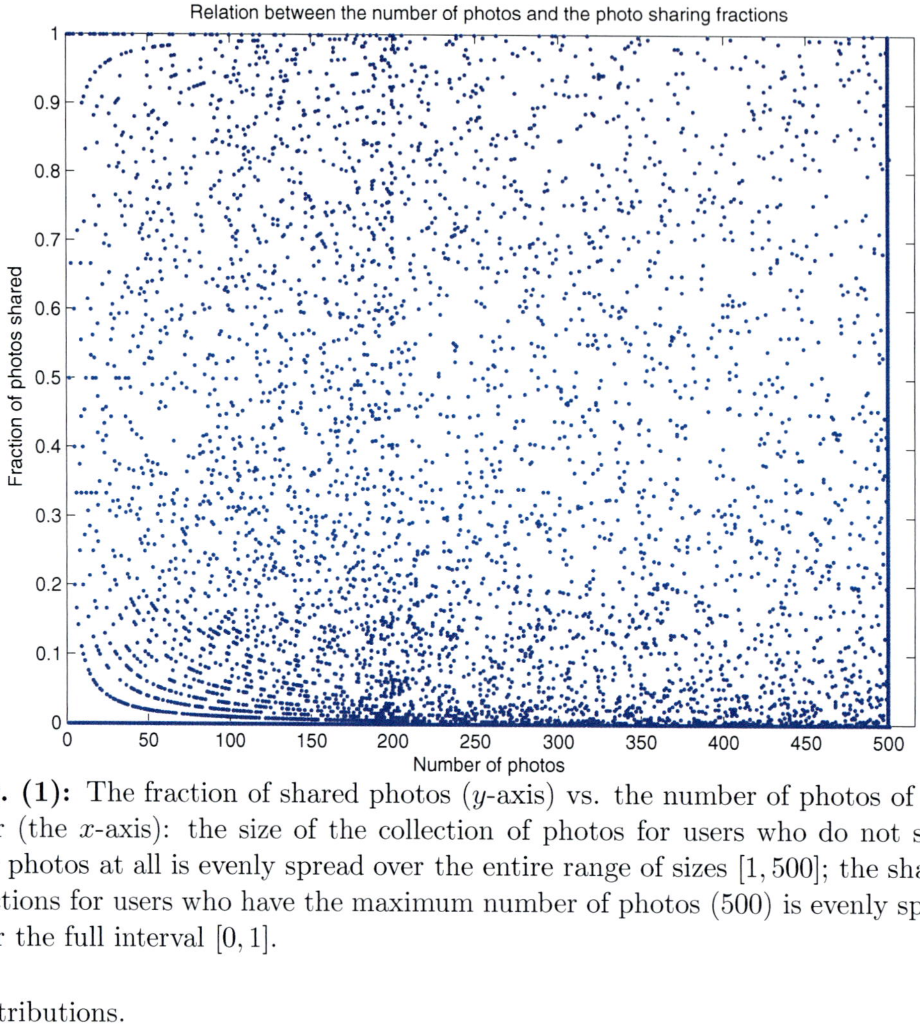

Fig. (1): The fraction of shared photos (y-axis) vs. the number of photos of each user (the x-axis): the size of the collection of photos for users who do not share any photos at all is evenly spread over the entire range of sizes $[1, 500]$; the sharing fractions for users who have the maximum number of photos (500) is evenly spread over the full interval $[0, 1]$.

contributions.

Thus, from a research perspective, Flickr Groups are interesting for several reasons. First and foremost, many of the groups act like content funnels, gathering in a single place - the group pool - references to photos that match a specific criterion, be it photographic technique, photographic subject, semantic subject, or aesthetic quality. Group administrators, and sometimes even regular group members, act as content filters. This is a great resource to tap into for the research community, and several studies have already used groups as a starting point for data collection [9, 10, 16].

Secondly, groups are natural paradigms of the "content+relations" model of social media. That means that not only there is content that is in one way or another consistent, but there is also information about relations between users. Several research groups have started to take advantage of this information in recent studies [5, 8, 11, 12, 13, 17, 18].

Finally, membership in a specific group also brings additional metadata if information about the group itself is included in the dataset, such as the group name, group size, or group type. Group names can be seen as commonly accepted tags by their respective members, or they can be used as groundtruth during evaluation of automatic analysis methods. This kind of metadata has also been exploited in several works [2, 3, 4, 9].

We will have a more in-detail look at these three different ways researchers have been taking advantage of group-related information in the following section.

3 Multimedia Analysis through Flickr Groups

We start off this section with a table summarizing the existing works which use, in one way or another, Flickr Groups. This list has been compiled by searching online and by manual inspection of the proceedings of the main conferences on multimedia, web and social media, and human-computer interaction. We list in Tab. (1) the reference, the approximate size of the dataset used, the task dealt with, the approach used for solving the task, and the way in which Flickr Groups were used.

Upon inspection, three major uses emerge:

- *groups as metadata*: membership to specific groups becomes metadata used by researchers to model user relations or image similarity, to quantify a user's degree of social participation, or simply to treat group names as additional textual data;
- *groups as funnels for data collection*: starting from certain Flickr groups, researchers gather images for model training with more accurate metadata, select users for in-depth studies of their behavior, or recruit users for ethnographic studies;
- *groups as a research domain on its own*: this is the case when groups themselves constitute a part of (or the totality of) the dataset. Researchers use information such as the number of members, the number of photos, the tags present in the group pool, or the name of the group in order to analyze, understand, or model Flickr Groups as entities of interest themselves.

Let us have a more detailed look at each particular usage of Flickr Groups.

Groups as metadata

As we mentioned earlier, the simple fact of being a member in a group can be used as metadata. In a study on tagging motivations, Nov *et al.* [15] examined the tagging behavior of users on Flickr. Starting from findings of previous studies

Tab. (1): Existing works in the literature that use, in one way or another, Flickr Groups. For display reasons, "M" indicates millions, and "K" thousands of items. Table is ordered by group usage and name of first author.

Paper	Dataset	Task	Approach	Group usage
Choudhury [3]	200 groups	predicting group activity over time	interaction metadata	data source
Choudhury [4]	925 groups, 15K images	recommending groups for new images	visual, textual, interaction	data source
Egger [5]	300 groups	extracting automatic hierarchy of groups	membership and group names	data source
Lerman [8]	13K images	personalizing image search	textual and social metadata	additional metadata
Negoescu [11]	10K groups, 8K users	automatic clustering of groups	textual and social metadata	data source
Negoescu [13]	8K groups, 6K users	modeling of groups and users	textual and social metadata	data source
Negoescu [12]	22K users, 51K groups, 6.9M images	analysis of sharing behavior	textual and social metadata	data source
Negoescu [14]	10K groups, 8K users	modeling of groups and users	textual and social metadata	data source
Prieur [17]	72K groups, 4.7M users	analysis of social interaction	metadata	data source
Lin [23]	52 groups, 50K images	modeling group theme evolution over time	visual, social, textual, temporal	data source
Chen [2]	600 groups	recommending groups and tags	visual content	content gathering source
Lerman [9]	55K users	analysis of content discovery	metadata	user selection
Miller [10]	10 users	analysis of photo sharing practices	user studies	user recruitment
Plangprasopchok [16]	21K users	constructing of folksonomies	sets and collection names	user gathering source
Nov [15]	237 users	analysis of tagging motivations	user studies	as measure of social presence
Singla [18]	2.1M users	detecting camera brand congruence	camera and temporal metadata	as prior for friendship strength
Van Zwol [20]	1.83M photos	analysis of social interaction	metadata	as measure of social presence
Wang [21]	103 groups	learning image similarity	visual content	as prior for image similarity, image gathering source

which suggest that social presence influences tagging behavior, the authors used multiple data sources in order to examine which motivations are associated with different tagging levels. One of their data sources were user studies, while for a more computational approach they used the number of Flickr groups a user belongs to as one of the social presence indicators, along with the number of contacts that the user has. Their findings show that, amongst other variables, the variance in tagging activity is best explained by the number of groups a user belongs to. Here, a relatively simple piece of information - the number of groups - helped establish statistically significant evidence to support qualitative research. In a closely related study, Van Zwol [20] tracked the evolution in the Flickr ecosystem of roughly 1.8 million photos uploaded within a 10 day period. The main question in this work is also aimed at understanding user behavior, but instead of targeting the producers of the content, it targeted the consumers (that is, the viewers), trying to identify the factors that explain photo popularity. One of the factors that correlates with the numbers of views a photo receives is the number of groups a photo is shared in. In this case too, metadata stemming from group membership helped verify the research hypothesis, namely that photo popularity is closely related to the social networking behavior of the users. The lesson from these two studies is that the number of groups a user belongs to is a good predictor of their behavior in other areas of the website, such as tagging activity and photo discovery.

In a different study, Singla and Weber [18] looked at Flickr's social network in order to determine whether social relations influence the brand of the camera a user owns. Their dataset included roughly 2.1 million users, and almost 44 milion user-user relationships. Their basic findings are that two users who have a link in Flickr are more likely to own the same brand of camera, with a probability of 0.27 as opposed to 0.19 for two random users. At the same time, the authors made an interesting assumption with respect to the strength of a relationship between two users, taking into account the number of common groups they belong to. Thus, the authors considered users who share a greater number of groups to be *closer* to each other than to other users they share less groups with. In their study however, there appears to be no correlation between the number of common groups and the chances of owning a same-brand camera. The use of group membership information as a measure of friendship strength remains nevertheless an interesting option, to be further explored in subsequent studies. Just as Singla and Weber [18] used overlapping groups as a measure of similarity for users, Wang *et al.* [21] used overlapping groups as a measure of similarity for images. The authors used the group membership information in order to solve the problem of image retrieval and organization in user collections that are not necessarily tagged. Their idea was to use images belonging to the same Flickr groups as training data for a classification algorithm that uses visual features, using images that share no groups at all with the training set as negative examples. For their experiments they used as starting point 130 groups that have specific interests, such as objects, like *aquarium* and *car*, specific scene types like *urban* and *sunset*, or abstract concepts like *Christmas* and *smiles*. For these 130 categories, the authors showed an improvement of the classification when the "Flickr similarity" is used as opposed to just visual features without any context.

We have seen in these examples a number of different ways in which the simple fact of belonging to a group can be used as additional information, either as a measure of sociability for the users themselves, or as measures of similarity for users or images sharing the same groups. Whatever the main task, taking into account such information has the advantage of being relatively simple from a computational point of view, and whenever possible it should probably be used.

Groups as funnels

A more straightforward way of using Flickr Groups is data gathering. Indeed, as certain groups tend to have very specific themes, they end up acting like content funnels. For example, as shown in Fig. (2), the *Everything GREEN!* group requires that any photo shared in the group by its contributing members (920 of them at the time of writing) contain something green. Similar groups can be found for nearly every color in the spectrum, as well as animal species, cars, trains, buildings, airplanes, airports, chairs, trees, leaves ... the list goes on and on. This plethora of *concept groups* has encouraged researchers to start using their photo pools as data sources.

This is for example the case for the work of Chen *et al.* [2] in which the authors proposed a group and tag recommender. The authors first defined a list of concepts, and then retrieved training data from Flickr by using photo-level and group-level searches. Their experiments showed that group-based training sets lead to better results when compared to photo-based ones, and this is most likely explained by the curating function of group moderators - users who make sure photos submitted to the group abide by the group rules. A photo tagged with concept "X" may or may not contain the specific concept (for instance Kennedy *et al.* [7] talked about a 50/50 chance of a concept being present in Flickr photos tagged with that concept), but when a photo is added to a group about concept "X" it is more likely to actually contain the concept due to group rules. It might therefore be more pertinent to gather content starting from groups matching the search term rather than from individual photo search results.

In a study on the ways people discover new content on Flickr, Lerman and Jones [9] have used three different sets of data: one coming from the most popular photos on Flickr, one from a random sample of photos, and a third one from the *Apex* group, a group dedicated, as the name implies it, to high quality photos. They concluded that most of a photo's popularity can be explained by what they called "social browsing", that is users who discover new content mostly through their social network of contacts. In this particular case, a very large group focused on exposing high quality photos was used as a starting point for content gathering.

Other authors have recently used groups as a starting point in user selection. Plangprasopchok and Lerman [16] attempted to construct a common folksonomy by aggregating shallow hierarchies created by many distinct Flickr users. To somehow limit the spread of concepts, they turned to Flickr Groups for user selection, gathering all members of 17 groups interested in a given category (insect photography). For each user the authors then collected information on their photo sets and collections - two photo management structures available in Flickr. Photos can be grouped in sets, and sets can be grouped in collections, therefore forming the shallow hierarchies the authors used for folksonomy extraction. Results seem to be promising, as the authors extract meaningful non-trivial hierarchies from this

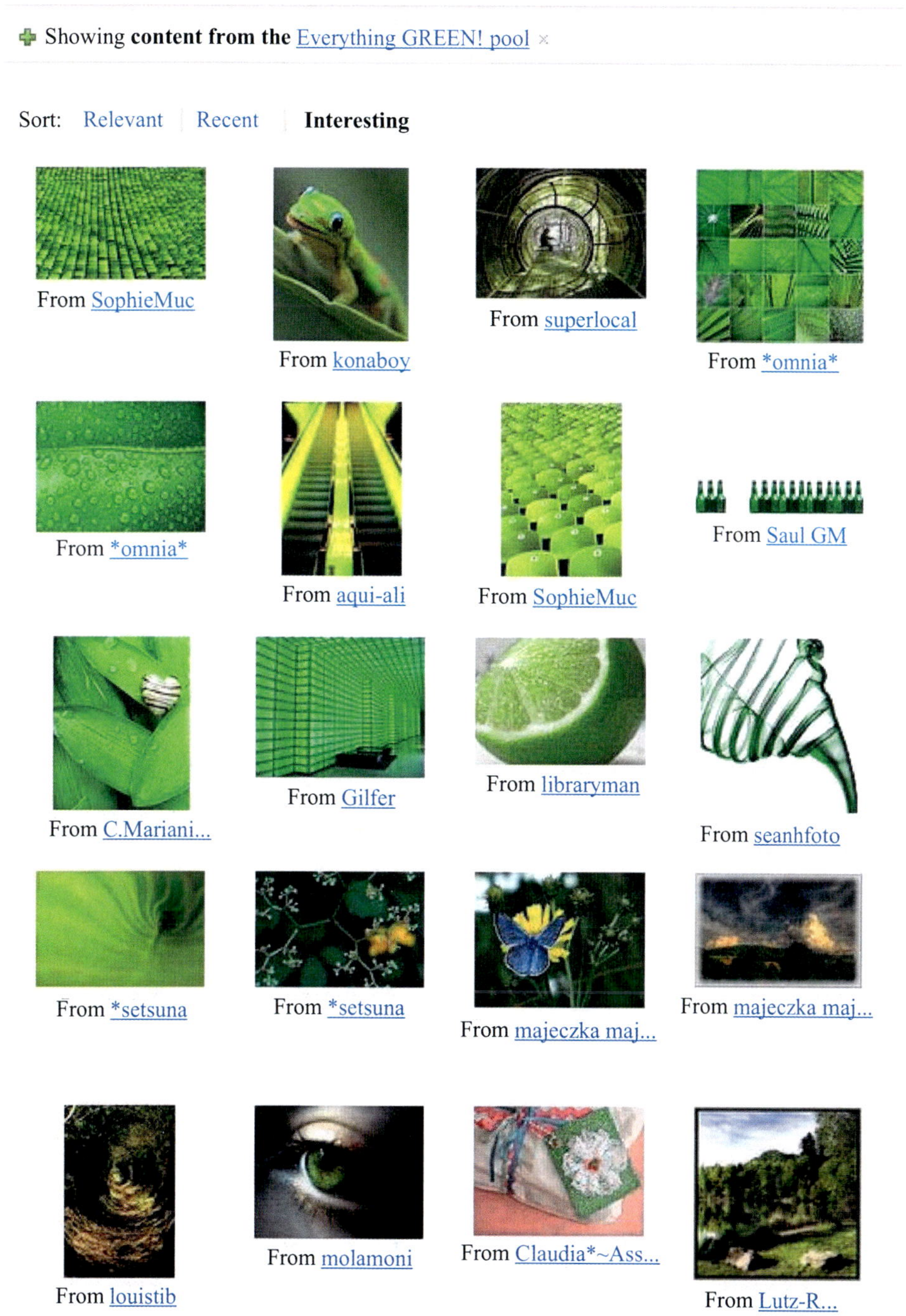

Fig. (2): A partial view of the photo pool for the group *Everything GREEN!*. Members are required to only post photos that contain at least one green element.

aggregation effort, with roughly 3200 concepts from data collected from over 21,000 users. A somewhat similar approach for user selection was also used by Miller and Edwards [10] in their ethnographic study on photo-sharing culture and practices of users of Flickr. Although at a much smaller scale - their work involved a user study with a group of 10 people, the authors made use of Flickr's groups in order to recruit participants in the study. The recruiting methods included word-of-mouth, email campaigns, Craiglist ads, and ads within a local Flickr group. It turned out that by far the most successful method was through the Flickr group - another indication that the social aspect is one of the driving forces of Flickr users. They describe a class of users they call *Snaprs* whose photo-sharing practices seem to be deeply tied to the way Flickr Groups work, for online sharing as well as offline activities.

In conclusion, whether looking at collecting a higher quality training set for image retrieval problems, or finding users interested in a certain theme or closely located geographically, Flickr Groups clearly provide an excellent starting point for research.

Groups as a subject of research

Last, but by no means least, we take a look at the research that makes use of groups as primary data source, and treats them as research entities in their own right. We left this discussion to the end as it is the widest spread use of Flickr Groups.

Prieur *et al.* [17] analyzed Flickr from data collected in 2006. They looked at basic statistics of the Flickr population and its communication patterns, and also looked at groups as a coordination tool. Their analysis, based on a sample of roughly 70,000 groups, seems to support the fact that groups are important community-building entities, and are used by users both as content pools and as social circles. In our own previous work [12], using a dataset of roughly 50,000 groups, we also analyzed Flickr users and groups from a participatory point of view. Our findings showed that users who shared photos in groups did so with roughly 30% of their photo collections, and they participated on average in 50 groups, showing the importance groups have for Flickr users. In the second part of our study we used a probabilistic topic model, namely Probabilistic Latent Semantic Analysis (PLSA), that enabled us to create a topic-based representation for groups. On a dataset of roughly 8,000 groups, each group was regarded as a text document defined by its composing words - the totality of the tags present in the group pool. In Tab. (2) and (3) we show example latent topics extracted from the model, along with groups that are highly probable within that topic, and also some of the photos found in the group pools for topics 1 and 12. Most topics in the model isolate a certain concept, illustrated here by three instances: topic 1 is about *Plants*, topic 3 is mainly about *New York City*, and topic 12 is about *Beach Landscapes*. The main advantage is that they are learnt automatically from the aggregated tags for all groups, with a

Tab. (2): Some of the topics in the PLSA model, characterized by their most probable tags (ranked by the probabilities of the tags given the topic, $P(t \mid z)$), and by their most probable groups (ranked by the probabilities of the topics given the group, $P(z \mid G)$) (taken from [12]).

Topic 1	
$P(t \mid z)$	**Tag**
0.0766	flower
0.0555	flowers
0.0550	nature
0.0431	ilovenature
0.0323	spring
0.0295	garden
0.0243	green
0.0221	yellow
0.0212	macro
0.0204	pink
0.0168	white
0.0136	plant
0.0126	blue
0.0122	purple
0.0112	red
0.0110	flora
0.0109	canon
0.0095	rose

Topic 1	
$P(z \mid G)$	**Group name**
0.9715	1-Plants World
0.9456	Flickr Gardens
0.8783	In my garden
0.8718	My Garden
0.8347	Daffodil World
0.8337	What plant is that?
0.8214	Gardening for Fun
0.8102	Garden Flowers
0.7993	grow
0.7377	Backyard Nature

Topic 3	
$P(t \mid z)$	**Tag**
0.1094	nyc
0.0767	newyork
0.0441	newyorkcity
0.0393	brooklyn
0.0384	gothamist
0.0363	manhattan
0.0354	montreal
0.0344	ny
0.0206	quebec
0.0119	canada
0.0101	urban
0.0099	york
0.0096	new
0.0091	coneyisland
0.0089	street
0.0083	city
0.0079	usa
0.0067	subway

Topic 3	
$P(z \mid G)$	**Group name**
0.9943	Mermaid Parade, 2007
0.9866	Coney Island Mermaid Parade
0.9849	Coney Island
0.9771	(718) Brooklyn
0.9224	N.Y.C.
0.9067	Curbed
0.8989	Gothamist
0.8988	NYC Social
0.8642	NYC from A to Zed
0.8623	The NYC Subway

Topic 12	
$P(t \mid z)$	**Tag**
0.0556	sky
0.0542	sunset
0.0460	clouds
0.0411	beach
0.0349	sea
0.0267	water
0.0248	ocean
0.0233	blue
0.0177	sun
0.0124	sand
0.0108	sunrise
0.0101	landscape
0.0089	cloud
0.0082	silhouette
0.0076	boat
0.0076	coast
0.0073	desert
0.0070	nikon

Topic 12	
$P(z \mid G)$	**Group name**
0.8866	Beaches & Sunset
0.8480	wave porn (pls nominate for best of)
0.8430	Fotos Caribe
0.8338	*I Love the Ocean/Sea* (Ocean Only, No People Shots)
0.8326	the sea and its spectrum
0.8126	Boating
0.8107	Sky and Sea
0.8070	Sea
0.8033	Caribbean perspective
0.8023	Atlantic Ocean

Tab. (3): Example photos from group pools, that are highly probable for topics 1 (top row) and 12 (bottom row), shown in Table (2) (taken from [12]).

photos from group *grow*, by *docman*(1), *Ben McLeod* (2,3), *gailf548* (4)

photos from group *Flickr Gardens*, by *Lorika13*, *egg.*, *annethelibrarian*, *Somerslea*

photos from group *Beaches & Sunset*, by *Mallmus*, *marj k*, *The Life of Bryan*, *cakecosas*

photos from group *Sea*, by *Martin Burns*, *mnadi*, *carf*, *Ennor*

global vocabulary of roughly 10,000 words. This topic-based representation can be used as a browsing tool for groups, or as a search improvement, particularly in a query expansion scenario, by going through the topic model and retrieving related tags based on the most likely topic for the search term.

Also dealing with the rather large amount of similar, competing groups, is the work of De Choudhury [3]. The author approaches group recommendation from a slightly different perspective, based not so much on the content itself, as similar groups will host similar content, but from a more social point of view: which is the group that will best reward a user's participation in it? To achieve this, the author proposed a method based on Hidden Markov Models to characterize groups' activity on two planes: content-related activity, such as uploads from users or the process of adding photos as favorites, and user-related activity, such as comments on each other's photos. A dataset of 200 groups and roughly 52,000 users was used for experiments which showed good correlation between the proposed activity prediction model and real group attributes tracked over a period of 30 days, such as the number of new members, the number of comments, the number of favorite images, and the number of new uploads. In a related study, De Choudhury *et al.* [4] also tried to recommend groups to users for a specific image, however in this case the recommendation took into account visual features of the image, textual tags, and user interaction through comments. Using roughly 15,000 images that belonged to 925 groups, the authors evaluated experimentally the predictive power of their model and found that, when social features were included in addition to the visual and textual ones, predictive performance improved.

Another study that considers Flickr Groups as a central research problem is our work [13] on modeling Flickr users and groups in a joint fashion. In this work we made the simplifying assumption that users and groups can eventually be seen as

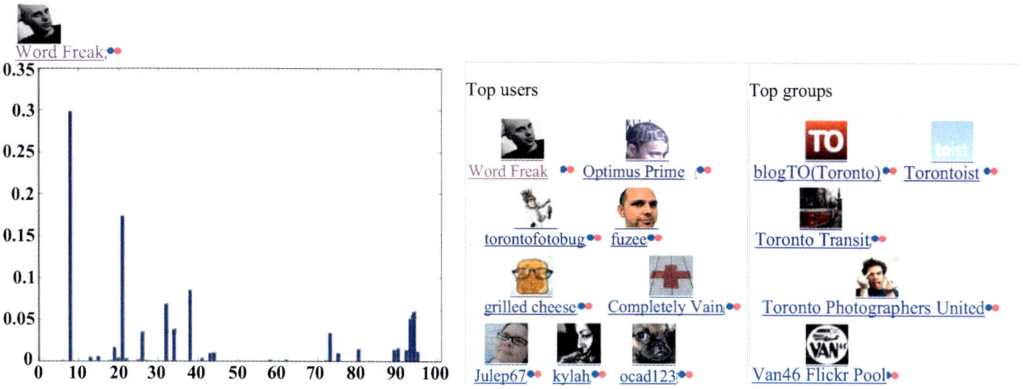

Fig. (3): A user's topic-based representation is shown on the left, with the topics' probability distribution. Based on this representation and a similarity measure, the most similar users and most similar groups are then displayed.

equivalent entities, as both have collections of photos and inherently tag vocabularies belonging to those photos. We learned a probabilistic topic model on the joint corpus of Flickr entities, much like we had already done with just groups in our previous work [12]. Each group and each user were seen as textual documents composed of their photos' aggregated tags, and the result of the model was a topic-based representation for users and groups alike. The joint model brings users and groups onto a common ground, and as such direct comparison is straightforward. We computed distances between all entities in our dataset of roughly 8,000 users and almost 11,000 groups and could thus simply rank all entities with respect to any other, obtaining recommendation lists of both groups and users. An example is shown in Fig. (3), where the "query user" and his topic-based distribution are shown on the left, the top recommended users in the middle, and the top recommended groups on the right. For a comprehensive study on joint modeling of Flickr groups and users we refer the reader to [14].

In a different direction, Lerman *et al.* [8] used a dataset collected from Flickr of roughly 13,000 images tagged with prototypical terms like *tiger*, *newborn* and *beetle*, on which they attempted to filter the search results based on the searching user's personal information, such as their list of contacts - other Flickr users - and their list of previously used tags. In addition, they explored integrating information from the groups the photos are submitted to in their tag-based model, considering the group name as a commonly agreed-upon tag. Personalization by contacts yielded significant improvement, although as search results are strictly filtered based on whether the images come from the user's social network, it is limited to content retrieval rather than content discovery. Personalization by tags used a topic model for each search set with 10 topics, and showed relative improvements over plain search as well. In this case, including group names as additional tags did not improve filtering results, on the contrary, it sometimes hurt. The authors believe this is mainly an effect of highly social groups, which do not necessarily have a focused photographic interest, and as such are rather noisy. This raises a question for the research community: how to know which groups can be useful in enriching a dataset, and when? This question was at least partially answered by Lin *et al.*[23] in a paper that tried to extract temporal patterns of themes of interest in Flickr Groups. The authors used visual features as well as social features in order to describe each group as a mixture of themes - each theme is a pattern of image content and context. Context in this case was information related to the owner of the photo, to the tags associated with the photo, and the timestamp of the photo upload. The authors used a dataset of 52 groups and roughly 50,000 images and evaluated their theme extraction method through a tag-prediction task, in which their method outperformed baselines that only used textual or visual features. From a user perspective, theme extraction can represent a novel way to browse group content. From a research perspective, knowing the rates at which a group's interest changes may become valuable metadata that describes the suitability of a given group for different tasks, like content gathering: the more stable a group's themes, the more chances of the content being homogeneous and suitable for training sets, and the more dynamic a group's themes, the higher the chances of mixed content.

We conclude with two recent works that deal with the lack of macro-structure related to Flickr Groups. At the time of writing, discovering new groups in Flickr was still a matter of searching by keywords or of serendipitous discovery while browsing someone else's photos. There is no hierarchy per se, nor any other kind of classification. In a study using a dataset of 300 groups, Egger *et al.*[5] used a membership-based measure they termed *GroupConnectivity* in order to perform community segmentation. This measure is simple to compute, as the fraction between the number of shared members of two groups and the total number of members of the smallest of the two groups. As such, this ratio is bounded by 0 if two groups have no members in common, and by 1 if all members of the smaller group are also members of a larger group. Taking this a step further the method builds, using the same measure of connectivity, a tree of groups. Their assumption was that larger groups are semantic parents of smaller groups with which they are highly connected. Through their experiments their assumption seemed to be generally confirmed, although some counterexamples were also found. In a similar study [11] we also looked at the problem of organizing Flickr Groups, by finding what we called *hypergroups*. Our approach was to use Latent Dirichlet Allocation, a probabilistic topic model, to describe each group as a mixture of topics of interest. We then computed a similarity measure based on the Jensen-Shannon divergence, and fed the similarity matrix into an Affinity Propagation (AP) [6] algorithm. The advantages of the AP clustering are manifold: (i) the number of clusters is determined automatically at run-time from the data points by message passing between all exemplars; (ii) at the end of the algorithm, each cluster "center" is an actual

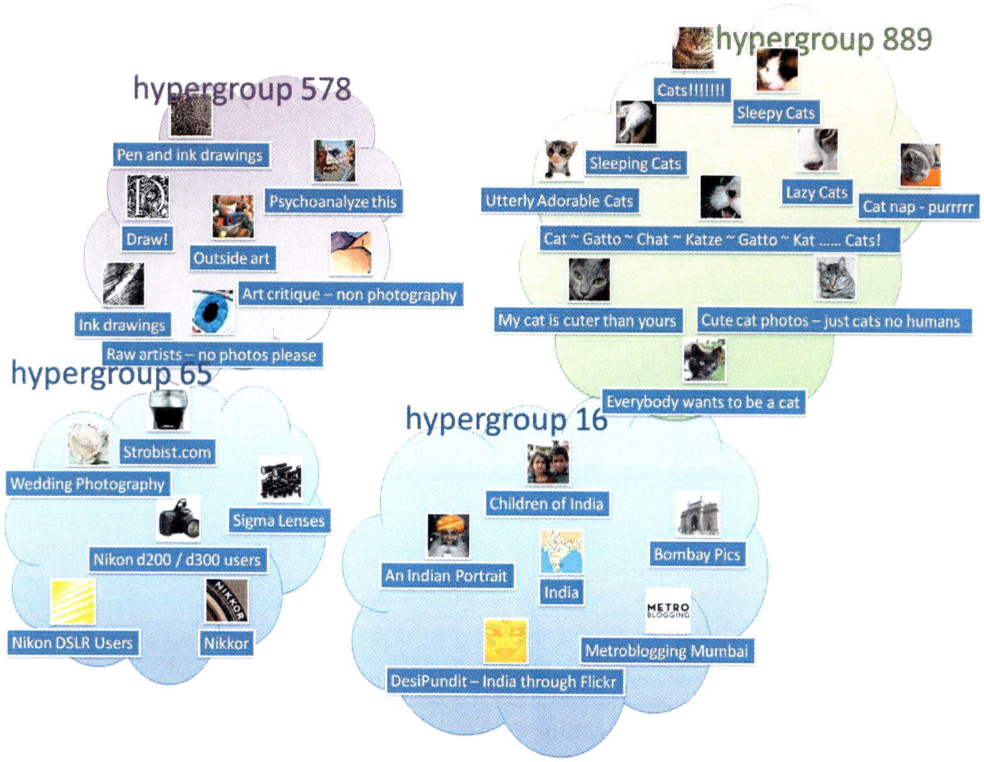

Fig. (4): Hypergroups obtained after clustering through Affinity Propagation. In hypergroup 65, *Strobist.com* is the Flickr group started by a hugely popular US based photographer, David Hobby, who happens to be a Nikon user. Hypergroups 16 and 889 leave no doubt about their member groups' interests. Hypergroup 578 brings together groups dedicated to art drawings and paintings, much less homogeneous from a group names perspective, but quite clearly homogeneous from an interest point of view (taken from [11]).

data point; (iii) the algorithm is fast to converge. In Fig.(4) we show clustering results on a dataset of over 10,000 groups. The hypergroups are generally homogeneous, and bring together groups that are not similar by name, but rather at a more abstract level, like for example *RUSTY and CRUSTY* and *Things that Moved.* For a human observer, making the link between things that moved and things that are rusty may be straightforward, but in the absence of keywords, this link is hard to find through a computer search. An even better example of the advantage brought by topic-based clustering is hypergroup 578, which corresponds to groups dedicated to art *except* photography. The group names are much less homogeneous, but quite clearly the hypergroup is homogeneous from an interest point of view.

4 Concluding Remarks

In this chapter we have reviewed the existing ways in which Flickr Groups have been used in research in order to either better understand the dynamics of online communities, to improve traditional multimedia problems such as image search, or to help users navigate Flickr Groups themselves. We have seen that, more often than not, including metadata stemming from the social activities of users is beneficial, be it in the form of user interaction through comments, views, and votes, or through membership in specific interest groups. In addition, from a computational point of view this kind of metadata is also almost always cheaper than the content itself (that is, visual features).

We also believe there are several new and interesting avenues to explore, as metadata gets richer and more social media websites will provide access to it. Understanding how this data can be used in order to enrich the user experience or facilitate exploration of ever growing content is of high relevance. Assuming that ways of federating user identities across multiple social media platforms become feasible, future work may investigate whether user behavior and metadata are consistent across social media platforms, or whether specific factors (such as system design and affordances) may impact the way users create, use, and annotate content.

We hope this short review of current research will help practitioners, researchers, and graduate students in social (multi)media processing to better understand the potential of rich communities like Flickr Groups.

Acknowledgements

This research has been supported by the Swiss National Science Foundation through the MULTI project. We also thank Marc Egger for sharing his figures.

5 References

[1] Morgan Ames and Mor Naaman. Why We Tag: Motivations for Annotation in Mobile and Online Media. In *SIGCHI*, 2007.

[2] Hong M. Chen, Ming H. Chang, Ping C. Chang, Ming C. Tien, Winston H. Hsu, and Ja L. Wu. Sheepdog: Group and Tag Recommendation for Flickr Photos by Automatic Search-based Learning. In *ACM Multimedia*, 2008.

[3] Munmun De Choudhury. Modeling and Predicting Group Activity over Time in Online Social Media. In *Proc of the 20th ACM Conf on Hypertext and Hypermedia*, 2009.

[4] Munmun De Choudhury, Hary Sundaram, Yu-Ru Lin, Ajita John, and Doree Duncan Seligmann. Connecting Content to Community in Social Media via Image Content, User Tags and User Communication. In *ICME*, 2009.

[5] Marc Egger, Kai Fischbach, Peter Gloor, Andre Lang, and Mark Sprenger. Deriving Taxonomies from Automatic Analysis of Group Membership Structure in Large Social Networks. In *Lecture Notes in Informatics*, 2009.

[6] Brendan J. Frey and Delbert Dueck. Clustering by passing messages between data points. *Science*, 2007.

[7] Lyndon S. Kennedy, Shih-Fu Chang, and Igor V. Kozintsev. To Search or to Label?: Predicting the Performance of Search-based Automatic Image Classifiers. In *ACM MIR*, 2006.

[8] K. Lerman, A. Plangrasopchok, and C. Wong. Personalizing Results of Image Search on Flickr. In *AAAI workshop on Intelligent Techniques for Web Personlization*, 2007.

[9] Kristina Lerman and Laurie Jones. Social Browsing on Flickr. In *ICWSM*, 2007.

[10] Andrew D. Miller and W. Keith Edwards. Give and Take: a Study of Consumer Photo-sharing Culture and Practice. In *SIGCHI*, 2007.

[11] Radu Andrei Negoescu, Brett Adams, Dinh Phung, Svetha Venkatesh, and Daniel Gatica-Perez. Flickr Hypergroups. In *ACM Multimedia*, 2009.

[12] Radu Andrei Negoescu and Daniel Gatica-Perez. Analyzing Flickr Groups. In *CIVR*, 2008.

[13] Radu Andrei Negoescu and Daniel Gatica-Perez. Topickr: Flickr Groups and Users Reloaded. In *ACM Multimedia*, 2008.

[14] Radu Andrei Negoescu and Daniel Gatica-Perez. Modeling Flickr Communities through Probabilistic Topic-based Analysis. *IEEE Transactions on Multimedia*, 2010.

[15] Oded Nov, Mor Naaman, and Chen Ye. What drives content tagging: the case of photos on flickr. In *SIGCHI*, 2008.

[16] Anon Plangprasopchok and Kristina Lerman. Constructing Folksonomies from User-specified Relations on Flickr. In *ACM WWW*, 2009.

[17] Christophe Prieur, Dominique Cardon, Jean-Samuel Beuscart, Nicolas Pissard, and Pascal Pons. The Strength of Weak Cooperation: a Case Study on Flickr. Retrieved on Jan 21, 2010 from http://arxiv.org/abs/0802.2317, 2008.

[18] Adish Singla and Ingmar Weber. Camera Brand Congruence in the Flickr Social Graph. In *WSDM*, 2009.

[19] Nancy A. Van House. Flickr and Public Image-sharing: Distant Closeness and Photo Exhibition. In *SIGCHI*, 2007.

[20] Roelof van Zwol. Flickr: Who is Looking. In *Proc. of the Intl. Conf. on Web Intelligence*, 2007.

[21] Gang Wang, Derek Hoiem, and David Forsyth. Learning Image Similarity from Flickr Groups Using Stochastic Intersection Kernel Machines. In *ICCV*, 2009.

[22] YouTube. Youtube Factsheet. Retrieved on Jan 21, 2010, http://www.youtube.com/t/fact_sheet, 2010.

[23] Yu-Ru Lin, Hari Sundaram, Munmun De Choudhury, and Aisling Kelliher. Temporal Patterns in Social Media Streams: Theme Discovery and Evolution using Joint Analysis of Content and Context. In *ICME*, 2009.

Internet Multimedia Search and Mining, 2013, 223-239

CHAPTER 9

Word2Image: A System for Visual Interpretation of Concepts

Haojie Li*
School of Software, Dalian University of Technology,
Tel: 86-411-87571638, Email: hjli@dlut.edu.cn
Jinhui Tang
School of Computer Science, Nanjing University of Science and Technology,
Tel: 86-25-84315635, Email: tangjh1981@acm.org
Guangda Li
School of Computing, National University of Singapore,
Tel: 65-65164091, Email: g0701808@nus.edu.sg
Tat-Seng Chua
School of Computing, National University of Singapore,
Tel: 65-65162505, Email: chuats@comp.nus.edu.sg

Abstract: Besides the use of traditional textual semantic description to convey the meanings of a certain word or concept, visual illustration is a complementary and often more intuitive way to interpret the concept. Thus the technique that converts word to image is desirable though it is very difficult. Since a concept usually has different semantic aspects, we need several correct and semantically-rich images to represent the concept under different context. In this chapter, we explore how to leverage the web image collection and existing knowledge resources to fulfill such task and develop a novel multimedia application system named *Word2Image*. Various techniques, including the correlation analysis, semantic and visual clustering are adapted into our system to produce the sets of high quality, precise, diverse

Xian-Sheng Hua, Marcel Worring & Tat-Seng Chua (Eds.)

and representative images to visually translate a given concept. The objective and subjective evaluations show the feasibility and effectiveness of our approach.

Keywords

Word2Image, Image Search, Social Media, Flickr, Semantic Aspect, Visual Translation, Multimedia Dictionary, Visual Saliency, Correlation Analysis, Tag Saliency

1 Introduction

The last few years have witnessed the explosive growth of video and image data on the Internet, along with the massive associated metadata, context and social information [1]. The large amount of multimedia resources on the web brings us new challenges to multimedia content analysis and retrieval; while at the same time, offers us great opportunities to evolve new multimedia applications [2, 3]. In this chapter, we present a novel system named *Word2Image*, to translate a word/concept into its visual counterpart with the sets of high quality, precise, diverse and representative images by leveraging the web image collection and knowledge resources.

A picture is worth a thousand words. This proverb reveals the importance of visualization in explaining a concept or word. Suppose someone is introducing the concept of an animal, such as *the elephant*, to a child. If he/she can provide some pictures of *elephant* to the child in the description, it will be more readily for the child to comprehend the meanings. Since manually finding such appropriate images is time consuming, we aims at developing a system that can automatically generate the sets of images to visually interpret a given word. Automatically linking image to word is very helpful for people to rapidly and conveniently acquire knowledge, but it also presents some challenging issues. First, the correctness of the linked images is critical; otherwise unrelated images will lead to misunderstanding. Second, since most word has different semantic aspects, the resulting set of images should be sufficiently diverse to represent these aspects. Third, the representative images should be selected from the image sets to reduce redundancy, i.e., we should present the compact and visual appealing images to users.

In recent years, digital image collections on the web have grown rapidly, and many image search engines including content-based and keyword-based systems, have been developed to help people access these resources. In the keyword-based engines, like Google [4] and AltaVista [5], when user types a keyword (or concept), the systems will return a large number of related images. Obviously, directly applying the search results is not an appropriate strategy for our application because the result list is not well organized and contains many irrelevant images. Moreover, since the images are crawled from all kinds of webpages, their quality is not ensured.

In this chapter, we develop a system named *Word2Image*, in which we use the community-contributed photo website *Flickr* [6] as the image resource, and employ various techniques to produce the sets of high quality, precise, diverse and representative images to visually translate a given word. *Flickr* is a growing photo sharing website. As at 1st August 2011, *Flickr* hosted over 6 billion photos, and the contributors continuously upload about 4.5 million premium photos per day to it. Different from other image collections, each photo in *Flickr* is loosely annotated with tags or metadata by the owner and other users, making it possible to perform the semantic analysis needed in *Word2Image*.

As depicted in Fig.(1), *Word2Image* works as follows. User inputs a concept or word, such as "elephant" from a specific domain such as "animal". Firstly, a large number of diverse and precise images are retrieved from *Flickr*, using heuristic rules and correlation analysis based on the pre-built domain model. Secondly, we extract salient keywords from tags and use them to represent the semantic features of images; the visual features are also extracted, and a hierarchical clustering method is applied to group the images into semantically and visually diverse topics using the two types of features. Thirdly, we select and rank representative images from the clusters based on their sematic and visual saliency. Finally, the representative images are presented to the user to visually interpret the given concept.

In the literatures, our work is related to image search result clustering, text-to-picture synthesis and applications on community-contributed web resources. In the multimedia research community, image clustering has attracted lots of attentions as it is a critical technique to help users digest large image collections. For example, Cai *et al.* [7] clustered web image search results using visual, textual and link analysis to discover the underlying topics. Gao *et al.* [8] simultaneously used the low-level visual features and surrounding texts in one framework based on tripartite graph model. *IGroup* system [9] first identifies some query-related semantic clusters based on web search result analysis. It then uses the cluster names to retrieve images and organizes the resulting images into a cluster structure to users. These three works are closely related to ours. However, they are all designed for clustering the image search results, addressing the diversity of results while our purpose is to give a visual explanation of word. Again, the precisions of results in these systems were not satisfactory and a large amount of junk images may mislead the understanding of the word. Zhu *et al.* [10] proposed a text-to-picture system that attempts to visually translate unrestricted natural language text by synthesizing a picture based on both the image parts and extracted keyphrases. Compared to this work, our system uses the sets of high quality real images to interpret a word, not just using one picture, thus it can better represent the diverse semantic aspects of the given word. Recently, Kennedy *et al.* [11] proposed to use *Flickr* to generate diverse and representative image search results for landmarks. They used visual clustering to find a landmark's diverse views and the results were encouraging. However, their work was limited to landmarks, and the semantic diversity was not considered. Our work can be seen a more general case.

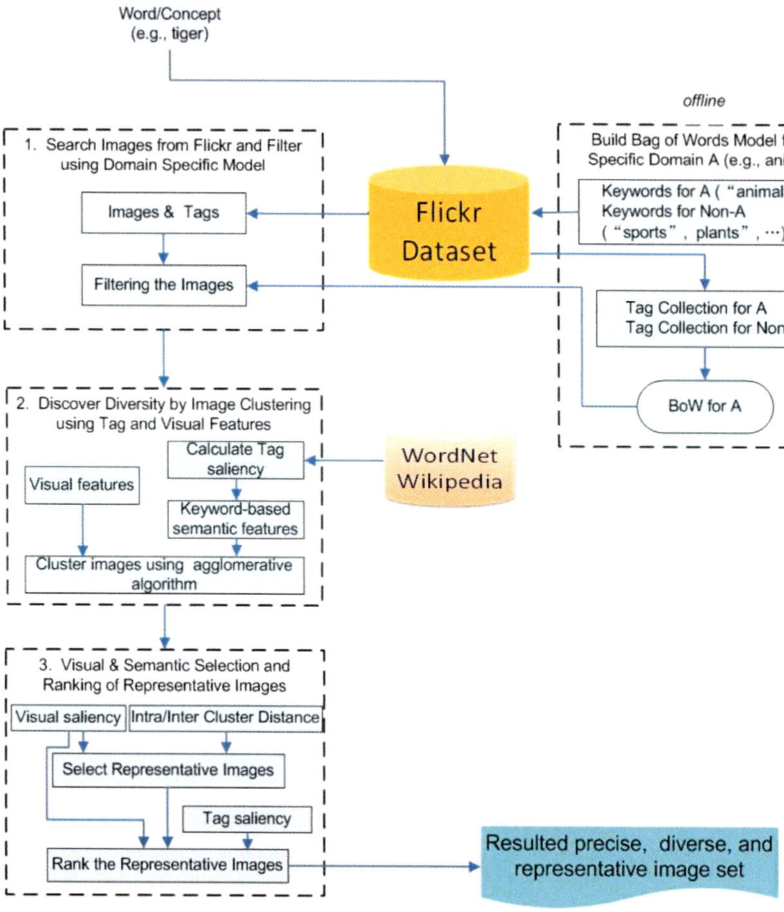

Fig. (1): The systematic flowchart of *Word2Image*.

2 Generating Diverse and Precise Image Set

As we have pointed out before, precision and diversity of images are two key requirements for the visual translation task. According to precision, we want the images to be correct; according to diversity, we want the images to be able to represent the different semantic aspects of the concept. Generally speaking, the state-of-the-art image search and processing techniques have much difficulty in meeting such requirements. In this chapter, we use *Flickr*, where the images are accompanied with some useful semantic cues. Such information includes: 1) image title along with several to dozens of tags added by the owner used to describe the content of image and 2) *metadata*, such as the photo's date and location, name of owner, etc. All these data and the images can be conveniently downloaded using *Flickr* API [6].

Heuristic for diversity

It is difficult to directly define diversity. However, we can expect that images coming from different groups, different users, even different time and locations will show sufficient variations in both semantic and visual characteristics. Therefore, in *Word2Image*, we uniformly sample images from different groups and users to ensure the diversity of resulting image sets.

Filtering strategy for precision

Generally, concept or word is polysemous. For example, "tiger" means a kind of *animal* in most cases; while in some context such as "tiger lily" it is referred to a kind of *plant*. Another example is "jaguar", which may means *animal*, *car* or *Mac OS* in different contexts. Therefore, if we issue a concept to the keyword-based image search engines, the returned results are usually mixed with several topics of the concept. In our application, since we want to visually explain specific sense of a concept, it is necessary to filter out the irrelevant images which belong to other senses of the concept. Here, we use the pre-built Bag of words (BoW) [12] domain/sense models to tackle this task.

Specifically, we first build domain model for given domain using the well-known TFIDF technique by mining the photo tags downloaded from *Flickr* by issuing keywords belonging to the given domain and other domains. As an example, the procedures for building the domain model for "animal" are given in the following 3 steps. 1) We collect photo tags of domain "animal" by issuing keywords like "animal", "animals", "tiger", "wolf", etc to *Flickr*. The keywords are removed from their respective tag collections to avoid bias on keywords when computing the TFIDF statistics. For example, we remove "tiger" from the photo tags obtained by issuing "tiger". 2)We collect photo tags of other domains such as "sports", "plant", "tool" and so on from *Flickr* like in Step 1). 3)With the tags collected from the domain "animal" and other domains, it is ready to build the BoW domain model of "animal" using the TFIDF technique. It is expected that the high frequency tags will either be semantically related to or have high co-ocurrence with the domain, thus we keep the top N tags and their frequencies to represent the given domain. We can also expect that if a photo is related to the specific domain, i.e., the specific sense of a concept, it should have a higher correlation score with the domain model. This motivates our criterion for filtering out unrelated images. Let the domain model of D be $M = \{w_i, p_i\}$, the word set of tags and the title of retrieved image I be $T = \{t_i\}$. Then the correlation score between I and domain D is defined as follows.

$$CorrScore(I, D) = \frac{\sum_{i=1}^{|M|}\{p_i * \ In(w_i, T)\}}{|T|} \tag{1}$$

where $In(w_i, T)$ equals to 1 if $w_i \in T$, otherwise 0.

We calculate the correlation scores for all the retrieved images and rank them according to the scores. It is clear that the top images are more related to the specific domain/sense. Thus we simply select the top K percent of images to interpret the given concept.

The use of prior domain/sense knowledge to filter out unrelated images is reasonable for our application, since when someone is introducing a concept to others, he must have in mind which topic of the concept he wants to explain.

3 Discover Diversity by Image Clustering

When we learn a word or concept (take "elephant" as the example), some related concepts like "zoo", "animal", are more helpful in capturing the meaning of the target than unrelated concepts like"sky","water". At the same time, we may care about the unique characteristics ("trunk", "tusk") or sub-concepts ("African elephant") of the target, namely, the semantic diversity of a word. Fortunately, the generated image set is diverse enough to include most of the topics of the word. Therefore, the visual translation system needs to discover these topics and group the images into the corresponding categories. Meanwhile, we also want the images of each category to be visually consistent. This function is performed by the semantic and visual clustering component.

The semantic representation of images

Text clustering is a well-studied subject in text mining research community [13]. But the existing methods cannot be applied directly to our system because each image has a varying number of tags ranging from a few to several dozens, which is too sparse as compared to documents. Moreover, different keywords in the images' tags and titles contribute differently to the discovery of topics. For example, "trunk" will dominate over "water" in finding interested topics for "elephant". In *Word2Image*, we first calculate the saliency of each keyword in the set of tags and titles and only the top M keywords are kept and used to represent each image with an M-dimensional vector.

Calculating the saliency score of keywords

Saliency is used to measure a keyword's importance in discovering the distinct topics of a given word (denoted as $\boldsymbol{w}$ from now on). Here keyword refers to words in the tag collection of retrieved images after filtering. There are many factors that influence the saliency of a keyword. Here we consider two kinds of information derived from statistics and knowledge sources. The former includes the keyword's TFIDF measure and its correlation with the given concept based on *Flickr*, and the latter comes from knowledge of *WordNet* [14] and *Wikipedia* [15]. Before the computation, each keyword is replaced with its stem using the Porter algorithm [16].

Keyword Frequency/Inverce Document Frequency(TFIDF)

This is similar to the traditional meaning of Term Frequency / Inverce Document Frequency (TFIDF). Intuitively, more frequent keywords will be more salient. However, keywords with higher document frequency (DF) will be too general and less informative. Hence, keywords with too high and too low DF are further filtered out. Finally, the TFIDF for a remaining keyword, K, is computed as:

$$TFIDF(K) = freq(K)log\frac{N}{N(K)} \quad (2)$$

where $freq(K)$ is the frequency of K in the tag collection of $\boldsymbol{w}$; N is the total number of images in the building of the domain model as above; and *N(K)* is the total number of images whose tags contain K.

Correlation with the Given Concept

Flickr's Related Tags is "a list of tags 'related' to the given tag, based on clustered usage analysis" [6]. For example, the top 10 related tags for "tiger" are "zoo, cat, animal, animals, nature, wildlife, bigcat, white, stripes, wild". It can be seen that these words are either semantically related to the concept or have high co-ocurrence with the concept. For a keyword K in the *Related Tags* of given concept $\boldsymbol{w}$, if $\boldsymbol{w}$ is also in the *Related Tags* of K, then we can deduce that K is closely related to $\boldsymbol{w}$, or a semantically interesting topic of $\boldsymbol{w}$. For example, "stripes" is the related tag of "tiger" while "tiger" is also the related tag of "stripes", and we know that "stripes" is a specific visual characteristics of "tiger". Thus, we can evaluate the correlation between K and $\boldsymbol{w}$ as follows.

$$Correlate(K, w) = \begin{cases} 1, & K \in RelatedTags(w) \ \wedge \ w \in RelatedTags(K) \\ 0, & otherwise \end{cases} \quad (3)$$

Hyponymy and Meronym with w

The hyponyms of a word reveal some of its important semantic aspects. For example, the hyponyms of "athlete" include "acrobat", "baseball player", "tennis player", "runner" and so on. Obviously, these keywords should be selected as distinct topics of "athlete". So, if a keyword is among the hyponyms of a target word, it will have higher saliency. This is similar with the meronyms of a word. For example, "tusk" and "trunk" are meronyms of "elephant", while they are also two important aspects of "elephant". Here $HM(K)$ is defined to indicate whether the keyword K is the hyponyms or meronyms of $\boldsymbol{w}$:

$$HM(K, w) = \begin{cases} 1, & K \in Hyponym(w) \ \vee \ K \in Meronym(w) \\ 0, & otherwise \end{cases} \tag{4}$$

where $Hyponym(w)$ and $Mernym(w)$ are respectively the hyponyms and meronyms of $\boldsymbol{w}$ and are obtained from *WordNet* [14].

2-gram Validation with Wikipedia

Some keywords can be concatenated with the given concept to form 2-gram phrases, such as the "African elephant", "Indian Elephant" etc for concept "elephant", which are some species of elephant and thus are of interests to us. However, not all of the concatenated phrases are helpful. We note that if a phrase is meaningful, it usually has an entry in the largest, collaboratively built encyclopedia *Wikipedia*. Therefore, we validate a 2-gram phrase obtained from a keyword K and $\boldsymbol{w}$ as follows.

$$Valid2Gram(K, w) = \begin{cases} 1, & Concat(K, w) \ or \ Concat(w, K) \ is \ an \ article \\ & title \ in \ Wikipedia \\ 0, & otherwise \end{cases} \tag{5}$$

where $Concat(w1, w2)$ is the concatenated phrase of $w1$ and $w2$.

Finally, the saliency score of K is calculated by combining the above four measurements with a simple fusion rule as follows.

$$\begin{aligned} Saliency(K) &= TFIDF(K) * (1 + Correlate(K, w)) * (1 + HM(K, w)) \\ &\quad *(1 + Valid2Gram(K, w)) \end{aligned} \tag{6}$$

Representing the semantic feature of an image using the keyword vector

Given the saliency score of each keyword, we use the top M keywords, $KEYWORD = \{K_1, K_2, \ldots, K_M\}$, as the text feature of each image. Thus the content of an image J can be represented as a M-dimensional saliency vector $V_J = (v_1, v_2, \ldots, v_M)$, where v_i is defined as:

$$v_i = \begin{cases} Saliency(K_i), & K_i \ is \ in \ the \ tags \ or \ title \ of \ image \ J \\ 0, & otherwise \end{cases} \tag{7}$$

As expected, the topic-related keywords for $\boldsymbol{w}$ are ranked at top positions. For example, the top 10 salient keywords for "elephant" are "africa, tusk, wildlife, trunk, zoo, india, safari, animal, asia, nature". Evidently, these keywords are more distinctive and informative in discovering the interesting topics of "elephant".

The visual representation of images

We extract two types of visual features to represent the visual contents of an image. These features are the 225-dimensional grid color moments (by dividing the image into 5×5 grids) and 108-dimensional Haar wavelet texture[17].

Cluster images using semantic and visual features

We normalize the semantic and visual feature vectors of each image before concatenating them to represent the overall content of the image. Let the overall feature vectors of two images be x_i and x_j, their similarity is calculated as $exp(-||v_i - v_j||^2)$.

Given the similarities between images, we apply the agglomerative algorithm [18] to hierarchically cluster the image set into semantically and visually consistent groups. Here the stopping criterion for clustering is controlled by the inconsistent coefficients [19]. Generally, it is difficult to determine the coefficients to get reasonable clusters. In our work we simply select a lower value, say 0.6 to make the resulting clusters more consistent.

After clustering, we obtain some interesting clusters for the given concept. Take "elephant" as the example again, the resulting clusters include topics like "africa-wild-zoo-animal", "africa-trunk-safari-tusk", "india-wildlife- temple-pachyderm", and so on.

4 Selecting and Ranking the Representative Images

Selection of representative images for each cluster

For each image cluster, we select representative images based on visual analysis. Two factors are considered in our work. They are the visual representativeness and visual saliency of images.

As in [11], representative images are expected to exhibit the following qualities: (1) representative images are highly similar to each other within the cluster, and (2) representative images are highly dissimilar to random images outside the cluster. Thus, we use two measurements, the intra cluster distance and the inter cluster distance, to estimate the visual representativeness of a image.

Given an image cluster $V = \{I_1, I_2, \ldots, I_N\}$, the intra cluster distance and inter cluster distance of its cluster member I_i are calculated as follows.

$$Intra(I_i) = \frac{\sum_{j=1}^{|N|} VisDist(I_i, I_j)}{N} \tag{8}$$

$$Inter(I_i) = \frac{\sum_{I_x \in \bar{V}} VisDist(I_i, I_x)}{|\bar{V}|} \tag{9}$$

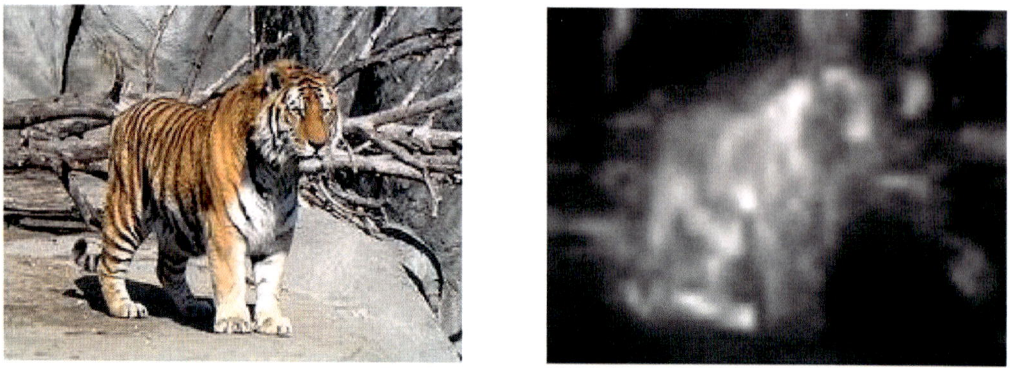

(a) (b)

Fig. (2): An image and its saliency map

where $VisDist(I_i, I_j)$ is the visual distance between image I_i and I_j, and $\bar{V}$ is the set of images outside the cluster V.

Besides the above two measurements, we propose to incorporate an additional visual saliency feature to rank the image's representativeness within its associated cluster. The similar idea of using visual saliency to find iconic images of a given object category has been exploited in [20]. Here, we also use it to measure the representativeness of an image with respect to a given object concept. This is based on the expectation that representative images should have large, at least medium size foreground objects which can be easily separated from the backgrounds. Computational attention model [21] is the most popularly used technique to find salient regions in an image by simulating the Human Visual System (HVS) which can filter the signals received by the HVS and select the important ones to be processed.

For each image, we first apply a graph-based visual saliency detection method [22] to generate a saliency map and then calculate its saliency score. The saliency map is an intensity image and the values of its pixels represent the visual saliency of the original image. Fig.(2) shows an input image and its saliency map. We can see that the saliency score of the object region is much higher than that of the background, implying that the computational attention model can be used to capture the focus of the image.

To calculate the saliency score of an image I, we use a center rectangle and its respective outer rectangle to compute the saliency contrast as in Fig.(3)(a). The center rectangle scans the image at different positions with different sizes, to locate an optimal position with optimal size that maximizes the following saliency score.

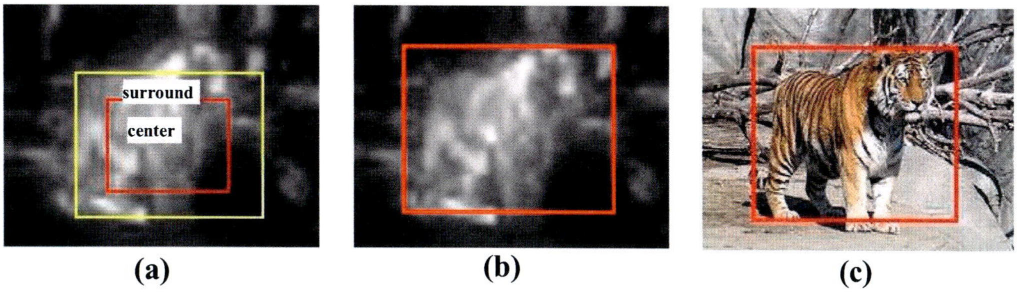

Fig. (3): The computation of saliency score of image. (a)center rectangle and outer rectangle used to compute saliency contrast; (b)the optimal center rectangle when the maximal saliency score is achieved; and c)the salient object.

$$\begin{aligned} VisSaliency(I) &= \max_{center}\{\frac{\sum_{(x,y)\in center} Sal(x,y) - \sum_{(x,y)\in surround} Sal(x,y)}{width\_center * width\_height} \\ &\quad * exp(-dist(center\_center, center\_image) \\ &\quad * exp(\frac{width\_center * height\_center}{width\_image * height\_image})\} \end{aligned} \tag{10}$$

where the last two terms are the position and size weights for the center rectangle; *Surround* is the band area between the outer rectangle and center rectangle; *dist*() is Euclidean distance function; and $Sal(x, y)$ is the value in position (x, y) of saliency map. In Fig.(3), (b) is the optimal center rectangle for calculating the saliency score, and (c) is the localized object derived from the center rectangle. It is clear that the center rectangle is effective in capturing the visual saliency of the image.

The three measurements of image I in cluster V: $Intra(I_i)$, $Inter(I_i)$ and $VisSaliency(I_i)$ are first normalized and the representativeness score of I is the linear combination of these three terms.

$$RepresentScore(I_i) = exp(Inter(I_i)) + exp(-Intra(I_i)) + exp(VisSaliency(I_i)) \tag{11}$$

Given the representativeness score of each image within each cluster, we can now select the image with the highest score as the representative one for the cluster.

Ranking of Representative Images

In this step, we rank the representative images selected from all the image clusters and present the top K images to users as the final images to visually translate the given concept.

We extract three scores from the representative images and their associated clusters to rank the images. The three scores are: (1) the cluster size, (2) the coherence of cluster in terms of semantic and visual characteristics, similar to the intra cluster distance measure aforementioned, and (3) the semantic and visual saliency of the image.

For the first score, it is obvious that a representative image will be more important if the associated cluster is larger. The second score is calculated as the variance of each cluster based on the semantic and visual distance between images within the cluster. For the third score, the visual saliency is the same as in Eq.(10); while the semantic saliency of a representative image is derived from its associated cluster. Each cluster is represented with top k salient keywords based on the saliency scores (see Eq.(6)) and frequencies of keywords. Then the semantic saliency of a cluster, i.e., a representative image, is estimated as the sum of saliency scores of the top k keywords.

The three scores are normalized and the ranking score of image I_i is calculated as:

$$RankScore(I_i) = exp(size(V)) + exp(-variance(V)) + exp(saliency(I_i)) \quad (12)$$

where $size(V)$ and $variance(V)$ are respectively the normalized size and variance of cluster V that image I_i belongs to; and $saliency(I_i)$ is the third score.

5 Experimental Results

We conduct experiments in the domain of "animal" to validate the effectiveness of the proposed *Word2Image* ; while it is straightforward to extend the method to other domains. We first randomly selected 31 animal concepts that include *tiger, elephant, jaguar, monkey, dolphin, shark, duck, crane, bear, leopard, zebra* and so on. We then built a domain model for "animal" using the TFIDF technique as mentioned before, where the values for parameters N, M, k are set as 300, 200 and 4 respectively. Next, we submitted these 31 concepts to *Flickr*, from which we collected up to 10,000 images together with their associated tags and titles for each concept.

Two types of evaluating methods are used to test the performance of *Word2Image*: objective evaluation and subjective evaluation. The objective evaluation addresses the precision of the result image set; while the subjective evaluation is based on user study, focusing on the diversity and representativeness of the result images.

Evaluation of precision

This evaluation is conducted to validate the effectiveness of the filtering strategy in improving the accuracy of image retrieval and the generation of representative images. In our experiments, we select the top 50% of the ranked images according to their correlation scores with the domain model as the filtering results. We first

Tab. (1): The average precision for image retrieval.

Tag based method	Filtering method
76.10	95.50

Tab. (2): The average precision for generating representative images.

	Tag based method	Filtering method
P@10	89.70	99.40
P@20	80.10	98.40

evaluate the strategy by comparing with the tag based image retrieval in *Flickr* (used as *baseline*). While it is difficult to label the ground truth for the large number of returned images, we use a sampling technique instead. We randomly sample 200 images from the crawled images and filtered images for each concept to represent the results of *baseline* method and *filtering* method respectively. These images are then judged manually as related or unrelated to the given concept. The performances in terms of average precision are tabulated in Tab.(1). The results show that the filtering technique is very effective in removing the unrelated images for given concepts.

The second test is to evaluate the performance of filtering strategy in improving the precision of the generated representative images. We use two measurements, the precision at generating top-10 (P@10) and top-20 (P@20) representative images from the images retrieved, to compare the *baseline* method and *filtering* method. The results are shown in Tab.(2), which clearly shows that the proposed correlation based filtering method is effective in improving the two precision measures as compared to the *baseline* method, which is the basic requirement of *Word2Image*.

Evaluation of diversity and representativeness

This experiment highlights the system's usability and performances in discovering diversity and representativeness. 21 student volunteers are invited to take part in the evaluation. Among the volunteers, there are 7 primary school students, 7 middle school students and 7 graduate students. The volunteers are required to submit the 31 concepts to the system and explore the top 10 resulting representative images for each concept. They are then asked to fill in an assessment form with 4 questions as shown in Tab.(3). Each question requires a numerical answer based

Tab. (3): Survey results from students on *Word2Image.*

Score / Assessment Questions	1	2	3	4	5
1) Do you think this system is useful in explaining the meaning of a word?	0	0	0	13	8
2) The coverage of the discovered topics	0	0	4	15	2
3) The representativeness of the representative images	0	0	2	16	3
4) Overall satisfaction with the system	0	0	3	16	2

Fig. (4): The resulted image set for *bear*

on the scale of: 1–strongly disagree, 2–disagree, 3–neutral, 4–agree, and 5–strongly agree.

The survey results are tabulated in Tab.(3). From the answers to question 1, we can see that such visual translation system is highly desirable for all the three types of users. The answers to question 2 reveal that *Word2Image* can successfully find out most of the interesting topics. This is attributed to the salient keyword detection and category clustering process. Results for two more examples: "bear" and "tiger", also support the answers. For "bear", *Word2Image* discovers topics such as "red bear", "polar bear", "panda", etc. For "tiger", the topics like "white tiger", "tiger stripes", "bengal tiger", etc, have been extracted. The answers to question 3 are as satisfying as expected due to the combination of visual saliency for the representativeness measuring and ranking. The resulting top 10 images for "bear" and "tiger" are shown in Fig.(4) and Fig.(5) respectively.

Fig. (5): The resulted image set for *tiger*.

6 Conclusions

In this paper, we introduced a novel multimedia application, *Word2Image*, which attempts to leverage the web image collection and knowledge resources to translate a concept into its visual counterpart using the sets of high quality, precise, diverse and representative images. The preliminary experimental results have demonstrated its usability and effectiveness. This is a step towards our ultimate goal of building a large scale multimedia dictionary, where multi-modality information including image, video, audio and text are integrated to help explain the concepts.

7 References

[1] Tat-Seng Chua, Jinhui Tang, Richang Hong, Haojie Li, Zhiping Luo, and Yan-Tao Zheng. NUS-WIDE: A Real-World Web Image Database from National University of Singapore. In *CIVR*, 2009

[2] Guangda Li, Zhaoyan Ming, Haojie Li, Tat-Seng Chua. Video reference: question answering on YouTube. In *ACM Multimedia*, 2009

[3] Zhiping Luo, Haojie Li, Jinhui Tang, Richang Hong, Tat-Seng Chua. ViewFocus: explore places of interests on Google maps using photos with view direction filtering. In *ACM Multimedia*, 2009

[4] Google image search engine, http://images.google.com/

[5] AltaVista image search, http://www.altavista.com/image/

[6] Flickr, http://www.flickr.com/

[7] D. Cai, X. He, Z. Li, W.Y. Ma, and J.R. Wen. Hierarchical clustering of www image search results using visual, textual and link information. In *ACM Multimedia*, 2004

[8] Bin Gao, Tie-Yan Liu, Xin Zheng, Qian-Sheng Cheng, Wei-Ying Ma. Web image clustering by consistent utilization of visual features and surrounding texts. In *ACM Multimedia*, 2005

[9] Feng Jing, Changhu Wang, et al. IGroup: web image search results clustering. In *ACM Multimedia*, 2006

[10] X Zhu, AB Goldberg, et al. A Text-to-Picture Synthesis System for Augmenting Communication. In *AAAI Conference on Artificial Intelligence*, 2007

[11] Lyndon S. Kennedy, Mor Naaman. Generating diverse and representative image search results for landmarks. In *International World Wide Web Conference*, 2008

[12] Lewis, David. Naive (Bayes) at Forty: The Independence Assumption in Information Retrieval. In *European Conference on Machine Learning*, 1998

[13] Berry, Michael W. Survey of Text Mining I: Clustering, Classification, and Retrieval. Springer-Verlag, New York, 2003

[14] Christiane Fellbaum WordNet: An Electronic Lexical Database. MIT Press, 1999

[15] http://en.wikipedia.org

[16] M.F. Porter An algorithm for suffix stripping. Program, 1980

[17] Sheng Tang, Jin-Tao Li, Ming Li, Cheng Xie, Yi-Zhi Liu, Kun Tao, Shao-Xi Xu TRECVID 2008 High-Level Feature Extraction By MCG-ICT-CAS. In *Proc. TRECVID Workshop*, 2008

[18] A. Jain and R. Dube. Algorithms for Clustering Data. Prentice-Hall, Englewood Cliffs, NJ, 1988

[19] Xiao-Yong Wei, Chong-Wah Ngo. Ontology-enriched semantic space for video search. In *ACM Multimedia*, 2007

[20] Tamara L. Berg and Alexander C. Berg. Finding Iconic Images. In *The 2nd Internet Vision Workshop at IEEE CVPR*, 2009

[21] Huiying Liu, Shuqiang Jiang, Qingming Huang, Changsheng Xu, Wen Gao. Region-Based Visual Attention Analysis with Its Application in Image Browsing on Small Displays. In *ACM Multimedia*, 2007

[22] J. Harel, C. Koch, and P. Perona. Graph-based visual saliency. In *Proc. Neural Information Processing Systems*, 2006

240 *Internet Multimedia Search and Mining,* 2013, 240-272

CHAPTER 10

Flickr Distance for Internet Multimedia Search and Mining

Lei Wu*

University of Pittsbugh, Tel: 1-412-624-8419, Email: leiwu@live.com

Xian-Sheng Hua

Microsoft Research, Email: xshua@microsoft.com

Abstract: In this chapter, we will introduce the Flickr distance (FD), which is used to measure the visual correlation between concepts. The relationship between concepts is a reflection of human perception, which is formed mainly based on the human visual information. Thus mining the conceptual correlation from visual information makes sense.

Flickr distance is calculated in two steps, concept modeling and concept distance estimation. In the first step, each concept is assumed to have multiple states, such as front views, side views, multiple semantics, etc., each of which is considered as a latent topic. For each concept, a collection of related images are obtained from the web, and then a latent topic visual language model (LTVLM) is built to capture these states. In the second step, the distance between two concepts is estimated by the Jensen-Shannon (JS) divergence between their LTVLM.

Different from traditional conceptual distance measurements, which are based on Web text documents, FD is based on the visual information. Comparing with the WordNet distance, FD can easily scale up with the increasing size of conceptual corpus. Comparing with the Google distance (NGD) and Tag Concurrence Distance (TCD), FD uses the visual information and can measure more kinds of conceptual relations properly. We apply FD to multimedia related tasks and find FD is more helpful than NGD. Based on FD, we also construct a large scale visual conceptual

***Correspondence Author:** Lei Wu, University of Pittsbugh; Email: leiwu@live.com.

Xian-Sheng Hua, Marcel Worring & Tat-Seng Chua (Eds.)

network (VCNet) to store the knowledge of conceptual relationship. Experiments show that FD is more coherent to human perception and can help boosting the performance of several applications over the existing methods.

Keywords

Flickr distance, conceptual similarity, visual language model, distance measurement, multimedia search, data mining, similarity search, image analysis, visual similarity, image annotation, image tagging, image retrieval

1 Introduction

Similarity measurements have been studied for decades and it remains a hot research topic especially in multimedia literature. There are quite a few important applications related to this theme, including indexing, ranking, clustering, annotation, and recommendation. These problems are directly related to two fundamental measurements, image similarity measurement and conceptual correlation measurement.

Image similarity measurement measures the similarity between two images based on their visual features. It does not actually measure the semantic relationship. This kind of similarity measurement can be used for near-duplicate detection, while it cannot be adopted in the applications where semantic level correlation is needed.

Conceptual correlation calculates the semantic distance between these two concepts. It is used for the semantic level correlation measurement. Currently, intensive research has been done on image similarity measurements, i.e. [1-4]. There are few works on measuring conceptual distance, which actually represents the relationship of two semantic concepts or keywords. Actually modeling the conceptual relationship can help improve the performance of many multimedia related applications.

Here conceptual distance needs to measure four kinds of common conceptual correlations, synonymy, similarity, meronymy and concurrence. Synonym denotes the same semantic concepts with different names, like football and soccer. Similarity denotes that two concepts are visually similar, i.e. horse and donkey. Meronymy denotes one concept is part of another, i.e. wheel and car. Concurrence denotes situations when two concepts appear simultaneously in daily life. Here human perception refers to these four types of conceptual correlation. The goal of designing Flickr distance is to simulate human perception on measuring conceptual correlations. The optimal solution is to generate the same results with human experts. However, it is hard to achieve. Here we try to generate a close correlation to human experts. We use "coherent coefficient" to measure this closeness.

As far as we know, there are currently three types of conceptual distance measurements. The first kind is generated by human experts, such as the WordNet Distance [5], which was developed by the Cognitive Science Laboratory of Princeton

University. It is widely used to exploit semantic relationship of common concepts. Since WordNet is defined by human experts, the semantic distance based on WordNet is very close to human perception. On the other hand, due to the same reason, it is hard to update the concept corpus with the increasing number of concepts on the Web. For example, there are 10^9 different online concepts on the photo sharing website like Flickr, and this number is still increasing every day, while WordNet only covers 150,000 concepts.

The second kind is generated by Web textual information, such as Normalized Google Distance (NGD)[6] and Tag Concurrence Distance (TCD)[7]. NGD was proposed by Cilibrasi and Vitányi to measure the conceptual distance by the Google page counts when querying both concepts to the Google search engine. It actually reflects how often two concepts will co-occur in the same web-pages. This distance costs little human effort and covers almost any concept on the Web.

However, NGD assumes the conceptual relationship only depends on the co-occurrence of these concepts among online textual documents. This assumption is simple, and cannot cover the cases of meronymy and concurrence, as shown in Tab.(1). The Tag Concurrence Distance (TCD)[7] directly applies the idea of Google distance to the tags. It treats the tag list of each image as a document, and calculates the TCD distance the same way as Google distance. This is a very intuitive way to measure the conceptual distance based on tags. The inverse of the mutual information between two tags can be further calculated as a distance between two different tags according to their association with the images. This distance reflects the frequency of two tags occurring in the same image. However, there is the problem of sparseness that many correlations are missing due to the incompleteness of tags. In Flickr, there are less than 10 tags per image. It is far less than the number of words in a typical web document. Therefore, many semantic relations may not be covered by this Tag Concurrent Distance.

The third kind is generated from the visual correlation, such as the proposed Flickr Distance (FD), which generates the latent topic visual language model (LTVLM) to represent each tag by analyzing the visual words correlation of its related images. Experiment shows this kind of distance is more coherent to human perception and can well represent all the four kinds of relationship.

Tab.(1) illustrates the distance measurements for the four kinds of relationship by different methods. We adopt three kinds of distances to measure four pairs of daily-life concepts. The NGD for both conceptual pairs "airport–airplane" and "Car–wheel" are larger than that for "airport–dog", which is somewhat against the human perception. However in the text domain, although the "airport" and "airplane" are concurrent, they are less likely to co-occur in the same textual web page. It is the same with "car" and "wheel". This illustrates that NGD may not represent all four kinds of relationship between concepts. The TCD can handle the concurrence relationship but still cannot represent Meronymy. FD can properly measure four kinds of relations.

In summary, WordNet distance which costs the human efforts is accurate but works for limited number of concepts. NGD and TCD methods cannot capture all four kinds of relationship between concepts. An example is illustrated in Tab.(1). The NGD method cannot properly measure the distance of "Concurrence" and "Meronymy" samples. The distance between "airplane" and "airport" is larger than the distance between "airplane" and "dog", which is against human knowledge. This problem is also with "Car" and "Wheel" pair. The TCD method also cannot properly measure the distance between "Meronymy" samples. The distance between "Car" and "Wheel" is also larger than that between "airplane" and "dog". Thus we propose the Flickr distance, which can be easily updated with the increasing concepts and can capture all kinds of conceptual relationship. We also apply FD to multiple multimedia tasks to compare with other commonly used distances, such as wordNet distance, NGD, and TCD.

Tab. (1): Illustration of NGD, TCD and FD. The first column shows the conceptual relationship. The second column listed some conceptual pairs. The third to the fifth columns are the conceptual distance under different measurements. Improper scores are marked in bold.

Relationship	Conceptual pair	NGD	TCD	FD
None	Airplane–dog	0.2562	0.8532	0.5151
Synonym	Football–soccer	0.1905	0.1739	0.0315
Similarity	Horse–donkey	0.2147	0.4513	0.4231
Concurrence	Airplane–airport	**0.3094**	0.1833	0.0576
Meronymy	Car–wheel	**0.3146**	**0.9617**	0.0708

The rest of the chapter is organized as follows. Section 2 overviews the problems and basic concepts in the chapter. Section 3 introduces the basic concepts of the concept representation. Section 4 discusses the difference kinds of concept distance measurements. Section 5 discusses the construction of visual conceptual network (VCNet) based on Flickr distance to represent the conceptual correlation. In Section 6 we demonstrate that the visual distance is more coherent to human perception than the text based distances (i.e. google distance, tag concurrence distance) by both subjective and objective experiments. We also provide some application scenarios to show that the Flickr distance is helpful to multimedia related tasks. Section 7 concludes the chapter.

2 Overview of Concept Distance

First of all, we will overview some of the basic concepts and problems in this task.

According to contemporary philosophy, a concept is a cognitive unit of meaning, which is divided into objects and abstract objects. Generally, an object is an entity that could be perceived by human sensors, like sense of sight or tactile organ. An abstract object is an abstract idea or mental symbol also named as the "unit of knowledge". Here the concept only refers to the objects, such as concrete objects, events, scenes, or motions. Since these concepts are frequently appeared and can be recorded by photos. Only the recordable concepts can be modeled and measured by our technology.

Each concept is related to some of the other concepts. For example, when talking about the concept "airplane", people always think about the "airport", or when we think of a "dog" and often can imagine the "head" and the "legs". This conceptual relationship embodies the distance between concepts in the semantic space, where semantically related concepts are closer to each other, i.e. "airplane" and "airport" is closer than "airplane" and "dog".

Concept is a semantic element in human perception, and the distance between concepts is also a measurement in human perception. It is difficult to calculate it directly. One of the possible means to measure this distance is to simulate the human perception. The perception is formed based on multiple information sources, such as from reading text documents, photos, videos, and verbal communications. The basic idea of measuring the conceptual distance is by data mining from a large pool of the visual knowledge.

Given two random concepts C_i and C_j, we try to calculate the semantical distance between them $d(C_i, C_j)$. There are several challenges in calculating the distance.

Firstly, the representation of the concept is a great challenge. With different representation models, the concepts C_i and C_j can be presented in different forms. While not all types of representations can be adopted to calculate the distance. Due to the computational complexity, the representation should be both differentiating and as simple as possible.

Secondly, the form of distance measurement is quite important. It is worth noting that the distance should meet some constraints, such as the triangular constraint. To ensure the concept distance does not conflict to each other, the distance measurement should also meet these constraints.

Finally, the conceptual distance measurement should be coherent to human perception. Here the distance measurement does not equal to the distance metric for low level visual features. The metric for low level features only measures the distance of the visual property such as color, texture, illumination, etc. The same semantic meaning can be represented by different types of features. Here the conceptual distance represents the distance between concepts in semantic space, which is evaluated by human perception.

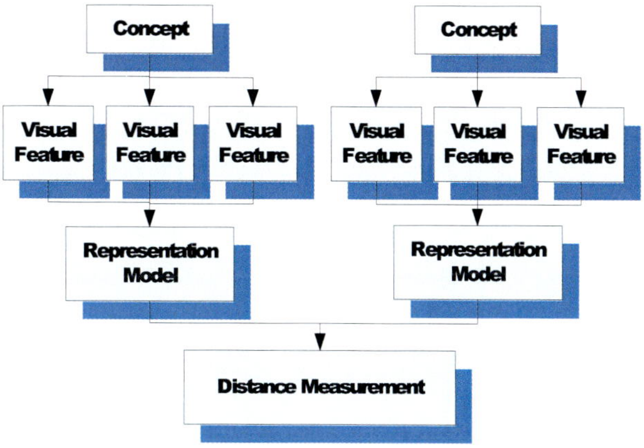

Fig. (1): Overview of the conceptual distance measurement task.

Fig.(1) shows the overview of the conceptual distance measurement task. In this task, we first try to search the related visual features for each concept. The visual features should be simple in order to handle a large-scale dataset. Then we model the concept by the latent topic visual language modeling technique based on a large collection of related and ordered visual features. This model is discriminant and efficient for large-scale dataset. Rather than just modeling the low-level feature for each image, the model also captures the statistical property of the semantic concepts. Finally, we will define a proper distance measurement to help calculate semantic relationship between concepts.

3 Concept Representation

Visual feature

Visual feature is defined as the global or local operations applied to an image to generate certain quantitative measurements, which are helpful for solving the computational tasks. According to the types of operations, the visual feature can be categorized into global feature and local feature. Global feature captures the property of the whole image, and local feature captures the property of local regions in the image.

Some commonly used global features include mean gray, gray histogram, image moment, texture histogram, etc. Each global feature can also be deemed as an operator L on the image I, denoted as $L(I)$. For example, let L_1 be the mean operator, and L_2 denotes the gray histogram, the mean gray and gray histogram features of given image I are represented by $L_1(I)$ and $L_2(I)$ respectively. These

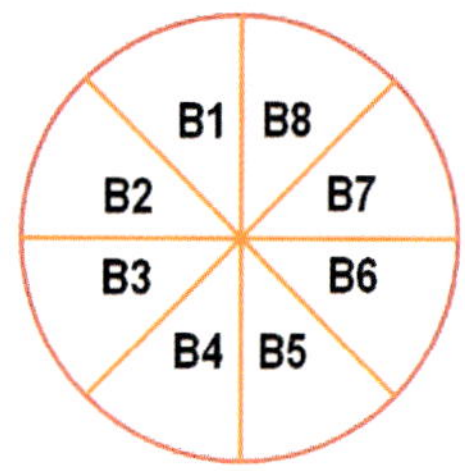

Fig. (2): 8-bin texture histogram.

operators can nest, i.e. mean of gray histogram of image I is represented by $(L_1 * L_2)(I)$. Lots of types of global features can be derived by nesting different operators.

If these operators are applied to the regions of the image, the local feature can be generated. For example, let $r_i, i = 1, \cdots, n$ be a series of regions in image I. The operator L on each of the regions $L(r_i)$ will be the local features. However, the main difference of local feature from global feature does not lie on the descriptor, but on the localization and segmentation of these local regions, which are called feature detection. The process specializes the informative regions, such as lines, edges, angle, and movements etc. Some most commonly used feature detection methods include Moravec corner detection [8], Harris and Stephens corner detection [9], multi-scale Harris operator [10], level curve curvature approach[11], Laplacian of Gaussian (LoG) [12], difference of Gaussians approach (DoG) [13], determinant of the Hessian (DoH) feature detection[14], hybrid Laplacian and determinant of the Hessian operator (Hessian-Laplace)[13], Wang and Brady corner detection[15], SUSAN corner detector [16], maximally stable extremum regions (MSER)[17], Affine-adapted interest point operator[13] etc. The well-known scale-invariant feature transform (SIFT) feature [18] is based on the DoG detection, with additional noise depression process and multi-scale keypoint descriptor.

In this chapter, we adopt a simple while effect texture gradient histogram feature.

A commonly used texture histogram is the 8-bin histogram. It divides the 2D space into 8 phases as shown in Fig.(2), denoted as $B_1, \cdots, , B_8$. The angle of each direction phase is set to be 45°. Then it calculates the direction of texture d at each pixel by Eq. (1)

$$d_{xy} = \arctan \frac{dy_{xy}}{dx_{xy}}; x = 1, \cdots, m; y = 1, \cdots, n \tag{1}$$

$$dx_{xy} = I_{xy} - I_{x+1,y} \tag{2}$$

$$dy_{xy} = I_{xy} - I_{x,y+1} \tag{3}$$

If the direction of texture lies in any of the 8 phases, the pixel is put into the corresponding bin, i.e. if $d_{xy} \in B_k$, then $\delta(I_{xy}, B_k) = 1$.

$$\delta(I_{xy}, B_k) = \begin{cases} 1, & d_{xy} \in B_k; \\ 0, & \text{otherwise.} \end{cases}$$

Finally, the texture histogram $H = [h_1, \cdots, h_8]$ of the image is formed by calculating the number of pixels in each bin.

$$h_k = \sum_{xy} \delta(I_{xy}, B_k)$$

The above texture histogram does not consider the gradient magnitude of the texture. An improvement is to weight the texture histogram by gradient magnitude $\mathbf{m}_{xy}$ of each pixel (Eq. (4)). The magnitude is calculated in Eq.(5).

$$h_k = \sum_{I_{xy} \in B_k} m_{xy} \tag{4}$$

$$m_{xy} = \sqrt{(dx_{xy})^2 + (dy_{xy})^2} \tag{5}$$

Comparing with mean gray and gray histogram, texture histogram contains more structural information. Since most objects and informative regions are lying on edges or corners, this feature is more discriminative for describing informative regions. However, it is sensitive to rotation. Suppose an object is rotated a little in the image, the texture histogram may be altered dramatically. We have also compared this feature with other local features, more detailed results can be found in [19]. Comparing with other features, texture gradient feature is one of the most robust features, and meanwhile the most efficient feature among all the robust features. Efficient is quite important since we are dealing with large-scale experiment. For this reason the rotation invariant texture histogram is used.

In order to make the texture histogram resistant to rotation, the average textural direction D of an image is firstly calculated.

$$D = \arctan \frac{\sum_{xy} dy_{xy}}{\sum_{xy} dx_{xy}} \tag{6}$$

$$dx_{xy} = I_{xy} - I_{x+1,y} \tag{7}$$

$$dy_{xy} = I_{xy} - I_{x,y+1} \tag{8}$$

Then the patch is rotated to make the average textural direction vertical pointing to the top. Starting from the average direction, eight direction phases are defined as $[B_1, B_2, \cdots, B_8]$. The angle of each direction phase is set to be 45°. Then the texture at each pixel is calculated and quantized into each bin by the same means as discussed previously. These quantized visual features are named *visual words* in the chapter.

Visual language model

The visual language model [20] adopts the uniformly distributed equal-sized patches to represent a concept (Fig.(3)). We believe the statistical property of a visual concept does not lie on the independent local features, but lie on the correlation between these dependent features, which can be deemed as a kind of local pattern. In other word, one local feature does not speak any semantic information, while a local pattern may contain some semantics. We use the conditional probability between the local features to represent such local pattern, and we adopt the uniformly distributed patches to facilitate calculate of the conditional probability between local features.

First, we assume that each word in the visual document is not independent, but correlated with all the other words in the document. However, when the size of the vocabulary is large, it is difficult to model so many relations. So we make the second assumption that visual words are generated in the order from left to right, and top to bottom. Each word is conditionally dependent on its previous words. In fact, we can also assume the visual words are generated from right to left, bottom to top, or from both directions. For simplicity, we only take the first assumption, which is enough to measure the visual word proximity.

The calculation of this conditional probability is still not efficient enough. Further inspired by 2D HMM[21, 22] used in face recognition and indexing, we make the third assumption that each patch depends only on its immediate vertical and horizontal neighbors. There may be some statistical dependency on remote visual words. The description of this dependency will make the model too complex to implement. In this paper, we would ignore the remote words dependency, just as the language model does for text classification. According to how much dependency information is considered in the model, we propose three kinds of visual language models, unigram, bigram and trigram. In unigram model, the visual words in an image are considered independent to each other. In bigram model, the proximity between two neighboring words is calculated, and in trigram model the words are assumed to depend on two immediate vertical and horizontal neighbors.

The training process will model the following conditional probability

$$p(w_{ij}|w_{00}w_{01}\cdots w_{mn}) = p(w_{ij}|w_{00}w_{01}\cdots w_{i,j-1}) \tag{9}$$

where w_{ij} represents the visual words of the patch at the i-th row and j-th column of the image. The calculation of this conditional probability is still not efficient enough. Inspired by 2D HMM [21] used in face recognition, the model assumes that each patch depends only on its immediate vertical and horizontal neighbors. Although there may be some statistical dependency on visual words with larger interval, the description of this dependency will make the model too complex to implement. This model ignores this kind of dependency, just as the language model does for text classification.

According to how much dependency information is considered in the model, there are three kinds of visual language models, i.e. unigram, bigram and trigram. In unigram model, the visual words in an image are regarded independent with each other. In bigram model, the dependency between two neighboring words is considered. And in trigram model a word is assumed to depend on both the word on the left and the word above it.

These three models are expressed in Eq. (10)-(12) respectively.

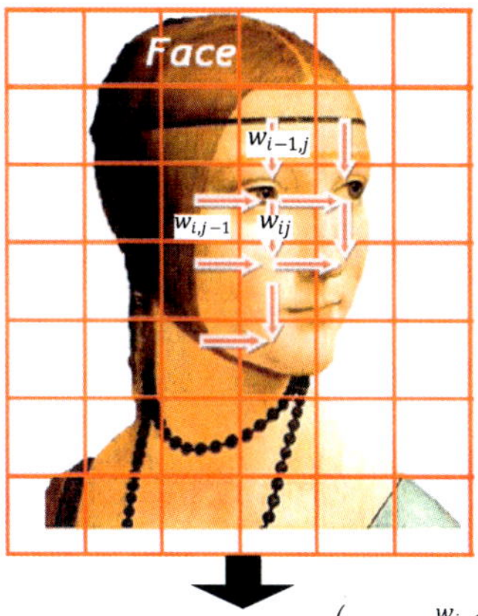

$$p(w_{ij}|w_{i-1,j}, w_{i,j-1}) = \frac{Count\begin{pmatrix} & w_{i-1,j} \\ w_{i,j-1} & w_{ij} \end{pmatrix}}{\sum_w Count\begin{pmatrix} & w_{i-1,j} \\ w_{i,j-1} & w \end{pmatrix}}$$

Fig. (3): Process of trigram language model training.

$$p(w_{ij}|w_{00}w_{01}\cdots w_{mn}) = p(w_{ij}) \tag{10}$$

$$p(w_{ij}|w_{00}w_{01}\cdots w_{mn}) = p(w_{ij}|w_{i-1,j}) \tag{11}$$

$$p(w_{ij}|w_{00}w_{01}\cdots w_{mn}) = p(w_{ij}|w_{i-1,j}w_{i,j-1}) \tag{12}$$

where w_{ij} represents the visual word at Row i, Column j in the word matrix. In the following, we will discuss in details about the training process for the three models.

Unigram Model

For each concept, a unigram model characterizes the distribution of individual visual words under the concept. In the training process, we calculate $p(w_i|C_k)$ using

$$p(w_i|C_k) = \frac{F_N(w_i|C_k)}{\sum_{w\in V} F_N(w|C_k)}, k = 1, 2, \ldots, K \tag{13}$$

To avoid zero probability which would cause the classifier to fail, we assign a small prior probability to each unseen word in the concept. Accordingly, the amount of this prior probability should be discounted from the probabilities of the words appearing in the concept, so that the sum of probabilities is 1. The smoothed words distribution is represented by Eq. (14).

$$p(w_i|C_k) = \begin{cases} \frac{F_N(w_i|C_k)\times(1-\frac{1}{N})}{\sum_{w\in V} F_N(w|C_k)}, & F_N(w_i|C_k) > 0; \\ \frac{1}{NR}, & otherwise. \end{cases} \tag{14}$$

where N is the total number of words in the training set and R is the number of words that do not appear in class C_k. This probabilistic model tells how likely a word appears in an image belonging to that concept.

Bigram Model

Unlike the unigram model, a bigram model assumes that each visual word is conditionally dependent on its left neighbor. So the training process is to learn the conditional probability by Eq. (15).

$$p(w_{ij}|w_{i,j-1}, C_k) = \frac{F_N(w_{i,j-1}, w_{ij}|C_k)}{F_N(w_{i,j-1}|C_k)} \tag{15}$$

$w_{i,j-1}$ is the left neighbor of $w_{i,j}$ in the visual words matrix. However, the bigrams are usually quite sparse in the probability space. The maximum likelihood estimation is usually biased higher for observed samples and biased lower for unobserved samples. Thus smoothing technique is needed to provide better estimation of the infrequent or unseen bigrams. Instead of just assigning a small constant prior probability, we adopt more accurate smoothing method [23], which combines back-off and discounting [24].

$$p(w_{ij}|w_{i,j-1}, C_k) = \begin{cases} \beta(w_{i,j-1}) \times p(w_{ij}|C_k), & F_N(w_{i,j-1}w_{ij}|C_k) = 0; \\ \hat{p}(w_{ij}|w_{i,j-1}, C_k), & otherwise. \end{cases} \tag{16}$$

$$\beta(w_{i,j-1}) = \frac{1 - \sum_{F_N(w_{i,j-1}w)>0} \hat{p}(w|w_{i,j-1}, C_k)}{1 - \sum_{F_N(w_{i,j-1}w)>0} p(w|C_k)} \tag{17}$$

$$\hat{p}(w_{ij}|w_{i,j-1}, C_k) = d_r \times \frac{F_N(w_{i,j-1}w_{ij}|C_k)}{F_N(w_{i,j-1}|C_k)} \tag{18}$$

Back-off method is represented in Eq. (16) (17), and discounting is represented in Eq. (18). If a bigram does not appear in the concept, back-off method is applied to calculate the bigram model from the unigram model. $\beta(w_{i,j-1})$ is called back-off factor. If bigram $w_{i,j-1}w_{ij} \in V$ appears in concept C_k, the discounting method is used to depress the estimation of its conditional probability. d_r is called the discounting coefficient.

$$d_r = \frac{r - b}{r} \tag{19}$$

$$b = \frac{n_1}{n_1 + 2n_2} \tag{20}$$

r is the number of times a bigram appears; and n_i is the number of visual words that appear i times in the concept.

Trigram Model

The above two modeling processes are almost the same as the statistical language models used in text classification, However, the trigram model for visual language is different from that for natural language processing. In text analysis, trigram is a sequence of three words $< w_{i-2}, w_{i-1}, w_i >$, while in visual document, which is a two dimensional matrix, we assume each word is conditionally dependent on its left neighbor and the word above it. So these three words form a trigram $< w_{i-1,j}, w_{i,j-1}, w_{ij} >$. The training process of a trigram model is illustrated in the following equation.

$$p(w_{ij}|w_{i-1,j}, w_{i,j-1}, C_k) = \frac{F_N(w_{i-1,j}w_{i,j-1}w_{ij}|C_k)}{F_N(w_{i-1,j}w_{i,j-1}|C_k)} \tag{21}$$

For the same reason with bigram model, discounting and back-off methods are also introduced for trigram model.

$$p(w_{ij}|w_{i-1,j}w_{i,j-1}, C_k) = \begin{cases} \beta(w_{i-1,j}w_{i,j-1})p(w_{ij}|w_{i,j-1}, C_k), & F_N(w_{ij}^3|C_k) = 0; \\ \hat{p}(w_{ij}|w_{i-1,j}w_{i,j-1}, C_k), & otherwise. \end{cases} \tag{22}$$

$$\beta(w_{i-1,j}w_{i,j-1}) = \frac{1 - \sum_{F_N(w_{i-1,j}w_{i,j-1}w)>0} \hat{p}(w|w_{i-1,j}w_{i,j-1}, C_k)}{1 - \sum_{F_N(w_{i-1,j}w_{i,j-1}w)>0} \hat{p}(w|w_{i,j-1}, C_k)} \tag{23}$$

$$\hat{p}(w_{ij}|w_{i-1,j}w_{i,j-1}, C_k) = d_r \times \frac{F_N(w_{i-1,j}w_{i,j-1}w_{ij}|C_k)}{F_N(w_{i-1,j}w_{i,j-1}|C_k)} \tag{24}$$

w_{ij}^3 represents the trigram $< w_{i-1,j}w_{i,j-1}w_{ij} >$. The spatial correlation between visual words is captured by the conditional probabilities of trigrams. In summary, the training procedure is as follows:

a. Divide each training image into patches;

b. Generate a hash code for each patch to form a visual document;

c. Build visual language models for each concept by calculating the conditional distribution of unigram, bigram and trigram.

The process of building trigram visual language model is illustrated in Fig.(3). It is worth noting that not all visual words are useful for classification. Therefore, we introduce a feature selection process during visual language training. Words are selected according to their term frequency (TF) and inverse document frequency (IDF).

$$tf_i^k = \frac{n_i}{\sum_j n_j} \tag{25}$$

$$idf_i = \log \frac{|V|}{|d : w_i \in d|} \tag{26}$$

where tf_i^k measures the frequency a word w_i appears in images belonging to concept C_k and idf_i reflects the frequency of word w_i in the dataset. The $tf - idf$ weight $tf_i^k \times idf_i$ evaluates how important the word w_i is to concept C_k. For each concept, we select the words with $tf - idf$ weight bigger than a threshold. And the words from different concepts are combined. This approach can depress the influence of random background and reduce the size of vocabulary.

Latent Topic Visual Language Model (LTVLM)

Visual language model can be used to represent a concept. However, some of the concepts may be quite complicated, i.e. various appearances in an images(front view/side view), multiple semantic meanings (apple for fruit/apple for computer). The simple visual language model may not handle such complicated situations, since we actually do not know what semantic meaning or appearance each concept possesses.

Here, we further incorporate the latent topic analysis into the VLM, naming it *latent topic visual language model (LTVLM)*. We define each appearance variation or semantic meaning of a concept as a latent topic z_i. We try to use the latent topic analysis method to help estimate the visual language model under each latent topic. The EM algorithm is adopted to analyze the visual language model under each latent topic. Since different variations are separately modeled, we generate a more precise statistical model for each concept. In the following, we will discuss specifically on the concept modeling process by latent topic trigram model (LTT).

LTT assumes that each tag on Flickr is a concept which corresponds to a subset of related images. LTT will firstly generate latent topic of the images with an EM procedure. For each topic, a visual language model is calculated to represent the semantics.

The latent topic VLM further estimates $P(w_{xy}|w_{x-1,y}^2, z_k^C)$, where z_k^C represents the kth appearance variation of concept C. This latent topic trigram modeling process can be formulated as follows.

$$\begin{aligned} &P(w_{xy}|w_{x-1,y}^2, d_j) = \sum_{k=1}^{K} P(w_{xy}|w_{x-1,y}^2, z_k^C)P(z_k^C|d_j) \\ &x = 1, \cdots, m;\ y = 1, \cdots, n;\ j = 1, \cdots, N. \end{aligned} \tag{27}$$

where d_j^C represents the jth image in the subset related to concept C. K is the total number of latent topics, which is determined by experiment. EM algorithm is adopted to estimate both parameters $P(w_{xy}|w_{x-1,y}^2, z_k^C)$ and $P(z_k^C|d_j)$. The object function of the EM algorithm is to maximize the joint distribution of concept and its visual word arrangement A_w.

$$maximize \quad p(A_w, C) \tag{28}$$

$$p(A_w, C) = \prod_{d_j \in C} \prod_{x,y} P(w_{xy}|w_{x-1,y}w_{x,y-1}, d_j) \tag{29}$$

In order to obtain analytically tractable density estimation, we propose a cross-updating scheme, in which we simultaneously estimate $P(w^3_{xy}|z^C_k)$ and $P(w^2_{x-1,y}|z^C_k)$. Then we calculate $P(w_{xy}|w^2_{x-1,y}, z^C_k)$ by (Eq. (36)). The E step and M step are performed as follows.

E step:

Given the current estimate of the parameters $P(z^C_k|d^C_j)$, $P(w^2_{x-1,y}|z^C_k)$, we estimate the expected value of the likelihood function Q_2 w.r.t the bigram distribution.

$$Q_2(z^C_k|d^C_j, w^2_{x-1,y}) \leftarrow P(z^C_k|d^C_j)P(w^2_{x-1,y}|z^C_k) \tag{30}$$

Then, we estimate the expected value of the likelihood function Q_3 and Q w.r.t the trigram joint distribution and conditional distribution respectively.

$$Q_3(z^C_k|d^C_j, w^3_{xy}) \leftarrow P(z^C_k|d^C_j)P(w^3_{xy}|z^C_k) \tag{31}$$

$$Q(z^C_k|d^C_j, w^3_{xy}) \leftarrow P(z^C_k|d^C_j)P(w_{xy}|w^2_{x-1,y}, z^C_k) \tag{32}$$

M step:

Update the parameters of the bigram model given each topic z^C_k and estimated likelihood function Q_2.

$$P(w^2_{x-1,y}|z^C_k) \leftarrow \frac{\sum_j n(d^C_j, w^2_{x-1,y})Q_2(z^C_k|d^C_j, w^2_{x-1,y})}{\sum_{x,y,j} n(d^C_j, w^2_{x-1,y})Q_2(z^C_k|d^C_j, w^2_{x-1,y})} \tag{33}$$

where $n(d^C_j, w^2_{x-1,y})$ represents the number of times bigram $w^2_{x-1,y}$ appears in the jth document in category C.

Update the parameters of the trigram model given each topic z^C_k and estimated likelihood function Q, Q_3.

$$P(w^3_{xy}|z^C_k) \leftarrow \frac{\sum_j n(d^C_j, w^3_{xy})Q_3(z^C_k|d^C_j, w^3_{xy})}{\sum_{x,y,j} n(d^C_j, w^3_{xy})Q_3(z^C_k|d^C_j, w^3_{xy})} \tag{34}$$

$$P(z^C_k|d^C_j) \leftarrow \frac{\sum_{x,y} n(d^C_j, w^3_{xy})Q(z^C_k|d^C_j, w^3_{xy})}{\sum_{x,y,k} n(d^C_j, w^3_{xy})Q(z^C_k|d^C_j, w^3_{xy})} \tag{35}$$

$$P(w_{xy}|w^2_{x-1,y}, z^C_k) \leftarrow \frac{P(w^3_{xy}|z^C_k)}{P(w^2_{x-1,y}|z^C_k)} \tag{36}$$

$$P(z_k^C|C) \leftarrow \sum_{d^C \in C} P(z_k^C|d^C, C)P(d^C|C) \tag{37}$$

The outputs are the conditional distributions of trigrams with respect to each latent topics, $P(w_{xy}|w_{x-1,y}^2, z_k^C)$, $k = 1, \cdots, K$.

4 Concept Distance Measurement

In the section we will introduce how to measure the concept correlation based on the concept models. Here the motivation of proposing such a concept distance is mainly for two reasons. First, the existing concept distances are not accurate in some cases. Second, Flickr distance analyzes the content of the images and is more suitable for multimedia related tasks, such as image annotation, tagging, visual concept clustering, etc.

Related distance measures

As is introduced previously, we aim to measure four kinds of concept relationship, synonym, similarity, meronymy and concurrence.

Before we go though the details of the proposed Flickr distance, we will discuss the drawback of some existing concept distance, i.e. WordNet distance, Google distance, and tag concurrence distance. Although these existing methods can be used to measure conceptual correlation, they fail to cover all these four kinds of relationship.

WordNet Distance

WordNet, which is generated by researchers in Princeton University, consists of a lexical database of over 70,000 concept entries. These concept entries are structured as a semantic hierarchical network. The nodes in the network are the concepts and the links in the network represent closeness of their relationship.

Rada, Mili, Bicknell, and Blettner [25] propose one simple measurement to calculate the distance between the concepts in WordNet by the shortest path between the two concepts in the network graph. The length of the path is calculated by counting the number of intervening nodes between the two concepts(nodes). They assumed that if two concepts have short path between each other in the network, they are close to each other.

One drawback with this distance measure is that it simply assumes that each link in the network has equal length, which is somewhat arguable. Some improvements to this distance were proposed by considering the density of each level in the hierarchical network. The calculation of the density weighted WordNet distance [26] is defined as follows.

$$WND(x, y) = \frac{d(x, y)}{D(x, y)}$$

where $d(x, y)$ represents the length of shortest path between x and y, and $D(x, y)$ is the local density between x and y. This local density could be estimated by many methods, such as the number of common words between x and y, the number of nodes within the sub-region where x and y are located, etc.

Google Distance

The second kind conceptual distance is generated by Web textual information, such as Normalized Google Distance (NGD)[6]. NGD was proposed by Cilibrasi and Vitányi to measure the conceptual distance by the Google page counts when querying both concepts to the Google search engine. It actually reflects how often two concepts will co-occur in same web-pages. This distance costs little human effort and covers almost any concept on the Web.

$$NGD(x, y) = \frac{max(\log f(x), \log f(y)) - \log f(x, y)}{\log N - min(\log f(x), \log f(y))} \tag{38}$$

where $NGD(x, y)$ represents the Normalized Google distance between concepts x and y. $f(x)$, $f(y)$, and $f(x, y)$ denotes the number of pages containing x, y, both x and y. N is the total number of web pages indexed by Google.

This kind of distance actually measures the symmetric conditional probability that a web page contains both concepts, and this probability is estimated by the co-occurrence of both concepts in all Web pages and is normalized by the frequency of each concept separately. For example, to calculate the Google distance between concepts "Google" and "Microsoft", firstly we calculate the number of web pages that contain "Google", which is 2,180,000,000. Then we calculate the number of web pages what contain "Microsoft", which is 481,000,000. After that we calculate the number of web pages that contain both, which is 142,000,000. Finally with Eq. (38), we get the NGD between "Google" and "Microsoft" is 0.1877.

Tag Concurrence Distance

The Tag Concurrence Distance (TCD)[7] directly applies the idea of Google distance to the tags. It treats the tag list of each image as a document, and calculates the TCD distance the same way as Google distance.

$$TCD(x, y) = \frac{max(\log f(x), \log f(y)) - \log f(x, y)}{\log G - min(\log f(x), \log f(y))} \tag{39}$$

where $f(x)$ and $f(y)$ are the numbers of images containing tag x and tag y respectively, and $f(x, y)$ is the number of images containing both x and y. These numbers can be obtained by performing search by tag on Flickr website using the tags as keywords. Moreover, G is the total number of images in Flickr. The concurrence similarity between tag x and tag y is then defined as

$$S(x, y) = \exp\{-TCD(x, y)\}$$

This is a very intuitive way to measure the conceptual distance based on tags. The inverse of the mutual information between two tags can be further calculated as a distance of two different tags according to their association with the images. This distance reflects the frequency of two tags occurring in the same image. However, there is the sparseness problem that many correlations are missing due to the incompleteness of tags. In Flickr, there are less than 10 tags per image. It is far less than the number of words in a typical web document. Therefore, many semantic relations may not be covered by this Tag Concurrent Distance.

Flickr Distance

All of the above conceptual distance measurements are based on the textual information, the visual information is ignored. In order to use visual information to calculate the concept distance, we propose the Flickr distance. Each concept corresponds to a visual language model, which consists of the trigram conditional distributions under different latent topics. Kullback-Leibler divergence (KL divergence) is a common measurement of the difference between two probability distributions. However, as it does not meet the constraint of triangular inequality, it is in fact not a strict metric. Based on KL divergence a more strict metric JS divergence is defined. This divergence is symmetric and its square root is demonstrated a strict metric. The visual correlation is defined as the inverse of average square root of the JS divergence between the latent topic VLMs.

Let $P_{z_i^{C_1}}$ and $P_{z_j^{C_2}}$ be the trigram distributions under latent topic $z_i^{C_1}$ and $z_j^{C_2}$ respectively. $z_i^{C_1}$ represents the ith latent topic of concept C_1. The K-L divergence between them is defined to be

$$D_{KL}(P_{z_i^{C_1}} || P_{z_j^{C_2}}) = \sum_l P_{z_i^{C_1}}(l) \log \frac{P_{z_i^{C_1}}(l)}{P_{z_j^{C_2}}(l)} \tag{40}$$

where $P_{z_i^{C_1}}(l)$,$P_{z_j^{C_2}}(l)$ correspond to the probability density of the lth trigram in these two distributions respectively. In the view of information theory, the L divergency is in fact a measurement of the mutual entropy between the two visual language models.

$$\begin{aligned} & D_{KL}(P_{z_i^{C_1}} || P_{z_j^{C_2}}) \\ &= -\sum_l P_{z_i^{C_1}}(l) \log P_{z_j^{C_2}}(l) + \sum_l P_{z_i^{C_1}}(l) \log P_{z_i^{C_1}}(l) \\ &= H(P_{z_i^{C_1}}, P_{z_j^{C_2}}) - H(P_{z_i^{C_1}}) \end{aligned} \tag{41}$$

where $H(P_{z_i^{C_1}}, P_{z_j^{C_2}})$ is the cross entropy of the two distributions, and $H(P_{z_i^{C_1}})$ is the entropy of $P_{z_i^{C_1}}$. According to the Gibbs' inequality, $D_{KL}(P_{z_i^{C_1}} || P_{z_j^{C_2}}) \geq 0$. It is zero if and only if $P_{z_i^{C_1}}$ equals $P_{z_j^{C_2}}$.

JS divergence is defined based on KL divergence to measure the distance metric between these visual language models (Eq. (42)).

$$D_{JS}(P_{z_i^{C1}}||P_{z_j^{C2}}) = \frac{1}{2}D_{KL}(P_{z_i^{C_1}}||M) + \frac{1}{2}D_{KL}(P_{z_j^{C_2}}||M) \tag{42}$$

$$M = \frac{1}{2}(P_{z_i^{C_1}} + P_{z_j^{C_2}}) \tag{43}$$

where M is the average of $P_{z_i^{C_1}}$ and $P_{z_j^{C_2}}$. It is demonstrated that the square root of the Jensen-Shannon divergence is a metric. Thus the Flickr distance between two concepts C_1 and C_2 is calculated as the average square root of the JS divergence between the latent topic VLM of concept C_1 and that of concept C_2.

$$D_{Flickr}(C_1, C_2) = \sqrt{\sum_{i=1}^{K}\sum_{j=1}^{K}\frac{1}{K^2}D_{JS}(P_{z_i^{C_1}}||P_{z_j^{C_2}})} \tag{44}$$

More generally, the conditional distribution of topics within each category can be used to weight the distance. This topic distribution is generated by the LTVLM.

$$D_{Flickr}(C_1, C_2) = \sqrt{\sum_{i=1}^{K}\sum_{j=1}^{K}P(z_i^{C_1}|C_1)P(z_j^{C_2}|C_2)D_{JS}(P_{z_i^{C_1}}||P_{z_j^{C_2}})} \tag{45}$$

Thus the visual correlation (VC) between two concepts C_1 and C_2 is inverse to the Flickr distance as Eq.(46), where δ is a very small constant ($\delta = 1$ in the experiment).

$$VC(C_1, C_2) = \frac{1}{\delta + \sqrt{D_{Flickr}(C_1, C_2)}} \tag{46}$$

5 Visual Conceptual Network

Based on the Flickr Distance, the visual correlation among concepts can be stored in a graph $G(V, E, W)$ naming visual conceptual network (VCNet), where concepts are nodes $v_i \in V, i = 1, \cdots, N$ and the semantic relationship between two concepts is the edge $e(v_i, v_j) \in E, i, j = 1, \cdots, N$. The visual correlation between the nodes is represented by the weight of the edge $w \in W$.

In Figure (4), only the top 10% of the strongest links are shown. If two concepts have large visual correlation, the edge between them is short; otherwise long. For a brief view of the conceptual network, we find the tags "mp3", 'MSN", "download", and "napster" form a clique in the network. This is coherent to our perception,

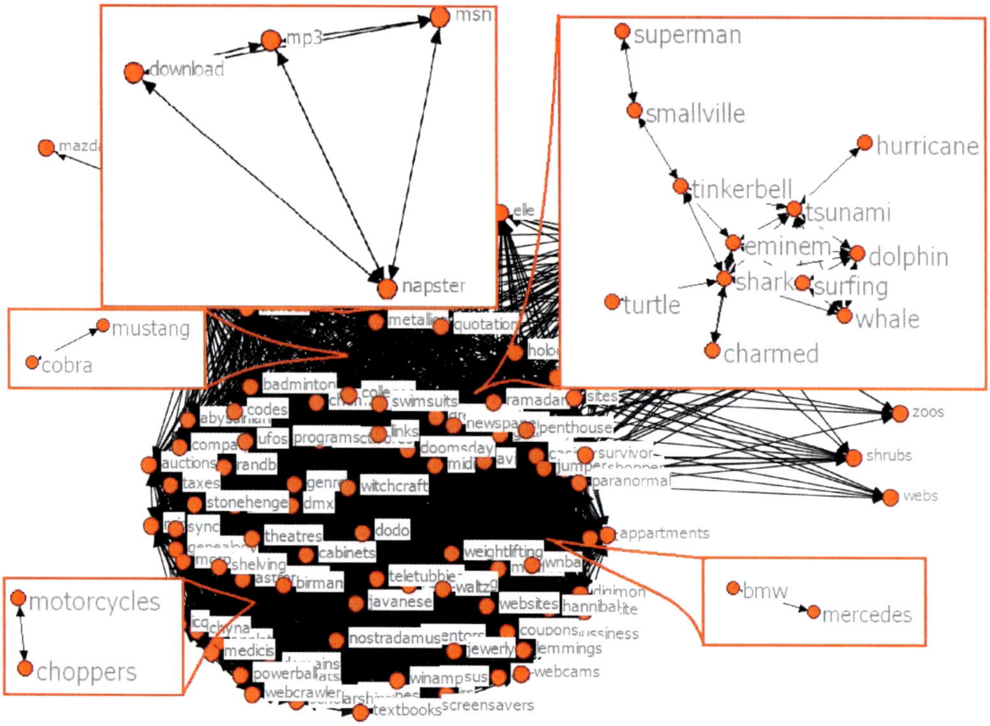

Fig. (4): The visual conceptual network over 1,000 popular Flickr tags.

since the same as MSN, napster is a kind of P2P software to help download mp3 from Internet, and it also provides messaging and online community services.

The visual conceptual network (VCNet) is useful in many multimedia related tasks, i.e. knowledge representation [27], multimedia retrieval [28], etc. This VCNet models the conceptual relationship in a graph manner like the WordNet. Besides, it can maintain a much larger and ever increasing corpus. Here we give a brief overview of the potential usages of VCNet, and more detailed experiments and application scenarios are elaborated in Section 6. One of the most direct applications of VCNet is the conceptual clustering. This task aims to cluster concepts (in image tags or descriptions) to help discover the main topic about a set of images. Using VCNet, concepts with semantic connections are more likely to be clustered together, which will be demonstrated in the experiment section. Another common application of VCNet is the content based web image/video annotation [29, 30], where the common paradigm is to annotate the images or video frame by classification. This is done by either considering the concepts are independent to each other[31, 32], or incorporating the conceptual relation into the model by using Google distance[33].

However, if the conceptual relation is modeled by VCNet, the annotation results will be further boosted (shown in Sect. 6). VCNet also has many other potential applications, such as query expansion [34], annotation refinement [35], etc. Any application which has ever used WordNet can now use the VCNet to scale up with the ever-increasing size of conceptual corpus.

Discussion

In this subsection, we would like to give the intuitive interpretation that Flickr distance can effectively measure the correlation between concepts.

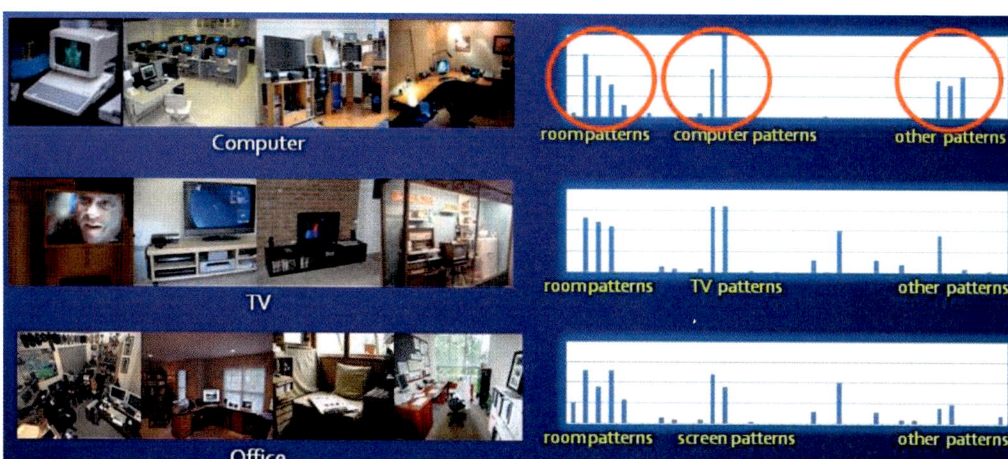

Fig. (5): Intuitive interpretation. If two concepts are synonymy, visually similarity, meronymy, or frequently concurrency, their visual feature distribution will share some patterns. These similar patterns will help measure the correlation between the concepts.

Fig.(5) gives some examples. For concept "computer", its VLM model actually is a distribution of all possible trigrams, among which there are patterns that reveal the characteristics of screens. There are also patterns to represent other related objects, such as the room, since computers are often placed in a room. Similarly, for concept "TV", there are also patterns for screens and rooms, and its particular patterns. For concept "office", there are mainly patterns for "room" and also some patterns for "screen" and other objects in the room. The JS distance is the difference between two distributions. As "computer" and "TV" shares similar patterns of "room" and "screen", their distance should be small, and similarly the distance between "office" and "TV", and distance between "office" and "computer" are also small. So this is an intuitive explanation why VLM divergence can estimate conceptual distance.

On the other hand, these samples show four kinds of relationships: "room" and "office" are Synonym. Screen of "TV" and screen of "computer" are visually correlated (Similarity). "TV"/"computer" typically will coexist with "room" (Concurrence). And "screen" is part of "TV" (Meronymy). So Flickr Distance can model all four kinds of conceptual relationships, some of which were not properly measured by traditional conceptual distances. Since FD adopts visual information not fully depends on tags, it can also work well even when the tags are incomplete. Or more clearly, if we can find similar patterns in the images associated with different concepts, the corresponding conceptual relationships can be discovered.

6 Experiments and Applications

In this section, we first demonstrate that the Flickr Distance is more coherent to human perception than NGD which are derived from textual correlation. This is illustrated by comparing the FD with NGD and TCD in both subjective and objective experiments. Then we construct and apply the VCNet in several scenarios, and show this conceptual network in visual domain is applicable and useful in multimedia related tasks. For simplicity, we denote the conceptual network generated with each distance measurement also as NGD, TCD, and FD.

Data description In this experiment, we choose Flickr as the data source. We randomly collected 3,000 tags from Flickr as a collection, and then manually selected 1,000 popular tags from the collection to conduct the experiment. Taking each tag as a query, the top 1,000 related images from the Flickr tag based search results are used to represent the its content.

In this experiments, we aim to demonstrate that the Flickr Distance is more coherent to human perception than the Google distance. For simplicity, we compare FD with NGD and TCD over the 1,000 tag dataset. Then we evaluate these two conceptual networks by both user study and WordNet results.

The evaluation can be conducted both subjectively and objectively. For subjective evaluation, we conduct a user study, in which users are required to score the correlation of each pair of related concepts according to their knowledge. Since the manually evaluation on the large scale conceptual network is too expensive and impractical, we also conduct the objective evaluation on larger test data. We take the WordNet as the ground truth, and compare average spectral coherence (ASC) of different conceptual networks to WordNet (WN). Although WordNet has some problems to scale up and update with the increasing of novel concepts on the web, it is a reasonable benchmark to evaluate the coherence to human perception, since it is generated by human experts.

Experiment I: Subjective user study

As an illustration, a portion of the 1,000 testing concepts are listed in Tab.(2). Three kinds of conceptual networks based on NGD, TCD, and FD are generated respectively.

Tab. (2): Illustration of the test concepts.

Concept list				
asian	eva	paris	simpsons	tinkerbell
birds	friends	scarface	snow	tsunami
bmw	fruit	sharks	soccer	tulips
bowling	golf	shower	softball	turtle
butterflies	hawaii	shrek	space	usher
charmed	horses	mercedes	spiderman	venus
choppers	hurricane	minnesota	spiders	volleyball
cross	lamborghini	motorcycles	sunset	whale
donkey	lingerie	mustang	surfing	wrestling
eminem	marijuana	paintball	tennis	...

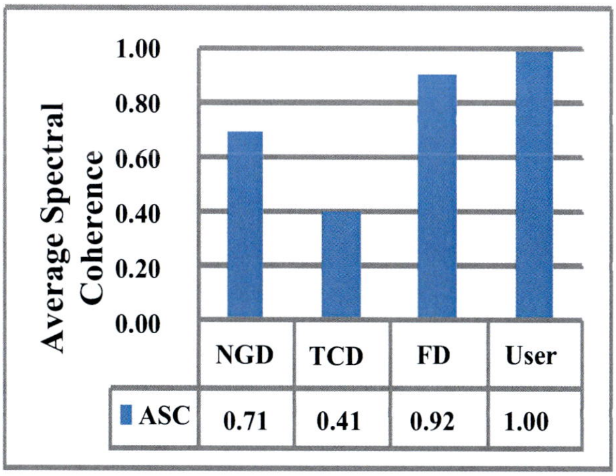

Fig. (6): Coherence to Human Score.

Tab. (3): Subjective user study. This table shows the relevance score for each pair of test concepts by NGD, TCD, FD and the average score given by 12 users. All scores are normalized to [0,5]. The last row is the average spectral coherence of each score to the user provided score.

Correlation score (normalized to [0,5])				
Conceptual pair	NGD	TCD	FD	User
BMW–Mercedes	0.18	4.01	1.88	1.60
charmed–Eminem	1.55	1.46	2.40	2.14
charmed–sharks	0.61	4.02	3.88	2.63
choppers–motorcycles	1.81	0.97	1.69	1.26
Cobra–Mustang	0.34	0.33	2.26	1.92
dolphin–Eminem	4.21	4.42	4.13	4.17
dolphin–sharks	0.50	2.16	2.14	1.93
dolphin–surfing	0.15	1.72	2.45	2.04
dolphin–tsunami	2.14	2.84	2.86	2.05
dolphin–whale	0.22	2.83	1.97	0.80
Eminem–sharks	2.17	2.97	4.44	3.73
Eminem–surfing	3.95	4.16	4.44	4.18
Eminem–Tinkerbell	0.87	0.18	3.64	2.73
Eminem–tsunami	1.61	2.57	4.29	4.09
football–soccer	0.03	1.90	1.67	1.54
hurricane–tsunami	1.86	3.32	1.74	1.68
sharks–surfing	3.30	4.05	2.35	2.04
sharks–Tinkerbell	4.39	1.38	4.44	4.19
sharks–tsunami	3.70	2.45	2.86	2.52
sharks–turtle	0.03	4.79	2.22	1.35
sharks–whale	0.94	3.62	1.93	1.17
Smallville–Superman	0.46	4.29	1.74	1.78
Smallville–Tinkerbell	2.18	2.15	3.08	2.79
surfing–tsunami	1.94	4.52	2.35	1.29
surfing–whale	2.89	0.16	2.45	1.81
tsunami–whale	0.17	3.72	2.61	1.94
Tinkerbell–tsunami	3.68	2.17	4.44	3.86
...	...	...	...	...
Average spectral coherence	0.71	0.41	0.92	1.00

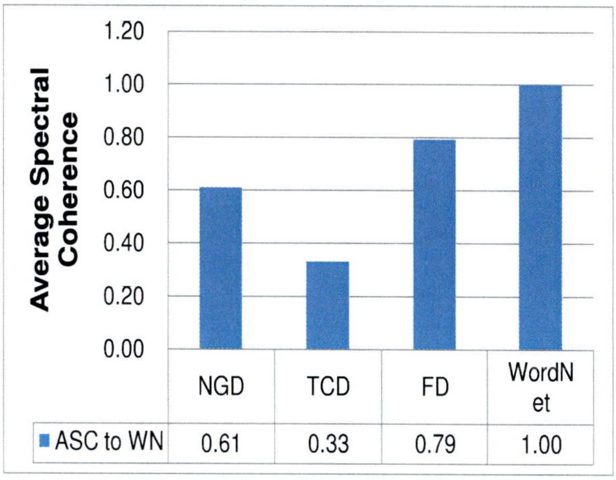

Fig. (7): Coherence to WordNet score.

To facilitate the evaluation, we extract 100 top relevant conceptual pairs from each conceptual network, and list the relevant score under each distance measurement as shown in Tab.(3). We then present these pairs to 12 independent users. For each conceptual pair, the users are required to give a score ranging from 0 to 5. The higher the score is, the more related the two concepts are according to the user's knowledge. By averaging the score from all the users, we get the average user score, which is shown in last column in Tab.(3). The coherence of scores provided by each method to the user provided scores are measured by the average spectral coherence (ASC), which is defined as follows:

$$C_{x,y} = \frac{|G_{xy}|^2}{G_{xx}G_{yy}} \tag{47}$$

where x and y are two sequences of scores. G_{xy} is the cross-spectral density between x and y, and G_{xx} and G_{yy} are the autospectral density of x and y respectively. The magnitude of the spectral density is denoted as $|G|$. ASC ranges from 0 to 1, and the larger ASC indicates the relevance score is more coherent to human perception. ASC of different methods on user score are shown in the last row in Tab.(3).

This subjective user study shows that the ASC of FD achieves 29.21% gain over the NGD, and 126.10% gain over the TCD. This shows that FD is more coherent to human perception.

Experiment II: Objective experiments

Superior to the subjective study, the objective evaluation can be conducted on relatively larger scale dataset.

To perform the objective experiment, we take the conceptual relationship in WordNet as the ground truth. The evaluation can only be conducted when both concepts in the pair appear in WordNet corpus. Thus there are 497 concepts that can be effectively evaluated by the WordNet ground truth. Conceptual networks based on NGD, TCD and FD are generated on these 497 concepts by the same means discussed in the above subsection. This dataset is much larger than commonly used dataset. Given enough ground truth and resource, the evaluation can be performed on even larger one. The average spectral coherence of each score to the score in WordNet is shown in Fig.(7).

This comparison (shown in Fig (7))(b) illustrates that FD outperforms NGD by 29.98% and outperforms TCD 139.06%. This result is almost the same with that of the subjective evaluation (Fig.(7)(a)).

Application I: Conceptual clustering

In this application scenario, we apply the Flickr distance based visual correlation on conceptual clustering. Conceptual clustering is widely used for topic detection and summarization. Since there are lots of tags and descriptions associated with web images, we are able to use conceptual clustering to detect the main topic of these images. However, the focus of the topic summarization in image may not be the same with that for the text. For example, the image is more likely to focus on the main object or scene, while in the text document it focuses more on the story or point of view of the author. Thus an applicable conceptual distance measurement for textual domain, i.e. Google distance, may not perform as well as the specific distance measurement for visual domain. Here we compare the conceptual clustering results of NGD, TCD, and FD.

Three groups of concepts are selected: Space related terms (4 concepts), Ball games (10 concepts), and Animals (9 concepts). We choose these concepts because all users agree that these concepts are grouped without ambiguous in the user study. In total there are 23 concepts in the experiment. The task is to group these concepts into clusters automatically. One of the key issues with conceptual clustering is the conceptual distance measurement. In most cases, WordNet is used to measure the conceptual distances. However, due to the limitation of WordNet lexicon, a large portion of concepts, i.e. famous movies, brand, game, sport star, singer, etc. are inextricable. In this experiment, we build two different networks between these concepts with Google distance and Flickr distance separately. Based on these two conceptual networks, spectral clustering is adopted to generate the conceptual clusters. We adopt spectral clustering rather than the commonly used K-means algorithm, because it is hard to calculate the cluster centers of these concepts in K-means algorithm, while the spectral clustering only use the relationship between the samples. The results of the conceptual clusters are shown in Tab.(4).

Tab.(4) shows that the Flickr distance based spectral clustering can effectively generate the conceptual clusters. After the conceptual clustering, we know the three categories of images are about space, animals, and ball games. The errors are

Tab. (4): Result of conceptual clustering. The bold font denotes the miss-clustered concepts.

Clustering by NGD			Clustering by TCD			Clustering by FD		
bears	**bowling**	baseball	moon	baseball	basketball	moon	bears	baseball
horses	dolphin	basketball	space	**donkey**	**bears**	saturn	dolphin	basketball
moon	donkey	football	Venus	softball	bowling	space	donkey	football
space	**saturn**	golf	**whale**	**wolf**	**dolphin**	venus	**golf**	**snake**
-	sharks	soccer	-	-	football	-	horses	soccer
-	snake	tennis	-	-	golf	-	sharks	bowling
-	**softball**	volleyball	-	-	**horses**	-	spiders	softball
-	spiders	-	-	-	**Saturn**	-	**tennis**	volleyball
-	turtle	-	-	-	**sharks**	-	turtle	-
-	**venus**	-	-	-	soccer	-	whale	-
-	whale	-	-	-	**spiders**	-	wolf	-
-	wolf	-	-	-	tennis	-	-	-
-	-	-	-	-	**turtle**	-	-	-
-	-	-	-	-	volleyball	-	-	-

marked in **bold** in Tab.(4). 6 out of the 23 total concepts are mistakenly clustered by NGD; 9 errors for TCD; and 3 errors in the result of FD. Comparing with the clustering results based on NGD and TCD, the results by FD are more promising.

Application II: Image annotation

Automatically annotating images is critical to web image retrieval and browsing. Most of the state-of-the-art image annotation approaches detect multiple semantic concepts in an isolated manner, which neglect the fact that the concepts may correlated to each other. The generative model of the annotation process can be represented as Eq. (48).

$$w^* = \arg\max_{w \in V} P(w, I_u) \tag{48}$$

where w is the annotation keywords, and w^* is the best suitable keyword. I_u represents the unlabeled image. This annotation process equals to maximizing the joint probability $P(w, I_u)$. The annotation performance may be further boosted with consideration of the conceptual relations.

Based on this motivation, the Dual Cross-Media Relevance Model (DCMRM) [33] is adopted and achieved well performance. This model assumes that the probability of observing the annotation keyword w and the images I_u are mutually independent given a keyword v, and the relevance model is represented as follows.

$$w^* = \arg\max_{w \in V} \sum_{v \in V} P(I_u|v)P(w|v)P(v) \tag{49}$$

where w and v are two annotation keywords. $P(I_u|v)$ denotes the probability of an untagged image I_u given a word v. $P(w|v)$ denotes the probability of a word w given a word v. In the DCMRM method [33], Google distance is adopted to calculate the $P(w|v)$, which is denoted by NGD-DCMRM for short in the following discussion. In contrast, we apply the Flickr distance to calculate the conditional probability $P(w|v)$, and the corresponding annotation method is denoted by FD-DCMRM.

For simplicity, we adopt the Flickr images associated to the top 79 most frequently used sample concepts (partially shown in Tab.(2)). Since there are 1,000 images for each concept, the dataset contains 79,000 images. 5-folds cross-validation is adopted, where 80% of the images are used for training and the rest images for testing. The performance is shown in Tab.(5).

Tab. (5): The comparison by precision@N.

	Prec@1	Prec@2	Prec@3	Prec@4
DCMRM	5%	4.00%	3.63%	3.38%
NGD-DCMRM	5.00%	10.5%	7%	6%
TCD-DCMRM	8.76%	12.23%	10.12%	12.87%
FD-DCMRM	5%	17.5%	14%	19.2%

Tab.(5) gives the precision@N (N=1, 2, 3, 4) of four different annotation methods. Precision@N measures the precision of annotation in the first N words. DCMRM [33] does not use the word relations and only use the correlation between images to annotate. NGD-DCMRM uses conceptual relations in the annotation process and measures the conceptual distance by NGD. TCD-DCMRM uses the TCD to calculate relations between keywords in the annotation. FD-DCMRM adopts the same annotation algorithm but with Flickr distance as the conceptual distance. The result shows that FD-DCMRM outperforms DCMRM, NGD-DCMRM and TCD-DCMRM on Prec@1,2,3,4. To further illustrate the advantage of using Flickr distance rather than Google distance in image annotation, we compare the total correct keywords annotated on the test dataset, consists of 1,000 test images. The result is shown in Figure (8). The number in horizontal axis denotes the evaluation is conducted on the first N keywords for each image (N=1, 2, 3, 4). The vertical axis represents the total number of correct keywords annotated to all the test images. This comparison shows Flickr distance based annotation method can generate more correct keywords, especially when annotating multiple keywords to each image. This also, in some aspects, demonstrates that Flickr distance is more helpful than Google distance in multimedia related tasks.

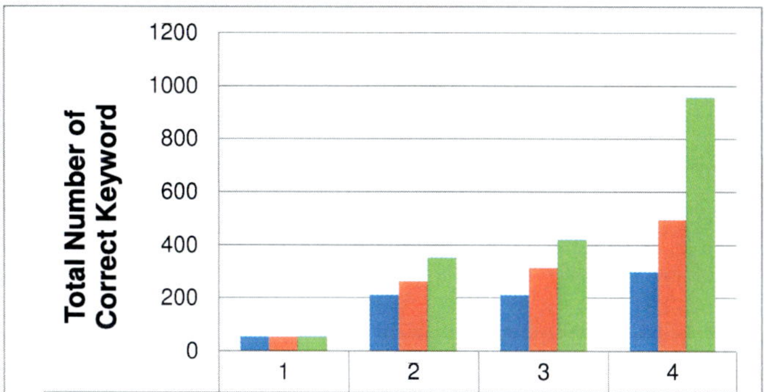

	1	2	3	4
NGD-DCMRM	55	212	212	301
TCD-DCMRM	57	264	317	497
FD-DCMRM	57	354	423	960

Fig. (8): The number of correct annotation words at first N words (N=1,2,3,4).

The computational cost of the proposed method lies on the training of VLM. The average time cost for each concept is about 1 minute. So 1,000 concepts cost around 17 hours at Intel(R) Xeon(R) CPU 2.66GHz 16G RAM. As the correlation matrix can be calculated offline, the computational time is not critical. Given the correlation matrix, the rest cost is the same with alternative approaches.

Application III: Social tagging recommendation

Social tagging allows all the users in a social network label the web resources with their own keywords and share with others. This labeling operation is named "tagging". Different from ontology based annotation; there is no pre-defined ontology or taxonomy in social tagging. Thus this task is more convenient for ordinary users.

Although social tagging is easy to perform, the user created tags contain much noise, such as ambiguous tags, misspelling tags, improper tags, due to the lack of effective recommendation. Tag recommendation will provide the related or more proper tags for the users to choose in tagging an image. The quality of tag recommendation is quite important [36] to final quality of tagging, since one reason users do not tag properly is because they cannot think of any proper tags [37].

One of the critical limitations in social tagging recommendation is the correlation measurement between the tags. Current recommendation is only based on the tag co-occurrence, while visual correlation is ignored in the recommendation process. In this experiment, we would like to demonstrate the usefulness of Flickr distance in the tag recommendation task.

Given the image and some of its initial user created tags, we would like to recommend a list of related tags which may be also applicable to the image. We denote the set of initial tags as $\mathcal{OT}$, and the set of remaining tags as $\mathcal{UT}$. The relevance of the tags is represented in two domains. The average tag co-occurrence in Flickr dataset is deemed as text domain correlation, and VCNet between tags is deemed as visual domain correlation. Then for these domains, we generate several ranking features $\{f_l\}_{l=1}^{3n}$ (n is the number of initial tags). The first n ranking features are based on NGD, and the following n by TCD, and the last n features by FD.

$$f_l(t_i, t_l) = W^s_{NGD}(t_i, t_l),\ t_l \in \mathcal{OT},\ t_i \in \mathcal{UT},\ l = 1, \cdots, n \tag{50}$$

$$f_{n+l}(t_i, t_l) = W^s_{TCD}(t_i, t_l),\ t_l \in \mathcal{OT},\ t_i \in \mathcal{UT},\ l = 1, \cdots, n \tag{51}$$

$$f_{2n+l}(t_i, t_l) = W^s_{FD}(t_i, t_l),\ t_l \in \mathcal{OT},\ t_i \in \mathcal{UT},\ l = 1, \cdots, n \tag{52}$$

where W^s_{NGD}, W^s_{TCD}, W^s_{FD} are the weights of t_i, t_l in the corresponding conceptual network. These ranking features of multi-domains are firstly used separately and then combined in the Rankboost framework [38], which considers only the order of instances and not scores, to generate the most related keywords for social tagging. Performance under different correlation features and their combinations are shown in Fig.(9).

We randomly select 10,000 images and associated 5,000 tags from Flickr as the test data, and the rest images and associated tags are used as the training data. To train the tag co-occurrence model, we count the co-occurrence frequency between every pair of tags from the collection, and then normalize them to $[0, 1]$. In the visual domain, we generate the ranking features based on VCNet. Then we combine these weak rankers from different domains using the Rankboost algorithm.

Each recommendation approach will generate an ordered list of relevant tags for each image. Then a group of volunteers are required to evaluate these recommended tags. If a tag is relevant to the image, it will be marked true; otherwise false. The average precision of the top 10 recommendations and the coverage over all correct recommendations are adopted to measure the performance of each recommendation method. The coverage is defined as the proportion of correct tags (including all correct tags by both methods and initial tags) that are recommended by the specific method. We adopt the coverage rather than the recall, because the recall is inapplicable for the recommendation task.

$$Coverage(m_i) = \frac{\#correct\,tags\,by\,method\,m_i}{\#correct\,tags\,in\,total} \tag{53}$$

Figure (9) compares the performance of the three methods. In Figure (9), "AP@10" is the average precision at top 10 recommendations, and "AC@10" is the average coverage at top 10 recommendations. We find FD outperforms NGD by 13.46% in precision and 19.24% in coverage, and outperforms TCD by 9.83% in precision and 11.43% in coverage. These results demonstrate the effectiveness of the Flickr distance and VCNet in tag recommendation task.

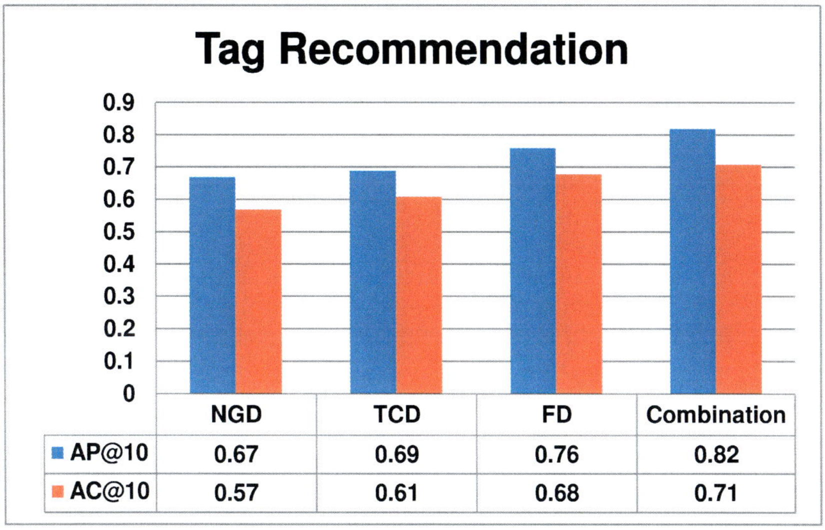

Fig. (9): Performance of the tag recommendation. The Flickr distance based tag recommendation outperforms Google distance based recommendation by 16% and outperforms tag concurrence based recommendation by 14%.

7 Conclusions

In summary, we discussed the Flickr Distance and its applications to Internet multimedia search and mining tasks in this chapter. The visual characteristic of the concepts is modeled by a novel latent topic visual language model. JS divergence between the LTVLM can be deemed as a measurement of the conceptual distance. Both subjective user study and objective experimental results show that Flickr distance is more coherent to human perception than text based distance, such as the Google distance, Tag concurrence distance, etc. Based on this novel visual correlation measurement, we construct VCNet to store the correlation between the tags on Flickr. Comparing with traditional WordNet, which is limited in conceptual corpus, VCNet can deal with far more concepts on the web and can be easily updated. Thus it is a good complement to WordNet in multimedia related applications. Furthermore, we apply the visual correlation measurement to conceptual clustering, image annotation, and tag recommendation. The results demonstrate that this novel Flickr distance and the corresponding VCNet are more helpful to multimedia tasks than the text based correlation measurement.

8 References

[1] J. A. Rodríguez-Serrano, F. Perronnin, G. Sánchez, and J. Lladós. A similarity measure between vector sequences with application to handwritten word image retrieval. In *CVPR*, 2009.

[2] L. Wu, L. Yang, N. Yu, and X.-S. Hua. Learning to tag. In *WWW*, 2009.

[3] L. Wu, S. C. Hoi, R. Jin, J. Zhu, and N. Yu. Distance metric learning from uncertain side information with application to automated photo tagging. In *ACM Multimedia*, 2009.

[4] L. Cao, J. Luo, and T. S. Huang. Annotating photo collections by label propagation according to multiple similarity cues. In *ACM Multimedia*, 2008.

[5] G. A. Miller and et.al. Wordnet, a lexical database for the english language. *Cognition Science Lab, Princeton University*, 1995.

[6] R. Cilibrasi and P. M. B. Vitanyi. The google similarity distance. *IEEE Transactions on Knowledge and Data Engineering*, 2007.

[7] D. Liu, X.-S. Hua, L. Yang, M. Wang, and H.-J. Zhang. Tag ranking. In *WWW*, 2009.

[8] H. P. Moravec. Obstacle avoidance and navigation in the real world by a seeing robot rover. Ph.D. dissertation, Stanford, CA, USA, 1980.

[9] C. Harris and M. Stephens. A combined corner and edge detection. In *Proceedings of The Fourth Alvey Vision Conference*, 1988.

[10] A. Baumberg. Reliable feature matching across widely separated views. In *CVPR*, 2000.

[11] L. Bretzner and T. Lindeberg. Feature tracking with automatic selection of spatial scales. *CVIU*, 1998.

[12] T. Lindeberg. Scale-Space Theory in Computer Vision. Springer, 1994.

[13] K. Mikolajczyk and C. Schmid. Scale & affine invariant interest point detectors. *International Journal of Computer Vision*, 2004.

[14] H. Bay, T. Tuytelaars, and L. Van Gool. Surf: Speeded-up robust features. In *ECCV*, 2006.

[15] W. Han and M. Brady. Real-time corner detection algorithm for motion estimation. *Image and Vision Computing*, 1995.

[16] S. M. Smith and J. M. Brady. Susan - a new approach to low level image processing. *International Journal of Computer Vision*, 1995.

[17] J. Matas, O. Chum, M. Urban, and T. Pajdla. Robust wide baseline stereo from maximally stable extremal regions. In *BMVC*, 2002.

[18] D. G. Lowe. Distinctive image features from scale-invariant keypoints. *International Journal of Computer Vision*, 2004.

[19] L. Wu, Y. Hu, M. Li, N. Yu, and X.-S. Hua. Scale-invariant visual language modeling for object categorization. *IEEE Transactions on Multimedia*, 2009.

[20] L. Wu, M. Li, Z. Li, W.-Y. Ma, and N. Yu. Visual language modeling for image classification. In *MIR*, 2007.

[21] H. Otluman and T. Aboulnasr. Low complexity 2-d hidden markov model for face recognition. *Proc. of IEEE Conference on International Symposium on Computer Architecture*, 2000.

[22] J. Li and J. Wang. Automatic linguistic indexing of pictures by a statistical modeling approach. *IEEE Transactions on PAMI*, 2003.

[23] P. Clarkson and R. Rosenfeld. Statistical language modeling using the CMU–cambridge toolkit. In *European Conference on Speech Communication and Technology*, 1997.

[24] S. Katz. Estimation of probabilities from sparse data for the language model component of a speech recognizer. *IEEE Transactions on Acoustics, Speech and Signal Processing*, 1987.

[25] R. Rada, H. Mili, E. Bicknell, and M. Blettner. Development and application of a metric on semantic nets. *IEEE Transactions on Systems Management and Cybernetics*, 1989.

[26] R. Richardson, A. F. Smeaton, A. F. Smeaton, J. Murphy, and J. Murphy. Using wordnet as a knowledge base for measuring semantic similarity between words. In *Proceedings of AICS Conference, Tech. Rep.*, 1994.

[27] W. Al-Khatib, Y. F. Day, A. Ghafoor, and P. B. Berra. Semantic modeling and knowledge representation in multimedia databases. *IEEE Transactions on Knowledge and Data Engineering*, 1999.

[28] T. S. Huang, C. K. Dagli, S. Rajaram, E. Y. Chang, M. I. Mandel, G. E. Poliner, and D. P. W. Ellis. Active learning for interactive multimedia retrieval. In *Proc. of the IEEE*, 2008.

[29] G.-J. Qi, X.-S. Hua, Y. Rui, J. Tang, T. Mei, and H.-J. Zhang. Correlative multi-label video annotation In *ACM Multimedia*, 2007.

[30] S.-F. Chang, D. Ellis, W. Jiang, K. Lee, A. Yanagawa, A. C. Loui, and J. Luo. Large-scale multimodal semantic concept detection for consumer video. In *Proc. of the international workshop on Workshop on multimedia information retrieval*, 2007.

[31] J. Jeon, V. Lavrenko, and R. Manmatha. Automatic image annotation and retrieval using cross-media relevance models. In *ACM SIGIR*, 2003.

[32] V. Lavrenko, R. Manmatha, and J. Jeon. A model for learning the semantics of pictures. In *NIPS*, 2003.

[33] J. Liu, B. Wang, M. Li, Z. Li, W.-Y. Ma, H. Lu, and S. Ma. Dual cross-media relevance model for image annotation. In *ACM Multimedia*, 2007.

[34] A. P. Natsev, A. Haubold, J. Tešić, L. Xie, and R. Yan. Semantic concept-based query expansion and re-ranking for multimedia retrieval. In *ACM Multimedia*, 2007.

[35] C. Wang, F. Jing, L. Zhang, and H.-J. Zhang. Content-based image annotation refinement. In *CVPR*, 2007.

[36] M. Ames and M. Naaman. Why we tag: motivations for annotation in mobile and online media In *SIGCHI*, 2007.

[37] S. Sen, S. K. Lam, A. M. Rashid, D. Cosley, D. Frankowski, J. Osterhouse, F. M. Harper, and J. Riedl. Tagging, communities, vocabulary, evolution. In *CSCW*, 2006.

[38] Y. Freund, R. Iyer, R. E. Schapire, Y. Singer, and G. Dietterich. An efficient boosting algorithm for combining preferences. In *Journal of Machine Learning Research*, 2003.

Internet Multimedia Search and Mining, **2013, 273-305**

CHAPTER 11

Geospatial Web Image Mining

Dirk Ahlers*
Norwegian University of Science and Technology, Tel: +47 735 90519,
Email: ahlers@dhere.de

Susanne Boll
University of Oldenburg, Tel +49 441 9722201, Fax: +49 441 9722202,
Email: susanne.boll@uni-oldenburg.de

Philipp Sandhaus
CEWE Color AG & Co. OHG, Tel: +49 441 404-3731,
Email: philipp.sandhaus@cewecolor.de

Abstract: One commonly asked question when confronted with a photograph is "Where is this place?" When talking about a place mentioned on the Web, the question arises "What does this place look like?" Today, these questions can not reliably be answered for Web images as they typically do not reveal their relationship to an actual geographic position. Analysis of the keywords surrounding the images or the content of the images alone has not yet achieved results that would allow deriving a precise location information to select representative images. Photos that are reliably tagged with labels of place names or areas only cover a small fraction of available images and also remain at a keyword level.

Results can be improved for arbitrary Web images by combining features from the Web page as image context and the images themselves as content. We propose a location-based search for Web images that allows finding images that are only implicitly related to a geographic position without having to rely on explicit tagging or metadata. Our spatial Web image search engine first crawls and identifies location-related information on Web pages to determine a geographic relation of the

***Correspondence Author:** Dirk Ahlers, Norwegian University of Science and Technology; Email: ahlers@offis.de.

Xian-Sheng Hua, Marcel Worring & Tat-Seng Chua (Eds.)

Web page, and then extends this geospatial reference further to assess an image's location. Combining context and content analysis, we are able to determine if the image actually is a realistic representative photograph of a place and related to a geographic position.

Keywords

Image Retrieval, Geospatial Search, Semantic Retrieval, Multimedia Retrieval, Image Analysis, Web Search, Geographic Web Information Retrieval, Context Analysis, Location Assessment, Location Classification, Photo Annotation

1 Introduction

The role of geographic location for images and the relation of Web information to a physical place have gained much attention in recent years. Web search is increasingly becoming "local", search engines not only index content by keywords but also by geographical locations. Users can have information mapped to a certain place or region of interest and search accordingly. Web image search, on the other hand, is mostly keyword-based or explores basic image features such as color or texture. A geospatial Web image search that works on unstructured Web pages with arbitrary images is not yet available. Searching for images related to a certain location quickly shows that Web images typically do not easily reveal their explicit relation to an actual geographic position. The geographic semantics of Web images are either not available at all or hidden somewhere within the Web pages' content. This lack of explicit location information also applies to the images contained in Web pages. Even though GPS has arrived at the consumer, the photos that actually have a location stamp or are geo-tagged cover only a tiny fraction of all Web images. Furthermore, such well-described images are mostly only available in social communities or on photography portals. Geotagged images are only seldomly found in general Web pages and thus only untagged images are found in the interesting asset of geospatially relevant Web pages. This poses an interesting challenge to the field of Web image retrieval, namely, the derivation of reliable location information for Web images from unstructured Web pages.

Currently, a Web search for photos of a certain well-known place name remains a keyword-based search of known geographic place names. This can work for known places, landmarks, or regions such as "New York" or "Singapore" but does not deliver a precise geo-reference for Web image content. We therefore need a spatial Web image search to enable users to search for images from a certain geographical coordinate or its spatial vicinity to complement geospatial Web search engines. This work therefore does not aim at the recognition of popular places or landmarks, but instead aims at "'local"' locations, providing illustrations even of places that are only of local interest. Such local locations may nevertheless be relevant to someone walking through the city, wanting an overview of a certain neighborhood, or looking for a certain building and requiring its visual description.

In this work, we develop a system for geospatial Web image search [1]. We aim at a general approach for common Web images that works beyond keyword-search and does not need prepared tags or annotations. We derive possible location information for those images that are contained in Web pages with an established spatial context. The mutual relation of a Web pages' text, location, its contained images, and associated metadata is a main driving force behind this approach. We employ our spatial search engine for a location-based geo-referenced search down to the address level [2]. It exploits the location information of a Web page that is not explicitly contained as metadata or other structured annotation but is rather an implicit part of the textual content. Based on this previously identified location of the Web page, we can identify representative photographic representations of the mentioned location. The potential propagation of this location to the images embedded in the page and its reliability is determined by content-based and context-based analysis. In a first step, an analysis of the Web pages identifies photographs, i.e., the image content relevant for a spatial image search for realistic depictions of places. Following the photograph identification, a location-relevance classification process evaluates image context and content to determine if the photograph is actually related to the location already identified for the Web page.

We evaluated and combined several heuristic approaches for analyzing and scoring relevant features. These are categorized into context and content information for both Web pages and embedded images. Feature classifiers are combined to achieve an overall assessment of an image's connection to a location. As a means to reduce the computational cost, classifiers' individual analyzers are ordered by their discriminatory ability and their computational cost to filter out non-promising images early, preferably even without the need to download them. Our test and evaluation show that, even though only a small fraction of the Web pages reveal photos that have a relation to the location, these can be well related to their geospatial context.

With a Web search that reliably finds georeferenced images from unstructured Web pages located at a certain geographic location or region, a large number of potentially geographically-related images on Web pages becomes available for spatial Web image search. This can be applied for a variety of interesting applications such as searching for images along a route when preparing a vacation, extending personal photo collections, gathering visual information about an area, or providing representative images for spatial search results.

2 Related Work

This work researches the connection of Web images and location from a unique angle. While the usual direction is to start from an image and examine its content and metadata (e.g. [21]) to estimate a location, our approach takes a different route in that it starts with a document as the image's context which already contains a known location and tries to extend and propagate it to matching images. Using Web pages as a special case of context and drawing the connection to the image content, our hybrid approach thus attacks the problem from both sides simultaneously. A large body of literature exists on techniques for image retrieval, geographic retrieval, Web search and various combinations thereof. The following examines the different fields of related work and compares and applies their findings to the goal of our approach.

Data sources for geospatial image search

Location is a fast growing topic in the Web today, generating huge interest for users and a growing number of location-aware data sources. GPS has arrived at the end-consumer; services such as Plazes, Dopplr, Yahoo! Fire Eagle, or Google Latitude allow users to share their own physical location. Users can use their location to start a local search or link their current location to their photos. Modern cameras with an integrated GPS-receiver can directly embed coordinates in a photo's EXIF metadata. However, such geo-located images are rare in the first place even in large photo collections and are even rarer in a general Web context. This lack of metadata is only partly due to loss of information in editing processes. Especially in the Web, images are often edited before publication and their EXIF information inadvertently destroyed. Regarding loss of metadata, [47] presents a system that captures metadata at media capture time and preserves it over the production process in a professional environment, which is therefore not yet suitable for common use and cannot address the current state of Web images. However, it is a complementary approach to metadata extraction and derivation on documents without systematically defined metadata.

A richer source for location-based images are Web 2.0 services that allow for organizing and sharing personal photo collections. They provide for an assignment of location-related information by manual tagging and annotation [43]. For example, Flickr (flickr.com) or other tag-oriented services allow adding names of locations to entities such as photos and to find photos tagged with the same placename. More intuitive to the user and more precise in the assignable location are services that provide means to drag digital content onto a map and by this manually geo-code the content: With Placeopedia (placeopedia.com) entries from Wikipedia can be associated with a geographic location and queried on a map; photos on Flickr or locr (locr.com) can also be positioned on a map to geocode them. Panoramio (www.panoramio.com) is a service entirely dedicated to collecting high-quality location-based images. These applications use collaborative efforts to manually geo-code image content and by this contribute to a localized search.

The massive amount of georeferenced images in these collections allows for interesting data mining approaches, for example, to identify places and sights of important landmarks [56, 66]. However, many successful approaches are based on a sufficiently dense distribution of well-tagged images of well-known places. Exploiting the long tail of photos of "less-interesting" locations is not as easy, either because some locations receive less interest or because images are less comprehensively tagged. Additionally, tagged media collections or prepared geocoded images cover only a very small fraction of images on the Web; many others still reside unrecognized on arbitrary Web pages.

A complementing approach to the long-tail of locations and their images can come from a different perspective. Several services are based on existing directories such as yellow pages. For their entries, the geographic location is known, enabling local search and visualization of results, e.g., on a 2D map. Such content is mapped by services such as Yahoo! Maps (maps.yahoo.com), Google Maps (maps.google.com), or MSN Live (maps.live.com), enabling map-based spatial search and visualization of results. By enhancing these entries with user-generated or specifically crawled content, images for these lcoations can become available. For example, Google Maps has created the ability for business owners to enhance their yellow pages entry with images of their business. Such images have the added value of being manually selected as representative images for a place, so they match the type of images our approach aims at. Their PlacePages further aggregates information about a specific location. This trend clearly emphasizes the demand for accompanying images to location information.

Geographic Web information retrieval

The field of Geographic Information Retrieval concerns itself with research towards extracting geographic meaning from unstructured documents and spatially indexing it. In many cases, the documents are the Web's textual resources. Central challenges in the field are the identification, extraction, and disambiguation of geographical entities as described in [5, 42, 44, 45]. Since textual clues for locations are often highly ambiguous, additional disambiguating terms are used to verify found locations. Such other features can be telephone numbers, state names, or similar. These features are verified against domain knowledge taken from gazetteers, geographic taxonomies detailing geographic coverage and location; placenames; physical, political, or demographic features etc. [23]. Further heuristics are used to aid in disambiguation and in improvement of retrieval performance in extracting geospatial entities. For example, when sufficient disambiguation terms are missing, larger locations may be preferred over smaller ones and locations near each other are often more probable than those with higher distance between them. Of specific interest to our work are those systems that aim to identify location references at a high granularity to pinpoint content to individual coordinates and not just a broad region. Exemplary geospatial Web search engines are presented in [49] and [42], addressing issues of extraction, indexing, and query processing.

The basis for the proposed geospatial Web image search is a location-based Web search engine we developed [1, 3] that employs geographically focused Web crawling and database-backed geoparsing at address-level granularity to spatially index Web pages and make them accessible to geospatial search.

Web image retrieval

Web image retrieval and classification aims to open up images on the Web for multimedia retrieval, often by textual queries that rather work on the surrounding content of the Web page than image content. Since the HTML code of a page provides rich context information for embedded images, most related approaches use text-based image retrieval as a basis by examining textual content such as surrounding text, image metadata, or take hints from the HTML code and especially its structure. Only secondarily, if at all, the actual Web image content is used. Similarly, current keyword-based Web image search engines such as Google Image Search (images.google.com) or Yahoo! Search (images.search.yahoo.com) employ mostly surrounding text features and the image name and path which allows for keyword-based queries. As an addition several approaches exist to combine traditional text-based queries with content analysis of images.

Looking at the field of image retrieval in general, [15] gives a good overview over current trends and approaches for image retrieval in general. An earlier work provides a good survey over the field on content-based image retrieval at *the end of the early years* [58] while [39] describes combinations of content- and context-based image retrieval specifically for photographs.

A survey and comprehensive discussion of existing technologies in Web image retrieval and how they address key issues in the field can be found in [33] along with application scenarios and a comparison of different existing systems. An early example for a system also considering the image content is ImageRover [57], combining text-based queries to provide initial example images following a content-based query-by-example approach to refine the result set. Other approaches combining text-based queries and content-based image similarity are [35, 38, 48]. Besides these works for general web image search more specialized approaches exist concentrating on specific domains (e.g. celebrity search by face recognition [6]).

Purely text-based Web image retrieval approaches are solely taking the HTML code into account to derive annotations for the images contained in the page. As one example, [61] uses an approach for image retrieval examining the attributes of the image tag itself, surrounding paragraph and title of the page. However, further examination of the the effectiveness of features [46] leads to the conclusion that the HTML source contains the most valuable initial clues, but that results improve if images themselves also are examined. Aiming to understand the role of an image on a Web page, [41] uses a range of features to assign roles to Web images. The features are taken from structural document data and image metadata but not from actual image content. Based on these features, various roles of Web images are derived and used to pre-process images for display on a mobile device. By means of structural analysis of HTML documents, [20] segments Web pages into semantic blocks. The authors propose that embedded images inherit the semantics from their surrounding semantic block. Other approaches consider both content and HTML context of an image for semantic annotation and clustering. An early work [16] uses the HTML content and a few selected image content features for Web image search. Building upon this work, [7] developed a classifier to distinguish images into two classes of either photographs or graphics using decision trees. The iFind system [22] considers context and content of images and examines their layout on a page for semantic annotation.

Aiming at a more intuitive presentation of Web multiple ambiguous image search results, approaches such as Igroup [30] as well as iFind [18] additionally consider the surroundings and the content of an image to organize Web image search results into semantically coherent clusters. The latter additionally examines the spatial layout of images on Web pages to identify nearness for groups of images. Closely arranged images are then considered to also be semantically related.

Content-based location detection

The use of only content-based image analysis to derive a location has produced some interesting results. Often, such systems are developed to work on known locations and are independent from Web pages. IDeixis [60] is a system to compare pictures taken by a mobile device to previously taken photos to initiate a search by finding similar photos. By combining image analysis and comparison methods, the most likely location of the given image can be determined. Image comparison is done rather naively by employing euclidian distance according to color histograms. Photo-to-Search [29] approaches a similar use case, but with an indexing and search system based on SIFT features provides a more sophisticated approach enabling for more accurate and faster search results. The PhotoTourism system [59] demonstrates how, with an extensive set of overlapping photographs of a place, a 3-dimensional reconstruction of that place is possible by estimating viewpoints of photographs and stitching them together for a 3D-scene working on image-based rendering.

In [21] the authors employ a large set of 6 million geo-tagged photos to determine the most probable location for a query image. For this the query image is compared according a number of content descriptors with indexed images in the data base build from the geo-tagged images and the most probable location is determined from the similarity to nearby images. A more recent work, but with a similar goal is presented in [13], where the authors employ a larger data set of 35 million photos and extend the approach by also considering temporal and textual features. [17] combines user tags and content-based features to determine a photograph's location. In [55] the authors introduce an approach to infer location information in a known urban area by matching building facades.

These approaches are relevant for our work as they show that location-recognition based on image content is possible in case the possible location is known and the retrieval scope is thus narrowed down. However, these systems require an already previously established collection of georeferenced images as the basis for comparison.

Landmark Recognition

Taking a complementary approach, annotated Web images can also be used to find places of interest and thus create a rich database of high-ranking places. Several groups have employed web images to extract popular world landmarks: The goal of *Tour the World* [66] is to build up a global landmark database by mining GPS-Tagged images from the net and online tour guides. Landmarks are extracted by unsupervised visual clustering of candidate images resulting in a database of currently 5312 landmarks from 1259 cities in 144 countries. [51] follows a similar goal by mining images from community photo collections and clustering these images in an unsupervised fashion regarding visual, textual and spatial proximity. Extracted landmarks are verified and semantically enriched by combining them with matching Wikipedia articles. [28] mines famous city landmarks from blogs with the help of a graph modeling framework, fusing context, content, and community information. [12] employs only tag and location information from community images to identify popular places of a specific area. [32] tries to find representative photos of places by analyzing large collections of community-contributed photos. The work leverages context information like location and tags as well as content-based features. An earlier work [26] solely works on the location information of the photos and their tags to find popular places and corresponding photos of a specific area or to also couple events and locations by more powerful algorithms [52]. This allows the visualization of photo's concepts by grouping them by their location and time.

Semantic Image Annotation

Many attempts have been made in the past to narrow the so-called *semantic gap* in image retrieval by trying to derive high-level semantic annotations from low-level image features. These attempts either try to identify specific kinds of objects in an image or try to categorize images according to semantic concepts. Most works rely on a combination of content-based features and supervised learning.

In the first group, one on the most heavily studied applications is face detection where [64] provides a comprehensive overview. Accordingly, other works focus on other object types such as on text characters [37], vehicles [34] or persons [9].

Considering the second group one can find many works trying to build classifiers for a limited number of categories. For example, [63] describes one of the first examples of simple concept detection by categorizing images as showing parts of a city or landscapes based on low-level image features. In a follow-up, [62] describes a hierarchical classification to detect high level concepts such as indoor or outdoor, city or landscape, sunset or forest etc. with high accuracy by performing supervised classification on the basis of low level features. A more recent contribution is [14] which tries to automatically tag or retag images according to general concepts and thus making them available to text based searches. A real time image annotation engine is presented in [36] and is available as a real-world system on the web (www.alipr.com). Work about inferring semantics by multimodal analysis of personal photo collections and their spatial and temporal properties was done by, e.g., our group in [54].

Regarding the relation of keywords and location, [25] analyzes the dependence of images and text on a page. [56] uses a combination of metadata and content-based retrieval methods in an approach for landmark clustering. With a strong geographic information retrieval background, [50] uses a combination of content-based image retrieval and text-based geographic retrieval to integrate a geographical facet into image search.

A lot of recent works concentrate on the location for semantic image annotation and it has been shown that location significantly improves image management and summarization [26]. [65] employs rough location and temporal information to improve semantic image region annotation. In [10] an approach is described to propagate semantic labels in image collections by similarity based on time and location. The authors of [40] present an interesting solution to enhance event recognition in photos by using the location information of photos to obtain corresponding satellite images and therefore being able to better categorize the surrounding scenery of the photo. [11] introduces Logistic Canonical Correlation Regression to geocode and semantically tag photos in photo community sites.

Following this line of work, we aim at an approach that can reliably derive a connection between images and their location, working on arbitrary images on the Web, useable on a Web-scale. The remaining open issue therefore is that explicit location information for Web pages and their images is given only for a small fraction of the Web, which leaves a large number of potentially geographically-related images on Web pages as yet unrecognised for spatial search. However, they could be uncovered by better use of implicit location information. This opens up a potential for other methods of location assessment and additional sources of data for geo-referencing Web images.

3 Geospatial Web search

Geospatial search allows querying for Web pages related to a certain given location. Most current search engines are already very efficient for keyword-based queries, but lack geospatial capabilities since the search for geospatial information poses some special requirements that they cannot completely fulfil. For example, certain location-based queries cannot be answered with a purely textual index, such as vicinity queries within a certain radius, results in a specific district of a city, or other geospatial constraints. Furthermore, the result presentation should consider and cater for the geospatial dimension.

Nowadays, location-based Web search and search services operating on prepared geo-referenced data receive widespread attention. This is consistent with the high relevance of location to the user. A study in 2004 [53] finds that as much as 20% of user's Web queries have a geographic relation while [31] estimates this at 5-15% for search on mobile devices. On the other hand, the Web contains a massive amount of resources that exhibit geospatial references. Web pages with the required location-related information include home pages of businesses, restaurants, agencies, museums etc. These are excellent sources to answer user's queries for relevant spatial information.

Even though these pages only represent an estimate of 10-20% of all Web pages [24, 27, 44], their relation to a physical location is a yet widely unused asset for an interesting set of location-based applications. The main goal of a spatial search engine is to properly discover and identify those Web pages that bear a relationship to a geographic location and process this information for a spatial search. For our own spatial Web search engine as presented in [1], we use common Web crawler and indexing technology and extended it with our own location specific components. The crawler is able to handle common content on the Web such as static or dynamic pages, scripts, or various media types. These are filtered to remove content not relevant to the scenario so that it mainly downloads textual Web content but no binary files. The image download is handled separately by our image classification steps to assure only potentially relevant images are downloaded. Our spatial crawler and indexer identify Web pages that exhibit a relation to a physical location, extract the desired information, and assign a geo-reference to the pages. They are designed to exploit the location information of a Web page that is not explicitly contained as metadata or structured annotation but is rather an implicit part of the textual content [2]. Based on our research in mobile pedestrian applications [8], we tailor our search to a mobile user who needs precise geo-references at the level of individual buildings.

The architecture detailed in Fig.(1) comprises the main components of our spatial Web search engine prototype, separated into function groups of crawling, indexing, and search. These groups are modeled after the general architecture for Web search engines, but are extended with spatial capabilities to support the spatial

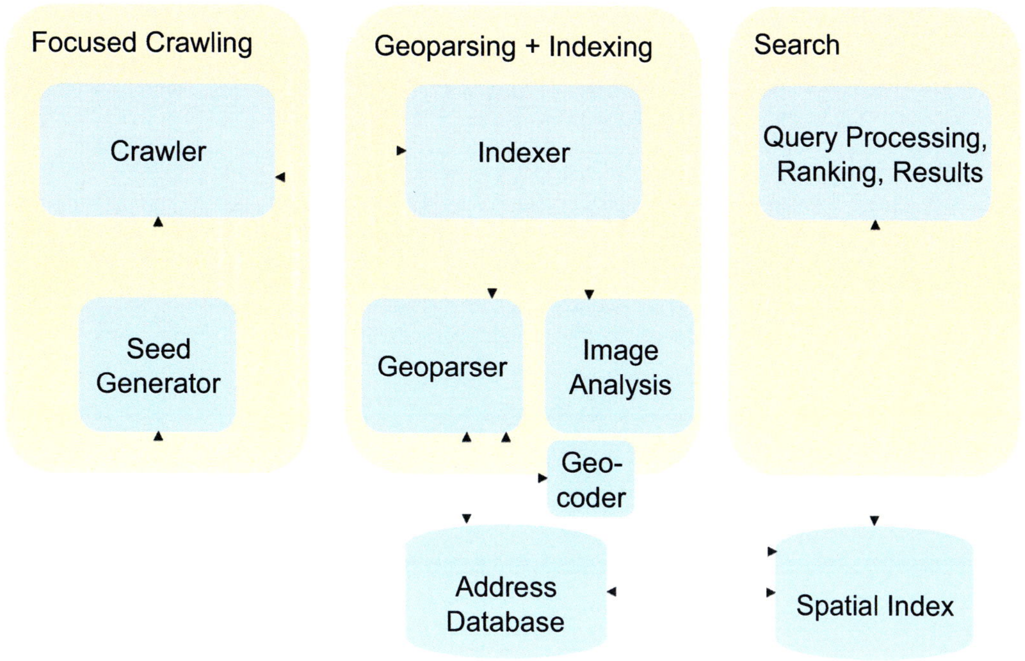

Fig. (1): Architecture of the spatial search engine.

search approach. The indexer can invoke several parsers; for this work we added an image analysis component. The architecture supports an efficient geographically focused crawling, meaning that the crawler aims at retrieving mostly only relevant pages [3]. For this, a seed generator feeds the focused crawler a number of seed URLs. These seeds are selected to be location-oriented and enable the crawler to start with pages that have a high relevance, i.e., that are themselves relevant to the desired location or act as hub to relevant local pages. The seeds alone, however, only form the starting point for focused crawling. A key aspect of focused crawling as opposed to general crawling is a feedback loop on downloaded documents to steer the crawler towards pages with the desired topic.

Besides the analysis of the textual Web content as known from search engines, a geoparser analyzes the page and tries to extract geographic information from it, if available. This extraction process is also supported by a gazetteer, i.e., a geographical thesaurus [23]. We use an address database to generate the gazetteer data at the required granularity of individual buildings to support the geoparser [2]. It can recognize multiple locations on a page; this is later used to analyze the images depending on their distance to potential multiple location references on a page. Whenever relevant location-related information is found it is notified to the indexer for a later geo-coding and insertion into a spatial index. At the same time the information about a location-information on a crawled Web page is fed back to the crawler to support the focused crawling. If the geo-parser determines one or multiple addresses on a page, each single address is geo-coded, i.e., the hierarchical textual description is mapped to a coordinate of latitude and longitude. The coordinate is then stored along with the textual address, the page and its URL in our spatial index. For this process, we use a commercially available address reference database to enable the geo-coding of found address to a geo-referenced position [4]. The index of the spatial search engine can then be used for the known keyword-based search now extended with spatial search capability.

Location references can be very diverse, ranging from mentions of countries, broad regions, or city names down to exact addresses. As our approach naturally restricts the amount of pages we can identify to those with precise geographical references, we might miss location-related photographs that are on pages without such references. On the other hand, as our location-based indexing delivers highly relevant and precise spatial information, this places the location-based Web image search on good grounds to deliver images at very high location granularity. The architecture and design of the location-derivation from Web pages has been presented in [1]. As one of several additional and supportive features for the geospatial Web search, this paper proceeds to examine its image-oriented aspects to enhance the search results by the extraction of representative images for the found results.

4 Web image location-assessment

While today an interesting set of semantic annotations can be derived from an image's content, a geographic location is usually not part of it. Apart from well-known geographic landmarks, existing annotations, or a prepared environment where images of all objects are already catalogued, a randomly chosen Web image showing some part of a town or some building cannot be processed by current techniques to pinpoint an actual location. This is of course different for images that come directly from a modern camera with GPS-information directly embedded in the EXIF metadata. However, such geo-located images are rare in the first place even in large photo collections and are even rarer in a general Web context. We therefore need other methods of location assessment and additional sources of data for geo-referencing Web images.

The goal of our spatial Web image search is to be able to automatically illustrate locations with relevant, representative images of themselves or their surroundings and for a given place to answer questions like "What does this place look like?" or "What is a representative image of this place?" by retrieving them from the Web. We aim to derive location-information for those images that are contained in Web pages that reveal some spatial context. As discussed in the literature [22, 25, 46], the proposed system will use a combination of content and context features from both Web page and images. The extension of spatial annotations from a page to its embedded images is made by the use of images in the content of a page. A page's spatial semantics are transitively extended to the embedded images which then will, to a certain degree and depending on detected features, inherit the location of the page, thus implementing a location relevance propagation. For this, the implicit location contained in some images has to be made explicit, which is both an extraction and a verification problem. It will have to examine different features from multiple aspects of an image such as its content, its context, available semantic annotations, and possibly other sources of information.

Fig. (2): Images and location on a sample Web page.

As one example of our approach, consider the Web page of a public library in Germany as shown in Fig.(2). The page features various images – surrounded by dashed lines – with the one in the center prominently displaying the library building. Its address – *Pferdemarkt 15, 26121 Oldenburg* – is present just to the right of the image and its name and city in some of the metadata such as keyword and title. A location-based image search focused on representative images of places should yield the photograph in the center. In the example, only this photograph should be retrieved since it is the only one descriptive of the location. The image analysis should be able to filter out all other, rather decorating images on the page. An analysis of the images' context and content should determine that only this one in fact has a location relevance and a strong connection to the specific location.

Method for location assessment

For the identification of a possible location-relation of images from Web pages, we propose a method for image location assessment based on processing chains. As mentioned before, using the Web page itself, only preliminary conclusions can be drawn about the image content of embedded images as no high-level annotations about these images exist and only keywords and structure of the HTML content is available. Thus, the content itself has to be taken into account as well. This is mirrored in the general process, which comprises two main logical components, a classifier for photographs and one for location relevance, respectively. These are arranged as weighted filter chains and utilize various criteria taken from the HTML content and metadata, the metadata of embedded images, image content, and the address previously found to arrive at a weighted classification result. This process is outlined in Fig.(3). The starting point is a Web page with an annotated known location from, e.g., our spatial search. This Web page is examined and all its image references are extracted. Each image is then analyzed and processed by a filter chain in the photo classification component. This analyzes each image to validate whether it satisfies the conditions to be considered a photograph. If the condition is met, the surrounding page as well as image features are input to the location classification. It examines image and Web page for hints towards a location reference, which are weighted and summarized. Some filters have can cast a veto on images where a direct negative classification is possible, effectively truncating the chain. Such cases can be 1x1 sized images, single-colored images etc. If a location could be reliably assigned, the process results in a geo-coded image. For both photograph classification and location classification, we utilize different information sources: the Web page itself, the HTML content surrounding the image, metadata of embedded images and their content, and the address previously found. With these criteria, we can have spatial information inherited and automatically annotate it to the images, based on a previously derived or known location of the Web page.

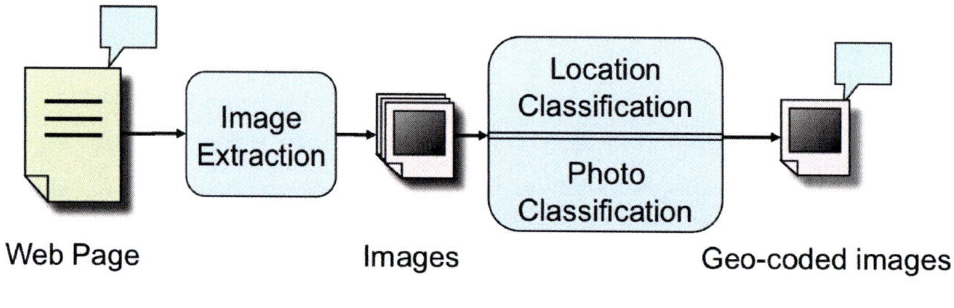

Fig. (3): Logical process of the location assessment.

Photograph classification

Images on Web pages are used for different reasons. Distinguishing their different roles supports filtering certain images by their roles. A first large group of images are those that serve an *illustrative* purpose: photographs, diagrams, graphics, sketches, titlebars, logos. A second group serves as *formatting objects*: bullets, borders, menu items, buttons, headings. Also, Web images can represent *advertisements* by means of banners, animated images or are used as "invisible" images used for *user tracking*. Other embedded media such as videos, flash or Java applets are outside the scope of this work since they have quite different semantics than images. We obviously miss some finer distinctions as needed by other approaches, but these classes suffice for the exclusion of non-location-bearing images according to our goal. Of the roles identified, we are only interested in photographs being the main bearers of visual location information. Such photographs serve illustrative purposes. Page authors use them with this in mind, and they clearly depict objects or scenery that is in most cases related to the text they accompany. This corresponds to the results of our initial surveys and probings.

Therefore, we developed methods to identify images with a high probability to be a realistic photograph of a place. To this end, we use different information sources and combine them into an overall classification by drawing on image metadata as well as image features. The different features and their relevance for photograph classification are discussed in the following. Each of these features alone is inconclusive, except in the direct negative case of a veto. Yet, in combination they yield satisfying results.

- *Image size* and *image ratio* is used to remove small images such as bullets, menu items and other formatting images as well as illustrative images that lack sufficient size or that have an unusual ratio that deviates too much from usual photos, in this case images with one side being less that 1/3 of the other. We found 100 pixels to be a good minimum size. This removes most advertisement banners, borders, rulers, headings etc. These filters are employed twice, once pre-download, if size information is available from the img-tag, and then post-download when size information is always available from the image itself.

- *size comparison* is an analysis over all images within a page to sort images according to their size. The assumption is that larger images often are more related to the content of a page. This can be observed in the case of news articles [19] which are illustrated with a teaser image, but can also – while with less weight – be used to search for photographs depicting locations. The analysis runs once in the pre-download phase, but since many images do not carry size information in the HTML source, is run again when all images of a page are downloaded. Since many images can already be removed by vetoes, its results may suffer from missing values and are thus weighted less.

- *filename comparison* is another page-scale analysis running only in the pre-download stage on the page content. Since image size information often is unavailable, it employs a different method to mainly detect formatting objects.

First, it counts *identical image* filenames within the page to identify images that have multiple occurrences in a page. Second, all filenames are compared to each other. By using editing distances, *similar filenames* can be grouped and images contained in a group weighted less since they are more likely to constitute formatting objects.

- *Color count and histogram analysis* is used to distinguish photographs with their high number of colors from illustrations or drawings. We calculate the ratio of used colors in an image to the maximum possible colors depending on file format. Black & white images are detected to be treated with different thresholds. For GIFs with the restricted palette of only 256 colors we cannot give a reliable threshold but rate them generally lower; JPGs and PNGs with 16777216 possible colors were found to need a minimum of 0.18% of possible colors to qualify as a photograph; black and white images were invariant for gifs, the other formats needed 0.0014% of possible colors. In the case of very few colors, images are most probably simple logos or similar and can receive a veto. Similarly, a histogram analysis aims at the same goal, but by using a greyscale histogram with its limited number of bins, it basically allows to work on a reduced palette, which can pool similar colors which often are present in jpeg-artifacts and might misguide a pure color count. The histogram therefore smoothes over such outliers and can provide a more aggregated view. For discrimination, bins are ordered by their value and the necessary number of bins to contain half the image's pixels are evaluated. Furthermore, if less than three bins are used, a veto discards the image.

- *Animation or transparency* in images usually indicates non-photographs. We also found many part-transparent click maps.

- *EXIF-data* in JPG files is a strong evidence for a photograph. Digital cameras today generate a multitude of camera-specific metadata such as camera type, focal length, flash usage, exposure etc. We use the fields of Flash (whether the flash fired), Model (the camera model) and ExposureTime as sufficient evidence that the image was taken by a digital camera and is thus a photograph. The reverse is not true; converting or manipulating images may destroy or remove the EXIF information.

- *Vertical edges* in above-average quantity can indicate photographs of a place showing buildings, pieces of architecture or trees. For our purposes, a modified Sobel filter operating on greyscaled images for edge detection was found to work best. However, this filter is biased towards urban buildings, facades, and other manmade structures. Since it is inconclusive for rural scenery, its weight is reduced.

- *Face detection* is used to distinguish mere snapshots of people at a location from images truly depicting the location itself. We found the number of such snapshots quite high and use this feature to focus on location-depicting photos instead of simply photos taken at the location.

Location-relevance classification

With the bearers of visual location information found to be in and around photographs, we have to make the connection to the actual location of the Web page. An image related to a location will exhibit certain characteristics which we exploit to create a set of measurements of how well the location of a Web page can be inherited by the images embedded in it.

Already knowing the location referenced on a Web page, we need to verify whether an image—or more precisely its content—is related to this location as well. We assume a certain intention of a Web page's author about images embedded in the pages. Images identified as illustrative do usually indeed often serve to visually describe the content present in the page—in our case, the location of the address present on the page or the referenced building or place. This relation is not always very clear and it is also not always present. Though, an image related to a location will exhibit certain characteristics which we exploit to create a set of measurements of how well a given location of a Web page can be inherited by the images embedded in it. To establish a relation of an image and an address on the Web page, we rely on content and structure of the page in question. From the photograph classification step, we know all photographs on the page; from our search engine, we also know the geographic location of a Web page as a full address including street, number, zip code, city name and also geo-coordinate. We assume this location reference does not necessarily stand for the entire page but rather may determine a location for at least part of the page decreasing in relevance by increasing distance from the location reference. Then, an image in the vicinity of an address has a higher probability for location relevance than one further away. Also, if we can identify a page as generally dealing with the location, it's probability to contain relevant images increases.

For the implementation of the location-relevance classification, we consider the distance of the image to each address on the page and the matching of image descriptors and key elements on the page to parts of the address. We use an in-page location keyword search. We interpret the given address as a small subsection of a geographic thesaurus. This allows for generalization of an address by traversing its hierarchy for keywords. We can broaden the search from full street address to only city or region. An address such as "*Escherweg 2, 26121 Oldenburg*" could be matched in decreasing levels of relevance as "*Escherweg, Oldenburg*" or "*Oldenburg*" alone. This truncation matching is already useful for searching the page, but absolutely necessary for searching features such as metatags, page title, or image attributes. They are very unlikely to contain full addresses, but will often contain at least the city name. This method also allows for more general approaches to describe location than just addresses. In theory, arbitrary topics could be searched this way. Matches of this search are rated by the amount of matched keywords and—where applicable—the distance from the image based on the DOM-representation of the document. The process would repeat for each location associated to a Web page.

The examined image tag attributes are *alt*, *title*, and *name*. These descriptive fields for an image may contain descriptions of the image contents and are therefore highly relevant as well as the *src* attribute for meaningful image or path names. The page's metatag fields *description*, *keywords* and *page title* as well as Dublin Core *DC.Subject*, *DC.Description* can hint that the page as a whole is concerned with the location and therefore contained elements receive a higher rating. Other well-known tags such as dc.coverage, geo.location or icbm coordinates were not encountered during our crawls and were therefore not included at this time. The set of evaluation features is presented in the following.

- *image-attributes* Checks whether a keyword appears within a textual, descriptive attribute of the image tag such as *alt*, *title* or *name*. These fields of an image may contain descriptions of the image contents and are therefore highly relevant.

- *DOM-Distance* Checks whether identified address keywords appear near the image on the page by using a DOM-representation of the HTML source. This decreases by distance to give text near the image a higher rating. Within many of the other systems discussed in Section 2, this is their only or major source for a similarity measure of keywords and image.

- *Source-Path* Checks the *src* attribute of an image for meaningful image file names or, to a lesser degree, path names.

- *Page title and metadata* Checks the page's metatag fields *description*, *keywords* and Dublin Core *DC.Subject*, *DC.Description*. This would mean that the page as a whole is concerned with the location and therefore the parts on it get a higher rating. These fields were selected for their possible general location relevance. Other well-known tags such as dc.coverage, geo.location or icbm coordinates were not encountered during our crawls and were therefore not included at this time.

Combining features for location assessment

The process shown before in Fig.(3) depicts two logical blocks for location assessment, photograph classification and location classification, each realised by an analysis chain. Inside each chain, several filters serially evaluate the aforementioned features, calculate a relevance score, and add an annotation for the assessed image.

With this partition into two processing chains it quickly becomes clear that this might not be the most efficient arrangement for use within a search engine, especially when the wanted images are rather rare. For applicability within a resource-constrained search engine, it is desireable to reduce the processing time, which is induced mainly by the need for analysis of features from the image file itself. Since we currently have no further need for images beyond those with a derived location, the solution is to reduce expensive image operations. The most expensive of these is the I/O overhead induced by the necessary download of images and to a lesser degree some image analysis steps such as face detection. However, for most analysis steps, the download and decoding of images is the major part of processing time. Therefore, the ability of the system to filter out unwanted and unpromising images has to be improved. This is achieved by adding a further result state to individual filters. While for the overall system, only the combination of multiple feature classifiers can provide reliable estimates on the positive classification for photograph or location, some features have the ability to directly judge an image as negatively classified for the overall chain. That is, a filter can have its own threshold below which the image is considered a non-match for the whole chain, making further processing unnecessary. Such filters are thus equipped with a veto ability for the remainder of the filter chains. This allows for a fast veto on unpromising images, freeing up performance for further processing.

Using the veto mechanism, the filter chains are rearranged from their logical arrangement of photograph and location classification into pre- and post-download operations on the images. Within each group, filters are ordered by their veto ability, discriminative ability, and computational expense. The resulting properties of the feature filters and their order is shown in Tab. (1). The stage column denotes whether a filter works before or after the download of images, i.e., on the html page or the image file; the scope denotes whether the filter works on image or Web page properties; and the classification indicates whether this goes into the location or photograph classification. The veto field indicates whether a specific filter can cast a veto on the processing. Note that the image size filter can be run twice, as often embedded images do not carry size attributes in the img-tag and size can only be evaluated when images are available after their download.

With the reordered chains, the location assessment is still mostly decoupled from the photo classification and run in the pre-download stage. Thus, if the evidence for location lies below a threshold, it is possible to abort the processing chain before the download as well, further improving efficiency. Furthermore, a cache of downloaded image's analysis results is kept so that once downloaded images can be reused if they appear in other pages again. Also, vetoed images are identified in subsequently analyzed pages and trigger a shortcut towards a faster veto. While Fig. (3) showed the logical arrangement of components, the reordered chains mandate an adapted

Tab. (1): Combination of evaluation features.

	stage, source		*scope*		*classification*		
feature	*pre-dl (html)*	*post-dl (image)*	*image*	*page*	*location*	*photo*	*veto*
image size/ratio	•	•	•			•	•
size comparison	•	•		•	(•)	•	
filename occurrence	•			•		•	•
filename similarity	•			•		•	
img-attributes	•		•		•		
DOM-distance	•		•		•		
source-path	•		•		•		
metadata	•			•	•		
animation/transparency		•	•			•	•
color count/histogram		•	•			•	•
EXIF-data		•	•			•	
edge detection		•	•		(•)	•	
face detection		•	•		(•)	•	

structure. The optimized process architecture with an arrangement of pre- and post-download filter sets is shown in Fig. (4). The page analysis extracts all image references from the page and feeds these to the pre-download operations, where unpromising images can be filtered out by their context features. The remaining image references are then downloaded, resulting in actual images which undergo the content.based classification steps and a relevance score evaluation. When the classification suceeds, the process results in geocoded photographs.

Formally, the assessment is defined as follows. Two actual chains *location* and *photo* are installed for location assessment and photograph detection respectively. These span the whole process, independent of the stage, as defined in Tab. (1). Let n be the number of feature filter modules in the chain. Each filter module $evaluation_i$ is assigned a weight w_i to express its relevance relative to other modules and allow for easy parameterization and tuning. The relevance score for an image img per chain is calculated by summing up the evaluation scores for each feature and noting potential vetoes:

$$relevance(img)_{chain} = \sum_{i=1}^{n} w_i \; evaluation_i(img) \tag{1}$$

$$veto(img) = \exists i \in 0..n \colon evaluation_i(img) = veto \tag{2}$$

For each chain, the final relevance score of an image is compared to an empirically determined threshold $threshold_{chain}$ to decide whether it is in or out of scope after checking for a veto:

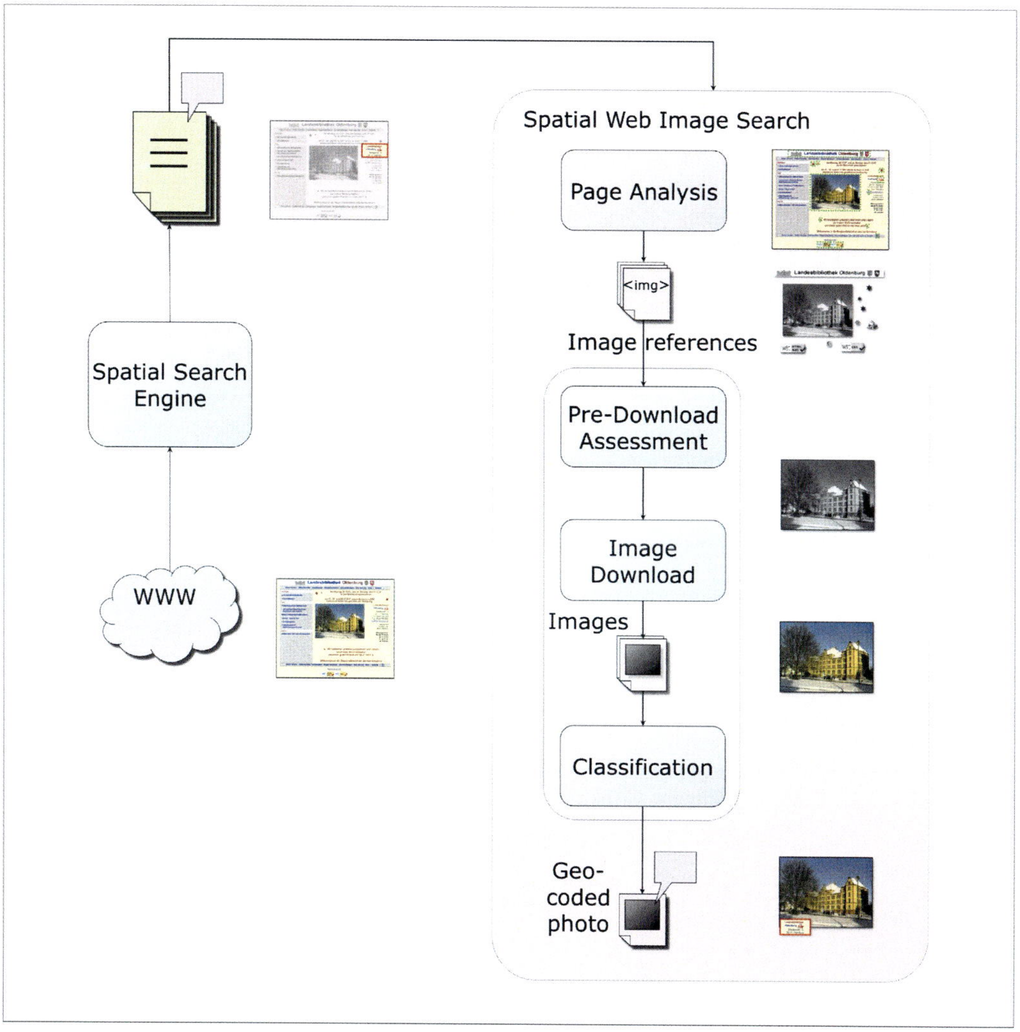

Fig. (4): Optimized process of the location assessment.

$$pass(img)_{chain} = \begin{cases} 0 & veto(img) = true \\ 1 & threshold_{chain} \leq relevance(img)_{chain} \\ 0 & otherwise \end{cases} \quad (3)$$

An image is classified as location-relevant if it passes both chains; its overall location score is given as $relevance(img)_{location}$ and the relation between image and location is established with the given relevance score value.

$$locRelevant(img) = pass(img)_{location} \wedge pass(img)_{photo} \quad (4)$$

Separating the classification into location classification and photograph classification allows setting different thresholds to pass the chain for the location classification and the subsequent photograph classification. This can be seamlessly integrated with the aforementioned separation into a pre- and post-download stage by simply collecting evaluation scores along the process and doing the calculation of the overall relevance at the end.

In the evaluation section, we will present the experimentation with different thresholds and discuss the quality of the results for different threshold values. The initial thresholds were determined experimentally with a known testset of images using the abovementioned features. During the experiments, we allowed each image to pass through each evaluation module to gather complete data. For later use, the veto mechanism and thresholds introduce efficient truncation for images which are rated well below passing thresholds in the assessment chains. With the location relation thus established, the image is associated with the location on the Web page and is accessible to spatial Web image search.

5 Evaluation

To evaluate our approach and assess its validity, we ran a series of test crawls on our system. These served to answer the questions of first, how reliable the photograph-classification is, and second, whether the overall location reference is correctly assigned. As a testset we chose a crawl of Rügen, Germany's largest island and a famous tourist area, and of the city of Oldenburg, Germany. The resulting testset comprises Web pages along with the addresses that were identified on them. Both regions deliver similar results, but the rural region of of Rügen has a slightly different composition of image types. We show the performance of photograph classification on a smaller testset and then present the location classification in a second step.

Evaluation of photograph classification

To create a small testset for the photograph classification we used a random sampling from our spatial index of 100 Web pages with an identified location relevance. Out of these, 78 pages could be used as 22 pages remained unreachable or had parsing problems. Within the remaining pages, we found 1580 images. Our photograph classification resulted in 86 images classified as photographs. Visual inspection of these images revealed that 69 were classified correctly. The remaining 17 images were misclassified graphics which still showed some of the relevant photographic features. 1538 images were classified as non-photographs and mainly comprised decorative items of Web pages. We also went through a visual inspection of these images and identified 1511 as classified correctly. The 27 falsely classified photographs contained only few colors or had untypical sizes or ratios such that their score fell beyond the threshold. The fact that we only found very few photographs is not surprising, as on the Web nowadays quite a lot of images are used for decorative purposes. This still means that $\approx 70\%$ of pages contained a photograph. Within this small testset, the achieved values for $precision \approx 0,80$ and $recall \approx 0,72$ are promising.

Evaluation of location classification

To draw meaningful conclusions for the location assessment, two larger crawls were performed. For the Crawl of Rügen, the testset was enlarged to 1000 pages. Of these, 857 pages could be examined. The result set of photographs confirmed a similar performance as before, but was not manually assessed. A resulting 618 combinations of photos with locations were analysed. Of the 74 images classified as having a location relevance we found 55 classified correctly and 19 with dubious or false results. Of the 544 images classified without location relevance, we have no exact values for the ratio of wrong classification. However, scanning these images seems to confirm that most of them are correctly classified; we estimate recall at above 0.7 and can calculate $precision \approx 0,7$ at a similar value. Examples of the images retrieved by our system are shown in Fig. (5). We find some well-related images *a-d*, some even from the interior of buildings, especially for holiday homes. However, some false positives and mismatches are also returned. Images *e* and *g* depict a location, but the connection to the found location is uncertain. For *g* we can assume that it is just a general landscape of the island. Some uncertainties could only be solved by in-depth linguistic analysis of the pages, some are unsolvable even by a human user. Clearly mis-classified is the illustrative graphic *f*. The sketch of a chapel *h* shows good location relevance but is not a photo. This shows an interesting capability of our system: The major part of images falsely classified as photographs were rated lower for location relevance than true photographs. Apparently the location classification compensates for some errors in the photograph detection.

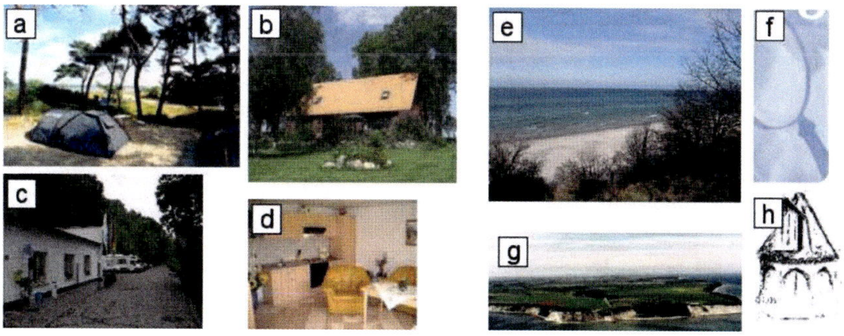

Fig. (5): Retrieved images Rügen, sample true positives (a–d) and false positives (e–h).

The results from the crawl of Oldenburg show similar results. A noteable difference is first the higher variance of images that were retrieved, manifesting in much more urban buildings instead of landscapes. Second, the images, especially the false positives, have a much higher variance in their types, ranging from actual buildings and interiors to products, people, or logos. Fig. (6) shows some characteristic results. Images *a–d* and *f* show broad exterior shots of buildings, two of of them museums *a* or banks *f*, other smaller houses of pharmacies or workshops. the latter is also shown in a more close-up shot in *g*. Finally, *g* is the interior of a church. These images are taken from different viewpoints regarding the building, but they all clearly show the building in question and can serve to illustrate the location of the respective Web page content. The false positives are rather varied, with *h* a collage from a museum, *m* a lasershow from a respective craftsman. *j*, *n* and *o* are general illustrative photographs. Interestingly, *i* shows a sports club in front of a landmark building and *l* shows another landmark, albeit on a CD cover. Finally, *k* shows a harbour location in a different city.

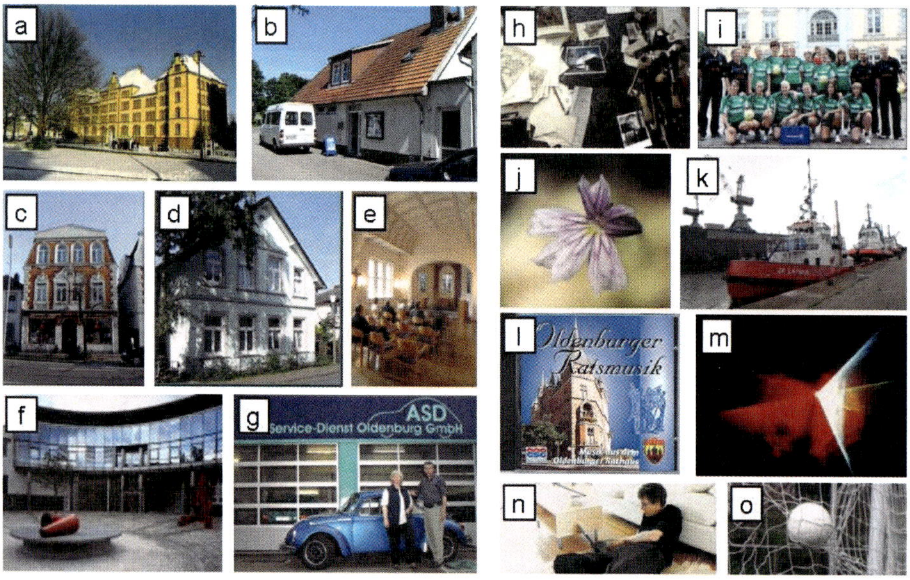

Fig. (6): Retrieved images Oldenburg, sample true positives (a–g) and false positives (h–o).

Performance evaluation

The performance evaluation was conducted for the crawl of Oldenburg, where more pages were made available. From a total number of 16,072 URLs, the system extracted 629,927 image references. Of these, 458,415 (73%) received a veto in the pre-download stage, a further 164,505 (26%) were vetoed afterwards. That left only 7007 images, a mere 1% of all image references, to receive an evaluation score. Manual random sampling showed no false negatives in the vetoed images but we cannot exclude that case completely. A run-time analysis examined the impact of individual filters. The arrangement of filters within a stage has a very low impact, as most performance is consumed by decoding an image and its previous download. Only the edge and face detection run slightly slower that other filters. However, this shows that the reordering into a two-stage-approach is very effective and can reduce the amount of downloaded images by over 70%.

Discussion of test sets and results

The evaluation shows that the approach is rather promising. However, some issues were encountered. The test set for the island Rügen covers a touristic but rural region. This leads to the problem that a lot of interesting sites do not have any kind of address and thus are not retrieved by the geospatial Web search in the first place. The famous chalk cliffs are an example for this difficulty. Furthermore a lot of images depicting Rügen are pure landscape-photos, which makes location validation difficult since the location cannot be exactly pinpointed. The testset for the urban region of Oldenburg exhibits different images where a lot of places actually have an address and are present in the result set. In this more urban environment most addresses lie within the city, while in a rural area, addresses can be in the countryside, leading to two different sets of photographs to be expected; one showing more buildings, the other more landscape-oriented photos. Our results show a slight decrease in reliability of our photo-detection for urban regions. By examining the filtered images, we recognized that the images from a more urban area contain much more graphics which are produced in a way that makes them more similar to photos. Another issue is the composition of the test set. It contained a lot of classifieds directory sites which mostly have no photos embedded, but often sport entensive graphics.

The system also discovers a substantial amount of maps on Web pages detailing location and directions for the referenced place. Other images that we aim to filter out, but which sometimes still appear in the results, comprise logos, products, people, etc. This can be further improved by respective filters. More difficult are some cases where the image does show a location, but it remains unclear whether it really shows the location present on the page. In a few cases, the location of the page and the one shown in the image are a definite mismatch, as evidenced, e.g., by mountains on the seaside. However, we were also able to recognize an interesting capability of our system: The majority of image falsely classified as photographs were rated with a lower score for location relevance than the real photographs. Apparently our location classification can compensate for some of the photograph classification errors and vice versa. This furthermore confirms our initial assumption that location and corresponding photos already relate to each other on the Web. This seems at least in part be due to the fact that page creators tend to use them in a certain way. In conclusion, the results and our chosen features show that context analysis for Web images in combination with content analysis can deliver useful results for detecting location-bearing photographs.

6 Future developments

As the results of the evaluation revealed, it remains challenging to determine if a photo actually carries a location-relation. Still, the results and our chosen features show that while context analysis for images alone is not sufficient, in combination with basic image content analysis it shows promising results in detecting location-bearing photographs. From this achieved state onward, several options are available to advance the system into different directions.

Improvements

A first advancement is of course the improvement of the existing system alongs its previously defined goals, to reliably propagate a Web page's location to embedded images for place illustration. This will include refining the parameters of the heuristics, analyzing in more detail to what extent the filters each influence the results and whether this could be exploited by using machine learning approaches. Since the current approach is rather exploratory, the results could be made more soundly founded by comparing different classification results by, e.g., decision trees, neural networks, SVMs etc. This could be supported by the use of more page and image features for the classification. Since the location of a page is already known, other sources could be used to indicate the type of area this location is in. Such information could be used to validate found images against an expectation for, e.g., rural areas, landscapes, or urban buildings. Such attempts to improve the location assessment would however require the use of content-based retrieval techniques. The aim then would be to better understand the content of images and their use and role on Web pages, which leads to further improvements as discussed in the next section.

Classification of illustrative images

A second development would be to turn some of the current misclassifications into new challenges. Instead of trying to remove them, they might actually be good results if only the question were framed a little different. This requires a redefinition of the notion of a "representative" image. A substantial amount of found images could be said to have a location relevance, but often rather because they have a very high relevance to the entity described on a Web page instead of depicting the location itself. So if the goal might not be to actually find a picture of a location but one that is characteristic for the described entity, a lot more opportunities open up. This is especially true since the actual amount of location-depicting images our approach finds is quite low.

A complimentary approach can be to extend the concept of image roles to be able to identify the type of photograph for more content-based image understanding. Some of the found images that are currently being discarded include driving directions (which still have a stong location aspect), logos, representative products, graphics design, characteristic tools, or pictures of individuals or groups These could be a valuable asset in some scenarios. For example, logos and similar images can serve as as mnemonic identifiers for entities. Similar to a favicon in a bookmark list, such images could be used to identify geospatial results on a map. These different semantics of images could be identified by image type classification using a content- and context-based hierarchical classification system.

The Web page context can be a further opportunity to feed specialized methods with additional data. These could work on basic characteristics of the underlying Web pages, such as the type of page or the type of entity described on them such as cultural entities, landmarks, restaurants, activities, shops, etc. Since different types of pages often carry different types of representative images, such knowledge could be gainfully used in a classification. A Web page about a person could then be illustrated with that very person, a shop with its logo or defining product. Depending on the type of entity, further preferences and expectations for image types could be defined. Complementing this development, the next section examines how the original goal of finding location-depicting images can be improved.

Geospatial images

Susan Sontag once famously wrote that "everything exists to end up in a photograph". Today, one might add, everything exists to ends up on the Web. But still, the exact extraction of what the "everything" in a given photo might be and, following, where it is located, still poses strong research challenges. Some of these challenges are currently being solved, as discussed in Section 2. Simultaneously, a growing number of sources for geospatial images exist. While in some cases these do not hold images georeferenced at a building level, they can still be used for a gainful advantage. First, the large amount of geospatially-enabled photo sharing sites such as flickr, locr, panoramio etc. can be used to find images from the position of interest and to try to match them to the current location and to a larger dataset, possibly identifying established logos or names of entities within some pictures. Another interesting source are large-scale high-resolution mappings of cities to retrieve images for pages without photographs. For example, Google Street View offers high-resolution street-level imagery in areas where coverage is available. Other navigation vendors have similar data, but usually do not release it. It can also be used to identify individual buildings and could be a suitable source to depict a building, museum, or landmark. For that, the individual boundaries of buildings and their spatial extent must be known and these then annotated in the image. At lower resolution, building or facade reconstruction from the oblique view of bird's eye imagery has been undertaken in several projects and can also provide low-resolution building and environment images. A use in car navigation systems could even benefit more from an abstract view of buildings for better visual integration. However, indoor images could not be retrieved this way and we remain dependent on the business owners to provide them on their pages. We were able to find an interesting set of such images, from recording studios over hotels or workshops to libraries or churches.

These are just some examples to demonstrate how rich datasources could be employed to retrieve spatially-enriched images. The main argument for the approach followed in this chapter is that the geospatial images on Web pages often better selected by the page's authors and therefore are better suited to be representative images for the page in question. However, to offset their rare occurrence, methods as described here can be employed for a more complete view over aggregated sources.

7 Conclusion

In this chapter, we presented an approach to automatically geo-reference images embedded in Web pages on the address level. Based on our work on location-based Web search, we presented our method and heuristics to propagate the location of a Web page and assign it to embedded photographs. We could show that a combined multi-source analysis of content and context is feasible for this task. Automatic location detection of images on unstructured Web pages now allows images to become part of the results of a geospatial Web search without previous manual tagging. The results of our evaluation are promising regarding classification and performance. However, for broad applicability, the approach lacks sufficient data in the form of geospatial Web images. To counter this effect, we also proposed several improvements. Depending on the application scenario, other types of images or other sources of data might be considered to gather representative images for a place. For such cases, the system described here could be adapted to arrive at a deeper understanding of representative Web images and their associated location.

Acknowledgements

We thank our students Sebastian Stockfleth for the initial implementation of the image search system and Timo Scheffler for substantial improvements and suggestions. Part of this research has been carried out as subproject of the Niccimon project and was supported by the State of Lower Saxony, Germany.

8 References

[1] D. Ahlers and S. Boll. Location-based Web search. In A. Scharl and K. Tochterman, editors, *The Geospatial Web. How Geo-Browsers, Social Software and the Web 2.0 are Shaping the Network Society.* Springer, 2007.

[2] D. Ahlers and S. Boll. Retrieving Address-based Locations from the Web. In *GIR '08: 5th Workshop on Geographic Information Retrieval*, 2008.

[3] D. Ahlers and S. Boll. Adaptive Geospatially Focused Crawling. In *CIKM*, 2009.

[4] D. Ahlers and S. Boll. On the Accuracy of Online Geocoders. In W. Reinhardt, A. Krüger, and M. Ehlers, editors, *Geoinformatik 2009, Osnabrück*, 2009.

[5] E. Amitay, N. Har'El, R. Sivan, and A. Soffer. Web-a-Where: Geotagging Web Content. In *ACM SIGIR*, 2004.

[6] Y. Aslandogan and C. Yu. Diogenes: A Web search agent for content based indexing of personal images. In *ACM SIGIR*, 2000.

[7] V. Athitsos, M. J. Swain, and C. Frankel. Distinguishing Photographs And Graphics on the World Wide Web. In *CAIVL*, 1997.

[8] J. Baldzer, S. Boll, P. Klante, J. Krösche, J. Meyer, N. Rump, A. Scherp, and H.-J. Appelrath. Location-Aware Mobile Multimedia Applications on the Niccimon Platform. In *IMA*, 2004.

[9] H. Bischof. Robust person detection for surveillance using online learning. In *Proceedings of the 2008 Ninth International Workshop on Image Analysis for Multimedia Interactive Services*, 2008.

[10] L. Cao, J. Luo, and T. S. Huang. Annotating photo collections by label propagation according to multiple similarity cues. In *ACM Multimedia*, 2008.

[11] L. Cao, J. Yu, J. Luo, and T. S. Huang. Enhancing semantic and geographic annotation of web images via logistic canonical correlation regression. In W. Gao, Y. Rui, A. Hanjalic, C. Xu, E. G. Steinbach, A. El-Saddik, and M. X. Zhou, editors, *ACM Multimedia*, 2009.

[12] W.-C. Chen, A. Battestini, N. Gelfand, and V. Setlur. Visual summaries of popular landmarks from community photo collections. In *ACM Multimedia*, 2009.

[13] D. J. Crandall, L. Backstrom, D. Huttenlocher, and J. Kleinberg. Mapping the world's photos. In *ACM WWW*, 2009.

[14] R. Datta, W. Ge, J. Li, and J. Z. Wang. Toward bridging the annotation-retrieval gap in image search by a generative modeling approach. In *IEEE Multimedia: Special Issue on Advances in Multimedia Computing*, 2007.

[15] R. Datta, D. Joshi, J. Li, and J. Z. Wang. Image Retrieval: Ideas, Influences, and Trends of the new age. *ACM Computing Surveys*, 2007.

[16] C. Frankel, M. J. Swain, and V. Athitsos. WebSeer: An Image Search Engine for the World Wide Web. Technical report, Chicago, 1996.

[17] A. Gallagher, D. Joshi, J. Yu, and J. Luo. Geo-location inference from image content and user tags. *Computer Vision and Pattern Recognition Workshop*, 2009.

[18] B. Gao, T.-Y. Liu, T. Qin, X. Zheng, Q.-S. Cheng, and W.-Y. Ma. Web image clustering by consistent utilization of visual features and surrounding texts. In *ACM Multimedia*, 2005.

[19] W. Gong, H. Luo, and J. Fan. Extracting informative images from web news pages via imbalanced classification. In *ACM Multimedia*, 2009.

[20] Z. Gong, L. H. U, and C. W. Cheang. Web image semantic clustering. In *ODBASE*, Lecture Notes in Computer Science, 2005.

[21] J. Hays and A. A. Efros. IM2GPS: estimating geographic information from a single image. In *CVPR*, 2008.

[22] X. He, D. Caia, J.-R. Wen, W.-Y. Ma, and H.-J. Zhang. Clustering and Searching WWW Images Using Link and Page Layout Analysis. *ACM Trans. on Multimedia Comput. Commun. Appl.*, 2007.

[23] L. L. Hill. Core Elements of Digital Gazetteers: Placenames, Categories, and Footprints. In *ECDL*, 2000.

[24] M. Himmelstein. Local Search: The Internet Is the Yellow Pages. *IEEE Computer*, 2005.

[25] M. Hughes, A. Salway, G. Jones, and N. O'Connor. Analyzing image-text relations for semantic media adaptation and personalization. In *SMAP*, 2007.

[26] A. Jaffe, M. Naaman, T. Tassa, and M. Davis. Generating Summaries and Visualization for Large Collections of Geo-Referenced Photographs. In *ACM MIR*, 2006.

[27] M. Jakob, M. Großmann, D. Nicklas, and B. Mitschang. DCbot: Finding Spatial Information on the Web. In L. Zhou, B. C. Ooi, and X. Meng, editors, *DASFAA*. Springer, 2005.

[28] R. Ji, X. Xie, H. Yao, and W.-Y. Ma. Mining city landmarks from blogs by graph modeling. In *ACM Multimedia*, 2009.

[29] M. Jia, X. Fan, X. Xie, M. Li, and W.-Y. Ma. Photo-to-Search: Using Camera Phones to Inquire of the Surrounding World. In *MDM*, 2006.

[30] F. Jing, C. Wang, Y. Yao, K. Deng, L. Zhang, and W.-Y. Ma. IGroup: Web Image Search Results Clustering. In *ACM Multimedia*, 2006.

[31] M. Kamvar and S. Baluja. A large scale study of wireless search behavior: Google mobile search. In *SIGCHI*, 2006.

[32] L. S. Kennedy and M. Naaman. Generating diverse and representative image search results for landmarks. In *ACM WWW*, 2008.

[33] M. L. Kherfi, D. Ziou, and A. Bernardi. Image Retrieval from the World Wide Web: Issues, Techniques, and Systems. *ACM Comput. Surv.*, 2004.

[34] Z. Kim and J. Malik. Fast vehicle detection with probabilistic feature grouping and its application to vehicle tracking. In *ICCV*, 2003.

[35] M. S. Lew. Next-Generation Web Searches for Visual Content. *IEEE Computer*, 2000.

[36] J. Li and J. Z. Wang. Real-time computerized annotation of pictures. In *ACM Multimedia*, 2006.

[37] R. Lienhart. Video OCR: a survey and practitioner's guide. *Video Mining*, 2003.

[38] G. Lu and B. Williams. An Integrated WWW image retrieval system. In *Proceedings of the AusWeb*, 1999.

[39] J. Luo, M. Boutell, and C. Brown. Pictures are not taken in a vacuum. *IEEE Signal Processing Magazine*, 2006.

[40] J. Luo, J. Yu, D. Joshi, and W. Hao. Event recognition: viewing the world with a third eye. In *ACM Multimedia*, 2008.

[41] T. Maekawa, T. Hara, and S. Nishio. Image classification for mobile web browsing. In *ACM WWW*, 2006.

[42] A. Markowetz, Y.-Y. Chen, T. Suel, X. Long, and B. Seeger. Design and implementation of a geographic search engine. In A. Doan, F. Neven, R. McCann, and G. J. Bex, editors, *WebDB*, 2005.

[43] C. Marlow, M. Naaman, D. Boyd, and M. Davis. HT06, Tagging Paper, Taxonomy, Flickr, Academic Article, To Read. In *HYPERTEXT*, 2006.

[44] K. S. McCurley. Geospatial Mapping and Navigation of the Web. In *ACM WWW*, 2001.

[45] Y. Morimoto, M. Aono, M. E. Houle, and K. S. McCurley. Extracting Spatial Knowledge from the Web. In *SAINT*, 2003.

[46] E. V. Munson and Y. Tsymbalenko. To Search for Images on the Web, Look at the Text, Then Look at the Images. In *Proceedings of the First International Workshop on Web Document Analysis*, 2001.

[47] F. Nack and W. Putz. Designing annotation before it's needed. In *ACM Multimedia*, 2001.

[48] M. Ortega-Binderberger, S. Mehrotra, K. Chakrabarti, and K. Porkaew. WebMARS: A Multimedia Search Engine, 2000.

[49] R. S. Purves, P. Clough, C. B. Jones, A. Arampatzis, B. Bucher, D. Finch, G. Fu, H. Joho, A. K. Syed, S. Vaid, and B. Yang. The Design and Implementation of SPIRIT: a Spatially Aware Search Engine for Information Retrieval on the Internet. *International Journal of Geographical Information Science*, 2007.

[50] R. S. Purves, A. Edwardes, and M. Sanderson. Describing the where – improving image annotation and search through geography. In G. Csurka, editor, *Proceedings of the workshop on Metadata Mining for Image Understanding (MMIU)*, 2008.

[51] T. Quack, B. Leibe, and L. Van Gool. World-scale mining of objects and events from community photo collections. In *CIVR*, 2008.

[52] T. Rattenbury, N. Good, and M. Naaman. Towards automatic extraction of event and place semantics from flickr tags. In *ACM SIGIR*, 2007.

[53] M. Sanderson and J. Kohler. Analyzing Geographic Queries. In *ACM SIGIR Workshop on Geographic Information Retrieval*, 2004.

[54] P. Sandhaus, A. Scherp, S. Thieme, and S. Boll. Metaxa – Context- and content-driven metadata enhancement for personal photo albums. In *Multimedia Modeling*, 2007.

[55] G. Schindler, P. Krishnamurthy, R. Lublinerman, Y. Liu, and F. Dellaert. Detecting and matching repeated patterns for automatic geo-tagging in urban environments. In *CVPR*, 2008.

[56] C. Schlieder and C. Matyas. Photographing a city: An analysis of place concepts based on spatial choices. *Computational Models of Place, Special Issue of Spatial Cognition and Computation: An Interdisciplinary Journal*, 2009.

[57] S. Sclaroff, M. La Cascia, and S. Sethi. Unifying textual and visual cues for content-based image retrieval on the World Wide Web. *Comput. Vis. Image Underst.*, 1999.

[58] A. W. M. Smeulders, M. Worring, S. Santini, A. Gupta, and R. Jain. Content-based image retrieval at the end of the early years. *IEEE Transactions on Pattern Analysis and Machine Intelligence*, 2000.

[59] N. Snavely, S. M. Seitz, and R. Szeliski. Photo Tourism: Exploring Photo Collections in 3D. *ACM Transactions on Graphics (TOG)*, 2006.

[60] K. Tollmar, T. Yeh, and T. Darrell. IDeixis – Image-based Deixis for Finding Location-Based Information. In *MobileHCI*, 2004.

[61] Y. Tsymbalenko and E. V. Munson. Using HTML Metadata to Find Relevant Images on the World Wide Web. In *Proceedings of Internet Computing*, 2001.

[62] A. Vailaya, M. Figueiredo, A. Jain, and H. Zhang. Image classification for content-based indexing. *IEEE Transactions on Image Processing*, 2001.

[63] A. Vailaya, A. Jain, and H. J. Zhang. On Image Classification: City Images vs. Landscapes. In *Proc. of the IEEE Workshop on Content-Based Access of Image and Video Libraries*, 1998.

[64] M.-H. Yang, D. J. Kriegman, and N. Ahuja. Detecting Faces in Images: A Survey. *IEEE Transactions on Pattern Analysis and Machine Intelligence*, 2002.

[65] J. Yu and J. Luo. Leveraging probabilistic season and location context models for scene understanding. In *CIVR*, 2008.

[66] Y.-T. Zheng, M. Zhao, Y. Song, H. Adam, U. Buddemeier, A. Bissacco, F. Brucher, T.-S. Chua, and H. Neven. Tour the world: Building a web-scale landmark recognition engine. In *CVPR*, 2009.

Internet Multimedia Search and Mining, 2013, 306-352

CHAPTER 12

Weighted Data Fusion for CBMIR

Peter Wilkins*
Centre for Sensor Web Technologies, Dublin City University,
Email: pete.wilkins@gmail.com
Alan F. Smeaton
Centre for Sensor Web Technologies, Dublin City University,
Email: alan.smeaton@dcu.ie

Abstract: In this chapter we present an overview of *data fusion*, and how it can be applied to the task of internet multimedia search, specifically content-based multimedia search. The chapter will primarily be focused on the *weighted* combination of ranked results from different retrieval experts, to formulate a final ranking for some given content-based information need. The types of data under examination in this chapter are *low-level* multimedia features, such as colour histograms, edge detection etc. The chapter reports an extensive series of experiments on a sizable collection of visual media and from these experiments a set of interesting and surprising results emerge.

Keywords

Data fusion, Query optimization, CBMIR, Image Retrieval, Video Retrieval, Evaluation, TRECVID, ImageCLEF, Multimodal, Query by example

---

***Correspondence Author:** Peter Wilkins, Centre for Sensor Web Technologies, Dublin City University, Ireland; Email: pete.wilkins@gmail.com.

1 Introduction

The availability of information resources on the internet has ushered in the 'Web 2.0' phenomenon, spearheaded by websites which are 'mashups'. These are websites which combine forms of data from multiple external sources in order to fulfill some form of information need. Often these forms of data will be multimedia, and allow for the creation of rich, informative sources of information. In many ways, the 'mashup' can be seen as an extension of an earlier web phenomenon, the meta-search engine which still exists today, as seen in a search service such as 'dogpile.com'. The meta-search engine takes in a single information query and combines the outputs of multiple other external search services to formulate a single response to that query. Both of these tasks, mashup and meta-search, are executing an operation known as *Data Fusion*.

Data fusion is defined as "the combination of evidence from differing systems" [1] with the aim of maximizing retrieval performance. In this chapter, we focus on data fusion, specifically with reference to multimedia search applications, where the types of data to be combined are considered to be very noisy. The fundamental purpose of this chapter is to demonstrate that even with very poor performing sources of data which are combined, retrieval performance through data fusion can achiever far greater results than over using single resources alone. Furthermore, the data fusion task we consider in this chapter is the combination of results from multiple search engines, that is each source of evidence is a ranked list of results, each of which is generated from some search service for the same information need.

On initial inspection, the data fusion task may appear relatively straightforward, namely to accept a query, issue it to search service 'a' and search service 'b' and merge the results. However there are many factors which impact upon the quality of this combination. For instance, how many results from each search service should be taken ? Is there a difference in quality between the search services, such that one service should be given a greater weight than another ? If so, how do we determine this weight ? Are the ranking metrics of each of the search services equivalent, or will they require some normalization first ? Should the combination be a summation of the scores assigned to each document, or its rank, and should this be a linear operation ? Each of these steps can impart significant performance benefits or degradations to retrieval performance. This chapter highlights each of these factors, and demonstrate the performance implications each factor brings.

Specifically let us define the type of system we are exploring in this chapter as a Content-Based Multimedia Information Retrieval (CBMIR) service, which is leveraging multiple 'low-level' search services, otherwise known as retrieval experts (i.e. each low-level search service is now referred to as a retrieval expert, or expert). The system will allow for 'query-by-example' (QBE), specifically multi-example QBE. A QBE query is one which allows a user to provide an example of what they are trying to find. For instance, in an image search engine, a QBE query image is submitted to that search engine such that the user's intent is to find images which are visually similar to the query image. We are also making the assumption in this chapter that each of the retrieval experts we use has indexed the same set of data. For instance if we have 1,000 images, we may have a color retrieval expert, and an edge histogram retrieval expert. Both of these experts provide a different interpretation of the source data, but both are operating over the same 1,000 images. Finally, in this chapter, our search service will operate over a *broad* domain, rather than a narrow domain [12]. This means that the system will be generalized and it makes no specific assumptions about the data it is operating on.

Other chapters in this book have used low-level features for tasks such as concept detection. In this chapter, we are using multiple low-level features directly for retrieval through weighted data fusion. There are several reasons for this. Firstly, the direct use of low-level features facilitates the QBE paradigm, which offers a unique vector for a user to search a collection. Secondly, traditional low-level features have *individually* provided very poor retrieval performance [12], however we will demonstrate that through ideal weighted combination with data fusion, that excellent performance is achievable. Finally, by using noisy, low-level features, they act as a proxy for a variety of information search services that a system-builder may wish to incorporate. As this chapter will not tailor the investigation towards any individual low-level expert, it means that a researcher or system-builder reading this book can take the approaches discussed and apply them to any form of ranked information resources which they may wish to combine.

Relationship to internet media search

Throughout this book the central theme has been the study and application of techniques to assist in internet media search, where we can imagine services which interface with some form of consumer media, such as Flickr. In this chapter we make a slight divergence from this area by operating within independent video databases which people may which to search. That is, we can imagine that we have a silo of digital video (for instance, archive news video) that we wish to search within. Whilst this is the data which is used in this chapter, the techniques and analysis discussed here are of wider application and indeed can be applied to the more general category of internet media search. For instance, new search services are appearing which call themselves 'reverse search engines', such as tineye.com, which are essentially content-based image search engines that allow for QBE. Other search services which may be developed could involve complex media searches, such as within blogs, where both the text and the images are analysed at a content-level, to allow for a richer vein of searching. In both of these instances we can see that the analysis of the data would involve several different types of content-analysis, and therefore for any retrieval task their successful combination. Such a combination is the focus of this chapter. When reading this chapter, the reader may consider each type of 'expert' to be atomic and as such the techniques discussed in this chapter can be considered broadly generic. The conclusions reached within this chapter however may have some specificity to the data which was used, however they will inform the reader of potential pitfalls to avoid, or at the very least investigate when constructing their system. Indeed the general study of 'data fusion' is widely applicable to many research domains, and the techniques used in data fusion can be considered as being independent of any particular type of data.

Within this book, the techniques described within the chapter titled "Cross-modality Indexing, Browsing and Search of Distance Learning Media on the Web (Arnon Amir, Kobus Barnard, and Alon Efrat)" describe alternative approaches to tackling the content-based search problems described within the present chapter.

The chapter is organized as follows. Following from this section, we will briefly examine data fusion itself providing some context and history for its use. Next in Section 3 we will provide an overview of the experimental framework used to generate our observations, and discuss the datasets, system and its resources used in this investigation. Section 4 will present our examination of data fusion and its variables, describing the variables which can be modified and their effect on performance. After this, Section 5 will present current approaches which use data fusion. Finally in Section 6 we will briefly examine related areas of research which can benefit from the observations presented in this chapter, followed by our conclusions.

Terminology

For reasons of clarity we will now formally define the terms used throughout the remainder of this chapter. We assume that a CBMIR system combines multiple retrieval experts together for queries which contain multiple components. For these definitions we use set and matrix notations, however our use of matrix notation is slightly unorthodox, as matrices typically contain numbers. In our notation, the matrices we define will contain ranked lists of documents. The use of matrix notation is for conceptual reasons to assist the reader in comprehending the number of variables at work.

Retrieval Expert A Retrieval Expert is treated as a black box – a service which processes a query and returns a ranked set of documents on a given collection. Formally our system will have Retrieval Experts $E = \{expert_1 \ ... \ expert_i\}$ where $1 \leqslant i \leqslant |E|$.

Query A Query within our context is a multi-modal request which describes an information need and is processed by the CBMIR system. A query may be comprised of text, multiple visual examples, etc. Within this context, each component of a query is treated as a separate query to be processed, e.g. a text component would go to the text expert, each individual visual component would go to visual experts. Therefore a Query Q is comprised of $\{query_1 \ ... \ query_j\}$

where $1 \leqslant j \leqslant |Q|$. As an example, if a user is searching for pictures of boats, the query may be the text 'boats' and two images of boats, therefore in this case the individual components of the query are $\{\text{'}boats', image_a, image_b\}$ otherwise referenced as $\{query_1, query_2, query_3\}$, each of which may be individually processed by the retrieval experts available. A multi-QBE query allows for a degree of query disambiguation. For instance, if a user wants to find images of a flower, but does not care about color, s/he can issue a query for a red flower and a yellow flower, indicating that they want a flower surrounded by green, but that the color of the flower itself is not as important [20].

Documents Documents in this context are the semantic unit of information that is indexed and retrieved. Typically the term refers to entire text documents or web-pages for ranking. In the case of MIR, the unit of retrieval can be a video, a 'shot' (i.e. a segment of video which is visually consistent), an audio recording, etc. The use of the term 'documents' will refer to any retrieval unit that can be handled by a CBMIR system.

Result Set A result set is the product of a unique pair of Retrieval Expert and Query $\langle expert_i, query_j\rangle$, which produces an ordered set of documents R such that $R = \{document_1 \ldots document_m\}$ where $1 \leqslant m \leqslant |R|$. Every unique pair $\langle expert_i, query_j\rangle$ produces a Result Set, which collectively form the matrix $\mathbf{RS} = [rs_{i,j}]\ i = 1 \ldots |E|, j = 1 \ldots j = |Q|$. The row index i represents experts, while column index j represents query components. Therefore, $rs_{i,j}$ represents the result set R generated by expert i and query component j.

Every $document_m$ in R will have associated with it a triple $\langle name, rank, score\rangle$ where $name$ is a unique identifier for the document, $rank$ is in the set $\mathbb{N}$ and $score$ is in $\mathbb{R}$. Every value of $rank$ will be unique in the set and it is desirable that every $score$ value is also unique, however depending on the ranking function this may not always hold. As the set R is ordered, the values of both $rank$ and $score$ will change monotonically as one iterates through the set. In order to compute a final response to a query, a set of coefficients is typically required so that we can give greater weight to those sets R which are likely to enhance retrieval performance.

Retrieval Coefficients We define a matrix of weights which are used to alter the impact of different $rs_{i,j}$ when they are combined into a single result. This matrix is **RC**, where $\mathbf{RC} = [rc_{i,j}]i = 1 \ldots |E|, j = 1 \ldots j = |Q|$. Individual coefficients have the properties $rc_{i,j} \in \mathbb{R}^+$ and $\sum rc_{i,j} = 1$. Every result set in matrix **RS** will have a corresponding entry in **RC**. For instance if no weighting was desired, all entries in **RC** would be set to the same value, thus providing a uniform weighting.

The final result set therefore, is some combination of the result sets rs_{ij} generated by pairs $\langle expert_i, query_j \rangle$ from sets E and Q, and application of the retrieval coefficients **RC**. Taking our previous example of finding images of boats with an CBMIR system which has available 3 retrieval experts (one text expert, two visual), we have potentially 5 result sets to combine into a single result set (one text result and four visual results), and up to 5 weights that can be applied.

To help illustrate the various approaches that different weighting schemes employ and how they impact upon retrieval, we will refer back to this section to help illustrate how various approaches may work. Defined in this section is an example CBMIR system and a multi-example query to it, as shown in Tab.(1).

In this example system, there are four retrieval experts (E) available within the system (where each of these experts is considered a black box with its own index and ranking function). We have also defined a query (Q) that is issued to the CBMIR system, which consists of the text "flowers", an image of a red flower and an image of a yellow flower. The system presented with this query, generates seven result sets (R), one for the text query, then six more from the two query images against the three visual experts. Technically there are more instances R than listed here, such as querying a visual expert with the text query, however this will produce a null set of results which for reasons of clarity we do not show here.

To summarise, we have defined within our CBMIR system, retrieval experts E, multi-part queries Q, individual result sets R and the matrix which contains all result sets **RS**. To weight each ranked list contained in the matrix **RS** we have the retrieval coefficients matrix **RC** which is used to weight each ranked lists so that they can be combined into our final response to a query.

$$E = \{expert_1 \ ... \ expert_i\}$$
$$Q = \{query_1 \ ... \ query_j\}$$
$$R = \{document_1 \ ... \ document_m\}$$
$$document_m \mapsto (name, rank, score)$$
$$\mathbf{RS} = [rs_{i,j}]_{|E| \times |Q|}$$
$$\mathbf{RC} = [rc_{i,j}]_{|E| \times |Q|}$$

2 Data Fusion

When we refer to *Data Fusion* we are conducting "the combination of evidence from differing systems" [1] with the aim of maximizing retrieval performance. This is a distinct from the *Collection Fusion* problem, which Voorhees *et al.* defines as the combination of "retrieval runs on separate, autonomous document collections that must be merged to produce a single, effective result" [2]. Fusion is an overloaded

Tab. (1): Example system and query, where there are 4 experts in the system and the query has 3 components.

Example System and Multi-Example Query			
E	*Expert Set*	Q	*Query Set*
$expert_1$	Text Expert	$query_1$	"Flowers"
$expert_2$	Colour Expert	$query_2$	
$expert_3$	Edge Expert	$query_3$	
$expert_4$	Texture Expert		
$\|E\|$	4	$\|Q\|$	3
Result Set matrix **RS**			
$rs_{1,1}$	"Flower" $\mapsto$ Text Expert	$rs_{3,2}$	 $\mapsto$ Edge Expert
$rs_{2,2}$	 $\mapsto$ Colour Expert	$rs_{3,3}$	 $\mapsto$ Edge Expert
$rs_{2,3}$	 $\mapsto$ Colour Expert	$rs_{4,2}$	 $\mapsto$ Texture Expert
		$rs_{4,3}$	 $\mapsto$ Texture Expert
Non-zero entries in matrix **RS** : 7			
Retrieval Coefficients matrix: **RC** rows i experts, columns j query components			
$\begin{pmatrix} rc_{1,1} & 0 & 0 \\ 0 & rc_{2,2} & rc_{2,3} \\ 0 & rc_{3,2} & rc_{3,3} \\ 0 & rc_{4,2} & rc_{4,3} \end{pmatrix}$			
Non-zero entries in matrix **RC** : 7			

term, within the multimedia processing community it can also refer to *Information Fusion* which includes activities such as the combination of various modalities such as the information from a visible light camera and an Infra-Red camera into a single signal [3].

Data fusion is the combination of multiple rank lists of documents returned from various retrieval experts, such that a single ranking is produced. Research into data fusion has been on-going since 1979, with observations about the overlaps in documents returned from different ranking models [4, 5, 6]. In particular, Saracevic & Kantor found that as result sets were being combined, that the probability of a document being judged as relevant increased monotonically as it appeared in more result sets. This led in turn to the hypothesis by Lee as to why data fusion works: "different runs might retrieve similar sets of relevant documents but retrieve different sets of nonrelevant documents" [7]. In other words, when we combine ranked lists of documents, there should be some degree of overlap in the relevant documents, but far less overlap in the non-relevant documents. Therefore when the scores or ranks of the relevant documents are combined, they are promoted higher in a final ranking. We can observe early implementations of this in the Garlic system developed by IBM which combined multiple information systems for retrieval through fuzzy sets [8]. For the interested reader, further texts on the data fusion hypothesis include McCabe *et al.* [9] and Beitzel *et al.* [10].

Within the domain of multimedia search there are two approaches within data fusion for the combination of data known as early fusion or late fusion [11], these are conceptually illustrated in Fig.(1). Early fusion is essentially the combination of data prior to indexing, meaning that data is first somehow aggregated, and then a ranking model is placed over this aggregated data. There are multiple examples of this type of system, such as combined document representations, classification tasks or learning to rank applications (some of which are discussed previously in this book). Therefore the combination of evidence through early fusion is typically handled in an 'indexing' phase. Late fusion instead assumes each source of data has associated with it some form of a ranking function, each of which can be independently queried. Once each source has been queried, the outputs of each of these queries can be aggregated together to form a final response to the initial query. Examples of late fusion include metasearch, and a majority of the text information retrieval experiments of combining ranked lists from different retrieval systems. Our choice of employing late fusion for our data fusion experiments means we do not need to explicitly model any particular source of data as that is the function of the retrieval expert associated with each source of data. This allows us to add or remove retrieval experts at any stage in the retrieval process, allowing for a relatively free environment in which to conduct our data fusion experiments. As such this is a generic approach which therefore has wide areas of application.

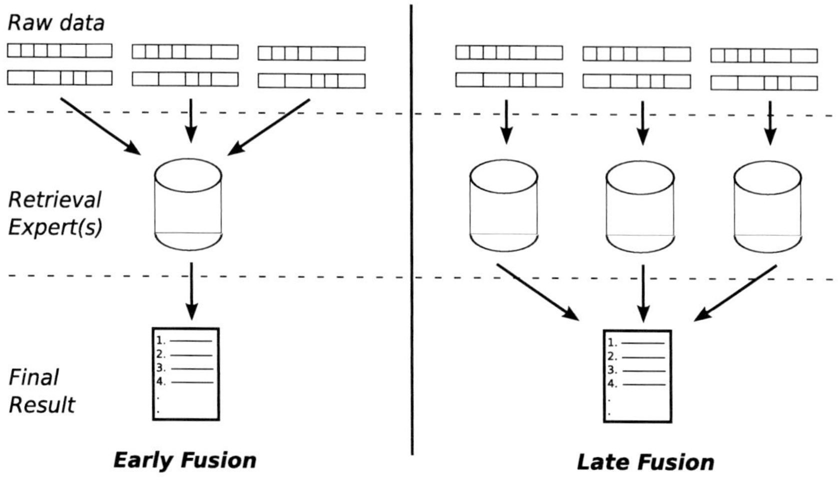

Fig. (1): Early vs. Late Fusion.

3 Experimental Setup

In this section we discuss our experimental framework for conducting our investigation into data fusion for multimedia retrieval. We begin first with a discussion of the retrieval experts which we use, followed by an overview of the data on which we conduct our experiments. Finally we discuss our experimental framework, which whilst unorthodox we believe is appropriate as it allows us to accurately observe the conditions under which weighted data fusion is successful for multimedia retrieval. First however we briefly describe the evaluation metrics used in this chapter, more details of which can be found in [13, 14].

In summary, the two fundamental concepts that underpin most metrics used in the evaluation of search problems are *precision* and *recall*. Let us assume we have built a retrieval system, and it processes an incoming query. For that query we return a subset of documents to answer that query. In such a scenario we have the entire set of documents which the system knows about, which we call the 'Collection' C. We have the subset of documents which were returned to the user, which we call n. We have as part of the collection the complete set of 'correct' (i.e. relevant) documents which answer the query, which we call R, and finally we have the subset of relevant documents which were returned to the user as part of n, which we refer to as r.

Precision is defined as the proportion of relevant documents contained in the set of documents which were returned to the user. We can expresses this as 'the number of relevant documents returned' divided by 'the total number of documents returned', or using the notation just defined:

$$Precision = \frac{r}{n} \tag{1}$$

So if we returned five documents to a user, and each of those five documents is relevant, then our value for precision would be 1. However, it may be for that query that there were in fact twenty documents which were of relevance to the user, but we only returned five. Precision did not capture this fact, that is the job of *recall*.

Recall is defined as the proportion of relevant documents returned to the user, out of all relevant documents contained in the collection. Using the notation we just defined:

$$Recall = \frac{r}{R} \tag{2}$$

Using the previous example, if we returned five relevant documents to the user out of a set of twenty relevant documents, then our recall value would be 0.25.

Both precision and recall can be considered as *set* based measures. That is there is no consideration given to the rank order that documents are returned in. Clearly for search problems if we are comparing two different search outputs, we would consider as better the search output which ranks its relevant documents higher in the ranked list.

The main evaluation measure we use is Average Precision (AP) which is designed with a bias of providing a better score for retrieval runs which rank relevant documents higher in a ranked list, over those which place relevant documents in lower rank positions, and is defined in Eq.(3).

$$AveragePrecision = \frac{\sum_{n=1}^{N} Precision(n) \cdot Relevance(n)}{|Relevant|} \tag{3}$$

In AP the function $Precision(n)$ is the precision at n documents and $Relevance(n)$ is a binary function which indicates if document n is relevant, variable N is the size of the ranked list and $|Relevant|$ is the *total* number of relevant documents in the *collection* under consideration. AP is the most common metric used in the evaluation of IR systems, however it provides a per *topic* score. Mean Average Precision (MAP) is a single scored metric which provides an indication of performance over an entire retrieval run, where a retrieval run consists of the results of multiple topics. MAP is simply the mean of all the AP scores in a retrieval run.

Alternative measures to AP exist, each of which has various advantages and disadvantages. A complete discussion of the evaluation metrics which could be used to evaluate search systems is out of the scope of this chapter, however the chapter "Evaluation of Multimedia Retrieval Systems" in Blanken *et al.* [14] provides a good overview.

Fundamental to all of these measures however, is the concept of a 'ground truth' otherwise known as 'relevance judgements'. A relevance judgement is a pairing of a query to a list of documents that are considered as relevant to that query. For instance, we may want to evaluate our system on how well it can find cats. That means we need to define the query 'cat' and manually label our search collection for positive instances of cats. Once done, we can then run repeated experiments where we can measure the performance of our system in finding 'cats'. The creation of relevance judgements is a research area within itself, for instance if you are searching over the entire web, it is clearly impossible to manually annotate every web page to determine if it is relevant to a query or not. However, that is the advantage of using 'test collections' such as we have used in this chapter for the purposes of system building and evaluation (see 3).

Retrieval experts

The extraction of low-level features from multimedia data is analogous to the extraction of terms from text documents and can be considered as part of an indexing phase in a CBMIR system. Low-level feature extraction is typically a fully automatic process. We use the phrase 'low-level' to describe these features as they impart no semantic or higher level understanding of the data, but rather they output either data patterns or statistics about the data being analysed. Low-level features are the foundation of most CBMIR systems upon which either more advanced features can be built or retrieval systems constructed from. Their independent use for retrieval however, particularly ad-hoc retrieval in unconstrained domains illicit poor performance [12]. In general there are three major types of multimedia data, images, audio and video. Images are a static form of data, whilst both audio and video have a temporal component.

In this chapter, we make use of both visual experts, and text experts whose data has been obtained either through transformations of an audio signal of some video data (through Automatic Speech Recognition (ASR)), or from attached annotations to some visual data. The majority of the visual experts we employ in this work are derived from the MPEG7 XM (eXperimentation Model), a reference implementation of features described in the MPEG7 standard [21]. The visual features we used include Color Layout, Color Moments, Color Structure, Scalable Color, Edge Histogram and Homogeneous Texture descriptors. Each of these also has an associated ranking metric which allows for the querying and generation of ranked lists by each of these features. Complete descriptions of these visual features can be found in Manjunath *et al.* [15]. For our text data we used a vector space model over this data to provide for retrieval functions, more details of which can be found in van Rijsbergen [13].

For illustrative purposes we conduct a simple experiment here where we measure the performance of each individual expert against each of our test corpora (discussed in the following subsection). The specifics of this test are that for each expert if there are multiple query components (e.g. the query contains multiple visual

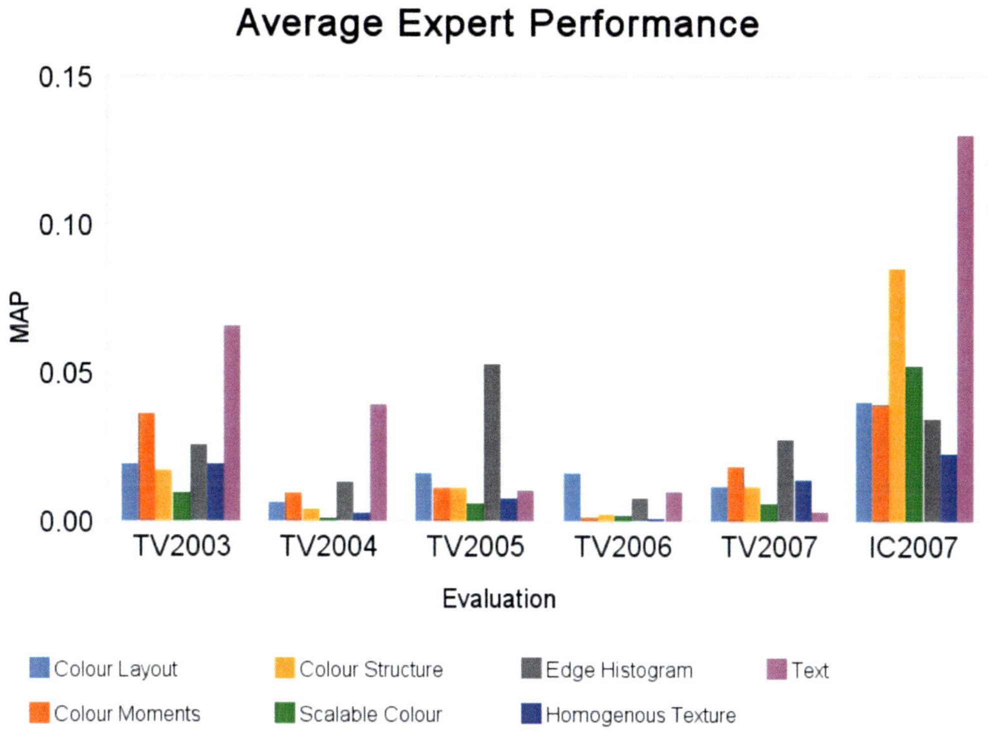

Fig. (2): Average individual expert performance.

examples), then the results of these are uniformly weighted and combined to provide an average indication of that expert's performance. The results of this experiment are presented in Fig.(2), with the x-axis representing the different test corpora which we will be using, and the y-axis representing Mean Average Precision (MAP). These results were generated by using MinMax normalization and CombSUM for combining multiple query-components within the one expert (i.e. as our queries are typically made up of three or more images, the result for a single expert is the aggregation of the results of those three queries for the one expert, the operators introduced here will be discussed in detail in the next section).

From this graph we can observe that individual retrieval experts perform very badly in terms of MAP across the majority of evaluation corpora, echoing previous research [12]. This is demonstrated by the majority of the results for each expert residing in the range 0.001 - 0.03 of MAP, which are very poor scores. Furthermore, we also note the performance variations which exist between experts, so whilst we have four color experts, in different retrieval scenarios, different experts perform better, indicating that it is beneficial to have multiple experts on hand and to combine their outputs.

We also note that there is significant performance shifts across corpora with different experts, demonstrating our motivation for experimenting on multiple corpora so as to gain more generalised knowledge of the behaviour of data fusion across a wide range of retrieval environments. This variation in performance though highlights the need for effective data fusion strategies, including the generation of appropriate weights for combination.

Data collections

For our experiments we are using what are known as 'test collections'. Test collections are standardized aggregations of data, queries and relevance judgements that allow for a uniform experimental environment. Basically, a standardized test collection allows us to more directly compare different systems, because it removes the impact that the data or the queries may have on performance. For instance, I may report that my system achieves excellent performance, but if my data collection consisted only of images of dogs, and my queries were about dogs, then it is not unexpected that I would achieve good performance. Standardized test collections provide a way in which multiple systems can be compared, by having all systems execute on the same data and the same sets of queries, and as such have lead to fundamental improvements in the evaluation of search systems. Of course questions remain that systems may become biased towards particular test collections (i.e. overfitting). In this work, we perform our experiments over six different test collections (which we refer to as experimental corpora), in an attempt to generalize our work.

The data on which we are experimenting comes from either collections of digital video, or annotated still photographs. As discussed earlier, we use the phrase 'document' to refer to any multimedia artifact used for retrieval. Digital video however introduces a temporal element into the retrieval process, and thus requires conversion into some discrete form to allow for retrieval. The element we use in this work is known as a 'shot', which is defined as a visually homogeneous segment of video which is of at least two seconds in duration. From the shot, 'keyframes' have been extracted, which are still images which represent the shot.

For our investigation into weighted data fusion for multimedia retrieval, we make extensive use of several benchmarking data collections. Five of these test corpora came from TRECVid [22] and are digital video collections, and one from ImageCLEF [23], a collection of travel photographs. These two campaigns share similar objectives as both seek to promote research in content-based retrieval by utilising common test collections and open, metrics-based evaluations. Within the five TRECVid corpora however we also have variation, with the data including mono and multilingual video, video from broadcast news and news magazine video.

TRECVid also defined the definition of the 'shot' and the meaning of extracted keyframes RKF and NRKF, details of which can be found in [22]. The following is a summary of our experimental corpora:

- **TRECVid 2003**: Approx. 60 hours of monolingual English news broadcasts. There are 72,624 total keyframes, of which 37,104 are 'NRKF' keyframes and 35,220 are 'RKF' keyframes. There are 138 topic images spread across 25 topics. Text evidence is provided through ASR transcripts. Abbreviated to 'TV2003'.
- **TRECVid 2004**: Approx. 70 hours of monolingual English news broadcasts. There are 48,818 total keyframes, of which 33,367 are 'RKF' keyframes and 15451 are 'NRKF' keyframes. There are 160 topic images across 24 topics, and text evidence is provided through ASR transcripts. Abbreviated to 'TV2004'.
- **TRECVid 2005**: Approx. 80 hours of trilingual news broadcasts in Arabic, Chinese and English, represented as 78,206 keyframes. Of these 45,765 are 'RKF' keyframes and 32,215 are 'NRKF' keyframes. Topics are represented by 228 topic images, across 24 topics. Text evidence is provided through ASR transcripts for English, whilst for the additional languages the ASR is run through an MT system. Abbreviated to 'TV2005'.
- **TRECVid 2006**: Approx. 160 hours of trilingual news broadcasts in Arabic, Chinese and English, represented as 146,497 keyframes. 'RKF' accounts for 79,848 keyframes whilst there are 66,844 'NRKF' keyframes. There are 169 topic images across 24 topics, text evidence is provided through ASR transcripts for English, whilst for the additional languages the ASR is run through an MT system. Abbreviated to 'TV2006'.
- **TRECVid 2007**: Approx. 50 hours of Dutch news magazine video, represented as 295,350 keyframes in total. Of these 19,702 are 'RKF' images, whilst for this collection we took the aggressive sampling strategy of extracting 'K-Frames', which make up the remaining 275,648 images. For the topics there were 205 topic images across 24 topics. The audio for this video was nearly all Dutch, so all text was first detected by ASR which was then run through an automatic Machine Translation (MT) process. Abbreviated to 'TV2007'.
- **ImageCLEFPhoto 2007**: 20,000 natural still images which form the IAPR TC-12 Benchmark and 180 topic images across 60 topics. Text evidence comes from well-formed, noise free text annotations which accompany each image. Abbreviated to 'IC2007'.

By using these multiple corpora, we introduce a degree of generality to our results and observations, as the data collections used in this chapter cannot be characterized as being of a mono-type, as we have observed in the performance of the retrieval experts in the previous subsection.

Experimental methodology

Given that the success or failure of any data fusion retrieval system is dependent upon the optimal generation of weights, and the manner in which those weighted documents are combined, it is essential that we know something about what the ideal distribution of weights for a query is, and what is the most effective manner in which to combine these documents.

In order to gain insights into what the ideal form of weighting for CBMIR data fusion is, and indeed how ranked lists should be combined, we need to deviate from the traditional empirical model typically used to evaluate new algorithmic advances. Traditionally we have some form of training data, either topics, data or both, some proposed model which we want to test and some form of parameters which require tuning and a set of evaluation metrics and relevance assessments. Also included in this model is a test set from which final results will be reported. The common sequence of events is that a model is first optimised on training data, then the optimised model is used on the test data. The final result typically reported is the outcome of the evaluation metrics run on the output of the model on the test data, where presumably the model has not been overfitted.

The major problem with the established empirical model is that of evaluation, where what we want to determine is *not* the comparison of competing models and their associated performance, but rather given a maximally performing model, what parameters were associated with it ? In data fusion tasks we will have a range of input sources of evidence, which we will then combine in some manner in order to compute a final response. The fundamental problem is that using the established empirical model, we could evaluate two different fusion systems, and after executing both having first trained on the training collection we can make the observation that system 'a' outperforms system 'b' by 15%. On the surface this seems fine, system 'a' has achieved a good performance improvement over system 'b'. However, this 15% is a *relative* increase, it is only meaningful when comparing the two systems under observation, and far less important when we do not know when given a fixed set of inputs, what the maximum achievable performance is. For instance, if system 'a' scored a MAP of 0.2, but the theoretical maximum attainable given the same inputs was 0.8, then the relative importance of system 'a's 15% improvement is diminished as there is clearly room for greater improvement. However, if the maximum was determined to be 0.21, then that 15% improvement is very significant.

A better use when determining what is the maximum performance for a fixed set of inputs, is to study the properties of this maximally performing model. Rather than being primarily concerned with the maximum performance MAP value, to flip this around such that given we have a model which achieves excellent performance,

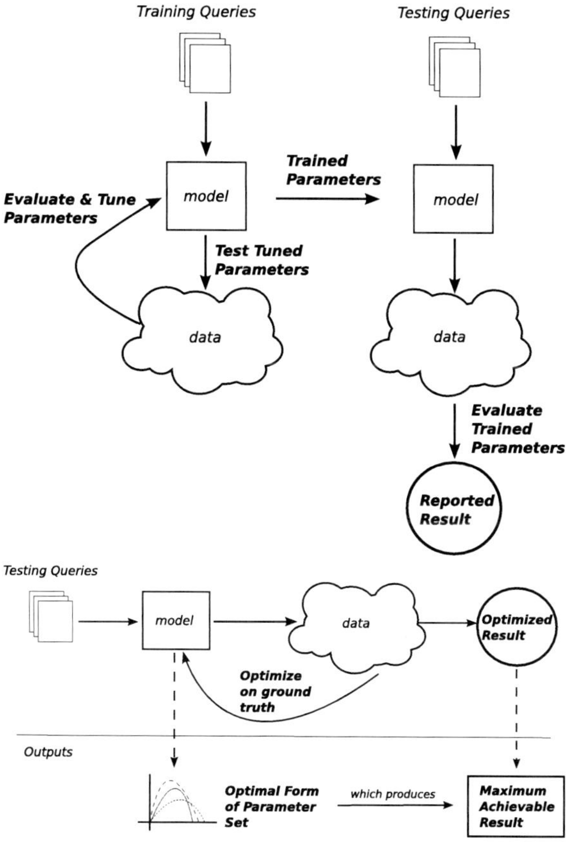

Fig. (3): Experimental Models, traditional model on the left, our empirical model on the right.

what are the properties of this model that led to this performance. In order to achieve this it necessitates optimisation directly on the test data. We are in fact not proposing any particular model for data fusion in this chapter, but rather we have created and observed the optimal model for this retrieval problem such that we can report on the properties of this model which future systems should seek to leverage. We illustrate these difference in Fig.(3), where the traditional model for algorithmic development is on the left, and the model used for these experiments where the objective is to study the optimal model and what parameters comprised it, on the right.

The objective of this chapter therefore is to study what are the variables which generate a maximally performing CBMIR data fusion system, and if there are any commonalities to these that can be discovered so as to inform the development of new data fusion algorithms and systems. The performance of these models is in themselves immaterial, it is these factors which we wish to identify and examine. In particular in this chapter, we examine the impact of combinational hierarchies upon performance, the distribution that an ideal form of weighting takes, the effect of different normalization strategies and the operators used for combining the ranked results. In other words we:

1. establish for any given query, what the ideal form of linear weighting is for that query. This allows us to identify and observe what form of weighting a data fusion algorithm should seek to emulate.

2. determine the capability of finding the ideal set of weights for any given query or set of retrieval factors which allows us to essentially freeze the impact that the weighting scheme has on retrieval performance. Therefore we can robustly test factors such as combination operators, normalisation approaches and combination levels, where for each as the ideal set of weights has been used we can cross-compare results knowing that the performance achieved is the best performance possible using that particular combination of factors.

No doubt at this point after mention of optimizing directly on the test set, alarm bells are ringing in several readers' minds, however we believe we have good justification for doing this. Whilst we have laboured the point as to why we are examining models optimized on the test data, we believe this is necessary as the approach is unorthodox, and inadequately justified can lead to the the results presented in this paper being dismissed out of hand. Furthermore, we emphasize at this point that the results presented here are empirically generated observations as to what constitutes ideally-weighted data fusion. We believe that these observations in several cases are unexpected and should form the foundation of the continued development of data fusion algorithms. This method however is clearly not appropriate for the testing of any new derived algorithm itself, as in so doing such an algorithm would be prone to overfitting.

Fundamental to implementing this experimental framework is the implementation of an appropriate optimisation framework. Several approaches were considered including standard grid searches and statistical approaches such as Expectation Maximisation. We selected the approach known as *coordinate ascent.* This approach was recently adapted for linear combination IR tasks, with direct optimisation on the relevance assessments by Metzler *et al.* [16], in whose work a complete description of the method can be found.

4 Exploration of Data Fusion Variables

In this section we discuss and examine weighted data fusion in detail. This section will identify the various components of a data fusion framework, and test each component to determine its impact upon retrieval performance. A difficulty in this explanation is that to test certain attributes, we have to lock down on others before we have explained them. Therefore if the reader is unfamiliar with some of the approaches used, s/he should jump to the appropriate sub-section to familiarise themselves. In each case, where one variable is being tested, the other variables were set to that which maximized performance except where otherwise noted.

The framework we are using for processing a weighted data fusion query is as follows:

1. Issue multi-part multi-expert query (i.e. $\{query_1 \ ... \ query_j\}$) against our retrieval experts (i.e. $\{expert_1 \ ... \ expert_i\}$).

2. For each generated result set, $rs_{i,j}$, normalize the documents within that set.

3. Determine what form of a combinational hierarchy is to be used, i.e. will result set be combined into a single set for each expert, for each query component, or will they be directly combined.

4. Based upon the previous step, apply an appropriate weight (either rc_i, rc_j or $rc_{i,j}$) to the candidate result sets.

5. Using the combination operators (either CombSUM or CombMNZ) combine the constituent parts into the final result.

This is a very high level overview of the data fusion operation, and as can be found in an implementation, several loops of this procedure may result in the final computation of a result. The order in which we iterate through these steps in this section is that first, we examine the ideal distribution of weights generated in optimal data fusion. Following this, we examine the impact of combinatorial hierarchies on retrieval performance. Next we examine the impact of the use of either CombSUM or CombMNZ, finishing by examining the impact different normalization strategies, based upon using the score or the rank, have on retrieval performance.

Optimal distribution of weights

In this sub-section we explore the form of an ideal weighting scheme so as to determine if any unique properties exist within it which may guide future data fusion algorithm development. In this experiment, we use score-based normalization through MinMax, with CombSUM for combining results, and we use a direct level of combination. As previously stated our mechanism for doing this is the execution of the coordinate ascent optimisation technique directly on our test corpora and relevance judgements. The first results of this process are presented in Fig.(4), which is a histogram of the distribution of the ideal weights generated over all corpora. The y-axis represents frequency, whilst on the x-axis, the assigned weights

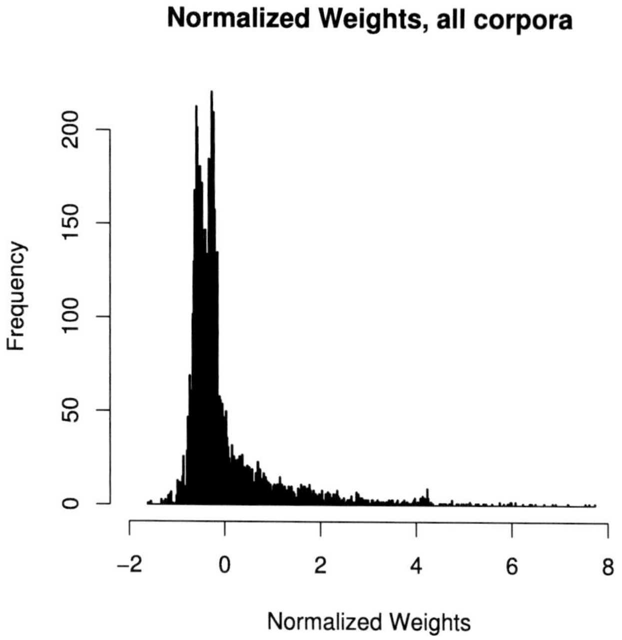

Fig. (4): Histogram of weight distribution, all corpora.

have been transformed into Z-Scores, to allow for cross-comparison between topics and corpora. Z-Scores (also known as standard score) shift and scale values to have a mean score of 0 and standard deviation of 1 allowing us to express a value in terms of how many standard deviations it is away from the mean. Therefore this normalisation allows us to examine how clustered the assigned weights are. For clarity, each *topic's* weights were normalized, meaning for each topic the average weight after normalization is 0. The results of the Z-Score's for each topic are aggregated into the presented graph and data.

From the histogram we can see demonstrated a highly positively skewed distribution, with a long tail of values extending up to Z-Score values of nearly 8σ. The shape of this distribution closely resembles that of a log-normal distribution, characterised by the extended positive tail. To further examine the skewness of the ideal weight distribution, we present various measures of central tendency in Tab.(2). From this we can see that whilst the mean of the weights is approximately 0 and the standard deviation has a value of 1, that the median value is less than the mean value, correlating with our positive skew observation. Furthermore, an examination of the quantiles reveals a very high degree of clustering with an extended tail, as the 75th quantile has a value of only 0.0036, whilst it isn't until the 90th quantile that values exceed 1.

This implies firstly, that whilst the distribution of weights has some properties of

Tab. (2): Measures of central tendency for ideal weight distribution, all corpora.

Mean	Median	σ	75 Quantile	90 Quantile
0.0004	-0.2978	1.0004	0.0036	1.1192

that of a normal distribution, such as a majority of the data points clustered around the mean and within the range $\pm 3\sigma$, there does exist a very definitive positive skew. Secondly, as part of this positive skew, approximately 10%-11% of the weights were assigned values $> 1\sigma$. This indicates that a minority of the pairs $\langle Expert_i, Query_j \rangle$ received the majority of a topic's weight.

The histogram presented is an amalgamation of the weights for all topics over all corpora. Without other evidence there remains the possibility that the effect presented is a corpora-specific event and that the weights are indeed more normally distributed. To account for this we present in Fig.(5) corpora-specific plots of the weight distributions in the form of quantile-quantile (Q-Q) plots. In each of these figures, the x-axis represents a theoretical normal distribution of weights, whilst the y-axis is the actual weight which was assigned. The dashed line displays the trend line of the weights if they were normally distributed.

Examining each of the six Q-Q plots, we can see that all of our experimental corpora follow the same distributional pattern, as each demonstrates a significant departure from a normal distribution, particularly once the normalised weights values exceed 1σ. The pattern shown in each plot is similar to what would be expected if the distribution of the weights was log-normal, again we can also see demonstrated in each plot, a positive skew.

Therefore, the ideal weighting form for data fusion constitutes a majority of pairs $\langle Expert_i, Query_j \rangle$ being assigned relatively low weights, whilst a handful of select pairs being aggressively weighted. Once again there remains the possibility that this observation whilst corpora-independent may be topic dependent. To explore this, we examined the distribution of weights within each topic for each corpora, the results of which are presented in Fig.(6).

In this figure there is a graph for each of our experimental corpora. We examined for every topic what proportion of pairs $\langle Expert_i, Query_j \rangle$ were assigned normalised weights greater that 1σ, and for these highly-weighted pairs, what the sum of their weights was, or in other terms, what proportion of the total weight did these highly-weighted pairs constitute.

Within each graph, the x-axis represents individual topics for each corpora. For every topic there are two bars, a yellow bar which represents the proportion of pairs $\langle Expert_i, Query_j \rangle$ which received weight greater that 1σ, and a blue bar which demonstrates what percentage of the total weighting did that represent. Taking

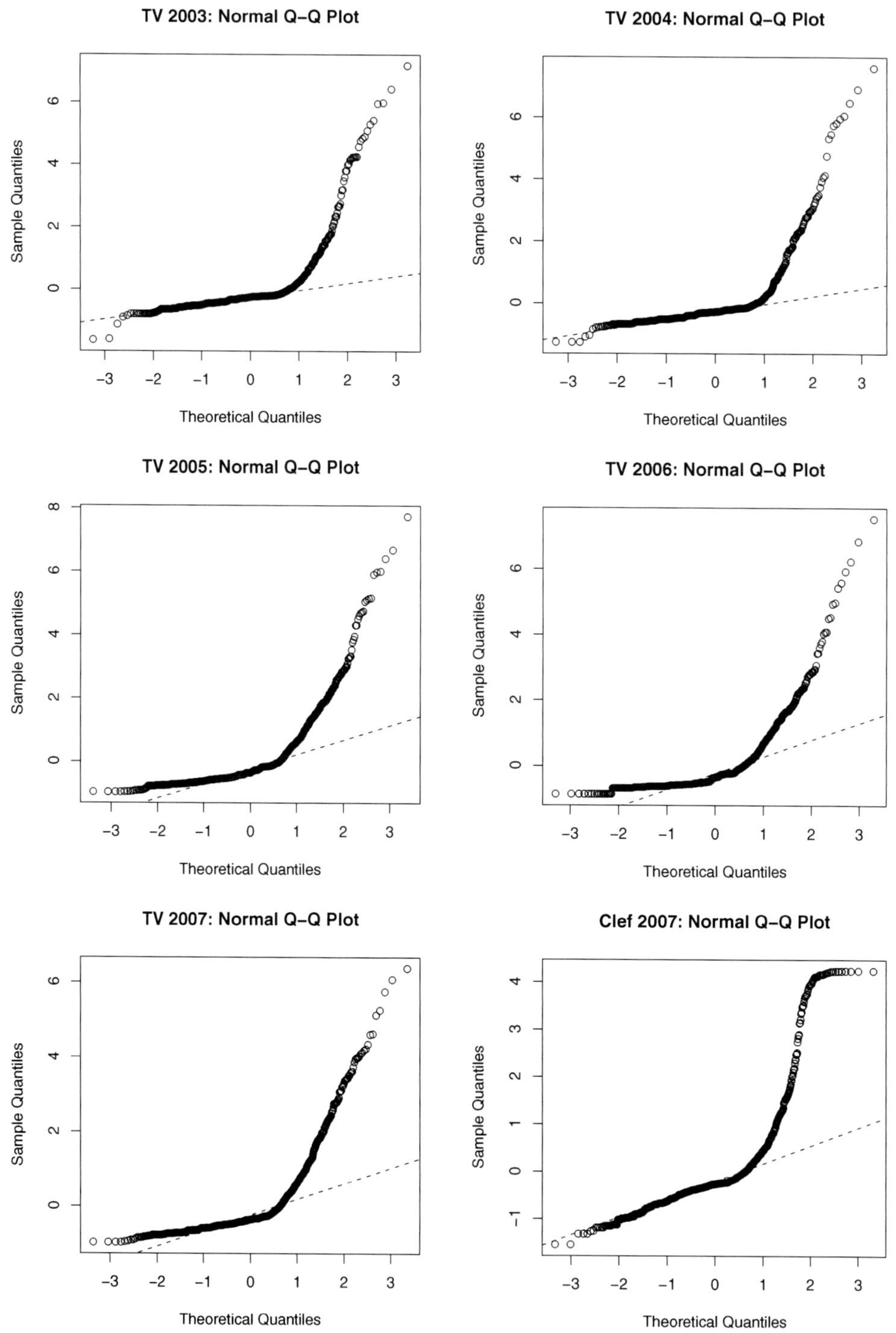

Fig. (5): Q-Q Plots of Weight Distributions.

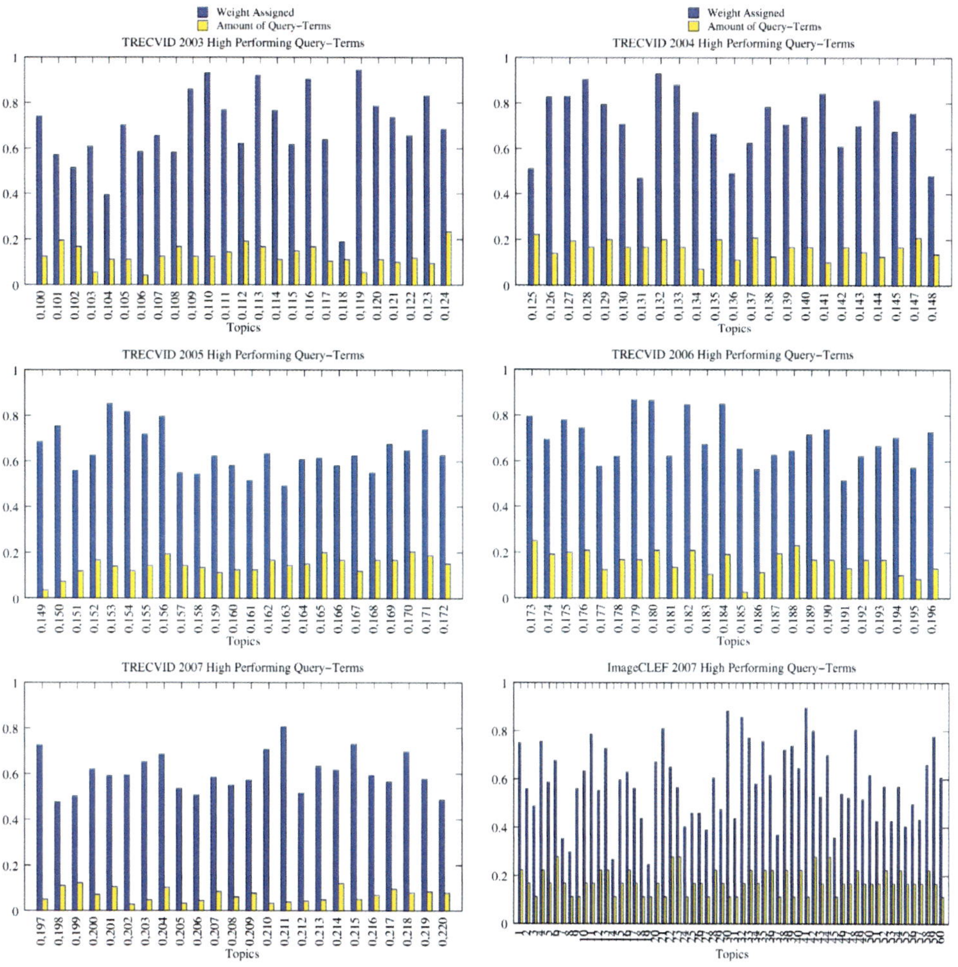

Fig. (6): Highly Weighted Pairs, all corpora.

as an example the first topic in corpora TRECVid 2003, we can see a yellow bar at approximately 16% and a blue bar at approximately 78%. This indicates that for topic '0100' in TRECVid 2003, 16% of the pairs $\langle Expert_i, Query_j \rangle$ used for that topic received 78% of the total weighting. From these graphs we can see that generally across topics the pattern remains the same, that between 10%-20% of the pairs $\langle Expert_i, Query_j \rangle$ used for that topic attracted between 60%-80% of the weight. Unlike our previous observations, these graphs were also generated from an optimisation process which used visual-only experts. This was selected so as to further determine if just one modality, i.e. text, was having a significant impact upon the distributions. From these results we can see that the general effect holds, that a minority of pairs attract a majority of the weight. The possibility does exist that even in this case, it may be one particular visual expert which is dominating the weighting and thereby causing the skewed weighting distribution.

Tab.(3) shows the breakdown of visual experts and the proportion of the weight assigned. There is a slight bias towards the Edge Histogram and to a lesser extent the Homogeneous Texture experts, however as there are only two texture but four colour experts, this bias can be accounted for. Taken together, the data presented in Fig.(6) and Tab.(3) shows that highly weighted $\langle Expert_i, Query_j \rangle$ are distributed across different experts.

Tab. (3): Distribution of Retrieval Experts in $\langle Expert_i, Query_j \rangle$ with $rc_{i,j} > 1\sigma$.

CL	CM	CS	SC	EH	HT
15%	17%	13%	13%	24%	18%

We have observed that the key to maximising AP is to correctly identify the salient pairs $\langle Expert_i, Query_j \rangle$ and ensure that these are highly weighted, rather than weighting the overall performance of any given retrieval expert. Therefore the task now is to test this observation to determine how robust it is. We devised a series of experiments that use only the highly weighted pairs $\langle Expert_i, Query_j \rangle$ to see if we still achieve good performance, or if the remaining lowly-weighted pairs contribute to maximising performance by boosting recall. For clarification, a highly-weighed pair $\langle Expert_i, Query_j \rangle$ is a pair whose weight rc_{ij} is greater than $+1\sigma$ of the mean weight for that topic.

However, before conducting these experiments, we first examine the impact of combination levels on retrieval performance, so that these observations can be tested and contrasted against the combination level experiments.

Combination levels

As previously illustrated, the CBMIR system which we are using in our work is capable of handling multiple retrieval experts and multi-example multi-modality queries. We have seen that each unique pair $\langle expert_i, query_j \rangle$ is able to generate a ranked result set $rs_{i,j}$. The objective of the CBMIR system is to combine all of these into a coherent single response. The nature of this setup is that it allows for hierarchical partitioning of the ranked results to facilitate this final combination. That is, systems may employ a multi-stage combination process, either to allow for easier training of weights to populate the weighting matrix **RC**, or because employing a combination hierarchy was accepted practice. For a late fusion CBMIR system, there are three basic levels of combination which could be employed, which we refer to as 'query level' combination, 'expert level' combination and 'direct level' combination. Each of these levels is illustrated in Fig.(7).

Earlier in our definitions of terminology, we stated that a CBMIR system could handle multi-example multi-modality queries, Q. The set Q defined a single search

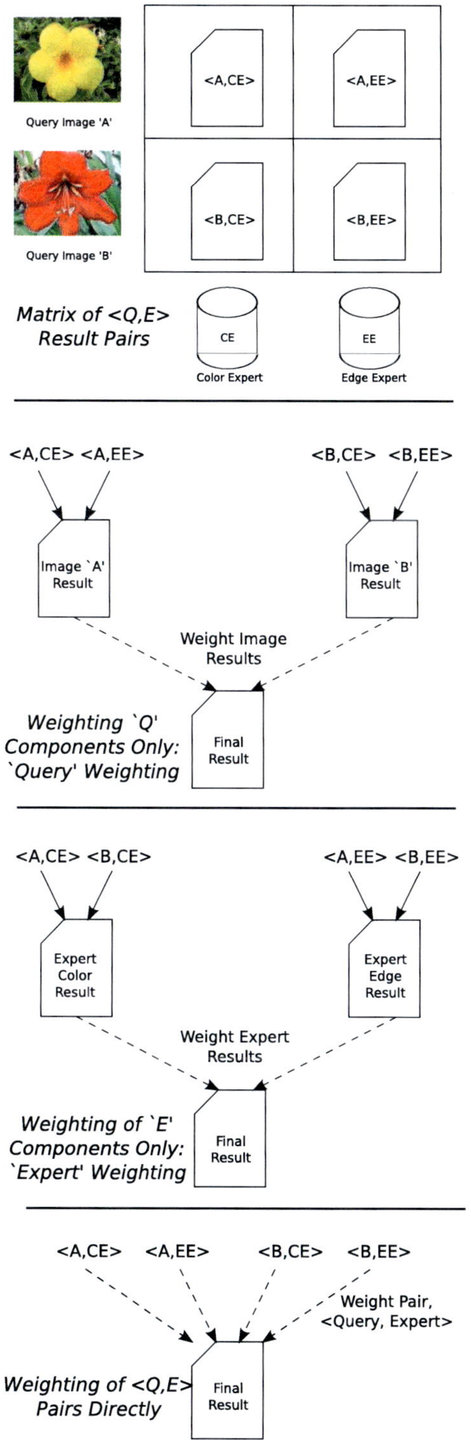

Fig. (7): Combination levels for single search, with 2 experts (E) and 2 query images (Q), giving 4 ranked lists (pairs $\langle Q_j, E_i \rangle$).

topic which the CBMIR system is to process. The example as given in Fig.(7), is that our query may be comprised of a yellow flower image and a red flower image and the intent of this query may be to find images of flowers regardless of colour [20]. In the example in Fig.(7) there are also two visual experts present, a colour expert and an edge expert. Applying our queries to the experts generates 4 result lists to be combined. Using our notation the four result set we have generated are:

$$\begin{aligned} E &= \{colour, edge\} \\ Q &= \{yellowflower, redflower\} \\ \mathbf{RS} &= \begin{pmatrix} colour, yellowflower & edge, yellowflower \\ colour, redflower & edge, redflower \end{pmatrix} \end{aligned}$$

Expert level combination

The first of the three levels we'll discuss is 'expert level' combination. For a specific expert ($expert_i$) we query against it all query components in Q, merging the results to produce for each expert, a single ranked list. Typically the combination of the individual results from an expert into a single result for that expert are uniformly weighted. Therefore, for every $expert_i$ we have one combined result set (rs_i). The final merger therefore is to combine each result set rs_i into a single response. In systems which implement this style of combination, it is at this level of aggregation that weighting would occur, that is each rs_i would be assigned a weight. This means that the number of weights which must be determined using this level of aggregation is $|E|$. To illustrate this with the example from Fig.(7), the result sets from pairs $\langle colour, yellowflower\rangle$, $\langle colour, redflower\rangle$ form one merged result set which is then weighted, whilst pairs $\langle edge, yellowflower\rangle$, $\langle edge, redflower\rangle$ form the other result set to be weighted. As there are two experts ($|E| = 2$), then two weights are used to calculate this query. Referring back to our result set matrix **RS** with individual elements $rs_{i,j}$, we can think of this approach as first aggregating the result sets in each column i, weighting each of these, then combining all instances of the columns rs_i into a single response.

Query level combination

If 'expert level' combination is the processing of the columns of the result set matrix **RS**, then 'query level' combination is the same processes except that we instead process the rows of matrix **RS**. Given a set of query components Q with members $query_j$, we combine with uniform weights the results of $query_j$ queried against every expert in E. Similarly to 'expert level' weighting, the aggregated result set for each $query_j$ is then weighted and combined to compute the final response to the query. Therefore, each rs_j is weighted, and the total number of weights used in tuning the system is $|Q|$. Illustrating this with our example from Fig.(7), there are two result sets rs_j, the first generated from a merger of the pairs $\langle colour, yellowflower\rangle$, $\langle edge, yellowflower\rangle$, and the second from the pairs $\langle colour, redflower\rangle$, $\langle edge, redflower\rangle$.

Direct level combination

Finally we have the "direct" level of combination, where if the 'expert level' of combination was the aggregation and weighting of columns rs_i, and 'query level' combination was the aggregation and weighting of rows rs_j, then 'direct level' is the direct weighting of each individual result set $rs_{i,j}$, in other words, processing the matrix **RS** directly without any intermediate levels of aggregation. This level specifies weights for every coupling of a query component and retrieval expert, meaning that using this approach, $|E| \times |Q|$ weights are required. Applying this to our example from Fig.(7), this means that the four pairs $\langle colour, yellowflower\rangle$, $\langle edge, yellowflower\rangle$, $\langle colour, redflower\rangle$ and $\langle edge, redflower\rangle$ each have their own weight.

Experiments with highly weighted pairs and combination levels

To test our observations we devised three experiments in order to (1) determine to what extent the highly-weighted pairs $\langle Expert_i, Query_j\rangle$ impact upon performance; (2) determine if the weighting of these pairs needs to be exact or if merely identification is enough; and finally, (3) determine the impact the remainder of the pairs $\langle Expert_i, Query_j\rangle$ which do not have much weight allocated to them have on performance. As a comparison we have also included two optimizations, "Query" level and "Expert" level optimizations. These represent the best performance achievable if we use existing data fusion methods (such as Query-Class approach, or single feature machine learning [24, 25]), and allow us to determine if our suggested strategies of targeted weighting of pairs $\langle Expert_i, Query_j\rangle$ rather than expert level weighting offers improvement.

- **(1σ) 1σ**: For each topic, only use highly-weighted pairs $\langle Expert_i, Query_j\rangle$ (i.e. pairs $\langle Expert_i, Query_j\rangle$ whose assigned value from optimization was $+1\sigma$ for the mean weight). The value of w_{ij} will be the value determined during optimization. This test will examine the impact of precisely weighted high-performing pairs $\langle Expert_i, Query_j\rangle$. It can be thought of as a high-precision experiment as for each topic we will be using only 5%-20% of the available ranked lists for that topic.

- **(1σU) 1σ Uniform**: Using only the highly-weighed pairs $\langle Expert_i, Query_j\rangle$, assign each a uniform weight. This will examine if just the identification of high-performing pairs $\langle Expert_i, Query_j \rangle$ is sufficient to yield performance increases, specifically determining if accurate weighting of pairs is required, or if they can be assigned a binary weight [0,1]. As the task of determining the optimal set w_{ij} is realistically only viable post-experiment, this experiment tests if realistic fusion approaches can be developed, as it does not require perfect weights, only identification of likely high performing pairs $\langle Expert_i, Query_j \rangle$.

- **(1σU-T) 1σ & Tail**: We extend experiment 1σ, by taking the remaining weight mass that isn't assigned to high-performing pairs and allocate it uniformly amongst the remaining pairs in **RC**. This experiment complements the previous, we assign a large weight to the high-performing pairs, whilst a low weight to the remainder. As the high-performing pairs constitute only 5%-20% of available pairs for a topic, this experiment is testing the impact of recall, i.e. can we include the remainder of the data without accurate weighting so as to increase our recall.

- **Expert Optimized**: We implement the "Expert" level of combination as is implemented by several data fusion approaches. Here we use the optimization approach as previously described so as to determine the near-optimal set of weights RC_i for "Expert" level combination. This demonstrates the best performance that can be expected using the same query images and experts as the previous experiments if we impose a combination hierarchy at the "Expert" level.

- **Query Optimized**: This experiment is as for "Expert" optimized, except that the weight set we are optimizing is RC_j, and demonstrates the best performance that can be achieved if we combine at the "Query" level.

For each experiment we include the minimum and maximum achieved for that corpus. The minimum is a 'Uniform' run, where all pairs $\langle Expert_i, Query_j \rangle$ are equally weighted, demonstrating the performance achieved if no weighting scheme at all is employed. The maximum is the fully optimized result, demonstrating the best performance that can be theoretically achieved. These two figures provide a lower and upper bound for data fusion performance comparisons, allowing us to make decisions using absolute observations with regard to the bounds, rather than relative observations by comparing only to existing data fusion approaches.

Our results are presented in Tab.(4). Each table presents the minimum (Uniform All), maximum (All Optimized) and results of the 5 experiments using MAP. For every experiment's MAP, we show in brackets how close that approach came to achieving the optimal performance. The MAP of each of the experiments, along with the maximum MAP, is graphed in Fig.(4). For each of our 5 runs we ran significance tests (partial randomization) with ρ 0.05. For the TRECVid benchmarks we found no significant difference between the 'Query' and 'Expert' levels of hierarchical combination, indicating that if hierarchical combination is employed and optimally weighted, there is no difference in between them. (However for ImageCLEF 'Expert' was significantly different.) For benchmarks TRECVid 2003 to 2006, all runs using highly weighted (1σ) pairs performed significantly better than the hierarchical combination approaches. For TRECVid 2007, only run 1σ was significantly different.

The graph presents a clear stratification of the results, particularly for benchmarks TRECVid 2003 to 2006. We can clearly see the very large discrepancy in performance between the hierarchical fusion approaches (at the bottom of the graph) versus the targeted weighting approaches in the middle. This separation illustrates the performance gains achievable by moving away from hierarchical combinations. Of exception is TRECVid 2007 and ImageCLEF 2007, where there is less of a difference in performance. These two benchmarks exhibit the greatest ratio of topic images to collection images – in the case of ImageCLEF one topic image for every 112 collection images. This indicates that recall plays a more prominent role in these evaluations, and that the selection of highly-weighted pairs may have been too restrictive to provide adequate topic coverage. This is reinforced by the run 1σU-T, which included all pairs $\langle Expert_i, Query_j\rangle$: it performed the best even though it used non-specific weights.

That is, the run 1σ highlights that using a subset of the highly weighted pairs $\langle Expert_i, Query_j\rangle$, very good performance can be achieved despite a reduction in potential recall by not using all pairs. Far more encouraging is the performance of runs 1σU and 1σU-T. Whilst run 1σ had value as an illustrative run, it is hard to conceptualize a data fusion algorithm that would create the exact optimal weights for these pairs. However, as runs 1σU and 1σU-T did not use the optimal weights, but rather only identified what the high-performing pairs 1σU and 1σU-T were (essentially a binary weighting), and still achieved excellent performance, it provides a clear direction for development of data fusion algorithms. These runs demonstrate that if methods can be developed to identify pairs $\langle Expert_i, Query_j\rangle$ that are likely to be highly weighted, then exact weighting is not required to obtain performance superior to that of methods which employ hierarchies.

Equivalence transformations

In this sub-section we examine the role of equivalence transformations and their impact on retrieval performance. To re-cap, equivalence transformations, or more generally 'normalisation', can be defined into two broad classes, score- and rank-based transformations. The objective of any of the normalisation approaches examined is to perform transformations on the set of $rs_{i,j}$ which are being combined, such that the effects of different factors like score ranges, numbers of retrieved results or score distributions does not adversely impact upon performance. Recall that in our candidate result sets to be combined ($rs_{i,j}$), each is comprised of documents m,

Tab. (4): Experimental Results, all corpora.

Legend	TRECVid 2003	TRECVid 2004	TRECVid 2005
Run	**MAP**	**MAP**	**MAP**
Uniform All	0.0593	0.0288	0.0646
Expert Level	0.0752 (61%)	0.0519 (47%)	0.0827 (59%)
Query Level	0.0776 (63%)	0.0543 (50%)	0.0850 (60%)
1σ Uniform	0.0966 (79%)	0.0738 (68%)	0.1037 (74%)
1σ Uniform & Tail	0.0958 (78%)	0.0764 (70%)	0.1109 (79%)
1σ	0.0989 (80%)	0.0770 (71%)	0.1108 (79%)
All Optimized	0.1224	0.1084	0.1407

Legend	TRECVid 2006	TRECVid 2007	ImageCLEF 2007
Run	**MAP**	**MAP**	**MAP**
Uniform All	0.0164	0.0422	0.1283
Expert Level	0.0299 (53%)	0.0655 (56%)	0.1648 (76%)
Query Level	0.0262 (47%)	0.0700 (60%)	0.1544 (71%)
1σ Uniform	0.0460 (82%)	0.0680 (58%)	0.1404 (65%)
1σ Uniform & Tail	0.0453 (80%)	0.0762 (65%)	0.1715 (80%)
1σ	0.0496 (88%)	0.0772 (66%)	0.1439 (68%)
All Optimized	0.0563	0.1175	0.2156

where $document_m \mapsto (name, rank, score)$. Score-based normalisation approaches alter the scores of documents to be combined, thereby allowing combination to occur utilising scores, whilst conversely rank-based transformations alter the ranks such that the rank of a document is what is used for combination.

Z-Score Score-based transformation converts the score of a document into the Standard Score [26] (Z-Score) within the $rs_{i,j}$ from which it came, the Standard Score being a measurement of how many standard deviations a score is from the mean score. This approach has no range restriction [27, 28].

$$Norm_{score(x)} = \frac{score_x - \mu}{\sigma} \tag{4}$$

Min-Max MinMax normalisation considers the best and worst scoring documents of a given $rs_{i,j}$ and assigns these scores of 1 and 0 respectively. Scores are then normalised within the range [0:1] [30].

$$Norm_{score(x)} = \frac{Score_x - Score_{min}}{Score_{max} - Score_{min}} \tag{5}$$

Tab. (5): Normalisation Results Comparison. n.b.* values for approach Z-Score are based on visual experts only.

	Score-Based		Rank-Based			
Year	Z-Score*	Min-Max	Borda	BordaMAX	RankMM	Reciprocal
TV2003	0.0095	0.1958	0.2127	0.2232	0.2206	0.1462
TV2004	0.0040	0.1524	0.1655	0.1774	0.1673	0.0892
TV2005	0.0117	0.1554	0.1654	0.1668	0.1670	0.1069
TV2006	0.0089	0.0846	0.0962	0.0989	0.0969	0.0645
TV2007	0.0195	0.1338	0.1433	0.1562	0.1459	0.0808
IC2007	0.0093	0.3148	0.3480	0.3678	0.3491	0.2503

Borda Borda ranked based transformation, given a set size of N the Borda transformation assigns a score of $N - x$, where x is the rank. As N is the size of the result set being transformed, it produces lower scores for result sets which do not contain many documents [19, 27, 29].

$$Norm_{score(x)} = N - rank_x \tag{6}$$

BordaMAX Extends Borda, where N becomes the value of the size of the largest result set being combined, which is then used for all result sets. This is to discount the bias against small result sets present in the standard Borda approach.

RankMM MinMax normalisation based upon ranks. Conceived as a middle ground between Borda and BordaMAX, RankMM normalises the range of ranks between [0:1].

Reciprocal Reciprocal rank is a rank transformation which is heavily biased towards the top ranked documents. The rank transformation is $\frac{1}{rank_x}$

For these experiments, documents were combined using CombSUM, CombSUM being a linear combination operator. With the exception of the Z-Score approach, all approaches combined both text and visual experts. Because the Z-Score approach does not perform any range restriction, we restricted this approach to visual expert only combination so that result set sizes would not be a factor. The results of our experiment are presented in Tab.(5).

From these results we can infer that rank-based approaches generally outperform any of the score-based approaches. The Z-Score method is a distinct failure with these data sets, and is excluded from further analysis. Likewise for the rank-based approaches, the Reciprocal method performs poorly, although nowhere near as bad as the Z-Score approach. The failure of the Z-Score approach is likely due to the lack of any range restriction of the scores being combined. This would have made the optimisation process problematic, as there would be no equivalence between the documents to be combined, meaning that any weight generated would be required to factor this in. In the case of the reciprocal method, its failure, whilst less severe than that of the Z-Score approach, highlights that the in-built aggressive weighting of the top ranked documents of any result set was too severe. Given that earlier we established that the ideal weights for expert combination take the form of a log-normal distribution, the optimisation process would have had to devise a weight which appropriately scaled the result sets to be combined whilst discounting against the heavily weighted top documents of each result set.

From our remaining four approaches, MinMax and the three Borda variants, we can see demonstrated that the score-based approach of MinMax is outperformed by all of the Borda based approaches. To compare the three Borda variants, we can observe that in terms of performance the standard Borda approach is the worst performer of the three. Given that the text expert often would not have returned the full 1,000 results, the standard Borda approach would have penalised this evidence. In terms of significance, the standard Borda approach is significantly worse than the BordaMAX approach, whilst for TRECVid corpora 2003-2006 there is no significant difference between it and the RankMM approach.

The BordaMAX approach appears to generally be the best performer, however there is no statistical difference between it and the RankMM approach for TRECVid corpora 2003 to 2006. Indeed in the case of TRECVid 2005 RankMM claims the top result. The main interpretation of this result is that rank-based approaches produce very successful results, but should not penalise result sets being combined which are of smaller size.

Whilst not a bad performer in itself, across all collections the MinMax approach is significantly worse than all of the Borda based approaches (with the exception of the standard Borda approach for TRECVid 2003, however in raw performance terms standard Borda is still superior). We note that the combination of results in this experiment used CombSUM. The question of why the score-based approach is less successful than the rank-based approaches we believe is due to the non-linear nature of scores and the application of linear weighting.

Given a result set $rs_{i,j}$, the sorted scores of this set are unlikely to exhibit a linear progression, and as such introduce a large degree of variability between the relative performance of individual documents. That is, given any two adjacent ranked documents in $rs_{i,j}$ the difference between the scores will vary considerably between pairs, whilst for ranks the difference between pairs will always be constant. Once a linear weight is then introduced, the impact of this weight will vary dependent on the value of the score to which it is being applied, whereas for rank approaches the impact of the weight is constant and predictable. This effect has been previously identified by [7], which termed the "independent weighting effect" which effectively introduces a second weight for combination. Upon reflection we can see that this observation is equally relevant for both the Z-Score and reciprocal approaches. In the case of the Z-Score approach, the independent weighting effect is present in the variation of the range which scores can take, whilst for the reciprocal approach it is evidenced in the aggressive weighting of highly ranked documents.

The question of the use of score or rank for data fusion is one which is not always fully considered by researchers. Many papers suggest that the use of scores is better than rank as they provide more information, such as the distribution of values or other variables [27, 31, 32], whilst many others would provide no justification at all, as described by Lee [7]. One reason for this is that much of the work in data fusion, particularly in the text domain, has been the non-weighted combination of similarly performing retrieval experts, where the scores (similarity values) once normalised have a degree of cross-comparability, as the experts from which they came are using similar retrieval techniques on the same types of index [10]. CBMIR alternatively combines experts of wildly varying performance from completely different indexing representations, and as such perhaps too much value is inferred onto the benefit of using scores from research experience found in text IR applications. Indeed as authors such as Robertson [33] and Dwork *et al.* [29] note that the score in many cases is just an artifact which is used for generating the ordering of a ranked list, the value of a score itself beyond this function is meaningless.

In Lee's work on data fusion he hypothesized that rank combination rather than score combination should perform better, given that scores are impacted by the "independent weighting effect". However experimentally he found that this is not the case [7], his work using normalised scores provides the better results. Croft[32] provides an interpretation of Lee's result:

> "This can be interpreted as evidence that the normalised score is usually a better estimator for the probability of relevance than the rank. Using the ranks is a more drastic form of smoothing that appears to increase error except when the systems being combined have very different scoring characteristics" [32].

This interpretation fits exactly to the characteristics of CBMIR, where as previously established we have very noisy sources of evidence being combined which vary wildly in performance.

Combination operators

Once the results from multiple ranked lists $rs_{i,j}$ have been normalised, they can then be combined to form a single ranked result for a given information need. In our discussion of the combination operators that can be used, we are assuming that one of the previously discussed transformations have been applied. If this is the case, then the combination approaches which we will now discuss can be applied to either the scores of a ranked list or to the rank of a ranked list. For convenience we will refer to a document's score when discussion combination approaches, however the normalised rank can be easily substituted and take the place of a score. The linear weighting of ranked lists and their subsequent combination has been proposed several times, with early work in linear weighting completed by Vogt *et al.* [34].

The more common approaches to combination of ranked lists is to use variants of linear interpolation. Fox and Shaw[30] in early work defined six approaches for linear combination, of which two have seen the most success, CombSUM and CombMNZ.

CombSUM

CombSUM is defined as the weighted sum of a documents score's in each of the result lists in which it appears. For instance, if we have our multi-part query Q and set of retrieval experts E, we will generate the matrix of result sets (ranked lists) **RS** and have along side it our weighting matrix **RC**. Given a document x, we examine each individual ranked list, $rs_{i,j}$, obtain the score of document x and apply the weight $rc_{i,j}$ to this score. The final score for document x therefore is the sum of each weighted instance of x occurring in the matrix **RS**. Formally this is described in Eq.(7).

$$CombSUM(score_x) = \sum_{rs_{i,j}}^{RS} (score_x \in rs_{i,j}) \times rc_{i,j} \tag{7}$$

CombMNZ

An alternative implementation developed by Fox *et al.* [30] is CombMNZ. CombMNZ extends CombSUM by introducing a variable which heavily weights documents that appear in more than one result set. This variable is the number of times that a document appears in result sets, i.e. the number of non-zero entries that a document has in the set of ranked lists to be combined (hence MNZ). In our terminology, this equates to the number of times a document x appears in a ranked list ($rs_{i,j}$) in our result list matrix **RS**. We define weighted CombMNZ in Eq.(8), where the weight has already been incorporated as part of the calculation of CombSUM.

$$CombMNZ(score_x) = CombSUM(score_x) \times \alpha \tag{8}$$

where α is the number of result sets in which a document was found, and $1 \leqslant \alpha \leqslant |\mathbf{RS}|$. Similar to some of the previous tools that we have examined, the choice of CombSUM versus CombMNZ is down to the intention of the system designer and the type of behaviour they would like present in the search system. CombMNZ

Tab. (6): CombSUM vs. CombMNZ for score & rank-based approaches.

	CombMNZ		CombSUM	
Year	Score	Borda	Score	Borda
TV2003	0.1720	0.1458	0.1958	0.2127
TV2004	0.1321	0.1258	0.1524	0.1655
TV2005	0.1329	0.1230	0.1554	0.1654
TV2006	0.0770	0.0701	0.0846	0.0962
TV2007	0.1157	0.1131	0.1388	0.1433
IC2007	0.2991	0.2861	0.3148	0.3480

aggressively promotes documents which occur in a majority of ranked lists to be combined, whereas CombSUM can be seen as a linear addition.

For this experiment, we will investigate the impact of CombSUM and CombMNZ on both score- and rank-based normalisation approaches. To test the score-based approach we use the MinMax score normalisation technique. For rank we use the standard Borda approach. The experts used for combination involve both text and visual experts and result sets $rs_{i,j}$ are truncated to 1,000 results. The results of this experiment are presented in Tab.(6).

There is little ambiguity in the presented results as we can quite clearly observe a constant ordering across all corpora with regards to performance. CombSUM using Borda normalisation is the most effective combination operator, whilst CombMNZ using ranks is consistently the worst performer.

However there is one curious artifact, which may explain the preponderance of data fusion literature which advocates the use of CombMNZ. From our results we observe that when scores (MinMax) rather than ranks are used, CombSUM achieves greater performance than CombMNZ once fully optimised. When CombMNZ is considered in isolation, score-based CombMNZ consistently outperforms rank-based CombMNZ, reversing the observation found with CombSUM. This result is of interest particularly when coupled with our previous observations about the popularity of using scores for data fusion in the research literature [7, 32]. In terms of significance, we found that for all instances, CombSUM performed better than CombMNZ with statistical significance.

Of interest however is this result of CombSUM and CombMNZ, particularly given the popularity that CombMNZ holds in data fusion, whilst in our experiments performing empirically worse. Lee's motivation for demonstrating the effectiveness of CombMNZ was an extension of the work of [6] where they observed that a document which appears in multiple ranked lists should be ranked higher. Lee saw CombMNZ as a mechanism which gave a boost in ranking to documents which

Tab. (7): CombSUM vs CombMNZ behaviour.

Doc.	E1	E2	E3	CombSUM	CombMNZ
a	0.8	0.0	0.9	1.7	3.4
b	0.6	0.3	0.6	1.5	4.5
CombSUM ranking				a > b	
CombMNZ ranking				b > a	

appeared in more lists.

Thinking of CombMNZ in terms of providing a boost to documents which appear in multiple lists gives an impression of a function which is positive, that it promotes documents up a ranked list. An alternative way however when thinking of CombMNZ is negative, that in fact the function's purpose is to *penalise* documents which do not appear in *all* ranked lists. We can illustrate this with a toy example given in Tab.(7).

In this table we have two documents, 'a' and 'b', and three experts 'E1 ... E3'. Document 'a' is only found in two of our three experts, however it is highly ranked positions in both of these experts. Document 'b' on the other hand is found in all three experts, but it appears around the middle of each experts result set. The combination behaviour of CombSUM and CombMNZ in this case produces two quite different orderings. CombSUM will rank document 'a' before document 'b', whereas CombMNZ will reverse the ranking putting 'b' before 'a' as it appears in all three of our result sets. The question for system builders becomes what sort of behaviour do they want present in their retrieval system ?

We believe that the CombSUM behaviour is more desirable, particularly considering that once any large number of result sets are to be combined through data fusion, that the probability of a document being found in every, or a majority of result sets, must decrease. This has been empirically justified in the results we have presented in this chapter for CombSUM and CombMNZ.

Discussion

In this section we explored the different ways data fusion can be implemented when combining multi-part queries from multiple retrieval experts. We observed that the best levels of performance can be achieved when specific instances of $rs_{i,j}$ can be identified and given greater weight. Two important caveats need to be mentioned at this point. Firstly, whilst we identified this attribute, the development of any technique to identify these instances of $rs_{i,j}$ at query-time is a non-trivial and significant research problem. Secondly, there remains the possibility that these observations may be more pronounced with the experimental corpora used in this investigation, specifically the news video collections. We could speculate that performance is more pronounced with these collections because there is a degree of redundancy in these collections (attributes such as advertisements), which may be having some form of an impact in our observations. We cannot discount this without further experimentation on more diverse corpora, however we believe that by using the six experimental corpora that we have, that a strong case can be made at the very least for further robust investigation.

5 Current Approaches for Weight Generation and Data Fusion

Here we present related work which currently addresses the data fusion problem and weight generation for multimedia applications. However, before proceeding we mention of two previous studies which have examined several of the issues we presented in this chapter, specifically work by McDonald and Smeaton [31] and by Yan and Hauptmann [35]. McDonald and Smeaton empirically compare combination approaches for score, rank and probability techniques. Their work evaluated these approaches by optimizing Mean Average Precision (MAP) on a training collection with multiple topics, then applying these generalized optimized parameters to a test set. Our work differs as our optimizations occur at the topic level (Average Precision), rather than the topic set level (MAP). Furthermore the fusion approaches detailed in [31] use a hierarchical approach which is likely to obscure the effect individual query images have on performance. Yan and Hauptmann [35] conduct experiments with TRECVid 2002 data to construct a theoretical framework for studying the upper bounds of combination functions. They found that linear forms of combination may be too restrictive for large numbers of experts to be combined effectively. However, like McDonald and Smeaton, this work examined combination at the expert level and as such did not delve down to the granularity of pairs $\langle expert_i, query_j \rangle$. Whilst there could be little argument that linear weighting could not be improved upon by non-linear weighting, the evidence we have presented in this chapter which uses linear weighting certainly indicates that very good performance could be extracted through linear weighting schemes.

Query independent weighting

Query Independent Weighting is one of the simplest methods that can be employed when combining retrieval experts. Popular in earlier research in CBMIR [19] because of its simplicity, query independent weighting is an empirical method which requires either a training corpus or domain knowledge of the collection being indexed. Weights are statically assigned for each expert in the system and do not change, regardless of the query being issued. For all queries being processed by the system, this single weight matrix, which weights only experts, is always used. Whilst relatively simple to execute, this method is only suitable when indexing data from a narrow domain [12].

Query-class weighting

Query-Class weighting can be seen as an evolution of query independent weighting as it directly addresses many of the failings of query independent weighting and as such has proven popular in the multimedia community. The central concept of this approach is that given a training collection and an appropriate set of training queries, query clusters (i.e. *query-classes*) can be found such that queries within each cluster share some similar 'properties' which differentiate them from other queries in the collection (where 'properties' may be artifacts such as semantic similarity, performance similarity, distance etc). By partitioning a set of training queries into discrete *query classes*, it is then possible to optimize for each *query-class* an instance of the weighting matrix **RC**, such that each class should have a different set of weights for combining retrieval experts. When a test/live query is then processed, it is first mapped to a *query-class* so that the relevant matrix **RC** can be applied for the retrieval experts used. As such, this provides a considerable improvement over query independent weighting, notably in the granularity of how experts can be weighted as every *query-class* has an associated weight matrix **RC**. Whilst the query independent approach only has one instance of **RC** to weight queries, in the *query-class* approach there are |*query-classes*| available for weighting. However like the query independent approach, our weighting matrix only weights at the expert level, not at the level of $\langle expert_i, query_j \rangle$, therefore we refer to these matrices again as $\mathbf{RC_i}$. Fig.(8) provides a high level overview of the *query-class* approach.

The *query-class* approach was initially developed by [36] for content-based video retrieval on the TRECVid corpora. Both share a degree of similarity in implementation as both statically define *a priori* the *query-classes* to be used by the system. [38] extend the initial approaches by automatically discovering *query classes* in a training set, free of any manual involvement. Their approach is based on the observation that the intent of *query class* weighting is to group queries together such that they share the same set of expert weights to achieve good performance. Therefore Kennedy *et al.* hypothesize that given a set of retrieval experts and training queries, that those queries which share similar performance variations between experts (where performance is measured by an evaluation metric, i.e. average precision) should belong to the same *query class*. One of the latest evolutions in the *query class* approach is provided by [53], whose work concentrates on creating dynamic *query-class* weighting during system operation, rather than the previously described approaches which learned classes from training data.

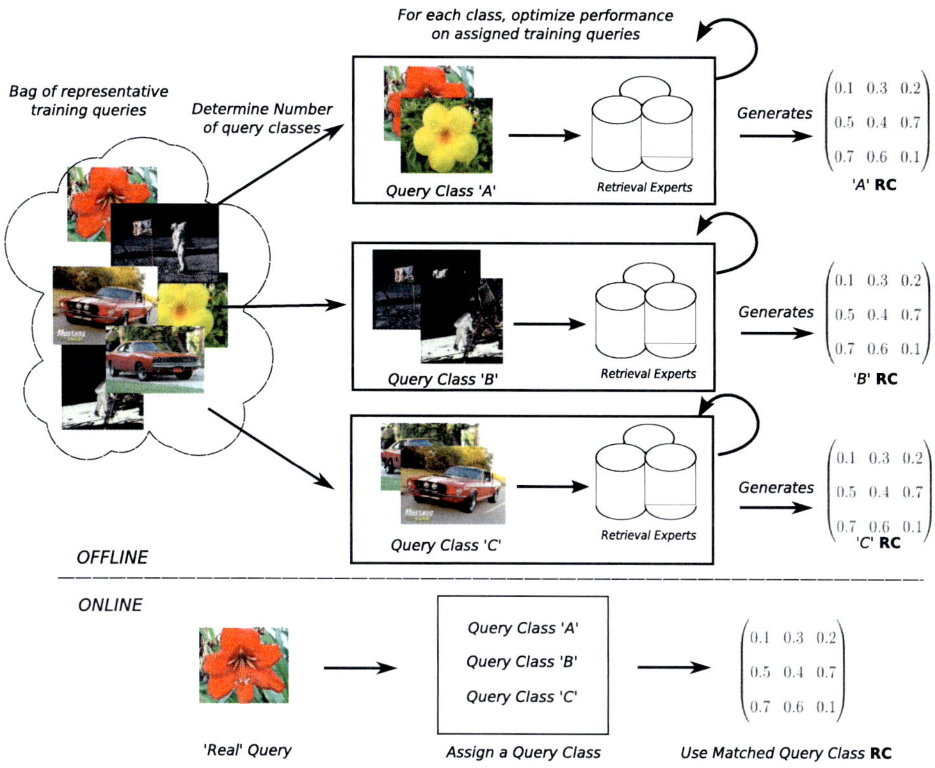

Fig. (8): Query class weighting.

Discriminative classification

Machine learning applications can be considered as techniques which discover structural patterns in data that allow us to explain and make predictions from that data [39]. They provide us with tools to help make sense of and to organize data. The field of machine learning is incredibly broad and a general review is outside the scope of this chapter. In this section, we restrict ourselves to a brief review of approaches which can be characterized as *supervised* and *discriminative*, that is approaches which require training data which has been manually labelled, and models which learn directly on the data provided to them.

Some of the challenges which apply to the use of machine learning approaches are the *class imbalance* problem and the *curse of dimensionality* [40]. These two problems are interrelated for the application of search. Put simply, the class imbalance problem for search is that often there are far more irrelevant than relevant items in a corpus, hampering classification as the classifier can be biased towards the larger of the imbalanced classes. Similarly, when learning from data, such as using visual feature vectors, that as the size of the feature vector grows, an exponential increase occurs in the size of the feature space, correspondingly requiring an increase in the number of examples we require in order to achieve a stable model [41, 42, 43].

[25] explicitly addresses the issue of multi-example, multi-feature search, such as the scenario defined by our example CBMIR system and query, making use of machine learning methods, specifically the use of Support Vector Machines (SVM) [49]. Natsev *et al.* conduct retrieval experiments using the TRECVid 2003 corpus and topics, where each topic contains not only a statement of the information need but also relevant visual examples. However, as traditional SVMs conduct discriminative classification, they require not only positive training samples (e.g. the visual example queries) but also negative training samples. Natsev *et al.* propose several mechanisms for generating 'pseudo-negative' examples, however the best approach was a random sampling of the collection. As TRECVid search topics are typically relatively complex information needs (e.g. find shots of George Bush walking versus a classification task of find outdoor shots), the actual number of relevant shots in a collection is relatively small. Natsev *et al.* refer to this as *bagging*, however it distinguishes itself from traditional machine learning *bagging* approaches as only the negative examples are randomly sampled, whereas in traditional *bagging* approaches, both classes are randomly sampled and multiple classifiers are built and averaged from these random samples. Therefore for each query, a modified bagging approach is conducted, where 10 'bags' are defined, each of which shares the same positive examples, but a random selection of negative examples. This learning process is conducted *per expert*.

[43] also address the issue of imbalanced and sparse learning instances for visual retrieval in multimedia search, by extending the work of [25]. Tešić *et al.* examine the modified bagging approach of [25] offering improvements to both the bagging approach itself and to the selection of the pseudo-negative examples.

6 Other Methods

In this section we briefly review other methods which have application for data fusion. We list these approaches under 'other methods' as they either occur after the initial retrieval process, or leverage aspects of the underlying data which we cannot for CBMIR.

Relevance feedback

Relevance Feedback has long been an area of active research within the information science community [44], dating back nearly 40 years [45]. The idea behind relevance feedback is that it can be difficult for a user to formulate a query to an Information System which will effectively capture what is being sought, but that a user presented with relevant information will recognize it. A system can use these user judgements to better refine the ranking presented to a user, typically in an iterative process. As such it is a valuable technique for bridging the information need of a user to a form that the system can better exploit.

Typically however, relevance feedback is an interactive process, or at the very least occurs after an initial ranking by an information system. Therefore for the purposes of this thesis, we do not consider relevance feedback as one of the approaches which we will examine in depth, as we are concerned with data fusion with regard to the generation of the best initial ranking. Whilst the study of relevance feedback does have some applicability to data fusion, as often multiple forms of evidence need to be combined, we state that the insights we obtain in this thesis can be applied to relevance feedback as a separate activity in order to improve it, and indeed relevance feedback can be applied to any of our techniques explored here in order to improve retrieval performance.

[44] conduct a thorough review of relevance feedback approaches in image retrieval, whilst [46] in their general review of image retrieval provides some additional updates to this work.

MARS, an early content-based multimedia retrieval system [47], implemented relevance feedback similar to what is found in many text retrieval systems. Using textures as the content-based feature, it uses a vector space representation and investigates both *tf.idf* and Gaussian normalization for determining the weight vector.

Machine Learning approaches feature prominently in image relevance feedback literature, their popularity due in part in being able to explicitly label non-relevant images, so as to achieve a better separation between relevant and non-relevant items [46]. [48] implement relevance feedback using a Support Vector Machine (SVM) [49]. Their paper demonstrates the usefulness of SVMs for the relevance feedback problem, but they highlight the need for multiple positive and negative examples to achieve good accuracy. [54] use an SVM with active learning. Rather than after each round of relevance feedback presenting to the user the top ranked relevant images from a static classifier, their approach is to present images for which the classifier is most uncertain and after each round the classifier determines new decision boundaries. This approach offered improvement over the use of regular SVMs. [50] addresses the class imbalance problem, that is for a typical relevance classification task there are far more non-relevant than relevant images. They build a modified SVM referred to as BSVM (Biased Support Vector Machine) which uses spherical hyperplanes to encompass relevant images. [51] also address the class imbalance problem, through using Semi-Supervised Learning (SSL) and dimensionality reduction in a method they term "Relevance Aggregation Projection (RAP)". The authors refer to the asymmetry problem in subspace CBIR machine learning, which is that images labeled as 'relevant' share some semantic properties, whilst 'non-relevant' images have no common properties, only that they differ from the relevant images. By performing dimensionality reduction and SSL they are able to capture nearby unlabeled data points to relevant points, thus leveraging the unlabeled data to improve classification accuracy. For clarity, the difference between active learning and SSL, is that in active learning, the user is required to annotate after each iteration, unlabeled data which a classifier is most unsure of, whilst in SSL, unlabeled data is assigned to relevant and non-relevant labels through transduction. The two approaches can be complimentary.

Query performance prediction

Query Performance Prediction is a related area of work which may have application in the task of weighted data fusion. The objective of query performance prediction is for any given query to a search service, determine how likely it is to provide good results to a user. The typical application for this is to identify queries which may perform poorly and are therefore good candidates for query reformulation [52]. The potential application for these approaches is that as they have some discriminating power to determine good from poor performing queries, they may be able to provide a good estimation for values of RC_{ij}.

7 Conclusions

In this chapter we conducted an empirical investigation into weighted data fusion and its impact on CBMIR retrieval performance. To achieve our observations we employed a non-conventional experimental model, which directly optimised retrieval performance on test corpora which were being examined. The major benefit of this approach was that for every subsequent experiment that was run within this framework, the ideal set of linear weights for data fusion was always used. This in effect held constant the effect of weighting on retrieval performance and allowed us to make robust observations as to the impact of different factors which effect the data fusion process.

The following observations were made in this chapter:

- The ideal weighting form for data fusion is a highly positively skewed distribution, where specific $rs_{i,j}$ in a topic are highly weighted, whilst the remaining results receive the remainder of the weight. We found that approximately 10%-20% of the result sets being combined in a query attracted 60%-80% of the weight when ideally weighted.

- Normalisation plays a crucial component in putting evidence into a form which allows it to be easily combined. For score-based normalisation we found that MinMax normalisation produces the best results. For rank-based normalisation we found that our BordaMAX or RankMM approaches produced the best performance. Overall we found that when ideal weighting is used, rank-based normalisation out-performed score-based normalisation.

- We examined the performance of the two most common combination operators, CombSUM and CombMNZ. Whilst CombMNZ is the most popular form of combination operator in text retrieval data fusion literature, we found that CombSUM clearly outperformed CombMNZ.
- Combination levels are often employed in data fusion approaches to make the task of combining evidence from sources more manageable. We found that combining at the 'expert' or 'query' level produced no difference in retrieval performance. Combining at the 'direct' level though produced a very large performance gain over combining results at any arbitrary level, greater than what was anticipated. Typically imposing a combination level restricted retrieval performance to between 50%-75% of what could be achieved with direct combination. This level of performance is better when we consider the first point of this list, that specific pairs correctly weighted drive retrieval performance. The direct level of combination is the only level of combination which allows for the specific weighting of pairs, and therefore is the most effective level of combination.
- We re-examined the early data fusion experiments of Lee, and found that contrary to reported results from text retrieval, when linearly weighted, CombSUM outperforms CombMNZ.

This chapter has explicitly examined many data fusion variables to a very fine level of detail and discovered several properties of data fusion which were masked by sub-optimal weighting being employed. Notable was the assumption that CombMNZ is the ideal form of evidence combination. From these observations, we find that many of the earlier examined algorithms for data fusion do not have properties which would allow for the full exploitation of the ideal data fusion form which we have observed in this chapter. Notably, none of the examined data fusion algorithms allows for the direct weighting of individual pairs $\langle Expert_i, Query_j \rangle$ at query time, with most data fusion approaches employing a combination level approach which aggregates results at the 'expert' level.

This indicates that significant gains can be made through the application of approaches such as saliency analysis to query images, so as to determine if there is a correlation between query images, and those which have been empirically shown to attract the most weight. Development of algorithms which are capable of identifying which pairs $\langle Expert_i, Query_j \rangle$ are likely to perform well, will generate retrieval performance which surpasses current unsupervised approaches.

8 References

[1] Belkin, N. J., Kantor, P., Fox, E. A., and Shaw, J. A. Combining the evidence of multiple query representations for information retrieval. *Information Processing*

Tab. (8): Summary of major findings.

Summary of Major Findings	
Ideal Weight Distribution	Highly Positively skewed Log-Normal.
Equivalence Transformations	
Score-based	MinMax
Rank-based	BordaMAX or RankMM
Overall	Rank superior with ideal weights.
Combination Operators	CombSUM outperforms CombMNZ.
Combination Levels	Direct-level far superior to alternatives.
High Impact Queries	Approx. 10% of query-components provide 80% of performance.

and Management, 1995.

[2] Voorhees, E. M., Gupta, N. K., and Johnson-Laird, B. Learning collection fusion strategies. In *ACM SIGIR*, 1995.

[3] Kludas, J., Bruno, E., and Marchand-Maillet, S. Information Fusion in Multimedia Information Retrieval. *Adaptive Multimedial Retrieval: Retrieval, User, and Semantics: 5th International Workshop*, 2007.

[4] McGill, M., Koll, M., and Noreault, T. An evaluation of factors affecting document ranking by information retrieval systems. Technical Report NSF-IST-78-10454 to the National Science Foundation (USA), 1979.

[5] Das-Gupta, P. and Katzer, J. A study of the overlap among document representations. *SIGIR Forum*, 1983.

[6] Saracevic, T. and Kantor, P. A study of information seeking and retrieving, iii: Searchers, searches, overlap. *Journal of the American Society for Information Science and Technology*, 1988.

[7] Lee, J. H. Analyses of multiple evidence combination. In *ACM SIGIR*, 1997.

[8] Fagin, R. Combining fuzzy information from multiple systems. In *PODS*, 1996.

[9] McCabe, M., Chowdhury, A., Grossman, D., and Frieder, O. System fusion for improving performance in information retrieval systems. In *ITCC*, 2001.

[10] Beitzel, S. M., Jensen, E. C., Chowdhury, A., Grossman, D., Frieder, O., and Goharian, N. Fusion of effective retrieval strategies in the same information

retrieval system. *Journal of the American Society for Information Science and Technology*, 2004.

[11] Snoek, C. G. M., Worring, M., and Smeulders, A. W. M. Early versus Late Fusion in Semantic Video Analysis. In *ACM Multimedia*, 2005.

[12] Smeulders, A. W. M., Worring, M., Santini, S., Gupta, A., and Jain, R. Content-based image retrieval at the end of the early years. *IEEE Transactions on Pattern Analysis and Machine Intelligence*, 2000.

[13] Van Rijsbergen, C. *Information Retrieval, 2nd edition.* Butterworth-Heinemann Newton, 1979.

[14] Blanken, H. M., Vries, A. P. d., Blok, H. E., and Feng, L. *Multimedia Retrieval (Data-Centric Systems and Applications).* Springer-Verlag New York, Inc., 2007.

[15] Manjunath, B., Salembier, P., and Sikora, T., editors *Introduction to MPEG-7: Multimedia Content Description Language.* Wiley, 2002.

[16] Metzler, D. and Croft, W. B. Linear feature-based models for information retrieval. *Information Retrieval*, 2007.

[17] Cooke, E., Ferguson, P., Gaughan, G., Gurrin, C., Jones, G., le Borgne, H., Lee, H., Marlow, S., Donald, K. M., McHugh, M., Murphy, N., O'Connor, N., O'Hare, N., Rothwell, S., Smeaton, A. F., and Wilkins., P. TRECVID 2004 Experiments in Dublin City University. In *Proceedings of TRECVID*, 2004.

[18] Amir, A., O Argillander, J., Berg, M., Chang, S.-F., Franz, M., Hsu, W., Iyengar, G., R Kender, J., Kennedy, L., Lin, C.-Y., Naphade, M., (Paul) Natsev, A., Smith, J. R., Tesic, J., Wu, G., Yan, R., and Zhang, D. IBM Research TRECVID-2004 Video Retrieval System. In *Proceedings of TRECVID*, 2004.

[19] Jeong, S., Kim, K., Chun, B., Lee, J., and Bae, Y. J. An effective method for combining multiple features of image retrieval. In *TENCON*, 1999.

[20] Jin, X. and French, J. C. Improving image retrieval effectiveness via multiple queries. In *Proceedings of the 1st ACM international workshop on Multimedia databases*, 2003.

[21] MPEG-7 Multimedia Content Description Interface. Standard No. ISO/IEC n?15938, 2001.

[22] Smeaton, A. F., Over, P., and Kraaij, W. Evaluation Campaigns and TRECVid. In *ACM MIR*, 2006.

[23] Clough, P., Grubinger, M., Hanbury, A., and Müller, H. Overview of the imageclef 2007 photographic retrieval task. In *Proceedings of the CLEF 2007 Workshop*, 2007.

[24] Yan, R. and Hauptmann, A. G. Probabilistic latent query analysis for combining multiple retrieval sources. In *ACM SIGIR*, 2006.

[25] Natsev, A. P., Naphade, M. R., and Tesic, J. Learning the semantics of multimedia queries and concepts from a small number of examples. In *ACM Multimedia*, 2005.

[26] McClave, J. T. and Sincich, T. *Statistics (10th Edition)*. Prentice Hall, 2006.

[27] Renda, M. E. and Straccia, U. Web metasearch: rank vs. score based rank aggregation methods. In *Proceedings of SAC*, 2003.

[28] Montague, M. and Aslam, J. A. Relevance score normalization for metasearch. In *CIKM*, 2001.

[29] Dwork, C., Kumar, R., Naor, M., and Sivakumar, D. Rank aggregation methods for the web. In *ACM WWW*, 2001.

[30] Fox, E. A. and Shaw, J. A. Combination of Multiple Searches. In *Proceedings of the 3rd Text REtrieval Conference (TREC-2)*, 1994.

[31] McDonald, K. and Smeaton, A. F. A comparison of score, rank and probability-based fusion methods for video shot retrieval. In *CIVR*, 2005.

[32] Croft, W. B. Combining approaches to information retrieval. *Advances in Information Retrieval*, 2000.

[33] Robertson, S. On score distributions and relevance. In *ECIR*, 2007.

[34] Vogt, C. C. and Cottrell, G. W. Fusion Via a Linear Combination of Scores. *Information Retrieval*, 1999.

[35] Yan, R. and Hauptmann, A. G. The combination limit in multimedia retrieval. In *ACM Multimedia*, 2003.

[36] Yan, R., Yang, J., and Hauptmann, A. G. Learning query-class dependent weights in automatic video retrieval. In *ACM Multimedia*, 2004.

[37] Chua, T.-S., Neo, S.-Y., Li, K.-Y., Wang, G., Shi, R., Zhao, M., and Xu, H. TRECVID 2004 search and feature extraction task by NUS PRIS. In *Proceedings of TRECVID*, 2004.

[38] Kennedy, L. S., Natsev, A. P., and Chang, S.-F. Automatic discovery of query-class-dependent models for multimodal search. In *ACM Multimedia*, 2005.

[39] Whitten, I. H. and Frank, E. *Data Mining: Practical Machine Learning Tools and Techniques; (2nd ed.)*. Morgan Kaufmann Publishers, 2005.

[40] Akbani, R., Kwek, S., and Japkowicz, N. Applying Support Vector Machines to Imbalanced Datasets. In *ECML*, 2004.

[41] Bellman, R. *Adaptive control processes: a guided tour.* Princeton University Press, 1961.

[42] Beyer, K., Goldstein, J., Ramakrishnan, R., and Shaft, U. When is nearest neighbor meaningful. In *ICDT*, 1999.

[43] Tešić, J., Natsev, A., Xie, L., and Smith, J. Data modeling strategies for imbalanced learning in visual search. In *ICME*, 2007.

[44] Zhou, X. S. and Huang, T. S. Relevance feedback in image retrieval: A comprehensive review. *Multimedia Systems*, 2003.

[45] Rocchio, J. J. Relevance feedback in information retrieval. In Salton, G., editor, *The SMART Retrieval System: Experiments in Automatic Document Processing*, Prentice-Hall Series in Automatic Computation, chapter 14, 1971.

[46] Datta, R., Joshi, D., Li, J., and Wang, J. Z. Image retrieval: Ideas, influences, and trends of the new age. *ACM Computing Surveys*, 2008.

[47] Rui, Y., Huang, T., and Mehrotra, S. Content-based image retrieval with relevance feedback in MARS. *ICIP*, 1997.

[48] Hong, P., Tian, Q., and Huang, T. S. Incorporate support vector machines to content-based image retrieval with relevant feedback. In *ICIP*, 2000.

[49] Vapnik, V. N. *The nature of statistical learning theory.* Springer-Verlag New York, Inc., 1995.

[50] Hoi, C.-H., Chan, C.-H., Huang, K., Lyu, M., and King, I. Biased support vector machine for relevance feedback in image retrieval. *Proceedings of the 2004 IEEE International Symposium on Neural Networks*, 2004.

[51] Liu, W., Jiang, W., and Chang, S.-F. Relevance aggregation projections for image retrieval. In *CIVR*, 2008.

[52] Cronen-Townsend, S., Zhou, Y., and Croft, W. B. Predicting query performance. In *SIGIR*, 2002.

[53] Xie, L., Natsev, A., and Tesic, J. Dynamic Multimodal Fusion in Video Search. In *ICME*, 2007.

[54] Tong, S. and Chang, E. Support vector machine active learning for image retrieval. In *ACM Multimedia*, 2001.

CHAPTER 13

Cross-modality Indexing, Browsing and Search of Distance Learning Media on the Web

Alon Efrat*
The University of Arizona, Email: alon@cs.arizona.edu
Arnon Amir
IBM Almaden Research Center, Email: arnon@almaden.ibm.com
Kobus Barnard
The University of Arizona, Email: kobus@sista.arizona.edu
Quanfu Fan
Research Staff Member (Exploratory Computer Vision Group), Tel: 1-914-784-6253, Email: qfan@us.ibm.com

Abstract: A large segment of people across the world have to search and browse the distance learning media, which calls for better indexing techniques. In this chapter, we introduce such an indexing technique by making full use of the slide channel. The slide channel is created by matching slides to video segments, and the video can be better indexed by mining the information in slide channel. Then we introduce several applications that benefit from the slide channel.

*Correspondence Author: Alon Efrat, The University of Arizona; Email: alon@cs.arizona.edu.

Xian-Sheng Hua, Marcel Worring & Tat-Seng Chua (Eds.)

Keywords

Cross-modality, Indexing, Distance Learning, data mining, slides, electronic presentations, Multimodality, backprojection, increased Accessibility, Slides

1 Cross Modality Indexing and the Slides Channel

Cross modality indexing is the indexing one modality of a multimodal stream using another modality, where the association between the modalities is represented by some mapping. A simple example is the use of speech recognition in video search. The indexing and search are performed on the audio channel while the "document" is a visual moving picture. In this example, the straightforward mapping between the two is temporal and, given the separated two channels, is determined by the time offset which aligns the two. The mapping may be more involved in the case of closed captions and speech. In this case, a complete sentence appears on the screen for a certain duration which may or may not cover the duration of the corresponding speech. In the case of live closed captions there is a delay between the voice and the captions. This requires an appropriate temporal model for mapping, or crossing between the modalities.

Snoek & Worring [23] gave the following definition to the term multimodality:

> **Definition 1:** *Multimodality* The capacity of an author of the video document to express a predefined semantic idea, by combining a layout with a special content, using at least two information channels.

Where the three main information channels, or modalities that Snoek & Worring propose are:

- Visual modality: contains the mise-en-scene, i.e., everything, either naturally or artificially created, that can be seen in the video document;
- Auditory modality: contains the speech, music,and environmental sounds that can be heard in the video document;
- Textual modality: contains textual resources that describe the content of the video.

We discuss multimodal content on the web in the context of indexing, browsing and search of distance learning media, and refer the reader to [23] for a survey of the other applications of cross-modality. We focus mostly on recorded media, although many of the techniques discussed below are also applied to live streaming of lectures. A special attention is given to electronic *slides* used in the lecture, and accessible to the system. Though they can be considered as either part of the visual channel (as they are seen in the video) or the textual channel (as they commonly contain text that describes the lecture content), we propose to acknowledge their unique nature, and consider them to be an independent channel, which we call the *"slides channel"*. The slides channel emerges once video segments are linked to the slides that were used in the presentation. Its is determined by the temporal correspondence — which slides (if any) appears in which frame of the video, and by the spatial correspondence — where in the frame the slide appears, and under which transformation. Once the temporal and spatial correspondences are found, text extracted from the slides can be used as semantic handles into the video content. The special characteristics of the slides channel are detailed below.

In Section 2 we motivate the methods developed here specifically for the important field of educational video. We discuss systems that do not use a slides channel and contrast them with the advantages of systems that time-align and link slides to video segments to improve video search and browsing. We also discuss manual, semi-automated, and automated methods to achieve this time alignment. In Section 3 we characterize the slides channel that is accessible once the alignment is available. Then in Section 4 we elaborate on how the multiple modalities enhance authoring of distance learning material by linking together multiple sources of knowledge, generating a dynamic presentation that a user can conveniently navigate. Finally, in Section 5 the capabilities that the slide channel enables for linking, retrieving, and accessing videos over the internet.

2 Indexing Distance Learning Materials

We open by discussing recent developments and the significance of distance learning video. According to a 2006 survey conducted by the Sloan Consortium [7], more than 96% of the largest educational institutions in the United States have on-line offerings, and nearly 3.2 million college students took at least one on-line course in the Fall 2005 term.

This trend suggests a future in which a much larger segment of people across the world will have access to distance learning opportunities. Distance learning is used by most large universities and corporations. In many cases, the content is created by video capture of lectures or presentations, and distribution is conducted by video streaming over the internet. The video quality, however, varies greatly. A high quality production with multiple cameras is costly and labor intensive. Low-cost video production, on the other hand, suffers in quality as a result of common problems such as inadequate illumination, significant color distortion, and images in video that lack clarity. Furthermore, reduced video quality affects readability of the text slides captured in the video, impairing learning ability of the viewer. Finally, the video stream is likely to lose the vibrant, interactive, and insightful context that exists in the lecture room.

Since the usage of the slides channel is central to this chapter, we discuss separately work that does not use this channel, and others that do use it.

Indexing distance learning media without using the slides channel

Systems for analyzing, indexing, searching and browsing educational videos have been studied extensively. Several of these systems deal with presentation slides. One of the earliest web-based browsing tools for educational videos is the Berkeley Lecture Browser [21], which provides access to streaming video and manually-synchronized slides. The Cornell Lecture Browser [20] is a similar tool, but uses automatic synchronization. The eClass system (originally known as Classroom 2000 [2]) uses an augmented "smart classroom" to capture white boards, slides, video and audio and create a virtual learning environment.

The CueVideo [3] system provides tools to quickly convert videotaped lectures or conference presentations into searchable on-line video proceedings, as well as automatic slide matching for topical indexing [24]. Other systems use information captured from whiteboards during lectures. However applying OCR to images of whiteboards is rather challenging. Instead, tracing the motion of the whiteboard marker can capture the temporal aspect of handwriting. See the recent book [16].

Web-based remote education systems, also referred as *e-learning* or *distance learning* systems, are significantly affecting the way people learn, teach and share knowledge. E-learning offers alternatives for those who cannot go to class and provides other advantages such as low cost, unlimited access of learning materials, and self-paced learning. Studies have reported that no significant differences are observed between the learning effectiveness of students learning over distance and students learning in classrooms [22].

Creating the slides channel: Matching slides to video frames

The specific task of synchronizing slides with video was first addressed by manually editing time stamps (e.g., the BMRC Lecture Browser [21]). Subsequently, the Classroom 2000 Project [2] introduced hardware to record time stamps during the presentation. Their ClassPad provided easy browsing and annotation of slides in the classroom for both teachers and students. Today, several commercial e-learning systems can deliver synchronized multimedia presentations over the Internet to end users where slides are displayed side by side with the video and the instructional content can be accessed directly through slides (e.g., the Mediasite system [18] and Microsoft Producer [19]).

The approach taken by Zhang *et al.* [5] approaches assumes that the RGB video signals from the lecturer's computer to the video projector can be "tapped", and the video frames can be matched against the slides' images. This is a rather reliable method, compared to methods that search for the slides in a video from a camera, as the signal has much less distortion. It also assumes the scenario common in, for example, conferences, in which lecturers use their own computers, while the projectors are usually fixed.

The approaches discussed so far typically require dedicated hardware and/or software systems that are engaged in advance of the presentation. This has two limitations. First, it adds some overhead on the capture process. Second, it does not help exploit the large stores of on-line video from disparate sources. To address this limitation, methods to automatically match slides-to-video frames have been proposed. Most of of the early work can be described as a two-step matching process: slide extraction followed by slide identification. For example, Mukhopadhyay *et al.* [20] developed a system for structuring multimedia content in which slides and audio information are automatically synchronized with video. The system relies on a fixed camera and a predetermined transformation established using the four corner points of the projector during the system installation. Adding flexibility, Sydeda-Mohmood [24] proposed locating slides in videos using an illumination-invariant descriptor built upon the background color of slides. This method can detect slides appearing anywhere in the frames. The spatial layout geometry of the identified slide regions is then exploited to recognize slides. Liu *et al.* [15] also detect quadrilaterals in frames to extract slide regions, but apply a different, pixel based, method to identify the slides.

Erol *et al.* [8] developed a method that links slide images captured during presentations to the source files that generate the slides. Their method first classifies slides into four different types, and depending on the type, the slide is recognized by combining one or more methods that include edge histogram matching, line profile matching, string matching and layout matching. More peripheral to our topic, we note that Behera *et al.* [4] developed a method to spot slide change events based on analyzing the visual stability of a sequence of frames. However, no further slide recognition is performed in that work. Finally, speech transcripts alone [28] and audiovisual features [6] have been exploited to synchronize slides with video. Most of the approaches described above have in common that they were developed to handle one particular type of video style.

The approach used in the SLIC (Semantically Linked Instructional Content) system [25], is distinct from previous approaches that begin with transformation estimation followed by slide identification. The method used by SLIC [9, 11] simultaneously solves for the transformation and slide identity. To do so, SIFT (Scale invariant feature transform) [17] keypoints extracted from both the slides and the video frames are matched subject to the constraint of consistent homography using RANSAC [12]. This approach is fully automatic and can handle video capture systems with few limits on the motion (pan, tilt, zoom and even motion) of the cameras.

To gain robustness, SLIC combines the spatial matching with camera event detection, and a dynamic HMM based on camera events. In addition, the spatial matching is done in several steps. In this first phase, frame-to-slide homographies (i.e., the projection transformation between the slides captured by camera and their original ones) are found for some slides (the easier ones) by keypoint matching. Using this information, all frames are classified into three categories: *full-slide* (the entire frame shows the slide content), *small-slide* (the frame contains both a slide area and a substantial portion of the scene back-ground), and *no-slide*. This classification, and associated homography estimates for all frames are then used to match all frames quickly using *local keypoint matching* which uses the estimated homographies to limit the possible matches to geometrically plausible ones. A second phase detects camera event between each pair of consecutive frames by using the computed homographies and the frame types classified in the first phase. Finally, in the third phase, the visual features, temporal information and the camera events are incorporated into a dynamic HMM to provide an optimal sequence of slides matching the frame sequence.

Besides being a very effective way to achieve the alignment, the homographies extracted while doing so have many uses. Note that the simultaneous method allows the homographies to be extracted even when the slide is zoomed in, and corners are not available. This is in contrast to the work of Gigonzac *et al.* [13] that focusses on video enhancement opportunities enabled by knowing the homographies, and uses detected corners to determine the homography.

The method developed by Wang and Kankanhalli [29] share with SLIC the usage of SIFT feature points and RANSAC. However, they place more emphasis on handling cases where the use of SIFT points alone creates problems. First, SIFT is defined on gray-scale level, so differences based on colors could be overlooked. Secondly, their system better addresses slides with animations, and, by using color gradients, also corrects slides that appear blurry. The latter case occurs for example when the camera is focused on the lecturer, and the screen is in the background. Similar to SLIC, after finding the matching keypoints, this methods also uses an HMM to further disambiguate the temporal matching — estimating which slide is shown during each video frame.

3 Characterizing the Slide Channel

The slides channel emerges once video frames are linked to the slides that were used in the presentation. Once this is done, text extracted from the slides can be used as semantic handles into the content. This is especially effective for two reasons. First, words can be extracted from the slides reliably compared with the obvious alternative of using automated speech recognition. This is especially true of technical words which are, ironically, the most important ones to get right. Second, slides are typically designed to summarize content, and words extracted from them are more likely to be good words for indexing.

The slides channel further enables segmenting the video into semantic chunks that are searchable and browsable by the extracted words. Further, for browsing, the images of the slides themselves provide effective icons for the chunk, as used in the SLIC system.

Finally, we consider the full use of the slides channel to include knowing the geometric mapping between the slide image in the frames, which is a linear transformation in homogeneous coordinates, specifically a homography [14]. Knowing this geometry means that user pointing gestures with respect to the video frame can be interpreted in the coordinate frame of the slide. Hence one knows, for example, what slide word is clicked, or which slide region should be magnified Further, slides can be backprojected into the video to improve its quality, or allow for better compression for studying the presentation with low bandwidth.

4 Applications of the Slides Channel

Video Browsing: Assisting a scholar in the browsing process is an excellent example in which cross-modality expresses itself:

We are accustomed to searching and finding text, or even presentation slides, on the web that are of interest to us. However, comparable capability in the case of video—notably educational videos—does not exist. The familiar (and sometimes awkward) process of finding textual information by retrieving many pages, and then sifting through the hits to find items of interest, completely breaks down in the case of video, even if transcripts are available and indexed. We usually have to either watch the video in its entirety or try fast-forwarding in our attempt to locate the information in which we are interested. More sophisticated video search tools, such as CueVideo [1], provide only modest help, and are not available to most users.

By presenting the slides to the students, and enabling them to browse through the slides and watch the video from the points at which these slides are discussed, SLIC is able to give the student efficient access to relevant material. Please refer to Fig.(2). This is helpful for a video of a single lecture, and even more so when the student is browsing slides of multiple lectures — e.g. an entire course. Moreover, a textual search of the text of the slides is far more accurate than a textual search of a transcript of the course.

Slide backprojection: The term *backprojection* in this context describes the process of substituting the slide image in the video frames with high resolution images from external slides. Subsequently, text and details of the slides that are too small and/or too blurry in the original video would appear much clearer and readable after backprojecting the slides. To successfully apply backprojection, the SLIC system relies on the high accuracy of homography described above between video frame pixels and external slide pixels. For each pixel $F_{i_{(x,y)}}$ in the frame region of frame i of the video, the system interpolates a color from the slide image S_j. Fig.(2) demonstrates the improvement in the quality and readability of the original frame (bottom), compared to the backprojected frame (top). Note that the projected slide region is sharper and the color is improved.

There are several ways in which backprojection can be accomplished. One is to generate a new video that the user can access, and treat it as if it is a "regular" video. This method enables careful adjustment of pixel colors. The method is simple from the user's standpoint. It can also assist in colors correction to best fit the original slide appearance. A slightly different method was presented in [30], based on sending to the user the (images of the) slides, the video of the lecture and the homography for each frame. An application on the client (user) side, for example SMIL (Synchronized Multimedia Integration Language) plays the video, while presenting the image of the slide as part of the frame seen by the user. The settings of the slide in the frame — its location and scales are determined by the homography. This method yields more visual artifacts, but yields a more detailed and sharper image. This method is more suitable for mobile applications, where low bandwidth limits the communication. It allows for higher compression while ensuring high quality where it is needed. The loss of detail from aggressive compression can be directed to less significant parts of the video such as the audience in the classroom, while the slide appearing in the video will stay sharp. Therefore, this technique significantly improves delivery and display of educational video in mobile devices with limited bandwidth availability and small screens such as PDAs or Smartphones.

Application to on-demand magnification: SLIC uses the slide-frame homographies to provide a magnifier utility, which provides a sharply magnified version of the slide region around a point clicked on by the user. This is very useful when the details of the slides appearing in the video are too blurry or too small. Notice that getting such detail from a slide image in some other window is often a poor alternative, as the user must then switch between the two and determine the correct location in the slide, losing the connection to the video context. Instead, in the SLIC system, once the user clicks on a specific point of the video player, its coordinates are back-transformed to the slide, providing the center of the region of (the image of) the slide of interest, which is then displayed with the desired enlargement factor. This is distinctly different than attempting to magnify the lower quality video and/or attempting to sharpen it (e.g. by the magnifying glass utility of Windows XP). With this approach, the only limitation on sharpness is the level of detail present in the original slide.

Laser Pointer Motion Semantics Laser pointers are frequently used by speakers in lectures to indicate a specific area of interest on a slide. Understanding where the laser pointer is directed on the video frame and hence the presentation slide can

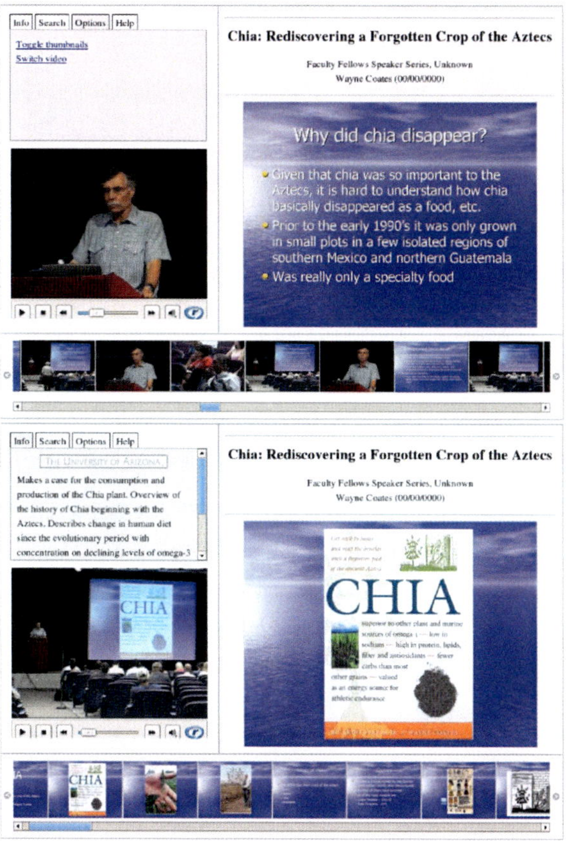

Fig. (1): Two ways of browsing videos [26]: a) by keyframes and b) by slides. Notice the difference at the bottom thumbnails slider. Slide changes provide a semantic video segmentation and are therefore more desirable for video browsing than keyframes extracted by shot boundary detection.

give us a good idea of what the main topic of focus is at that instant in time. The detection of laser pointer light is therefore of value for a good system for searching and browsing lectures.

In [30] the authors describes how to track the laser pointer robustly, and the spectrum of applications it enables. Since input video comes from external sources, scene brightness and color is unknown and frame differencing is used to remove these variations. For each frame of the video, a second frame is computed as the difference between the corresponding frame and a pixel-wise average of a set of proceeding frames in the original video. A median filter on brightness approximately equal in size to the laser pointer is then passed over each frame of the difference video. The brightest pixel from the resulting image is then selected. Curve fitting is used both for noise filtering and as input for following steps.

Fig. (2): Comparison between the original video frame, vs. frame after backprojection of the slide. The later is clearly much more readable.

The applications of the tracking include: (i) Seeking the instance in the video where a queried keyword is *emphasized* by the lecturer, and (ii) it is also used for enhancing, changing background colors, or enlarging ("zooming-in") portions of the relevant slides. The enlargement effect is especially useful for displaying on a small screen (e.g. smartphones) or helping visually impaired students.

5 Cross-Modality and the Internet.

All applications mentioned in the previous section fail to utilize the real potential of studying in an environment so rich of data as the internet. Seeing the variety of data sources on the web, we face two challenges. One is how to be an efficient consumer of this data, so a student watching an educational video could follow links that we would embed in the video and in the video browser, accurately finding most-relevant resources. The second challenge is to be good providers of the data withing videos created by ourselves and others in the community. Having the video deposited and accessible for view does not go far enough. We want to ensure that interested scholars can find exactly what they are looking for. What is more, we want the scholar to have easy access to video on their topic in alternative contexts (e.g., math presented in the context of math classes, versus application oriented discussion) and styles of presentation. The search for relevant video segments should not be harder than a search for relevant documents. As an analogy, we do not expect a scholar to need to skim through an entire online document that we have created when she seeks only a small portion of it. So, why should we expect her to listen to an entire lecture if she only needs knowledge from a short segment?

We show next how the usage of the "slide channel" can address both challenges.

Linking and Selectively Browsing Educational Videos from Multiple Sources: Once an educational video is processed by a system like SLIC, it can be linked to other online-available educational materials. First, keywords extracted from the video's slides form searchable terms that can be linked, for example, to standard internet sources such as Wikipedia and electronic books. Results could be further filtered and refined using speech recognition tools and context similarity. These links are embedded in the videos so that students browsing them can efficiently link to keyword-based content.

Second, the matching can link to other relevant educational videos that are available online. These videos may be located, for example, on the educational channels of Youtube, through Google searches of publicly available lectures, or via contributions to a repository that could potentially be formed by SLIC users willing to share videos with one another. Given the universe of potentially relevant videos, we have two tasks: to identify which videos are substantively relevant, and to automatically link to segments of relevant videos with appropriate supplementary content. Both tasks are easier if slides on which videos are based are separately available, since matching slides to other slides is much more robust than matching videos directly. Thus it seems quite feasible to make use of the slides channel, even without having the slides available as a separate data source. Here slides would be extracted and linked simultaneously. This is a research direction that we are actively pursuing.

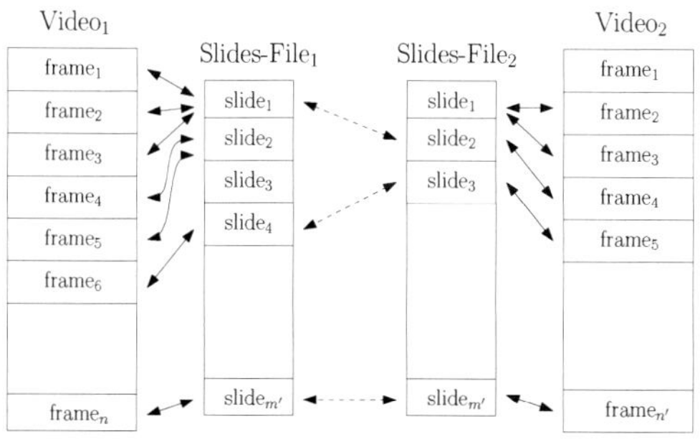

Fig. (3): This example demonstrates the potential of accurately linking frames of different videos once each video is linked to its slides file. Here we assume that the matching between $Video_1$ to $Slides\text{-}File_1$, and between $Video_2$ to $Slides\text{-}File_2$ are computed using for example SLIC, while the matching between $Slide\text{-}File_1$ and $Slide\text{-}File_2$ is computed based on textural and image matching. Hence implicitly obtaining the matching between $Video_1$ to $Video_2$. So for example in this illustration $frame_6$ in $Video_1$ is matched to $frame_5$ in $Video_2$.

Once slides are matched, the cross-modality nature of the materials provide data that is used to rank the overall relevance of a particular video. The two sets of slides from the original video and the target online video are then matched to each other. From these slide-matchings, we are capable of directly matching video segments, and embedding links within the material the user is browsing.

Making Videos Accessible via Internet Search Engines By piggybacking SLIC search mechanisms onto common search engines such as Google or Bing, content indexed by SLIC can be made widely and seamlessly available to internet searchers. Currently, a user searching for educational content will at best receive a link to powerpoint slides, if available on the web, or less commonly, a link to an entire video whose metadata happens to contain the search term. The user must then manually browse the slides and/or video to find relevant content, a tedious and potentially fruitless endeavor. The slides channel from SLIC solves the problem of indexing and locating relevant content by leveraging the natural partition of a video into meaningful *video segments* based on the slides the video contains.

SLIC can be extended to enable accurate search for video segments stored within the SLIC from anywhere on the web. A user can simply submit a query, and receive an appropriate video segment, with the accompanying slide in reply. The mechanism that allows search engines to index SLIC content is that each video has a website with meta-data indexing video segments and the text of the associated slide. Once a search engine such as Bing or Google invokes a SLIC webpage, the website in turn retrieves the text of the query from the search engine, and passes the query to SLIC. Next, SLIC uses its internal query mechanism to find the most appropriate video segment and play it. From the user's perspective, this process is transparent: she simply enters a query in a search engine, and is taken directly to the relevant segment of the SLIC website, where the video will begin automatically playing. The user will also be able to see and browse neighboring segments, and enjoy the other useful properties of SLIC mentioned above. In short, a searcher anywhere on the web can be just one click away of viewing otherwise difficult to locate and highly relevant educational content.

6 References

[1] Cuevideo. In *http://www.almaden.ibm.com/projects/cuevideo.shtml*

[2] G. D. Abowd, C. G. Atkeson, A. Feinstein, C. E. Hmelo, R. Kooper, S. Long, N. N. Sawhney, and M. Tani. Teaching and learning as multimedia authoring: The classroom 2000 project. In *ACM Multimedia*, 1996.

[3] A. Amir, G. Ashour, and S. Srinivasan. Automatic generation of conf. video proceedings. In *Journal of Visual Communication and Image Representation, JVCI Special Issue on Multimedia Databases*, 2004.

[4] A. Behera, D. Lalanne, and R. Ingold. Looking at projected documents: Event detection document identification. In *ICME*, 2004.

[5] Y. R. C. Zhang, J. Crawford and L. He. An automated end-to-end lecture capturing and broadcasting system. In *ACM Multimedia*, 2005.

[6] Y. Chen and W. J. Heng. Automatic synchronization of speech transcript and slides in presentation. In *ISCAS*, 2003.

[7] T. S. Consortium. Maing the grade: Online education in the united states, 2006. In *http://www.sloan.org/publications/survey/survey06.asp*, 2006.

[8] B. Erol, J. J. Hull, and D. Lee. Linking multimedia presentations with their symbolic source documents: algorithm and applications. In *ACM Multimedia*, 2003.

[9] Q. Fan, A. Amir, K. Barnard, R. Swaminathan, and A. Efrat. Temporal modeling of slide change in presentation videos. In *ICASSP*, 2007.

[10] Q. Fan, K. Barnard, A. Amir, and A. Efrat. Accurate alignment of presentation slides with educational video. In *ICME*, 2009.

[11] Q. Fan, K. Barnard, A. Amir, A. Efrat, and M. Lin. Matching slides to presentation videos using sift and scene background matching. In *MIR*, 2006.

[12] A. Fischler, M. and C. Bolles, R. Random sample consensus: A paradigm for model fitting with applications to image analysis and automated cartography. *Comm. of the ACM*, 1981.

[13] G. Gigonzac, F. Pitie, and A. Kokaram. Electronic slide matching and enhancement of a lecture video. *IET Conference Publications*, 2007.

[14] R. Hartley and A. Zisserman. *Multiple View Geometry in Computer Vision.* Cambridge University Press, 2000.

[15] T. Liu, R. Hjelsvold, and R. Kender, J. Analysis and enhancement of videos of electronic slide presentations. *ICME*, 2002.

[16] M. Liwicki and H. Bunke. *Recognition of Whiteboard Notes: Online, Offline and Combination.* World Scientific Pub Co Inc, 2008.

[17] D. Lowe. Distinctive image features from scale-invariant keypoints. *International Journal of Computer Vision*, 2004.

[18] MediaSite. In *http://www.mediasite.com*, 2004.

[19] MSproducer. Microsoft producer: - a capturing and authoring tool for distance learning. In `http://www.microsoft.com/windows/windowsmedia/technologies/producer.mspx`, 2003.

[20] S. Mukhopadhyay and B. Smith. Passive capture and structuring of lectures. In *ACM Multimedia*, 1999.

[21] J. M. Rowe, L. A. andGonzelez. Bmrc lecture browsers. In `http://bmrc.berkekey.edu/frame/projects/lb/index.html`, 1999.

[22] T. Russell. *The No Significant Difference Phenomenon as Reported in 355 Research Reports, Summaries and Papers.* North Carolina State University Press, 1999.

[23] C. Snoek and M. Worring. Multimodal video indexing: A review of the state-of-the-art. *Multimedia Tools and Applications*, 2005.

[24] T. F. Syeda-Mahmood. Indexing for topics in videos using foils. In *CVPR*, 2000.

[25] J. Torkkola, Q. Fan, R. Swaminathan, A. Winslow, K. Barnard, A. Amir, A. Efrat, C. Gniady, and S. Fong. The slic video browsing system demo. `http://vision.cs.arizona.edu/SLIC`, 2005.

[26] ——. The slic video browsing system demo. `http://vision.cs.arizona.edu/SLIC`, 2005.

[27] B. Triggs, P. McLauchlan, R. Hartley, and A. Fitzgibbon. Bundle adjustment – A modern synthesis. In *Vision Algorithms: Theory and Practice*, ser. LNCS, W. Triggs, A. Zisserman, and R. Szeliski, Eds. Springer Verlag, 2000.

[28] F. Wang, C.-W. Ngo, and T.-C. Pong. Synchronization of lecture videos and electronic slides by video text analysis In *ACM Multimedia*, 2003.

[29] X. Wang and M. Kankanhalli. Robust Alignment of Presentation Videos with Slides. In *PCM*, 2009.

[30] A. Winslow, Q. Tung, Q. Fan, J. Torkkola, R. Swaminathan, K. Barnard, A. Amir, A. Efrat, and C. Gniady. Studying on the move-enriched presentation video for mobile devices. *IEEE INFOCOM Workshops*, 2009.

Internet Multimedia Search and Mining, 2013, 367-396

CHAPTER 14

Web Music Indexing and Search

Lie Lu*
Dolby Laboratories, Tel: +86-10-59103052, Fax: +86-10-59103001
Email: llu@dolby.com

Zhiwei Li
Microsoft Research Asia, Tel: +86-10-59173195, Fax: +86-10-88097306
Email: zli@microsoft.com

Abstract: This chapter presents music indexing schemes by exploiting and utilizing two data sources: surrounding text on web pages and metedata describing music attributes. We first present a framework to index and organize web music by discovering its inherent structure attributes with trustworthy domain knowledge. In this approach, layered LSI spaces are first built to represent the hierarchically structured domain knowledge, music object representation is then constructed through hyperlink analysis, and the structure attributes of a music object is finally discovered by matching against the domain knowledge. This approach also indicates a new way to organize dispersive information on the Surface Web by using trustworthy Deep Web knowledge. We further present our work on enhancing music indexing with automatic music annotation, which attempts to automatically annotate a music object with a set of semantic labels (tags) to create metadata describing its attributes and to facilitate music search, organization, and recommendation. Besides modeling music annotation as a multi-label binary classification task, we also attempt to discover the correlation between semantic labels and present an approach to collective music semantic annotation.

Keywords

Music indexing, music search, automatic music annotation, collective annota-

***Correspondence Author:** Lie Lu, Dolby Laboratories; Email: llu@dolby.com.

Xian-Sheng Hua, Marcel Worring & Tat-Seng Chua (Eds.)

tion, deep web, knowledge space building, layered LSI, web object, web object representation, confidence propagation, multi-label classification

1 Introduction

Searching for music and related information is popular in daily life. Considerable efforts have been investigated in both research community and industry to build music search engines. To facilitate music search, music needs to be indexed first. In general, two major data sources (and correspondingly, two methodologies) can be applied for music indexing:

1. The surrounding text of a music object on a web page, including the related information such as anchor text. Various user generated contents (UGC) can be also used to index music, such as users' music reviews in a forum. This set of data provides description of a music object to some extent, however, it is usually not well-organized, noisy, and insufficient to represent music attributes.

2. The metedata or tags that directly describe music attributes, such as artist, genre, melody, and emotion. This kind of data usually needs manual creation, either by users (such as Last.fm) or by experts (such as Pandora.com). However, manual metadata creation is expensive and not scalable. Alternatively, automatic music annotation through content-based analysis gains more and more attention in recent years for music indexing and search.

Meanwhile, the term "music search" can refer to different applications, scenarios or methodologies that in turn define the data sources that can be used for music indexing. Some typical examples include,

1. General web music search: search music dispersed on the Web, which is usually unstructured and lacks of sufficient information describing music. This application is considered in this chapter, by structuring the surrounding text on the Web and automatic music metadata generation.

2. Vertical music search: search music through one or multiple dedicated music databases. In this application, music is usually well-structured, typically in a hierarchical structure including artist, album, and track. With the structured data, music search can be as straightforward as keyword matching.

3. Implicit music search: search music without an explicit query. One typical example is music recommendation. In this application, the listening history of a user plays an important role in modeling his personalized profile. A number of technologies, such as collaborative filtering and content-based music similarity measure, are developed.

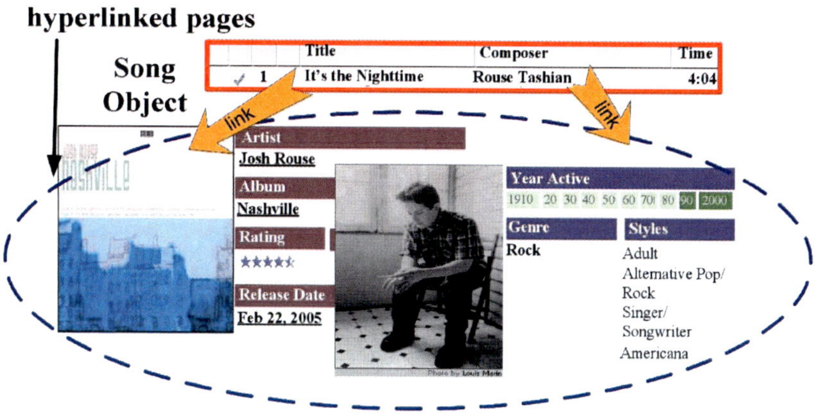

Fig. (1): An example of "music object".

Traditional web music search engines use surrounding text to index music, by employing similar indexing methods as those used in general web search. For example, when a music object (e.g. a hyperlink pointing to a MP3 file) is detected in a web page, a number of words (typically twenty) appearing before and after the music object, including the title of the web page and the anchor text, are extracted as the "descriptions" of the music object. These words can be efficiently indexed by the inverted list technology [39], and accordingly, a search engine can be deployed based on keyword matching. However, keyword-based search may not satisfy user's requirement. For example, one uses the query "Beatles" to search for Beatles' albums and songs, instead of the web pages containing the query term. It implies that, a real "music object oriented" indexing scheme is expected, and more structured and intelligent search results are preferred.

To index a "music object" embedded in a web page, besides the surrounding text on the web page, its neighboring (hyperlinked) pages also provide useful complementary information. Fig. (**1**) illustrates an example of music object with the description of its album and performer in the hyperlinked web pages. Moreover, music objects usually lie in a hierarchical structure, for example, as Fig. (**2**) shows, in a structure of artist-album-song(track). Such a structure provides a potential way to organize music resources distributed dispersedly on the Web.

In "Deep" Web sites, such as All Music Guide (AMG) (http://www.allmusic.com), music is usually well organized and presented in a hierarchical structure, where each node in the structure is described by an individual web page and the hierarchical relationship between them is preserved by a hyperlink. However, in most "Surface" Web, the structure information is not explicitly presented. Thus, a natural idea is that, the structured domain knowledge (such as those presented in the Deep Web) can be utilized to identify the "structure attributes" of the music objects on the

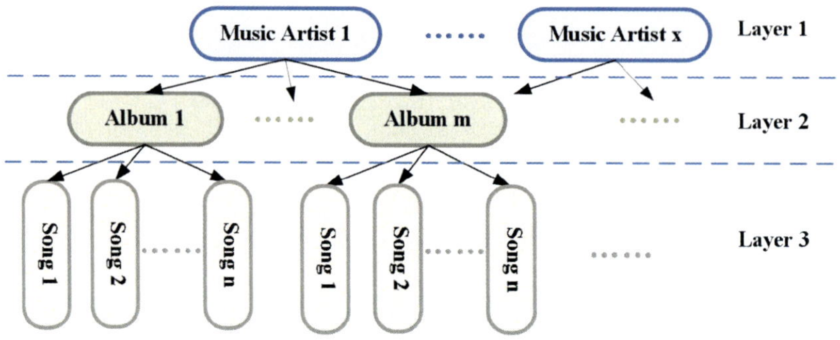

Fig. (2): Hierarchical structure of music objects, which includes three layers: artist, album and song.

surface Web and organize the search results in such a structure. For convenience, we use "structure attributes" to indicate the position (or level) of a music object in the structured hierarchy and the related information that can be identified, such as its artist, album, and song title. In addition, we use "knowledge document" in the coming sections to indicate the description of a music object in a document of the domain knowledge (e.g. a Deep Web page).

To facilitate web music object search, in this chapter, we present a general framework to index music on the surface web and organize them based on the discovered (implicit) structure attributes, based on the hierarchically structured domain knowledge. There are two major difficulties: 1) Lack of information. The information surrounding a music object is usually noisy and insufficient to represent the music object. It is critical to enrich the description of the target music object and prune the noisy information. 2) Difficult to identify the structure attributes. Even with sufficient information, it still leaves a difficult problem to extract the structure information. Although some hierarchical clustering methods are proposed to detect a semantic structure, the obtained hierarchy is usually not meaningful to a domain-specific object [3]. It also meets some traditional obstacles like polysemy and synonymy due to various word usages in different web pages. Moreover, the traditional wrapper-based information extraction approaches [21] are not suitable in this application, since a wrapper is usually specialized to only one kind of web pages but cannot be adapted to diverse surface web pages. To deal with these problems, we present a non-clustering and non-wrapper approach to music indexing, by integrating hyperlink analysis and domain knowledge. Hyperlink analysis is used to enrich the textual description of the music object, and domain knowledge is used to prune noise and identify structure attributes.

Besides surrounding text and hyperlinks on web pages, an alternative way to enrich the description of music objects, as mentioned above, is to exploit and utilize music metedata or tags. While common editorial metadata, such as artist, album and track, provides a good entry to browse music, more intelligent tags describing key music attributes, such as genre, instruments, tempo, melody and emotion [17], can greatly help music indexing, organization and search. These tags also open the possibility to search music in new ways. Compared with traditional music search that usually uses title, album or artist as a query, with these tags available, we can search music based on genre, select music based on tempo and rhythm, or organize music based on emotion. For example, one can choose light music with soft volume and slow tempo when he wants to relax, and one can also choose music with strong rhythm and beat for his workout at gymnasium. However, this kind of data is usually hard to obtain. The most straightforward way is manual annotation. For example, Pandora.com assigns each song up to 400 musical characteristics obtained by trained music analysts to help users discover new music they like. However, manual annotation is usually tedious, expensive and time consuming. As an alternative way, automatic music annotation through content-based analysis gains more and more attention in recent years.

Automatic music annotation attempts to automatically annotate a music object by a set of semantic labels (words or tags) which best describe its attributes, through music signal processing and music-label modeling. Current approaches to automatic music annotation can be basically divided into two categories: *non-parametric* and *parametric*. Non-parametric methods model the text-audio relations implicitly. For example, Slaney [30] created separate hierarchical models in the acoustic space and text space, and linked two spaces for annotation and retrieval. Cano and Koppenberger [4] proposed an approach to predict semantic words based on nearest neighbor classification. On the other hand, parametric methods explicitly model the text-audio relations. For instance, Whitman *et al.* [36, 37] trained a one-versus-all discriminative model for each semantic word, based on which each audio frame can be classified. Turnbull *et al.* [33] built a generative model for each semantic word, and calculated a multinomial distribution over the word vocabulary for each song. Eck *et al.* [8] used AdaBoost to predict the strength of the occurrence of each social tag on a large audio data set.

The methods abovementioned achieved good results by modeling the text-audio relations, however, they share two drawbacks. First, taxonomy is lacked to organize the semantic labels. One consequence is that: a song is not guaranteed to be annotated from all the meaningful music attributes, so that tags from some attributes may dominate while tags from other attributes may be missed. Second, in the previous methods, semantic labels are modeled individually, that is, the methods only build text-audio relations, but ignore the text-text relations between two labels. However, some labels do have strong correlation, and this information can be investigated to improve annotation schemes. For example, "hard rock" and "electronic guitar" tend to co-occur in the annotation of a song, while "happy" and "minor key" are rare to co-occur. To address these issues, in this chapter, we present an approach to *collective* music annotation with a set of category-based semantic vocabulary.

The rest of this chapter is organized as follows: a framework of web music indexing is first presented, including a layered indexing scheme of hierarchical domain knowledge, music object representation through hyperlink analysis, and inherent structure attribute detection with confidence propagation. Next, automatic music annotation is presented to enhance web music search, where a collective annotation scheme is attempted. Subsequently, evaluation on representative music data sets is presented, and the related work and conclusions are given at the end.

2 Web Music Indexing

Fig. **(3)** illustrates the framework of web music indexing: using the structured domain knowledge to index and organize the music dispersed on the web. This framework is adapted from our previous work [35] on "web object" indexing. For generality, we still use the term "web object" in this framework, however it is clear that the web object is meant to be a music object in the context. The framework is mainly composed of three steps: knowledge space building, web object representation, and web object indexing. In the first step, Layered Latent Semantic Indexing (Layered LSI) spaces are built from the hierarchically-structured domain knowledge for further use in web object representation and identification. In the second step, a target web object is represented in the Layered LSI spaces, through hyperlink analysis and noisy page/word pruning. In the third step, the structure attributes of a web object is identified by matching against the domain knowledge, in the Layered LSI spaces as well. Although the presented framework emphasizes on utilizing the domain knowledge and its hierarchical structure, the approach is also feasible for non-hierarchical structure, which can be considered as a special case of hierarchical structure with the layer number equal to one.

Knowledge space building

Both the web object description and knowledge documents are text on the webpage. However, they are usually edited by different authors. This fact leads to their different term spaces. In order to address this problem, in our approach, Latent Semantic Indexing (LSI) is used to index the knowledge documents. In some degree, LSI is capable to deal with polysemy and synonymy problems as indicated in text retrieval applications [7].

Moreover, as shown in Fig. **(2)**, a knowledge source is usually hierarchically structured (tree-like), where each layer has a different semantic concept and thus has a different term space. For instance, the typical three layers in music domain represent the concepts of artist, album, and song, and the term "Beatles" is more probable to appear at the "artist" layer, but less at the "album" or "song" layer.

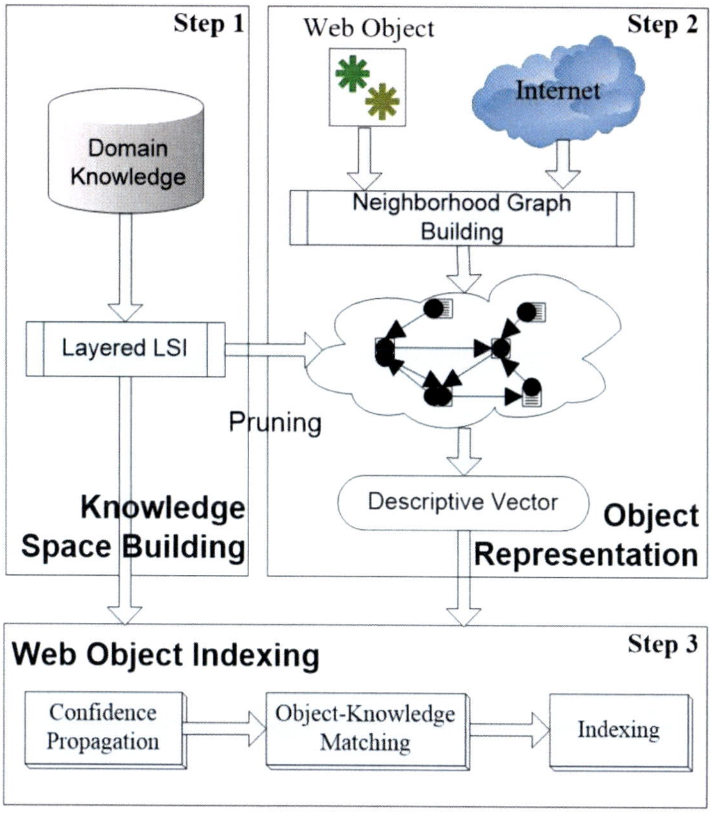

Fig. (3): The framework of web object indexing.

In addition, the scale of the term space at each layer is also different. If all the layers are indexed together into one LSI space, the layer with smaller term space will be overwhelmed by the larger one. It implies that the term importance in the small-scale layer will be unfairly reduced. Therefore, in our approach, each layer is indexed independently and Layered LSI spaces are finally composed.

To build the Layered LSI spaces, the knowledge documents are tokenized to construct a term-document co-occurrence matrix, where TFIDF is used as the weighting function in the co-occurrence matrix, as:

$$\text{TFIDF}(w) = f(w) \cdot \log \frac{N}{|D(w)|} \tag{1}$$

where w denotes a term, $f(w)$ represents the term frequency, N is the dimension of the term space, and $D(w)$ stands for the set of documents that contain term w. Supposing there are c layers in the knowledge source and the weighted term-document matrix in each layer is denoted as $A_i, (i = 1, ..., c)$, each matrix can be decomposed by SVD as,

$$A_i = U_i \Sigma_i {V_i}^T \tag{2}$$

The largest k singular values are subsequently selected to construct the latent semantic space of A_i, denoted as A_i^k,

$$A_i^k = U_i^k \Sigma_i^k {V_i^k}^T \tag{3}$$

The built semantic spaces will be used for both domain knowledge representation and web object representation and indexing. In these two steps, all the web pages describing the target web object are mapped to the Layered LSI spaces. It helps remove irrelevant words that are out of domain. As mentioned above, each layer of domain knowledge has its unique semantics and term space. From this point of view, when a web page is projected to a layer of the LSI spaces, in some degree, only the words that accord with the corresponding semantics are amplified, while other irrelevant words are suppressed or removed.

Web object representation

The preliminary information of a web object can be found from its surrounding text or the corresponding web block [3]. However, the information is usually insufficient to describe the web object and may also contain many noisy words. In order to enrich the web object representation, a neighborhood graph around the web object is constructed with hyperlink analysis, where neighborhood pages are considered since they usually help verify or complement the information about the web object.

Fig. (4) illustrates an example neighborhood graph, where the web page or the web block containing the target web object is taken as the graph center, and all the related web pages are "connected" to each other according to their hyperlinks. It is an undirected graph with each web page taken as a node and each hyperlink as an edge, and can be efficiently built by the approach proposed in [14]. In the following sections, the web page (or web block) containing the target web object is referred to as "container" for simplicity, and a page linked to the container is called "neighborhood page".

In general, the fewer steps (hyperlinks) a neighborhood page takes to connect to the container, the more closely it is related to the target web object. Therefore, the layer number of the graph, which determines how far the webpages are considered, is an important factor in web object representation. With a larger layer number, more pages are included to describe the web object, but more irrelevant (noisy) information is also introduced. The noisy pages do not contribute to our task and will even lead to "topic drift" [2], such as the "contact us" page and "how to buy" page. They are necessary to be removed for further processing.

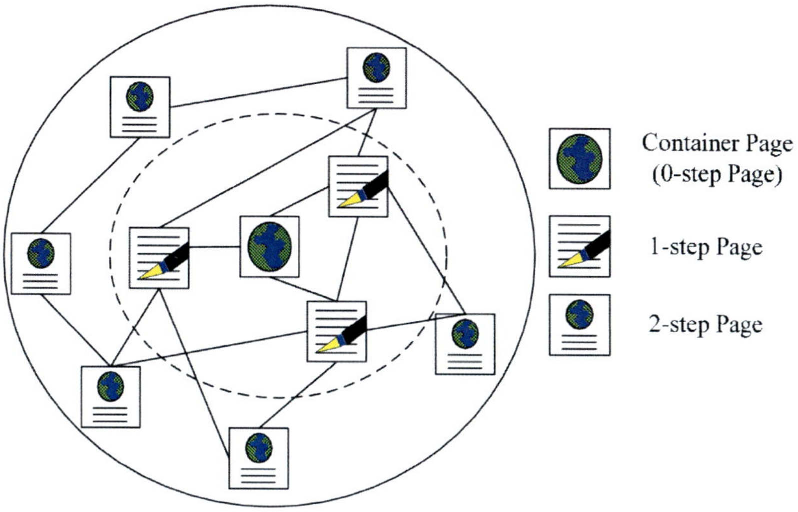

Fig. (4): A 2-layer neighborhood graph with 1- and 2-step pages.

To remove the noisy pages, the similarity between each neighborhood page and the container is calculated, assuming the page that is similar to the container is more relevant to the web object. In our approach, a cosine measure is applied in each layer's LSI space. The similarity in the jth-layer represents the confidence that the corresponding page has mutual semantics with the container from the viewpoint of the jth-layer. Intuitively, the pages with small similarity can be considered as noisy pages [2] and removed, with an experimentally determined threshold called *cutoff* percentage. With the measured similarities in different layers, a candidate set of noisy pages is obtained from each layer. Since different pages have different semantics and may get different confidences in different layers, only the intersection of these candidate sets is considered as noisy pages and pruned from the neighborhood graph.

Once the noisy pages are removed in the neighborhood graph, we can integrate the textual information from all the pages to give a better representation of the web object. In our approach, the weighted centroid of the neighborhood graph is used as the representation vector of the web object, which is defined as,

$$C = \sum_{D_i \in G} w_i D_i \tag{4}$$

where G is the pruned neighborhood graph, D_i is a web page in G, and w_i is the weight of the web page D_i. This weight is set according to the path steps from the corresponding web page to the container. A general rule is, the fewer steps the page takes, the higher weight it is assigned. In our method, the weight is experimentally defined as the following formula and then normalized to one,

$$w_i \propto \frac{1}{\log(d_i + 2)} \tag{5}$$

where d_i is the corresponding path steps, and the constant "2" is heuristically set in order to avoid zero in the denominator.

Web object indexing

To this end, the structure attributes of the target web object can be extracted by discovering the best matched knowledge document. For this purpose, the similarity between the web object representation and each knowledge document in each layer is calculated, using cosine measure as well. One straightforward way to find the best matched document is to sort the obtained similarity scores in the corresponding target layer. However, a potential problem of this method is that the unavoidable noise may greatly harm the accuracy. To deal with this issue, the hierarchical structure of domain knowledge is utilized, and each candidate document in the target layer is reranked by cross-verification with its relatives (including ancestors and offspring). For example, as Fig. (**5**) shows, the confidence of the node T (a candidate document) is reranked by considering the confidence score from its ancestors (node 1-2) and offspring (node 3-7). This process is called *confidence propagation*. The confidences from the relatives actually represent the similarity between the candidate document and the target web object in the corresponding semantic layers. The final score is thus cross-verified from various semantic layers.

The confidence propagation from the relatives of a candidate document can be divided into two directions, propagating from its ancestor (root) nodes (top-down), and propagating from its offspring nodes (bottom-up), as Fig. (**5**) illustrates. In the top-down propagation, confidence scores of the upper-layers in the path from the root to the candidate document are directly summed up. It is feasible since the corresponding path is unique. However, from its offspring, the bottom-up propagation path is not unique. If the scores of all the paths from the candidate document to its offspring are also summed up, the candidate document with lots of offspring would be over-weighted. Therefore, an average score is chosen: the candidate document with a "big" subtree is "punished" by dividing the number of its children.

The math expression of confidence propagation is shown in Eq. (**6**), which sequentially combines the information from the upper and lower layers, as well as

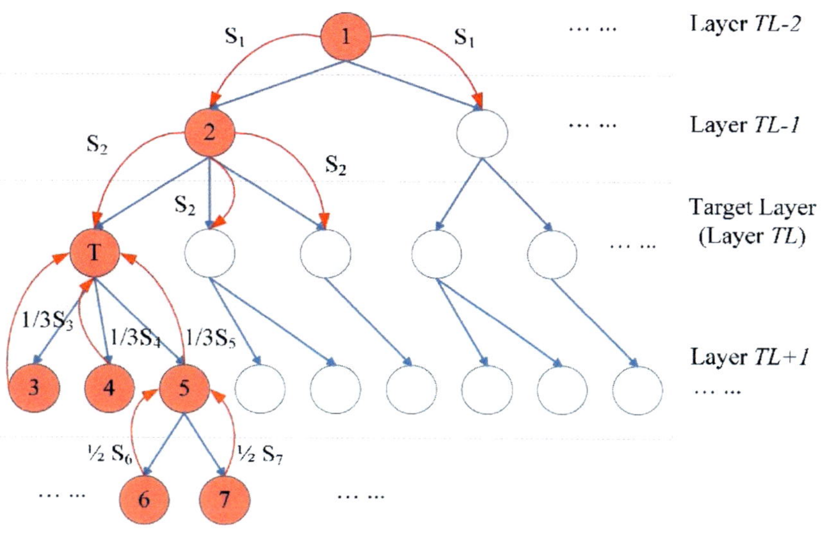

Fig. (5): Web object matching and confidence propagation.

normalizes information coming from lower layers.

$$\begin{aligned} D(r_i) &= s(r_i) + \sum_{k \in par(r_i)} D(k), 1 \leq i < TL \\ U(r_i) &= s(r_i) + \sum_{k \in chi(r_i)} \frac{U(k)}{NC(r_i)}, TL \leq i < L \\ S(r_{TL}) &= s(r_{TL}) + \sum_{k \in par(r_{TL})} D(k) + \sum_{l \in chi(r_{TL})} \frac{U(l)}{NC(r_{TL})} \end{aligned} \quad (6)$$

where $s(\cdot)$ and $S(\cdot)$ represents the original and updated confidence of a document; $U(\cdot)$ and $D(\cdot)$ means the propagated confidence from bottom-up and top-down, respectively; r is a knowledge document and its subscript represents its semantic layer; L is the layer number of domain knowledge and TL is the target layer; $par(\cdot)$ and $chi(\cdot)$ stands for the set of parents and children of a document, and $NC(\cdot)$ is the number of its children. After confidence propagation, the candidate document with the highest similarity score $S(r_{TL})$ is chosen as the optimal document that best describes the structure attributes of the target web object.

Once the web object is matched with a knowledge document, the trust-worthy domain knowledge can be used to extract the structure attributes of the web object for further music indexing and organization. It can be divided into two cases:

1. If the domain knowledge is fully-structured, such as a database, the keys of each record (entry) can be used to represent the structure attributes of the

web object. For example, if a song object is matched with a record in a database where the corresponding metadata, such as artist, album, genre, and the release year, is available as keys of the record, these metadata can be used to index the song as "index terms". Furthermore, based on the structure of the domain knowledge, the keys of the *related* records can also be used to describe and index the target web object.

2. If the domain knowledge is not a structured database, for example, the knowledge document is not a record but a plain text, the text is chosen to better describe the web object. Traditional indexing schemes in text retrieval can be used to index the web object.

3 Enhancing Music Indexing with Automatic Music Annotation

The above method utilizes the surrounding information of a music object and uses domain knowledge to discover its structure attributes. On the other hand, the content of the music signal can be analyzed to discover more semantic music attributes, such as genre, rhythm, tempo, instruments and emotion, which can be further used to enrich the music description. While manual annotation of music attributes is expensive and tedious, automatic music annotation provides a more scalable way and becomes an important direction in the field of music information retrieval.

The main objective of automatic music annotation, briefly, is to select a subset of tags or labels that best describe the attributes of a given music object from a semantic vocabulary. A semantic vocabulary lists all the tags or labels that can be used for semantic annotation. Currently there is not a standard vocabulary, and most researchers build their own vocabularies. Cano and Koppenberger [4] used the taxonomy provided by WordNet (http://wordnet.princeton.edu/wn2.0). Whitman and Rifkin [36] extracted about 700 words from web documents associated with artists. Turnbull *et al.* [33] extracted 135 musically relevant words spanning six semantic categories from song reviews. These vocabularies are usually large enough to cover various aspects of music attributes. However, due to the large vocabulary, it is usually hard to avoid preference over words when acquiring the ground truth annotations.

Another problem is that there lacks of a music-related taxonomy to organize the semantic labels. Music has a number of important aspects affecting music perception, such as genre, instrumentation, emotion, and tempo. The semantic labels used for music annotation can be naturally divided into groups corresponding to these aspects. However, in most of the annotation methods, the labels are not structurally organized. For example, Turnbull *et al.* [33] calculated the posterior

Tab. (1): The vocabulary contains 50 quantized labels and spans 10 semantic categories. Each song is annotated by labels from each category with a number limitation.

Category	**Words**	**Num**
Genre	Blues, Country, Electronica, Folk, Funk, Gospel, HardRock, Jazz, Pop, Punk, Rap, R&b, Rock-roll, SoftRock	1-2
Instrument	Acoustic guitar, Acoustic piano, Bass, Drum, Electric guitar, Electric piano, Harmonica, Horn, Organ, Percussion, Sax, String	1-5
Texture	Acoustic, Electric, Synthetic	1-2
Vocal	Group, Male, Female, No	1-2
Affective	Positive, Neutral, Negative	1
Arousal	Strong, Middle, Weak	1
Rhythm	Strong, Middle, Weak	1
Tempo	Fast, Moderato, Slow	1
Tonality	Major, Mixed, Minor	1
Production	Studio, Live	1

probability of each label word in the vocabulary given a song, and selected a constant number of labels (with the largest posterior probability) to annotate the song. One consequence is that it cannot guarantee that a song is annotated from each aspect of music attributes, and cannot avoid two words contradictive to each other are both chosen to annotate the same music object.

In this chapter, we build a simplified (but still general) vocabulary from a list of web-parsed musically relevant words. 50 commonly used labels are manually selected and quantized, covering 10 semantic categories (aspects) to describe characteristics of music signals. Tab. ((**1**)) lists the vocabulary. Using this vocabulary, each song is annotated by labels from every category with a label number limitation. It solves the problem that the labels in some semantic aspects are missed in the annotation of a music signal if the vocabulary is not organized as categories. It is noticed that multiple labels can be selected from the categories of genre, instrument, texture, and vocal, while the labels in the other categories are exclusive with each other.

It is also noted that, as mentioned previously, some labels in the vocabulary have strong correlation, either *positive* or *negative*. For example, "Genre.HardRock" and

"Arousal.Strong" tend to co-occur frequently (with a positive correlation), while "Tonality.Major" and "Affective.Negative" tend rarely to co-occur (with a negative correlation).

To measure the correlation between two labels (X, Y), the normalized mutual information (NormMI) is used, as

$$\text{NormMI}(X, Y) = \frac{I(X, Y)}{\min\{H(X), H(Y)\}} \quad (7)$$

where $I(X, Y)$ is the mutual information between X and Y

$$I(X, Y) = \sum_{x \in \{+1, -1\}} \sum_{y \in \{+1, -1\}} P(x, y) \log \frac{P(x, y)}{P_X(x) P_Y(y)} \quad (8)$$

and $H(x)$ is the entropy of label X defined by

$$H(X) = - \sum_{x \in \{+1, -1\}} P_X(x) \log P_X(x) \quad (9)$$

Here $+1$ or -1 is the value representing the presence or absence of a label. The probability $P_X(x)$, $P_Y(y)$, and $P(X, Y)$ can be estimated from a training set.

NormMI(X, Y) has the following properties:

1. $0 \leq \text{NormMI}(X, Y) \leq 1$;
2. $\text{NormMI}(X, Y) = 0$ when X and Y is statistically independent;
3. $\text{NormMI}(X, X) = 1$.

NormMI considers label correlation only, and is irrelevant to the distribution of an individual label. The larger the NormMI is, the stronger the correlation is (either positive or negative). Tab. ((**2**)) lists several selected label pairs with high NormMI values. These correlations will be investigated in music annotation.

In the following sections, we will first present the music features used in music-label modeling, and then present the schemes of music annotation .

Audio feature extraction

Each song is first divided into frames by a sliding window (20ms-length with 10ms-overlap). Tempo estimation and beat tracking are performed, based on which a song is further divided into beat-aligned segments, and each segment contains a number of successive frames. A bag of beat-level feature vectors are extracted to represent a song. Each feature vector contains two sub feature sets: timbre feature and rhythm feature, as

Tab. (2): Selected label pairs with high normalized mutual information. The label pairs in the first five rows are from the same semantic category and negatively correlated, and those in the last five rows are from different categories.

Word pair	NormMI
(Production.Live, Production.Studio)	1.00
(Vocal.Female, Vocal.Male)	0.79
(Tonality.Major, Tonality.Minor)	0.69
(Tempo.Fast, Tempo.Moderato)	0.62
(Rhythm.Middle, Rhythm.Strong)	0.56
(Genre.Electronica, Texture.Synthetic)	0.25
(Arousal.Weak, Rhythm.Weak)	0.24
(Instrument.AcousticGuitar, Texture.Acoustic)	0.23
(Instrument.Drum, Rhythm.Weak)	0.23
(Genre.HardRock, Instrument.ElectricGuitar)	0.19

Timbre Features For each audio frame, three classes of spectral features are calculated, including Mel-frequency cepstral coefficient (MFCC), spectral shape feature and spectral contrast feature. The spectral shape feature, including brightness, bandwidth, rolloff, and spectral flux, is commonly used in genre classification [34]. The spectral contrast feature, which was originally proposed in [18] and shown successful in different applications [23, 24], is used as a complement of MFCC on the sub-band information. These three classes of features constitute a 47-dimensional frame-level feature vector. Finally, the mean and standard deviation of the frame-level timbre features in each beat-aligned segment compose a beat-level timbre feature vector, which is 94-dimensional.

Rhythm Features Rhythm is also an important characteristic of music. In our approach, a 20-second window (with current beat-segment sitting in the middle) is used in rhythm feature extraction. Following [24], eight rhythm features are extracted, including average tempo, average onset frequency, rhythm regularity, rhythm contrast, rhythm strength, average drum frequency, drum amplitude, and drum confidence.

By concatenating these two sub feature sets , a 102-dimensional beat-level feature vector is extracted for each beat segment. Furthermore, Mean and Variance Normalization (MVN) is applied for feature normalization, and Principle Component Analysis (PCA) is employed to reduce the dimensionality of the feature vector to 65, reserving 95% of its energy.

The reason of using beat-level features is that a beat is a basic unit in music presentation, and it covers a relatively long period so that it can represent some high-level music characteristics which would be helpful for the annotation task. Besides, beat-level features are more compact than the frame-level features to represent a song, which hence results in a lower computational complexity.

Music semantic annotation

Given a vocabulary $\mathcal{V}$ consisting of $|\mathcal{V}|$ word labels $w_i \in \mathcal{V}$, and a song s represented by a bag of T real-valued feature vectors $\mathcal{X} = \{\mathbf{x}_1, \cdots, \mathbf{x}_T\}$, the goal of music semantic annotation is to find a set $\mathcal{W} = \{w_1, \cdots, w_A\}$ of A words best describing the song. It is convenient to represent the set $\mathcal{W}$ as an annotation vector $\mathbf{y} = (y_1, ..., y_{|\mathcal{V}|})$. Here y_i is a binary variable, valued 1 or -1 to represent "presence" or "absence" of label w_i. Accordingly, a training dataset $\mathcal{D}$ can be represented as a collection of song-annotation pairs $\mathcal{D} = \{(\mathcal{X}_1, \mathbf{y}_1), \cdots, (\mathcal{X}_{|\mathcal{D}|}, \mathbf{y}_{|\mathcal{D}|})\}$.

In general, this annotation problem can be addressed by maximum *a posterior* (MAP). That is, the best annotation is the annotation vector with maximum posterior probability: $\hat{\mathbf{y}} = \arg\max P(\mathbf{y}|\mathcal{X})$ [33]. In existing methods, the labels are treated independent, so that the posterior probability of an annotation vector can be decomposed into the multiplication of the posterior probability of each label as

$$P(\mathbf{y}|\mathcal{X}) = \prod_i^{|\mathcal{V}|} P(y_i|\mathcal{X}) \propto \prod_i^{|\mathcal{V}|} p(\mathcal{X}|y_i)P(y_i) \tag{10}$$

Assuming that feature vectors $\mathbf{x}_1, \cdots, \mathbf{x}_T$ are independent, then

$$p(\mathcal{X}|y_i) = \prod_t^{T} p(\mathbf{x}_t|y_i) \tag{11}$$

where T is the number of feature vectors in the bag $\mathcal{X}$. The likelihood $p(\mathbf{x}_t|y_i)$ can be estimated using a parametric model such as a GMM from the training data. The prior probability $P(y_i)$ can be estimated as well or set to a uniform distribution as usual.

However, as mentioned above, the labels are not independent. Their correlation can be investigated to collectively annotate the target music. In the following sections, two collective approaches are exploited: a GMM-based method, and a Conditional Random Field (CRF)-based method.

GMM-based collective annotation

If the labels are not independent, the joint posterior probability $P(\mathbf{y}|\mathcal{X})$ cannot be decomposed into single label posteriors. Instead, we approximate it using the multiplication of single label posteriors and label-pair posteriors.

$$P(\mathbf{y}|\mathcal{X}) \sim \prod_i^{|\mathcal{V}|} P(y_i|\mathcal{X}) \left(\prod_j^{|\mathcal{E}|} P(y_{e_j^1}, y_{e_j^2}|\mathcal{X}) \right)^{\alpha} \tag{12}$$

$$\propto \prod_i^{|\mathcal{V}|} p(\mathcal{X}|y_i)P(y_i) \left(\prod_j^{|\mathcal{E}|} p(\mathcal{X}|y_{e_j^1}, y_{e_j^2})P(y_{e_j^1}, y_{e_j^2}) \right)^{\alpha} \tag{13}$$

where $\mathcal{E}$ is a set of selected label pairs that have large normalized mutual information, e_j^1 and e_j^2 are the two labels in the pair, α is a tradeoff parameter balancing label posteriors and label-pair posteriors, which is set to 1 in our experiment. Although the right part of Eq.(12) is not the exact decomposition of $P(\mathbf{y}|\mathcal{X})$, it represents the intuitive idea that the annotation should not only maximize the posterior probabilities of individual labels, but also consider the posteriors of the correlated label pairs.

In our implementation, we trained a 8-kernel GMM to model the feature distribution of each label or each label pair. With these models, the computation of the likelihood $p(\mathcal{X}|y_i)$ and $p(\mathcal{X}|y_{e_j^1}, y_{e_j^2})$ is straightforward based on Eq.(11), assuming the feature vectors are independent.

CRF-based collective annotation

Conditional Random Field (CRF) was proposed by Lafferty *et al.* [22] to segment and label sequence data such as natural language. It is an undirected graphical model, where the nodes represent label variables and the edges represent relations between labels. Compared with Hidden Markov Model (HMM), an advantage of the CRF model is that it relaxes the strong independence assumptions. A general CRF can naturally model arbitrary dependencies between features and labels. Ghamrawi and McCallum [10] proposed two multi-label classification models based on CRF, which directly parameterized the correlation among labels and features.

Generally, given a sample $\mathbf{x}$ and its output label vector $\mathbf{y}$, using the multi-label classification CRF models, the posterior probability $p(\mathbf{y}|\mathbf{x})$ can be written as

$$p(\mathbf{y}|\mathbf{x}) = \frac{1}{Z(\mathbf{x})} \exp\left(\sum_k \lambda_k f_k(\mathbf{x}, \mathbf{y}) + \sum_l \mu_l g_l(\mathbf{x}, \mathbf{y}) \right) \tag{14}$$

where $Z(\mathbf{x})$ is the normalizing factor. $f_k(\mathbf{x}, \mathbf{y})$ and $g_l(\mathbf{x}, \mathbf{y})$ are two predefined real-valued functions, corresponding to a node (one label) and an edge (a label pair) respectively. They are usually referred to as *features* of CRF. In principle, any real-valued function of sample $\mathbf{x}$ and label $\mathbf{y}$ can be treated as a CRF feature. For example, it can be the frequency of a phrase in a text document, or one dimension of the beat-level feature vector in a music signal. λ_k and μ_l are the parameters to be estimated to maximize Eq.(14) using training data, where k and l enumerate the indexes of CRF features, as following

$$k \in < r_i, y_j >: 1 \leq i \leq |R|, 1 \leq j \leq |\mathcal{Y}| \tag{15}$$

$$l \in < r_i, y_j, y_{j'} >: 1 \leq i \leq |R|, 1 \leq j, j' \leq |\mathcal{Y}| \tag{16}$$

where R is a set of music features (to avoid confusion, we refer to f_k and g_l as CRF features), and $r_i \in R$ is one feature component; $|\mathcal{Y}|$ is the size of the label vector, and y_j is a label variable. It can be seen that each f_k corresponds to a pair consisting of a label and a music feature, and each g_l corresponds to a triplet consisting of a label pair and a music feature.

Note that k in Eq.(15) enumerates all the nodes, and l in Eq.(16) enumerates all the edges. Therefore, Eq.(14) corresponds to a full connected graph, where $\sum_k \lambda_k f_k(\mathbf{x}, \mathbf{y})$ represents the overall potential of nodes, and $\sum_l \mu_l g_l(\mathbf{x}, \mathbf{y})$ represents the overall potential of edges. However, in practice, not all the label pairs have close relations, and only those with strong correlations needed to be considered. That is, the edges of the CRF graph are sparse. Suppose the number of edges is E, and all the label variables have C possible values (in our case, $C = 2$, representing the presence and absence of each label), then the number of parameters to be estimated in total is $|R||Y|C + |R|EC^2$.

In Eq.(16), the potential of edges are feature-dependent. It can also be degenerated to feature-independent as

$$l \in < y_j, y_{j'} >: 1 \leq j, j' \leq |\mathcal{Y}| \tag{17}$$

In this case, the number of parameters to be estimated in total is $|R||Y|C + EC^2$. In order to reduce the computational complexity, we adopt this degenerated CRF model in our implementation.

As for the music feature set R, beat-level features cannot be used directly since here we are not modeling a temporal sequence. Instead, we treat each song as one sample, and a 115-dimensional song-level feature vector is calculated. It consists of two parts: a 65-dimensional vector that is the mean of the beat-level features, and a 50-dimensional vector, with each dimension representing the likelihood of a song given an semantic label in the vocabulary, calculated using Eq.(11). The 50-dimensional vector can also be seen as a song representation in an anchor space [1], where each anchor represents one of the 50 semantic labels in the vocabulary.

4 Experiments

In this section, the two schemes presented above are evaluated on representative testing datasets. We first evaluate the approach to web music indexing with a set of

Tab. (3): The details of the collected domain knowledge documents.

Type	#Documents	#Overall
Artist	1599	
Album	4635	32513
Song	26279	

webpages crawled from the Web, and then evaluate the method of automatic music semantic annotation with a set of collected western pop songs.

Evaluation on web music indexing

In this experiment, the music domain knowledge is collected from a deep Web site, All Music Guide (AMG), where we downloaded artist pages, album pages, and song pages, and organized them into a three-layered, tree-like structure, in which each layer represents artist, album, and song respectively, as shown in Fig. **(2)**. A specific HTML parser is developed to re-build up the knowledge hierarchy from the crawled pages, and extract specific keywords, such as artist, album, and genre. The details of the collected pages are shown in Tab. (**(3)**). Overall, there are 32513 pages, including 26279 song pages, 4635 album pages and 1599 artist pages. Layered LSI spaces are further built from these pages. For comparison, A non-layered LSI space is also built by combining all the documents at the three layers. In the field of text retrieval, many researchers reported that keeping 100 - 300 dimensions is a good tradeoff between performance and computation complexity of LSI. In our experiment, the dimension of LSI space is set to 200 accordingly.

To collect testing music objects, we first collected the top queries from the search logs of AMG in one week, which includes hundred of songs, albums and artists. Then, we submitted valid queries into Google and crawled the returned web pages. In the crawled pages, only those containing hyperlinks pointing to music files are labeled as music object pages. A 2-layer neighborhood graph is built for each music object. We do not consider 3-step pages (that is in the third layer), since the number of web pages increase explosively while a majority of them are irrelevant to the target music object. We also limit the total page number under 500 in neighborhood graph building, in order to reduce the computational complexity. Tab. (**(4)**) shows the details of the testing music objects, where we manually divide the music objects into three class: artist object, album object, and song object (corresponding to the webpage describing artist, album, and song), in order to compare the indexing performance of music objects at different layers in the hierarchy.

To measure the accuracy of our approach, web music indexing is viewed as a ranking/retrieval task, that is, the knowledge document is ranked according to its

Tab. (4): The details of music objects in the testing set.

Object Type	#Objecct	#Average Pages
Artist	30	457
Album	50	460
Song	200	373

similarity to the target music object, and the averaged top N precision is used as an evaluation metric, as

$$P(N) = \frac{\sum_{q_i \in Q} |q_i \cap R_i^N|}{|Q|} \tag{18}$$

where Q is the set of testing music objects and q_i is one music object, R_i^N is the top N results corresponding to query q_i, and $|\cdot|$ is the count of a set. In our experiment, P@1, P@5, and P@10 are evaluated.

In the following subsections, we first evaluate the overall accuracy of the proposed approach with various settings, and then evaluate the effectiveness of each module in the proposed framework.

Overall performance

This experiment evaluates the overall performance of the proposed approach, combining domain knowledge representation using Layered LSI spaces, neighborhood graph building and pruning, and hierarchical web object matching. There are two critical parameters in the experiment: the number of graph layer and the cutoff percentage in the construction of the neighborhood graph. Fig. **(6)** illustrates the result of P@5 on song object indexing, with regard to various graph layers and cutoff percentages, where the graph layer is chosen as 1 or 2, and the cutoff percentage ranges from 25% to 100%, with an interval of 5%.

The result shows that more than 80% of the song objects can be correctly identified in the returned top 5 knowledge documents, with cutoff set to 60% in 1-layer graph and 85% in 2-layer graph. It also shows that, when the cutoff percentage increases, the performance first increases as more noisy information is pruned, and then decreases when relevant information is also filtered out with a large cutoff. Compared with 1-layer graph, the 2-layer graph gains 4% absolute improvement. However, a majority (85%) of pages in the 2-layer graph are considered as noise and removed. Although it means some waste of page crawling and parsing, in the following experiments, we keep using 2-layer graph (including container, 1-step and 2-step pages) with optimal cutoff 85% as our default setting, in order to get higher performance.

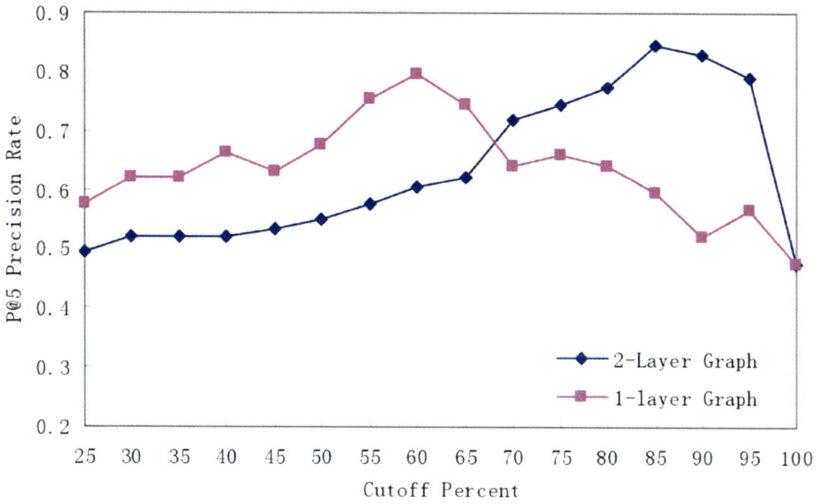

Fig. (6): Overall performance with respect to various graph layers and cutoff percentages.

Since the performance of our approach heavily depends on the sufficiency of the descriptive information of the song object, in order to evaluate the performance on different song objects, we manually classify them into three sets, including 'self-descriptive', 'multi-page descriptive' and 'non-descriptive'. The 'self-descriptive' object contains sufficient information in its container page to tell its structure attributes; the 'multi-page descriptive' object has to be identified jointly from the container and neighborhood pages; and the 'non-descriptive' object does not have sufficient information in its neighborhood graph. Fig. **(6)** illustrates the performance corresponding to these three sets of song objects. It shows that the performance on the self-descriptive set first increases and then is almost stable when the cutoff percentage grows, while the performance on multi-page descriptive set has an increasing phrase and a decreasing phrase, with the optimal cutoff at 85%. It actually reflects the tradeoff between pruning noisy information and incorporating complementary information in the neighborhood pages. As for the performance of non-descriptive set, it is as poor as expected, with accuracy less than 20%.

Looking into each module

We first evaluate the effectiveness of the Layered LSI spaces, by comparing three alternative options, including 1) Layered LSI on domain knowledge, 2) one-layer LSI on domain knowledge, and 3) no domain knowledge and no LSI (that is, comparing pages in the neighborhood graph directly as in [2]). The comparison result in Fig. **(7)** shows that the Layered LSI indexing scheme performs best. It is about

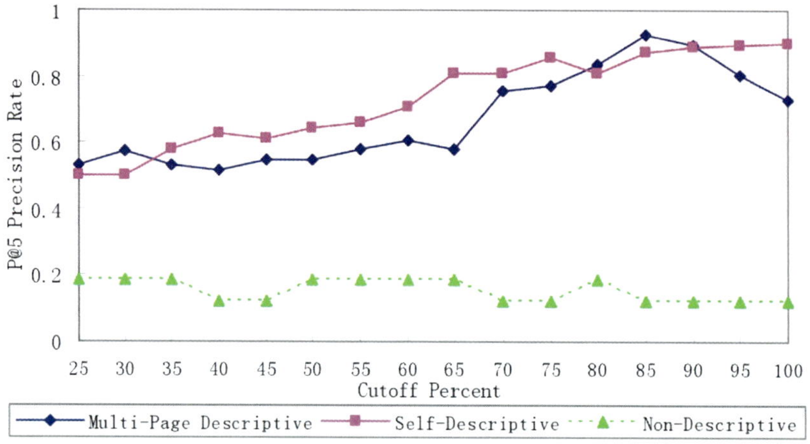

Fig. (7): Precision on different sets of song objects.

5% higher than "no LSI", and about 3% better than one-layer indexing. The result verifies that using domain knowledge can provide better web object representation and the layered indexing can achieve high performance.

The neighborhood graph is built to enrich the description of the target music object. It is especially suitable for those multi-page descriptive music objects, as mentioned above. Fig. (**8**) illustrates the performance of multi-page descriptive music object indexing, by comparing 1-layer neighborhood graph (with optimal cutoff at 60%), 2-layer neighborhood graph (with optimal cutoff at 85%), and without neighborhood graph (only with the container page). It shows that the performance is dramatically improved by using neighborhood pages. For example, the P@1 and P@5 are almost doubled after using 1-layer graph or 2-layer graph.

Confidence propagation is performed in music object matching to rescore the similarity between a candidate document and the target music object. Fig. (**10**) illustrates the performance comparison between the schemes with and without confidence propagation. It shows that, with confidence propagation, the precision (P@1, P@5 and P@10) is consistently improved by around 5%-7%.

To explore the performance on music objects at different layers of the knowledge hierarchy, we also evaluate the performance on album objects and artist objects. The detailed comparison is illustrated in Fig. (**11**). The result shows that the performance on artist and album objects is much higher than that of song objects, especially the P@1. There are two reasons. First, in music domain, the number of artists or albums are relatively smaller while the terms used to describe artists or albums are usually much more than those of songs. In other words, there is more information that can be used to distinguish artists and albums. Second, information in song page is usually not sufficiently discriminative. With a neighborhood graph,

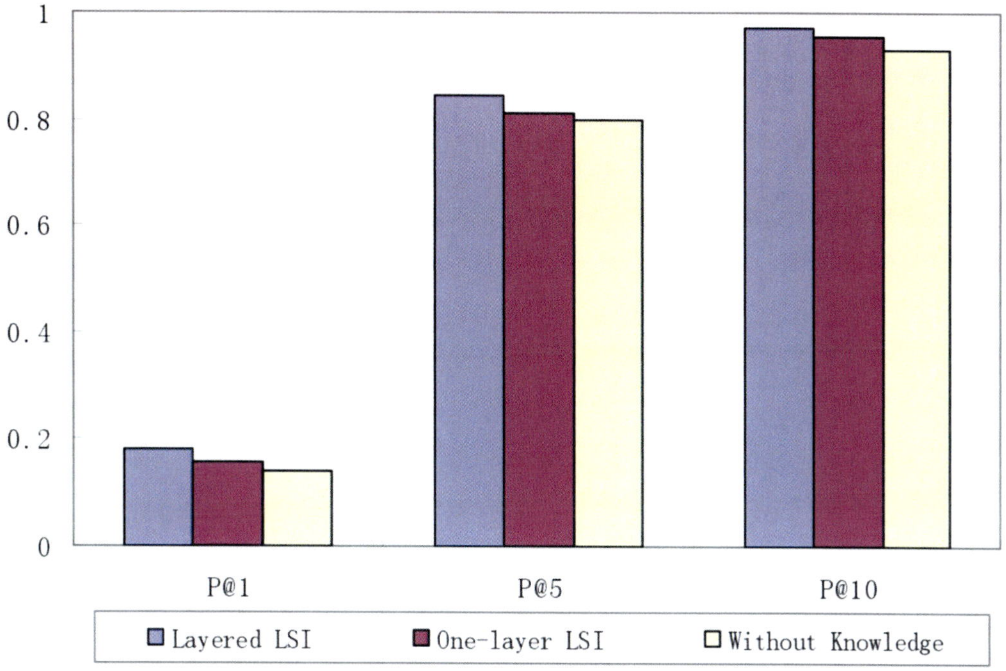

Fig. (8): Precision comparison on different LSI indexing approaches.

the description of a song object usually has a large overlap with the songs from the same album. As a result, it is usually difficult to discriminate the songs from the same album, while it is relatively easy to identify an album or an artist object. Therefore, the P@1 of song objects is lower than that of album and artist objects. Interestingly, the P@10 is very similar among them since an album typically has about 10 songs.

Evaluation on automatic music annotation

In this section, different methods of automatic music annotation are compared, including two presented collective annotation methods and two individual annotation methods: the individual GMM-based method with Eq.(10), and the individual CRF-based method that does not consider the edges (or label pairs) in the graph. The experimental data set consists of 4,951 Western popular songs, each of which was manually annotated with semantic labels from the vocabulary shown in Tab. ((**1**)). 25% of the songs are randomly selected as the training set and the left as the test set. For the collective methods, 49 label pairs (with NormMI values larger than 0.1) are chosen to be modeled.

These methods are evaluated from both *category*-based and *song*-based aspects.

Tab. (3): The details of the collected domain knowledge documents.

Type	#Documents	#Overall
Artist	1599	32513
Album	4635	
Song	26279	

webpages crawled from the Web, and then evaluate the method of automatic music semantic annotation with a set of collected western pop songs.

Evaluation on web music indexing

In this experiment, the music domain knowledge is collected from a deep Web site, All Music Guide (AMG), where we downloaded artist pages, album pages, and song pages, and organized them into a three-layered, tree-like structure, in which each layer represents artist, album, and song respectively, as shown in Fig. (**2**). A specific HTML parser is developed to re-build up the knowledge hierarchy from the crawled pages, and extract specific keywords, such as artist, album, and genre. The details of the collected pages are shown in Tab. ((**3**)). Overall, there are 32513 pages, including 26279 song pages, 4635 album pages and 1599 artist pages. Layered LSI spaces are further built from these pages. For comparison, A non-layered LSI space is also built by combining all the documents at the three layers. In the field of text retrieval, many researchers reported that keeping 100 - 300 dimensions is a good tradeoff between performance and computation complexity of LSI. In our experiment, the dimension of LSI space is set to 200 accordingly.

To collect testing music objects, we first collected the top queries from the search logs of AMG in one week, which includes hundred of songs, albums and artists. Then, we submitted valid queries into Google and crawled the returned web pages. In the crawled pages, only those containing hyperlinks pointing to music files are labeled as music object pages. A 2-layer neighborhood graph is built for each music object. We do not consider 3-step pages (that is in the third layer), since the number of web pages increase explosively while a majority of them are irrelevant to the target music object. We also limit the total page number under 500 in neighborhood graph building, in order to reduce the computational complexity. Tab. ((**4**)) shows the details of the testing music objects, where we manually divide the music objects into three class: artist object, album object, and song object (corresponding to the webpage describing artist, album, and song), in order to compare the indexing performance of music objects at different layers in the hierarchy.

To measure the accuracy of our approach, web music indexing is viewed as a ranking/retrieval task, that is, the knowledge document is ranked according to its

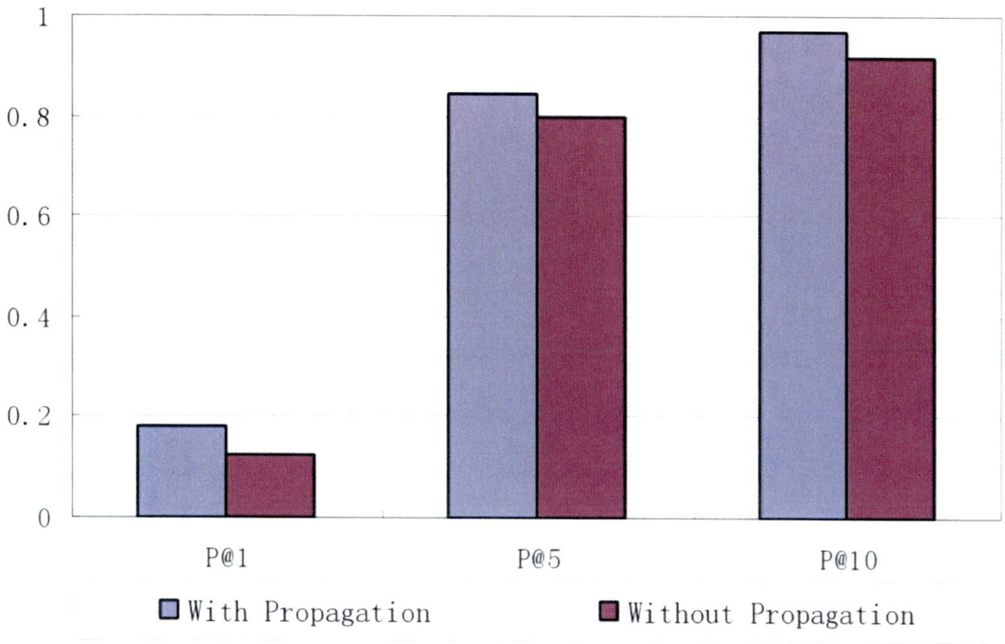

Fig. (10): Performance comparison between schemes with and without confidence propagation.

However, the performance improvement from individual models to collective models is marginal. Although the level of improvement accords with the experiments in [10], we need to further discover the reasons and exploit possible solutions. One possible reason is that, while each label is modeled individually in the individual modeling methods, the "correlated" labels share a number of songs in their training set (since each song has multiple labels). This makes the trained models of the "correlated" labels are also "correlated", or in other words, the correlation is implicitly modeled.

5 Related Work

Previous work on object-oriented indexing can be traced back to the framework of image retrieval proposed by Harmandas [14], in which a model for Web image retrieval is presented, by combining the text content and hypertext in neighborhood graph. However, it did not consider the underlying structures of web objects. Using a connective cluster of web pages to improve web search is also addressed in some work. Kleinberg's HITS [20] is an early important effort using link analysis to rank documents, however it only depends on in/out-degrees of links. Bharat *et al.* [2]

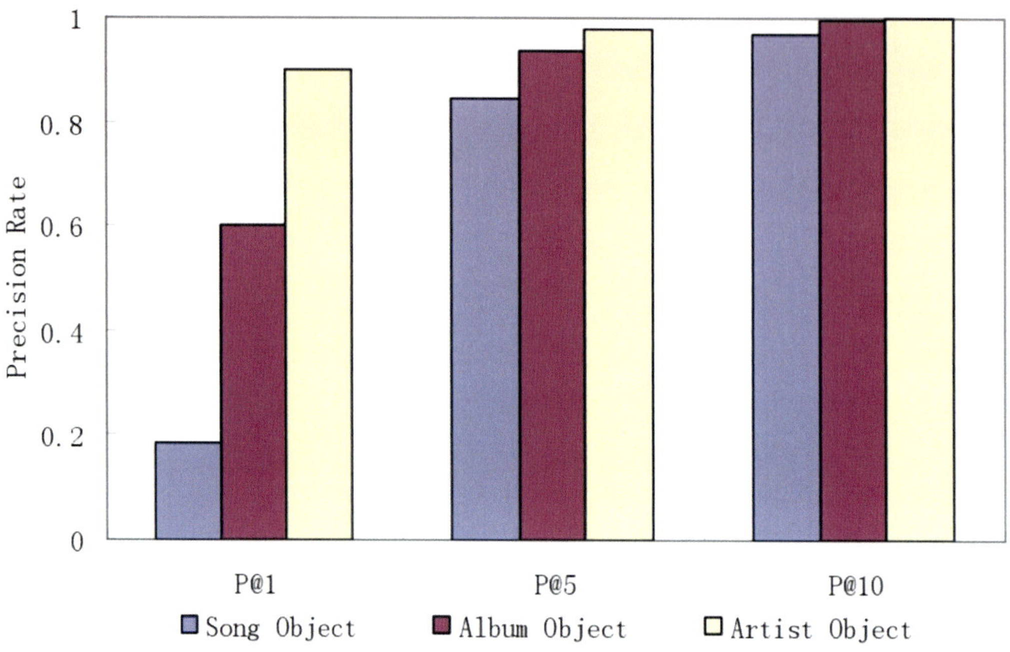

Fig. (11): Performance on music objects at different layers.

identified a problem of HITS: topic drift, and proposed to resolve it by content analysis in local graph. This modification achieved a remarkable better precision in topic distillation application. By manipulating the weights of pages, Chang *et al.* [5] created customized authority by adding more weights to the documents that users have interest. Recently, researchers proposed to use connective analysis to improve term weighting scheme in hyperlink environment [32]. However, none of them considered using domain knowledge to improve the combination of link analysis and content analysis. Similar to our work (matching music object representation in knowledge database), "DB+IR" [6, 16, 28] was proposed in the database domain to use unstructured query to search structured database. Different from traditional Structure Query Language (SQL) technologies, "DB+IR" regards database records as plain text, and use IR technologies to index and search database. Some researchers also proposed to improve search precision by using the structure of database, such as XSearch [6] which utilized the structure of XML DOM tree, and proposed to use Inverse Leaf Frequency (ILF) to punish common terms in leaf nodes.

Various approaches to music information retrieval are related to music semantic annotation, such as tempo estimation, beat tracking, music genre classification, music key detection, and music emotion classification. A number of methods on these topics were reported in the proceedings of ISMIR (http://www.ismir.net/),

Tab. (5): Average per-category performance on each semantic category in the vocabulary. For each cell, three numbers are listed in the order of "Precision / Recall / F-measure". It is noted that, for the bottom 6 semantic categories, precision, recall and F-measure are the same, and hence written as one number.

%	Individual GMM	Collective GMM	Individual CRF	Collective CRF
Overall	60.7/**61**.0/60.8	61.2/**61**.0/61.1	68.0/60.5/64.0	**68**.4/**61**.0/**64**.5
Genre	43.4/**50**.9/46.9	44.5/50.2/47.2	54.2/40.9/46.6	**55**.4/41.8/**47**.7
Instrument	54.3/53.5/53.9	54.9/**53**.8/54.3	72.8/48.4/58.1	**72**.9/48.6/**58**.3
Texture	73.2/**71**.8/72.5	74.0/71.7/72.8	75.1/71.0/73.0	**75**.2/71.0/**73**.1
Vocal	76.5/71.3/73.8	76.7/71.2/73.8	**80**.6/84.3/82.4	**80**.6/**85**.4/**82**.9
Affective	46.8	**47.5**	42.1	43.1
Arousal	56.5	56.6	57.0	**58.5**
Rhythm	63.0	62.3	64.0	**64.5**
Tempo	59.2	59.4	**63.3**	63.0
Tonality	56.9	57.4	**60.4**	60.1
Production	93.0	93.0	94.5	**94.6**

Tab. (6): Performance of song annotation, comparing with four methods.

%	Precision	Recall	F-measure
Individual GMM	60.9	61.4	60.9
Collective GMM	61.4	61.4	61.2
Individual CRF	68.1	60.9	64.0
Collective CRF	**68**.5	**61**.3	**64**.4

a conference dedicating to music information retrieval. Tempo and beat detection is a fundamental step to characterize music rhythm. Various algorithms of tempo induction were proposed and many of them were compared and discussed in [13]. For example, Klapuri [19] induced tempo and time signature through an HMM process based on per-band "accent signals". As a subsequent step, Goto *et al.* [12] implemented a real-time beat tracking system based on a multiple-agent architecture, and Scheirer [29] proposed a beat tracking system using a bank of band-pass filters and parallel comb filters. Researchers also focused on various music classification tasks, such as to identify music genre, key, or emotion. These topics can be considered as music annotation on one specific music attribute (with a limited vocabulary). Tzanetakis *et al.* [34] presented a music genre classification system using the features of timbre texture, rhythmic content and pitch content. Jiang *et al.* [18] developed a similar algorithm to classify music into classical, pop, jazz and rock, by using octave-based spectral contrast. Pye [27] used Gaussian Mixture Model (GMM) and Mel-Frequency Cepstral Coefficients (MFCC), to classify music into six genres, including blues, easy listening, classical, opera, dance and indie rock. In another direction, Lu *et al.* [24] proposed an approach to classify music into four emotion categories, using a set of timbre features and rhythm features. Since emotion category is usually ambiguous and sparse, Yang *et al.* [38] employed a regression approach to map each music clip to a 2D (arousal-valence) emotion space. Music key identification was also studied, such as the work in [11, 26], where *chroma* feature was extracted to represent a song and matched against existing chroma profiles corresponding to 24 major and minor keys.

6 Conclusion and Discussion

To summarize, this chapter presents two complementary methods to improve music indexing and search: 1)use the trustworthy domain knowledge to discover the inherent structure attributes of the music dispersed on the surface web; and 2) through music signal processing and machine learning, automatically annotate music with a set of musical-related attributes and tags to enrich music metadata and music description. These two methods provide complementary information for music indexing and can be effectively combined together to provide a better indexing scheme. With this information available, we can build several interesting features for music search engines, such as search result clustering, music information aggregation, music filtering, and music recommendation.

As a future work, we will consider to exploit more related music information such as users' review, and associate it with the corresponding music object. It would be helpful if we can summarize the reviews from different users. Music search is both a personal and a social behavior, if we can learn the music preference of a specific user or his friends, it helps to find more music he may like and enhance user experience on music sharing and new music discovery. We will also consider to support different kinds of queries besides artist, album and track. Searching music based on genre, emotion, and tempo/rhythm will greatly help users to find suitable music to listen to in specific contexts or for specific purposes, such as jogging, relaxing, reading, and dancing.

7 References

[1] A. Berenzweig, D.P.W. Ellis, and S. Lawrence. Anchor Space for Classification and Similarity Measurement of Music. In *ICME*, 2003.

[2] K. Bharat, and M. R. Henzinger. Improved Algorithms for Topic Distillation in a Hyperlinked Environment. In *SIGIR*, 1998

[3] D. Cai, S. Yu, J. Wen, and W.-Y. Ma. VIPS: a Vision-based Page Segmentation Algorithm. *MSR-TR-2003-79*, 2003

[4] P. Cano, and M. Koppenberger. Automatic Sound Annotation. In *Proc. IEEE Workshop Mach. Learn. Signal Process*, 2004.

[5] H. Chang, D. Cohn, and A. McCallum. Creating customized authority lists. In *ICML*, 2000.

[6] S. Cohen, J. Mamou, Y. Kanza, and Y. Sagiv. XSEarch: A Semantic Search Engine for XML. In *VLDB*, 2003

[7] S. Deerwester, S. Dumais, et. al. Indexing by Latent Semantic Analysis. *Journal of the American Society for Information Science*, 1990

[8] D. Eck, P. Lamere, T. Bertin-Mahieux, and S. Green. Automatic Generation of Social Tags for Music Recommendation. In *NIPS*, 2007.

[9] S. Essid, G. Richard, and B. David. Instrument Recognition in Polyphonic Music based on Automatic Taxonomies. In *IEEE Trans. Audio, Speech and Lang. Process*, 2006.

[10] N. Ghamrawi, and A. McCallum. Collective Multi-label Classification. In *CIKM*, 2005.

[11] E. Gómez. Tonal Description of Polyphonic Audio for Music Content Processing. In *INFORMS Journal on Computing, Special Cluster on Computation in Music*, 2006.

[12] M. Goto and Y. Muraoka. Beat Tracking based on Multiple-agent Architecture: A Real-time Beat Tracking System for Audio Signals. In *Int. Conf. on Multi Agent Systems*, 1996

[13] F. Gouyon, A. Klapuri, S. Dixon, M. Alonso, G. Tzanetakis, C. Uhle, and P. Cano. An Experimental Comparison of Audio Tempo Induction Algorithms. *IEEE Trans. on Audio, Speech and Language Processing*, 2006.

[14] V. Harmandas, M. Sanderson, and M. D. Dunlop. Image retrieval by hypertext links. In *SIGIR*, 1997

[15] K. P. Han, Y. S. Pank, S. G. Jeon, G.C. Lee, and Y. H. Ha. Genre Classification System of TV Sound Signals Based on a Spectrogram Analysis. *IEEE Transactions on Consumer Electronics*, 1998

[16] V. Hristidis, and Y. Papakonstantinou. DISCOVER: Keyword Search in Relational Databases. In *VLDB*, 2002

[17] D. Huron. Perceptual and Cognitive Applications in Music Information Retrieval. *ISMIR*, 2000.

[18] D.N. Jiang, L. Lu, H.J. Zhang, J.H. Tao, and L.H. Cai. Music Type Classification by Spectral Contrast Features. In *ICME*, 2002.

[19] A. Klapuri, A. Eronen, and J. Astola. Analysis of the Meter of Acoustic Musical Signals. In *IEEE Trans. Speech and Audio Processing*, 2006

[20] J. Kleinberg. Authoritative Sources in a Hyperlinked Environment. In *Journal of the ACM*, 1999

[21] N. Kushmerick Wrapper Induction for Information Extraction. In *IJCAI*, 1997

[22] J. Lafferty, A. McCallum, and F. Pereira. Conditional Random Fields: Probabilistic Models for Segmenting and Labeling Seqeunce Data. in *ICML*, 2001.

[23] Y.X. Liu, Q.L. Xiang, Y. Wang, and L.H. Cai. Culttural Style based Music Classification of Audio Signals In *ICASSP*, 2009

[24] L. Lu, D. Liu, and H.J. Zhang. Automatic Mood Detection and Tracking of Music Audio Signals. In *IEEE Trans. on Audio, Speech and Lang. Process*, 2006.

[25] G. Peeters. Time variable tempo detection and beat marking. in *ICMC*, 2005.

[26] G. Peeters. Chroma-based Estimation of Musical Key from Audio-Signal Analysis In *ISMIR*, 2006.

[27] D. Pye. Content-Based Methods for the Management of Digital Music. in *ICASSP*, 2000.

[28] B. Y. Ricardo, and M. P. Consens. The continued saga of DB-IR integration. In *VLDB Tutorial*, 2004

[29] E. D. Scheirer. Tempo and Beat Analysis of Acoustic Musical Signals. In *Journal of Acoustical Society of America*, 1998

[30] M. Slaney. Mixtures of Probability Experts for Audio Retrieval and Indexing. In *ICME*, 2002.

[31] H. Soltau, T. Schultz, Martin Westphal and Alex Waibel. Recognition of Music Types. in *ICASSP*, 1998

[32] K. Sugiyama, K. Hatano, M. Yoshikawa, and S. Uemura. Refinement of TF-IDF Schemes for Web Pages using their Hyperlinked Neighboring Pages. In *Proc. the fourteenth conference on Hypertext and Hypermedia*, 2003

[33] D. Turnbull, L. Barrington, D. Torres, and G. Lanckriet. Semantic Annotation and Retrieval of Music and Sound Effects. In *IEEE Trans. Audio, Speech and Lang. Process.*, 2008.

[34] G. Tzanetakis, and P. Cook. Musical Genre Classification of Audio Signals. In *IEEE Trans. Speech and Audio Process*, 2002.

[35] M.Y Wang, Z.W Li, L. Lu, W.Y. Ma, and N.Y Zhang. Web Object Indexing Using Domain Knowledge. In *Proc. SIGKDD*, 2005

[36] B. Whitman, and R. Rifkin. Musical Query-by-Description as a Multiclass Learning Problem. In *IEEE Workshop Multimedia Signal Process*, 2002.

[37] B. Whitman, and D.P.W. Ellis. Automatic Record Reviews. In *Proc. ISMIR*, 2004.

[38] Y.H. Yang, Y.C. Lin, Y.F. Su, and H.H. Chen. A Regression Approach to Music Emotion Recognition. In *IEEE Trans. Audio, Speech adn Language Processing*, 2008.

[39] J. Zobel and A. Moffat. Inverted Files for Text Search Engines. In *ACM Computing Surveys*, 2006.

Internet Multimedia Search and Mining, 2013, 397-414

CHAPTER 15

Video Recommendation

Tao Mei*
Microsoft Research Asia, Tel: 86-10-59173036, Fax: 86-10-8286 8529, Email: tmei@microsoft.com

Kiyoharu Aizawa
University of Tokyo, Tel: 3-5841-6651, Fax: 03-5841-6693, Email: aizawa@hal.t.u-tokyo.ac.jp

Abstract: This chapter is intended to introduce the basic techniques for general recommender systems, as well as specific research for video recommendation, which have become interesting and important topics in video search and mining. We will first define video recommendation and survey three principle approaches to video recommendation, i.e., collaborative filtering, content-based, and hybrid approaches. We will also discuss the connection and difference between video recommendation and search. Then, we will introduce several recent exemplary systems for recommendation, including: (1) "graph-based video recommendation" which builds random work graph based on user-video pairs [5], (2) "contextual video recommendation by multimodal relevance and user feedback" which does not require a large collection of user profiles [30, 43], and (3) "consumer generated video recommendation" which discusses ranking distances for recommendation and proposes an edit-distance for ranking [22]. The first system uses collaborative filtering-based recommendation approach, while the latter two belong to content-based recommendation.

Keywords

Video recommendation, collaborative filtering, content-based recommendation, graph-based recommendation, user generated videos, video search and mining, VideoSense,

***Correspondence Author:** Tao Mei, Microsoft Research Asia, China; Email: tmei@microsoft.com.

Xian-Sheng Hua, Marcel Worring & Tat-Seng Chua (Eds.)

user feedback, consumer generated video, user profiles

1 Introduction

The proliferation of digital capture devices and the explosive growth of online videos have led to the countless private video collection on local computing devices, such as personal computers, cell phones, and personal digital assistants (PDAs), as well as the huge yet increasing public videos on the Internet [7]. For example, the most popular video sharing site, Youtube [44], drew 5 billion U.S. online video views in July 2008. As a result, online delivery of video content has surged to an unprecedented level. This trend has brought a wide variety of online video services, such as search, editing, sharing, management, advertising, and so on. It is natural to imagine that today's online users always face a daunting volume of video contents—be it from video sharing or blog content, or from IPTV and mobile TV. There is an increasing demand of video recommendation services which can push the "interesting" or "highly related" contents to targeted people at every opportunity. Video recommendation is able to release users' efforts on manually filtering out the unrelated content and finding the most interesting videos, according to their current viewing content, preferences, historical behaviors, or their friends with similar tastes.

This chapter is intended to introduce the basic techniques for video recommendation. We will first briefly introduce the general recommendation approaches. We then categorize the approaches to video recommendation. Specifically, we present several recent exemplary systems for video recommendation, including: (1) "graph-based video recommendation" which builds random walk graph based on user-video pairs [5], (2) "contextual video recommendation by multimodal relevance and user feedback" which does not require a large collection of user profiles [30, 43], and (3) "consumer generated video recommendation" which discusses ranking distances for recommendation and proposes an edit-distance for ranking [22]. We conclude this chapter with a list of future works and possible extensions.

2 General Recommendation

The earlier research on recommendation began in the mid-1990s [19], in which a recommender system is defined as to estimate *ratings* for the unseen items by a user. Examples of the items in the recommendation include books, CDs, products at Amazon [3, 25], movies by MovieLens [32], news or events in CNN [12], etc. Resnick *et al.* has given a more general definition as to ones in which "people provide recommendations as input, which the system then aggregates and directs to appropriate recipients" [35]. There are three major types of approaches commonly used in traditional recommender systems [1]:

- *Collaborative filtering* which predicts preference of a given user based on the ratings of the users whose tastes are similar to the given user [16]. For example, in a movie recommendation application, to recommend movies to user u, the collaborate filtering recommender system tries to find the "peers" of user u whose tastes are similar to u (e.g., rate the same movies similarly), and recommend the movies that are most liked by the "peers."

- *Content-based* recommendation which predicts the interest of a user on an item based on the similarity between the given item description and the user profile or between the given item and the items which the user has already rated [18]. For example, in a movie recommendation application, to recommend movies to user u, the content-based recommender system tries to understand the commonalities among other movies rated by user u in the past, and recommends the movies that have a high degree of similarity to whatever the user's preferences.

- *Hybrid* recommendation in which both of the above approaches are used [24].

In general, collaborative filtering focuses more on user-user relationship but less on properties of recommended items, and hence, it often requires enough users and their profiles. On the other hand, content-based recommendation focuses more on item-user relationship but less on influence of other users.

Besides the above categorization of recommender systems, Burke also summarized the techniques in traditional recommenders using another three dimensions as follows [9].

- *Demographic-based* recommendation: to collect sufficient users' information from diverse sources such as interactive responses and users' homepages, create relationship among users based on this information, and finally make recommendations like *collaborative* recommendation.

- *Utility-based* recommendation: to let users input a "utility function" to directly describe their needs.

- *Knowledge-based* recommendation: to aggregate the knowledge not only from average users but also from the experts in a specific area for recommendation. An example of this approach is Encyclopedia system [14].

To summarize, the first dimension proposed by Burke (i.e., demographic-based recommendation) heavily rely on a sufficient collection of user profile, while this information is not required in the latter two.

3 Video Recommendation

Challenges in video recommendation

The most straightforward way for video recommendation is to directly apply the methods for general recommendation in previous section to video domain. However, we still need to investigative domain-specific approach to video recommendation due to the following reasons.

- Traditional collaborative filtering recommenders rely on a sufficient collection of user information, i.e., user profile or the "utility function" which explicitly indicates user interest or need. However, when surfing web videos, most users browse anonymously. As a result, a video recommender should deal with the absence of user information. On the other hand, it is not easy to choose a general "utility function" that can satisfy all kinds of users. Therefore, conventional collaborative filtering-based recommendation techniques can not be directly applied to video.

- Traditional content-based recommenders reply on the precise description of item, so that it can estimate the description of users based on the rated items. However, there are usually very few textual descriptions or too much noisy textual information associated with a video on the web [34, 43]. For example, the average number of terms per video on Youtube is $3 \sim 5$ [33]. Directly applying content-based techniques to video would result in false alarms of the recommended videos, since the noisy textual words cannot precisely describe the visual content. For example, using conventional cosine distance based on the associated words would fail to capture the similarity between two video items. Before we adopt any content-based recommendation techniques for video, it is desired to introduce more accurate textual information or reduce existing noise via visual content analysis.

- Video is different from traditional recommended items like product and book. A video is a sequence with a huge amount of images and rich visual information. To understand a video, users need to pay much time for consuming the content. For example, a user may skip, fast forward, pause to see detail, and so on, while watching a video. Capturing these user behaviors on videos will help us understand user intent or need, which in turn would make the recommender more user-targeted. Furthermore, a video recommendation system also needs a user-friendly interface to facilitate video browsing and searching. For example, a compact but visually appealing visualization of video content would help user understand the video at a quick glance [31].

From the above observations, we can see that video is quite different from traditional recommended items. A recommendation system dedicated to video has to be designed by considering the characteristics of video.

Commercial video recommendation systems

Many existing video-oriented sites, such as YouTube [44], Bing Video [6] and Yahoo! Video [42], have already provided recommendation services. Fig.(1) shows some representative recommendation systems. Though no details of the algorithms in these systems are available, it is likely that most of them recommend videos only based on the relevance derived from textual information (such as query and keywords) or collaboratively based on user preference (if he/she is a registered user). As a result, the recommended videos are generally related to the associated text rather than the video content. However, the user-provided tags (i.e., keywords and surrounding text) are typically incomplete and noisy. The heavy reliance on these tags will lead to the recommended videos not reach the content of the clicked video. On the other hand, in many real cases, a user visits a Web page anonymously and is less likely to provide his/her profile. Therefore, a recommendation method without the assumption of a large collection of user profiles is highly desired. Moreover, few of existing recommendation systems take users' click-through (e.g., which part of video has been watched differently, the transition between two clicked videos, etc.) into consideration. It still remains a challenging problem to leverage the video content and user click-though for a more effective recommendation.

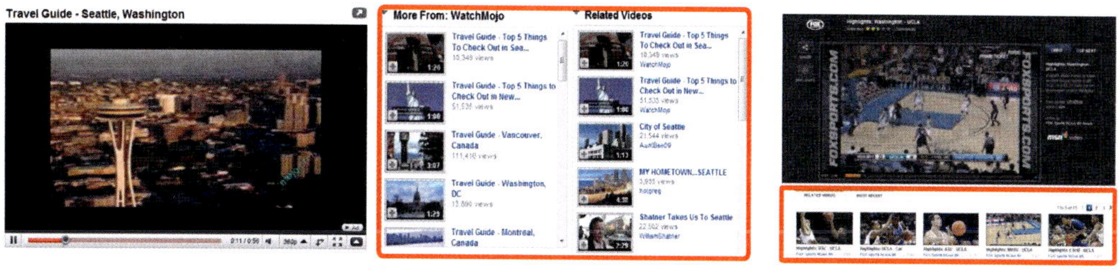

(a) (b)

Fig. (1): The representative existing video recommender systems: (a) Youtube [44], (b) Microsoft's Bing Video Search [6]. The "Related Videos" in the highlighted rectangles will appear as the recommended videos after the current videos are viewed. The recommended videos are generally related to the associated text rather than the video content.

Research on video recommendation

There exists rich research on video recommendation [5, 17, 19, 22, 26, 27, 30, 37, 38, 43]. Analog to the research on general recommendation, these works can be summarized into three categories: 1) collaborative filtering-based approach [5, 19, 37], 2) content-based approach [8, 17, 22, 26, 27, 30, 38, 43], and 3) hybrid approach which combined the first two approaches in a single framework [10].

The collaborative filtering-based approaches compare a users's ratings of videos with those of hundreds of others, find people who share similar preferences, and then recommend unseen videos that these similar people have viewed or rated. In the collaborative filtering video recommender systems, there is an assumption that a sufficient collection of user ratings or profiles is available. For example, Hill *et al.* designed an email interface to collect data on how a virtual community functions (i.e., person, item, rating, correlation among persons) from Oct. 1993 to May 1994 [19]. Then, given a user, the system recommended unseen videos rated by a group of similar persons. Setten *et al.* proposed to use different social filtering methods to predict user interest based on other users' information, and designed a combination of prediction technique [37]. Baluja *et al.* built a user-video graph which represented the co-view information among different users [5]. The recommendation was performed by a graph propagation in which the label of each node is obtained from its neighbors. We will introduce this method in more details in the next section. The challenge in collaborative filter-based recommendation is that users tend to visit a Web page or a video site anonymously, and hence, it would be challenging to get user profile or ratings for a particular video item in a real system.

The content-based approaches, on the other hand, recommend unseen video items to a given user based on the video contents which he/she has rated or directly based on his/her profile. The estimation of the relationship between the unseen videos and user interest is based on similarity between those unseen videos and the videos rated or viewed by this user. The challenge in this kind of recommendation is the content-based similarity between different videos, which is expected to be able to represent user interest toward those videos. For example, the Open Video Project generated video recommendations by a process of spreading activation on the basis of co-download patterns derived from download log data [8]. A co-download was defined as the same user downloading a pair of videos within a short time slot. Then, a co-download network was generated in which the activation value of video was propagated throughout the network. The videos were recommended to the user, ranked according to their final activation values. The VCSR system recommended videos that are similar with user profile based on the textual similarity [38]. The textual information about a video is derived using Optical Character Recognition (OCR) over video frames. Luo *et al.* presented a topic network navigation interface to let users select news topic of interest interactively [26, 27]. The news topic is minded from different modalities (i.e., audio, closed captions, and video) through a synchronization module. The news videos are recommended according to their importance and representativeness scores based on user selection. In this way, the system is able to provide personalized news video recommendation. Gantner applied

Bayesian Personal Ranking (BPR) to video recommendation [17]. The performance of a matrix factorization model optimized by BPR was evaluated on a collection of BBC videos. Yang *et al.* presents a novel contextual video recommendation system called VideoReach, based on multimodal content relevance and user feedback [30, 43]. An online video was represented by different modalities (i.e., visual and audio track, as well as associated texts such as query and keywords). The recommended videos are relevant to current viewing in terms of multimodal relevance. They also considered that different parts of videos are with different degrees of interest to a user, as well as different features and modalities have different contributions to the overall relevance. The recommended videos are also relevant to current users in terms of user feedback based on relevance feedback technique. Irie *et al.* introduced degree-of-edit (DoE) ranking to estimate how much a consumer generated video (CGV) is edited as a ranking measure for CGV recommendation [22]. We will also discuss the latter two as exemplary systems in the next.

It is worth noting that an alternative to video recommendation is to adopt the techniques used in the domain of video search [13, 40]. However, the tasks of video search and video recommendation are different. Video search aims to find the videos that exactly "match" the given query. In other words, the "relevance" in video search usually indicates exact "match," while it indicates not only "match" but also with common "interest." Such interest can be derived from collaborative ratings from a set of users with the similar profiles or rating the same videos, or from user click-through. In addition, the query in a search system is typically a list of keywords or together with an example of image (although query by example is not yet realized to any search engine so far), while the query in a recommender system is a video document clicked or searched by a user with certain interest and click-though. This query may consist of visual-aural content and textual information associated with this video. Therefore, multimodal content relevance, as well as user feedback, should be taken into account for video recommendation. Tab.(1) lists the comparisons between video search and recommendation systems. It can be concluded that video recommendation is more general than video search as it involves collaborative rating and interest, as well as click-through data. In addition, the query for a video recommender system could be more diverse than that in a video search system. Some say that recommendation technology represents the new paradigm of search: interesting items find the user instead of the user explicitly searching for them. In an article published in CNN Money, Fortune magazine writer Jeffrey M. O'Brien, writes: "The Web, they say, is leaving the era of search and entering one of discovery. What's the difference? Search is what you do when you're looking for something. Discovery is when something wonderful that you didn't know existed, or didn't know how to ask for, finds you."

In the next, we will discuss three exemplary video recommendation systems: user-video co-view graph-based recommendation which is a collaborative filtering approach [5], as well as VideoReach [30, 43] and Degree-of-Edit Ranking-based video

Tab. (1): Comparisons between video search and video recommendation. "√" denotes "used" while "×" denotes "not used."

	Keyword query	Visual-aural query	Relevance	Collaborative rating	Collaborative interest	Click-thru
Video Search	√	×	√	×	×	×
Video Recomm.	√	√	√	√	√	√

recommendation systems [22] which belong to content-based approaches.

Exemplary systems

1. User-video graph-based recommendation: a collaborative filtering-based approach

The user-video graph-based recommendation is a kind of collaborative filtering-based approach [5]. The goal is to create a personalized page of video recommendations that provides users with recommended videos tailored to their viewing habits. A user-video graph was built to represent the co-view pattern through the user-video bipartite graph. Fig.(2) shows the co-view graph in which a user u is connected to a video v if: (1) u and v have a short path between them, (2) u and v have several paths between them, or (3) u and v have paths that avoid high-degree nodes. The idea of recommending videos commonly co-viewed with a user's watched videos is abstracted as finding the labeled nodes with multiple short paths from the user node.

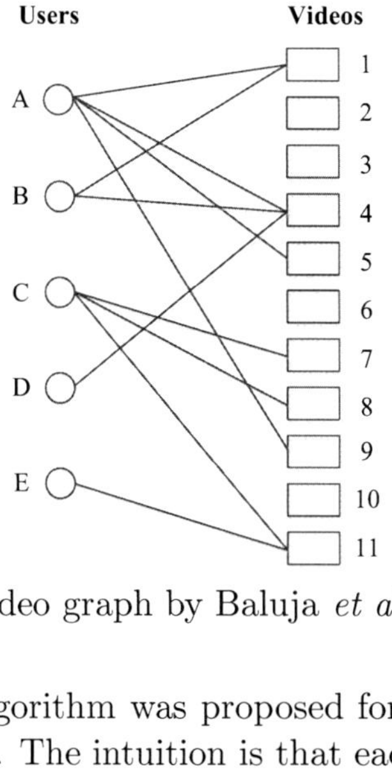

Fig. (2): User-video graph by Baluja *et al.*, courtesy [5].

An so-called *adsorption* algorithm was proposed for the propagation of the labels of each node in the graph. The intuition is that each node carries some labels, forwards the labels to its neighbors, who, in turn, forward them to their neighbors, and so on. The adsorption algorithm is a very general framework for classification and learning when there are some labeled objects and a rich graph structure that underlies the universe of labeled and unlabeled objects. The authors present three different but equivalent interpretations for this algorithm, i.e., adsorption via averaging, adsorption via random walks, and adsorption via linear system.

The experiments were conducted over a collection of live user views of videos from Youtube [44] in the period of three months in 2007. After some preprocessing, 1.1 million users and 1.3 million videos, corresponding to 12.5 million watches, are used in the experiment. Using *precision-recall* curve and *Precision@Top* 1 as the evaluation metrics, the *adsorption* method for recommendation outperforms some existing approach like global and local popularity.

2. VideoReach: a content-based approach

VideoReach is a video recommendation system that uses multimodal relevance and user feedback [30, 43]. It is designed based on the fact that users tend to visit a video site anonymously, and therefore it is usually difficult to get user profile. Moreover, user click-through history of certain videos can tell the underlying his/her interest and thus can be leveraged to find the video targeted to the user [20]. For example, user's browsing behavior (e.g., the staying duration) on a specific video indicates whether this video is of interest.

The input of VideoReach system is a video document $\mathbf{D}$, which is represented by textual, visual and aural documents as $\mathbf{D} = (D_T, D_V, D_A)$. Given an online video document $\mathbf{D}$ clicked by a user, the task of video recommendation is expressed as finding a list of videos with the best relevance to $\mathbf{D}$. Since different modalities have different contributions to the relevance, we use $(\omega_T, \omega_V, \omega_A)$ to denote the weights of textual, visual and aural document, respectively. Thus a video document can be further represented by

$$\mathbf{D} = \mathbf{D}(D_T, D_V, D_A, \omega_T, \omega_V, \omega_A) \quad (1)$$

Similarly, the document of a single modal D_i ($i \in \{T, V, A\}$) can be represented by a set of features and the corresponding weights:

$$D_i = D_i(\mathbf{f}_i, \omega_i) \quad (2)$$

where $\mathbf{f}_i = (f_{i1}, f_{i2}, \ldots, f_{in})$ is a feature set from modality i. $\omega_i = (\omega_{i1}, \omega_{i2}, \ldots, \omega_{in})$ is a set of corresponding weights. Let $\mathcal{R}(D_x, D_y)$ denotes the relevance of two video documents D_x and D_y. The relevance between video document D_x and D_y in terms of modality i is denoted by $\mathcal{R}_i(D_x, D_y)$, while the relevance in terms of feature f_{ij} is denoted by $R_{ij}(D_x, D_y)$.

Fig.(3) illustrates system framework of VideoReach. To obtain multimodal relevance between two video documents, the relevance in terms of a single modality

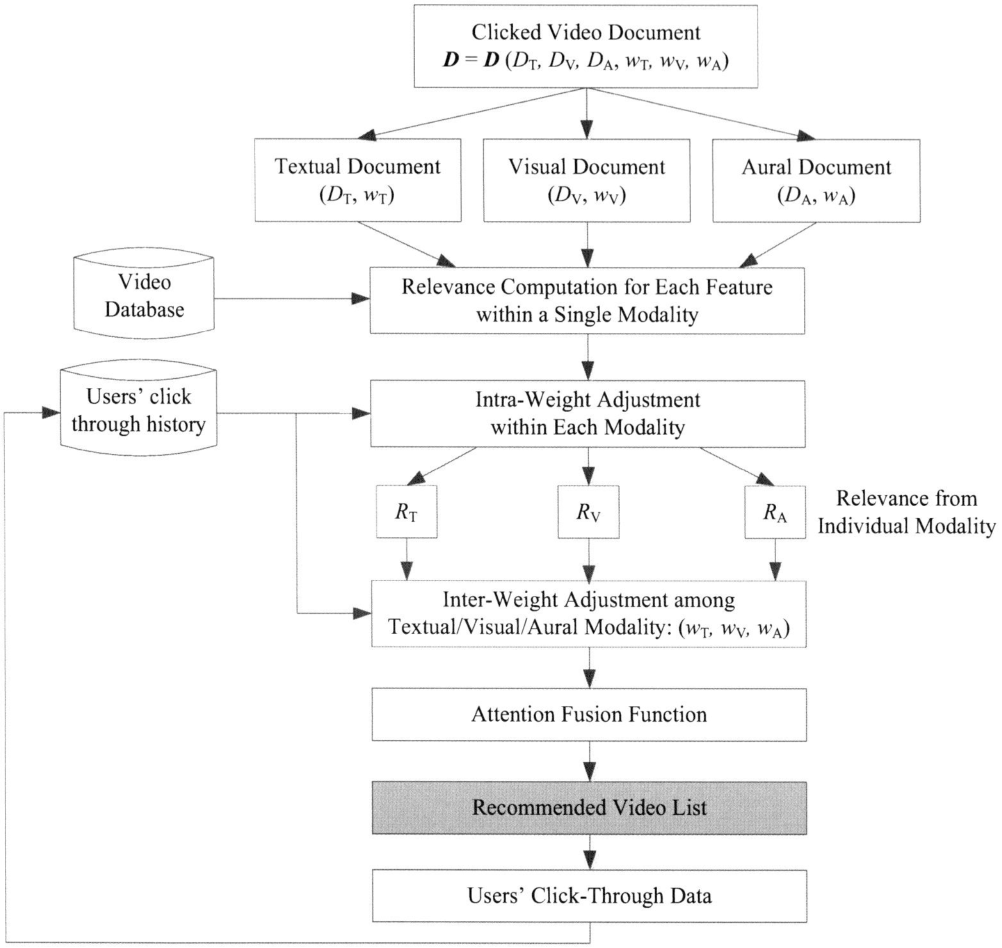

Fig. (3): The framework of VideoReach by Mei and Yang *et al.*, courtesy [30, 43].

is first computed by weighted linear combinations of relevance between features. Then relevance of single modality $R_i(\cdot)$ is fused using attention fusion function (AFF) with the weights proposed in [21]. The intra-weights ω_{ij} within each modality i and inter-weights ω_i among different modalities are adjusted dynamically using relevance feedback [36].

Different methods are adopted to compute the relevance $R_i(\cdot)$ for modality i ($i = \{T, V, A\}$). For example, a vector space model is used to measure the textual similarity between two video documents based on the surrounding texts [4]. The visual relevance is measured by normalized color histogram, motion intensity and shot frequency (the average number of shots per second), which had proved to be effective to describe visual content in many existing video retrieval systems [19]. The aural document is described by the average and standard deviation of aural tempos among video shots. Average aural tempo represents the speed of music or audio, while standard deviation indicates the change frequency of music style. The aural relevance of two video documents is defined based on L_1 distance on the feature space.

Once the relevance is obtained, the problem is then how to combine the relevance from different modalities. Although linear combination is a straightforward method for fusion, it is not consistent with human's attention response. The AFF to simulate human's attention characteristics is adopted as it is applicable when two properties are satisfied: *monotonicity* and *heterogeneity* [21]. Since different features should have different weights, the 3-dimensional AFF with weights is used to get a final relevance. For two video documents D_x and D_y, the final relevance is computed as

$$\mathcal{R}(D_x, D_y) = \frac{R_{avg} + \frac{1}{2(n-1)+n\gamma}\sum_i |n\omega_i \mathcal{R}_i(D_x, D_y) - R_{avg}|}{W} \tag{3}$$

where

$$R_{avg} = \sum_i \omega_i \mathcal{R}_i(D_x, D_y) \tag{4}$$

$$W = 1 + \frac{1}{2(n-1)+n\gamma}\sum_i |1 - n\omega_i| \tag{5}$$

and $i \in \{T, V, A\}$. n is the number of modalities ($n = 3$), ω_i is the weight of individual modality to be detailed later, γ is a predefined constant.

There are two remaining problems before using AFF: (1) how to obtain the intra-weights ω_{ij} within modality i, and (2) how to decide the inter-weights ω_i for modality i. It is observed that users' click-through data usually tell a latent instruction to the assignment of weights, or at least a latent comment on the recommendation results. If a user opens a recommended video and closes it within a short time (i.e. less than 15 seconds), probably this video is a false recommendation. Such kind of video is called "negative" example. On the other hand, if a user views a recommended video for a relative long time, this video is probably a true recommendation, since this user is rather interested in this recommendation. Such kind of video is called "positive" example. With "positive" and "negative" examples, relevance feedback [36] is an effective solution to automatically adjusting the weights of different inputs.

The adjustment of intra-weights ω_{ij} is to obtain the optimal weight of each kind of feature within an individual modality. Among the returned list, only positive examples indicated by a user are selected to update intra-weights as follows

$$\omega_{ij} = \frac{1}{\sigma_{ij}} \tag{6}$$

where $i \in \{T, V, A\}$, σ_{ij} is the standard deviation of feature f_{ij}, whose corresponding document D_i is a positive example. The intra-weights are then normalized between 0 and 1.

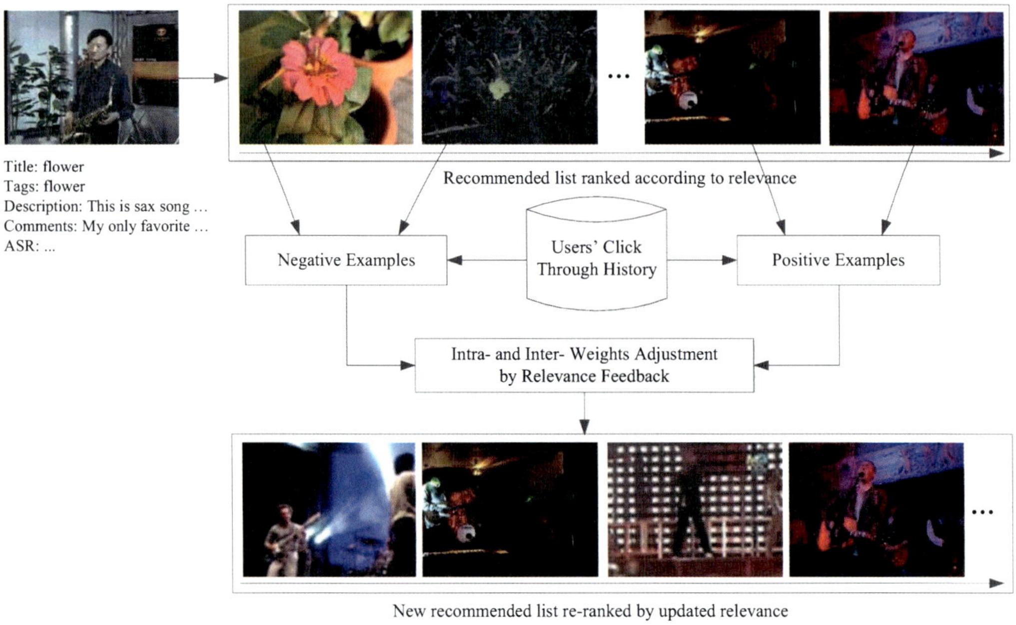

Fig. (4): The procedure of weight adjustment in VideoReach, courtesy [43].

The adjustment of inter-weights ω_i is to obtain the optimal weight of each modality. For each modality, a recommendation list $(D_1, D_2, \ldots, D_K)$ is created based on the individual relevance from this modality, where K is the number of recommended videos. We first initialize $\omega_i = 0$, and then update w_i as follows

$$\omega_i = \begin{cases} \omega_i + 1, & \text{if } D_k \text{ is a ``positive'' example} \\ \omega_i - 1, & \text{if } D_k \text{ is a ``negative'' example} \end{cases}$$

where $i \in \{T, V, A\}$ and $k = 1, \ldots, K$. The inter-weights are then normalized between 0 and 1.

Fig.(4) shows the procedure of intra- and inter- weight adjustment in VideoReach. For an input video document, the system first generated a recommended list to a user according to current intra- and inter- weights; then from this user's click-through, classified some videos in the list into "positive" or "negative" examples, and updated the historical "positive" and "negative" lists which were obtained from previous users' click-through; finally, the intra- and inter- weights were updated based on the new "positive" and "negative" lists, and were used for the next user.

3. Degree-of-Edit ranking: a content-based approach

As the consumer generated videos (CGV) increased dramatically with the recent widespread use of video sharing sites, the retrieval and recommendation of these

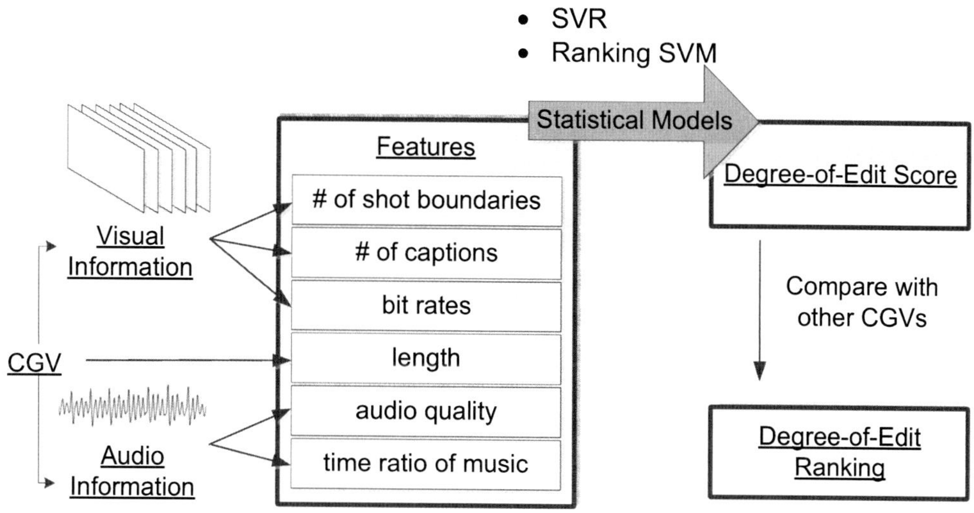

Fig. (5): The framework of DoE ranking-based CGV recommendation by Irie *et al.*, courtesy [22].

CGV have become an important issue. Irie *et al.* in [22] claimed that edited CGVs tend to be with high quality and more attractive for many users, and proposed degree-of-edit (DoE) ranking as a ranking signal for recommending CGVs. The work focused on investigating "how much a CGV is edited" via visual and audio content analysis. Given a CGV, the authors proposed to extract a set of visual and audio features and leverage Support Vector Regression (SVR) and Ranking Support Vector Machine (RSVM) to predict the DoE scores. The CGVs are then recommended according to the DoE scores. Fig.(5) shows the flowchart of their approach.

The features include the following six kinds of visual and audio signals:

- length of the video,
- the number of shot boundaries,
- audio quality,
- average bit rates,
- the number of inserted captions,
- time ratio of music part to entire video.

The six features are input to a statistical learning model to estimate the DoE ranking. The authors also compared the performances using SVR and RSVM on a collection of 22,795 CGVs from ClipLife [11]. The values output by a model are taken as the DoE score of a CGV, and the CGVs in the set of initial retrieved results are rearranged in a decreasing order of their DoE scores. It is observed that RSVM outperforms SVR in terms of rank correlation. They also compared different recommendation strategies based on DoE scores and found that combining the ranking by the times viewed and the DoE score achieved the best performace.

4 Conclusions and Future Challenges

We have summarized the research on video recommendation into collaborative filtering-based, content-based, and hybrid categories. As content-based recommendation does not hold the assumption that a sufficient collection of user profile is required, it has been the predominant approach to video recommendation in recent years. However, with the popularity of social networks and mobile devices in our daily lives, video recommendation systems are expected to be designed by leveraging the contexts from social networks and mobile devices. The current video recommendation systems could be extended in the following ways.

- Leveraging video content analysis (e.g., object recognition [15], concept detection [19], affective/emotion analysis [23, 46], video genre classification [45]) for content-based video recommendation. As we discussed in Section 3 that the surrounding text can hardly describe video content, the heavily reliance of textual information for video recommendation will lead to significant false alarm of the videos that are truly interesting. However, one can perform visual recognition techniques to recognize some predefined vocabularies or classify videos into some categories. Then, we can recommend users the videos which are much more relevant.

- Mining context from mobile devices, social networks, query logs, or click-through data. As mentioned in [20], user's browsing behaviors are strong clues to represent his/her interest. Social networks build strong relationship among millions of users. Mobile devices can be used to mine user profiles easily as there are much more contexts on them. Context-based recommendation would be one of the next trends of recommendation. For example, one can recommend local videos to users based on their GPS locations.

- Efficient recommendation visualization tools for video recommendation. We need an efficient browsing tool that enables users to quickly go through or understand those recommended videos. For example, VideoCollage [31, 39] and news topic network techniques both present compact visualization for a particular video or a group of videos. Another way for visualization is let users interactively select recommended videos so that the recommendation systems can learn user interest dynamically.

- Using novel user feedback. For example, Xu *et al.* designed a system that recommends online videos via commodity eye-tracking [41]. The system is able to track a user's attention time over online videos, which is obtained via a data mining process and based on data captured by a vision-based commodity eye-tracking device. The attention time is a strong indication of user interest. There is a possibility to use physiological signals to estimate user's interest [2].

- Less-intrusive recommendation by psychology analysis. Another issue is what is the best time for recommendation when a user is watching current video. As video is a long sequence, it would be better if the recommended content appears (either besides or within the original video) at the less-intrusive time slot. For example, VideoSense represents the first attempt to find the least-intrusive and high discontinuity points in a video [29].

5 References

[1] G. Adomavicius and A. Tuzhilin. Toward the next generation of recommender systems: A survey of the state-of-the-art and possible extensions. *IEEE Transactions on Knowledge and Data Engineering*, 2005.

[2] K. Aizawa, K. Ishijima, and M.Shiina. Summarizing wearable video. In *ICIP*, 2001.

[3] Amazon. http://www.amazon.com/.

[4] R. Baeza-Yates and B. Ribeiro-Neto. *Modern Information Retrieval.* Addison Wesley, 1999.

[5] S. Baluja, R. Seth, D. Sivakumar, and et al. Video suggestion and discovery for youtube, taking random walks through the view graph. In *ACM WWW*, 2008.

[6] Bing Video. http://video.bing.com/.

[7] S. Boll. MultiTube—where multimedia and web 2.0 could meet. *IEEE Multimedia*, 2007.

[8] J. Bollen, M. L. Nelson, R. Araujo, and G. Geisler. Video recommendations for the open video project. In *Proceedings of the ACM/IEEE-CS joint conference on Digital libraries*, 2005.

[9] R. Burke. Hybrid recommender systems: Survey and experiments. *User Modeling and User-Adapted Interaction*, 2002.

[10] C. Christakou and A. Stafylopatis. A hybrid movie recommender system based on neural networks. In *International Conference on Intelligent Systems Design and Applications*, 2005.

[11] Cliplife. http://cliplife.jp/.

[12] CNN. http://www.cnn.com/.

[13] A. Efrat, A. Amir, K. Barnard, and Q. Fan. *Cross-modality Indexing, Browsing and Search of Distance Learning Media on the Web.* Book Chapter of Internet Multimedia Search and Mining, X.-S. Hua, M. Worring, and T.-S. Chua (Ed). Bentham Science Publishers Ltd., 2010.

[14] Encyclopedia. http://www.encyclopedia.com/.

[15] L. Fei-Fei, R. Fergus, and P. Perona. One-shot learning of object categories. *IEEE Transactions on Pattern Analysis and Machine Intelligence*, 2006.

[16] F. Fouss, A. Pirotte, J. M. Renders, and M. Saerens. Random-walk computation of similarities between nodes of a graph, with application to collaborative recommendation. *IEEE Transactions on Knowledge and Data Engineering*, 2007.

[17] Z. Gantner, C. Freudenthaler, S. Rendle, and L. Schmidt-Thieme. Optimal ranking for video recommendation.

[18] M. Gibas, G. Canahuate, and H. Ferhatosmanoglu. Online index recommendations for high-dimensional databases using query workloads. *IEEE Transactions on Knowledge and Data Engineering*, 2008.

[19] W. Hill, L. Stead, M. Rosenstein, and G. Furnas. Recommending and evaluating choices in a virtual community of use. In *Proceedings on Human Factors in Computing Systems*, 1995.

[20] J. Hu, H.-J. Zeng, H. Li, C. Niu, and Z. Chen. Demographic prediction based on user's browsing behavior. In *ACM WWW*, 2007.

[21] X.-S. Hua and H.-J. Zhang. An attention-based decision fusion scheme for multimedia information retrieval. In *Proceedings of IEEE Pacific-Rim Conference On Multimedia*, 2004.

[22] G. Irie, K. Hidaka, T. Satou, A. Kojima, and K. Aizawa. A degree-of-edit ranking for consumer generated video retrieval. In *ICME*, 2009.

[23] G. Irie, K. Hidaka, T. Satou, T. Yamasaki, and K. Aizawa. Latent topic driving model for movie affective scene classification. In *ACM Multimedia*, 2009.

[24] T. Iwata, K. Saito, and T. Yamada. Recommendation method for improving customer lifetime value. *IEEE Transactions on Knowledge and Data Engineering*, 2008.

[25] G. Linden, B. Smith, and J. York. Amazon.com recommendations: item-to-item collaborative filtering. *IEEE Internet Computing*, 2003.

[26] H. Luo, J. Fan, and D. A. Keim. Personalized news video recommendation. In *ACM Multimedia*, 2008.

[27] H. Luo, J. Fan, D. A. Keim, and S. Satoh. Personalized news video recommendation. In *Multimedia Modeling*, 2009.

[28] T. Mei, X.-S. Hua, W. Lai, L. Yang, and et al. MSRA-USTC-SJTU at TRECVID 2007: High-level feature extraction and search. In *TREC Video Retrieval Evaluation Online Proceedings*, 2007.

[29] T. Mei, X.-S. Hua, and S. Li. VideoSense: A contextual in-video advertising system. *IEEE Transactions on Circuits and Systems for Video Technology*, 2009.

[30] T. Mei, B. Yang, X.-S. Hua, L. Yang, S.-Q. Yang, and S. Li. VideoReach: An online video recommendation system. In *ACM SIGIR*, 2007.

[31] T. Mei, B. Yang, S.-Q. Yang, and X.-S. Hua. Video collage: Presenting a video sequence using a single image. *The Visual Computer*, 2009.

[32] MovieLens. http://www.grouplens.org/taxonomy/term/14.

[33] E. Moxley, T. Mei, X.-S. Hua, W.-Y. Ma, and B. S. Manjunath. Automatic video annotation through search and mining. In *ICME*, 2008.

[34] E. Moxley, T. Mei, and B. S. Manjunath. Video annotation through search and graph reinforcement mining. *IEEE Transactions on Multimedia*, 2010.

[35] P. Resnick and H. R. Varian. Recommender systems. *Communications of the ACM*, 1997.

[36] Y. Rui, T. S. Huang, M. Ortega, and S. Mehrotra. Relevance feedback: A power tool for interactive content-based image retrieval. *IEEE Transactions on Circuits and Systems for Video Technology*, 1998.

[37] M. V. Setten and M. Veenstra. Prediction strategies in a TV recommender system – method and experiments. In *ACM WWW*, 2003.

[38] C.-C. Tsai, C.-I. Chung, Y.-T. Huang, C.-H. Shen, Y.-C. Wu, and J.-C. Yang. VCSR: Video content summarization for recommendation. In *IEEE International Conference Advanced Learning Technologies*, 2007.

[39] Y. Wang, T. Mei, J. Wang, and X.-S. Hua. Dynamic video collage. In *Multimedia Modeling*, 2010.

[40] P. Wilkins and A. Smeaton. *Weighted Data Fusion for Content-Based Multimedia Information Retrieval.* Book Chapter of Internet Multimedia Search and Mining, X.-S. Hua, M. Worring, and T.-S. Chua (Ed). Bentham Science Publishers Ltd., 2010.

[41] S. Xu, H. Jiang, and F. C. C. Lau. Personalized online document, image and video recommendation via commodity eye-tracking. In *ACM Conference On Recommender Systems*, 2008.

[42] Yahoo! http://www.yahoo.com/.

[43] B. Yang, T. Mei, X.-S. Hua, L. Yang, S.-Q. Yang, and M. Li. Online video recommendation based on multimodal fusion and relevance feedback. In *CIVR*, 2007.

[44] YouTube. http://www.youtube.com/.

[45] X. Yuan, W. Lai, T. Mei, X.-S. Hua, and X.-Q. Wu. Automatic video genre categorization using hierarchical svm. In *ICIP*, 2006.

[46] S. Zhang, Q. Tian, S. Jiang, Q. Huang, and W. Gao. Affective mtv analysis based on arousal and valence features. In *ICME*, 2008.

CHAPTER 16

Visual Query Suggestion for Internet Image Search

Zheng-Jun Zha*
Institute of Intelligent Machines, Chinese Academy of Science, Hefei, China Tel: 86-551-65591136, Email: junzzustc@gmail.com
Linjun Yang
Microsoft Research Asia, Tel: 86-10-88097306, Email: linjuny@microsoft.com
Meng Wang
Hefei University of Technology, Email: eric.mengwang@gmail.com

Abstract: Query suggestion is an effective approach to bridge the *Intention Gap* between the users' search intents and queries. Most existing search engines are able to automatically suggest a list of textual query terms based on users' current query input, which can be called Textual Query Suggestion. This chapter introduces a new query suggestion scheme named Visual Query Suggestion (VQS) which is dedicated to image search. VQS provides a more effective query interface to help users to precisely express their search intents by joint text and image suggestions. When a user submits a textual query, VQS first provides a list of suggestions, each containing a keyword and a collection of representative images in a dropdown menu. Once the user selects one of the suggestions, the corresponding keyword will be added to complement the initial query as the new textual query, while the image collection will be used as the visual query to further represent the search intent. VQS then performs image search based on the new textual query using text search techniques, as well as content-based visual retrieval to refine the search results by using the corresponding images as query examples.

***Correspondence Author:** Zheng-Jun Zha, Institute of Intelligent Machines, Chinese Academy of Science, Hefei, China; Email: junzzustc@gmail.com.

Xian-Sheng Hua, Marcel Worring & Tat-Seng Chua (Eds.)

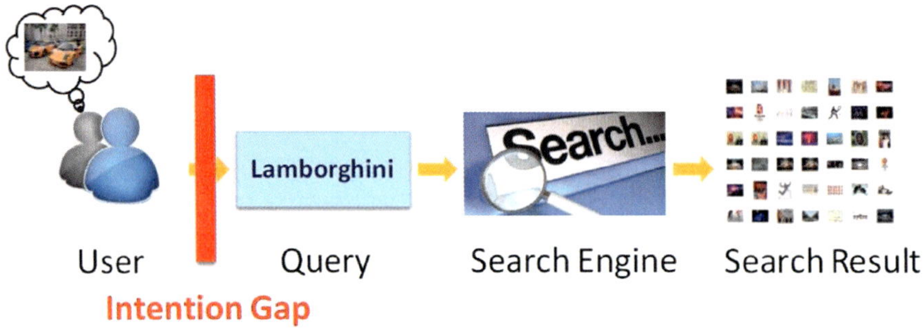

Fig. (1): "Intention Gap": the gap between user's search intent and the query.

Keywords

query suggestion, visual query suggestion, keyword suggestion, image suggestion, joint keyword-image suggestion, search intention, intention gap, ambiguous query, image search, textual query suggestion

1 Introduction

With the rapid advances in both hardware and software technologies, large collections of images have been made available on the Internet. To help users find the desired images, image search has been intensively studied [7, 17, 22]. Many popular search engines (e.g., Google Image Search, Microsoft Bing Image Search, and Yahoo! Image Search) have developed technologies that allow users to search Internet images.

Most of the existing popular search engines allow users to formulate the query as a list of keywords. However, it is not trivial for users to clearly express their search intents in keywords. There are times and situations when users can imagine what they desire, but are unable to express this desire in precise wording [7, 9]. For example, when we see a Lamborghini car in the street, we want to search for some images about it without knowing its model. What query can we use to express this intent? We probably input "Lamborghini" as the query. This query however is overly general and cannot express the intent clearly, since there is a range of Lamborghini cars with difference models. Moreover, keyword queries are usually ambiguous especially when they are short (one or two words) and thus cannot reflect users' intents precisely. For example, the query "apple" covers several different topics: fruit, computer, and smart-phone etc.. Overall, there is usually a gap between the users' search intents and the queries, called *Intention Gap*, due to the incapability of keyword queries to express users' intents precisely (see Fig. (1)). This *Intention Gap* often leads to unsatisfactory search results. As illustrated in

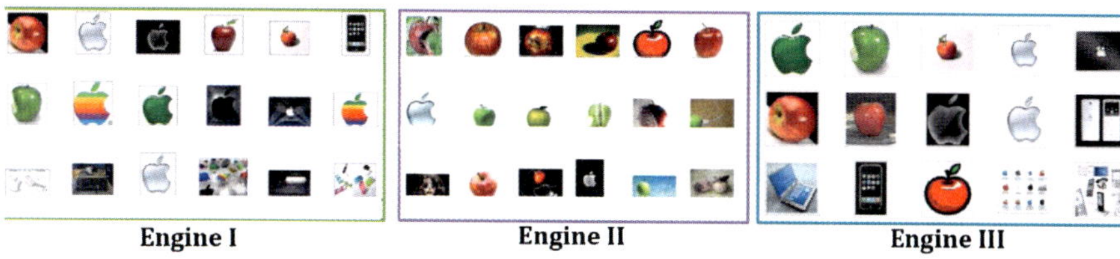

Fig. (2): The search results of ambiguous query "apple" from three popular image search engines: Engine I, II, and III. It is observed that the search results are mixed with different prototypes of "apple."

Fig. (2), search engines return results for "apple" mixed with "apple"—the fruit, "apple"—the computer, and "apple"—the smart-phone (We use Engine I, II, III to represent three popular image search engines to preserve anonymity.). Such results are unsatisfactory since users typically prefer search results that could be aligned with their interests, rather than those mixed with diverse categories. Therefore, showing images from one or more categories in which users are truly interested is much more effective and efficient than just returning images from all interpretations.

One promising solution to bridge the *Intention Gap* is suggesting a list of queries based on users' inputs, called query suggestion, which aims to help users to formulate precise queries to deliver their search intents clearly. Query suggestion technique has embarked on a dramatic evolution in recent years. Although this evolution is still underway, we can summarize trends of query suggestion for Internet image search into two generations in terms of information carrier for users: textual and visual query suggestion. Many textual query suggestion methods, which suggest a list of keywords based on users' current queries, have been proposed in information retrieval committee and simply adopted for image search. Recently, researchers argue that image can better help users to express their search intents, and therefore providing visual (i.e., image) query suggestion is a more natural way for image search than only showing textual query terms(see Fig. (3)).

In this chapter, we will briefly review textual query suggestion approaches and elaborate the research advance in visual query suggestion.

2 Textual Query Suggestion

A wealth of textual query suggestion techniques have been proposed to address the *Intention Gap* problem in information retrieval committee. A commonly adopted solution is to find keyword suggestions from documents retrieved by the initial query [3, 16, 25, 26]. For example, Xu *et al.* [25] and Lam *et al.* [16] extracted keywords from top-ranked documents that were regarded as the relevant results of the initial query. Carpineto *et al.* [3] proposed to select the keywords that maximized the divergence between the language model defined by the top-ranked

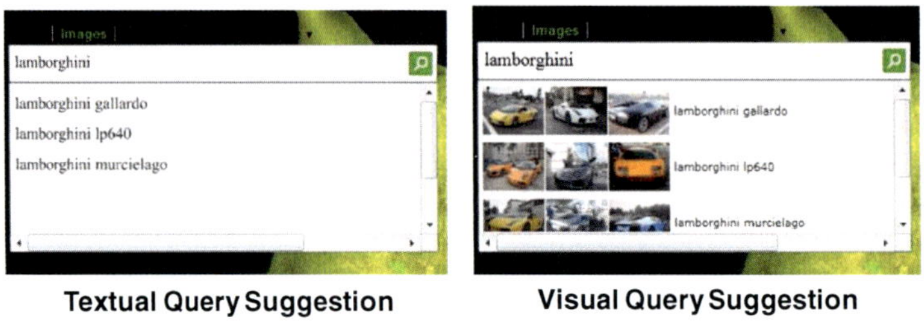

Fig. (3): Comparison between conventional Textual Query Suggestion (TQS) and Visual Query Suggestion (VQS). TQS suggests a list of keywords, while VQS suggests not only the keywords but also the visual examples for the keywords.

documents and that defined by the entire document collection. Recently, Yu *et al.* [26] selected the keywords from vision-based segments of Web pages to deal with the multiple topics residing problem.

Another solution to textual query suggestion is to mine "wisdom of the crowds" from search logs [4, 5, 6]. For example, Huang *et al.* [4] extracted query pairs that frequently co-occur in same search sessions. The extracted queries were then used as suggestions for each other. Jones *et al.* [5] and Fonseca *et al.* [6] mined session data for query pairs that were usually adjacent in same sessions.

Some other works tend to find similar queries from click-through data, which is usually represented as a bipartite graph with the vertices on one side corresponding to queries and on the other side to clicked URLs. Groups of similar quires, which share a large number of clicked URLs, are obtained through a clustering process over the click-through data. The similar queries are then used as suggestions for each other. For example, Beeferman *et al.* [1] adopted a hierarchical agglomerative clustering method to find similar queries in an iterative way. Wen *et al.* [24] used a density-based clustering method that exploits both query content and click-through information. Baeza-Yates *et al.* [20] adopted k-means algorithm to discover similar queries.

Recently, textual query suggestion technique has been applied for Internet image search, while popular image search engines such as Google, Yahoo!, and Microsoft Bing search also provide textual query suggestion functionality. However, textual query suggestion only suggest a list of keywords based on users' current queries. As we know, compared with text, image carries more information that can be perceived more quickly, just like an old saying, "*an image is worth a thousand words.*" Moreover, there are times and situations when textual query suggestion is unable to help users to specify their search intents. For example, as illustrated in Fig. (3), textual query suggestion technique may suggest a list of Lamborghini models for the query "Lamborghini." These suggestions however are useless for the users who have no knowledge of Lamborghini models, since they do not know which model is the one they desire. In this case, if some visual examples are associated with suggested models, the users can exactly know which model is the desired one and thus can reformulate a better query that expresses the search intent more clearly.

Motivated by the above observations, we argue that images can better help users specify their search intents, and therefore providing visual (i.e., image) query suggestion is a more natural way for image search than only showing textual suggestions. If a list of joint visual-textual queries is offered, not only the ambiguity can be reduced in query formulation but also a better matching between the original text query and images can be achieved. In this way, users would have better search experience. In the next section, we will introduce the recent research advance in visual query suggestion [28, 30].

3 Visual Query Suggestion

Fig. (4) shows the entire procedure of query suggestion for image search in the visual query suggestion system [28, 30]. When a user is typing a query, VQS system provides a list of suggestions each containing both representative image and keyword in a dropdown menu, which is quickly responsible for the user's operation. Once the user chooses one keyword-image suggestion from the list, VQS system expands the initial query with the corresponding keyword. This results in a composite query, with which VQS system performs image search using text-based search techniques. Then, VQS system regards the corresponding image suggestion as *query example* and refines the initial search results by leveraging visual information, which is useful to improve text-based image search [11, 12, 18, 29]. The re-ranked results are then presented, which meet the user's intent much better. The main contributions of this paper can be summarized as follows:

System overview

Fig. (5) illustrates the framework of the Visual Query Suggestion system, which contains three components, i.e., query suggestion mining, suggestion presentation, and image search with query suggestion. In query suggestion mining module, we discover both image and keyword suggestions in order to help users to express the search intents more clearly. Specifically, the keyword-image suggestions are generated by exploiting the knowledge from a popular photo-sharing Website: Flickr (Flickr: http://www.flickr.com/). Flickr contains more than two billion photos that are tagged by billions of tags (keywords). Discovering keyword-image suggestions from these plentiful images associated with abundant keywords is rational and advantageous in the following two aspects: (1) the suggestions can be generated without performing search for the initial query. This leads to the proposed method being more efficient; and (2) the suggestion mining approach will not suffer from the unsatisfactory search results of the initial query and thus can offer more effective suggestions. A two-step approach is developed to discover the keyword-image

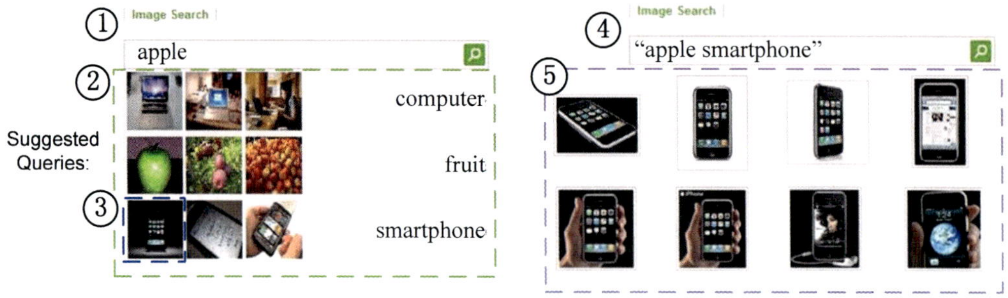

Fig. (4): The procedure of image search with visual query suggestion. User can interactively: (1) submit an keyword query; (2) browse the keyword-image suggestions provided by VQS system; and (3) select one suggestion to specify the search intent. Then, VQS system: (4) expands the original query with the corresponding keyword; (5) performs image search based on the new query in (4) using text search techniques, preforms content-based visual retrieval to refine the search results by using the corresponding images as *query example*, and returns the final search results.

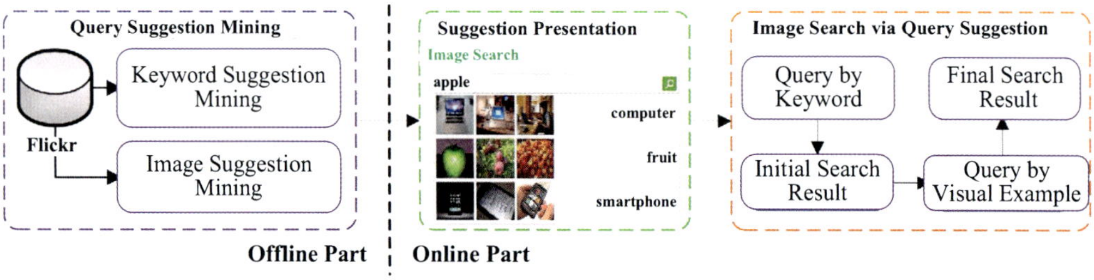

Fig. (5): System framework of VQS. VQS contains three components: (1) query suggestion mining: discovering both image and keyword suggestions for user's current query; (2) suggestion presentation: showing the keyword-image suggestions in a dropdown menu; and (3) image search with query suggestion: performing image search using text search techniques and refining the search results by using the selected image suggestion as *query example*.

suggestions. The first step involves a statistical method that can suggest keywords (i.e., tags) to reduce the ambiguity of the initial query . In the second step, for each keyword suggestion, we first collect the images associated with both the initial query and the suggested keyword, and cluster these images, with each cluster representing one aspect of the combined query. We then select the most representative images from these clusters to form the image suggestions.

Keyword suggestion generation

Given an ambiguous query Q (i.e., a keyword or a list of keywords), our goal is to find a set of keywords $\mathcal{S}_Q$ from the whole set of keywords $\mathcal{S}$. These keywords should be able to resolve the ambiguity of Q. Therefore, they should satisfy the following two properties [23]:

- **Relatedness**: Each of the selected keywords $q \in \mathcal{S}_Q$ is inherently related to the initial query Q;
- **Informativeness**: The selected keywords $\mathcal{S}_Q$ are informative enough such that they can reflect different aspects of the initial query Q.

A good example of an ambiguous query is "apple," since it has various meanings. For the query "apple," the keywords "fruit," "computer," "smartphone" are all good suggestions because they are inherently related to "apple" and reflect the different aspects of "apple."

A probabilistic formulation is developed to addresses the above two properties simultaneously. The relatedness between $q_i \in \mathcal{S}_Q$ and Q is calculated based on their co-occurrence, which is defined as the following conditional probability [21].

$$p(q_i|Q) = \frac{I(q_i \cap Q)}{I(Q)}, \tag{1}$$

where $I(Q)$ denotes the number of images associated with Q, and $I(q_i \cap Q)$ is the number of images associated with both q_i and Q. The relatedness between q_i and Q is then computed as

$$R(q_i, Q) = f\big(p(q_i|Q)\big), \tag{2}$$

where $f(\cdot)$ is certain monotonically increasing function. We define $f(\cdot)$ as the standard sigmoid function in the experiments. Accordingly, the relatedness between a keyword set $\mathcal{S}_Q$ and Q is given by

$$R(\mathcal{S}_Q, Q) = \sum_{q_i \in \mathcal{S}_Q} R(q_i, Q). \tag{3}$$

To address the second property, we find a set of keywords $\mathcal{S}_Q$ that can diversely reflect various aspects of the initial query Q. Each keyword $q_i \in \mathcal{S}_Q$ should be informative enough such that it is able to reflect one facet of Q. Meanwhile, this facet should be different from those characterized by other keywords $q_j \in \mathcal{S}_Q \backslash \{q_i\}$. We assume that q_i and q_j reflect two different aspects of Q if appending q_i or q_j to Q can result in very different distribution over the remaining keywords $q \in \mathcal{S} \backslash \{q_i, q_j\}$. That is to say, q_i and q_j can resolve the ambiguity of Q if the distribution $p(q|Q \cup \{q_i\})$ and $p(q|Q \cup \{q_j\})$ are quite different [23]. For example, given the query "apple," the keywords co-occurring with {"apple," "fruit"} and those with {"apple," "computer"} are quite different. Therefore, appending "fruit" or "computer" to "apple" leads to two different distributions, i.e., $p(q|\text{"}apple,\text{"}\,\text{"}fruit\text{"})$ and $p(q|\text{"}apple,\text{"}\,\text{"}computer\text{"})$. Here, we use the symmetric Kullback-Leibler (KL) divergence [15, 23] to measure the distribution difference between $p(q|Q \cup \{q_i\})$ and $p(q|Q \cup \{q_j\})$ as

$$\widetilde{KL}(q_i||q_j) = KL(q_i||q_j) + KL(q_j||q_i), \tag{4}$$

where

$$KL(q_i||q_j) = \sum\nolimits_q p\big(q|Q \cup \{q_i\}\big) \log \frac{p(q|Q \cup \{q_i\})}{p(q|Q \cup \{q_j\})}. \tag{5}$$

Accordingly, we define the informativeness of $\{q_i, q_j\}$ with respect to Q as

$$D(q_i, q_j, Q) = g\big(\widetilde{KL}(q_i, q_j)\big), \tag{6}$$

where $g(\cdot)$ is a monotonically increasing function. The informativeness of a keyword set $\mathcal{S}_Q$ can be measured as $\sum_{q_j, q_k \in \mathcal{S}_Q} D(q_j, q_k, Q)$.

Afterwards, we can seek for the keyword suggestions $\mathcal{S}_Q$ for the query Q by solving the following problem:

$$\mathcal{S}_Q^* = \arg\max_{\mathcal{S}_Q} \Big\{ \frac{\lambda}{N} \sum_{q_i \in \mathcal{S}_Q} R(q_i, Q) + \frac{(1-\lambda)}{C_N^2} \sum_{q_j, q_k \in \mathcal{S}_Q} D(q_j, q_k, Q) \Big\} \tag{7}$$

where $N = |\mathcal{S}_Q|$ is the number of the selected keywords. λ $(0 \leqslant \lambda \leqslant 1)$ is a tradeoff parameter.

However, it is computationally intractable to solve Eq. (7) directly since it is a non-linear integer programming (NIP) problem [2]. Alternatively, we resort to a greedy strategy which is simple but effective in solving NIP problem. The process is illustrated in Algorithm 2. In real-world problems, most keywords $q \in \mathcal{S}$ are not related to Q. Therefore, we can only consider the keywords with large $R(q, Q)$ in Algorithm 2. This will further accelerate the suggestion generation process. With the discovered keywords $\mathcal{S}_Q$, we move our effort to generate the image suggestions in the next section.

Image suggestion generation

As aforementioned, VQS system provides not only keyword suggestions but also image suggestions. Consider a suggested keyword q for the query Q, we firstly collect the images associated with both q and Q from Flickr image set. The representative images are then selected to form the image suggestions for keyword q. Here, we adopt the Affinity Propagation (AP) method to find a small number of representative images that can accurately represent the corresponding keyword suggestion [8].

Algorithm 2 Keyword suggestion generation

Input: $\mathcal{S}$, Q
Output: $\mathcal{S}_Q^*$
Initialization: set $\mathcal{S}_Q^* = \emptyset$
1: **for each** iteration t **do**
2: $\mathcal{S}_Q^* = \emptyset$, $L(\mathcal{S}_Q^{(t)}) = 0$;
3: randomly select the first keyword q from $\mathcal{S} \setminus \mathcal{S}_Q^{(t)}$;
4: $\mathcal{S}_Q^{(t)} = \mathcal{S}_Q^{(t)} \cup \{q\}$;
5: select the next keyword q_i from $\mathcal{S} \setminus \mathcal{S}_Q^{(t)}$ by solving
$\arg\max_{q_i} L(q_i) =$
$\arg\max_{q_i} \left\{ \lambda R(q_i, Q) + \frac{(1-\lambda)}{|\mathcal{S}_Q^{(t)}|} \sum_{q_j \in \mathcal{S}_Q^{(t)}} D(q_i, q_j, Q) \right\}$
$L(\mathcal{S}_Q^{(t)}) = L(\mathcal{S}_Q^{(t)}) + L(q_i)$;
6: **if** $\Delta L(\mathcal{S}_Q^{(t)}) > e$ where e is a threshold **do**
$\mathcal{S}_Q^{(t)} = \mathcal{S}_Q^{(t)} \cup \{q_i\}$, go to step 5;
else
end this iteration;
end if;
7: **end for**
return $\mathcal{S}_Q^* = \arg\max_t L(\mathcal{S}_Q^{(t)})$

Based on the collected image set $\mathcal{I} = \{I_i\}_{i=1}^N$ for (Q, q), and the similarity measure $s(I_i, I_j)$ between two images, our goal is to cluster $\mathcal{I}$ into M $(M < N)$ clusters, each represented by the most representative image called "exemplar". In affinity propagation, all the images are considered as potential exemplars [8]. Each of them is regarded as a node in a network. The real-valued message is recursively transmitted via the edges of the network until a good set of exemplars and their corresponding clusters emerge. Let $\mathcal{I}_e = \{I_{ei}\}_{i=1}^M$ denote the final exemplars and $e(I)$ represent the exemplar of image I. In brief, the AP algorithm propagates two kinds of information between images: 1) the "responsibility" $r(i, j)$ transmitted from image i to image j, which measures how well-suited I_j is to serve as the exemplar for I_i by simultaneously considering other potential exemplars for I_i , and 2) the "availability" $a(i, j)$ sent from candidate exemplar I_j to I_i, which reflects how appropriately I_i chooses I_j as exemplar by simultaneously considering other potential images that may choose I_j as their exemplar. This information is iteratively updated by

$$\begin{aligned} r(i,j) &\leftarrow s(I_i, I_j) - \max_{j \neq j'} \left\{ a(i, j') + s(I_i, I_{j'}) \right\}, \\ a(i,j) &\leftarrow \min\{0, r(j,j)\} + \sum_{i' \notin \{i,j\}} \max\left\{0, r(i', j)\right\}. \end{aligned} \tag{8}$$

The "self-availability" $a(j, j)$ is updated by

$$a(j, j) \leftarrow \sum_{i' \neq j} \max \{0, r(i', j)\}. \tag{9}$$

The exemplar $e(I_i)$ of image I_i is chosen as $e(I_i) = I_j$ by solving

$$\arg\max_j \{r(i, j) + a(i, j)\}. \tag{10}$$

The original AP algorithm that uses fully connected network may lead to a high computational cost of $O(N^2T)$, where T is the number of iterations. A solution to this problem is to perform AP on a sparse network [14]. This can be accomplished by constructing a sparse graph $\mathcal{G} = \langle \mathcal{V}, \mathcal{E} \rangle$, where $\mathcal{V}$ is the image set and $\mathcal{E}$ represents the edges between images. Here, we construct the graph using the k-nearest neighbor strategy [10]. However, when we perform AP on a sparse graph, each data point can and only can be the exemplar of $(k + 1)$ data points. In other words, there are at least N/k exemplars. which is much more than expected. To address this problem, we adopt an edge refinement method proposed in [14], which is summarized in Algorithm 3. In each iteration, multiple exemplars may be merged into one cluster. The AP performed on the re-constructed graph may generate fewer exemplars. Once the number of exemplars is reduced to a desirable value, the iteration can be ended. The final exemplars are regarded as the image suggestions.

Algorithm 3 Image suggestion generation

Input: $\mathcal{I}$, $\mathcal{G}$
Output: $\mathcal{I}_e$
Initialization: set $\mathcal{G}^{(0)} = \mathcal{G}$
1: **for each** iteration t **do**
2: Generate $\mathcal{I}_e^{(t)}$ with AP on $\mathcal{G}^{(t-1)}$, $\mathcal{I}_e = \mathcal{I}_e^{(t)}$;
3: Construct $\mathcal{G}^{(t)}$ based on $\mathcal{I}_e^{(t)}$ and $\mathcal{G}^{(t-1)}$
(1) for each $I_i \in \mathcal{I}_e^{(t)}$, if I_i is the exemplar of I_j, then an edge between I_i and I_j is added;
2) for I_k,$I_l \in \mathcal{I}_e^{(t)}$, if there are two data points I_m, I_n that are the neighbor to each other and satisfy $e(I_m) = I_k$ and $e(I_n) = I_l$, then I_k, I_l are connected by an edge;
(3) for $I_k, I_l \in \mathcal{I}_e^{(t)}$, if they are connected in (2), then all data points that choose I_k as exemplar are connected to I_l, and vice versa.
4: **end for**
return $\mathcal{I}_e$

Image search via joint keyword-image suggestion

After the user chooses a keyword-image suggestion, the keyword is appended to the initial query. This results in a composite query, with which VQS system performs image search using text-based search techniques. However, due to the mismatch between the image content and the associated text, the performance of text-based image search is usually unsatisfactory. On the other hand, the user-selected image suggestion inherently reflects the user's search intent and the visual content of the image is potentially useful to improve text-based image search [11, 12, 18, 29].

Therefore, we propose to refine the text-based search results by exploiting visual information. A re-ranking method is developed to re-rank the returned images according to the visual similarities between them and the selected image suggestion. It is worth noting that the system is extensible as any other re-ranking algorithm can be easily integrated. Suppose there are K visual modalities (e.g., color, shape, and texture), we first calculate the visual similarities $\mathcal{S}_k = \{s_{ki}\}_{i=1}^N$ between the returned images and the user-selected image suggestion I_q on the k-th modality, where N is the number of returned images. Then, all the K visual information are aggregated to refine the initial search results through the following equation.

$$\begin{aligned} r_i &= \alpha_0 r_{0i} + \sum_{k=1}^{K} \alpha_k s_{ki}, \\ s.t. \quad & \alpha_0 + \sum_{k=1}^{K} \alpha_k = 1, \quad i = 1, \cdots, N \end{aligned} \tag{11}$$

where r_{0i} denote the initial relevance score between the query and the image I_i, which is generated by text-based search method [19]. r_i is the refined relevance score, α_0 and α_k are the weighting parameters used to modulate the textual and visual information. Since the similarities over different modalities may vary significantly, the visual similarities $\{s_{ki}\}_{i=1}^N$ over each modality are normalized such that s_{ki} is with zero mean and unified variance. The initial relevance scores $r_{0i}$are also normalized in the same way.

After obtaining the final relevance scores $\mathcal{R} = \{r_i\}_{i=1}^N$, the VQS system presents the images sorted by the relevance scores with a descending order.

4 Performance Evaluation

We conducted extensive experiments and evaluations, including both subjective and objective evaluations, as well as the comparison between the proposed VQS and three popular image search engines. We first evaluated the performance of query suggestion provided by VQS system, and then investigated the performance of image search via VQS.

Tab. (1): Sample initial queries used in the experiments.

Initial Query	
airshow	animal
apple	building
camping	car
disaster	flag
flight	flower
fruit	game
insect	panorama
Paris	plant
portrait	road
scenic	season
sky	sports
sunset	travel
weather	

Data and methodologies

To generate keyword-image suggestions, We used Flickr images as our database. Flickr is the most popular image sharing sit that allows users to upload, share, and tag their photos. We have collected 3 million Flickr images, which were associated with about 15 million keywords in total. To evaluate the performance of image search with visual query suggestions, one popular image search engine (i.e., Engine III) was adopted as the baseline search engine. We used Engine III to retrieve images with each initial query and the corresponding renewed query, which is the combination of the initial query and the keyword suggestion. The top 1,000 returned images of each query are crawled to construct the experimental data set . To obtain the ground truth of the relevance orders of the returned images, we resorted to a manual labeling procedure. Specifically, each image was labeled as three relevance levels with respect to the query: level 2—"highly relevant," level 1—"relevant," and level 0—"irrelevant." We invited 20 subjects to manually label the relevance levels of these returned images. Each image was labeled by at least three subjects. The ground truth is obtained through the majority voting of subjects' labeling.

To represent the image content, we extract three types of visual features, including (1) 225-dimensional block-wise color moment based on 5-by-5 division of the image, (2) 128-dimensional wavelet texture, and (3) 75-dimensional edge distribution histogram [19]. The visual similarity between two images is calculated as $\exp(-||x_i - x_j||^2)$, where x_i is the feature vector of image I_i. The monotonically increasing function $f(\cdot)$ in equation 2 and $g(\cdot)$ in equation 6 are defined as the sigmoid function, i.e., $f(x) = g(x) = \frac{1}{1+e^{-x}}$. The tradeoff parameter in equation 7is

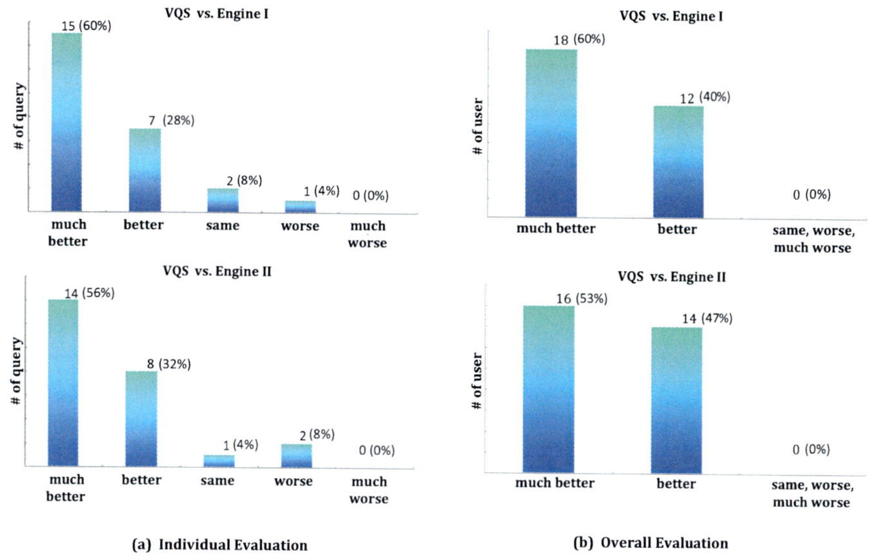

Fig. (6): Comparison results between VQS and existing image search engine I and II from the 30 "professional" users.

empirically set to 0.7. All the tradeoff parameters in equation 11 are set to $\frac{1}{K+1}$.

Suggestion quality evaluation

We conducted two user studies to evaluate the VQS. The first study aimed to compare VQS with two existing query suggestion services provided by Engine I and Engine II. While the second study evaluated the usefulness of VQS.

Two groups of users were invited, including 30 "professional" users and 10 "average" users. The "professional" users here refer to the users who are familiar with image search. The 30 "professional" users included 28 graduate students and two researchers. All of them had the experience of using image search engines more than once per week. The "average" users refer to the users who are not familiar with image search. The 10 "average" users covered a wide variety of backgrounds, such as sales people, marketing people, teachers, government officers and so on. In total, there were 40 users including 30 males and 10 females. Their ages range from 21 to 55.

To facilitate the evaluation and comparison, we selected 25 representative queries (see Tab.(1)) from the query log of Engine III. These queries belong to different types such as scene, object, and event. For each query, we selected four keyword suggestions and three image suggestions for each keyword. As a result, there were 300 ($25 \times 4 \times 3$) pairs of initial query and keyword-image suggestion for evaluation.

The users were required to submit the 25 queries one-by-one to the three image search systems, i.e., Engine I, Engine II, and the VQS system. Then, they were asked to provide the following evaluations:

- **Individual evaluation** We compared VQS with Engine I and Engine II separately. Based on the observation of the suggestion service of VQS, Engine I(II) for each query, participants were asked to give a score from "2" to "-2," which indicates that VQS performs much better, better, closely, worse, and much worse than Engine I(II), respectively.
- **Overall evaluation**: Similarly, evaluators were also asked to give the overall comparisons between VQS and existing image search engines. They were asked to choose one from the five options: VQS performs "much better," "better," "same," "worse," and "much worse" than Engine I(II).

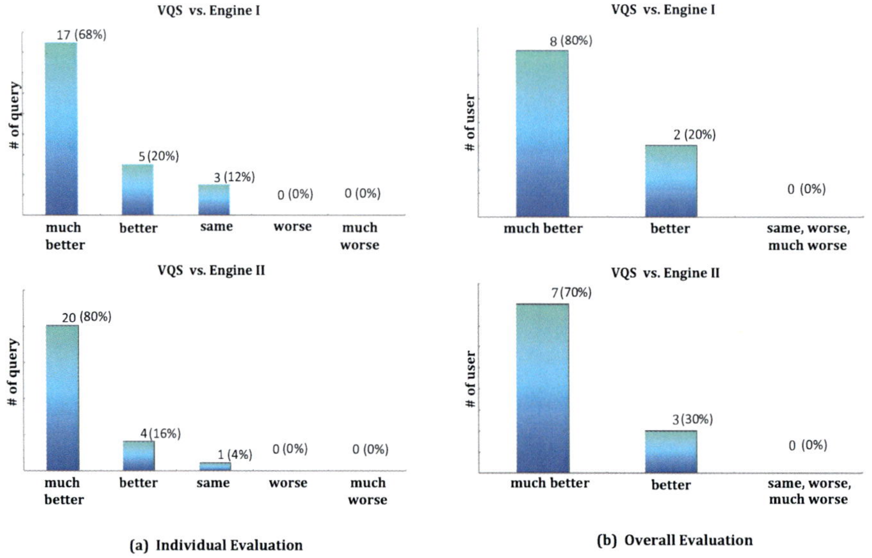

Fig. (7): Comparison results between VQS and existing image search engine I and II from the 10 "average" users who are not familiar with image search.

The results from 30 "professional" users are illustrated in Fig. (6). Fig. (6) (a) provides the average numbers of the queries with the score "2," "1," "0," "-1," or "-2" from the 30 participants. Compared to Engine I, the VQS system performs much better over 15 queries, better over 7 queries, closely over two queries, and worse on only one query. Compared to Engine II, the VQS system provides much better suggestions for 14 queries and better suggestions for eight queries. Fig. (6) (b) shows the overall evaluation. All the 30 users consider VQS system outperforms existing image search engines. Specifically, 60% and 53% users reported

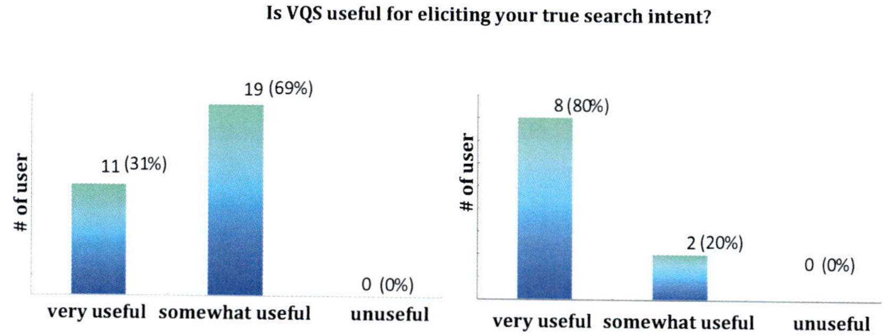

(a) "Professional" User (b) "Average" User

Fig. (8): Evaluation result of the usefulness of VQS.

that the query suggestions of VQS system are much better than those of Engine I and Engine II, respectively. shows the evaluation result from the 10 "average" users. They considered that VQS system performs much better than Engine I on 17 queries, better on 5 queries, and closely on 3 queries, while they thought VQS system performs much better than Engine II over 20 queries, better over 4 queries, and closely over 1 query. In the overall evaluation, all of them thought VQS system outperforms existing image search engines.

To evaluate the usefulness of VQS system, participants were invited to answer the question "Is VQS useful for eliciting your true search intents?" They were asked to choose one from three options: "very useful" "somewhat useful," and "unuseful." Fig. (8)(a) shows the evaluation results from the 30 "professional" users. The VQS system was regarded to be very useful by 30% users and be useful to the remaining 70% users. As indicated in Fig. (8)(b), eight out of the 10 "average" users considered VQS system is very useful and the remaining two thought it is useful.

From the above user studies, we can find that the proposed VQS system outperforms existing popular image search engines and it is useful for better eliciting the search intents of users.

Search performance evaluation

We evaluate the performance of three search strategies:

- **IQ**: searching images using the initial query;
- **IQ+KS**: searching images using the combined query consisting of the initial query and the keyword suggestion;
- **IQ+KS+IS**: re-ranking the returned images of IQ+KS based on the selected image suggestion.

The average performance over the 25 queries is reported for the evaluation.

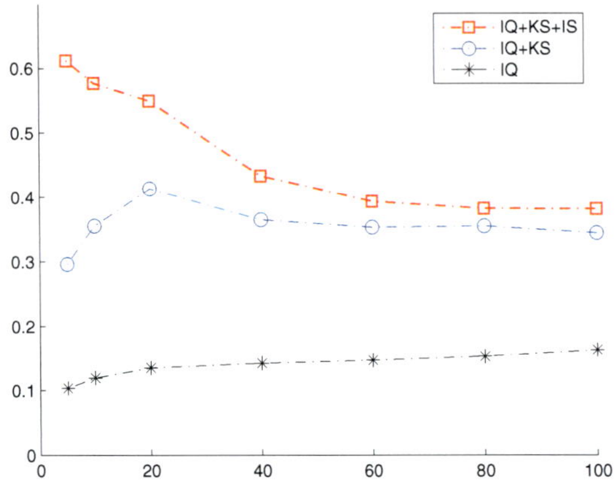

Fig. (9): Comparison of NDCG@k for three search strategies: searching images using IQ, IQ+KS, and IQ+KS+IS.

We adopt the Normalized Discounted Cumulative Gain at top k (NDCG@k) as the evaluation metric, which is calculated by

$$NDCG@k = \frac{1}{Z}\sum_{n=1}^{k}\frac{2^{s(p)}-1}{\log(1+p)} \tag{12}$$

where $s(p)$ is the function that represents reward given to the retrieved image at position p, Z is a normalization term derived from the perfect ranking of top k images so that it can normalize NDCG@k to be [0, 1].

Fig. (9) shows the performance comparison of the three approaches (i.e., IQ, IQ+KS, and IQ+KS+IS) with respect to the rank position k. We can see that IQ leads to unsatisfactory performance due to the Intention Gap between user's search intent and the initial query. By appending keyword suggestion to the initial query and searching images with the renewed query, IQ+KS represents the search intent more clearly and thus outperforms the IQ strategy. By further specifying the search intent using image suggestion and leveraging visual information, the IQ+KS+IS strategy gets the best performance.

5 Conclusions

In this chapter, we have briefly reviewed textual query suggestion technique and introduced a novel visual query suggestion approach dedicated to Internet image search. Unlike textual query suggestion only suggests a list of keywords, visual query suggestion provides both keyword and image suggestions simultaneously. It is able to help users specify and deliver their search intents in a more precise and efficient way. Extensive experiments have been conducted to evaluate the VQS system against three popular image search engines. The experimental results show that VQS system outperforms these engines in terms of the quality of query suggestions and search performance.

6 References

[1] Doug Beeferman and Adam Berger. Agglomerative clustering of a search engine query log. In *ACM SIGKDD*, 2000.

[2] Stephen Boyd and Lieven Vandenberghe. Convex optimization. *Cambridge University Press*, 2004.

[3] Claudio Carpineto, Renato De Mori, Giovanni Romano, and Brigitte Bigi. An information-theoretic approach to automatic query expansion. *ACM transactions on Information Systems*, 2001.

[4] Chien-Kang Huang, Lee-Feng Chien, Yen-Jen Oyang. Relevant term suggestion in interactive web search based on contextual information in query session logs. *Journal of the American Society for Information Science and Technology*, 2003.

[5] Rosie Jones, Benjamin Rey, Omid Madani, Wiley Greiner. Generating query substitutions. In *ACM WWW*, 2006.

[6] Bruno M. Fonseca, Paulo Golgher, Bruno Possas, Berthier Ribeiro-Neto, Nivio Ziviani.. Concept-based Interactive Query Expansion. In *ACM CIKM*, 2005.

[7] Ritendra Datta, Dhiraj Joshi, Jia Li , and James Z. Wang. Image retrieval: ideas, influences, and trends of the new age. *ACM Computing Surveys*, 2008.

[8] Brendan J. Frey and Delbert Dueck. Clustering by passing messages between data points. *Science*, 2007.

[9] Richard Gerrig and Philip Zimbardo. *Psychology and Life (16 Edition)*. Allyn & Bacon, 2001.

[10] Daniel Heesch and Stefan M. Rger. Nnk networks for content-based image retrieval. In *ECIR*, 2004.

[11] Winston H. Hsu, Lyndon S. Kennedy, and Shih-Fu Chang. Video search reranking via information bottleneck principle. In *ACM Multimedia*, 2006.

[12] Xinmei Tian, Linjun Yang, Jingdong Wang, Yichen Yang, Xiuqing Wu, Xian-Sheng Hua. Bayesian Video Search Reranking. In *ACM Multimedia*, 2008.

[13] Yuan Liu, Tao Mei. CrowdReranking: exploring multiple search engines for visual search reranking. In *Proceedings of ACM International Conference on Research and Development in Information Retrieval*, 2009.

[14] Yangqing Jia, Jingdong Wang, Changshui Zhang, and Xian-Sheng Hua. Finding image exemplars using fast sparse affinity propagation. In *ACM Multimedia*, 2008.

[15] S. Kullback and R.A. Leibler. On information and sufficiency. *Annals of Mathematical Statistics*, 1951.

[16] Adenike M. Lam-Adesina and Gareth J. F. Jones. Applying summarization techniques for term selection in relevance feedback. In *ACM SIGIR*, 2001.

[17] Michael S. Lew, Nicu Sebe, Chabane Djeraba, and Ramesh Jain. Content-based multimedia information retrieval: state of the art and challenges. *ACM Transactions on Multimedia Computing, Communications and Applications*, 2006.

[18] Yuan Liu, Tao Mei, and Xian-Sheng Hua. CrowdReranking: Exploring multiple search engines for visual search reranking. In *ACM SIGIR*, 2009.

[19] Tao Mei, Xian-Sheng Hua, Wei Lai, Linjun Yang, Zheng-Jun Zha, Yuan Liu, Zhiwei Gu, Guo-Jun Qi, Meng Wang, Jinhui Tang, Xun Yuan, Zheng Lu, and Jingjing Liu. MSRA-USTC-SJTU at TRECVID 2007: High-level feature extraction and search. In *TREC Video Retrieval Evaluation Online Proceedings*, 2007.

[20] Ricardo Baeza-Yates, Carlos Hurtado, and Marcelo Mendoza. Query recommendation using query logs in search engines. In *Proceedings of International Conference on Extending Database Technology*, 2004.

[21] Börkur Sigurbörnsson and Roelof van Zwol. Flickr tag recommendation based on collective knowledge. In *ACM WWW*, 2008.

[22] Arnold W.M. Smeulders, Marcel Worring, Simone Santini, Amarnath Gupta, and Ramesh Jain. Content-based image retrieval at the end of the early years. *IEEE Transactions on Pattern Analysis and Machine Intelligence*, 2000.

[23] Kilian Weinberger, Malcolm Slaney, and Roelof van Zwol. Resolving tag ambiguity. In *ACM Multimedia*, 2008.

[24] Ji-Rong Wen, Jian-Yun Nie, and Hong-Jiang Zhang. Clustering user queries of a search engine. In *ACM WWW*, 2003.

[25] Jinxi Xu and W. Bruce Croft. Query expansion using local and global document analysis. In *ACM SIGIR*, 1996.

[26] Shipeng Yu, Deng Cai, Ji-Rong Wen, and Wei-Ying Ma. Improving pseudo-relevance feedback in web information retrieval using web page segmentation. In *ACM WWW*, 2003.

[27] Huanhuan Cao, Daxin Jiang, Jian Pei, Qi He, ZZhen Liao, Enhong Chen and Hang Li. Context-Aware Query Suggestion by Mining Click-Through and Session Data. In *ACM SIGKDD*, 2008.

[28] Zheng-Jun Zha, Linjun Yang, Tao Mei, Meng Wang, Zengfu Wang. Visual Query Suggestion. In *ACM Multimedia*, 2009.

[29] Shiliang Zhang, Qi Tian, Gang Hua, Qingming Huang, Shipeng Li. Discriptive Visual Words and Visual Phrases for Image Applications. In *ACM Multimedia*, 2009.

[30] Zheng-Jun Zha, Linjun Yang, Tao Mei, Meng Wang, Zengfu Wang, Tat-Seng Chua, Xian-Sheng Hua Visual Query Suggestion: Towards Capturing User Intent in Internet Image Search. *ACM Transactions on Multimedia Computing, Communications and Applications*, 2010.

CHAPTER 17

Image Search by Color Sketch

Jingdong Wang*
Microsoft Research Asia, Tel: +86(10) 59173786, Email: jingdw@microsoft.com
Yinghai Zhao
University of Science and Technology of China, Tel: +8613716398968, Email: yinghai.zhao@gmail.com
Xian-Sheng Hua
Microsoft Research, Tel: +1 (425) 4214405, Email: xshua@microsoft.com

Abstract: Most existing Web image search engines exploit the text information associated with images (e.g., from the surrounding text, or image title) to index images. It is still difficult and challenging to search images into the image content. Tagging is a solution, but is limited in some specific styles or types (e.g., dominant color, clip art, line drawing, or photo). In this chapter, we present a new interactive image search system, which enables users to interactively indicate the search intention, how the colors are spatially distributed in desired images, by scribbling a few color strokes or dragging an image and highlighting a few regions of interest in an intuitive way. Moreover, we propose an effective scheme to mine the latent search intention from the user's input. Experimental results demonstrate the effectiveness and efficiency of the proposed system.

Keywords

Image search, color sketch, intention map, image content, interactive image search, QBIC, spatial correspondence, spatial relation, contextual color map,color similarity, spatial occurrence

***Correspondence Author:** Jingdong Wang, Microsoft Research Asia; Email: jingdw@microsoft.com.

Xian-Sheng Hua, Marcel Worring & Tat-Seng Chua (Eds.)

1 Introduction

With the rapid development of commercial image search engines, people can easily get a large amount of images by inputting a text query. However, existing search engines return search results only using the relevance of text information (e.g., the surrounding text) of images with the text query. This does not meet with users' requirement because a handful of keywords are generally insufficient for characterizing an image. Visually different images may have the similar keywords, or visually similar images could be labeled by very different keywords. If a person seeks an image with visual characteristics that cannot be easily expressed in keywords, they generally result in scrolling through large numbers of results in search of desired images.

To help users search images, existing popular Web image search engines have provided search options to filter image search results, according to tags associated with images. One common search option is the pornographic content filter, which eliminates most inappropriate material by checking whether the image comes from adult sites or detecting the image content. Some image search engines also support search options, e.g., image size (small, medium, large, icon, wallpaper, and so on), layout (square, wide, and tall), types (photo, clip art, and line drawing), color (color and gray), and whether an image includes only faces, head and shoulders, or others.

Recently, Google image search released a new search option, which can be viewed as a filter by a dominant color, i.e., searching images that contains a specific color, such as red, pink, or green. But this search option is limited in that it cannot describe the spatial distribution of colors in an image. The spatial distribution of colors, called color map in this chapter, in some sense can describe the semantic meaning. For example, for the query "flower", a color map, with the red color in the middle and the green color around the red color, can describe an image with the semantic meaning that the red flower is in the middle and surrounded by green leaves. For the query "Brooke Hogan" (an American singer, actress, model, and television personality), a color map, with the red color on the bottom, may mean to find Brooke Hogan walking on the red carpet.

In this chapter, we present a novel image search technique, image search by color sketch, which enables end-users to intuitively indicate the search intent on the spatial distribution of colors for promoting images matching the specified color map. To use the technique, end-users merely sketch a few color strokes in a blank canvas, or drag an image to the blank canvas and mask the color regions of interest, to roughly show the desired spatial distribution of colors. Our system mines and formulates the search intent from the user's input, and rerank image search results to help users find desired images.

For example, given image search results shown in Fig. (1)(a), users may be interested in images with blue sky on the top and green grasses on the bottom. But it is difficult to only use a text query to meet such requirement; it is time-costly

(a) (b) (c)

Fig. (1): Image search by color map. (a) shows the original search results, (b) shows the target color map, and (c) shows the refined results.

to scroll search results to manually find such images; it is also difficult to merely use example images to indicate the requirement because the intent from example images is ambiguous and not easily automatically mined. Using our system, we can have reordered top 24 results as shown in Fig. (1)(c) according to the target color map sketched by some user, e.g., as shown in Fig. (1)(b).

2 Related Work

There are many efforts that have been made to refine image search results. There exist two types of refinement methods, including visual reranking [8, 10], and implicit intent based search [3]. Visual reranking is to reorder images only according to image visual content, but it does not present a way to introduce users' intent into refinement. Intentsearch [3], which is very similar to query-by-example, tries to make use of users' intent, but the intent is given in an implicit way by selecting several images, and has to be carefully mined, which is very difficult in practice. Other online systems include Tiltomo (`http://www.tiltomo.com/`), and GazoPa (`http://www.gazopa.com/`). Differently, the method proposed in this chapter aims to deliver an explicit way to allow users to express the intent, specifically, sketching a color map, and reorder the images according to the consistency of the colors and their spatial map between target color map and images.

In the conventional query by image content (QBIC) image retrieval methods (a literature survey can be found from [4, 18]), color content has been investigated. We will review the most relevant techniques that specify the query by providing color strokes or dependently on the colors. Almost all these methods represent the whole image with little ability of distinguishing the spatial relation of different colors. Those methods roughly consist of two types: global color feature and color spatial correspondence.

The simple technique is to allow users to merely select colors of interest or input a color image and return the images according to the global color feature [16]. Some online applications based on this technique have been delivered, e.g., multicolor search lab (`http://labs.ideeinc.com/multicolour/`) and Color Fields Experimental Colr Pickr (`http://www.krazydad.com/colrpickr/`). However, this technique only makes use of the frequency feature (histogram) of target colors to rank the images, without using any spatial information.

Color based retrieval by sketch, instead, allows users to scribble a color image, which provides the color-spatial information. This kind of method is usually to view the sketched image as an example image and directly evaluates the similarity by matching the most pronounced slabs of colors, i.e., spatial correspondence. More attention on this topic has been paid to pursuit fast retrieval techniques, including fast wavelet based matching [9, 20], sequenced multi-attribute tree [15], filtering out some irrelevant images [2], multi-precision querying [12], and etc. There are some Web application examples, such as Retrievr (`http://labs.systemone.at/retrievr/`) that is implemented using the fast multiresolution technique [9], and hermitage Web site (`http://www.hermitagemuseum.org/fcgi-bin/db2www/qbicLayout.mac/qbic?selLang=English`) that is based on IBM's query by image content [6]. Those methods only take into account spatial correspondence of individual colors across images, but without exploring spatial relation among different colors as a factor for similarity evaluation.

Besides, VisualSEEk [19], another color content based image retrieval method, tries to utilize spatial relation between colors to help image retrieval. But there are several differences between it and our approach. 1) They have different capability to make use of spatial relation. The capability of VisualSEEk is limited in that it adopts 2D string to approximate the spatial relation, while ours is direct to exploit the spatial relation using a set of spatially-relational colors. 2) They have different map representation. VisualSEEk's spatial relation representation is a little complicated and is not suitable for real applications, while our representation is more compact, more efficient and effective for ranking, and hence more practical. 3) Our approach has the extra ability to deal with the uncertainty of target color map, which reduces the user's labor of specifying it.

There are some other relevant techniques. The sketch-based image retrieval system [1, 13, 14] (e.g., GazoPa similar image search `http://www.gazopa.com/`) also provides a mechanism for users to sketch an image, but differently the shape consistency between sketched image and images in the database is adopted to search the images. The spatial distribution information among objects is also exploited for image retrieval [7, 5], but the information is represented by a complicated graph model, leading to the difficulty of evaluating the similarity between the representations in both the accuracy and the computation.

Contributions

In this chapter, we present a novel image search system, image search by color sketch. A novel scheme is introduced to represent the color map with a set of spatially-relational colors. This representation is very sufficient to represent the color map, particularly for the target color map which is composed of only a few color strokes. Some powerful image representations, e.g., spatial pyramid matching [11], multi-precision histogram [12], and so on, are essentially unsuitable to represent the target color map since there are only a few color strokes instead of a whole image. Moreover, the proposed color map representation makes the similarity evaluation more powerful. The proposed novel similarity evaluation scheme takes into consideration color spatial correspondence across images, which is exploited in the conventional image retrieval techniques based on query by image content, and additionally the spatial relation of different colors within an image is even investigated to compare the images, which is less investigated in the conventional methods. Furthermore, the proposed method does not need the user to specify the target color map accurately, and our method offers a scheme to deal with the roughness. Besides, a convenient interactive interface is presented to allow users to sketch target color map flexibly.

Organization

The remainder of this chapter is organized as follows. Section 3 presents the color map extraction method. Section 4 gives the similarity evaluation scheme. Section 5 introduces the target color map specification mechanism. Section 6 reports experimental results to demonstrate the proposed approach. Finally, Section 7 concludes this chapter.

3 Color Map Extraction

The proposed color map extraction process, consists of two steps: extract representative colors for each cell and concatenate them into spatial maps with each corresponding to the same quantized color.

Representative colors

We divide the image uniformly into $g \times g$ grids. For each grid (x, y), we aim to find dominant colors, $\mathcal{C}_{xy} = \{\mathbf{c}_{xy}^i\}$, to represent the colors in this grid. The dominant colors are found as follows. We calculate the frequencies for all the quantized colors appearing in this grid, and sort them according to their frequencies. We select the colors corresponding to the first k largest frequencies such that $f_{i-1} < 2f_i$, $\forall i \leqslant k$ and $i \neq 1$. In our experiment, we find that $g = 8$ works well. After extracting the colors in each grid, we find the representative colors for the whole image by unifying the representative colors of all the cells,

$$\mathcal{C} = \cup_{xy}\mathcal{C}_{xy}.$$

As preprocessing, we first transform the RGB (red, green, blue) color space into the HSV (hue, saturation, value) space, which is then quantized into $n_h \times n_s \times n_v$. In this chapter, $n_h = 12$ $n_s = 4$, and $n_v = 4$, and then there are totally 192 quantized colors. The finer quantization for the hue channel is reasonable and works well because it is observed that human is perceptually more sensitive to hue variance. For each grid, in addition, we preform a median filtering to smooth the images on the HSV color space.

Color map

For each color $\mathbf{c} \in \mathcal{C}$, we introduce a term, spatial map, to indicate whether one color appears in one grid, and compute it as a binary vector $\mathbf{l}$ of dimension $g \times g$ such that

$$l_k = \begin{cases} 1 & \text{if } \mathbf{c}^i_{xy} = \mathbf{c}, \ \exists \mathbf{c}^i_{xy} \in \mathcal{C}_{xy}, \\ 0 & \text{else,} \end{cases}$$

where k is one dimensional index corresponding to two dimensional indices (x, y). Intuitively, if color $\mathbf{c}$ appears in grid (x, y), the corresponding entry l_k is set to be 1, and 0 otherwise. Then in summary, the color map of the image is defined as a set of colors and associated spatial map, and written as $\mathcal{I} = \{(\mathbf{c}_t, \mathbf{l}_t)\}_{\mathbf{c}_t \in \mathcal{C}}$. This whole algorithm for color map extraction is easily implemented, and the computational cost is also very cheap, which will be justified in the experiment part. Moreover, the extracted color map feature is an effective feature and is proved very valuable with the combination of the proposed similarity evaluation scheme that will be presented in Section 4.

Since the spatial map, $\mathbf{l}$, is a binary vector, we can represent it in a compact manner by several byte variables, i.e., $[b_1 \ \cdots \ b_n]^T$ with $n = \lceil \frac{g^2}{8} \rceil$, which will bring fast similarity evaluation by using a precomputed lookup table. For convenience, we still use the binary vector $\mathbf{l}$ in the following presentation.

4 Color Map Similarity Evaluation

In this section, we present the similarity evaluation scheme between target color map and image color map. Suppose image color map is denoted as $\mathcal{I} = \{(\mathbf{c}_k, \mathbf{l}_k)\}$, and target color map is denoted as $\mathcal{Q} = \{(\mathbf{c}_q, \mathbf{l}_q)\}$. We made an investigation from user experience on the latent meaning for matching between target color map and image color map, and analyzed that it includes two aspects, spatial correspondence compatibility and spatial relation consistency. Therefore, we define the similarity

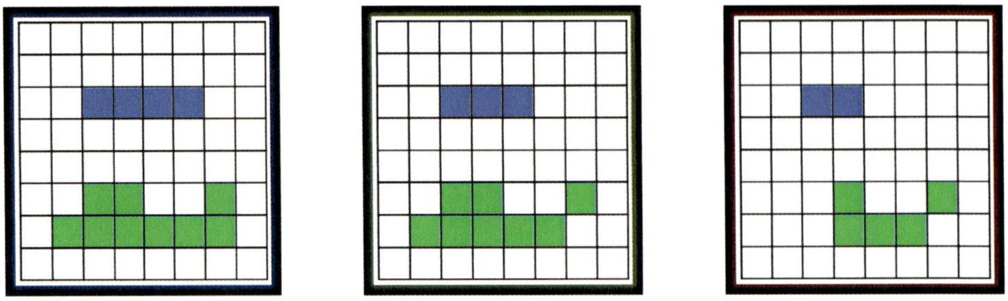

(a) (b) (c)

Fig. (2): Illustration of color spatial correspondence compatibility. (a) target color map, (b) color image 1, and (c) color image 2.

from those two points: 1) Color spatial correspondence compatibility. It takes into account the similarity of individual colors within the associated spatial areas between target color map and image color map; 2) Color spatial relation consistency. It exploits the consistency of spatial relations of different colors between target color map and image color map. In addition, to tolerate the roughness of target color map, we define another similarity: 3) Contextual color map similarity. It aims to complement the roughness of target color map, which makes users specify target color map quite conveniently.

Spatial correspondence compatibility

This subsection defines the similarity, called color spatial correspondence compatibility, to measure the accordance of each individual color appearance on the associated areas between target color map and image color map. Let's see an illustrative example in Fig. (2) to justify this compatibility measure. Figs. (2)(a), (2)(b) and (2)(c) show the target color map, color image 1, and color image 2. It is implied that color image 1 in Fig. (2)(b) is more compatible to the target color map Fig. (2)(a) as the overlapped area for target colors (blue and green) between target color map and color image 1 shown in Fig. (2)(b) is larger than the one between target color map and color image 2 shown in Fig. (2)(c).

Following this observation, we define such a color spatial correspondence compatibility measure. For each individual color in target color map, we compare its spatial map and the spatial maps of all the colors in the image, aggregate their similarities with the color similarity as the weight, and get the compatibility for this specific individual color map between it and the image. Then, we can obtain the overall compatibility by adding the compatibilities together. Mathematically,

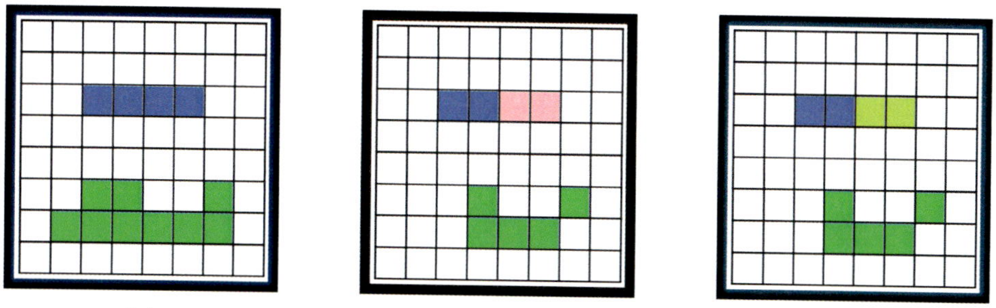

(a) (b) (c)

Fig. (3): Illustration of color spatial relation consistency. (a) target color map, (b) color image 1, and (c) color image 2.

this process is formulated as

$$\begin{aligned} s_a(\mathcal{Q}, \mathcal{I}) &= \sum_{q|\mathbf{c}_q \in \mathcal{C}_q} \frac{1}{Z_q} s_a((\mathbf{c}_q, \mathbf{l}_q), \mathcal{I}) \\ &= \sum_{q|\mathbf{c}_q \in \mathcal{C}_q} \frac{1}{Z_q} \sum_{k|\mathbf{c}_k \in \mathcal{C}_i} \text{sim}(\mathbf{c}_q, \mathbf{c}_k)\, \text{sim}(\mathbf{l}_q, \mathbf{l}_k), \end{aligned} \tag{1}$$

where $\mathcal{C}_q$ and $\mathcal{C}_i$ are the representative color sets for target color map and image color map, Z_q, a normalization variable, is equal to one norm of $\mathbf{l}_q$, $\|\mathbf{l}_q\|_1$, $s_a((\mathbf{c}_q, \mathbf{l}_q), \mathcal{I})$ is to evaluate the compatibility between the individual color map, $(\mathbf{c}_q, \mathbf{l}_q)$, and the whole image color map $\mathcal{I}$, $\text{sim}(\mathbf{c}_q, \mathbf{c}_k)$ is the color similarity between $\mathbf{c}_q$ and $\mathbf{c}_k$, $\text{sim}(\mathbf{l}_q, \mathbf{l}_k)$ is the spatial occurrence consistency between $\mathbf{l}_q$ and $\mathbf{l}_k$. The details of these two similarities will be discussed later.

Spatial relation consistency

This subsection defines another similarity to take into consideration the spatial relation of different colors between target color map and image color map. Let's consider the example in Fig. (3) to demonstrate the necessity of the color spatial relation consistency, in which color image 1 in Fig. (3)(b) is different from color image 2 in Fig. (3)(c) only in two cells. Merely using the compatibility evaluation in Eq. (1), it is not easy to differentiate the two images as this similarity measure may lead to the similar (even same) scores. However, common sense tells us that color image 1 is more similar to target color map because the aqua color in color image 2, appearing in the grids corresponding to the grids with target blue color in target color map, is more similar to the green color, which is one target color in the bottom scribbled grids of target color map. This case is called here the spatial relation inconsistency of different colors.

Therefore, we introduce a color spatial relation consistency measure. Intuitively, it is preferred that the color, appearing in the image region corresponding to one target color region, should be less similar to other target colors, otherwise it will be in conflict with the user intent in color spatial relation. Hence, we check the spatial map associated with each target color to compute the spatial consistency between it and image color map, and accumulate them together to obtain the overall consistency score. Mathematically, this spatial relation consistency is defined as

$$\begin{aligned} s_s(\mathcal{Q},\mathcal{I}) &= \sum_{q|\mathbf{c}_q\in\mathcal{C}_q} \frac{1}{Z_q} s_s((\mathbf{c}_q,\mathbf{l}_q),\mathcal{I}) \\ &= \sum_{q|\mathbf{c}_q\in\mathcal{C}_q} \frac{1}{Z_q} \sum_{k|\mathbf{c}_k\in\mathcal{C}_i} \operatorname{asim}(\mathbf{c}_q,\mathbf{c}_k,\mathcal{C}_q)\operatorname{sim}(\mathbf{l}_k,\mathbf{l}_q) \\ &= \sum_{q|\mathbf{c}_q\in\mathcal{C}_q} \frac{1}{Z_q} \sum_{k|\mathbf{c}_k\in\mathcal{C}_i} [\min_{q'|\mathbf{c}_{q'}\in\mathcal{C}_q, q'\neq q} (\operatorname{sim}(\mathbf{c}_q,\mathbf{c}_k) - \operatorname{sim}(\mathbf{c}_{q'},\mathbf{c}_k))\operatorname{sim}(\mathbf{l}_k,\mathbf{l}_q)], \end{aligned} \quad (2)$$

where $Z_q = \|\mathbf{l}_q\|_1$, $\operatorname{asim}(\mathbf{c}_q,\mathbf{c}_k,\mathcal{C}_q)$ is the similarity between target color $\mathbf{c}_q$ and color $\mathbf{c}_k$, adjusted by all the target colors $\mathcal{C}_q$. Combining it with the spatial occurrence consistency $\operatorname{sim}(\mathbf{l}_k,\mathbf{l}_q)$, the measure will reflect the consistency degree between the spatial relations of target colors in target color map and the ones of colors in the image.

Contextual color map similarity

Practice shows that users often present a rough target color map. Thus it is insufficient for color map similarity evaluation to only involve the scribbled regions in target color map. Let's see an example in Figs. (4)(b) and (4)(c). It is clear that their similarities using the above two measures are the same if target color map is given as shown in Fig. (3)(a). However, common sense will tell us that color image 2 in Fig. (4)(c) is more similar than color image 1 in Fig. (4)(b).

Therefore, we propose a scheme to "generalize" target color map. We propagate target color map by viewing the scribbled grids as seeds. Specifically, we adopt the front propagation algorithm [17] to propagate the seeded colors. To differentiate the propagated color map from the original color map, we assign different weights to the propagated grids according to their distances from the seed grids. For computational efficiency, we assign only two different weights for the propagated maps, i.e., set the weight as 0.25 for the near maps, and 0.125 for the far map. Fig. (4)(a) shows a propagation example, in which the weights are depicted by the color saturation. Let's denote the propagated weighted color map as $\bar{\mathcal{Q}} = \{(w_q, \mathbf{c}_q, \bar{\mathbf{l}}_q)\}$ with excluding the original scribbled grids. For example, in the propagated target color map in Fig. (4)(a), the propagated blue grids is represented by two types of components, with different weights and spatial maps for the same color. The similarity, w.r.t. the propagated color map, is defined as

$$s_c(\mathcal{Q},\mathcal{I}) = s'_a(\bar{\mathcal{Q}},\mathcal{I}) + s'_s(\bar{\mathcal{Q}},\mathcal{I}), \quad (3)$$

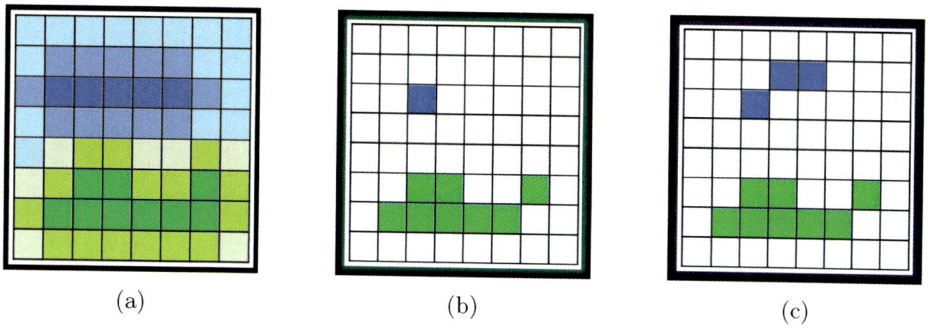

Fig. (4): Illustration of contextual color map similarity. (a) propagated target color map, (b) color image 1, and (c) color image 2.

where $s'_a(\bar{\mathcal{Q}}, \mathcal{I})$ is contextual color spatial correspondence compatibility, and $s'_s(\bar{\mathcal{Q}}, \mathcal{I})$ is contextual color spatial relation consistency. They are defined as follows,

$$s'_a(\bar{\mathcal{Q}}, \mathcal{I}) = \sum\nolimits_{q|\mathbf{c}_q \in \bar{\mathcal{C}}_q} \frac{w_q}{Z_q} s_a((\mathbf{c}_q, \bar{\mathbf{l}}_q), \mathcal{I}), \tag{4}$$

$$s'_s(\bar{\mathcal{Q}}, \mathcal{I}) = \sum\nolimits_{q|\mathbf{c}_q \in \bar{\mathcal{C}}_q} \frac{w_q}{Z_q} s_s((\mathbf{c}_q, \bar{\mathbf{l}}_q), \mathcal{I}), \tag{5}$$

where Z_q, $s_a((\mathbf{c}_q, \bar{\mathbf{l}}_q), \mathcal{I})$, and $s_s((\mathbf{c}_q, \bar{\mathbf{l}}_q), \mathcal{I})$ are same defined as the previous two subsections, and $\bar{\mathcal{C}}_q$ is the weighted representative color set for the propagated target color map.

Overall similarity measure

After obtaining all the above three measures, the whole similarity between $\mathcal{I}$ and $\mathcal{Q}$ is formulated as follows

$$s(\mathcal{Q}, \mathcal{I}) = \alpha_a s_a(\mathcal{Q}, \mathcal{I}) + \alpha_s s_s(\mathcal{Q}, \mathcal{I}) + \alpha_c s_c(\mathcal{Q}, \mathcal{I}), \tag{6}$$

where α_a, α_s and α_c are the weights for different similarity measures. We assign a less weight to $s_c(\cdot, \cdot)$ since it is a generalized one. In our experiments, we find it performs well when $\alpha_a = \alpha_s = 2 \times \alpha_c$.

Color similarity and spatial occurrence consistency

Color similarity

The color similarity is evaluated in the HSV color space. According to the physical meaning of the HSV colors, the distance between $\mathbf{c}_i$ and $\mathbf{c}_j$, $d(\mathbf{c}_i, \mathbf{c}_j)$, is defined as

$$\sqrt{(s_i \cos h_i - s_j \cos h_j)^2 + (s_i \sin h_i - s_j \sin h_j)^2 + (v_i - v_j)^2},$$

where $[h_i \; s_i \; v_i]^T = \mathbf{c}_i$ and $[h_j \; s_j \; v_j]^T = \mathbf{c}_j$. Then, we can define the color similarity as

$$s(\mathbf{c}_i, \mathbf{c}_j) = (1 - d(\mathbf{c}_i, \mathbf{c}_j)/d_{\max})^{\beta}, \tag{7}$$

where $d_{\max} = \max_{mn} d(\mathbf{c}_m, \mathbf{c}_n)$ and $\beta = 2$ in our experiment.

Experiences show that human is more sensitive to the H (hue) color channel. Hence we should pay more attention on this H channel, and define the similarity over the H channel,

$$s(h_i, h_j) = 1/\sigma\sqrt{2\pi} \exp(-(h_i - h_j)^2/(2\sigma^2)), \tag{8}$$

where $\sigma = \frac{\pi}{3}$ with h's range being $[0, 2\pi]$. This assignment of σ makes the similarity between different colors with larger difference of H channel much smaller. Then, the overall color similarity is as the following

$$\mathrm{sim}(\mathbf{c}_i, \mathbf{c}_j) = s(h_i, h_j) \times s(\mathbf{c}_i, \mathbf{c}_j). \tag{9}$$

As mentioned before, we have quantized the HSV space into $12 \times 4 \times 4$ colors, i.e., totally 192 colors. We precompute their similarities according to Eq. (9) and store them in a lookup table of size 192×192. In this manner, we reduce the computation cost by only looking up this table instead of expensive online computation.

Spatial occurrence consistency

The spatial occurrence consistency between spatial maps is very straightforward and evaluated by the inner product, $\mathrm{sim}(\mathbf{l}_q, \mathbf{l}_k) = \mathbf{l}_q^T \mathbf{l}_k$. As mentioned before, $\mathbf{l}$ is a binary vector with entries equal to 0 or 1, and represented by a byte variable vector $[b_1 \; \cdots \; b_n]^T$. Hence the inner product can be fast evaluated by the *and* operation as the following

$$\mathbf{l}_q^T \mathbf{l}_k = \sum\nolimits_{i=1}^{n} \mathrm{count}(b_{qi} \wedge b_{ki}), \tag{10}$$

where the basic operation $\wedge$ is *and* operation on byte variables, and $\mathrm{count}(\cdot)$ is the number of set bits. There are total 256 different values for a byte variable. To avoid online computation, we precompute a lookup table of size 256×256, in which each entry is the number of set bits of the *and* result for two byte variables.

5 Target Color Map Specification

The proposed interface for target color map specification consists of two modules: target color selection and target map sketching.

Target color selection

The target color selection scheme provides color palettes and allows the user to pick up a target color. Our main work on this color palette focuses on how to generate a color palette. We provide three color selection schemes.

1. Standard color palette. We organize the colors without using the information from image search results.

2. Color palette from image search results. We mine image search results, and present the most-frequent colors to form a color palette.

3. Color palette from an example image. We generate a color palette directly using an example image selected from search results. Specifically, the user can drag an image as the color palette, and then pick up the colors from the image.

Target map sketching

After selecting the target color, the user then can sketch the target map. We provide three specification schemes.

1. Free-scribbling. The user can freely draw strokes to indicate the target spatial map.

2. Template map. The user can select an target map from a set of templates.

3. Map from an example image. The user can select an example image from search results, and draw on this image to indicate the target color map.

6 Experiments

To evaluate the proposed approach, we crawled images from the photo sharing engine, flickr, and image search engines (e.g., Google, Microsoft Bing, Yahoo!). For each engine, we crawled top 1000 images from the returned images for a specific text query. There are totally 51 queries, which are selected from top popular queries such that those cover different types of queries, such as object, scene, portrait and etc.

We collected target color maps from the users. We recorded the color maps when the users playing our system, and sampled some color maps for our experiments. Then we asked users to help label the ground truth. To differentiate different relevance degrees, we adopted a graded relevance scale, and use four levels from level 0 to level 3. Level 3 corresponds to the most relevant, and level 0 the least relevant. We asked 5 users to manually label the relevance level for each target color map, and then selected the most frequent level as the final level for each image. To avoid any bias on the labeling, those users were selected such that they have no special knowledge on image search and are initially unknown about the proposed technique.

To evaluate the performance, we use the normalized discounted cumulative gain (nDCG) measure. DCG measures the usefulness, or gain, of a document based on its position in the result list. The gain is accumulated cumulatively from the top of the result list to the bottom with the gain of each result discounted at lower ranks. Two assumptions of DCG measure are that highly relevant documents are more useful when appearing earlier in a search engine result list (have higher ranks) and that highly relevant documents are more useful than marginally relevant documents, which are in turn more useful than irrelevant documents. Comparing a search engine performance from one query to the next cannot be consistently achieved using DCG alone, so the cumulative gain at each position (p) should be normalized across queries. This is done by sorting documents of a result list by the ground truth, producing an ideal DCG at position p. Mathematically, nDCG at position p is calculated as

$$\mathrm{nDCG}(p) = \mathrm{DCG}(p)/\,\mathrm{IDCG}(p), \tag{11}$$

$$\mathrm{DCG}(p) = \sum\nolimits_{i=1}^{p} r_i/\log_2(i+1), \tag{12}$$

where r_i is the graded relevance of the result at position i, and calculated as $r_i = 2^{c_i} - 1$, with c_i the ground truth level of the image at position i, IDCG(p) is an ideal DCG at position p. The nDCG values for all queries (all target color maps in our experiments) can be averaged to obtain a measure of the average performance for many queries.

Sensitivity analysis

In this subsection, we conducted experiments to show the performance variance with the grid dimension varying. We report and analyze the effects of the grid dimension on several aspects: computational cost for color map feature extraction, computational cost for similarity evaluation and ranking performance.

For the computational cost of feature extraction, we average all the computational time over all the images. Ranking cost herein is the whole time cost from the time when the ranking process starts to the time when the ranked results are obtained. In other words, the whole process includes the analysis of target color map, similarity evaluation between target color map and images, and sorting procedure. The computational costs for feature extraction and image ranking are depicted in Fig. (5)(a). From this figure, it can be seen that the extraction time cost is almost stable and that time cost increase for image ranking is stable when grid dimension is from 1 to 8 and time const increase is much bigger when grid dimension is changed from 8 to 32.

We also show nDCG performance variance with grid dimension changing, which is shown in Fig. (5)(b). This figure shows the performance when rank positions $\{5, 10, 20 \cdots 200\}$ are considered. From this figure, it can be observed that the performance is improved when the grid dimension increases till 8 and that the performance is deteriorated a little when the grid dimension is chosen as 16 or 32.

This deterioration is because in this case the color map representation is too detailed and makes the distinctive map characteristics ambiguous.

In our application, feature extraction is offline, and ranking is online. From the perspective of a real application, a proper grid dimension should be carefully selected so that the following properties are satisfied 1) the online ranking is conducted on the fly, 2) the performance is satisfactory, and 3) the offline feature extraction is not expensive. According to Fig. (5) and the above analysis, we conclude that it is better that grid dimension is selected to be 8. Then, the average computational costs for color map extraction and image ranking are about 44 ms and 17 ms, respectively. In the following , all the experimental results are reported using grid dimension 8.

We move to the last issue, storage cost for the color map feature. It is better that the storage cost is cheap in that color map feature extraction is performed when the image is crawled and is stored as metadata. In our implementation, we store the color map feature color by color. Specifically, we store the color index, followed by the spatial map feature, for each color. The map feature can be directly saved as 8 bytes. However, from the statistics in our experiment, we observed that on average each spatial map (binary vector of length 64) only has 6.3 ones. Therefore, we use a byte variable to indicate the index for the entry valued as one, which will reduce the storage cost from 8 bytes to 6.3 bytes. Moreover, the largest value for the grid index is 63, which leaves the top two bits of a byte variable unused. We can use those bits to separate the map feature of different colors. In other words, we store the color index (1 byte), followed by the corresponding spatial map feature (several bytes), and particularly, for the last map feature of each color we store it after increasing it by 64, which will be used as a flag to separate different colors. By comparison, this color-by-color scheme costs lower storage than grid-by-grid scheme that may need to store the color number and indices for each grid. In summary, our scheme only needs to store the color indices $\{\mathbf{c}_i\}_{i=1}^n$ and the map features $\{\mathcal{F}_i\}_{i=1}^n$ with $\mathcal{F}_i = \{f_j\}_{j=1}^{m_i}$ and m_i the number of ones, so the total storage cost is $n + \sum_{i=1}^n m_i$. From the statistics, $n = 15.67$, $\sum_{i=1}^n m_i = 98.65$, and the total cost is 114.32 bytes.

Quantitative evaluation

In this subsection, we would like to present quantitative evaluation of our approach, by investigating the effects of different components in the similarity evaluation formulation and comparing it with several related methods.

Effects of three components

The color map similarity measure is composed of three components: spatial correspondence compatibility, spatial relation consistency, and contextual color map similarity. To investigate their effects on the performance clearly, we divide target color map into several categorizes, which makes it clear where and how each

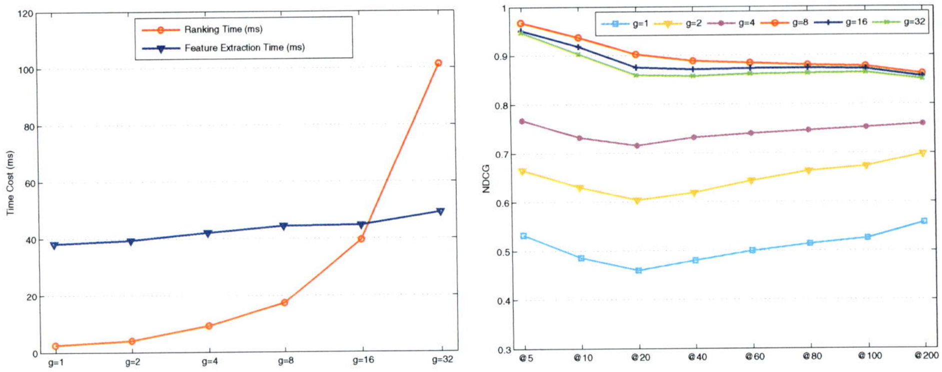

(a) (b)

Fig. (5): Sensitivity to grid dimension. (a) shows the extraction cost and online ranking cost with different grid dimensions, and (b) shows the nDCG performance with different grid dimensions.

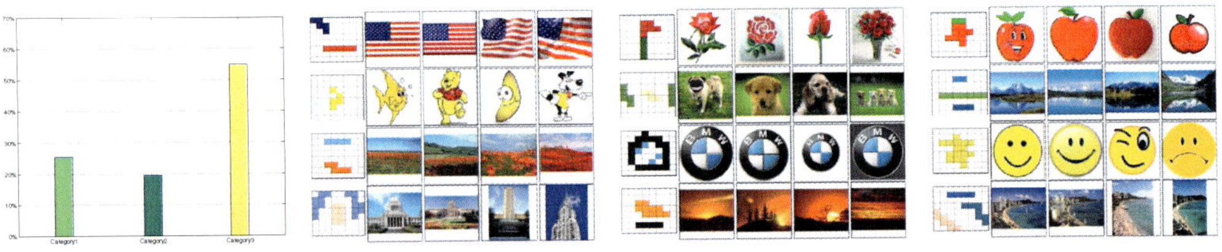

(a) (b) (c) (d)

Fig. (6): Target color map categorization. (a) shows the statistics of different categories. (b), (c) and (d) show target maps of three categories and their corresponding images of interest.

component works. It should be noted that the target color map are collected from the users that do not know anything about three components, i.e., they scribble the target color maps for those image search results without any special hints that favor the three components. Hence, the ratios of different categorizes reflect the practice, without specially designed for our approach. The target color map categorization is shown in Fig. (6). From Fig. (6)(a), it can be observed that realistic target maps indeed cover those three categories. Figs. (6)(b), (6)(c) and (6)(d) visually illustrate different categories.

To justify those three components, we perform a serial of experiments using different combinations of the three components over four types of data sets: three categories and the whole data set. For convenience, we denote color spatial correspondence compatibility as SCC, color spatial relation consistency as SRC, and contextual color map similarity as CSS. We consider four combinations, SCC, SCC + SRC, SCC + CSS, and SCC + SRC + CSS. The first combination inspects the effect of the basic color map similarity measure, the second and third combinations

Tab. (1): Comparison of our approach with two representative related techniques.

	Our approach	VisualSEEk	Multi-resolution
spatial correspondence	Y	Y	Y
spatial relation	Y	Y	N
robustness to roughness	Y	N	N

aim to examine the effects of SRC and CSS, respectively, and the final combination is actually the proposed approach. Such experimental results are shown in Fig. (7), from which we can have the following observations:

1. Fig. (7)(a) shows the performance over the first category of target color maps. It can be observed that in such a case the basic component SCC is sufficient since the performances of all the methods are almost the same.

2. Fig. (7)(b) shows the performance over the second category. This figure discloses that in some case the second component, SRC, makes effects.

3. Fig. (7)(c) shows the performance over the third category. The comparison that SCC + CSS has the similar performance with SCC + SRC +CSS shows that CSS actually makes the key role of performance improvement.

4. Fig. (7)(d) shows the performance over the whole data set. SCC + SRC + CSS, i.e., the proposed approach, gets the best performance.

Comparison

It is novel to refine image search results using color map sensitive feature. But some existing techniques using color information in content based image retrieval, can be applied to image search result refinement. To justify the superiority of the proposed approach, we perform a quantitative comparison with two representative techniques, visualSEEk [19] and the multi-resolution based method [9].

The comparison over the whole data set is shown in Fig. (8). It can be observed that our approach is the best and that the multi-resolution based method gets the worst performance. Some analysis is given as follows. Our approach is superior over VisualSEEk at least in two aspects: 1) The color map representation has larger ability to represent the spatial relation; and 2) Our similarity measure is more capable to discriminate the spatial relation consistency and hence is more compatible with users' intent. Compared with the multi-resolution based method, our approach exploits both spatial correspondence and spatial relation, while the multi-resolution based method only considered the color spatial correspondence. Tab. (1) summarizes their differences.

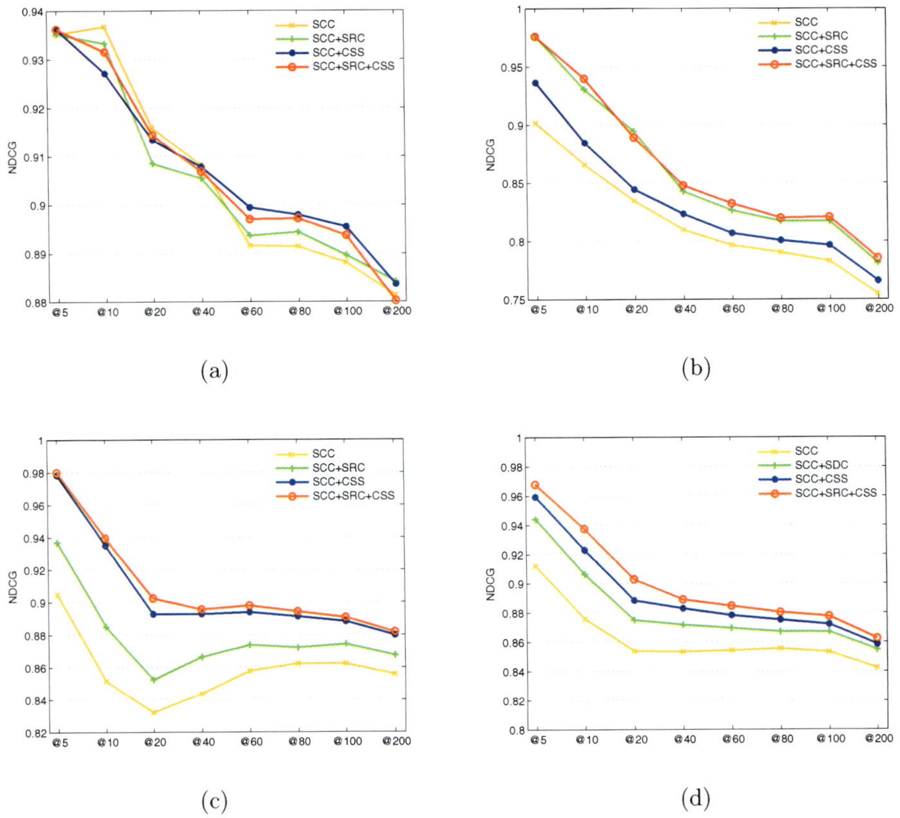

Fig. (7): Illustration of effects of different components. (a), (b) and (c) show the performance over three categories of data sets. (d) shows the performance over the whole data set.

Visual comparison

In this subsection, we present the visual results to compare the proposed approach and the conventional method that only considers the spatial correspondence.

In Fig. (9), we present a visual comparison to show that our approach has the ability to distinguish different color spatial relations. Fig. (9)(a) shows the original top ten images corresponding to the query "beach". Figs. (9)(b) and (9)(c) show two target color maps from the users. It should be noted that these two target color maps have the same colors but different spatial relation. For the target color map in Fig. (9)(b), the user hopes that the yellow sand appears in the bottom left and the blue sky appears in the top right. The top ten images of our approach and the approach only exploiting spatial correspondence are shown in Fig. (9)(d) and Fig. (9)(e), respectively. We can see that the images in Fig. (9)(d) meet with the user's intent, i.e., the yellow sand appearing in the bottom left and the blue

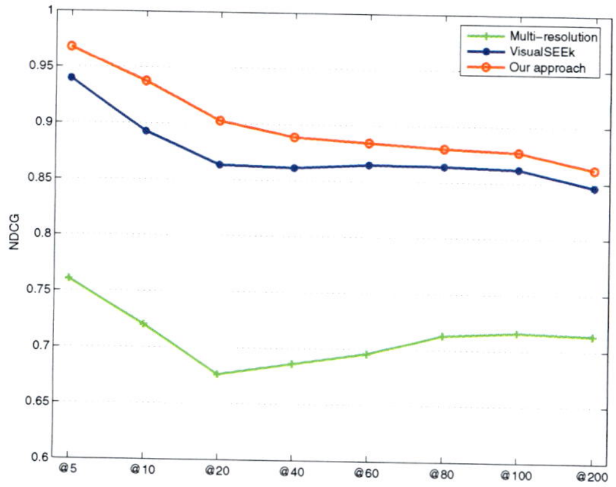

Fig. (8): Quantitative comparison with two representative related techniques.

sky appearing in the top right, while the ninth and tenth images in Fig. (9)(e) are not consistent with the requirements. For the target color map in (9)(c), our results shown in Fig. (9)(f) are very satisfactory, and obviously are better than the results in Fig. (9)(g). In the results based on spatial correspondence shown in Fig. (9)(g), the third, fourth, and fifth images are not consistent with the user's requirements. This comparison shows that our approach is superior over the spatial correspondence based method and can distinguish different spatial relations even with the same colors.

We present two additional visual comparisons shown in Fig. (10) to demonstrate that our approach can be applied to an interesting application, dominant color query. By specifying a single color map, the user intends to find the images that the whole image has such color tones. Figs. (10)(a) and (10)(d) show the target color maps from the users over two image search results corresponding to "mountain" and "grass". Figs. (10)(b) and (10)(e) show the results of our approach, and Figs. (10)(c) and (10)(f). It can be observed that our results are better. The superiority benefits from that contextual color map similarity which in some sense handle the roughness of the target color map. It should be noted that some other method without exploiting the spatial information, e.g., color histogram over the whole image, can obtain the similar results. But with this experiment, we want to show that among the methods exploiting the spatial information, our approach can also perform better over such cases than other methods.

In addition, we present an experiment with the target color map from an example image, as shown in Fig. (11). Figs. (11)(a) and (11)(b) show the selected example image and the specified color map. Fig. (11)(c) show the original and refined results, respectively.

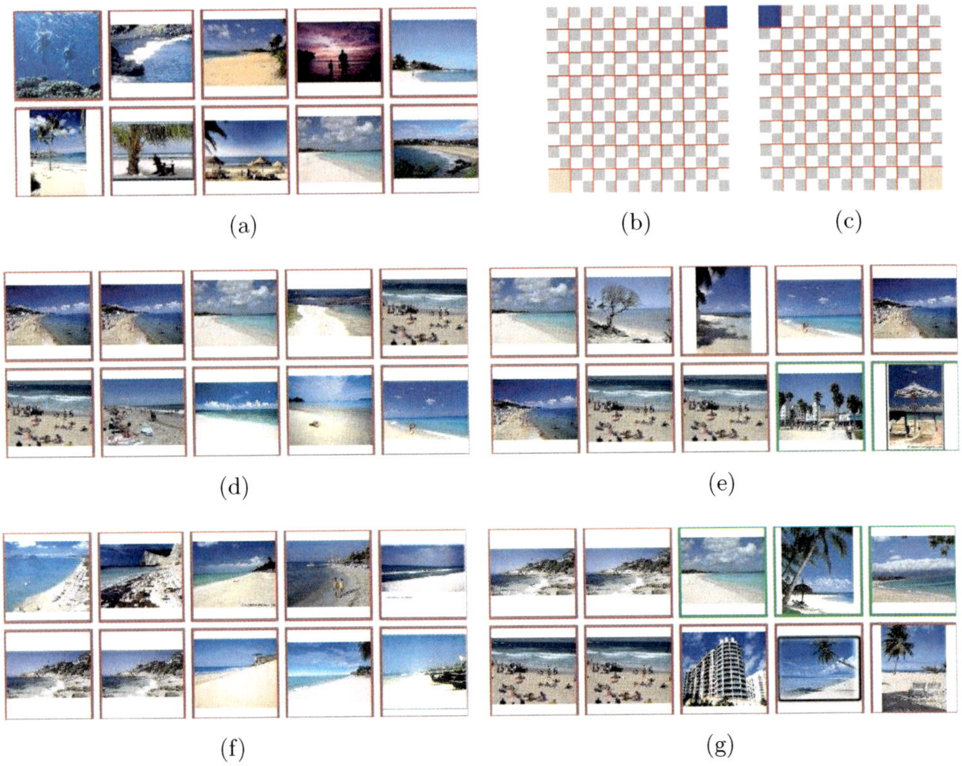

Fig. (9): Visual comparison between our approach and the spatial correspondence based approach. (a) shows the original top 10 images. (b) and (c) show two target color structures with the same colors and different spatial maps. (d) and (f) show the top 10 images of our approach, corresponding to the two target color maps. (e) and (g) show the top 10 images of the spatial correspondence based approach. It can be easily observed that the results of our approach meet with the target color map and are better.

User study

In this subsection, we present the user study for the target color map specification mechanism. The mechanism consists of two main modules: color selection and map sketching. For color selection, we present three schemes: 1) stand color palette, 2) color palette from image search results, and 3) color palette from an example image. We collect the feedbacks from 20 users. Those users are unknown of our system at the beginning and then are trained to use our system. After two days of using our system, the users are asked to give scores for each scheme and the combinations of schemes according to the convenience and frequencies of using them. The score is from level 1 to level 5, and level 5 is the best score. The average scores of all the combinations of schemes is shown Fig. (12)(a). From this figure,

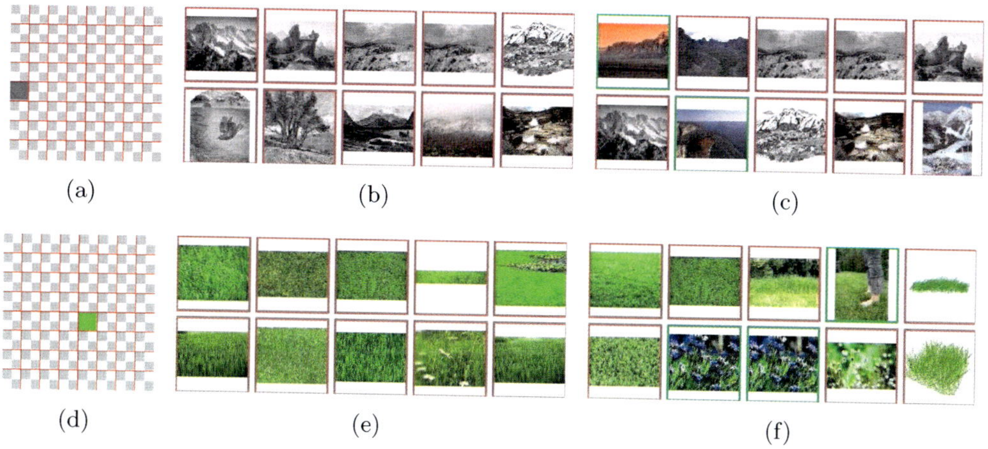

Fig. (10): Visual comparisons for single color query.

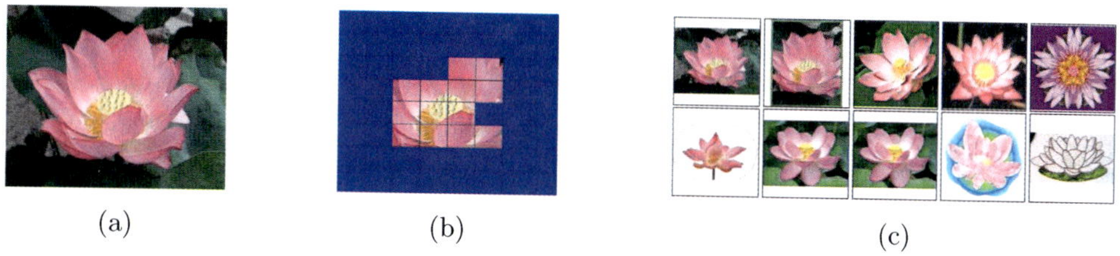

Fig. (11): Visual results with the target color map from an example image. (a) shows the selected image, (b) shows the specified color map, in which the center region without superposing blue color corresponds to target color map, (c) shows the refined results.

it can be observed that the combination of three schemes are most useful and that color palette from an example image is most attractive among the tree individual schemes. From this sense, the color selection scheme is successful. For target color map specification, we deliver three schemes: a) free-scribbling, b) template structures and c) map from images. We perform a similar user study, and the result is shown Fig. (12)(b). The overall scores show that the map sketching interface is also very convenient.

7 Conclusion

In this chapter, we propose a novel interactive image search system, image search by color map, to meet with users' intent on the colors and their spatial distribution. The proposed approach is superior over the conventional color based image retrieval method that only utilizes the spatial correspondence information because our approach additionally exploits the spatial relation of colors within an image to comparing and is robust to the roughness of target color map specified by the user.

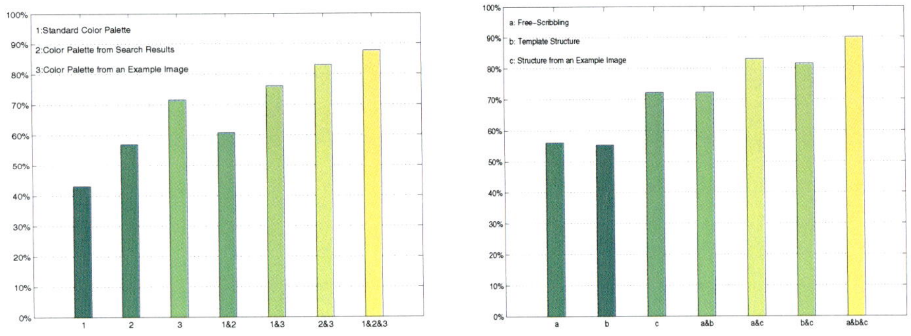

(a) (b)

Fig. (12): User study for color selection and map sketching interfaces. (a) shows average scores for different combinations of color selection schemes, and (b) shows average scores for different combinations of map sketching schemes.

The experimental results over real image search results demonstrate the efficiency and effectiveness. More visual examples and the release on Microsoft Bing image search could be found from `http://research.microsoft.com/en-us/um/people/jingdw/searchbycolor/`.

8 References

[1] A. D. Bimbo and P. Pala. Visual Image Retrieval by Elastic Matching of User Sketches. *IEEE Transactions on Pattern Analysis and Machine Intelligence*, 1997.

[2] T.-S. Chua, K.-L. Tan, and B. C. Ooi. Fast Signature-Based Color-Spatial Image Retrieval. In *ICMCS*, 1997.

[3] J. Cui, F. Wen, and X. Tang. IntentSearch: Interactive On-line Image Search Re-ranking. In *ACM Multimedia*, 2008.

[4] R. Datta, D. Joshi, J. Li, and J. Z. Wang. Image retrieval: Ideas, influences, and trends of the new age. *ACM Comput. Surv.*, 2008.

[5] J. Fauqueur and N. Boujemaa. Mental image search by boolean composition of region categories. *Multimedia Tools Appl.*, 2006.

[6] M. Flickner, H. S. Sawhney, J. Ashley, Q. Huang, B. Dom, M. Gorkani, J. Hafner, D. Lee, D. Petkovic, D. Steele, and P. Yanker. Query by Image and Video Content: The QBIC System. *IEEE Computer*, 1995.

[7] C.-S. Fuh, S.-W. Cho, and K. Essig. Hierarchical Color Image Region Segmentation for Content-Based Image Retrieval System. *IEEE Transactions on Image Processing*, 2000.

[8] W. H. Hsu, L. S. Kennedy, and S.-F. Chang. Reranking Methods for Visual Search. *IEEE Multimedia*, 2007.

[9] C. E. Jacobs, A. Finkelstein, and D. Salesin. Fast Multiresolution Image Querying. In *SIGGRAPH*, 1995.

[10] Y. Jing and S. Baluja. Pagerank for Product Image Search. In *WWW*, 2008.

[11] S. Lazebnik, C. Schmid, and J. Ponce. Beyond bags of features: Spatial pyramid matching for recognizing natural scene categories. In *CVPR*, 2006.

[12] S. Lin, M. T. Özsu, V. Oria, and R. T. Ng. An extendible hash for multi-precision similarity querying of image databases. In *VLDB*, 2001.

[13] S. Matusiak, M. Daoudi, T. Blu, and O. Avaro. Sketch-Based Images Database Retrieval. In *Multimedia Information Systems*, 1998.

[14] B. M. Mehtre, M. S. Kankanhalli, and W. F. Lee. Shape Measures for Content Based Image Retrieval: A Comparison. *Inf. Process. Manage.*, 1997.

[15] B. C. Ooi, K.-L. Tan, T.-S. Chua, and W. Hsu. Fast Image Retrieval Using Color-Spatial Information. *VLDB*, 1998.

[16] N. Sebe and M. S. Lew. Color-Based Retrieval. *Pattern Recognition Letters*, 2001.

[17] J. Sethian. *Level Sets Methods and Fast Marching Methods.* Cambridge University Press, 2nd edition, 1999.

[18] A. W. M. Smeulders, M. Worring, S. Santini, A. Gupta, and R. Jain. Content-based image retrieval at the end of the early years. *IEEE Transactions on Pattern Analysis and Machine Intelligence*, 2000.

[19] J. R. Smith and S.-F. Chang. VisualSEEk: A Fully Automated Content-Based Image Query System. In *ACM Multimedia*, 1996.

[20] J. Z. Wang, G. Wiederhold, O. Firschein, and S. X. Wei. Content-Based Image Indexing and Searching Using Daubechies' Wavelets. *Int. J. on Digital Libraries*, 1997.

INDEX

A

Xian-Sheng Hua, Marcel Worring & Tat-Seng Chua (Eds.)

B

C

D

E

F

G

H

I

J

K

L

M

N

O

P

Q

R

S

T

U

V

W

Made in the USA
Las Vegas, NV
09 May 2026

46612111R10288